www.wadsworth.com

wadsworth.com is the World Wide Web site for Wadsworth and is your direct source to dozens of online resources.

At *wadsworth.com* you can find out about supplements, demonstration software, and student resources. You can also send email to many of our authors and preview new publications and exciting new technologies.

wadsworth.com
Changing the way the world learns®

THE WADSWORTH CONTEMPORARY ISSUES IN CRIME AND JUSTICE SERIES

Todd Clear, Series Editor

✳

The Invisible Woman

Gender, Crime, and Justice

Second Edition

JOANNE BELKNAP
University of Colorado—Boulder

WADSWORTH
✳ ™
THOMSON LEARNING

Australia • Canada • Mexico • Singapore • Spain
United Kingdom • United States

HV
9950
.B45
2000

WADSWORTH
THOMSON LEARNING

Executive Editor, Criminal Justice: Sabra Horne
Developmental Editor: Terri Edwards
Assistant Editor: Ann Tsai
Editorial Assistant: Cortney Bruggink
Marketing Manager: Jennifer Somerville
Project Editor: Jennie Redwitz
Print Buyer: April Reynolds
Permissions Editor: Joohee Lee

Production Service Coordinator: Andrea Bednar, Shepherd Incorporated
Copy Editor: Carol Hoke
Illustrator: Rod Wiese
Cover Designer: Joan Greenfield
Cover Image: Daniel Proctor/Photonica
Cover Printer: Webcom Ltd
Compositor: Shepherd Incorporated
Printer: Webcom Ltd

For permission to use material from this text, contact us by
Web: http://www.thomsonrights.com
Fax: 1-800-730-2215
Phone: 1-800-730-2214

Wadsworth/Thomson Learning
10 Davis Drive
Belmont, CA 94002-3098
USA

For more information about our products, contact us:
Thomson Learning Academic Resource Center
1-800-423-0563
http://www.wadsworth.com

International Headquarters
Thomson Learning
International Division
290 Harbor Drive, 2nd Floor
Stamford, CT 06902-7477
USA

UK/Europe/Middle East/South Africa
Thomson Learning
Berkshire House
168-173 High Holborn
London WC1V 7AA
United Kingdom

Asia
Thomson Learning
60 Albert Street, #15-01
Albert Complex
Singapore 189969

Canada
Nelson Thomson Learning
1120 Birchmount Road
Toronto, Ontario M1K 5G4
Canada

Library of Congress Cataloging-in-Publication Data
Belknap, Joanne.
    The invisible woman : gender, crime, and justice / Joanne Belknap.—2nd ed.
       p. cm.—(The Wadsworth contemporary issues in crime and justice series)
    Includes bibliographical references and index.
    ISBN 0-534-54209-3
    1. Sex discrimination in criminal justice administration—United States. 2. Female offenders—United States. 3. Women—Crimes against—United States. 4. Policewomen—United States. I. Title. II. Contemporary issues in crime and justice Series.

HV9950 .B45 2000
364'.082'0973—dc21   00-063333

*This book is dedicated with the deepest gratitude
and affection to my two favorite gender benders:
Casey Belknap-Summers and R. S. Summers*

*I would also like to dedicate this book to all the women
and girls who have taken part in my various studies*

✳ Contents

IV   WOMEN WORKERS

*

Foreword

As editor of the Wadsworth Contemporary Issues in Crime and Justice Series, I am delighted to announce the publication of the second edition of *The Invisible Woman: Gender, Crime, and Justice,* by Joanne Belknap. The Contemporary Issues series is devoted to furthering our understanding of important issues in crime and justice by providing an in-depth treatment of topics that are neglected or insufficiently discussed in today's textbooks. *The Invisible Woman* is an excellent example of the kind of work the series was designed to promote.

It is common knowledge that the criminal justice system has been growing for over two decades. Most people also know that women make up a small minority of felony offenders—about 20% of felons, and about 9% of prisoners. What is not well—known is that for more than a decade, the growth rate of female offenders has been higher than that of males. And among victims, women are more numerous than they are among offenders; about 40% of the victims of violent crime are women.

Despite these figures, the criminal justice system is geared toward men, not women. When state and federal legislatures establish their penal codes, they tend to have in mind male offenders, and when courts establish their sentencing guidelines, they base them upon men. Correctional programs in prison and supervision policies in the community are developed with men in mind. In this way, women—as clients of the criminal justice system—are truly invisible: when laws are passed and policies are established, it is typically the case that nobody will ask how they will eventually affect the women offenders who are coming through the criminal justice system in increasing numbers.

The problem in criminology is even more basic. The traditional theories of the causes of crime have been developed largely on studies of men, largely with male offenders in mind, and have been predominantly tested by studies of men. But the factors that may explain why a 15-year-old young man runs afoul of the law may not apply very well to a 15-year-old young woman, and the factors that influence adult male offenders into and out of their criminal careers may not apply in the same way to adult women.

Women are also invisible as victims. In recent years, great strides have been made to include victims as people of standing in the criminal justice process. But when women are victimized, especially by men, a host of special circumstances often apply that the criminal justice system has been slow to recognize. Women are often victimized by intimates, and when a woman becomes a victim, it often leads to later criminal behavior as one natural consequence of the circumstances of her victimization.

However, as the criminal justice system has grown, it has become more open to the special circumstances of women. In part, this has been a result of increasing employment of women in professional roles that previously had been dominated by men: police, prosecutors, correctional officers, and others. As women have been more active in the professions of criminal justice, there has been an emergence of interest in the special problems facing women as clients and victims. Further, women who have joined the justice professions have blazed new professional trails for those who will follow, fighting open and covert job discrimination and facing intolerant thinking from those who think men deserve certain types of positions, not women. But although the slow opening of doors for women as professionals has magnified the human face of the field, they still represent a minority: among law enforcement employees, one-fourth are women; but only 10% of uniformed officers are women, and in corrections, almost 30% of employees are women, but only about 20 are line correctional officers.

Complex questions arise regarding women and criminal justice policy. On the one hand, the criminal justice system needs to find ways to recognize the special circumstances faced by women as offenders, the special needs represented among women victims, and the unique opportunity for advancing the profession that comes form opening doors to women. But these new policies face a tough standard, since the most significant tradition of the criminal law is "equal treatment under law." The argument that women have unique needs and circumstances has for many years been used as a rationale to treat women unfairly under the law, to apply misogynistic legal and program practices and to justify paternalistic justice strategies—to the disadvantage of the very women who were being given "special" treatment. The contemporary challenge is not whether to recognize the differences represented by women as clients and workers, but how to incorporate policies that are fair and effective when considering the relevant differences regarding women in these roles and circumstances.

That is why I am delighted to include *The Invisible Women* as a book in the series. No other book is as effective in its analysis of the special issues regarding women in the network of crime and justice. Professor Belknap, a lifelong advocate for women's issues and a talented analyst of the criminal justice system, has written a superb book. Those readers who are inclined to think about women and criminal justice from a reform perspective will find much to support their views and will obtain a wealth of important analysis that will shape how they see the tasks ahead. For those of you who have never really thought about women in crime and justice-for those to whom these women have been for too long invisible—this book will change forever your understanding of this essential aspect of crime and justice.

Todd R. Clear
Series Editor

✳

Preface

I was about 9 years old when my mother brought my brothers, my sister, and me to a large toy store to buy one of my older brothers "The Visible Man" for his birthday. For weeks he had been looking forward to owning the model, which was a clear plastic statue that stood about a foot high, came apart, and had removable internal organs as well as a skeleton. All of us were fascinated with this concept, but then a funny thing happened when we got to the store. "The Visible Woman" seemed infinitely more interesting than the "The Visible Man." Not only did she seem more dimensional, but she had two different stomachs: a nonpregnant stomach and a pregnant stomach. There were more parts to play with, and there was also a little fetus that could be put inside of her large, round tummy. Apparently my brother also decided she was more interesting because he picked her instead of the "The Visible Man." I certainly found her more fascinating than my stick-thin Barbie doll with conical breasts, whom I could never imagine looking like. "The Visible Woman" looked human, strong, *and* female.

When I decided to write a book on women and crime, I was struck by the recurring theme of women's and girls' everyday invisibility in society, in crime, and in the crime-processing system. If women are represented, it is often in stereotypical, passive, or sexual images. I remembered the model my brother had gotten for his birthday and how the "visible" woman seemed strong, fascinating, and real. The title of this book reflects the focus on women's invisibility while the contents attempt to make them visible with descriptions of the lives, experiences, and strengths of real women.

I think of the many women I have met in prison who are forgotten in society and in the crime-processing system; sadly, these women are often forgotten by their young children as well. When I visit or interview women and girls in prison, I am often struck by how normal they seem, not scary and repulsive as represented in the media (if they are represented at all). These women face deplorable conditions and desperate situations. Who will look after their children? Can they get counseling to deal with the incest and battering in their pasts? Can they get decent dental care? Can they get mammograms for breast lumps? Are their lawyers really working on their appeals? Can they get tampons or sanitary pads when they are menstruating? The strength of many of these women under these conditions is humbling. Given that women are the fastest-growing segment of the U.S. prison population, these problems are becoming more profound.

In writing the preface for this book, I also think of the women police officers and jail and prison guards I have interviewed and met, who have reported intensely hostile working environments, created by some of their male co-workers and supervisors. Often, even in those cases where the women felt sufficiently empowered to formally report their experiences to officials within the organization, nothing was done to the offending men. One ex-policewoman who spoke to one of my classes reported some of the worst sexual harassment experiences I had ever heard. She had considerable documentation of the numerous ways and times her male co-workers and supervisor had violated the sexual harassment laws, including displays of pornographic pictures with her face pasted on them and taped obscene phone calls to her home. Unfortunately, this woman was further victimized when she brought these offenders to court on sexual harassment charges. The male judge agreed with the defense attorney that the case should be a mistrial because this 39-year-old woman also reported having been raped when she was 16. Apparently, she had already been allotted her one "credible" rape.

This book documents not only the high rates of sexual abuse of girls and women but also the increased likelihood of women survivors of child sexual abuse being sexually victimized again as adults. This book also traces the unfair treatment that sexual abuse victims often experience in the crime-processing system. The original and revictimization rates of females have long been ignored or misunderstood; thus it is hardly surprising that official responses to these victims are often lacking at best and damaging at worst.

Regarding the invisibility of women victims, I think about my classes in which women have regularly written in their journals about incest, stranger and date rapes, sexual harassment at jobs they needed to keep, and the battering and stalking by boyfriends, ex-boyfriends, husbands, and ex-husbands. These women, understandably, rarely feel comfortable discussing these victimizations in classes, yet often do.

When women are made visible, it is often in stereotypical and offensive ways. For instance, one of my students had been battered by her second husband, who shot and killed her first husband (who had come to help her) in front of her children. When her batterer went to trial for the murder, she was asked about her sexual history. Not only is the rate of woman battering unrecognized in society, but the many useless responses to women's cases (such as in my student's case) is also unknown. This book describes the high rates of woman battering, as well as a crime-processing system that has been reluctant to take action against batterers. Moreover, it presents the risks of battered women being murdered by their batterers or killing their batterers in self-defense and subsequently spending many years or life in prison. In our society, these women are essentially invisible.

NEW TO THIS EDITION

This Second Edition is updated, and the sheer volume of new works since I wrote the First Edition speaks to the advancement of feminist criminology in recent years. These changes offer hope: Research on violence against women and girls and research on female offenders are being conducted at an unprecedented rate. Both are due to the feminist movement in general and the growing number of feminist scholars who are able to pursue careers conducting feminist research in criminology and other fields. Two important outgrowths of the feminist movement that affected the massive changes in this book are (1) the Violence Against Women Act (VAWA) funding for programs and research on battering, rape, and stalking; and (2) funding and encouragement by the Office of Juvenile Justice Delinquency and Prevention (OJJDP) to support research on and programming for delinquent girls. Thus, the significant increase in feminist scholars and the ability to make one's career as a feminist criminologist, along with huge funding increases for research on female victims and offenders, have made an important mark that is reflected in the changes between the First and Second Editions of this book. The interest in and funding for women working in the criminal processing system as police, guards, and lawyers have not changed nearly as significantly since the First Edition of this book was written, and that is reflected in this Second Edition. Also, it is important to remember that everyone who receives VAWA or OJJDP funding to research violence against or offending of women and girls is not necessarily conducting feminist or pro-feminist research. Indeed, there has been a backlash against the support for feminist research that manifests itself as exaggeration or misrepresention of women's use of violence/abuse in intimate partner relationships and women's and girls' use of violence in "every day" offending.

Like my brother's toy model, women in society and the crime-processing system are often invisible, but they are also often strong and capable. The chapters ahead focus on the theme of women's invisibility, and the book concludes on a note of hope and optimism regarding changes that have advanced the visibility and status of women and girls in the crime-processing system.

ACKNOWLEDGMENTS

I am very grateful to my friends and family members who have aided in a multitude of ways in writing both this and the First Edition. Some of my friends are some of my harshest critics, but their remarks have been constructive. It is difficult to mention these folks in any kind of order, so I am listing them alphabetically: Leslie Alexandria, Barbara Belknap, Bonnie Berry, Barbara Bloom, Bonnie Cady, Lynette Carpenter, Meda Chesney-Lind, Sandy Dangler, Helen Eigenberg, Edna Erez, Lynette Feder, Jackie Gibson-Navin, Steve Graham, Donna Hale, Violet Hall, Janet Jacobs, Christina Johns, Andrea Kornbluh, Mike Ma, E. Gail McGarry, Jane Menken, Joanne Meyerowitz, Merry Morash, Sharon Peters, Sheila Peters, Susan Ransbottom, Claire Renzetti, Cris Sullivan, Pat Swope, Anna Vayr, Pat Van Voorhis, and Patti Witte.

I'd also like to thank the reviewers of the Second Edition for their helpful comments: Nawal Ammar, Kent State University; Dana Britton, Kansas State University; Nanette Davis, Western Washington State University; Michael Hallett, Middle Tennessee State University; and Vickie Jensen, California State University—Northridge.

I am grateful to my colleagues in both sociology and women's studies at the University of Colorado, where the leadership has been terrific and where feminist scholarship is appreciated (a new experience for me). I am also grateful to some of the students here who made my life much easier through their fine work, in particular, Amy Leisenring, Heather Melton, and Jenn Roark. Finally, I am grateful to my women's studies colleagues at the University of Cincinnati, my saving grace in that job. Robin Sheets, the director until her death last July, was a mentor, leader, and friend. Although it is sad beyond words to think of her death, I still benefit from how she mentored, how she led, and how she showed sisterhood.

PART I

✳

Introduction

1

✳

The Emergence
of Gender
in Criminology

> The need for feminism arises from the desire to create a world
> in which women are not oppressed. If there is no term or focus,
> no movement which incorporates the struggle against sexism,
> women run the risk of becoming invisible.
>
> (JOHNSON-ODIM, 1991, 319)

This book presents the current state of women and girls in criminology (the study of crime) and criminal justice (the processing of victims and offenders). Whereas criminology is concerned with developing theories on what causes crime, criminal justice focuses on workers in the criminal justice system and the ways decisions are made about victims and offenders. To understand the current state of women and girls and the way in which gender relates to crime and criminal justice, it is first necessary to comprehend the historical evolution of the status of women and girls in the home, society, and the workplace. Therefore, this book includes relevant historical factors that have affected the status of women and girls in crime today. Finally, this book examines successes in effecting change for women and girls as victims, offenders, and professionals in the criminal justice system.

The term *criminal justice* is most often used to describe the practices of workers in the system (such as police, judges, and prison staff), as well as the formal processing and treatment of crime victims and offenders. This book replaces the term *criminal justice* with the term *crime processing,* given that there is little evidence that the criminal "justice" system is either just or fair in its treatment of women victims, offenders, and workers, particularly for women and girls of color and poorer women and girls. Indeed, the lack of justice for women and girls, especially the more marginalized, is the focus of this book.

The purpose of this chapter is to expose readers to an overall view of the important concepts behind women (and girls) and crime. These significant concepts include a presentation of women's invisibility in criminology and crime-processing studies, relevant concepts and definitions, and an understanding of how the images of women and girls in society have affected their experiences as victims, offenders, and professionals in society and in the crime-processing system.

INVISIBILITY OF WOMEN
AND GIRLS IN CRIME

The major areas covered in this book are (1) women and girls as offenders, (2) women and girls as victims, and (3) women professionals working in the crime-processing system. As stated previously, a common characteristic of women and girls in these areas is their invisibility. This section briefly explains how women's experiences have been denied or ignored. Moreover, this section discusses how women and girls do not always fit neatly into one of the three categories: offenders, victims, and professionals in the crime-processing system. Rather, a great deal of overlap exists. For example, many times when I have interviewed women police officers, they have spoken about being abused by their husbands or ex-husbands. One jail guard I interviewed told me she was an incest survivor. Many of the delinquent girls and women in prison that I have met report astounding rates of victimization including incest, date rape, stranger rape, and intimate partner battering. When I interviewed an incarcerated girl once and asked whether she believed any childhood events had led to her offending, she reported that she just didn't cope the same after she saw her uncle shoot her father and he died with his head in her lap. Thus, my own and many other researchers' work (covered in this book) has found a significant blurring between the victim and offender categories in women's and girls' lives, and many women working in the crime-processing system have histories of victimization.

Any discussion on the invisibility of women and girls in the study of crime must address the current resistance to this topic in academic research as well as in the classroom. Historically, women and girls as both victims and offenders were usually left out of the studies or, if included, were typically done so in very sexist and stereotypic ways. In conducting the research for this book, I often found it frustrating to search through mainstream journals (and some books) to find out whether women and/or girls were included in the research questions or samples. For example, studies with male-only samples rarely identified this in the title, whereas studies with female-only or female and male samples almost consistently reflected this in their titles. If women were excluded from the study, then most authors perceived no need to include "male" in the title. Similarly, Naffine (1996, 20) notes with some alarm that "it is still possible to study criminal men scientifically without referring to their sex" in mainstream U.S. and British criminology texts. Moreover, a feminist analysis of education in "criminal justice" departments noted that although feminism has had clear effects on the curriculum, pedagogy, and campus climate, "it has not been enough to transform criminology/criminal justice education so that gender is a central organizing theme. Feminist criminology/criminal justice education seems to remain at the margins of the 'male-stream' [a reflection that 'mainstream' is really about males]" (Renzetti, 1993, 219).

On a more positive note, it is clear that significant pro-feminist changes are occurring. Not only are "women and crime" courses more routinely offered and required, but academia is also producing more feminist scholars (women and men), and for the past decade, criminal justice and sociology departments increasingly recruit "feminist criminologists." The advances in research on women offenders in recent years is unprecedented. Although we still have much to learn, this book describes the historical as well as the more recent research in and the great contributions to understanding both the risks for offending and also the gender differences and similarities in the processing, treating, and punishing of offenders. Research on violence against women and girls has also increased almost exponentially in recent years. This is in part due to the increased number of women and feminists in academia but has been greatly aided by the implementation of the federal Violence Against Women Act of 1994. Congress passed this act, which in 1994 was signed into law by President Clinton. A provision of the act authorizes the attorney general to make monies (totaling over $120 million) available, starting in 1996, to research violence against women. Research on violence against women, therefore, has been funded at an unprecedented rate since this act, which was recently renewed. Another example of the "boom" of research in the area of violence against women and girls is the development of the journal *Violence Against Women* in 1995. The editor, Claire Renzetti, was soon so overwhelmed and impressed with the large number of high-quality manuscripts submitted to the journal that in 1999 she doubled the number of issues published per year (from four to eight). Unfortunately, the research on women working in the criminal-processing field has not experienced such a significant increase in research and attention. However, this area, too, has had some meaningful increase, which is reported in this book.

Women and Girls as Offenders

Most criminology theories are concerned with the etiology of crime and thus focus on factors related to offending, primarily male juvenile offending. Until the late 1970s, it was highly unusual for these studies to include girls (or women) in their samples. Although gender is the strongest factor indicating a person's likelihood to break the law, these (almost exclusively male) researchers rarely thought it was necessary to include women or girls in their samples. The irony is that "sex, the most powerful variable regarding crime has been virtually ignored" (Leonard, 1982, *xi*). Leonard goes on to say that criminology theories were constructed "by men, about men" and explain male behavior rather than human behavior. Furthermore, "[e]xploring why women commit fewer crimes than men (if indeed they do) could arguably provide clues for dealing with men's criminality" (Morris, 1987, 2).

When the researchers did include girls in their samples, it was typically to see how girls fit into boys' equations. That is, rather than include in the study a means of assessing how girls' lives might be different from boys' lives, girls' delinquency has typically been viewed as peripheral and unnecessary to understanding juvenile offending and processing. Thus, these theories failed to address gender differences in criminal behavior (Leonard, 1982; Morris, 1987). Whereas social class, access to opportunities to learn crime, and area of residence in a city have been used to explain boys' likelihood of turning to crime, the causes of girls' criminality have rarely been examined until recent years. Additionally, criminological theory historically tended to view women as "driven" to crime because of biological influences, whereas men were viewed as turning to crime due to economic or sociological forces. For instance, Shaw and McKay's (1969, 365) book *Juvenile Delinquency and Urban Areas* devotes only a few pages to girls' delinquency and then implies it is mostly sexual— associated with the "hunting ground" these girls live in, which is composed of dance halls, massage and bath establishments, movie theaters, and so on. Chapter 2 in this book discusses how the early criminologists (such as Cesare Lombroso, Otto Pollack, W. I. Thomas, and even Sigmund Freud) emphasized biology to explain women's criminality.

Thus, girls' delinquency was seen as neither interesting nor important until the past couple of decades. Similarly, theory has traditionally placed boys in the center. Feminist theories not only attempt to focus women more centrally, but they include how the inequalities between the sexes can differentially affect male and female experiences and behaviors. Furthermore, feminist theory has been increasingly committed to examining how factors such as racism, classism, and heterosexism, in addition to sexism, are useful for understanding gender differences and discrimination dynamics. Fortunately, particularly in the last few years, research assessing the "causes" of women's criminality has grown rapidly. This research, presented mostly in the next chapter, offers new and exciting (although sometimes depressing) ways of understanding women's crime. Moreover, the feminist research contributing to the understanding of why some girls commit crimes is making a significant impact in understanding why some *boys* commit crimes. For example, traditional strain theory never measured incest as a source of strain that might lead to delinquency for either girls or boys. In the late 1970s and early 1980s, three studies were published on the high rates of victimizations in offending girls' and women's lives (Chesney-Lind and Rodriguez, 1983; James and Meyerding, 1977; Silbert and Pines, 1981). Since then, many other studies report that incest and other childhood victimizations increase the likelihood of subsequent offending not only for girls and women (e.g., Arnold, 1990; Chesney-Lind and Shelden, 1992; Coker et al., 1998; Gilfus, 1992; Klein and Chao, 1995; Lake, 1993; Owen, 1998) but also for boys and men (e.g., Dembo et al., 1992; Dodge et al., 1990; Widom, 1989a, 1989b).

Another aspect of the invisibility of female offenders is the "correctional" institutions provided for women and girls. The prisons and delinquent institutions for women and girls, both historically and presently, vary drastically from those for boys and men, mostly to the disadvantage of girls. Moreover, historically, treatment and punishment issues/opportunities differed vastly for women based on race (Freedman, 1981; Rafter, 1985). The excuse for the lack of research on institutions housing women offenders, as well as the lack of training, vocational, educational, and counseling programs available to incarcerated women, is that women make up a small percentage of offenders. This lack of interest in and opportunities for women and girls is particularly disturbing given that their incarceration rate is growing much faster than men's (e.g., Immarigeon and Chesney-Lind, 1992; Kline, 1993; Mumula and Beck, 1997).

Women and Girls as Victims

Current research on victimization rates and fear of crime often fails to account for the ways that victimization and fear of victimization differ between the sexes. Some scholars have noted that society and the legal system often fail to distinguish "normal" heterosexual sex from rape, with the assumption that male dominance, and even violence, is acceptable sexuality (Edwards, 1987; McLean, 1988; Smart, 1989). The crimes that women and girls are most likely to experience—sexual victimization (rape) and woman battering (domestic violence)—not only are the most underreported, but also are abusive and humiliating, and often violent and dangerous. Yet researchers still frequently inform us that women are "oddly" more afraid of crime while being less vulnerable to victimization (see Stanko, 1990, 1992). Research, however, has established that the discrepancy between women's low rates of reported victimization and high levels of fear can be explained by disproportionately high rates of serious acquaintance victimizations (Stanko 1990; Young 1992). Moreover, most young women and girls grow up with strong messages about dangerous men lurking in alleys and behind bushes; thus, in a sense, women are trained to fear crime (see Madriz, 1997).

Another "gendered" form of victimization that is rarely recognized is "corporate" or "organizational" victimization. Gerber and Weeks's (1992) overview of this topic highlights a number of examples. First, they note that *sweatshops* and other factory-type jobs have numerous instances of "accidents" from poor working conditions and that the victims of these accidents are predominantly women. Second, they discuss the intrauterine birth-control device called the "Dalkon Shield," which was proved to be linked to "illness, sterility, spontaneous abortions, birth defects, and deaths" (ibid., 1992, 333). Notably, although a considerable amount has been written about this as "white-collar" and "corporate" crime, the fact that women were the primary victims was rarely recognized. Furthermore, Gerber and Weeks (ibid.) point out that some oral contraceptives (e.g., Depo-Provera and Ovulen) for women are related to breast and uterine cancer, yet the manufacturers fail to inform the consumers, or if the U.S. Food and Drug Administration (FDA) does not allow them to distribute them in the United States, they do so in other, usually Third World countries. Third, Gerber and Weeks (ibid.) discuss how some on-the-job hazards, such as carpal tunnel syndrome and overexposure to video display terminals, are disproportionately experienced by women workers given their prominence in clerical and factory work. Finally, they note that although a gender analysis of "brown lung" disease has not been conducted, this affliction appears to be disproportionately experienced by women.

Another example of corporate violence against women is provided in an in-depth study of silicone breast implants (Rynbrandt and Kramer, 1995). Rynbrandt and Kramer (ibid.) identify Dow Corning (the largest supplier of silicone breast implants), plastic surgeons, and "an apparently indifferent government" as the key players in allowing this dangerous procedure, which has been used in over two million women in the United States since 1964. These scholars document that the FDA approved these implants despite inadequate research assessing their safety. In 1991, rather than recalling the procedure until adequate safety testing could be conducted, they simply called for more testing. "The committee argued that they chose not to end or restrict silicone implants—despite the suspected risks—because they were a public health necessity both after cancer surgery and simply to enlarge breasts" (ibid., 209). (In actuality, 75–85 percent of breast implants were for cosmetic desires rather than for reconstructive surgery after breast cancer.) Despite the FDA's significant lack of concern for examining the safety of breast implants before approving them, the encouraging aspect of this battle is the role of the media and individual women who came forward to file lawsuits against Dow Corning and other companies. More specifically, when the government did not act responsibly, fortunately some journalists did by reporting what was really happening to women. For example, internal memos from Dow Corning regarding some of their staff who feared the implants were unsafe were "leaked" to the press. This was followed by Dow Corning releasing documents in 1992 indicating that they had known for more than two decades "that the implants could leak and that the gel could cause health problems" (ibid., 212). In March 1994, implant manufacturers agreed to a $4 billion class action settlement (ibid.). Thus, the press and individual women banding together to sue these companies in civil court resulted in actions taken against these irresponsible corporations. Croall's (1995, 233) overview of women's victimization in the corporate world in England addresses most of the types of abuses noted earlier, but she also includes two more types: (1) the "big business" of the "slimming industry" and (2) the high rates of sexual abuse and sexual exploitation women workers face with co-workers. The "slimming industry" examples cover the questionable and often inadequately tested weight-loss products that are harmful. Her example of sexual harassment at work as a form of corporate crime is certainly an interesting and important point.

Finally, a current practice that may well end up being classified as a form of organizational crime is the practice of paying women to undergo drug treatment in order to harvest their eggs for infertile couples. The women most sought after for their eggs are young, white college women, given the (racist and classist) desire for many of these couples to have white and potentially smart babies. To date, little is known about the long-term effects of this very intrusive medical procedure of harvesting eggs. Indeed, it may be that the heavy drug treatment used to produce numerous eggs (temporarily "throwing" these women into menopause) may increase these "donors'" chances not only of ovarian cancer but also of infertility problems themselves later on (Mead, 1999).

Women as Professionals in the Crime-Processing System

The final major area of women and crime covered in this book is women's employment in the crime-processing system. The three major types of employment opportunities in crime processing include prisons and jails, policing, and the law. Part IV of this book examines historical and current issues for women correctional officers, policewomen, and women lawyers and judges. All of these women have faced considerable resistance to employment in the crime-processing field. This resistance is based primarily on the attitude that women are unsuitable because working with male offenders requires "macho" men. The 1970s, when Title VII (a 1972 amendment to the 1964 Civil Rights Act) was enacted, proved crucial for women's professional entrance to the crime-processing system. Unfortunately, women's advancement in both numbers and rank has been slow. Despite current efforts by law schools and police departments to hire more women, the numbers of women in these occupations are still quite low, as are the number of women working in men's penal institutions, which make up the majority of correctional facilities. This persisting low representation of women in crime-processing jobs is due to the lack of adequate training and education necessary to support them and is further aggravated by the resistance they sometimes meet from male administrators and co-workers. Finally, it has been noted that not only are women working in the crime-processing system "invisible" in these systems and in the research until recently, but women criminologists have also been invisible, with historical accounts of criminology often ignoring women scholars' contributions to the field (Laub and Smith, 1995).

Blurring of Boundaries of Women's Experiences in Crime

In addition to acknowledging the invisibility of women offenders, women victims, and women working in the crime-processing system, it is important to recognize the overlapping of these categories in many women's experiences. As was stated earlier, my research on women working as police officers and in jails included numerous disclosures by these workers of having survived incest, extrafamilial child sexual abuse, stranger rape, and woman battering in intimate relationships. (A number of the women police officers discussed battering perpetrated by their police officer husbands.) Moreover, given the high rates of women in general who experience male violence (some statistics suggest as many as half of all women in the United States; see Chapters 6 through 8), it would be difficult to have women working in the crime-processing system who hadn't been victimized. Although this hasn't been empirically studied, women's victimization experiences may be related to their desire to work in the crime-processing system.

There is growing documentation that delinquent girls and women prisoners have disproportionately high records of victimization, usually incest, rape, and battering preceding their offending behaviors (e.g., American Correctional Association, 1990; Arnold, 1990; Belknap and Holsinger, 1998; Carlen, 1983; Chesney-Lind and Rodriguez, 1983; Daly, 1992; Fletcher and Moon, 1993; Immarigeon, 1987a, 1987b; Lake, 1993; Sargent et al., 1993). Many of these accounts suggest that the likelihood that prior victimization, offending (especially prostitution, running away, and drug offenses), and subsequent incarceration are interrelated (Arnold, 1990; Carlen, 1983; Chesney-Lind and Rodriguez, 1983; Daly, 1992; Gilfus, 1992; Lake, 1993, Owen, 1998). Recent research has identified running away from home and drug use as women's and girls' means of coping with and surviving abuse in their homes. Thus, the "escape" options open to women and girls who are being sexually and/or physically victimized are often illegal.

U.S. prisons house many battered women survivors who killed their batterers as a last resort (e.g., Browne, 1987; Richie, 1996). Although the crime-processing system has historically failed to respond to battered women as victims, it has responded harshly to them as "offenders." However, these women rarely have any criminal record before the murder, they are almost always the ones who notify the police of the murder, and the murder almost always occurs during a battering incident in which the victim is acting in self-defense (see Maguigan, 1991). These women typically receive longer sentences than men who kill their wives (Schneider and Jordan, 1981). In the late 1980s and early 1990s, governors from Ohio, Illinois, Maryland, and Texas received considerable press for commuting the sentences of women who had served time after killing their abusive partners in self-defense.

As discussed earlier, women victims, offenders, and professionals in the crime-processing system have historically remained invisible. Because of the shame associated with sexual abuse and battering, these crimes are not routinely reported to crime-processing authorities, research interviewers, or even family members and health-care officials. Similarly, offending women have remained invisible because, until recently, they made up less than 5 percent of the prison population. Finally, roles for women professionals were largely nonexistent until the 1970s. The goal of this book is to make issues surrounding women and crime more visible, to trace the changes in society and the crime-processing system that have occurred, and to propose changes that still need to occur. But first, to understand these issues, it is important to have an understanding of feminism and the difference between sex and gender.

SEX VERSUS GENDER

Differences between men and women have been divided into two categories: sex differences and gender differences. Sex differences are biological differences, including differences in reproductive organs, body size, muscle development, and hormones. Gender differences, on the other hand, are those that are ascribed by society and that relate to expected social roles. Examples of gender differences include clothing, wages, child-care responsibilities, and professions. Most differences between men and women are gender differences, which are determined by society; they are not biologically determined. Moreover, socially based differences are rooted largely in inequality (MacKinnon, 1990). Because society creates these inequalities, society must also be the solution to restructuring the images and opportunities of women and men (and girls and boys) in order to achieve equality.

Women's and men's different roles historically have been viewed as "biologically based and unalterable." More recently, however, feminists assert that "women's roles are learned and socially determined" (Klein, 1984, 3). Thus, it is important to examine and acknowledge how sex differences influence gender differences. For instance, when only boys are allowed to take part in sports programs, girls are prevented from exercising their bodies and becoming strong. It is necessary to acknowledge that even in the traditional sense, some women are stronger than some men. Also, the relative differences in men's and women's times for running marathons, shorter running events, and swimming have significantly decreased since the 1930s, possibly due to girls' and women's increased access to exercise and training for sports (Fausto-Sterling, 1985). In fact, between 1964 and 1984, women's marathon times decreased by more than one-and-one-half hours, whereas men's times decreased by only a few minutes (ibid.). In addition to women holding the records in marathon swimming, the first woman ever "allowed" to swim the English Channel (in 1926) "not only astounded the world by succeeding at all, but she broke the men's record by two hours!" (ibid., 218).

West and Zimmerman (1987), in a classic article called "Sex and Gender," call for the need to understand three phenomena: sex, sex category, and gender. They define sex as "a determination made through the application of socially agreed upon biological criteria for classifying persons as males or females" (ibid., 127). Thus, they point out that even sex is not immutable and that it is *socially agreed upon biological criteria*. It is useful to have this discussion in terms of hermaphrodites. That is, even biologically it is not always clear what sex someone is, and the pattern has been to have the doctor decide at birth in those "questionable" cases. *Sex category* placement of individuals in society "is established and sustained by the socially required identificatory displays that proclaim one's membership in one or the other category [male or female]" (ibid., 127). The process of sex categorization, then, is the ongoing identification in everyday life of persons as boys or girls or men or women based on factors such as their dress or bearing. One does not need a chromo-somal test to assume one's sex; rather, we assume that someone's sex is what it appears to be "unless we have a special reason to doubt" it (ibid., 133). Thus, "while sex category serves as an 'indicator' of sex, it does not depend on it" (West and Fenstermaker, 1995, 20).

Gender, according to West and Zimmerman (1987, 127), "is the activity of managing situated conduct in light of normative conceptions of attitudes and activities appropriate for one's sex category. Gender activities emerge from and bolster claims to membership in a sex category." Therefore, West and Zim-merman (ibid., 129) argue that "gender is not a set of traits, or a variable, nor a role, but the product of social doings of some sort. . . . We claim that gen-der itself is constituted through interactions. . . . Our object here is to explore how gender might be exhibited or portrayed through interaction, and thus be seen as 'natural,' while it is being produced as a socially organized achievement." Thus, West and Zimmerman (ibid.) examine the construction of gender as individual but also heavily "socially organized." Gender is not simply an individual attribute but rather is accomplished through interactions with others. Indeed, they view gender "both as an outcome of and a rationale for various social arrangements and as a means of legitimating one of the most fundamental divisions in society [the differences between males and females]" (ibid., 126). They explain how these socially constructed differences appear to be a biological given:

> Doing gender means creating differences between girls and boys and women and men, differences that are not natural, essential, or biological. Once the differences have been constructed, they are used to reinforce the 'essentialness' of gender. (ibid., 137)

In later work, West and Fenstermaker (1995) attempt to examine "doing difference" by examining how race and class fit in with "doing gender." They point out the vast complexities in this endeavor, particularly in terms of attempting to determine how people are perceived and how they experience situations based on where they "fit" in the categories of race, sex, and class. Their approach, however, has been criticized for "treating gender as the most fundamental, theoretical category and then 'adding' on race and class. They lay out their theoretical argument within a gender-only framework and then gen-eralize this argument to race and class" (Collins et al., 1995, 493).

Acker (1990) emphasizes the need to examine not just the individual but to also acknowledge that organizational structure is gendered. She states that if an organization or any other analytical unit is "gendered," this does not mean that gender is simply an addition to ongoing processes that are gender neutral. Rather, a gendered organization is one in which control, identity, meaning, actions, emotions, and advantage are patterned by distinguishing between male and female (and masculine and feminine). Acker (ibid.) notes some interacting processes by which gendering occurs, including (1) the construction of divi-

Table 1.1 The Five Elements That Distinguish Feminist Thought from Other Types of Social and Political Thought

- Gender is not a natural fact but a complex social, historical, and cultural product; it is related to, but not simply derived from, biological sex differences and reproductive capacities.
- Gender and gender relations order social life and social institutions in fundamental ways.
- Gender relations and constructs of masculinity and femininity are not symmetrical but are based on an organizing principle of men's superiority and social and political—economic dominance over women.
- Systems of knowledge reflect men's views of the natural and social world; the production of knowledge is gendered.
- Women should be at the center of intellectual inquiry, not peripheral, invisible, or appendages to men.

SOURCE: Kathleen Daly and Meda Chesney-Lind. 1988. "Feminism and Criminology." *Justice Quarterly* 5:504.

sions along gender lines (e.g., allowed behaviors, power, and office space); (2) the construction of images and symbols that reinforce these gender divisions (e.g., dress, the media, and technical skills); and (3) interactions among workers that portray submission or dominance (e.g., men taking more "turns," asking questions, making comments, and interrupting more).

Court cases on sex discrimination have historically confused sex and gender differences, often ruling to the disadvantage of women on the basis that cultural/societal (or gender) differences are "immutable" (Rhode, 1989, 3). That is, legal discourse has historically failed to distinguish sex from gender differences, viewing both as inherent, not recognizing the role society plays in perpetuating gender inequalities. In fact, some scholars believe that most societies, including the United States, are invested in perpetuating gender distinctions (Epstein, 1988, 120). Daly and Chesney-Lind (1988, 504) clearly delineate the importance of gender and a feminist approach (see Table 1.1).

Inherent in this distinction between sex and gender are the concepts of sexism and patriarchy. Sexism refers to oppressive attitudes and behaviors directed at either sex; that is, sexism is discrimination or prejudice based on gender. In practice, the discrimination, prejudice, and negative attitudes and behaviors based on sex and gender are directed primarily at women (that is, women are not as "good" as men, women exist for the sexual pleasure of men, women are defined by their beauty, and so on).

Patriarchy, on the other hand, refers to a social, legal, and political climate that values male dominance and hierarchy. Central to the patriarchal ideology is the belief that women's nature is biologically, not culturally, determined (Edwards, 1987). What feminists identify as gender differences (for example, the ability to nurture children), therefore, are often defined as sex differences by the patriarchy. The patriarchal social structure of modern times is not as strong as it once was. Nevertheless, MacKinnon (1989) notes that the state operates from men's standpoint; the laws are consistent with men's experiences. Patriarchy and its privileges, then, remain as part of the defining quality of the culture and thus of criminology and crime processing. Indeed, feminist legal scholar Carol Smart (1989) is so concerned that the existing legal system is so inherently patriarchal that she questions the whole concept advanced by some feminist legal scholars known as *feminist jurisprudence.* Jurisprudence is the philosophy or science of law. Smart (ibid., 69) argues that the concept of jurisprudence presumes that basic principles of justice, rights, or equity underpin all aspects of law. She maintains that a primary limitation of constructing a feminist jurisprudence "is that it does not de-center law. On the contrary, it may attempt to change its values and procedures, but it pre-serves law's place in the hierarchy of discourses which maintains that law has access to truth and justice." Thus, she believes that the legal system is too entrenched in patriarchal presumptions to allow any type of meaningful changes. "The search for feminist jurisprudence is generated a feminist chal-lenge to the power of law as it is presently constituted, but it ends with the cel-ebration of positivistic, scientific feminism which seeks to replace one hierarchy of truth with another" (ibid., 89). Still, others advocate for "feminist or woman's law" in order to "describe, explain and understand women's legal position, especially for the purpose of improving women's position in the law and society" (Dahl, 1986, 240).

It is often assumed that changes made to advance gender equality will result in unfairness to men. This view not only is used to justify opposition toward equality but also ignores the fact that changes may benefit men. For instance, Cincinnati Bell Telephone was brought to court for failure to hire women to work on telephone poles. The court upheld that such a practice was discrim-inatory, which caused Cincinnati Bell to devise new and improved equipment so that women could more easily perform the job. Such innovations included making lighter ladders and tools with improved torque that required less mus-cle power. The male workers responded, "Why didn't you do this a long time ago?" Such changes made the job open to a wider range of male workers as well as female workers. This is similar to the point made earlier that the fem-inist research on the causes of women's criminality has helped us to better understand male criminality as well (e.g., the risk of childhood victimization as a precursor to delinquency).

As stated earlier, some women are physically stronger than some men. Even so, exceptionally strong women historically have been denied access to "men's" jobs that require physical strength. Unfortunately, such dedication to exclusively male occupations is not restricted to jobs associated with high use of physical strength. Traditionally, women have faced obstacles in their efforts to enter fields associated with strong mental abilities such as science, engineer-ing, law, and medicine. Ironically, women's so-called tender susceptibility has barred them from prestigious professions "but not from grueling and indeli-cate occupations like factory and field labor" (Rhode, 1990, 200). Only in the past couple of decades has women's access to traditionally male jobs become more commonplace.

Understanding the distinction between sex and gender informs us that most differences between men and women and boys and girls are societally based (gender), not biologically determined (sex). Although this is encouraging in that we are more likely to be able to change society than we are to alter biology, this book examines how gender differences are strongly entrenched in tradition and have negatively affected the lives of women and girls, including in the crime-processing system. Furthermore, sex differences, such as the ability to become pregnant, have also worked to women's disadvantage in many law cases.

WHAT IS FEMINISM?

Feminism and feminists recognize that gender inequalities exist in society, and they value change that enhances gender equality. While the perspectives of feminism are numerous, the approach has been to attempt to answer the "woman question(s)," where "partial and provisional answers intersect, joining together both to lament the ways in which women have been oppressed, repressed, and suppressed and to celebrate the ways in which so many women have 'beaten the system,' taken charge of their own destinies, and encouraged each other" (Tong, 1989, 1–2). Although the first "unmistakably feminist voices were heard in England in the seventeenth century," feminist philosopher Alison Jaggar states:

> In a sense, feminism has always existed. Certainly, as long as women have been subordinated, they have resisted that subordination. Sometimes the resistance has been collective and conscious; at other times it has been solitary and only half-conscious, as when women have sought escape from their socially prescribed roles through illness, drug and alcohol addiction, and even madness. (1983, 1)

Black feminist bell hooks defines feminism simply as "the struggle to end sexist oppression" (1984, 26). She compares patriarchy to racism and other forms of oppression and points out that for sexism to end, racism and other forms of oppression cannot remain intact. Feminism, therefore, is part of the larger movement to end domination in all of its forms (hooks, 1990). The aim of feminism

> is not to benefit solely any specific group of women, any particular race or class of women. It [feminism] does not privilege women over men. It has the power to transform in a meaningful way all our lives. (hooks, 1984, 26)

Unfortunately, a number of myths have damaged the concept of feminism as a legitimate issue and approach. Journalist Susan Faludi (1991) documents in her book *Backlash* how the media and politicians sometimes exaggerate or manipulate statistics and incidences in order to condemn feminism and keep women in gender-specified roles. Daly and Chesney-Lind (1988) identify three myths about feminism: (1) Feminism lacks objectivity; (2) feminist analysis narrowly focuses on women; and (3) there is only one feminist perspective. Regarding charges that feminism lacks objectivity, Daly and Chesney-Lind (1988) point out that men and nonfeminists are no more objective about gender issues than are women and feminists. The problem is that too often "men's experiences are taken as the norm and are generalized to the population" (ibid., 500). With regard to the criticism that feminism focuses too narrowly on women, in fact, feminist analysis does not ignore men and masculinity; rather, men are included in—but are not the center of—the analysis. Obviously, it is necessary to examine masculinity and men's lives and viewpoints in order to fully understand women's lives (ibid.). "The irony is that feminist scholarship is characterized as being only about women or as hopelessly biased toward women, when in fact the project is to describe and change both men's and women's lives" (ibid., 501).

Feminist theory, overall, "is a woman-centered description and explanation of human experience and the social world. It asserts that gender governs every aspect of personal and social life. . . . Also, feminist theory is activist and seeks social change to end the neglect and subordination of women" (Danner, 1989, 51). An examination of feminist analysis quickly establishes that there are many feminist perspectives. The five major strains of feminist theory are liberal, Marxist, socialist, radical, and postmodernist feminism. The origins of liberal feminism can be traced back to the late eighteenth century with Mary Wollstonecraft's publication *A Vindication of the Rights of Women* and later John Stuart Mill's article "The Subjection of Women." Fundamentally, liberal feminists argue that women's access to equality in education and employment, or the "public world" in general, is blocked by customary and legal constraints (Tong, 1989). Gender justice, therefore, requires that the rules to the "game" are fair and that no one's civil rights and economic opportunities are disadvantaged in playing the "game" (ibid.).

Marxist feminists, on the other hand, are most concerned with inequalities set up in a capitalist society. They believe that abolition of a class society, where the means of production are shared and wealth is not owned by a few, will liberate women because they won't be economically dependent on men. Marxist feminists do not view women's oppression as a result of individuals' intentional actions but rather as due to the political, economic, and social structures of capitalism (ibid.). Marxist feminism is most concerned with work-related inequities and has advanced understanding of the trivialization of women's work in the home (especially raising children) and the boring, poorly paid jobs women have predominantly occupied (ibid.).

The socialist and radical feminist theories are largely reactions to Marxist feminism. In particular, socialist feminism purports that class alone fails to explain women's subjugation; thus, both class and the patriarchy must be examined as dual systems of domination (ibid.). "Without overthrowing the economic system of capitalism, as socialists and communists organize to do, we cannot liberate women *and* everybody else who is oppressed" (Wong, 1991,

290). Gender and class play equal roles in explaining women's oppression (Tong, 1989). Socialist feminists criticize Marxist feminists for implying that the abuse women suffer from men is inconsequential compared with what the proletariat (worker) endures from the bourgeoisie (the production managers and owners) (ibid.).

Radical feminists, also disillusioned with Marxist feminism, first organized in the 1960s and 1970s. Radical feminism was also a result of women active in the "New Left" antiwar and civil rights movements being treated as "second-class" citizens within these movements (Donovan, 1985). Unlike Marxist feminists, radical feminists believe that patriarchy is central to women's oppression. Radical feminism points out that Marxist feminism's focus on work-related concerns has left little room to address other feminist issues, particularly reproductive freedom and violence against women (Tong, 1989). Radical feminism is also more apt than the other strains of feminism to hold individual men, rather than society, responsible for oppressing women (ibid.).

Finally, postmodernist feminism argues against socialist feminism's "unrealistic" goal to synthesize feminism and find one theory to explain women's oppression (ibid.). Rather, postmodernists propose that because women's experiences differ based on class, race, sexual, and cultural lines, feminist theory should reflect this (Gagnier, 1990). For example, legal scholar Angela P. Harris (1990, 588) warns against the practice of *gender essentialism:* "[t]he notion that there is a monolithic 'women's experience' that can be described independent of other facets of experience like race, class, and sexual orientation. . . ." Furthermore, Harris (ibid., 589) states that "feminist essentialism paves the way for unconscious racism." She reports on the harm in essentialism:

> In my view, however, as long as feminists, like theorists in the dominant culture, continue to search for gender and racial essences, black women will never be anything more than a crossroads between two kinds of domination, or at the bottom of a hierarchy of oppressions; we will always be required to choose pieces of ourselves to present as wholeness. (ibid.)

Crenshaw (1989) elaborates on this approach, arguing that there is a tendency to treat race and gender as mutually exclusive categories of experience and analysis, with the result that law suits addressing discrimination are defined "by white women's and Black men's experiences" (p. 143).

> Black women sometimes experience discrimination in ways similar to white women's experiences; sometimes they share very similar experiences with Black men. Yet often they experience double-discrimination— the combined effects of practices which discriminate on the basis of race, and on the basis of sex. And sometimes, they experience discrimination as Black women—not the sum of race and sex discrimination, but as Black women. (ibid., 149)

Johnson-Odim (1991) discusses the necessity of addressing Third World women's needs in defining feminist and women's needs. She exams women living in the Third World as well as what she refers to as "Third World women

living in the Western World." She therefore defines the former as residents of
" 'underdeveloped'/overexploited geopolitical entities" and the latter as
"oppressed nationalities from these world areas who are now resident in 'developed' First World countries" (ibid., 314). Regardless of whether these Third
World women are living in the Third World or are residents in the First World,
Johnson-Odim argues that these women's needs for change are far greater than
simply gender equality.

> The point is that factors other than gender figure integrally in the op-
> pression of Third World women and that, even regarding patriarchy,
> many Third World women labor under indigenous inequitable gender
> relationships exacerbated by Western patriarchy, racism, and exploitation.
> For Third World women resident in the West, race and class, along with
> gender, have been indivisible elements in their oppression. (ibid., 321)

In an analysis of "lesbians and the law" in Canada, Eaton (1990) effectively
highlights some of the additional legal (as well as social) forms of discrimination experienced by lesbians, compared to their heterosexual sisters. Moreover,
Eaton's overview is very applicable to "lesbians and the law" in most Western
countries, and much of the legal and social homophobic responses to lesbians
are also experienced by gay men. Some of the examples of additional oppression experienced by lesbian (relative to "straight") women are: (1) they cannot
legally marry nor can they reap the social and legal benefits from this institution (e.g., health benefits, legal rights, and so on); (2) lesbians are more at risk
of being labeled as "sexual aggressors" (particularly in terms of sexual relationships with "straight" women); (3) women who divorce husbands and identify themselves as lesbians risk losing the custody of their children (a significant
reason to keep women with young children "closeted"); and (4) lesbians have
less legal protection for basic human rights (e.g., in acquiring and maintaining
housing, employment, and services).

Rosemarie Tong concludes her book on feminist thought by relating that
although these various approaches to feminism are at times confusing and
splintered, "feminist thought permits each woman to think her own thoughts.
Apparently, not the truth but the truths are setting women free" (1989, 238).
Despite the various frameworks of feminist thought presented in this section,
it appears that all of the feminist perspectives presented here are increasingly
adopting the need for inclusion of many women's experiences and recognizing that gender intersects with race/ethnicity, class, sexuality, national identity,
religion, and other forms of oppression. This is certainly true of socialist feminism (Danner, 1989, 51). Or, as Naffine (1996, 29) states in her book on feminism and criminology, it is "apparent that none of the divisions between the
different styles of feminism stand firmly."

For the purposes of this book, I described these various types of feminism
to clarify that "not all feminists think alike." On the other hand, there is a
common thread among feminists: Men and women should be treated equally
but frequently are not. Although many find the word *feminist* too "political,"
the tendency is to wrongly reduce it to mean "man hating." It is hoped that

readers of this book who fall into that category were enlightened by this section documenting what feminism is, the ways it has grown (particularly in becoming more inclusive regarding race, class, and sexuality), and the overview of "feminist" problems that this book addresses. Naffine notes that despite the differences between some of the "feminisms," they all have one thing in common:

> The animating force of their scholarship is both political and intellectual. It is to think about women's lives in new ways, and so improve the lives of women. All of these feminist criminologies have therefore helped us to see crime differently—with greater intellectual rigour and with a sharpened sense of the political significance of the purposes and methods of criminology. (ibid.)

It is also hoped that readers will see ways that feminist changes potentially help men and boys, too.

WHAT IS FEMINIST METHOD?

It is useful to follow a discussion on feminist theory with a brief section on feminist method. This is because it is useful to recognize that not only does feminist theory distinguish itself from many theories (other than Marxist and radical theories) in its efforts to be applied and actually result in changes in society, but that in many senses, feminist theory purports a variety of means of collecting data, particularly in terms of hearing women's voices. For example, Maher (1997) writes in her book on women crack users that she was partially motivated to conduct her research because of the ways these women were presented as "monsters" in the media: "I want to present the accounts of a group of women we hear much about but little from. . ." (ibid., x). Additionally, it is important to address that feminist theory and methods are not designed to understand women exclusively. Notably, to fully address male offending, it appears very useful to use feminist theory and applications of masculinity to explain males' risk of offending. Instead, it appears that research on crime has attempted to design theories to explain boys' and men's criminality and then tried to "fit" them to girls and women (also known as "the add-women-and-stir approach" and "the generalizability problem") (see Daly and Chesney-Lind, 1988; Naffine, 1996).

> The maleness of crimes is true of the United States of America, of Britain, of Australia and indeed of all Western countries. Men are the vast majority of violent and non-violent offenders. . . . In view of this remarkable sex bias in crime, it is surprising that gender has not become *the* central preoccupation of the criminologist, rather than an afterthought. Surely it would be natural to ask the "man question": what is it about men that makes them offend and what is it about women that makes them law-abiding? (ibid., 6)

The focus on method in criminology has been "empirical criminology," or rather, how can we scientifically understand such important criminological and criminal processing questions as "Why do (some) people commit crimes?" "What policies best deter offenders from future offending?" "How are decisions made by the police, prosecutors, judges, parole review boards, and others?" "Who frequently do different types of crimes occur?" "What increases people's chances of victimization?" and "How can victims of crimes best heal?" We can approach answers to these research questions empirically (scientifically) through a number of means. Feminist methods might mean coming up with more sensitive questions to quantify a rate or determining how best to interview women and girls about the questions that need to be asked. Concerning the issue of more sensitive questions, for example, it was common before the 1980s to measure rape occurrence as the number of rapes reported to the police. Feminist researchers later began asking the women, knowing that many rape victims do not report their victimizations to the police. Next it became apparent that asking women whether they have been raped "lost" a number of rapes, given that many women and girls do not define their experiences so that they legally "fit" the definition of rape as "rape." Now it is known that the best method to capture rape rates is to ask women whether they have been "forced to have sex" rather than simply asking "Have you been raped?" The former wording captures a far more accurate measure of rape.

An important intersection in the recently forthcoming research on gender and crime in the past 25 years is that, given the relative newness research in this area, particularly from a feminist perspective, much of this research is exploratory in nature. That is, the researcher may not have a formed hypothesis but may instead be trying to determine what questions need to be asked. Exploratory research is more consistent with qualitative methods than quantitative methods. At the same time, many scholars minimize or decry qualitative findings as "unscientific" and "ungeneralizable." Although quantitative data collection and analysis are preferred to determine rates of particular phenomena and ways in which various phenomena may or may not be related to each other, without collecting extensive qualitative data we may not even know which variables to include in quantitative models.

For example, while I was conducting focus groups with incarcerated girls in Ohio, I was initially unsure about the types of questions to ask. I had some ideas from the existing research, but given the sexist nature of much of it (including the many that did not even include girls in the sample), it was difficult to figure out exactly what we wanted to "count." After conducting numerous focus groups across the state with both the girls and those who work with them, the research team formed much better ideas about "what to count." For example, we noticed that many of the girls had at least one parent who was dead, many had witnessed horrible violence (such as a parent being murdered), and many faced sexism in their schools. Thus we used the existing research *and* the findings from our qualitative focus groups to design a detailed quantitative survey that we then distributed to over 500 youth around Ohio (Holsinger, Belknap, & Sutherland, 1999).

Another example of the need for qualitative and exploratory research can be seen in the research on woman battering. Since the early 1980s this research has largely been conducted with little or no victim/survivor input. My own research has been "guilty" of this in that I asked the police or used police records to determine police responses to battered women and batterers (e.g., Belknap, 1995; Jones and Belknap, 1999) with no accounting of victims' accounts of *their* experiences. This is not necessarily "wrong" unless it is the *only* type of research on the police processing of battering cases that exists, which is somewhat true until recent years. Some of the qualitative studies giving domestic violence victims' "voice" in more recent years exemplify the ways that the criminal-processing system sometimes *limits* women's attempts to leave their batterers and gain safety (e.g., Erez and Belknap, 1998; Websdale, 1995a, 1995b; Websdale and Johnson, 1997). The traditional police data research rarely documented ways the police and other personnel were remiss in processing these cases. Similarly, the exploratory research on woman offenders offers lengthy qualitative quotes from these women and provides unprecedented insight into their lives and incarceration experiences (e.g., Artz, 1999; Owen, 1998; Richie, 1996).

Finally, feminist research methods perhaps more than any other method, have attempted to focus on the relationship between the researcher and those studied:

> The reason that feminist scientific work represents an improvement
> on the older methods is that feminists have generally been more self-
> reflective than orthodox criminologists. They have been conscious of
> the political goals of their inquiry, and they have explored the methods
> which are more sensitive to the effects of the relationship between inves-
> tigator and investigated. (Naffine, 1996, 31)

EFFECT OF SOCIETAL IMAGES
ON WOMEN IN CRIME

It is difficult to understand how women victims, offenders, and professionals are viewed and treated in the crime-processing system without first understanding the images of women in society. Rafter and Stanko (1982) have identified six images of women that influence how they are perceived in the crime-processing system and in society as a whole when they offend, are victimized, or work in crime-processing jobs. Rafter and Stanko's (ibid.) first image is woman as the *pawn of biology,* where women are viewed as "gripped by biological forces beyond [their] control" (ibid., 3). For example, when Walter Mondale selected Geraldine Ferraro as his running mate during the 1984 presidential election, numerous journalists and others made observations such as "What if he dies and she becomes president? She might go through menopause and get us involved in a nuclear war." Similarly, women's menstruation and premenstrual syndrome have often been inappropriately used to explain women's behavior or even used as reasons why women should not be allowed to be astronauts. Regarding the practice, both historically and currently, to limit women's opportunities due to their "unpredictable mood swings," Karlene Faith (1993, 46) points out the irony of this given the "overwhelming evidence that male angers and mood swings present significantly more danger to other people."

The second image of women offered by Rafter and Stanko (1982) is woman as *impulsive and nonanalytical,* where women are perceived to act illogically and intuitively. A person with these perceived characteristics is unlikely to be hired as a professional, particularly to deal with crime or important court cases. The third image, women as *passive and weak,* implies that women are easy prey for victimization, will blindly follow criminal men into a life of crime, and as professionals are incapable of assuming authority. Rafter and Stanko's (ibid., 3) fourth image, women as *impressionable and in need of protection,* implies that women are "gullible and easily led astray." Again, this stereotype makes women appear inadequate for crime-processing jobs. Furthermore, it is less likely to be available as a "loop hole" for a lesser sentence if the offender is of color than if she is white. Rafter and Stanko's (ibid.) fifth image, the *active woman as masculine,* views any women who break from stereotypical passive roles as deviant and likely to be criminal. This woman is also likely to be viewed as lesbian (whether she is or not); thus, she is prey to the hostility and discrimination associated with homophobia in society. The active woman as masculine is consistent with two of the images Karlene Faith (1993) identified of "unruly women" in films and movies. Specifically, Faith discusses how strong women in movies are depicted as "masculine" and how lesbian characters are often presented as "villains." Rafter and Stanko's final image, the criminal woman as *purely evil,* implies that it is worse for women than for men to be criminal because women not only are breaking out of law-abiding boundaries but, perhaps more important, are stepping out of stereotypical gender role boundaries. One of Faith's (ibid.) categories of depictions of women in popular film, "devil woman," is analogous to Rafter and Stanko's (1982) criminal woman as purely evil. Faith's (1993) "devil woman" films are those where offending girls and women have close links with the devil (e.g., *Rosemary's Baby* (1968), *The Exorcist* (1973), or are just simply evil (e.g., *The Bad Seed* (1956)).

Criminology research has also helped to reinforce stereotypes of women and girls, which affects their assessment in society and the crime-processing system. For instance, the concept of "victim precipitation," used by Hans Von Hentig, Menachem Amir, and Marvin E. Wolfgang, has largely been used to see how women (and men) "attract" victimization. Whether it is to reinforce myths that women who wear certain clothes are "asking to be raped" or that women who stay in battering relationships are "masochistic," victim precipitation models have often been used to deny women's real risk of victimization while at the same time blaming them for this victimization.

Feminist research on other images includes acknowledgment that women's lives have been dichotomized into "madonnas" or "whores" (Feinman, 1986).

This model asserts that women are often assigned to either a madonna category, where they are sweet and passive and produce children, or to a whore category, which includes any women who don't follow the prescribed societal role defined by the madonna category (ibid.). Young (1986) challenges the madonna/whore typology to the extent that it may apply only to white women. She claims that where the madonna/whore dichotomy implies a good girl/bad girl dichotomy, categories for women of color include no "good girl" categories. Instead, she views African-American women as falling into four categories, all of which are negative. The amazon is seen as inherently violent and capable of protecting herself; the sinister sapphire is vindictive, provocative, and not credible; the mammy is viewed as stupid, passive, and bothersome; and the seductress is sexually driven and noncredible as a victim or professional (ibid.). DeFour (1990) discusses the additional ramifications for women and girls of color regarding sexual harassment. She argues that these women may be more at risk of sexual harassment victimization, yet receive the least serious responses, due to societal portrayals of them as "very sexual" and "desiring sexual attention" more than their white sisters. She points to cultural myths portraying Hispanic women as "hot-blooded," Asian women as "exotic sexpots," and Native American women as "devoted to male elders" (ibid., 49). These limited categories are damaging for women of color. The categories also fail to account for the diversity among women and how identical behaviors (such as engaging in sexual activity or committing crimes) can be viewed quite differently based on whether a man or woman is "acting out" the behavior.

It is useful to examine the images of women and crime in the popular media using specific examples. One example is that two movies (that were released about the same time) about women offenders were reviewed by the public and the media very differently. Specifically, the movie *Pretty Woman* received numerous accolades as a romance and a "fun" movie. The movie portrayed a sex worker who married one of her patrons. One could argue that the effect of this "feel good" movie on girls would be "Wow! Prostituting results in finding handsome, wonderful husbands!" which is hardly the message mainstream U.S. culture supports. About the same time period as *Pretty Woman,* the film *Thelma and Louise* was released. This movie depicted women taking a road trip where one shoots and kills a man trying to rape the other in a parking lot. The woman who shoots fears (it would seem legitimately, given information provided later in this book) that she is going to receive serious prison time for killing this rapist. This results in the two women trying to evade the police. Despite a significant amount of public acclaim for this film, a significant number of people, including journalists, portrayed this as a "bad" message for girls. Notably, the reviews for *Pretty Woman* never came to that conclusion. One could argue that the overall message is that it is acceptable to be a prostitute but not to shoot a man trying to rape your friend. Another example, raised by a man in one of my courses, regarded hypocrisy in television warnings. He described how one night when he was watching T.V., there were numerous warnings about an upcoming "Different World" episode dealing with date rape, suggesting that perhaps children should not watch it or that the content might be offensive to some viewers. On the same channel, the same evening, a movie was broadcast showing teenage boys spying on women taking showers through a peep hole in the wall. No warnings were made to the viewers that this movie contained potentially offensive material.

A final example of images of criminal as gendered is the way the recent "school shootings" have been portrayed in the media. These shootings have been committed exclusively by white boys, and the targets have disproportionately been girls (Steinem, 1999). However, the media fail to identify this as gendered. Additionally, after the inundating images we get of males of color as violent offenders in the media, little has been made of these boys' race/ethnicity. After the Columbine High School shootings in Colorado in 1999, journalists were asking, "What's wrong with our children?" (Steinem, 1999). It seems a better question would be, "What's wrong with how we're raising our boys? Why do we have so many of these school shootings? Why are girls the main target?"

Finally, in our discussion of popular images of women and girls, it is useful to remember that girls and women who merely fail to adhere to stereotyped gender norms, regardless of whether their appearance or actions are in fact criminal, are often viewed as offensive simply for violating the gender norm. Karlene Faith refers to such women as "unruly":

> The unruly woman is the undisciplined woman. She is renegade from the disciplinary practices which would mold her as a gendered being. She is the defiant woman who rejects authority which would subjugate her and render her docile. She is the offensive woman who acts in her own interests. She is the unmanageable woman who claims her own body, the whore, the wanton woman, the wild woman out of control. She is the woman who cannot be silenced. She is a rebel. She is trouble. (Faith, 1993, 1)

DIVERSITY AMONG WOMEN

One of the many challenges for feminism in general and feminist criminology in particular is the paradox of acknowledging diversity among women while claiming women's unity in experiences of oppression and sexism (Daly and Chesney-Lind, 1988, 502). Historically, feminist scholarship has focused too strongly on the lives and experiences of European American (Anglo or white), largely middle-class, women. This focus has failed to account for the diversity in women's experiences and backgrounds and the importance of race and class in particular in discussing women's and girls' experiences. "Experience of racial prejudice, for example, is an integral part of 'being Black' and Black women's experiences of crime and in the criminal justice system obviously differ from white women's because of this" (Morris, 1987, 15).

Feminist legal theorists have proposed the concept of multiple consciousness: that we are often born with more than one identity (Harris, 1990; Matsuda, 1989). Multiple consciousness is a "process in which propositions are constantly put forth, challenged, and subverted" (Harris, 1990). A reason for this challenge and subversion, according to Harris (ibid., 585), is the phenomenon (discussed previously) referred to as "gender essentialism," in which women's experiences are "isolated and described independently of race, class, sexual orientation, and other realities of experience." Similarly, Asian American legal scholar Mari J. Matsuda (1989, 7) describes how legal training in most law schools includes "training the students out of the muddle-headed world where everything is relevant and into the lawyer's world where the few critical facts prevail." Matsuda describes how this training results in bifurcated thinking, separating what one believes is relevant from what one's legal training has taught is relevant. This involves "shifting back and forth between consciousness as a Third World person and the white consciousness required for survival in elite educational institutions" (ibid., 8). Further, a woman of color may feel more able to bring up issues of male violence in a law or criminal justice class where the professor is a white woman instead of a white man, but she may not feel that she can safely bring up issues of racism as well as male violence. Or a woman of color attorney may feel able to bring up her client's racism experiences before a man of color judge but feel less comfortable discussing her client's sexism experiences relevant to the case. Hence, multiple consciousness is the result. However, multiple consciousness as a method "encompasses more than consciousness-shifting as skilled advocacy. It encompasses as well the search for the pathway to a just world" (ibid., 9). Matsuda closes with this information:

> I cannot pretend that I, as a Japanese American, truly know the pain of, say, my Native American sister. But I can pledge to educate myself so that I do not receive her pain in ignorance. And I can say as an American, I am choosing as my heritage the 200 years of struggle by poor and working people, by Native Americans, by women, by people of color, for dignified lives in this nation. I can claim as my own the Constitution my father fought for at Anzio, the Constitution that I swore to uphold and defend when I was admitted to the bar. It was not written for me, but I can make it my own, using my chosen consciousness as a woman and person of color to give substance to those tantalizing words "equality" and "liberty." (ibid., 10)

Finally Ruth Chigwada-Bailey (1997, 25) notes. "The various intersections between race, gender, and class oppression—and other differentiating characteristics—affect how and when *all* women experience sexism."

In the same vein, this book hopes to make women's and girls' lives visible as victims, as offenders, and as professionals in the crime-processing system, while acknowledging that women's and girls' experiences may differ based on their race, class, sexual preference, national origin, and other personal characteristics.

It is important to note the more recent identification of *hate crimes* as a social problem and the subsequent studies on this. There is some debate by both scholars and activists as to whether "sex/gender" should be one of the target-group categories of hate-crime victimizations, under the assumption that women and girls are battered and raped because they are female. Regardless of one's feelings about which groups should be legally protected in hate-crime legislation (e.g., racial minorities, lesbian/gay/bisexual/transgendered persons, persons with disabilities, religious minorities, and so on), it seems clear that women in these proposed subgroups are at more risk of hate-crime victimization (including rape and murder) than women who do not fit into these categories (e.g., Brenner, 1995; Ferber, 1998; Jenness and Broad, 1997; Levin and McDevitt, 1997). A particularly chilling account is Claudia Brenner's (1995) autobiography about her experiences of being shot and witnessing her partner's murder while camping because a male camper who saw them from a distance was angry they were lesbians. In addition to physical victimization, another significant form of hate crimes in most hate-crime legislation is the destruction of property (e.g., painting swastikas on synagogues, painting racial or homophobic slurs on people's homes or businesses, and so on). In 1994 some students at the University of New Mexico took, hid, and defaced with offensive slogans and symbols over 100 books in the gender and gay studies section of the library (Hood and Rollins, 1995).

SUMMARY

This chapter presented the numerous ways that women's and girls' experiences as victims, offenders, and professionals in the crime-processing system have been made invisible. The concepts of sex, gender, feminism, and patriarchy were explored. Finally, this chapter discussed the importance of not assuming a monolithic experience for women and girls and the reasons race, class, sexual preference, and other variables must be considered when discussing and researching women's and girls' experiences and behaviors.

REFERENCES

Acker, Joan. 1990. "Hierarchies, Jobs, Bodies: A Theory of Gendered Organizations." *Gender and Society* 4:139–158.

American Correctional Association. 1990. *The Female Offender: What Does the Future Hold?* Arlington, VA: Kirby Lithographic Company.

Amir, Menachem. 1971. *Patterns in Forcible Rape.* Chicago: University of Chicago Press.

Arnold, Regina. 1990. "Processes of Victimization and Criminalization of Black Women." *Social Justice* 17:153–166.

Artz, Sibylle. 1999. *Sex, Power and the Violent School Girl.* New York: Teachers College Press.

Belknap, Joanne. 1995. "Law Enforcement Officers' Attitudes about the Appropriate Responses to Woman Battering." *International Review of Victimology* 4(1):47–62.

Belknap, Joanne, and Kristi Holsinger. 1998. "An Overview of Delinquent Girls: How Theory and Practice Have Failed and the Need for Innovative Changes." Pp. 31–64 in *Female Crime and Delinquency: Critical Perspectives and Effective Interventions,* edited by R. T. Zaplin. Gaithersburg, MD: Aspen Publishing, Inc.

Blee, Kathleen. 1991. *Women of the Klan: Racism and Gender in the 1920s.* Berkeley, CA: University of California Press.

Brenner, Claudia. 1995. *Eight Bullets.* Ithica, NY: Firebrand Press.

Browne, Angela. 1987. *When Battered Women Kill.* New York: Free Press.

Carlen, Pat. 1983. *Women's Imprisonment: A Study in Social Control.* London: Routledge and Kegan Paul.

Chesney-Lind, Meda, and Noelie Rodriguez. 1983. "Women under Lock and Key." *Prison Journal* 53:47–65.

Chesney-Lind, M., and R. G. Shelden. 1992. *Girls, Delinquency and Juvenile Justice.* Pacific Grove, CA: Brooks/Cole.

Chigwada-Bailey, Ruth. 1997. *Black Women's Experiences of Criminal Justice.* Winchester, England: Waterside Press.

Coker, Ann L., Nilam J. Patel, Shanthi Krishnaswami, Wendy Schmidt, and Donna I. Richter. 1998. "Childhood Forced Sex and Cervical Dysplasia among Women Prison Inmates." *Violence Against Women* 4(5):595–608.

Collins, Patricia Hill, Lionel A. Maldonado, Dana Y. Takagi, Barrie Thorne, Lynn Wever, and Howard Winant. 1995. "On Fenstermaker's 'Doing Difference.'" *Gender and Society* 491–505.

Crenshaw, Kimberle. 1989. "Demarginalizing the Intersection of Race and Sex: A Black Feminist Critique of Antidiscrimination Doctrine, Feminist Theory, and Antiracist Politics." *University of Chicago Legal Forum* 14:139–167.

Croall, Hazel. 1995. "Women's Victimization and White-Collar Crime." Pp. 227–245 in *Gender and Crime,* edited by R. E. Dobash, R. P. Dobash, and L. Noaks. Cardiff: University of Wales Press.

Dahl, Tove Stang. 1986. "Taking Women as a Starting Point: Building Women's Law." *International Journal of the Sociology of Law* 14:239–247.

Daly, Kathleen. 1992. "Women's Pathways to Felony Court." *Review of Law and Women's Studies* 2:11–52.

Daly, Kathleen, and Meda Chesney-Lind. 1988. "Feminism and Criminology." *Justice Quarterly* 5:497–538.

Danner, Mona J. E. 1989. "Socialist Feminism: A Brief Introduction." Pp. 51–54 in *New Directions in Critical Criminology,* edited by B. D. MacLean and D. Milovanovic. Vancouver: The Collective Press.

DeFour, Darlene C. 1990. "The Interface of Racism and Sexism on College Campuses." Pp. 45–52 in *Ivory Power: Sexual Harassment on Campus,* edited by M. A. Pauludi. Albany, NY: State University of New York Press.

Dembo, R., L. Williams, W. Wothke, J. Schmeidler, and C. H. Brown. 1992. "The Role of Family Factors, Physical Abuse, and Sexual Victimization Experiences in High-risk Youths' Alcohol and Other Drug Use and Delinquency: A Longitudinal Model." *Violence and Victims* 7(3):245–266.

Dodge, Kenneth A., John E. Bates, and Gregory S. Pettit. 1990. "Mechanisms in the Cycle of Violence." *Science* 250:1678–1683.

Donovan, Josephine. 1985. *Feminist Theory.* New York: Frederick Ungar.

Eaton, Mary. 1990. "Lesbians and the Law." Pp. 109–131 in *Lesbians in Canada,* edited by S. D. Stone. Toronto: Between the Lines.

Edwards, Anne. 1987. "Male Violence in Feminist Theory: An Analysis of the Changing Conception of Sex/Gender

Violence and Male Dominance."
Pp. 13–29 in *Women, Violence, and
Social Control,* edited by J. Hanmer
and M. Maynard. Atlantic Highlands,
NJ: Humanities Press International.

Epstein, Cynthia F. 1988. *Deceptive Distinc-
tions: Sex, Gender, and Social Order.*
New Haven, CT: Yale University
Press.

Erez, Edna, and Joanne Belknap. 1998.
"In Their Own Words: Battered
Women's Assessment of Systemic
Responses." *Violence and Victims*
13(3):3–20.

Faith, Karlene. 1993. *Unruly Women: The
Politics of Confinement and Resistance.*
Vancouver: Press Gang Publishers.

Faludi, Susan. 1991. *Backlash: The Unde-
clared War against Women.* New York:
Doubleday.

Fausto-Sterling, Anne. 1985. *Myths of
Gender: Biological Theories about Women
and Men,* 2nd ed. New York: Basic
Books.

Feinman, Clarice. 1986. *Women in the
Criminal Justice System,* 2nd ed. New
York: Praeger.

Ferber, Abby L. 1998. *White Man Falling:
Race, Gender, and White Supremacy.*
Lanham, MD: Rowman & Littlefield.

Fletcher, Beverly R., and Dreama G.
Moon. 1993. "Introduction."
Pp. 5–14 in *Women Prisoners: A Forgot-
ten Population,* edited by B. R.
Fletcher, L. D. Shaver, and D. G.
Moon. Westport, CT: Praeger.

Freedman, Estelle. 1981. *Their Sisters'
Keepers: Women's Prison Reform in
America, 1830–1930.* Ann Arbor:
University of Michigan Press.

Gagnier, Regenia. 1990. "Feminist Post-
modernism: The End of Feminism or
the Ends of Theory?" Pp. 21–32 in
*Theoretical Perspectives on Sexual Differ-
ence,* edited by D. L. Rhode. New
Haven, CT: Yale University Press.

Gerber, Jurg, and Susan L. Weeks. 1992.
"Women as Victims of Corporate
Crime." *Deviant Behavior* 13:325–347.

Gilfus, Mary E. 1992. "From Victims to
Survivors to Offenders: Women's

Routes of Entry and Immersion into
Street Crime." *Women and Criminal
Justice* 4:63–90.

Harris, Angela. 1990. "Race and Essentialism in Feminist Legal Theory."
Stanford Law Review 42:581–615.

Holsinger, Kristi, Joanne Belknap, and
Jennifer L. Sutherland. 1999. "Assess-
ing the Gender-Specific Program and
Service Needs for Adolescent Females
in the Juvenile Justice System: Final
Report." Office of Criminal Justice
Services, Columbus, OH.

Hood, Jane C., and Stephen Rollins.
1995. "Some Didn't Call It Hate."
Violence Against Women 1(3):228–240.

hooks, bell. 1984. *Feminist Theory: From
Margin to Center.* Boston: South End
Press.

———. 1990. "Feminism: A Transfor-
mational Politic." Pp. 185–196 in
*Theoretical Perspectives on Sexual Differ-
ence,* edited by D. L. Rhode. New
Haven, CT: Yale University Press.

Immarigeon, Russ. 1987a. "Women in
Prison." *Journal of the National Prison
Project* 11:1–5.

———. 1987b. "Few Diversion Programs
Are Offered Female Offenders."
Journal of the National Prison Project
12:9–11.

Immarigeon, Russ, and Meda Chesney-
Lind. 1992. *Women's Prisons: Over-
crowded and Overused.* San Francisco.
National Council on Crime and
Delinquency.

Jaggar, Alison M. 1983. *Feminist Politics
and Human Nature.* Totowa, NJ: Rowman & Allanheld.

James, Jennifer, and Jane Meyerding.
1977. "Early Sexual Experiences and
Prostitution." *American Journal of
Psychiatry* 134(12):1381–1385.

Jenness, Valerie, and Kendal Broad. 1997.
*Hate Crimes: New Social Movements and
the Politics of Violence.* Hawthorne,
NY: Walter de Gruyter.

Johnson-Odim, Cheryl. 1991. "Common
Themes, Different Contexts: Third
World Women and Feminism."
Pp. 314–327 in *Third World Women*

and the Politics of Feminism, edited by C. T. Mohanty, A. Russo, and L. Torres. Bloomington, IN: Indiana University Press.

Jones, Dana A., and Joanne Belknap. 1999. "Police Responses to Battering in a Pro-Arrest Jurisdiction." *Justice Quarterly,* 16(2):249–273.

Klein, Ethel. 1984. *Gender Politics.* Cambridge, MA: Harvard University Press.

Klein, Hugh, and Betty S. Chao. 1995. "Sexual Abuse during Childhood and Adolescence as Predictors of HIV-Related Sexual Risk during Adulthood among Female Sexual Partners of Drug Users." *Violence Against Women* 1(1):55–76.

Kline, S. 1993. A profile of female offenders in state and federal prisons. *Female Offenders: Meeting the Needs of a Neglected Population* (pp. 1–6). Laurel, MD: American Correctional Association.

Lake, E. S. 1993. An exploration of the violent victim experiences of female offenders. *Violence and Victims* 8(1):41–51.

Laub, John H. and Jinney S. Smith. 1995. "Eleanor Touroff Glueck: An Unsung Pioneer in Criminology." *Women and Criminal Justice* 6(2):1–22.

Leonard, Eileen B. 1982. *Women, Crime, and Society.* New York: Longman.

Levin, Jack, and Jack McDevitt. 1997. *Hate Crimes: Rising Tide of Bigotry and Bloodshed.* New York: Plenum Press.

MacKinnon, Catherine. 1989. *Toward a Feminist Theory of State.* Cambridge: Harvard University Press.

————. 1990. "Legal Perspectives on Sexual Difference." Pp. 213–225 in *Theoretical Perspectives on Sexual Difference,* edited by D. L. Rhode. New Haven, CT: Yale University Press.

Madriz, Esther. 1997. *Nothing Bad Happens to Good Girls,* Berkeley, CA: University of California Press.

Maguigan, Holly. 1991. "Battered Women and Self-Defense: Myths and Misconceptions in Current Reform Propos-

als." *University of Pennsylvania Law Review* 140:379–486.

Maher, Lisa. 1997. *Sexed Work: Gender, Race and Resistance in a Brooklyn Drug Market.* Oxford: Clarendon Press.

Matsuda, Mari J. 1989. "When the First Quail Calls: Multiple Consciousness as Jurisprudential Method." *Women's Rights Law Reporter* 2:7–10.

McLean, Sheila A. M. 1988. "Female Victims in the Criminal Laws." Pp. 195–215 in *The Legal Relevance of Gender,* edited by S. McLean and N. Burrows. Atlantic Highlands, NJ: Humanities Press International.

Mead, Rebecca. 1999. "Eggs for Sale: Annals of Reproduction." *The New Yorker Magazine.* August 9:56–65.

Morris, Allison. 1987. *Women, Crime, and Criminal Justice.* Oxford: Basil Blackwell.

Mumola, Christopher J., and Allen J. Beck. 1997. *Prisoners in 1996.* Bureau of Justice Statistics. U.S. Department of Justice, June, 15 pp.

Naffine, Ngaire. 1996. *Feminism and Criminology.* Philadelphia: Temple University Press.

Owen, Barbara. 1998. *In the Mix: Struggle and Survival in a Women's Prison.* Albany, NY: State University of New York Press.

Rafter, Nicole H. 1985. *Partial Justice: Women in State Prisons 1800–1935.* Boston: Northeaster Press.

Rafter, Nicole H., and Elizabeth A. Stanko. 1982. "Introduction." Pp. 1–28 in *Judge, Lawyer, Victim, Thief: Women, Gender Roles and Criminal Justice,* edited by N. H. Rafter and E. A. Stanko. Stoughton, MA: Northeastern University Press.

Renzetti, Claire M. 1993. "On the Margins of the Mainstream (Or They Still Don't Get It, Do They?): Feminist Analyses in Criminal Justice Education." *Journal of Criminal Justice Education* 4:219–249.

Rhode, Deborah L. 1989. *Justice and Gender: Sex Discrimination and the Law.* Cambridge, MA: Harvard University Press.

————. 1990. "Definitions of Difference." Pp. 197–212 in *Theoretical Perspectives on Sexual Difference,* edited by D. L. Rhode. New Haven, CT: Yale University Press.

Richie, Beth E. 1996. *Compelled to Crime: The Gender Entrapment of Black Battered Women.* New York: Routledge.

Rynbrandt, Linda J., and Ronald C. Kramer. 1995. "Hybrid Nonwomen and Corporate Violence." *Violence Against Women* 1(3):206–227.

Sargent, Elizabeth, Susan Marcus-Mendoza, and Chong Ho Yu. 1993. "Abuse and the Woman Prisoner." Pp. 55–64 in *Woman Prisoners: A Forgotten Population,* edited by B. R. Fletcher, L. D. Shaver, and D. B. Moon. Westport, CT: Praeger.

Schneider, E. M., and S. B. Jordon. 1981. "Representation of Women Who Defend Themselves in Response to Physical or Sexual Assault." In *Women's Self-Defense Cases: Theory and Practice,* edited by E. Bochnak. Charlottesville, VA: Michie Company Law Publishers.

Shaw, C., and H. McKay. 1969. *Juvenile Delinquency and Urban Areas.* Chicago: University of Chicago Press.

Silbert, Mimi H., and Ayala M. Pines. 1981. " Sexual Child Abuse as an Antecedent to Prostitution." *Child Abuse and Neglect* 5:407–411.

Smart, Carol. 1989. *Feminism and the Power of Law.* London: Routledge & Kegan Paul.

Stanko, Elizabeth A. 1990. *Everyday Violence: How Women and Men Experience Sexual and Physical Danger.* London: Pandora.

————. 1992. "The Case of Fearful Women: Gender, Personal Safety and Fear of Crime." *Women and Criminal Justice* 4:117–136.

Steinem, Gloria. 1999. "Supremacy Crimes." *MS. Magazine.* August/September:45–47.

Tong, Rosemarie. 1989. *Feminist Thought.* Boulder, CO: Westview Press.

Von Hentig, Hans. 1948. *The Criminal and His Victim.* New Haven, CT: Yale University Press.

Websdale, Neil. 1995a. "An Ethnographic Assessment of the Policing of Domestic Violence in Rural Eastern Kentucky." *Social Justice* 22:102–122.

Websdale, Neil. 1995b. "Rural Woman Abuse: The Voices of Kentucky Women." *Violence Against Women* 1:309–338.

Websdale, Neil, and B. Johnson. 1997. "The Policing of Domestic Violence in Rural and Urban Areas: The Voices of Battered Women in Kentucky." *Policing and Society* 6:297–317.

West, Candace, and Sarah Fenstermaker. 1995. "Doing Difference." *Gender and Society* 9:8–37.

West, Candace, and Don H. Zimmerman. 1987. "Doing Gender." *Gender and Society* 1:125–151.

Widom, Cathy S. 1989a. "Child Abuse, Neglect, and Adult Behavior: Research Design and Findings on Criminality, Violence, and Child Abuse." *American Journal of Orthopsychiatry* 59(3):355–367.

Widom, Cathy S. 1989b. "The Cycle of Violence." *Science* 244:160–166.

Wolfgang, Marvin E. 1958. *Patterns in Criminal Homicide.* Philadelphia: University of Pennsylvania Press.

Wong, Nellie. 1991. "Socialist Feminism: Our Bridge to Freedom." Pp. 288–296 in *Third World Women and the Politics of Feminism,* edited by C. T. Mohanty, A. Russo, and L. Torres. Bloomington, IN: Indiana University Press.

Young, Vernetta D. 1986. "Gender Expectations and Their Impact on Black Female Offenders and Victims." *Justice Quarterly* 3:305–327.

————. 1992. "Fear of Victimization and Victimization Rates among Women: A Paradox?" *Justice Quarterly* 9:419–442.

PART II

✳

Female Offending

2

✳

Critiquing
Criminological Theories

Despite the public's obsession with crime, despite the morbid fear
it arouses, despite the endless volumes written to account for it, sex,
the most powerful variable regarding crime, has been virtually ignored.

(LEONARD, 1982, XI)

Criminology, it seems, is mainly about academic men
studying criminal men and, at best, it would appear that
women represent only a specialism, not the standard fare.

(NAFFINE, 1996, 1)

Criminology is not unique among academic disciplines in its historical exclusion of females from most research questions (see Fausto-Sterling, 1985; Morris, 1987; Smart, 1976; Spender, 1981). Most criminological theories explain why some males, but not females, break the law. Additionally, it has been pointed out that theoretical criminology has been constructed by men and about men (Leonard, 1982; Messerschmidt, 1993; Naffine, 1996). There are two important implications of focusing solely on males' experiences: (1) The theories and findings are really theories and findings about male crime, and (2) we must question the validity of any "general" theory if it does not also apply to women (Morris, 1987, 2).

Rasche (1975) identifies three reasons or excuses why females have been consistently neglected in studies of criminal behavior. First, women make up a small percentage of prisoners (approximately 7 percent, currently). Second, research on female offenders is more likely to be opposed by correctional authorities and by the women themselves than research on male prisoners. In my own and other researchers' experiences, the most threatening aspect of "breaking into" the prisons to do research on women is related to deplorable health care. A number of scholars (including me) have had to remove questions about health care from their surveys and interviews in order to distribute them or have simply been told they cannot do the study given the questions on health care. Another limitation other scholars and I have faced in our research on incarcerated females is the prison authorities allowing questions on the prisoners' prior victimizations before coming to prison but not allowing any questions regarding abuse they experienced *while in prison*. Rasche's (ibid.) third reason/excuse that there is relatively little research on female offenders is that women have generally been deemed insignificant as a topic of interest. In short, the lack of attention to female offenders is largely a result of not defining female offending as a significant social problem.

Historically, the neglect of female crime stands in stark contrast to the extensive amount of research that has been devoted to deviations more consistent with stereotypical aspects of women's lives: maternal deprivation, insanity, and mental breakdowns (Smart, 1976). Further, female lawbreakers historically (and to some degree today) have been viewed as "abnormal" and as "worse" than male lawbreakers—not only for breaking the law but also for stepping outside of prescribed gender roles of femininity and passivity.

Recently the amount and nature of attention to female criminality have begun to change. One reason is that the number of women in prison has increased at an unprecedented rate—indeed, at a pace much greater than male imprisonment (e.g., Acoca and Austin, 1996; Kline, 1993; Pollock-Byrne, 1990). During the 1980s, the number of women in U.S. prisons *tripled* (Church, 1990; Fletcher and Moon, 1993; Immarigeon and Chesney-Lind, 1992; Kline, 1993), while the corresponding increase in males' incarceration rates "only" doubled for the same time period (Kline, 1993). A review of the Bureau of Justice's statistics data indicates that the gender gap in the increasing rate of imprisonment is growing. Specifically, Acoca and Austin's (1996) account of these federal data reports that women's incarceration rates in the United States *almost quadrupled* (increased 386 percent) between 1980 and 1994, while men's rates "only" doubled (increased 214 percent). Moreover, they report that 1 out of every 130 women in the United States (or 794,100 women) were in prison or jail or on probation or parole in 1994. In 1996 alone, there was a 9.1 percent increase in women's incarceration in the United States, while the corresponding increase in men's imprisonment was 4.7 percent (Mumola and Beck, 1997, 5).

Feminists and the women's movement have also helped at least some scholars redefine criminological research as pertaining to females as well as males. Although there still exists a tendency for studies on offenders to be conducted solely on males, grant-giving institutions and journal editors are more likely to request a legitimate explanation as to why a sample would be all male. In short, although there is a great deal of catching up to do in order to understand, respond to, and explain female criminality, important strides have been made in recent years.

This chapter discusses the various schools of criminological theories developed in this and the last century: traditional, strain and subcultural, differential association, labeling, social control, Marxist/radical, and women's liberation/emancipation. During the periods in which these theories developed, studies often either routinely ignored women or viewed them through a stereotypical lens.

THE TRADITIONAL, POSITIVIST STUDIES

The traditional, or original, studies of female criminality were conducted between the end of the nineteenth century and the middle of the twentieth century. The most prominent researchers included Cesare Lombroso and William Ferrero (1895), W. I. Thomas (1923, 1967), Sigmund Freud (1933), and Otto Pollak (1950, 1961). These studies were grounded in the belief that biological determinism accounts for female criminality: Whereas men are rational, women are driven by their biological constitutions. The classical studies were informed by four main assumptions: (1) Individual characteristics, not society, are responsible for criminal behavior; (2) there is an identifiable biological nature inherent in all women; (3) offending women are "masculine," which makes them incompetent as women and thus prone to break the law; and (4) the differences between male and female criminality are due to sex, not gender, differences. The classical theorists, not surprisingly, have been accused of viewing women as turning to crime because of their "perversion of or rebellion against their natural feminine roles" (Klein, 1980, 72). In addition to the sexist nature of the classical studies, they have been classist, racist, and heterosexist, focusing on wealthy, white, married women as the "feminine" standard. These theorists' works are reviewed in the following sections.

The Atavistic Female Offender

Cesare Lombroso, who studied both incarcerated men and women in nineteenth-century Italy, is often referred to as the "father" of criminology. In addition to moving the study of criminology from the domain of legal and social science experts to the domain of biologists, physicians, and psychologists who embraced his positivist approach, Lombroso has been influential in setting the stage for a sexist, racist, and classist view of female criminality. He dismissed the effects of socialization or social-structural constraints as important determinants of criminal behavior. Instead he focused exclusively on the physical and psychological makeup of the individual in determining criminal behavior. Inherent in his approach was the assumption that women are driven by their biological inferiorities, including a madonna/whore duality, where women are either good or bad:

> Implicit in the madonna/whore duality is women's subservience to men, who assumed the role of protectors of the madonna and punishers of the whore. . . . A good woman is a loyal, submissive wife who serves her husband, and for this she is honored and protected. The evil woman, on the other hand, destroys man and brings pain and ruin. (Feinman, 1986, 4)

Lombroso and (his son-in-law) Ferrero's (1895) now-discredited book *The Female Offender* explains female criminality through atavism. Atavism is a concept that defines all deviant behavior as a "throwback" to an earlier evolutionary stage in human development. Thus, in his early theorizing, "Lombroso firmly maintained that deviants are less highly evolved than 'normal' law abiding citizens" (Smart, 1976, 31). Lombroso and Ferrero concluded that women offenders showed less degeneration than men simply because women had not evolved as much as men. Despite their perceived slower evolution, however, women were viewed as less likely than men to be criminal.

In their search for degeneration and atavism, Lombroso and Ferrero measured and documented incarcerated women's craniums, heights, weights, hair color (and baldness), moles, and tattoos. Smart (ibid.) offers a critical analysis of Lombroso and Ferrero's work. "Significantly, although they found some signs of so-called degeneration, like misshapen skulls or very thick black hair," observes Smart (ibid., 31), "the offenders in their study did not fit well into the theory of atavism." Lombroso and Ferrero also assumed that criminal behavior was a sex, not a gender, trait. This led to the tenuous assumption that a woman exhibiting criminal tendencies "is not only an abnormal woman, she is biologically like a man" (ibid., 33). Finally, Smart (ibid.) has criticized Lombroso and Ferrero's analysis for assuming that middle-class women's inactive and dependent roles in nineteenth-century Europe were "natural." This view fails to acknowledge the varied roles of women in other places and times.

Given this context, it is hardly surprising that kleptomania, a biological "explanation" of middle-class, white women's shoplifting, was identified in the late nineteenth century as a "uterine ailment" (Abelson, 1989). More recently, in the 1970s and 1980s, PMS (premenstrual syndrome) was often characterized as a biological problem of all women. This reinforced cultural stereotypes and implications about women's "place" and was even used as a defense in trials of women accused of murder (see Rittenhouse, 1991). Thus, the marks of biologism and women continue to linger.

The Unadjusted Girl

W. I. Thomas's work, published in the books *Sex and Society* (1907) and *The Unadjusted Girl* (1923, 1967), was heavily influenced by Lombroso, although Thomas was more liberal. Thomas advanced Lombroso's work to define criminality as "a socially induced pathology rather than a biological abnormality" (Smart, 1976, 37). Similar to Lombroso and Ferrero, however, Thomas viewed differences in males' and females' likelihood to become "politicians, great artists, and intellectual giants" as a result of sex rather than gender, thus overlooking the strong societal restrictions of women during that era (ibid.). An example of a "sex" difference that Thomas attributed to women was the inclusion of more varieties of love in their nervous systems:

> [Thomas] argued that it was this additional and intense need to give and feel love that leads women into crime, particularly sexual offenses like prostitution. The prostitute, he argued, is merely looking for the love and tenderness which all women need, but the means by which she seeks satisfaction are not socially approved. (ibid., 39)

Again, these assumptions completely deny the socialization of women and girls and the very real constraints on their opportunities. The reality is very different from what Thomas suggests, given that most sex workers are driven into this occupation due to the lack of well-paying legitimate occupations. This relates to the film *Pretty Woman* (discussed in Chapter 1), that is, that sex workers are simply "looking for love." It also, like the film, suggests that women find "love and tenderness" in prostitution, which could not be farther from the truth.

Further, Thomas "equated female delinquency with sexual delinquency," confusing "promiscuity" with crime; notably, this kind of logic never occurs in studies of male crime (Heidensohn, 1985, 117). The disadvantaged position of women and girls in society was of little importance to Thomas in his accounting of male and female differences. His later work, however, acknowledged that women were property of men, and he departed from social Darwinism to examine the complexity of the interaction between society and the individual (Klein, 1980).

Thomas's analyses of class and sexuality are overly simplistic. He views class, sex, sexuality, and crime as related to each other. According to Thomas, middle-class women are invested in protecting their chastity and thus commit few crimes; poor women, on the other hand, long for crime in the manner of a new experience. In fact, he believed that delinquent girls manipulate males into sex as a means of achieving their own goals. Thus, Thomas favors psychological over economic motivations to explain female criminality. Given that Thomas was writing in an era of mass illness and starvation, the choice to ignore economic deprivation as a potential cause of female crime is rather remarkable (ibid.).

Anatomy as Destiny

Psychiatrist Sigmund Freud's attempts to explain female behavior center around the belief that women are anatomically inferior to men—hence, Freud's infamous "penis envy" approach to explaining female behavior. To Freud, the healthy woman experiences heterosexual sex as a receptor, where sexual pleasure consists of pain, while the sexually healthy man is heterosexual and aggressive and inflicts pain (Klein, 1980).

Thus, the deviant woman is a woman who wants to be a man, and she will only end up neurotic in her fruitless search for her own penis. "Women may be viewed," says Klein (ibid., 72) of this psychological explanation, "as turning to crime as a perversion of or rebellion against their natural feminine roles." Included in this analysis is a glorification of women's duties as wives and mothers, and, in turn, the view that treatment involves "helping" deviant women adjust to their "proper," traditional gender roles (ibid.). Again, in addition to the obvious sexism, Freud's theories are fraught with racism, classism, and heterosexism: "Only upper- and middle-class women could possibly enjoy lives as sheltered darlings. Freud sets hegemonic standards of femininity for poor and Third World women" (ibid., 89).

As recently as 1977 Freud's approach to understanding male v. female offending was used to guide a study that focused on the relationship between fire, urination, and phallus (Felthous and Yudowitz, 1977). Keep in mind that the authors were serious about testing Freud's assertion that yet another way that penis-envy plays out is that women are excluded from the manly act and long to be able to distinguish a fire by urinating on it. The authors claim that although sociopathology "is a considered a male disorder, . . . behavior associated with sociopathology can also be regarded as sex-linked" (ibid., 270). (The authors found that enuresis, firesetting, cruelty to animals, and violent behavior, while all occurring less frequently among male than female offenders, "the presence of these items can be expected to convey comparable significance in both male and female subjects" (ibid., 274).

Behind the Mask

Although Otto Pollak's (1950, 1961) study of female criminality, *The Criminality of Women,* was published more than a half century after Lombroso and Ferrero's work, it has been closely linked with their approach. Like Thomas, Pollak believed that sociological factors, in addition to biological factors, have some relevance in crime determination. To Pollak, however, the fundamental influences on female criminality are biology and physiology; he thus repeats many of the assumptions and prejudices encountered in Lombroso and Ferrero's and Thomas's works (Smart, 1976).

The major thrust of Pollak's analysis is the "masked" nature of female criminality. He assumes that male and female crime rates are similar. In part, claims Pollak, female crime is "masked" by the supposedly chivalrous or lenient treatment of women in the crime-processing system. But Pollak's main point is that women are better at hiding their crimes.

He emphasizes the "deceitful" nature of women, using as supporting evidence females' ability to hide the fact that they are menstruating or having orgasms and their inactive role during sexual intercourse. Pollak fails to consider, however, that women's inactive role during heterosexual sex may be culturally rather than biologically determined. Further, women's training in acquiescence to men, particularly during sex, could account for the fact that women were not hiding orgasms but rather were not experiencing them.

Smart compares Pollak's analysis to Eve's deceit with Adam (in the *Bible*), where women are viewed as evil and cunning:

> It is Pollak's contention that women are the masterminds behind criminal organizations; that they are the instigators of crime rather than the perpetrators; that they can and in fact do manipulate men into committing offenses whilst remaining immune from arrest themselves. (ibid., 47)

Again, Pollak's analysis fails to account for the power imbalance between men and women. His discussion is based purely on speculation, with no empirical evidence. Rather, he is convinced that a great deal of female criminality is undetected and thus unreported.

Legacy of the Positivist Theorists

The enduring effects of the positivists can be viewed in the research on female criminality that was published in the 1960s and 1970s. Similar to Pollak, Gisela Konopka (1966) portrays women in her book *The Adolescent Girl in Conflict* as the instigators of crime. Her main point is that women and girls are driven to crime because of emotional problems, specifically loneliness and sexuality (Klein, 1980). Economic and social explanations are ignored at the expense of explaining female criminality through physiology and psychology.

Similarly, Vedder and Somerville (1970) stress the importance of the female as criminal instigator in *The Delinquent Girl*. Not only do they claim that female delinquency is simply a result of maladjustment to the "normal" female role, but they also ignore the causal importance of social and economic factors. Most disquieting, they attribute high rates of delinquency among black girls to "their lack of 'healthy' feminine narcissism"—an explanation with racist overtones (Klein, 1980, 99). Following this logic, they see therapy as the solution to female delinquency and ignore the need to address the potentially criminogenic social and economic constraints in which many delinquent girls are enmeshed. Finally, in their book *Delinquency in Girls,* Cowie, Cowie, and Slater (1968) use masculinity, femininity, and chromosomes to explain female criminality. "In this perspective, the female offender is different physiologically and psychologically from the 'normal' girl," in that she is too masculine; she is rebelling against her femininity (ibid., 101).

Thus, in the positivist school, because women's behavior was believed to be largely biologically determined, the complexity of women's criminal behavior was reduced to a challenge of the traditional gender role—a role that was not rooted in nature but societally specified. The positivists assumed that the girl or woman who defied the prescribed gender role had a problem, and thus they were blind to the possibility that there was a problem with the prescribed role that women, regardless of resources or situation, are expected to fulfill. Indeed, it has been recognized recently that there is not one societally prescribed role for all women but that "appropriate" gender roles vary depending on a woman's race and class and that a dominant patriarchy does not affect all women the same (Rice, 1990).

STRAIN AND SUBCULTURAL THEORIES

Drawing on Durkheim's anomie (state of normlessness) theory, Robert Merton (1938, 1949) has been credited with developing strain theory. A refreshing departure from biological determinism, Merton's premise is that strain and frustration occur when individuals are taught the same goals in their culture but are denied equal access to legitimately attain these goals. For example, the values of educational success and upward mobility are ingrained in U.S. culture, but not all citizens have the means of achieving these shared values. There are a number of criticisms of strain theory, but the most important—and the one that applies most to girls—is that this framework has examined strains primarily in terms of class inequalities, comparing the strains of the working class to the middle class and then only of boys. Approaches that focus on poverty as an explanation of criminal behavior, while preferable to biological explanations, frequently ignore that "[f]emales constitute the most impoverished group of every Western society, yet females commit by far the least crime" (Faith, 1993, 107).

Delinquent Boys

In his book *Delinquent Boys,* Albert Cohen (1955) adapted Merton's strain theory to explain the development of delinquent gangs among working-class boys in the United States. In Cohen's analysis, boys have broad and varied goals and ambitions, whereas girls' narrow ambitions center around males: dating, dancing, attractiveness, and, generally, acquiring a boyfriend or husband.

> The message from Cohen is manifest. Men are the rational doers and achievers. They represent all that is instrumental and productive in American Culture. Women's world is on the margins. Women exist to be the companions of men and that is their entire lot. . . . While men proceed with their Olympian task of running all aspects of the nation, women perform their role of helpmate. (Naffine, 1987, 11–12)

Cohen thus believes that girls have not adopted the competitive, spirited, successful goals depicted as the "American dream."

A strength of Cohen's (1955) is his addressing the construction of gender *for boys,* in that his work vividly depicts the masculinity of boy delinquents. That is, he is likely the first theorist to actually pay attention to the construction of masculinity, and he drew on Freud to do so. In contrast, he devotes only four pages of his book to girl delinquents. He portrays them as boring and colorless and as expressing their delinquency through sexual promiscuity (Mann, 1984; Naffine, 1987). Cohen thus joins the disturbing tendency in criminological theory to link inextricably girls' criminality and sexuality, while ignoring or implicitly applauding the identical sexual conduct of boys.

In short, Cohen believes that boys have the "real" strains of employment and income in their lives, whereas girls' only strain is to marry well. Cohen was so confident of the accuracy of this stance on girls that he saw no need to confirm his hypothesis through data collection. Interestingly, it has been argued that Cohen's approach to explaining male delinquency has "fallen into disfavor" among criminologists, while in "the literature on women it has yet to be seriously contradicted" (Naffine, 1987, 14). An exception to this is Campbell's (1987) study of Puerto Rican female gang members. She rebuffs Cohen's belief that girls' delinquency is acted out through sexuality, instead claiming that gang membership for females, like males, is a means of fulfilling their identities in an environment plagued with classism, racism, and sexism. Another exception is a study by Joe and Chesney-Lind (1995) of racially diverse gang members in Hawaii. They found that both boys and girls join gangs primarily to resolve boredom and for the sense of social solidarity it provides in an otherwise hostile environment. Similar to Campbell (1987), they note that these youth live in communities "racked by poverty, racism, and rapid population growth" (1995, 427). Indeed, Joe and Chesney-Lind report that, for both boys and girls, gang membership serves as an "alternative family" for these youth who are often neglected and/or abused in their homes. Notably, the strains of neglect and abuse in one's family and daily experiences with poverty and racism are not the types of strains examined in the traditional theories.

Delinquency and Opportunity

Cohen's (mis)portrayal of female delinquents was reaffirmed in Cloward and Ohlin's (1960) *Delinquency and Opportunity*. In Cloward and Ohlin's opportunity theory, boys were viewed as having legitimate struggles to attain the "American dream," whereas girls encounter only frivolous concerns, such as finding boyfriends. Cloward and Ohlin, however, took a different twist in their version of strain theory, which is known as opportunity theory. In this version, the focus was to explain that delinquent subcultural values and gangs served as a collective solution to the frustrations that lower-class urban males experienced in schools and in terms of bleak job prospects. Again, females were left out of the model.

The subculture, often represented by gangs, not only gave juveniles a sense of belonging but also provided them with opportunities to learn illegitimate means to achieve success. (Subcultural theories have been criticized for implying that crime occurs exclusively among the poor [Leonard, 1982].) Cloward and Ohlin's approach is almost identical to Cohen's, concerning male versus female delinquency:

> The delinquent subculture is therefore a male solution to an exclusively male problem. Females are neither pressured to achieve the major success goals of their society nor offered a delinquent outlet for their frustrations. The horizons of the female are confined to the family. The limited nature of their offending, its predominantly sexual nature, reflects this narrow set of concerns with personal relationships. (Naffine, 1987, 15)

Cloward and Ohlin, as well as other strain theorists, failed to recognize that females also experience unequal opportunities. "Indeed, logically, one might expect women to have a higher crime rate than men since their opportunities are more limited" (Morris, 1987, 76). On the other hand, females may also have less access to illegitimate means than males (a less delinquent subculture than males, for example), which would account for their lower crime rates (Harris, 1977). Bottcher's (1995) study of the siblings of incarcerated boys reported that her findings are consistent in some ways with opportunity theory "with the ideas that opportunities are determined structurally and distributed inequitably in society, and that social and economic opportunities affect delinquency (1995, 53). As expected, many of the siblings of both sexes lacked characteristics associated with social and economic success.

> Yet in equally limiting environments, the study revealed an organization of gender that produced different options and limitations for each group. Females had more chance to concentrate their efforts with fewer distractions, but often they had the limitation of caring for children on their own at a relatively young age. Males had the opportunities that freedom provides—a wider range of activity, of association, and of movement— but they also had the greater risk of accidents, conflict, peer pressure, and delinquent activity, at a time before they could make more mature judgements (Bottcher, 1995, 53–54).

Females and Strain

In 1964 Ruth Morris was the first scholar to focus strain theory on girls as well as boys. She viewed girls as slightly more dimensional than did her predecessors: Girls were not interested just in husband hunting but were also concerned with other affective relationships, such as with family members. Morris found that girls, delinquent and not, were faced with less subcultural support and more disapproval for delinquency than boys, and she believed this might explain girls' lower delinquency rates. Furthermore, delinquent girls were more likely than delinquent boys to describe their families as unhappy.

It is instructive that studies in the late 1960s and 1970s found that girls' efforts to find mates were not related to their delinquency rates (Sandhu and Allen, 1969) and that the patterns of boys' and girls' delinquent behavior were quite similar, except that boys' rates were higher (see Naffine, 1987, 18). Research on gender differences in the role of youth subcultures (often measured as gangs) tends to confirm that boys' subcultures are more prone to delinquency than girls' subcultures (Esbensen and Huizinga, 1993; Joe and Chesney-Lind, 1995; Lerman, 1966; Morash, 1983, 1986; Morris, 1964, 1965; Rahav, 1984; Thompson et al., 1984). However, research addressing whether strain/blocked opportunity is more, less, or equally related to boys' and girls' delinquency rates has been inconsistent. Some studies report that strain is more relevant in predicting girls' than boys' delinquency (Datesman et al., 1975; Segrave and Hastad, 1983); another study notes that strain is more influential in predicting boys' than girls' delinquency (Simons et al., 1980); and still others claim that strain similarly influenced girls' *and* boys' delinquency rates (Cernkovich and Giordano, 1979; Figueira-McDonough and Selo, 1980; Smith, 1979). Yet another study reported that strain variables were related in the opposite direction as expected for white females but in the expected direction for African-American females (Hill and Crawford, 1990). Although the findings are inconsistent regarding the applicability of strain theory to females:

> [t]he weight of the evidence produced by researchers into strain has probably tended more to contradict than to confirm Cohen's formulation. There is little here to justify the claim that the sexes react differently to impeded goals or indeed that their aims do not correspond. Theorists are therefore perverse in their belief that women's behavior is more uniform and conventional than men's because women are not subjected to the stresses of the male role. (Naffine, 1987, 23)

Overall, the findings are quite mixed regarding whether strain, as it is traditionally defined, affects boys' and girls' delinquency similarly or differently. Given the more recent research, discussed in the prior chapter and in more detail later in this one, assessing the strain of child abuse (e.g., nonsexual physical, sexual, and neglect) that is related to boys' and girls' subsequent offending, it seems the traditional measures of strain were grossly lacking when not including child abuse and neglect as means of strain. Moreover, the traditional strain theories appeared to be more invested in addressing blocked legitimate economic opportunities, while ignoring the strain of experiencing poverty, racism, and sexism on a daily basis.

DIFFERENTIAL ASSOCIATION THEORY

Edwin Sutherland, first alone and then in collaboration with Donald Cressey, developed the theory of differential association in the classic text *Principles of Criminology* (1939, 1966). Sutherland's attempt was to move away from poverty as the major explanation of crime; however, he also attacked Freud and other individual theorists. The basic tenet of differential association theory is that criminal behavior is learned, just as any other behavior is learned. Thus, one's group association is instrumental in determining whether one becomes delinquent.

Although Sutherland and Cressey agree with Cohen's contention that there is unequal access to success in the United States, they depart from Cohen's belief that all classes have internalized the same goals (that is, the goals of middle-class males). Further, Sutherland and Cressey claim that criminal subcultures are not unique to frustrated working-class male youths; people of all classes, including white-collar workers, can and do partake in criminal behavior. Similarly, whereas Cohen defines a U.S. culture that excludes women and girls, Sutherland and Cressey's perspective is not so exclusively male in theory and is presented as a general non-sex-specific theory (Naffine, 1987).

Despite Sutherland and Cressey's promise of a non–sex-specific theory, they rarely address girls. And where girls are briefly mentioned, they are seen as uniform and homogeneous. Again, girls are treated as peripheral and insignificant to the mainstream culture. Thus, Sutherland and Cressey's gender-neutral approach exists only in words, not in content. What is additionally disturbing is how easily accepted Sutherland and Cressey's view of males as "free to engage in a range of behaviors" is contrasted with the view of girls as belonging in the family (Naffine, 1987). Further, girls' perceived tendency toward abiding the law is portrayed as dull, rather than as positive and moral (Naffine, 1987).

Despite this neglect, researchers have examined the relevance of differential association theory for an explanation of girls' criminality. One of the initial applications of differential association theory to include both girls and boys found that girls were similar to boys in both their frequency of delinquent behaviors and their connections with delinquent companions (Clark, 1964). In contrast, while finding support for differential association theory and a strong relationship between delinquent friends and delinquent behavior for both boys and girls, Hindelang (1971) reported that females had fewer delinquent friends and less delinquent behavior than boys.

Another study of delinquent girls found that they were significantly influenced by their peers and in fact were more influenced by other girls than they were by the boys who were peers (Giordano, 1978). "In other words, the more a girl thought her female friends approved of crime, the more likely she was to offend" (Naffine, 1987, 37). A study of adult heroin users, on the other hand, found that white males reported more benefits from both legal employment and illegal subcultures than African-American males and females and white females (Covington, 1986). In conclusion, although Sutherland and Cressey ignored females in their research, their theory potentially provides insight into gender differences and similarities in delinquent involvement.

Feminist criticisms of differential association theory have centered mainly on Sutherland and Cressey's decision to avoid discussing females in any meaningful way (see Leonard, 1982; Naffine, 1987). Some feminists have suggested, however, that differential association theory is a useful way of examining male and female delinquency rates and of explaining gender differences. Two points are important.

First, girls' relatively lower crime rates may largely be a result of the constraints they experience compared to boys. For example, at least traditionally, girls have been expected to stay closer to home, are more likely to have curfews, are more likely to be disciplined (particularly for minor infractions and sexual experimentation), and are generally provided less freedom than their brothers and other boys. The differential socialization, then, of boys and girls is believed to significantly affect gender behavior differences (see Hoffman-Bustamante, 1973; Morris, 1987). The second point is that the increase in girls' delinquency rates in the last couple of decades might be explained by females' increased freedom. Even Cressey (1964) asserted that where there is greater equality between the sexes, the crime-sex ratio is likely to be lower.

LABELING THEORY

Labeling theory is concerned with the process by which deviant labels are applied and received. Specifically, labeling theory speculates about how people are "branded" with a deviant, delinquent, or criminal label, and the effect of the label on future behavior. It has been suggested that being treated as deviant may relate more to "the kind of person" one is than to her or his particular behavior (Schur, 1984). For example, labeling theory proposes that some people are more likely to be labeled criminal because of their race, sex, class, and so on. Moreover, labeling theory posits that once someone is labeled delinquent or criminal, she or he may accept this label unquestioningly and continue on in crime because of this.

Numerous researchers helped advance the concepts behind labeling theory (see Erikson, 1962; Kitsuse, 1962; Lemert, 1951), but perhaps the most famous is Howard Becker (1963) in his research on jazz and dance musicians in the book *Outsiders*. Becker's work is admirable in many ways, particularly his efforts "to enter the world of the deviant to find out how it worked by seeing it from the vantage point of those who lived there, from the viewpoint of those labeled deviant" (Naffine, 1996, 40). He collected his data through participant observation, playing the piano professionally with his subjects. Consistent with the theorists discussed thus far, however, Becker devotes his analysis almost exclusively to men musicians. When women are examined in Becker's work, it is most frequently as the wives of the men, and in these instances these women are portrayed as boring, laughable, and "square." Thus, while Becker used innovative and in-depth methods to really get to know and understand the male musicians, his approach to studying the women "remained highly orthodox" (Naffine, 1996, 41). The women are seen only through the lens of the male musicians and are depicted as nags who threaten the livelihood of the band by trying to convince their husbands to get "real" jobs. When women musicians are given any attention in Becker's analysis, it is only as sex objects, not as legitimate musicians—an all-too-familiar approach to studying nonconforming and criminal women (Naffine, 1987). In the work of Becker and many others, conforming women are portrayed as boring and spineless, whereas criminal men are seen as creative and exciting.

When labeling theory analysis is applied to women and girls, a key issue is whether there are gender differences in how offenders are labeled. Thus, the possibility that girls may be less likely than boys to be labeled or viewed as delinquent might also help explain their lower rates. Or perhaps women/girls are labeled more harshly for some crimes, while men/boys are discriminated against for others.

Research on these issues has revealed inconsistent findings regarding police and court actions. Some studies found no gender differences, some found preferential treatment for men/boys, others found preferential treatment for women/girls, and still others found that women/girls were treated more harshly for some crimes and men/boys were treated more harshly for others. Controlling for the amount of delinquency, one study showed that children, especially girls from mother-only homes, were more likely to be officially labeled delinquent than those from two-parent homes (Johnson, 1986). In addition to helping explain women's and girls' criminality, labeling theory may also be helpful in explaining the current strong trend in increasing rates of women's imprisonment, despite their persistently low crime rates:

> [C]onditions that previously protected women from the pernicious effects of labeling have declined. With this, women are more likely to be subject to the stigma of official labeling. The result, according to labeling theory, is an increased likelihood that their criminal involvement will become deeper and more intractable. (Leonard, 1982, 84)

Another interesting point in examining gender differences in labeling is Morris's (1987) contention that women are more likely to be labeled mentally ill than men, and men are more likely to be labeled criminal than women. Accordingly, "mental illness is presented as both an alternative to and an explanation of crime" (ibid., 55). Similarly, whereas men may be more likely to be labeled "criminal," women are more likely to be labeled "deviant" or labeled in general (for example, they are called nags and bitches and are described as promiscuous and hysterical).

> [W]omen do not really have to engage in specific acts in order to be defined and responded to as deviant. Physical appearance—and in a sense perhaps even the mere condition of "being" a woman—can lead to stigmatization. (Schur, 1984, 190)

In a historical overview of how women's "madness" has been related to crime, Frigon (1995, 29) summarizes: "The female offenders, of course, were the antithesis of ideal femininity." Punishing females (and to some degree, males) for not conforming to their "appropriate" gender roles has a long history. Frigon (ibid.) traces the historical manifestations of this, for example the execution of hundreds of thousands of lesbians and thousands of gays for heresy in fifteenth- and sixteenth-century France during the Roman Catholic Inquisition. Other examples include the long history of executing women charged as "witches." Thus, a distinction for the criminal female appears to falls into "mad" (mentally ill, including the rejection of culturally prescribed gender roles) and "bad" (just pure evil) (see Frigon, 1995).

Anthony Harris (1977) questions this investment in stereotyping women into roles of inherently conforming. He views this stereotyping as functional in a patriarchal society; it is a means to keep women out of prison and where they "belong"—home cleaning the house and raising the children. Furthermore, stereotyping African-American ghetto males as inherently criminal is functional in perpetuating the myth that they fail to contribute to society in any way (Harris, 1977). Fox (1977) discusses how women are controlled by the relentless pressure to be labeled "nice." This informal societal control is so effective that females are less likely than males to need the formal criminal label (Hagan et al., 1979).

Naffine (1987) is concerned with how women are represented in the works of Harris, Fox, and Becker. All three authors, she observes, fail to view women with any sense of intention and purpose. She points out that Fox and Harris are more descriptive than explanatory. Naffine is troubled that even Harris's and Fox's portrayals, albeit less sexist than Becker's, fail to allow

> for the sort of individualism and glamour described by Becker when the male was the subject of interpretation. . . . While labeling theorists may be right in claiming that men have more freedom than women to deviate, they have developed their arguments about the socialized woman to a point at which her humanity has been extinguished. (1987, 88)

SOCIAL CONTROL THEORY

The theories discussed thus far have focused on what makes people break the law. Taking a different approach, the social control theories are more concerned with explaining what compels most of society to abide by the law. This section discusses such theories.

Social Bond Theory

Travis Hirschi (1969), in his book *Causes of Delinquency,* focuses on what motivates people to obey laws. His theory, social bond or control theory, examines four categories of "social bonds" that prevent people from acting on their criminal desires: attachment, commitment, involvement, and belief. A person's likelihood to offend will be related to her or his ties to (1) conventional people, especially parents; (2) conventional institutions and behaviors in her or his employment and recreation; and (3) the rules of society. Although the theory was described as non-sex-specific, it changed in its application. Thus, to test his hypotheses, Hirschi analyzed only the responses of white school boys. He found that, indeed, the boys with stronger conventional ties were less likely to report delinquency.

Given that Hirschi switched the approach of studying crime from "Why do people offend?" to "Why don't people offend?" it has been suggested that studying females—or, at least, including females in the sample—would have made more sense because most research suggests that they are more law abiding than males (Naffine, 1987). Interestingly, Hirschi began his study with males and females.

> Indeed Hirschi explains, in some detail, his empirical method for eliminating bias from his samples by referring to both male and female cases. Then, unaccountably and without comment, he discards his female respondents and the research project becomes a study of social control as it applies to the male. From this one can infer that professional criminologists regard it as perfectly right not to cater for the female experience in

the tests of their theory, even when that theory is presented as non-sex-specific. (Naffine, 1987, 66)

Or, as Mann points out:

> Travis Hirschi stratified his samples by race, sex, school, and grade. He included 1,076 black girls and 846 nonblack girls; but in the analysis of his data Hirschi admits "the girls disappear," and he adds, "Since girls have been neglected for too long by students of delinquency, the exclusion of them is difficult to justify. I hope I return to them soon." He didn't. (1984, 263)

Additionally, where delinquent boys were often celebrated and revered in prior theory focusing on why some people (boys) commit crimes, in Hirschi's approach the conforming (law-abiding) boy becomes ennobled. This is particularly noteworthy given the image of conforming girls in research testing the other theories; they are depicted as lifeless, boring, and dependent. In the prior studies asking "Why do people offend?" the criminal boy was portrayed as exciting, instrumental, and masculine. In Hirschi's approach, the noncriminal boy becomes lauded as responsible. In fact, it has been pointed out that men who conform are labeled "successful," whereas there is little or no reward for conforming women (Schur, 1984). "What all this seems to indicate is a profound criminological tendency to devalue the female and value the male even when they are doing precisely the same things" (Naffine, 1987, 67).

Social control theory was advanced by Michael Gottfredson and Travis Hirschi in *A General Theory of Crime* (1990). This "general" theory purports to explain criminal behavior as a function of individual self-control; it predicts that individuals with low selfcontrol are more prone to criminal behavior. General theory has been criticized, however, for (1) ignoring gender as a significant power relationship, (2) dismissing and misrepresenting male violence against women, and (3) ignoring feminist research on gender divisions within families (Miller and Burack, 1993). An exception to this was a test of this theory by David C. Rowe and his colleagues (1995) who used a variety of scales to measure delinquency, parental control, parental affection, rebelliousness, and so on in both girls and boys. In short, they report that the same factors motivating/causing male delinquency also cause female delinquency and that the causes of the differences between boys and girls in their offending ("between sex differences") are the same factors that cause differences *among* boys and differences *among* girls ("within sex differences") (Rowe et al., 1995).

Research on Social Control Theory

Research on social control theory has been fairly extensive. A study of African-American and white girls and boys in California found that although introducing social control variables (measuring attachment to conventional people) greatly decreased the gender differences in reported delinquency rates, these social ties did not completely eliminate or explain boys' higher offending rates (Jensen and Eve, 1976). Another test of social control theory found that although conventional ties predicted both girls' and boys' offending, this relationship was stronger for boys (Hindelang 1973). A study of girl delinquents measuring social bonding as attachment to school and education found that, although these factors played a role in determining delinquency rates, their effect was minimal (Torstensson, 1990). Another study of high school students found that similar "bond variables" influenced both girls and boys (Figueira-McDonough et al., 1981). A study of men and women (adults), on the other hand, found that even women with weak conventional ties were more law abiding than men, thus implying that conventional ties alone do not explain women's greater conformity (Smith, 1979).

A number of studies attempted to determine social control within the family, such as the effects of parental and sibling interactions and behaviors. A study following female delinquents over time found strong evidence that dysfunctional families increase the likelihood that girls will proceed from committing status offenses as youths to committing criminal offenses as adults (Rosenbaum, 1989). A study comparing parents' and their children's drug use found, for both daughters and sons, more support for social learning theory (that is, modeling and evaluating behaviors of significant others) than for social control theory (Dembo et al., 1986). Another family study found that social control theory better explained female delinquency than male delinquency. The study also found that some parental behaviors influenced daughters' delinquency, while other parental behaviors influenced sons' delinquency (Cernkovich and Giordano, 1987). Notably, another study found that the number of sisters a girl or boy has exerts no impact on her or his delinquency rate; however, the more brothers a boy has, the greater the likelihood that he will become delinquent, and the more brothers a girl has, the less likely that she will become delinquent (Lauritsen, 1993). A recent study on gender as social control to explain gender differences in delinquency reported gender-related life conditions that contributed to these differences. Specifically, Bottcher's (1995) study of the siblings of incarcerated boys reports that social structure of gender is a major form of social control, specifically through activities and definitions of the youth. The following diagram represents Bottcher's (1995) findings on gender differences in youths' activities and definitions:

Activities
- *range:* Boys typically operate in a wider arena and spend more time away from home, largely due to fewer home responsibilities than their sisters.
- *timing:* Boys are more able than girls to be out of their homes late at night.
- *pace:* Boys move faster, farther, and more freely and engage in more activities than girls.
- *focus:* Girls have more focused activities, particularly social activities, than boys; girls tend to have a smaller circle of friends than boys; boys are more able to avoid parental responsibilities than girls; and girls' focus on their children and a single boyfriend (at least at one time) seemed to shield them from delinquency.

Definitions

- *self-definitions:* Boys are more self-centered, competitive, are bolder and more macho than girls.
- *peer pressures:* Most youth spend most of their time in sex-segregated leisure time, and boys are more responsive to peer pressure in committing crimes.
- *societal definitions:* Boys are more likely labeled by the police than girls, and some crimes are more acceptable when committed by one sex than another (e.g., a boy stealing a car).
- *physical differences:* Boys' greater strength and running speed make them better able to commit crimes; parents are stricter with daughters than sons because of fear of pregnant daughters.
- *meanings of crime:* Girls commit fewer crimes than boys because they are smarter than the boys; boys are more bold and "showy" in the commission of their crimes.

Power-Control Theory

Hagan and his colleagues (1985, 1987) built on social-control theory through the development of power-control theory. One of the few theories to explicitly include gender, this theory joins class theory with research on gender and family relationships:

> Central to our extension of power-control theory is a conceptualization of class and family that focuses on power relations in the workplace and the home. A key premise of our extended theory is that positions of power in the workplace are translated into power relations in the household and that the latter, in turn, influence the gender-determined control of adolescents, their preferences for risk taking, and the patterning of gender and delinquency. (Hagan, 1987, 813)

Hagan (ibid.) found a greater gender difference in delinquency rates in patriarchal homes, where the mother had a lower status than the father, than in egalitarian homes, where parents had equivalent status or the mother was the only parent. Thus, this approach asserts that the gender-power makeup in the parents' relationship influences their daughters' subsequent delinquent behavior. Or rather, in a home where there is less sexism in the parents' roles, there should theoretically be fewer gender differences between sons' and daughters' behaviors. An assumption of this theory is that daughters from egalitarian homes are socialized, like their brothers, to engage in risk-taking behaviors, and because risk-taking behavior is associated with delinquency, girls from the more egalitarian homes will be more delinquent than their "sisters" from traditional, patriarchal homes.

The research by Hagan and his colleagues confirmed this belief, as did the research in a similar study (Singer and Levine, 1988). Another study found, however, that although both maternal and paternal support were effective in reducing delinquency, girls were more affected by maternal support and boys were more affected by paternal support (Hill and Atkinson, 1988). A related study reported that although girls' delinquency rates were more influenced than boys' by family risk factors—such as marital discord, marital instability, and discipline—the gender stereotypes did not always fit (Dornfeld and Kruttschnitt, 1992). Yet another study with a more detailed measure of parents' power structure did not find that parents' relative equality affected the sons' or daughters' delinquency rates; rather, these rates were related to the family's social class and the negative sanctions from the father (Morash and Chesney-Lind, 1991). Finally, another replication found no class-gender variations, yet gender differences by race were consistent with the theory: Gender differences were greater for whites than for African-Americans (Jensen and Thompson, 1990). The explanation offered for this difference was that "white families may be more 'patriarchal' than black families" (1990, 1016). As Kruttschnitt's (1996, 139) review of the tests of power-control theory states: "[E]mpirical tests of this theory have not supported it with any consistency."

Still other studies have tried to integrate sex, social bonds (conventional ties), and masculinity/femininity. Generally, "masculine" girls did not have weakened conventional ties (Norland et al., 1981; Thornton and James, 1979). Although one study found that males reported more delinquency than females in four types of crimes (violent, property, drugs, and status), controlling for "masculinity" reduced the effect of sex on delinquency rates. Further, although scoring high on "masculinity" was related to both sexes' increased reported delinquency, this was particularly true for males (Cullen et al., 1979). Notably, another study found that girls who were neither "masculine" nor "feminine" had the weakest conventional ties and the highest delinquency rates (Loy and Norland, 1981). A study that did not set out to test Hagan's (1988) power-control theory reported that the findings were consistent in a general way with this theory. Bottcher's (1995) interviews with sisters and brothers of incarcerated boys suggest that girls have stronger informal social controls than boys in their families, and are more aggressively controlled by social service and law enforcement professionals. She points out that in contrast to Hagan's theory, both the girls and the boys in her study reported that the increased familial control of girls was due to the effort to monitor the girls' (and not the boys') sexual activities. She concludes that, for the high-risk youth in her study, the parental control cited by Hagan "is a very limited component of the social control that gender encompasses" (ibid., 53).

Although not specifically a test of social control or power control theory, Jang and Krohn (1995) attempted to determine whether the role of gender for delinquents varies over youthful development. They were interested in testing two contradictory models. First, Gottfredson and Hirschi's "sex-invariant model" assumes that gender differences are predisposed at young ages and do not change over a youth's childhood, thus gender differences in delinquency are stabile over adolescence. Second, the "sex-variant model" assumes that "the causes of behaviors change over time and that the development pace at which boys and girls are socialized can vary," thus "differences in male and female delinquency can vary substantially over adolescence" (ibid., 196–197).

Jan and Krohn tested these models using a sample of urban African–American youth and reported: "[S]ex differences in delinquency tend to vary as the subjects grow older, rather than remain constant as the invariance thesis posits. Specifically, sex differences in delinquency peak at the age of 15 and thereafter decline with age. We also find that parental supervision significantly explains sex differences in delinquency for younger adolescence, but not for older adolescence" (Jang and Krohn, 1995, 195).

In summary, social control theory applied to women and girls has inconsistent findings. Although women and girls tend to have stronger conventional ties and lower offending rates than men and boys, the social ties are generally insufficient to explain the gender differences in criminal behavior. Furthermore, women's increased attachment to conventional ties and decreased delinquency rates cannot be explained simply by their "femininity" or "masculinity."

MARXIST/RADICAL THEORIES

In the late 1960s in the United States and early 1970s in Britain, a more radical perspective entered the ring of criminological theories (Naffine, 1996). "Conflict theory" is grounded in Marxism. Although Marx himself wrote very little about crime, his perspective on class struggle and on social relations under capitalism are the basis for conflict or Marxist criminology.

Conflict theory proposes that rather than looking at the offender, we should focus on society, particularly lawmakers and powerful interests. This criminology begins with the assumption that laws are biased, reflecting the needs of the upper class, and thus enforcement of these laws is inevitably unjust. Crime itself is politicized and defined by the powerful elite. The key to solving the crime problem, then, is changing the economic system (Bonger, 1969), and this is highly political in nature.

The Marxist or radical perspective on criminology was crystallized and even renamed the "new criminology" and "critical criminology" with the publication of Ian Taylor, Paul Walton, and Jock Young's books of the same names (*The New Criminology* [1973] and *Critical Criminology* [1975]). Other criminologists have also helped develop this perspective (see Gordon, 1973; Platt, 1975; Quinney, 1972, 1975; Schwendinger and Schwendinger, 1970). The "new criminologists" viewed society as two-tiered—with harmful wealthy capitalist men beyond the arm of the law and working-class men offenders who should be regarded as "resistors" to the "real criminals" (the capitalists) and thus should be viewed with appreciation and sympathy (Naffine, 1996, 44). The most common criticism of the "new criminology" is that it is overly simplified and generalized (Leonard, 1982, 161). In addition to ignoring gender in general, and female offenders, specifically, another feminist criticism of the "new criminologists" has been their either outright ignoring of the crimes of rape and domestic assaults or documenting them uncritically (Naffine, 1996, 45).

Marx and his early followers rarely addressed the topics of crime and women, and the "new criminologists" have been roundly criticized for continuing to ignore women (Heidensohn, 1985; Klein and Kress, 1976; Leonard, 1982; Morris, 1987; Naffine, 1996). The same charge has been made regarding Marxist legal scholars (Rhode, 1990). Indeed, in her book on the construction of women in criminology, Naffine does not discuss the Marxist approach except in a footnote:

> A Marxist approach is not included in this volume for the simple reason that the Left has shown little specific interest in the female offender. In the mid–1970s, there were rallying calls about the need to revitalize the study of female crime within a radical critique of society. . . . Unfortunately they have yet to generate a recognizably Marxist account of the subject. (1987, 134–135)

Similarly, Morris states:

> Taylor, Walton and Young (1973), for example, argue that only the acceptance of Marxist methods can fill the "blank spots" left by other attempts to construct social theories of deviance. They are unaware of their own "blank spot": women. There is not one word on women in their text and, despite a sharp critique of criminology, they do not notice the relevance or applicability to women of the theories reviewed. (1987, 11)

The new criminologists also often fail to recognize that economic factors alone cannot explain gender differences in criminal behavior; they require a political analysis as well (Leonard, 1982). In a refreshing departure from the numerous accounts of critical criminology that fail to address the "woman question," Dorie Klein and June Kress (1976) wrote an insightful article discussing how the status of women and sexist oppression were relevant to radical criminology. Other Marxist-feminist accounts declare that sexism is directly tied to capitalism, governing economic, social, and legal aspects of our lives (Messerschmidt, 1988; Rafter and Natalizia, 1981).

Leonard's (1982) more dated writings are kinder in critique, allowing that it may be simply that the "new criminology" is so new that it has not had a chance to address women, although she expresses concern that even this radical approach will continue to overlook women. A book on radical criminology published in the late 1980s, however, devoted only five pages to women and gender (Lynch and Groves, 1989). In the late 1980s, some of the radical criminologists attempted to return to the "realism" of empirical criminology and to accept the claims of feminists and some working-class people that, indeed, much of the crime is harmful (Naffine, 1996, 63). These "left idealists" then transformed and renamed themselves "left realists" (ibid.). However, while the left realists claim to be sensitive to feminist accounts of crime, Naffine (ibid., 64) describes their approach as "naive." Naffine (ibid.) cites work by Young and Rush (1994) pointing out that the left realists are concerned with crime in the public arena (read: street crime committed by men against men), reducing the frequently hidden crimes against women (e.g., rape and battering).

In summary, consistent with less liberal approaches, the new criminologists have been equally guilty of omitting women and girls from their theories and analyses, despite the powerful potential of gender and sexual stratification in society to explain criminal behavior and processing. It is hoped the more recent influx of feminists into the radical organizations within criminology will help change this.

WOMEN'S LIBERATION/ EMANCIPATION HYPOTHESIS

As we have seen, traditionally, criminological theory showed only a passing interest in explaining the offending and the system's crime processing of females. All changed in 1975, however, with the publication of Freda Adler's *Sisters in Crime* and Rita Simon's *Women and Crime*. These books, particularly Adler's, received a great deal of attention regarding their hypothesis that the women's "liberation" movement is linked to the female crime rate.

Also called the "emancipation hypothesis," this approach suggests that the feminist movement, although working toward equality for women, increased the female crime rate. Although similar overall, Adler and Simon parted ways concerning the types of crime the women's movement was expected to affect. Adler proposed that the violent crime rate would increase because of women's "liberation." In contrast, Simon proposed that only the property crime rate would increase with women's "liberation." Simon suggested further that women's violent crime would decrease because women's frustrations with life would diminish as they gained access to new work and educational opportunities.

Naffine (1987) summarizes some of the assumptions present in the women's "liberation" theory: (1) Feminism brings out women's competitiveness; (2) the women's movement has opened up structural opportunities to increase places where women can offend; (3) women have fought and won the battle of equality; (4) feminism makes women want to behave like men; and (5) crime itself is inherently masculine. There are obvious problems with these assumptions. Even the most plausible assumption—that feminism has opened up women's structural opportunities—loses credibility when faced with statistics showing that women have not achieved equality in high-paying and managerial professions (see Chapter 9). These assumptions, and liberation theory in general, have been soundly criticized for being wrong and also for misusing and manipulating statistics and their interpretations in efforts to prove that gender equality breeds female crime (see Crites, 1976; Feinman, 1986; Leonard, 1982; Morris, 1987; Naffine, 1987; Smart, 1976, 1982). A study published in 1983 on incarcerated violent females reported these women to be generally "traditional," "feminine" (*not* "feminist"), and "conformist" in terms of sex-roles, hardly the hard-core feminists Adler's (1975) theory predicted (Bunch et al., 1983).

Another problem with the "emancipation" or "liberation" hypothesis is that it predicts the opposite of previous strain and class theories: that crime will increase with an improvement of opportunities. This implies an underlying fundamental difference between male and female criminality. The theories discussed thus far, when they accounted for class—as they often did—hypothesized that crime would increase with blocked or worsened economic opportunities (see Steffensmeier and Streifel, 1992).

Most important, however, the hypothesis that women's violent crime rates are catching up with men's is questionable. (This topic, comparing men's and women's criminality, will be addressed more fully in the following chapter.) Besides Adler, most research on the relationship between women's violent crime rate and the women's movement has found that females' violent crime rate has remained relatively stable since the 1970s (see Feinman, 1986; Steffensmeier, 1980). On the other hand, research on property crimes, particularly larceny and petty property crimes, has shown that women's rates have increased since the feminist movement of the 1970s (for example, Box and Hale, 1983, 1984; Chilton and Datesman, 1987; Smith and Visher, 1980; Steffensmeier and Streifel, 1992).

The increase in women's property crime rates, however, is more likely a result of the changing economic situation than the strength of the feminist movement. "The absence, rather than the availability, of employment opportunity for women," observes Naffine (1987, 88) "seems to lead to increases in female crime, for when times are good, the offending of women stabilizes rather than escalates." Thus, the "feminization of poverty," the increased number of women (with and without dependents) living in poverty, is a better predictor of women's criminality—and then, of property crimes—than is the strength or weakness of the feminist movement. The "liberation" hypothesis is particularly ironic because the feminist movement has probably had a greater effect on middle-class, white women than on those women most vulnerable to arrest: poor and unemployed women of color (Smart, 1982). In fact, the types of crime for which women were increasingly arrested after the women's movement of the 1970s, prostitution and offenses against the family (such as desertion, neglect, and nonsupport), are crimes not "altogether compatible with the view of the emancipated female" (Steffensmeier and Allan, 1988).

It has also been found that general sentencing patterns of men and women alike (for example, "get tough on crime" eras) have done more than the feminist movement to increase females' official crime rate reported by the police (Box and Hale, 1984). Furthermore, if the women's movement has had any negative effect on women's criminality, it is that women now appear to be more likely to have their behaviors defined as criminal or delinquent by judges and police officers (Curran, 1984; Morris, 1987). Notably, researchers specifically examining the effect of young women's adherence to feminist ideals (for example, regarding women and work and gender roles in the family) report that pro-feminist women and girls are no more likely to report aggression and criminal or delinquent behavior than their more traditional sisters (Figueira-McDonough, 1984; McCord and Otten, 1983). Finally, feminist scholar

Josefina Figuera-McDonough (1992) proposes an approach to studying gender differences in delinquency by starting with a *community structure* model, acknowledging that poor communities can have strong informal groups. She states that we need to understand (1) the salience of informal controls and (2) the spread of normative gender equality in reproducing gender differences in delinquency. Kruttschnitt's careful overview of tests of Adler's and Simon's hypothesis concludes:

> Simply put, the continuing evidence of stability in women's rates of violent offending combined with the lack of evidence that gender-role socialization was related to female offending . . . led scholars to focus on a new set of explanatory hypotheses which would address the increases in property offending among women. These hypotheses focus on the economic marginalization, drug use, and changes in formal social control . . . Although empirical support for these hypotheses is better grounded than it was for the liberation or opportunity theories, they have yet to be formally integrated into an explanatory model of female offending or of gender differences in offending. (1996, 137)

BIOSOCIAL AND EVOLUTIONARY PSYCHOLOGICAL THEORIES

A more recent attempt to explain aggressive behavior, particularly violence against women, is through biosocial and evolutionary psychological theories. An example of this is a 1993 book, *Sexual Aggression,* edited by Gordon N. Hall, Richard Hirschman, John Graham, and Maira Zragoza. In setting the stage for the rest of the book, the authors state in the first sentence that "sexually aggressive behavior is a biopsychosocial phenomenon that is primarily engaged in by males" (1993, 1). The biosocial and evolutionary psychology advocates are in some manner making new waves about how we cannot ignore biology in the commission of crimes. Although throughout the book some of the authors claim to integrate the biosocial approach with feminist theory, the result is basically that biology, with a smattering of sociological forces, predicts why females are victims and males are offenders. This context is that rape is significantly explained (or my fear is that it is *excused*) by such biological forces as sex drives and hormones. In one chapter of this book, Ellis uses natural selection to explain that our gender roles are a result of our biological dispositions, whereby men gain by being "pushy" about sex and women gain by showing such feminine traits as "coyness" and "hesitancy" (1993, 23). Ultimately, Ellis claims that males compete with each other for access to female sex partners whereas females compete with each other to find the best male who can provide for their offspring. Ellis (ibid., 24) believes that males do not rape because they want to dominate females, but they use these dominating and aggressive rape behaviors simply in their efforts to "copulate." This perspective is not only insulting to girls and women, viewing them as pathetic, needy competitors for male attention, but it is also insulting to boys and men, viewing them as incapable of controlling their biological urges (Belknap, 1997). Although some other areas support this new wave to use biology as a "cause" of crime (e.g., Booth and Osgood, 1993; Wrangham and Peterson, 1996), other books offer more progressive and insightful efforts to question the use of biology to explain male aggression against females (e.g., Small, 1996; Talyor, 1996).

A book edited by Kaj Bjorkqvist and Pirkko Niemela (1992), entitled *Of Mice and Women: Aspects of Female Aggression,* is a review and compilation of recent studies by leading scholars addressing gender differences and similarities in aggressive behavior. In this book, a chapter by Benton (1992, 46) concludes: "The majority of evidence indicates that in the general population differences in aggressiveness reflect the level of testosterone only to a limited extent, if at all. There is no reason to suggest that testosterone causes the behavior of males and females to differ markedly." Other chapters in this book are convincing in their overview of scientific research, maintaining that "too much" is being made of biological differences between males and females in attempts to "explain away" cultural differences. Indeed, a chapter on "biology and male aggression" concludes: "Finally, we can look forward to the day when the myth that male animals are more aggressive than females can no longer be used by those who would argue that war is the product of biology rather than culture" (Adams, 1992, 24). Indeed, in the introductory chapter the editors state: "There is no reason to believe that women overall should be less motivated to be aggressive than men" (Bjorkqvist and Niemela, 1992, 14). Rather, they claim that males' and females' *style* differences in aggressive behavior depend on culture, age, and situations. They view *modes* of female aggression as dependent on learning and social norms, not biology. They conclude: "Female aggressive behavior may accordingly be described as resulting from a complex combination of cultural, situational, and individual-specific factors. The cognition of frustration, as well as its emotional experience, function as triggers of aggression, while learned scripts determine the mode, or pattern, of behavior" (ibid., 15). Similarly, Mary B. Harris's (1996) extensive overview of her own and others' research on this topic concludes that aggressive behavior is more consistent with *social learning,* including cultural norms and specific experiences, than it is with biological factors.

> Although it would be foolish to deny that biological factors can affect aggressive behaviors, the studies described above suggest that sociocultural variables, such as cultural norms and gender role stereotypes, previous experiences with aggression, attitudes toward the aggression of others, and judgements of the justifiability of retaliation, are even more important influences on aggression. (Harris, 1996, 141)

FEMINIST AND PRO-FEMINIST THEORIES

Messerschmidt's Masculinities and Crime Theories

James Messerschmidt's (1993) rethinking of feminist theory focuses on structured action and gendered crime. Messerschmidt addresses the impact of gender not only on women's criminality but also on men's. He defines social structures as "regular patterned forms of interaction over time that constrain and channel behavior in specific ways" (1993, 63). Messerschmidt identifies three social structures as important to understanding our gendered society: the gender division of labor, gender relations of power, and sexuality. Moreover, class, race, and gender relations are interconnected to a number of social structures and thus are related to social actions.

To Messerschmidt, masculinity is key to explaining criminality. This is consistent with Naffine's (1996) contention that feminism, particularly using masculinity to assess why males behave more criminally than females, is useful for studying male as well as female offending. Messerschmidt carefully examines how race, class, and gender interact within various social structures that encourage the preponderance of criminality perpetrated largely by young males. Accounting for differences among males, Messerschmidt describes how middle-class white males can use power structures, such as a good education and respectable careers, to establish masculinity and provide for themselves and their families. Lower-class males and males of color have fewer legitimate options, however, and thus are more likely to use crime and delinquency to prove masculinity. Accounting for gender differences, it is far more important for males than for females to show power or to need to prove masculinity. Regarding sexuality, more respect is accrued to heterosexuals than to lesbians and gay men, and, as discussed in Chapter 4 of this book, consensual (hetero) sexuality is more permissible in society and the crime-processing system when it is by males than when it is by females. Messerschmidt effectively uses these variables of class, race, and sexuality to explain rape causality, the differential treatment of males and females who are sexually active, and participation in various crimes and offenses ranging from sexual harassment to robbery and homicide.

This new approach to studying crime causation is appealing in that it accounts for both males and females, as well as the impact of gender, race, and class. Furthermore, it explains crime and criminal processing within the important social structures that shape society and the individuals in it.

Life Course Theory   A recent theoretical approach that is consistent in many respects with a pro-feminist method is the "Life Course Development Model." This approach theorizes that various life events, particularly those during childhood and adolescence, affect one's risk of offending behavior. Thus, various developmental stages are "age specific," making offending behavior age associated (see Loeber, 1996). Indeed, adolescence is identified as a particularly "at risk" time given the angst of puberty, changing schools, and peer pressure. In this sense, crime is viewed as a network of various causal factors. One aspect of the life course approach is that independent variables become dependent variables over time. For example, delinquency decreases one's chance of doing well in school, which in turn, becomes a predictor for (re)turning to crime. Some of the key variables assessed in much of the life course research include antisocial behavior, intelligence, and income levels, as well as general criminal, delinquent, and deviant behaviors. Thus, a focus of some life course research is to assess whether antisocial behavior is continuous over an individual's life ("life course persistent") or whether there are periods of antisocial behaviors, usually limited to adolescence ("adolescence-limited") (Moffitt, 1993). The life course approach, then, examines "pathways through the age-differentiated life span," acknowledging different life stages, turning points, and transitions in individuals' lives (Elder, 1985). Therefore, this research tends to be longitudinal in nature (collecting data about individuals' lives over time).

The life course perspective, then, is a developmental perspective, focusing on individuals' behavioral changes from birth until death, the "social development over the full life course; specifically developmental processes from childhood and adolescence through adulthood" (Laub and Lauritsen, 1993, 236). Over the course of most individuals' lives, the formal and informal social controls vary, particularly the informal controls such as the family, school, and work, and these changes are largely age-specific (Laub and Lauritsen, 1993). That is, most children do not have jobs, so we cannot examine that control for them, but their schools and parents typically have less control over them as they age, at the same time that they are usually increasingly influenced by their peers. In their work with the life course model, Sampson and Laub (1990) identify two hypotheses: first, that childhood antisocial behaviors predict problems in adult development, and second, that social bonds to work and family in adulthood explain changes in crime and development over the life span. They also identify two central concepts to the life perspective: trajectories and transitions. *Trajectories* have to do with life's "pathways" or development lines over the life span including a persons' work life, marriage, parenthood, self-esteem, and criminal behavior. *Transitions,* on the other hand, are "specific life events that are embedded in trajectories and evolve over shorter time spans (e.g., first job or first marriage)" (ibid., 610). Sampson and Laub (ibid.) view one's social bonds in adulthood as potentially modifying events on the trajectory to criminal behavior. That is, stabile and supportive social bonds (through attachment to a spouse, job stability, and commitment to occupational goals) in adulthood may ameliorate childhood experiences, setting one on the path to crime.

As stated previously, in many ways the life course perspective is seemingly pro-feminist in nature: It purports to address significant childhood and adult experiences and to view how these, particularly social bonds, are related to delinquent, criminal, and deviant behavior. Indeed, the research conducted from the life course perspective on boys/men has generally found considerable support for it. *In practice,* to date, this research has less information to offer on girls and women. First, to date this research has focused almost exclusively on males (Laub and Sampson, 1993; Loeber, 1996; Moffitt, 1990,1993; Nagin, Farrington, and Moffitt, 1995; Sampson and Laub, 1990; Stattin and Magnusson, 1991). In some sense this is "excusable" given that the researchers are dealing with existing longitudinal data sets that began data collection in times when there was significantly less interest in females and gender. On the other hand, it is somewhat remarkable how little effort is made in the existing studies to mention how this research might apply to girls and women or the seeming lack of interest in it given that it is rarely or never mentioned as a limitation of the research. One exception is Farrington's (1992) discussion of three large-scale longitudinal British data sets. At least one of the three data sets he discusses has both males and females. Unfortunately, Farrington barely addresses any findings about the women and gender differences. Another article on the life course provides no empirical data but stresses the need for comparative studies across countries or even allowing for various structural locations within a country (including the United States) as important "next steps" for the life course perspective (Laub and Lauritsen, 1993). Unfortunately, the authors appear to be interested in race and class only as "structural location" variables, not mentioning gender. Therefore, similar to most of the theories addressed thus far in this chapter, although the theory might be meaningfully applied to girls and women, it does not appear to be happening. Or, as Kruttschnitt (1996, 141) states: "Failing to address how family and peer influences on delinquency change for males and females over the course of adolescence limits our ability to predict and explain the gender-crime relationship."

An exception to this is a study by Sommers and Baskin (1994). They briefly refer to life course research but claim their study "considers factors identified by previous works in integrated theory in order to understand pathways into violent offending for a specific sample of serious women offenders" (ibid., 469). They collected "life event histories" through interviews with 85 women arrested or incarcerated for violent crime in New York City, distinguishing between "early" and "normal/later" onset into offending and using self-report data. Notably, 60 percent reported an early onset of violent behavior, with 10 as the average age of becoming involved in street fighting. There were no significant differences between the early and normal onset groups in terms of family background, largely because both sets "grew up in multiproblem households" with high rates of both experiencing and witnessing violence in the home. The neighborhood the woman grew up in, however, was significant. Girls raised in neighborhoods with high concentrations of poverty were more likely both to have an early onset into violent behavior and to report sexual and physical abuse by a stranger. Schooling was also significant, with the early onset offenders dropping out of school at a younger age than normal/late onset offenders. Another significant distinction between the early and normal/late onset violent offending females was initiation into and addiction to drugs. The early onset women were more likely than the normal/late women to have started using alcohol and marijuana at a younger age (typically before they turned 9 years old) and younger when they became addicted to more powerful drugs (ibid., 478).

Another point worth mentioning about the life course studies is that in addition to being sexist, they are often heterosexist. Social ties as adults appear to be exclusively measured in terms of marriage and divorce. Also, although many of the life course studies claim to address variables loosely labeled "family diversity" or "poor family functioning," there is no mention of parental abuse or other types of abuse of these children and how this may influence their social bonds and subsequent delinquent and criminal behavior.

Feminist Pathways Research   Research, at least since 1977, has increasingly used women's and girls' voices to determine "life course" events that place girls (and women) at risk of offending. Unlike the longitudinal data collected over time on individuals by the life course researchers (or using such existing data sets), this research typically collects data at one point in time, usually interviewing incarcerated women (and sometimes girls) about their lives, often pointedly asking or at least attempting to determine "how did you end up being an offender/delinquent?" However, not all of these studies use incarcerated populations, indeed the earliest ones used self-identified prostitutes "on the street" (as well as some incarcerated prostitutes). Thus, the feminist pathways research attempts to gain data that are quasi-longitudinal by asking girls and women to discuss their lives and attempt to sequence major events (e.g., abuse by parents, school experiences, delinquent and criminal behavior, and so on).

Although the term "pathways" is used in this book and some of the more recent writings describing this phenomenon, this label did not exist in the earlier and even some of the later studies reported in this section. Also, grouping the studies in this "feminist pathways" section is a bit tenuous. For example, the "pathways" approach is very consistent with the Life Course Theory, the Cycle of Violence Theory, and the Intergenerational Transmission of Violence Theory, none of which claim to be "feminist." Furthermore, I am not sure that all of the scholars whose research is presented in this section personally identify as "feminists" or view their research as "feminist." Additionally, not all of these studies use "women's and girls' voices." For example, Daly used presentence investigation reports, and Widom used official reports. Despite these differences, it is hoped that the reader will see the common theme in what is included as "feminist pathways research" in this book: research that attempts to examine girls' and women's (and sometimes men's and boys') histories, allowing them, when possible, "voice" in order to understand the link between childhood and adult events and traumas and the likelihood of subsequent offending.

The first "feminist pathways" study I have found was a combination of data collected from two studies on prostitutes, both involving self-report data from questionnaires, interviews, and ethnographic field observations of prostitutes contacted on the street and in jail (James and Meyerding, 1977). The first data set, Study 1, was collected between 1970 and 1972 and included 72 adult and 20 adolescent prostitutes. The second data set, Study 2, was collected between 1974 and 1975 and included 136 prostitutes. The researchers, Jennifer James and Jane Meyerding, compared their data on prostitutes to existing "normal" population rates reported in publications, in an attempt to determine whether the prostitutes' rates of early/childhood sexual experiences differed from the "normal" (nonprostitute) population. As the researchers expected, the prostitutes reported more problematic sexual experiences than reported by the "normal" population: "The prostitutes had in common many negative experiences not found or found less often in other populations of young women. These include incestuous and/or coerced sex, lack of parental guidance, intercourse at a young age, and few or no meaningful relationships with males" (ibid., 1977, 1381). These scholars go on to speculate how these childhood experiences could lead to prostitution, and they postulate three factors that "may have influenced them toward accepting prostitution as a lifestyle" (ibid., 1384). First, they see the lack of parental monitoring and guidance leading to the increased likelihood of early and casual sexual intercourse. Second, the young woman or girl learns that sex both adds to and detracts from her social status: She has a new found "power" with males, but her nonvirgin status "makes her unacceptable to the majority of the culture" (ibid.). Third, rape and incest experiences are emotionally destructive. Although James and Meyerding's final analysis omits what many scholars say about some of these street prostitutes now, that they have little or no choice but to prostitute, their perspective into the double-standard of males' and females' acceptable sexual agency is insightful and particularly profound given when it was written:

> Because the range of acceptable sexual behaviors is much narrower for women than for men, and because women more than men are judged (by themselves and others) on the basis of their sexual desirability and behavior, sexual experiences may be a more important factor in a woman's development of self-identity. A woman who views herself as sexually debased or whose sexuality is more than normally objectified may see prostitution as a 'natural'—or as the only—alternative. (ibid.)

The second "feminist pathways" study was likely one by Mimi H. Silbert and Ayala M. Pines (1981), who used word of mouth and Public Service Announcements to recruit their sample. They interviewed 200 current and former prostitutes in the San Francisco Bay area. The sample ranged in age from 10 to 46, with an average age of 22. This impressive sample was also racially diverse: 69 percent white, 18 percent Black, 11 percent Hispanic, 2 percent Native American, and 1 percent Asian American. Although two-thirds of the sample came from middle or higher-income families, almost 90 percent reported their financial situation at the time of the interview as "just making it" or "very poor" (ibid., 408). Silbert and Pines's profound findings include:

- Three in five participants (60 percent) reported being sexually abused before the age of 16 (although most were first abused at much younger ages) by an average of two sexual abusers each.

- Two-thirds of the sexual abuse victims were abused by fathers or father figures (step-fathers, foster fathers, and mothers' common-law husbands).

- "Only" ten percent of the victims were sexually abused by strangers.

- The sexual abuse frequently led to running away from home, which led to prostitution and other street work.

- When asked why they started prostituting, nine-tenths said it was because they were hungry, needed money, and had no other options available to them. (ibid., 410)

The third feminist study examining women's/girls' pathways to offending, published in 1983 by Meda Chesney-Lind and Noelie Rodriguez, used intensive interviews with 16 incarcerated women. Among their findings was the prevalence of severe nonsexual child abuse experienced by ten of the women, where violence included extreme brutality with homes devoid of affection and security. Similar to Silbert and Pines (1981), nine-tenths of the women reported involvement in prostitution, and for most this was an outgrowth of running away from home and started in their teens. Also similar to Silbert and Pines (1981), their reasons for becoming prostitutes were "largely financial" (55). Half of the women reported having been raped as children, and three-fifths reported some form of child sexual abuse victimization. Chesney-Lind and Rodriguez (1983) also reported how subsequent drug dependency was related to further entanglement with the law.

Ironically, a few studies coming out about this time, although not designed to address how childhood traumas and other experiences may be "pathways" to offending, actually report some statistics consistent with this hypothesis/theory. Earlier in this chapter, under the section on Freud, a 1977 study of women's jealousy of men's ability to extinguish fires through urinating on them was discussed as a means to show how ludicrous some of the theorizing has been *and* the impact of Freud. However, findings the authors collected in this study are supportive of the gendered pathways approach. This study of 31 female and 19 male prisoners found that the incarcerated women were significantly more likely than the men to report physically injurious punishments by their fathers, deviant paternal punishments, and abandonment by one or both parents before the age of 10 (Felthous and Yudowitz, 1977). An article published in 1983, designed to examine the impact of varied sex roles on individual women's criminal behavior, interviewed with 90 women in a maximum-security prison. In addition to findings that challenged the assumptions that women can't commit a crime without a man showing them how, the study reported that half of the women reported seriously traumatic health (including mental health) histories, 37 percent reported extreme physical violence in the homes where they grew up, and 62 percent had been victims of crimes such as rape, aggravated assault, and robbery (Bunch et al., 1983).

A major contributor to the understanding of childhood traumas and sub-sequent offending is Cathy Spatz Widom. One study, comparing the juvenile and adult offense records of more than 1,500 persons who had and had not been abused as children, found that abused and neglected girls were signifi-cantly more likely than their nonabused/neglected counterparts to have both formal adult and formal juvenile criminal records (Widom 1989). The abused/neglected girls, however, were no more likely than the nonabused/neglected girls to have a record for *violent* crimes. In another publication, Rivera and Widom (1990) reported that girls who were abused or neglected were at an increased risk for arrest for a violent crime while still a juvenile, although abused and neglected boys were not more likely than nonabused/nonneglected boys to face arrests for violent crimes. Most recently, Widom (1995) examined 908 individuals who at the age of 11 years or younger had victimization cases of child abuse (physical or sexual) or neglect processed through the courts between 1967 and 1971. The sample then added nonabused and nonneglected youth with similar characteristics who were "matched" on other characteristics as a control group.

> At the time they were chosen for the study, none of them had as yet engaged in delinquent or criminal behavior. The major aim of this analy-sis was to determine whether sexual abuse during childhood puts victims at greater risk for criminal behavior later in life than do the other types of [childhood] maltreatment [nonsexual physical abuse and neglect]. (ibid., 3)

Given that the data collection relied solely on officially reported child abuse and neglect cases, it is likely that the abuse and neglect cases represented only the most serious and extreme abuse and neglect cases (ibid., 4).

As expected, Widom (ibid.) found that individuals who experienced child-hood abuse (physical or sexual) or neglect were more likely than their nonabused and nonneglected counterparts to be arrested later in life. Indeed, slightly over one-quarter (26 percent) of the youth who experienced abuse and/or neglect were arrested as juveniles, and about the same percent (29 per-cent) were arrested as adults. Although childhood sexual abuse victimization placed an individual at increased risk of future arrests, these childhood abuse survivors were no more likely to be arrested later in life than the individuals who experienced no (officially reported) sexual abuse but experienced (offi-cially reported) physical abuse and/or neglect. However, individuals officially designated as "sexual abuse plus" victims, those who experienced sexual abuse *plus* physical abuse and/or neglect as a child, were at the greatest risk of being arrested for running away. *A significant finding of this study was that childhood sex-ual abuse victims were far more likely to be arrested for prostitution than their nonsex-ually abused counterparts.* (However, arrests for running away did not significantly predispose youth to prostitution arrests.) Additionally, careful analysis was conducted to determine the individual effects of three types of abuse: any sexual abuse, any physical abuse, and any neglect. Notably, "any sexual abuse" had the greatest impact on the likelihood of being arrested for prostitution, and "any non-sexual physical abuse" had the greatest impact on the likelihood of being arrested for rape or sodomy. Stated alternatively, regarding the link between childhood abuse types and subsequent "sex crimes" offending, of the three types of childhood victimizations (sexual, physical, and neglect), childhood sexual abuse has the greatest impact on subsequent prostitution offending, and (nonsexual) physical childhood abuse has the greatest impact on the likelihood of committing rape or sodomy. Unfortunately, these statistics lump females and males together, so we don't know how these dynamics may have varied by gender.

Regina A. Arnold (1990) conducted intensive interviews, participant observation, and questionnaires with 60 African-American women prisoners. Similar to the previous "pathways" studies, Arnold (ibid., 154) explains how these women were labeled and processed as deviants and delinquents as young girls "for refusing to accept or participate in their own victimization." This refusal led to their structural dislocation from three primary socialization institutions: the family, the educational system, and occupational systems. This dislocation, in turn, led to their entry into "criminal life." Arnold effectively discusses how patriarchal families and family violence, economic marginality, racist teachers, and a poor educational system individually and collectively produce environments leading to the criminalization of girls, where they are alienated in their own homes, schools, and communities. Furthermore, Arnold (ibid.) reports that these women and girls often "self-medicate" with drugs in attempts to numb the pain from their violent experiences and pasts.

Margaret Shaw's (1991) study surveying women in Canadian prisons, convicted of both violent and nonviolent offenses, found that 68 percent reported having been physically abused at some time in their lives, and 53 percent reported sexual abuse experiences at some point. These rates were higher for the Aboriginal women: 90 percent reported physical victimization at some point, and 61 percent reported sexual victimization. "Some said that they had 'got over' what occurred, others that they felt they needed a great deal of help" (Shaw, 1995, 125). Shaw discusses how their physical and sexual victimization histories were not the only life experiences they reported that might be related to their criminal acts and behaviors:

> [S]eventy-five percent had an involvement with substance abuse, 66 percent had no work skills or regular legitimate employment, [and] almost half had severe disruption in their early lives. The Aboriginal women in particular have a history as victims of racism, violence in the home and on the street, dependence on drugs and alcohol from a very young age, being sent to institutions or white foster homes with sometimes as many as forty-seven different placements before the age of fifteen or sixteen. For some women, although not all, their contact with society has been one of violence and punishment almost all their lives. (ibid., 126)

Mary E. Gilfus (1992) also conducted intensive interviews with incarcerated women. The life histories of the 20 women she interviewed were analyzed in an attempt to understand their entries into street crime. Similar to the pathways studies presented thus far, these women also reported patterns of victimization to offending. Many of these women's survival skills to avoid victimization were criminal: running away from home, using drugs, and prostitution. The women were from economically disadvantaged backgrounds, particularly the African-American women. In addition to abuse and poverty, prevalent in the women's childhoods, were educational neglect and extremely troubling school experiences. The Black women reported significant racial violence in their childhoods, including a girl who had witnessed her uncle murdered by two white men. The victimization, then, led to offending, which led to *revictimization* in their lives on the street, including rape, assault, and attempted murder. Many of the women in Gilfus's (ibid.) sample also reported experiencing battering by their intimate male partners in adulthood, as well.

Kathleen Daly (1992) examines both male and female offenders but focuses on women's distinct pathways to lawbreaking. Specifically, she uses felony court presentence investigation reports (PSIs) as biographies of offending women. Daly identifies five categories of women: street women, harmed-and-harming women, battered women, drug-connected women, and "other." Although there is considerable overlap between the women's experiences (for example, battering victim/survivor, alcohol and drug abuse, and abuse or neglect as children), each category identifies a specific feature that brings the woman to felony court.

Daly's *street woman* category draws on Eleanor M. Miller's (1986) work and book of the same title. The street woman has typically experienced significant amounts of physical and psychological damage as a child or adult, and she hustles on the street to "eke out a living" (Daly, 1992, 37). Street women often support their drug habits by prostitution, selling drugs, and stealing, which is usually what brings them to court. Daly's second category, the *harmed-and-harming woman,* on the other hand, is characterized by abuse and neglect as a child, which led to "acting out" and being labeled a "problem child." Alcohol often leads to her becoming violent, and she may be drug-addicted. The harmed-and-harming woman's inability to cope with a certain situation, such as feeling someone "did her wrong," is what brings her to court. Also, unlike the street woman, the harmed-and-harming woman is not living on the streets and hustling, and she harms others because she is angry.

Daly's (ibid.) third category of women's pathways to lawbreaking is the *battered woman.* This woman is either currently in, or has just ended, a relationship with a violent man. Although women in some of Daly's other categories were also battered, being involved with a violent man is what brings the women in the battered-woman category to court. The "crime" for which the battered woman goes to court is typically harming or killing the abusive man during an assault on her. Daly's *drug-connected woman,* on the other hand, uses or sells drugs as a result of her relationships with her male intimate, children, or mother. Her drug experiences are recent, and like the battered women, she does not tend to have much of a criminal record. For example, of the women Daly classified as "drug-connected," one woman allowed her boyfriend to use her apartment to sell drugs, and another stole and pawned her parents' silverware to support her and her husband's drug habit.

Daly's (ibid.) final category, which she simply labels *other,* can best be defined as economically motivated. Either greed or a pressing economic circumstance motivated the crimes. Other women do not have a history of abuse or problems with drugs or alcohol. For example, Daly describes a woman who embezzled over $125,000 although she and her husband had no major debts. Daly believes that the street woman pathway to crime is probably more common in the misdemeanor than the felony courts but offers the remaining four categories of pathways as a means to "argue for a more multi-dimensional portrait of why women get caught up in crime" (ibid., 45).

One of the most profound studies addressing "pathways" to crime is Beth E. Richie's (1996) research focusing on African-American battered women in prison (although she also collected data from white battered and African-American nonbattered women in prison). In this work, Richie used "life-history interviews" to elicit women's voices. Ultimately, she develops her theory of *gender entrapment* in an attempt to understand the "contradictions and complications of the lives of the African-American battered women who commit crimes" (ibid., 4). More specifically, gender entrapment involves understanding the connections between (1) violence against women in their intimate relationships, (2) culturally constructed gender-identity development, and (3) women's participation in illegal activities. Two of the many important contributions of Richie's (ibid.) research are her dispelling of myths about battered women regarding "why they stay" and her investigation into the impacts of race and racism. For example, a major finding is that the African-American battered women appeared to have had a more privileged childhood family environment (e.g., felt loved and important) than the white battered women and the African-American nonbattered women. Richie (ibid.) suggests this "heightened status" in their families of origin is what makes these women vulnerable to entrapment when they become involved with batterers: They have become disappointed with their experiences in the public sphere where they encountered racism instead of a heightened status, thus they refocus their goal on obtaining the perfect nuclear family. When the battering starts, they hold an optimism about being able to "fix" things. In addition to reporting how battered women are "trapped by the violence" in their abusive intimate partner relationships as adults, she also reports "six paths to crime," reported in Figure 2.1.

The goal of Joan W. Moore's (1999) study of Latino/a gang members and their families in East Los Angeles was to understand gang membership in terms of major themes relating to the family, including immigration and ethnicity, parental economic status, and the climate of the homes in which the gang members were raised. Ethnic identity was reported as confusing for many of these youth, as they were virtually all born in the United States, yet were raised by their parents and treated by racist whites as if they were Mexican. (For the parents, the Mexican identity was positive; for racist whites, it was negative.) For both girls and boys, the racist experiences with whites could lead to fights.

Pathways Associated with African American Battered Women

- *Women Held Hostage* This pathway involved women whose intimate partner batterers used extreme violence against them to keep them hostage and isolated, and these women were frequently charged in the deaths of their children that were committed by their batterers.

- *Projection and Association* This pathway involved battered women who committed violent crimes against men other than their batterers, where the new men served as "proxies" for their batterers, as projected or symbolic retaliation for past abuse.

- *Poverty* These were women arrested for property or other economically motived crimes (e.g., burglary, forgery, robbery, and possession of stolen property).

Pathways Associated with both African American and White Battered Women

- *Sexual Exploitation* Although many of the women reported prostitution or sex-for-drugs experiences, this pathway involved women who ended up in prison due to illegal sex work. Notably, their batterers often forced/coerced them into the prostitution which landed them in prison, and the women in this category had higher rates of child and adulthood sexual abuse histories.

- *Fighting Back* This pathway involved battered women who committed offenses (arson, other property offenses, or assaults on their batterers) in the context of an assault against them by their batterers. The women did not deny their actions but viewed them more as "self-defense" than as crimes.

Pathways Equally Associated with African American Battered Women, White Battered Women, and African American Non-battered Women

- *Addiction* Women whose primary offense landing them in prison was a drug offense. For the African American battered women, the drug use usually followed a battering incident, and drugs were used as a way to "reconnect" with the batterer (e.g., to create emotional intimacy). Indeed, some African American women indicated that their drug use/addiction started with being forced to take drugs by their batterers. The non-battered African American women reported more voluntary initiation into drug use. A White battered woman reported her arrest for selling drugs was due her attempt to be able to afford to leave her batterer.

FIGURE 2.1 Richie's Incarcerated Women's Six Paths to Crime

SOURCE: Richie, Beth E. 1996. *Compelled to Crime: The Gender Entrapment of Battered Black Women.* New York: Routledge.

For both sexes, the households in which they were raised were more reflective of "poverty" than of the traditional extended Mexican families, and their parents were usually poorly educated. Although fathers were far more likely than mothers to work outside the home, most of the parents "did not hold very good jobs" (ibid., 163). Notably, girls (44 percent) were far more likely than boys (19 percent) to report that their mothers worked outside the home. *Despite these patterns of poverty, Moore reports that the emotional climate of the family during childhood was a far better predictor of youth in this area to join a gang than were the strains of poverty and immigrant life.*

Moore (ibid., 165) reports that many of the gang members' families were not particularly happy, and some were "acutely unhappy." Moreover, one-third of the male members and forty percent of the female members reported seeing their fathers beat their mothers. When asked about their reaction to their fathers' abuse of their mothers, about half of the females and two-thirds of the males "withdrew in fear" (ibid., 167). Notably, the females were more likely than the males to try to intervene and stop their fathers' abuse of their mothers or to fight their fathers themselves. About half of the males and two-thirds of the females were clearly afraid of their fathers, often "with good reason" (ibid., 168). Girls were also more likely to be afraid of their mothers than were boys, and consistent with other research, girls tended to be far more restricted than their brothers by their parents. Females were more likely than males to describe their parents as strict and to say their parents enforced rules with them. Although a few male members of the sample reported inappropriate sexual advances made to them as children, 29 percent of the females reported incest, usually perpetrated by a father but also by uncles, brothers, and grandfathers. Although Moore (ibid., 174) found that both male and female gang members report common experiences with "troubled" families, "clearly more women than men came from troubled families. They were more likely to have been living with a chronically sick relative, one who died, one who was a heroin addict, or one who was arrested. In fact, a large majority of the [gang] women had a relative die or be arrested [when they were children]" (ibid.).

Candace Kruttschnitt's (1996) overview of research on gender and crime includes "exposure to parental deviance" in the rubric of social learning theory. However, in many senses what she discusses is relevant for life course or pathways research as well. Specifically, she examines two aspects of parental deviance: exposure to parental violence including harsh discipline and the effects of parental deviance on their children's offending.

> In both cases there is evidence that gender modifies the outcomes. In the case of parental violence, girls who have been abused or neglected in their families or those who have witnessed family violence are less likely to engage in violent or aggressive behaviors . . . or to have an arrest record for substance use than comparable boys . . . Interestingly, however, there is some evidence of higher rates of depression among maltreated girls than boys. (ibid., 140)

In a recent book, *"In the Mix": Struggle and Survival in a Women's Prison,* Barbara Owen writes about her carefully conducted study of women in the largest women's prison in the world: the Central California Women's Facility (CCWF). This research included almost 300 face-to-face interviews with women prisoners. Although Owen's (1998) intention in the research had not been to report on these incarcerated women's life histories, she makes a compelling argument that understanding these life histories is essential for understanding women prisoners. She carefully addresses how women prisoners' life histories explain not only how they ended up in prison but also how these histories, including childhood abuses in intimate partner victimization (domestic violence), are related to how they experience prison. Specifically, Owen (ibid.) identifies five significant phenomena in the "pathways to imprisonment": (1) the multiplicity of abuse; (2) early family life; (3) children; (4) the street life; and (5) spiraling marginality. The *multiplicity of abuse* is consistent with the other research reported in this section, in that the women in Owen's study report numerous types of physical, sexual, and emotional abuse. For example, about 70 percent of the women experienced *ongoing* physical abuse under the age of 18 (usually perpetrated by a father, step-father, or mother), and 62 percent experienced *ongoing* physical abuse at age 18 and older (usually perpetrated by a spouse or boyfriend). About 40 percent reported *ongoing* sexual abuse under the age of 18 (usually perpetrated by a father, step-father, or other male relative), and 40 percent reported *ongoing* sexual abuse over the age of 17 (usually perpetrated by a spouse, partner, or boyfriend). In her discussion of *children* as a pathway of women to prison, Owen states:

> Relationships with children are central to the lives of many of the women at CCWF. The presence of children in the lives of these women shapes their pre-prison experience, as well as how they serve their time. . . . These relationships, however, often duplicate the disorder and disorganization of their own childhoods, bringing these problems full circle. (ibid., 54–55)

In the discussion of the third pathway to prison, *street life,* which Owen (ibid.) identifies, she emphasizes that although most of the women did *not* experience gang activity or youthful incarcerations, for some of the women their "disordered" lives included early histories of juvenile crimes and gang membership. Owen (ibid.) found that once a girl/woman was involved with street life, she moved farther from attachments to conventional ties. Owen's (ibid., 61) final category of women's pathways to crime, *spiraling marginality,* is related to the related intersection of substance abuse and street life:

> For women on the economic and social margins, looking to escape home lives or simply looking for excitement unavailable through the conventional world, the fast life becomes a reasonable survival option. This life is shaped by the overlapping dimensions of drug use, crime, and, often, violence. The pathway to imprisonment is shaped by choices made by women looking for excitement or lucrative hustles or otherwise unable to make it in the traditional world. Once again, these data also suggest that the prime motivation for most women's crime is economic, psychological, and social survival. . . . The most often cited reason for not working was substance abuse problems. . . . The second most often cited reason for not working was "made more money from crime and hustling," with child care responsibilities a close third. (ibid., 61)

In this discussion of feminist research on the pathways to crime, focusing largely on the victimization-to-offending trajectory, it is important to note Lisa Maher's (1997) feminist critique of both the traditional (non- or antifeminist) *and* feminist research. Maher claims that the approaches to women's involvement in crime dichotomizes their agency. One approach (the more traditional approach) tends to ignore the gendered, classed, and raced world in which most female offenders exist, viewing them as "active subjects" seeking criminal opportunities with "over-endowed" agency (ibid., 1). The other approach, consistent with feminist pathways modeling, is in many ways the extreme opposite. Maher criticizes this approach for denying women any agency:

> . . . . where women are portrayed as the passive victims of oppressive social structures, relations and substances, or some combination thereof. Women are cast as submissive objects, serving as mere automata for the reproduction of determining structures. Constituted by and through their status as victims, they are devoid of choice, responsibility, or accountability; fragments of social debris floundering in a theoretical tide of victimage. (ibid.)

SUMMARY

Theories attempting to explain the etiology of criminal behaviors (and reactions by the crime-processing system) have proposed biological, psychological, social, political, and economic causes. The earliest theories focused on biology and the individual, whereas more recent theories have focused on the societal, economic, and political sources of crime. Most of these theories were developed to explain male criminality. Until Adler's women's "liberation" theory, most theorists made little attempt to account for female criminality. When they did, their hypotheses were fraught with sexist stereotypes, often defining female crime in terms of sexuality. The findings of this research are inconsistent; it is still unclear how males' and females' socialization and responses by the criminal-processing system differ and how these may affect their crime and delinquency rates.

In 1975, for the first time, a theory was developed to explain women's criminal behavior: women's "liberation" theory (Adler, 1975; Simon, 1975). Unfortunately, this theory was based on erroneous assumptions about the feminist movement, and statistics and their interpretations were often misleading. It is vital that future theory building and theory testing examine "pathways" to crime, sexuality, family factors, social and economic status, same-sex friendships, and mixed-sex friendships as equally relevant (or in the case of sexuality, perhaps irrelevant) for studies of both males and females (Campbell, 1990). Future theory building cannot assume, moreover, that women or girls as a group behave similarly to each other. For example, recent research applying various theories to white and African-American women found that social–psychological variables were more related to white than to African-American women's involvement in crime, whereas African-American women's crime rates were more affected by structural forces (Hill and Crawford, 1990).

Although there is a renewed interest in biology to determine gender differences in crime and to explain men's violence against women, at the same time, some of the new feminist and pro-feminist theories are offering exciting ways to assess how both girls' and boys' life experiences (e. g., experiences with abuse, schools, peers, and so on) are likely related to their subsequent offending. Unfortunately, the life course research, to date, rarely includes women in the sample, and even the research on men, though promising, does not appear to adequately assess childhood abuse variables. However, it offers the potential to enhance understanding of girls' trajectories into crime if girls and women are included in the samples and childhood victimizations and experiences can be validly measured. To date, the most useful data regarding understanding girls' and women's, and perhaps boys' and men's, entries into delinquency and crime, are the pathways models. Although they are considered somewhat "new," studies confirming a pathways model date back to the 1970s and have consistently suggested the need to understand the role of childhood and adulthood traumas as precursors to offending.

REFERENCES

Abelson, Elaine S. 1989. "The Invention of Kleptomania." *Signs* 15:123–143.

Acoca, Leslie, and James Austin. 1996. *The Crisis: Women in Prison.* The National Council on Crime and Delinquency, February.

Adams, David. 1992. "Biology Does Not Make Men More Aggressive than Women." Pp. 17–26 in *Of Mice and Women: Aspects of Female Aggression,* edited by K. Bjorkqvistand and P. Niemela. San Diego: Academic Press.

Adler, Freda. 1975. *Sisters in Crime: The Rise of the New Female Criminal.* New York: McGraw-Hill.

Arnold, Regina A. 1990. "Women of Color: Processes of Victimization and Criminalization of Black Women." *Social Justice* 17(3):153–166.

Becker, Howard S. 1963. *Outsiders: Studies in the Sociology of Deviance.* New York: Free Press.

Belknap, Joanne. 1997. "Variations in Perspectives and Quality in Three Books on Rape." *Criminal Justice Review* 22(1):77–84.

Benton, David. 1992. "Hormones and Human Aggression." Pp. 37–48 in *Of Mice and Women: Aspects of Female Aggression,* edited by K. Bjorkqvistand and P. Niemela. San Diego: Academic Press.

Bjorkqvist, Kaj, and Pirkko Niemela (Eds.). 1992. *Of Mice and Women: Aspects of Female Aggression.* San Diego: Academic Press.

Bjorkqvist, Kaj, and Pirkko Niemela. 1992. "New Trends in the Study of Female Aggression." Pp. 3–16 in *Of Mice and Women: Aspects of Female Aggression,* edited by K. Bjorkqvistand and P. Niemela. San Diego: Academic Press.

Bonger, Willem. 1969. *Criminality and Economic Conditions.* Bloomington: Indiana University Press.

Booth, Alan, and D. Wayne Osgood. 1993. "The Influence of Testosterone on Deviance in Adulthood." *Criminology* 31(1):93–118.

Bottcher, Jean. 1995. "Gender as Social Control." *Justice Quarterly* 12(1):33–58.

Box, Steven, and Chris Hale. 1983. "Liberation and Female Criminality in England and Wales." *British Journal of Criminology* 23:35.

———. 1984. "Liberation/Emancipation, Economic Marginalization, or Less Chivalry: The Relevance of Three Arguments to Female Crime Patterns in England and Wales, 1951–1980." *Criminology* 22:473–498.

Brown, Beverly. 1990. "Reassessing the Critique of Biologism." Pp. 41–56 in

Feminist Perspectives in Criminology, edited by L. Gelsthorpe and A. Morris. Buckingham, England: Open University Press.

Bunch, Barbara J., Linda A. Foley, and Susana P. Urbina. 1983. "The Psychology of Violent Female Offenders: A Sex-Role Perspective." *The Prison Journal* 63:66–79.

Campbell, Anne. 1987. "Self Definition by Rejection: The Case of Gang Girls." *Social Problems* 34:451–466.

———. 1990. "On the Invisibility of the Female Delinquent Peer Group." *Women and Criminal Justice* 2:41–62.

Cernkovich, Stephen, and Peggy Giordano. 1979. "A Comparative Analysis of Male and Female Delinquency." *The Sociological Quarterly* 20:131–145.

———. 1987. "Family Relationships and Delinquency." *Criminology* 25:295–321.

Chesney-Lind, Meda, and Rodriguez, Noelie. 1983. Women under Lock and Key. *Prison Journal* 63:47–65.

Chilton, Ronald, and Susan K. Datesman. 1987. "Gender, Race, and Crime: An Analysis of Urban Trends, 1960–1980." *Gender and Society* 1:152–171.

Church, George. 1990. "The View from behind Bars." *Time Magazine* Fall 135:20–22.

Clark, S. M. 1964. "Similarities in Components of Female and Male Delinquency: Implications for Sex-Role Theory." P. 217 *in Interdisciplinary Problems in Criminology,* edited by W. C. Reckless and C. L. Newman. Columbus: Ohio State University.

Cloward, R. A., and L. E. Ohlin. 1960. *Delinquency and Opportunity: A Theory of Delinquent Gangs.* New York: Free Press.

Cohen, Albert K. 1955. *Delinquent Boys: The Culture of the Gang.* New York: Free Press.

Covington, Jeanette. 1986. "Self-Esteem and Deviance: The Effects of Race and Gender." *Criminology* 24:105–138.

Cowie, John, Valerie Cowie, and Eliot Slater. 1968. *Delinquency in Girls.* London: Heinemann.

Cressey, Donald. 1964. *Delinquency, Crime, and Differential Association.* The Hague: Martinus Nijhoff.

Crites, Laura. 1976. *The Female Offender.* Lexington, MA: D. C. Heath.

Cullen, Francis T., Kathryn M. Golden, and John B. Cullen. 1979. "Sex and Delinquency." *Criminology* 17:301–310.

Curran, Daniel J. 1984. "The Myth of the 'New' Female Delinquent." *Crime and Delinquency* 30:386–399.

Daly, Kathleen. 1992. "Women's Pathways to Felony Court: Feminist Theories of Lawbreaking and Problems of Representation." *Review of Law and Women's Studies* 2:11–52.

———. 1994. *Gender, crime and punishment.* New Haven: Yale University Press.

Datesman, Susan, Frank Scarpitti, and Richard Stephenson. 1975. "Female Delinquency: An Application of Self and Opportunity Theories." *Journal of Research in Crime and Delinquency* 12:107–123.

Dembo, Richard, Gary Grandon, Lawrence La Voie, and William Burgos. 1986. "Parents and Drugs Revisited: Some Further Evidence in Support of Social Learning Theory." *Criminology* 24:85–103.

Dornfeld, Maude, and Candace Kruttschnitt. 1992. "Do the Stereotypes Fit? Mapping Gender-Specific Outcomes and Risk Factors." *Criminology* 30:397–420.

Elder, Glen H. 1985. "Perspectives in the Life Course." Pp. 23–49 in *Life Course Dynamics,* edited by G. H. Elder. Ithaca, NY: Cornell University Press.

Ellis. 1993. in *Sexual Aggression: Issues in Etiology, Assessment, and Treatment,* G. N. Hall, R. Hisrchman, J. Graham, and M. Zragoza (Eds). Washington, DC: Taylor and Francis.

Erikson, Kai T. 1962. "Notes on the Sociology of Deviance." *Social Problems* 9:309–314.

Esbensen, Finn-Aage, and David Huizinga. 1993. "Gangs, Drugs, and Delinquency in a Survey of Urban Youth. *Criminology* 31:565–590.

Faith, Karlene. 1993. *Unruly Women: The Politics of Confinement and Resistance.* Vancouver: Press Gang Publishers.

Farrington, David P. 1992. "Criminal Career Research in the United Kingdom." *British Journal of Criminology* 32(4):521–536.

Fausto-Sterling, Anne. 1985. *Myths of Gender: Biological Theory about Women and Men.* New York: Basic Books.

Feinman, Clarice. 1986. *Women in the Criminal Justice System,* 2nd ed. New York: Praeger.

Felthous, Alan R., and Bernard Yudowitz. 1977. "Approaching a Comparative Typology of Assaultive Female Offenders." *Psychiatry* 40:270–276.

Figueira-McDonough, Josephine. 1984. "Feminism and Delinquency: In Search of an Elusive Link." *British Journal of Criminology* 24:325–342.

———. 1992. "Community Structure and Female Delinquency Rates: A Heuristic Discussion." *Youth and Society* 24(1):3–30.

Figueira-McDonough, Josephine, William H. Barton, and Rosemary C. Sarri. 1981. "Normal Deviance: Gender Similarities in Adolescent Subcultures." Pp. 17–45 in *Comparing Female and Male Offenders,* edited by M. Q. Warren. Beverly Hills, CA: Sage.

Figueira-McDonough, Josephine, and E. Selo. 1980. "A Reformulation of the 'Equal Opportunity' Explanation of Female Delinquency." *Crime and Delinquency* July: 333–343.

Fletcher, Beverly R., and Dreama G. Moon. 1993. "Introduction." Pp. 5–14 in *Women Prisoners: A Forgotten Population,* edited by B. R. Fletcher, L. D. Shaver, and D. G. Moon. Westport, CT: Praeger.

Frigon, Sylvie. 1995. "A Genealogy of Women's Madness." Pp. 20–48 in *Gender and Crime,* edited by R. E. Dobash, R. P. Dobash, and L. Noaks. Cardiff: University of Wales Press.

Fox, G. L. 1977. " 'Nice Girl': Social Control of Women through a Value Construct." *Signs* 2:805.

Freud, Sigmund. 1933. *New Introductory Lectures on Psychoanalysis.* New York: W. W. Norton.

Gilfus, Mary E. 1992. From Victims to Survivors to Offenders: Women's Routes of Entry and Immersion into Street Crime. *Women and Criminal Justice* 4:63–90.

Giordano, Peggy C. 1978. "Girls, Guys, and Gangs: The Changing Social Context of Female Delinquency." *Journal of Criminal Law and Criminology* 69:126–132.

Gordon, David. 1973. "Capitalism, Class, and Crime in America." *Crime and Delinquency* 19:163–186.

Gottfredson, Michael R., and Travis Hirschi. 1990. *A General Theory of Crime.* Stanford: Stanford University Press.

Hagan, John, A. R. Gillis, and John H. Simpson. 1985. "The Class Structure of Gender and Delinquency." *American Journal of Sociology* 90:1151–1178.

Hagan, John, John H. Simpson, and A. R. Gillis. 1979. "The Sexual Stratification of Social Control: A Gender-Based Perspective on Crime and Delinquency." *British Journal of Sociology* 30:25.

———. 1987. "Class in the Household: A Power-Control Theory of Gender and Delinquency." *American Journal of Sociology* 92:788–816.

Hall, Gordon N., Richard Hisrchman, John Graham, and Maira Zragoza (Eds.). 1993. *Sexual Aggression.* Washington, DC: Taylor and Francis.

Harris, Anthony. 1977. "Sex and Theories of Deviance: Toward a Functional Theory of Deviant Type-Scripts." *American Sociological Review* 42:3–16.

Harris, Mary B. 1996. "Aggression, Gender, and Ethnicity." *Aggression and Violent Behavior* 1(2):123–146.

Heidensohn, Frances M. 1985. *Women and Crime: The Life of the Female Offender.* New York: New York University Press.

Hill, Gary D., and Maxine P. Atkinson. 1988. "Gender, Familial Control, and Delinquency." *Criminology* 26:127–149.

Hill, Gary D., and Elizabeth M. Crawford. 1990. "Women, Race, and Crime." *Criminology* 28:601–626.

Hindelang, M. 1971. "Age, Sex and Versatility of Delinquent Involvement." *Social Problems* 21:471.

———. 1973. "Cases of Delinquency: A Partial Replication and Extension." *Social Problems* 21:471.

Hirschi, Travis. 1969. *Cases of Delinquency.* Berkeley: University of California Press.

Hoffman-Bustamante, Dale. 1973. "The Nature of Female Criminality." *Issues in Criminology* 8:117–136.

Immarigeon, Russ, and Meda Chesney-Lind. 1992. *Women's Prisons: Overcrowded and Overused.* San Francisco: National Council on Crime and Delinquency.

James, Jennifer, and Jane Meyerding. 1977. "Early Sexual Experiences and Prostitution." *American Journal of Psychiatry* 134(12):1381–1385.

Jang, Sung Joon, and Marvin D. Krohn. 1995. "Developmental Patterns of Sex Differences in Delinquency among African American Adolescents: A Test of the Sex-Invariance Hypothesis." *Journal of Quantitative Criminology* 11(2):195–222.

Jensen, Gary J., and Raymond Eve. 1976. "Sex Differences in Delinquency." *Criminology* 13:427–448.

Jensen, Gary F., and K. Thompson. 1990. "What's Class Got to Do with It? A Further Examination of Power-Control Theory." *American Journal of Sociology* 95:1009–1023.

Joe, Karen A., and Meda Chesney-Lind. 1995. " 'Just Every Mother's Angel': An Analysis of Gender and Ethnic Variations in Youth Gang Membership." *Gender and Society* 9(4):408–431.

Johnson, Richard E. 1986. "Family Structure and Delinquency: General Patterns and Gender Differences." *Criminology* 24:65–84.

Kitsuse, John I. 1962. "Societal Reaction to Deviant Behavior: Problems of Theory and Method." *Social Problems* 9:247–256.

Klein, Dorie. 1980. "The Etiology of Female Crime: A Review of the Literature." Pp. 70–105 in *Women, Crime, and Justice,* edited by S. K. Datesman and F. R. Scarpitti. New York: Oxford University Press.

Klein, Dorie, and June Kress. 1976. "Any Woman's Blues: A Critical Overview of Women, Crime, and the Criminal Justice System." *Crime and Social Justice* 5:34–49.

Kline, Sue. 1993. "A Profile of Female Offenders in State and Federal Prisons." Pp. 16 in *Female Offenders: Meeting the Needs of a Neglected Population.* Laurel, MD: American Correctional Association.

Konopka, Gisela. 1966. *The Adolescent Girl in Conflict.* Englewood Cliffs, NJ: Prentice-Hall.

Kruttschnitt, Candace. 1996. "Contributions of Quantitative Methods to the Study of Gender and Crime, or Bootstrapping Our Way into the Theoretical Thicket." *Journal of Quantitative Criminology* 12(2):135–161.

Laub, John H., and Janet L. Lauritsen. 1993. "Violent Criminal Behavior over the Life Course: A Review of the Longitudinal and Comparative Research." *Violence and Victims* 8(3):235–252.

Laub, John H., and Robert J. Sampson. 1993. "Turning Points in the Life Course: Why Change Matters to the Study of Crime." *Criminology* 31(3):301–325.

Lauritsen, Janet L. 1993. "Sibling Resemblance in Juvenile Delinquency." *Criminology* 31:387–410.

Lemert, Edwin M. 1951. *Social Pathology: A Systematic Approach to the Theory of Sociopathic Behavior.* New York: McGraw-Hill.

Leonard, Eileen B. 1982. *Women, Crime, and Society: A Critique of Criminology Theory.* New York: Longman.

Lerman, Paul. 1966. "Individual Values, Peer Values and Subcultural Delinquency." *American Sociological Review* 33:219–235.

Loeber, Rolf. 1996. "Developmental Continuity, Change, and Pathways in Male Juvenile Problem Behavior." Pp. 1–28 in *Delinquency and Crime,* edited by J. David Hawkins. New York: Cambridge University Press.

Lombroso, Cesare, and William Ferrero. 1895. *The Female Offender.* London: Fisher Unwin.

Loy, P., and S. Norland. 1981. "Gender Convergence and Delinquency." *Sociological Quarterly* 22:525.

Lynch, Michael J., and W. Byron Groves. 1989. *A Primer in Radical Criminology,* 2nd ed. New York: Harrow and Heston.

Maher, Lisa. 1997. *Sexed Work: Gender, Race and Resistance in a Brooklyn Drug Market.* Oxford: Clarendon Press.

Mann, Coramae Richey. 1984. *Female Crime and Delinquency.* Montgomery: University of Alabama Press.

McCord, Joan, and L. Otten. 1983. "A Consideration of Sex Roles and Motivations for Crime." *Criminal Justice and Behavior* 10:3–12.

Merton, Robert K. 1938. "Social Structure and Anomie." *American Sociological Review* 3:672–682.

———. 1949. *Social Theory and Social Structure.* Glencoe, IL: Free Press.

Messerschmidt, James W. 1988. "From Marx to Bonger: Socialist Writings on Women, Gender, and Crime." *Sociological Inquiry* 58:378–392.

———. 1993. *Masculinities and Crime.* Lanham, MD: Rowman & Littlefield.

Miller, Susan L., and Cynthia Burack. 1993. "A Critique of Gottfredson and Hirschi's General Theory of Crime: Selective (In)Attention to Gender and Power Positions." *Women and Criminal Justice* 4:115–134.

Moffitt, Terrie E. 1990. "Juvenile Delinquency and Attention Deficit Disorder: Boys' Development Trajectories from Age 3 to Age 15." *Child Development* 61:893–910.

———. 1993. "Adolescence-Limited and Life-Course-Persistent Antisocial Behavior: A Developmental Taxonomy." *Psychological Review* 100(4):674–701.

Moore, Joan W. 1999. "Gang Members' Families." Pp. 159–176 in *Female Gangs in America: Essays on Girls, Gangs and Gender,* edited by M. Chesney-Lind and J. M. Hagedorn. Chicago: Lakeview Press.

Morash, Merry. 1983. "Gangs, Groups, and Delinquency." *British Journal of Criminology* 23:309–335.

———. 1986. "Gender, Peer Group Experiences, and Seriousness of Delinquency." *Journal of Research in Crime and Delinquency* 23:43–67.

Morash, Merry, and Meda Chesney-Lind. 1991. "A Re-Formulation and Patriarchal Test of the Power Control Theory of Delinquency." *Justice Quarterly* 8:347–378.

Morris, Allison. 1987. *Women, Crime and Criminal Justice.* Oxford: Basil Blackwell.

Morris, Ruth R. 1964. "Female Delinquency and Relational Problems." *Social Forces* 43:82–88.

———. 1965. "Attitudes toward Delinquency by Delinquents, Non-Delinquents and Their Friends." *British Journal of Criminology* 5:249–265.

Mumola, Christopher J., and Allen J. Beck. 1997. *Prisoners in 1996.* Bureau of Justice Statistics. U.S. Department of Justice, June, 15 pp.

Naffine, Ngaire. 1987. *Female Crime: The Construction of Women in Criminology.* Sydney, Australia: Allen and Unwin.

————. 1996. *Feminism and Criminology.* Philadelphia: Temple University Press.

Nagin, Daniel S., David P. Farrington, and Terrie E. Moffitt. 1995. "Life-Course Trajectories of Different Types of Offenders." *Criminology* 33(1):111–138.

Norland, Stephen, Randall C. Wessel, and Neal Shover. 1981. "Masculinity and Delinquency." *Criminology* 19:421–433.

Owen, Barbara. 1998. *In the Mix: Struggle and Survival in a Women's Prison.* Albany, NY: State University of New York Press.

Platt, Anthony. 1975. "Prospects for a Radical Criminology in the U.S." Pp. 95–112 in *Critical Criminology,* edited by I. Taylor, P. Walton, and J. Young. London: Routledge and Kegan Paul.

Pollak, Otto. 1950. *The Criminality of Women.* Philadelphia: University of Pennsylvania Press.

————. 1961. *The Criminality of Women.* New York: A. S. Barnes.

Pollock-Byrne, Joycelyn M. 1990. *Women, Prison, and Crime.* Pacific Grove, CA: Brooks/Cole.

Quinney, Richard. 1972. "The Ideology of Law: Notes for a Radical Alternative to Repression." *Issues in Criminology* 7:1–35.

————. 1975. *Criminology: Analysis and Critique of Crime in America.* Boston: Little, Brown.

Rafter, Nicole H., and E. M. Natalizia. 1981. "Marxist Feminism: Implications for Criminal Justice." *Crime and Delinquency* 81–98.

Rahav, Michael. 1984. "Norm Set and Deviant Behavior: The Case of Age-Sex Norms." *Deviant Behavior* 5:151–179.

Rasche, Christine. 1975. "The Female Offender as an Object of Criminological Research." Pp. 9–28 in *The Female Offender,* edited by A. M. Brodsky. Beverly Hills: Sage.

Rhode, Deborah L. 1990. "Feminist Critical Theories." *Stanford Law Review* 42:617–638.

Rice, Marcia. 1990. "Challenging Orthodoxies in Feminist Theory: A Black Feminist Critique." Pp. 57–69 in *Feminist Perspectives in Criminology,* edited by L. Gelsthorpe and A. Morris. Buckingham, England: Open University Press.

Richie, Beth E. 1996. *Compelled to Crime: The Gender Entrapment of Battered Black Women.* New York: Routledge.

Rittenhouse, C. Amanda. 1991. "The Emergence of Premenstrual Syndrome as a Social Problem." *Social Problems* 38:412–425.

Rivera, B., and Cathy S. Widom. 1990. "Childhood Victimization and Violent Offending." *Violence and Victims* 5(1):19–35.

Rosenbaum, Jill L. 1989. "Family Dysfunction and Female Delinquency." *Crime and Delinquency* 35:31–44.

Rowe, David C., Alexander T. Vazsonyi, Daniel J. Flannery. 1995. "Sex Differences in Crime: Do Means and Within-Sex Variation Have Similar Causes?" *Journal of Research in Crime and Delinquency* 32(1):84–100.

Sampson, Robert J., and John H. Laub. 1990. "Crime and Deviance over the Life Course: The Salience of Adult Social Bonds." *American Sociological Review.* 55:609–627.

Sandhu, Harjit S., and Donald E. Allen. 1969. "Female Delinquency: Goal Obstruction and Anomie." *Canadian Review of Sociology and Anthropology* 5:107–110.

Schur, Edwin M. 1984. *Labeling Women Deviant: Gender, Stigma, and Social Control.* New York: McGraw-Hill.

Schwendinger, Herman, and Julia Schwendinger. 1970. "Defenders of Order or Guardians of Human Rights?" *Issues in Criminology* 5:123–157.

Segrave, Jeffrey O., and Douglas N. Hastad. 1983. "Evaluating Structural and

Control Models of Delinquency Causation." *Youth and Society* 14:437–456.

Shaw, Margaret. 1991. *Survey of Federally Sentenced Women: Report to the Task Force on Federally Sentenced Women on the Prison Survey* (User Report 1991–4: Ottawa, Ministry of the Solicitor General).

———. 1995 "Conceptualizing Violence by Women." Pp. 115–131 in *Gender and Crime,* edited by R. E. Dobash, R. P. Dobash, and L. Noaks. Cardiff: University of Wales Press.

Shover, N., S. Norland, J. James, and W. Thornton. 1979. "Gender Roles and Delinquency." *Social Forces* 58:162.

Silbert, Mimi H., and Ayala M. Pines. 1981. "Sexual Abuse as an Antecedent to Prostitution." *Child Abuse and Neglect* 5:407–411.

Simon, Rita. 1975. *Women and Crime.* Lexington, MA: D. C. Heath.

Simons, R. L., M. G. Miller, and S. M. Aigner. 1980. "Contemporary Theories of Deviance and Female Delinquency: An Empirical Test." *Journal of Research in Crime and Delinquency* 17:42.

Singer, Susan J., and Murray Levine. 1988. "A Power-Control Theory, Gender, and Delinquency." *Criminology* 26:527–547.

Small, M. 1996. *Female Choices: Sexual Behavior of Female Primates.* Ithaca, NY: Cornell University Press.

Smart, Carol. 1976. *Women, Crime and Criminology: A Feminist Critique.* London: Routledge and Kegan Paul.

———. 1981. "Criminological Theory: Its Ideology and Implications concerning Women." Pp. 6–17 in *Women and Crime in America,* edited by L. H. Bowker. New York: Macmillan.

———. 1982. "The New Female Offender: Reality or Myth?" Pp. 105–116 in *The Criminal Justice System and Women,* edited by B. R. Price and N. J. Sokoloff. New York: Clark Boardman.

Smith, Douglas A. 1979. "Sex and Deviance: An Assessment of Major Sociological Variables." *Sociological Quarterly* 20:183.

Smith, Douglas A., and Christy A. Visher. 1980. "Sex and Involvement in Deviance/Crime: A Quantitative Review of the Empirical Literature." *American Sociological Review* 45:691–701.

Sommers, Ira, and Deborah R. Baskin. 1994. "Factors Related to Female Adolescent Initiation into Violent Street Crime." *Youth and Society* 25(4):468–489.

Spender, Dale. 1981. *Men's Studies Modified.* Oxford: Pergamon Press.

Stattin, Hakan, and David Magnusson. 1991. "Stability and Change in Criminal Behaviour Up to Age 30." *The British Journal of Criminology* 31(4):327–346.

Steffensmeier, Darrell J. 1980. "Sex Differences in Patterns of Adult Crime, 1965–1977: A Review and Assessment." *Social Forces* 58:1080–1108.

Steffensmeier, Darrell J., and Emilie A. Allan. 1988. "Sex Disparities in Arrests by Residence, Race, and Age: An Assessment of the Gender Convergence/Crime Hypothesis." *Justice Quarterly* 5:53–80.

Steffensmeier, Darrell J., and Cathy Streifel. 1992. "Time-Series Analysis of the Female Percentage of Arrests for Property Crimes, 1960–1985: A Test of Alternative Explanations." *Justice Quarterly* 9:77–104.

Sutherland, Edwin. 1939. *Principles of Criminology,* 3rd ed. Philadelphia: J. B. Lippincott.

Sutherland, Edwin, and Donald Cressey. 1966. *Principles of Criminology.* Philadelphia: J. B. Lippincott.

Taylor, Ian, Paul Walton, and Jock Young (Eds.). 1973. *The New Criminology: For a Social Theory of Deviance.* New York: Harper and Row.

———. (Eds.) 1975. *Critical Criminology.* London: Routledge and Kegan Paul.

Taylor, T. 1996. *The Prehistory of Sex.* New York: Bantam Books.

Thomas, W. I. 1907. *Sex and Society.* Boston: Little, Brown.

———. 1923. *The Unadjusted Girl.* Boston: Little, Brown.

———. 1967. The Unadjusted Girl. New York: Harper and Row.

Thompson, William E., Jim Mitchell, and Richard A. Dodder. 1984. "An Empirical Test of Hirschi's Control Theory of Delinquency." *Deviant Behavior* 5:11–22.

Thornton, W. E., and J. James. 1979. "Masculinity and Delinquency Revisited." *British Journal of Criminology* 19:225.

Torstensson, Marie. 1990. "Female Delinquents in a Birth Cohort: Some Aspects of Control Theory." *Journal of Quantitative Criminology* 6:101–115.

Vedder, Clyde, and Dora Somerville. 1970. *The Delinquent Girl.* Springfield, IL: Charles C. Thomas.

Widom, Cathy S. 1989. "The Cycle of Violence." *Science* 244:160–166.

———. 1995. Victims of Childhood Sexual Abuse—Later Criminal Consequences. Research in Brief, National Institute of Justice, U.S. Department of Justice.

Wrangham, R., and D. Peterson. 1996. *Demonic Males: Apes and the Origins of Human Violence.* New York: Houghton Mifflin.

Young, Alison, and Peter Rush. 1994. "The Law of Victimization in Urban Realism." In *The Futures of Criminology,* edited by David Nelken. London: Sage.

3

✳

The Frequency
and Nature of Female
Offending

Perhaps the least contentious proposition one
can advance within the discipline of criminology
is that women are more law-abiding than men.

(NAFFINE, 1987, 1)

As stated in Chapter 2, female crime has not historically been defined as a social problem. This is one reason criminologists and others have consistently left females out of their research models and study samples. Male crime, on the other hand, has been taken far more seriously, and male offenders are often seen as the "real" offenders. There is some truth to this: Studies consistently show not only that females generally commit fewer crimes than males but also that their offenses tend to be less serious and violent in nature.

This chapter draws on prior and current research and data in order to assess female offending. However, for a complete understanding of the studies and data, female offending must be examined and understood in a number of contexts:

1. The nature of female offending: the types of crimes women and girls commit

2. The extent of female offending: the frequency with which women and girls commit crimes

3. Gender comparisons in offending: how the nature and frequency of female and male offending compare

4. Changes over time in the extent, nature, and gender differences in offending

DESCRIPTION OF OFFENDING

The nature of offending, for the purposes of this book, addresses the type and seriousness of the offense. The extent of offending, on the other hand, is the frequency with which various offenses are committed. The term *offending* rather than *crime* is used, given that many of the studies are of youth and status offenses, behaviors that are not considered crimes when adults commit them (for example, truancy, drinking alcohol, and running away).

Offending rates are measured a number of ways. Typically, the rate is the number of offenses per 100,000 people in the population. Other measures of offending rates include giving high school students self-report surveys asking them how often (if ever) they participate in various offenses, or conducting interviews with sample participants. Whatever the structure for collecting offending rates, these rates are used to examine the extent and nature of offending at one point in time or over a period of time (if conducted repeatedly).

Table 1 presents data on 1998 arrests in the United States. Almost 22 percent of the arrests that year were of females, thus about one in five arrests. About 17 percent of all violent index crime arrests were of females, and this was highest for aggravated assaults (20 percent). Females' arrests constituted slightly over one-tenth of the arrests for murder and nonnegligent manslaughter, one-tenth of robbery arrests, and 1 percent of rape arrests. Almost 30 percent of property index crime arrests were of females, with the largest percent, 35 percent, for larceny-theft. Female arrests made up between 12 and 16 percent of the arrests for burglary, motor vehicle theft, and arson (see Table 3.1).

Table 3.2 presents the top ten arrests for females and males. Males and females had the same offenses as their top four offenses: larceny-theft, nonindex crime assaults, drug abuse violations, and driving under the influence. Drug abuse was the number one arrest offense for males, while larceny-theft was for females. Still, females constituted only about one-third of the total larceny-theft arrests. Males and females had the same sixth, seventh, and eighth arrest offenses: disorderly conduct, liquor law violations, and aggravated assaults, respectively. While drunkenness was the fifth most common arrest for males, it was the tenth most common arrest for females. Burglary and vandalism were the ninth and tenth most common arrest offenses for males but did not make the females' "top ten" arrest list. On the other hand, fraud, the fifth most common arrest offense for females, and running away, the ninth most common arrest offense for females, did not make the males' "top ten" arrest list. Notably, running away was the only offense on the females "top ten" list

Table 3.1 U.S. Arrests in 1998 by Sex[a]

Offense	FEMALES		MALES	
	Percent	(n)	Percent	(n)
Total Crimes	21.8%	(2,245,890)	78.2%	(8,049,239)
Total Index Crimes	25.6	(454,732)	74.4	(1,319,371)
Violent Index Crimes	16.8	(81,072)	83.2	(400,206)
Murder & Nonnegligent manslaughter	11.2	(1,385)	88.8	(10,950)
Forcible rape	1.2	(269)	98.8	(21,635)
Robbery	10.0	(8,744)	90.0	(78,385)
Aggravated assault	19.6	(70,674)	80.4	(289,218)
Property Crime Index	28.9	(373,660)	71.1	(919,165)
Burglary	12.5	(29,066)	87.5	(204,369)
Larceny-theft	34.7	(326,058)	65.3	(614,185)
Motor vehicle theft	15.7	(16,746)	84.3	(90,257)
Arson	14.7	(1,790)	85.3	(10,354)
Selected Non-Index Offenses				
Other assaults[b]	22.4	(211,998)	77.6	(735,598)
Drug abuse violations	17.5	(193,491)	82.5	(915,297)
Weapons (carrying, possessing, etc.)	7.9	(10,685)	92.1	(125,364)
Prostitution & commercialized vice	57.8	(39,627)	42.2	(28,909)
Running away	58.2	(68,170)	41.8	(48,919)

[a]The data presented in this table include *all* arrests, combining juvenile and adult arrests.

[b]"Other assaults" include assaults that are not the "aggravated assaults" classified under the violent crime index. "Other assaults" are classified under the nonindex offenses.

SOURCE: U.S. Department of Justice (1999) *Crime in the United States 1998: Uniform Crime Reports.* Federal Bureau of Investigation, U.S. Government Printing Office. (Data for this table collected from Table 42, page 227.)

where they constituted more than half of the arrests (females were 58 percent of running away arrests).

Furthermore, males' and females' offense rates can be compared to determine whether there are gender differences in the extent and nature of offending and whether these differences have changed over time. The patterns of offending rates over time (especially of females) received increased attention with the advent of Adler's (1975) and Simon's (1975) "liberation" hypothesis. This hypothesis suggests that rather than stable differences between the sexes (Option A) or gender–divergence (increasing differences) between the sexes (Option B), gender–convergence (Option C) is likely to occur over time (see Figure 3.1). Gender-stability is any pattern over time where the differences between female and male rates are relatively stable. They co-vary: Female and male rates rise and fall together. Thus we would expect that in an era of "get tough on crime" policies or in times of economic depression, men's and women's crime rates would be equally affected. With gender-divergence the disparity in offending rates between the sexes increases over time, with gender differences growing. Gender-convergence, consistent with the "liberation"

**Table 3.2 Top Ten Crimes in the U.S. in 1998
Resulting in Arrests, by Sex[a]**

FEMALES		MALES	
Offense	**(% of arrests that are female)**	**Offense**	**(% of arrests that are male)**
1. Larceny-theft	(34.7%)	1. Drug abuse violation	(82.5%)
2. Other assaults[b]	(22.4%)	2. Driving under the influence	(84.4%)
3. Drug abuse violation	(17.5%)	3. Other assaults[b]	(77.6%)
4. Driving under the influence	(15.6%)	4. Larceny-theft	(65.3%)
5. Fraud	(45.8%)	5. Drunkenness	(87.2%)
6. Disorderly conduct	(23.3%)	6. Disorderly conduct	(76.7%)
7. Liquor law violations	(21.4%)	7. Liquor law violations	(78.6%)
8. Aggravated assault	(19.6%)	8. Aggravated assault	(80.4%)
9. Running away	(58.2%)	9. Burglary	(87.5%)
10. Drunkenness	(12.8%)	10. Vandalism	(84.8%)

[a]The data presented in this table include *all* arrests, combining juvenile and adult arrests. This table excluded the variable listed in the source called "all other offenses (except traffic)," given the vagueness of this variable. Had we included this variable, it would have been the most frequent offense type for both males ($n=2{,}148{,}906$, 79.5%) and females ($n=553{.}976$, 20.5%).

[b]"Other assaults" include assaults that are not the "aggravated assaults" classified under the violent crime index. "Other assaults" are classified under the nonindex offenses.

SOURCE: U.S. Department of Justice (1999) *Crime in the United States 1998: Uniform Crime Reports.* Federal Bureau of Investigation, U.S. Government Printing Office. (Data for this table collected from Table 25, page 16.)

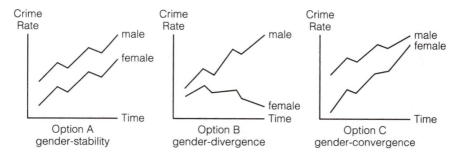

FIGURE 3.1 Examples of Comparing Gender-Offending Patterns Over Time

hypothesis, occurs any time that the distance between males' and females' rates is decreasing and their offending rates are becoming similar.

To address the existence of support for the "liberation" hypothesis, that the feminist movement has increased both gender equality and female offending, this section also presents studies evaluating gender patterns in offending over time and then draws on current U.S. arrest data to examine this. Specifically, this section draws on the concepts of gender-stability, gender-divergence, and gender-convergence (described at the beginning of this chapter) in order to analyze offending patterns over time.

Despite the "liberation" hypothesis, most researchers have agreed that women's crime rates have basically stayed the same except in the areas of less serious property crimes (Leonard, 1982; Naffine, 1987; Steffensmeier, 1981, 1993; Steffensmeier and Cobb, 1981; Steffensmeier and Streifel, 1992) and drugs. It is acknowledged that there are cyclical patterns of policies against crime, where an abundance of "get tough on crime" policies often result in increases in arrests and imprisonment rates, although there may be no corresponding increase in actual offending behavior. Overall, there is very little evidence for gender-convergence in crime rates. Indeed, there is some indication that women's overall proportion of homicide arrests has *decreased* in recent years (Gauthier and Bankston, 1997; Steffensmeier, 1993).

A study following arrest rates in Toronto from 1859 to 1955 showed gender-stability in offending; overall, the patterns of males' and females' arrests increased and decreased at the same times (Boritch and Hagan, 1990). Although men had much higher violent crime arrests, the long-term pattern suggested that violent crimes were decreasing for both sexes and that the drop in arrest rates was particularly acute for women. Crimes of public order, such as drunk and disorderly conduct and vagrancy, constituted the largest proportion of both female and male crime. Following these crime rates over time indicated gender-convergence. However, the researchers concluded that official statistics may be a better indicator of criminalization practices than of criminal behavior. Furthermore, females' arrest rates decreased with corresponding increases in their economic opportunities (ibid.).

Numerous studies conducting gender-offense comparisons over time in the United States have found overall gender-stability, with the limited evidence of gender-convergence usually for less serious property crimes and alcohol and drug use (Canter, 1982; Chilton and Datesman, 1987; Giordano et al., 1981; Steffensmeier, 1993; Steffensmeier and Cobb, 1981; Steffensmeier and Steffensmeier, 1980). A study of juvenile offending over time, however, found no evidence of gender-convergence (Ageton, 1983). Thus, where gender-convergence appears to exist, it can be largely explained by (1) changes in law-enforcement practices, (2) the worsening economic position of women (the feminization of poverty), (3) changes in data collection methods, and (4) inflation in the small base of women's crimes (Canter, 1982; Chilton and Datesman, 1987; Giordano et al., 1981; Steffensmeier, 1993; Steffensmeier and Cobb, 1981; Steffensmeier and Steffensmeier, 1980). If the gender gap in offending is closing, it appears to be for less serious property crimes, and possibly for drug use.

A more recent analysis of Uniform Crime Reports (UCR) data shows that although girls' arrests increased dramatically (by 250 percent) during the

1960s and early 1970s, this was largely due to the "baby boomers" hitting the high-risk age group. Although the percentage of females committing larceny increased some, this was temporary (Chesney-Lind and Shelden, 1992). Studies from other countries have provided more indication of gender-convergence. Statistics from Canada suggest that although the changes from the 1960s to 1989 are inconsistent and largely for nonviolent offenses, gender-convergence occurs in property crimes (G. Campbell, 1990). A study using official statistics in England and Wales from 1965 to 1975 found large proportional increases in female criminality, particularly violent offenses, but pointed out that these findings were suspect because of a small base and fluctuations in women's crime rates in earlier periods (the 1930s and 1940s) (Smart, 1982).

Table 3.3 presents the arrest trends by sex between 1989 and 1998. Total females' and males' percentage changes over this time period are reported, as well as juvenile males' and females' arrests for this time period. The final column of this table is my estimation of what pattern is suggested by the percentage changes (C = convergence, D = divergence, and S = stability). "Eyeballing" these data suggests that convergence is the most common pattern, but it is important to keep in mind that (looking back at Table 1 for 1998), males still make up by far the bulk of arrests for these offenses, over three-quarters of the arrests for almost all of the offenses (except 71 percent of total property index crime arrests, 42 percent of prostitution and commercialized vice arrests, and 42 percent of running away arrests). Divergence is suggested regarding the total murder and nonnegligent manslaughter arrests (females' decreased 26 percent and males' decreased 20 percent). Males' percent of running away arrests decreased more than females', suggesting that this typically female-related offense is becoming more so when measured by arrest changes. Gender-stability was indicated regarding forcible rape arrests and weapons arrests.

Some studies have made a concerted effort to account for racial as well as gender differences in offending rates over time. However, there is no pattern in these studies' findings. One reported gender-divergence among both African-American and white juvenile populations (Laub and McDermott, 1985); another reported gender-stability in larceny rates, although white men and women of color now have similar rates (Chilton and Datesman, 1987). Another study claimed that gender-stability appeared to be the pattern for whites, but gender-convergence was apparent for some offense types for people of color (Smith and Visher, 1980). Finally, another study reported overall gender-convergence, especially for white misdemeanor offenses but gender-divergence for felonies perpetrated by African-Americans (Farnworth et al., 1988). Thus, although it appears to be important to account for race in assessing gender offending patterns over time, to date it is unclear how race and sex interact in the overall gender-convergence, gender-stability, and gender-divergence patterns.

Table 3.3 U.S. Arrests Trends By Sex, 1989–1998

	PERCENT CHANGE FEMALES		PERCENT CHANGE MALES		SUGGESTED PATTERN[a]	
Offense	Total Females	(Females under 18)	Total Percent	(Males under 18)	Total Sample	(Youth under 18)
Total Crimes	**+27.5**	**(+50.3)**	**+2.3**	**(+16.5)**	C	C
Total Index Crimes	**+3.9**	**(+24.6)**	**-18.9**	**(-17.0)**	C	C
Violent Index Crimes	**+52.9**	**(+64.3)**	**-1.9**	**(+8.3)**	C	C
Murder & Nonnegligent manslaughter	-26.0	(-8.1)	-19.5	(-24.0)	D?	C
Forcible rape	-13.7	(-8.7)	-16.8	(-2.6)	S	S
Robbery	+2.9	(+18.7)	-14.0	(+8.1)	C	C?
Aggravated assault	+67.3	(+79.7)	+4.5	(+11.2)	C	C
Property Crime Index	**-2.8**	**(+21.3)**	**-24.7**	**(-21.1)**	C	C
Burglary	-2.1	(+7.8)	-32.1	(-24.8)	C	C
Larceny-theft	-3.2	(+24.5)	-20.2	(-14.4)	C	C
Motor vehicle theft	+1.9	(-1.6)	-34.7	(-43.8)	C	C
Arson	+5.3	(+24.3)	-7.9	(+8.1)	C	C
Selected Non-Index Offenses						
Other assaults[b]	+98.0	(+125.4)	+30.0	(+51.5)	C	C
Drug abuse violations	+25.9	(+113.4)	+18.4	(+82.0)	C?	C
Weapons (carrying, possessing, etc.)	-11.5	(+69.8)	-13.3	(+11.4)	S	C
Prostitution & commercialized vice	-13.3	(-21.2)	+16.0	(+17.1)	C	C
Running away	-1.2	(-1.2)	-9.5	(-9.5)	D?	D?

[a]The suggested pattern is the author's estimation, given the percentage changes over time, whether the gender-offending patterns over time suggest stability (S), divergence (D), or convergence (C).

[b]"Other assaults" include assaults that are not the "aggravated assaults" classified under the violent crime index. "Other assaults" are classified under the nonindex offenses.

SOURCE: U.S. Department of Justice (1999) *Crime in the United States 1998: Uniform Crime Reports.* Federal Bureau of Investigation, U.S. Government Printing Office. (Data for this table collected from Table 33, page 215.)

THE IMPORTANCE OF HOW CRIME RATES
ARE MEASURED AND THE ROLES
OF GENDER, AGE, RACE, AND CLASS

Chapter 2 pointed out how criminological theories have tended to be sex-blind, either completely ignoring females or viewing them through a stereo-typical lens that usually distorts women's and girls' real-life experiences. Any analysis of gender must avoid a similarly restricted view by accounting for differences *among* females based on their age, race, and social class (see Simpson, 1991). First, age is important because it has been well documented that there are relatively few "career criminals." Most people who break the law do so roughly between the ages of 15 and 24. Second, race is vital to understanding offending rates because of limited legitimate opportunities available to many people of color, as well as their increased risk of being labeled "criminal." Third, it is important to recognize that one's social class affects one's opportunities and treatment in our society. Class also affects the likelihood that one will turn to crime for survival, and similarly limits one's abilities to pay bond and to pay for a good attorney. Finally, the type of data used—official reports, victimization surveys, or self-reported offending—may influence the representation of offending rates. This is partially because most offending goes undetected by the juvenile and adult crime-processing systems, but also because official reports are apt to reflect bias, particularly in the forms of racism, classism, and sexism.

One of the most popular data sets used to assess crime rates in the United States is the Uniform Crime Reports (UCR). These reports summarize the yearly arrests from police departments in the entire country. Thus the UCR data are a measure of *arrests* and therefore do not include crimes unknown and unreported to the police, nor do they include reported offenses for which the police choose not to arrest or are unable to arrest (e.g., there is insufficient evidence, or they cannot find or identify a suspect). Unfortunately, the reports do not control for social class. Nor do they control for race and sex at the same time, making it impossible to track African-American women, white women, African-American men, and so on. Official statistics such as the UCR, court convictions, and imprisonment rates rely on the crime-processing system actors' perceptions of whether a crime occurred. Theoretically, police arrest and judges and juries convict only when they believe there is a strong likelihood that a person committed a crime. Thus, a major threat to the validity of using official statistics of crime rates is that discrimination may distort the statistics. For example, if Hispanic women are more likely than white women to be arrested for the same offense, the official statistics would exaggerate Hispanic women's offending relative to white women. Thus, it is not clear whether race, class, sex, and age differences represented by official statistics reflect different rates of offending or, rather, differential (discriminatory) processing of offenders.

Lewis's (1981) review of the research found that although African-American women have been disproportionately incarcerated, analyses have failed to control systematically for sex and race, thus making it impossible, until recently, to determine how African-American women compare to white women, African-American men, and so on. This problem has historically been even worse regarding people of color other than African-Americans, particularly non–African-American women of color. In fact, it was common until quite recently to combine Latinos and Native Americans with whites in crime-processing statistics. Additionally, research on racial differences has focused almost exclusively on white and Black offenders, ignoring other racial and ethnic groups. At any rate, Lewis's (ibid, 93) review of research found that "correctional" statistics suggest that Black women "display somewhat greater involvement with violent and other personal crimes than white women." However, she also cautions that when examining arrest records or other data to compare various races' offending patterns, it is important to control for age because the higher rate of African-American to white females' violent crime rates might partially be explained by the fact that the African-American population as a whole is younger (and thus in a higher-risk age group) than the white population (ibid.). On the other hand, the age difference between African-Americans and whites cannot by itself, according to Lewis, explain the offending differences between white and Black women; these analyses must also consider economic deprivation, gender status inequality, socialization, gender role expectations, and racism.

> Black women, then, display gender role behavior, a social status and a crime pattern, all of which contradict acceptable feminine behavior, as defined by the dominant society. They tend to be assertive, function as unmarried heads of household and be convicted for violent person crimes. In short, they epitomize the type of deviant women the criminal justice system is committed to punish. (ibid., 102)

The importance of controlling for factors such as race and age, as well as the type of crime, can be seen in various studies. A study using national self-report data of women 18 to 23 years old found that although there were no significant differences between Black and white women in the composite crime rate, when the types of crime were broken down, white women reported significantly more drug use than Black women, and Black women reported more involvement in major property and assault crimes than white women. Furthermore, that Black women were more likely to report acquiring income from illegal activities suggested their increased economic vulnerability relative to white women (Hill and Crawford, 1990). Another study of female arrests found few racial differences overall, but white women were more likely than Black women to be arrested for serious property crimes, and Black women were more likely than white women to be arrested for gambling, assault, family offenses, and violent crimes (Steffensmeier and Allan, 1988). Thus, these studies are not in agreement on racial/ethnic differences in female offending, particularly regarding serious property offenses. This indicates the need for more research in the area of the relationship between race/ethnicity and female offense rates by type of offense. For example, Kruttschnitt (1996,

141) states that ignoring racial variations in gender comparisons of of "presumes that Blacks and Whites are similarly situated in social life influenced by the same risk factors" and therefore is "short-sighted."

Turning to the importance of age, a study of arrested females in a southern U.S. city found that women under 18 were involved mostly in petty property offenses and were rarely arrested for drugs/alcohol or sex work; women 18 to 30 had high property and violent crime offense rates and the highest sex work (prostitution) rates; and women over 30 were minimally involved in sex work but had high rates of drug/alcohol arrests (Wolfe et al., 1984). A study of England and Wales found that while 3 percent of offenses committed by girls 10 to 14 years old were violent crimes against the person, this rose to 8 percent for girls 14 to 17 years old (Morris, 1987). Kruttschnitt's (1996, 139) careful review of existing studies reports that "the age-crime relationship may not be gender invariant," meaning that there exist gender differences depending on age. For example, the ratio of male-to-female offending varies significantly depending on the age-group examined, and factors such as age at initiation into offending, age at which one escalates to more serious offending, and age at which offenders stop offending, all vary by gender (ibid.).

Unfortunately, data gatherers in both official statistics and many self-report studies are either unwilling or unable to account for class differences, so little is known about this seemingly powerful variable. However, those studies that have controlled for race, gender, class, and age often find that these are important predictors of offending behavior, as well as treatment by the crime-processing system. Research has shown that making simple racial or gender comparisons is less useful than controlling for both race and sex to see how the experiences of women from different races compare and how men and women of the same race compare. It is important to emphasize the danger in relying solely on official crime-processing statistics (e.g., police and court records), in that they may be a better reflection of bias than offending. Researchers should also use self-report surveys and interviews to present a more valid measure of offending.

The data collected thus far on female offenders, both juvenile and adult, indicate some important patterns. Although it is important to keep in mind that these data largely reflect *officially* collected statistics, they are probably a better indicator of girls and women *detained* by the police and formally processed by the system than of actual offending (including both officially detected and undetected breaking of the law). The typical adult female offender is young (usually under age 30), of color, undereducated, a single mother, poor, and a social service client (Sarri, 1987; Wolfe et al., 1984).

FEMALE OFFENDING IN CONTEXT

This section discusses the findings from various studies regarding the extent and nature of female offending and how it compares to male offending. Some studies were conducted solely on females (Figure 3.2), whereas others included both females and males in their samples. First, some important concepts related to

- 3.2 million women were arrested in 1998, accounting for 22 percent of all 1998 arrests. Juvenile females were twice as likely as adult females to be arrested.
- Women account for about 14 percent of violent offenders (about 2.1 million female offenders per year) based on victims' self-reports. Approximately 28 percent of female violent offenders are juveniles.
- For males, there is about one violent offender for every nine males 10 years old or older, a per capita rate six times that of women.
- Three out of four violent female offenders commit a simple assault.
- Three-fourths of the victims of women's violent offending are other women, and two-thirds of these women knew their offenders.
- The rate of women's murders per capita has declined since 1980.

FIGURE 3.2 A Profile of Female Offending in the U.S.

SOURCE: Greenfeld, Lawrence A., and Tracy L. Snell. 1999. *Women Offenders*. Bureau of Justice Statistics: Special Report. U.S. Department of Justice, December, p. 4.

gender differences in crime are presented. Then, descriptions of female offenders and a comparison of female and male offenders are presented for various types of offenses. The following section discusses gender patterns over time.

Concerning the extent of female crime in both the United States and Canada, women constitute about 15 percent of people arrested by the police (G. Campbell, 1990; Mann, 1984). Regarding the nature of women's offending, the crimes for which females are most strongly represented are sex work, running away, larceny/theft, fraud, and forgery/counterfeiting (Leonard, 1982). Although the concepts of the extent and nature of female crimes are relatively straightforward, making gender comparisons and examining changes over time are more complicated. Gender comparisons in offending are commonly evaluated by determining which offenses are gender-related and which are gender-neutral (see Smart, 1976). Whereas gender-related crimes are more likely to be committed by one sex than the other, gender-neutral crimes are equally likely to be committed by either sex. Given males' higher propensity to offend, the majority of crimes are male gender-related, but especially rape and other violent crimes. The most common example of a female gender-related crime is sex work.

Even if the legal code has progressed to define crimes as gender neutral (not specifying "penis," "female," and so on), which makes either sex equally culpable of committing the same offense, the enforcement of the law may continue to be gender specific (see Morris, 1987). For example, the sex work law may be changed to include male prostitutes or to go after clients as well as prostitutes, but the police and judges may continue to disregard these male offenders because they do not fit their stereotypes of offenders. In fact, it is likely that the police are even less likely to detect the male offenders because they do not picture them in these roles. Stereotypical assumptions about women, then, affect assumptions about the crimes they commit. For example, because the stereotype is that women shop and women use marriage to exchange sex for security, shoplifting and sex work are viewed as extensions of women's "normal" roles (Morris, 1987, 29–30).

Historically, legal codes have often not allowed that males could be prostitutes (similar to rape laws that did not allow that males could be victims). Additionally, both in law and in practice, the sanctioning of prostitutes (who are typically female) is much more rigorous than the sanctioning of prostitutes' clients (who are typically male, regardless of the prostitute's sex).

One assumption about the gendered nature of offending has been that when females commit crimes, it is in the role of followers where males are the "leaders." Research indicates that although the gendered nature of being a follower, leader, or conspirator varies by the type of crime, generally, women act alone about 20 to 30 percent of the time (Alarid et al., 1996; Bunch et al., 1983). One study of women in prison found that 70 percent reported planning their crimes themselves, and 30 percent worked with another woman (Bunch et al., 1983). Thus, "the final portrait is not necessarily one of women playing a supportive role to men" (ibid., 71).

Finally, before addressing gender representation in specific offenses, a more recently recognized phenomenon is that of battered women who commit crimes with their batterers, often under duress and extreme pressure (see Walker, 1993, 239). In some of these cases, if the male codefendant (batterer) is unknown to the legal system, the woman may take the entire blame. Similarly, there are cases of women sentenced to prison for unknowingly perpetrating a crime designed by their intimate male partners or helping them in order to avoid risking their own or their children's well-being. The majority of these offenses involve selling drugs (see Tyson, 1993).

Sexuality

There has been a concerted effort to control females' sexuality, both socially and legally, which has resulted in a double standard. For example, terms such as *promiscuous, loose,* and *nymphomaniac* are rarely applied to males. In fact, males are often expected to be sexually active, regardless of their marital status. Females, on the other hand, are often expected to be chaste or at least to limit themselves to one male partner. "A 'good' girl is never sexual, although she must be sexually appealing, while a healthy boy must prove his masculinity by experimenting sexually" (Chesney-Lind, 1974). Given the homophobia in our culture, it is unclear with whom the "healthy" boys are supposed to have sex. Although female sexuality has received increased latitude since the 1970s, women and girls still experience more social constraints on their sexuality than boys and men do. Current research documents the difficult time that girls still have in "doing desire," particularly when compared to their male peers (Alder, 1998; Tolman, 1994). Indeed, Alder examines this in the context of processing sexually active girls as "delinquents" and argues that "practices which seek to protect girls by denying their sexuality and independence may not ultimately be in the girls' best interests" (1998, 81).

One female gender-related "offense" can best be labeled "promiscuity." This is a useful example of how official statistics fail to reflect the actual behavioral representations in society. That is, both females and males engage in voluntary sex. Although males engage in more voluntary sex than females, female juveniles are more often labeled with promiscuity "sex offenses" than males are. Many of the status offenses are directly or indirectly tied to both voluntary and abusive sexuality such as being sexually active (directly tied) or running away from home (indirectly tied). The status offenses of "running away" in the United States and "being in moral danger" in the United Kingdom are strongly related to sexual "promiscuity" (Smart, 1976). Many girls (and boys) who run away from home are running away from sexual victimization, or incest. In fact, 20 percent of girls and 7 percent of boys seeking help from runaway and homeless centers report sexual abuse as a reason for their predicament; 9 percent of girls and 2 percent of boys who are runaways report sexual abuse by a parent (U.S. Department of Health and Human Services, 1991).

Many runaways experience sexual victimization and/or are coerced or forced into sex work after leaving home. One study of runaways found that 38 percent of boys and 73 percent of girls reported sexual abuse (McCormack et al., 1986). Moreover, although sexually abused runaway boys are no more delinquent/criminal than nonsexually abused runaway boys, sexually abused girl runaways are more likely than nonsexually abused girl runaways to be arrested, to be placed in jail, and to participate in a violent act (ibid.). Thus, not only are females and males labeled differently for consensual sexual activity, but sexual abuse appears to have a more detrimental effect on the subsequent delinquency of runaway females than of runaway males.

The crime-processing system, which has historically failed to respond to incest victims in the home, has diligently responded to girls who have run away from home. Girls have been labeled and severely punished for running away, regardless of the circumstances motivating their flight. The system's processing of these "offenders" is covered in more detail in Chapter 4.

The issue of sex work (or prostitution) is discussed throughout this chapter, in particular in the section on drugs given the link that often occurs between these types of offending. However, it is also useful to discuss it in terms of sexuality, in that the crime of prostitution is women and girls selling sex. Thus, women and girls "giving" sex via "promiscuity" is wrong and often deemed illegal (particularly for girls), and selling sex most certainly is. Suh (2000, 147) makes a powerful point in her analysis of how "the social construction of Asian women as prostitutes can be traced both to the process of U.S. economic globalization that brought labor from Asia and to the gendered exclusion of Asian permanent residents." More specifically, she describes how in the late 1800s prostitution was listed as an occupation in the official census, and the forces to criminalize it are strongly related to the "xenophobic drive to exclude Chinese from this country [the U.S.]:"

> In the late nineteenth century, U.S. mining and railroad companies recruited from China men who were not permitted to bring their families. Through the activities of recruiters who lured or kidnapped women and brought them to the United States, Chinese women in prostitution be-

came institutionalized. They became targets of rhetoric about Asians' lack of morality. . . . Thus, the social construction of Asian women as prostitutes can be traced both to the process of U.S. economic globalization that brought labor from Asia and to the gendered exclusion of Asian permanent residents. (Suh, 147)

Suh (ibid., 156) points out the ramifications of this history today, regarding Asian women who marry U.S. military men who subsequently abuse them. If these women leave these abusive men before they are considered citizens, in a time when benefits for immigrants are decreasing, and they are forced into work in the sex (or drug) industry for survival, this clearly limits their ability to apply for citizenship and the benefits they should have received through citizenship or marriage.

Juvenile Offending

It is important to recognize that both female and male offending, particularly of serious crimes, is relatively rare, and most juvenile offenses are minor, without a clear victim (Chesney-Lind and Shelden, 1992). When girls do commit crimes, it is typically for less serious offenses than boys (Chesney-Lind, 1987). However, one study of over 15,000 Stockholm youth found that 30 percent of males and 16 percent of females had a conviction by the time they were 30 (Andersson, 1990). Although females were less likely to have a large number of convictions, both females' and males' prior convictions influenced the likelihood of their future criminal involvement (ibid.).

A study that followed females committed to the California Youth Authority in the 1960s found that the average age of offending onset was 14 and that two-thirds of the girls entered the system via a status offense arrest (Warren and Rosenbaum, 1986). A majority of those women arrested as youth had a number of arrests, and they continued to be arrested into adulthood. The primary offense for half of the sample was a property offense, sex work was the primary offense for 20 percent, and drugs were the primary offense for 13 percent (ibid.). Another study of women found that legal intervention as a juvenile was predictive of becoming an alcoholic (Miller et al., 1989). Of utmost importance is the potentially powerful negative impact of the status offense labeling of girls. Do the labels help make criminals? Although more research is needed in this area, this chapter and the next discuss the important role of status offenses in controlling and affecting girls' lives.

U.S. data from UCR statistics on youth found that while the overall male–female arrest ratio is 4:1, the biggest gender gap is in serious property crimes (11:1) and violent crimes (9:1) (Chesney-Lind and Shelden, 1992). However, even larceny theft, often strongly associated with the "female" offense of shoplifting, is committed predominantly by males (3:1); one-fifth of boys' and one-fourth of girls' arrests are for shoplifting. Status offenses, particularly "running away," continue to play a much bigger role in girls' than boys' arrests: One-fifth of girls' arrests and one-twentieth of boys' arrests are for running away (ibid.). Larceny/theft and running away have constituted the bulk of girls' delinquency arrests, accounting for approximately half of all female arrests since 1965 (ibid., 10). Boys, on the other hand, are more eclectic in the types of offenses they commit, and they have a greater rate of offending (Belknap and Holsinger, 1998; Chesney-Lind and Shelden, 1992).

Uniformity in female and male juvenile offending is most apparent in (1) less serious offenses, (2) self-report studies, and (3) more recent studies. This suggests that official statistics are a better indication of crime-processing system labeling than actual offending rates and that girls' and boys' offending is most likely to portray gender-convergence for minor offenses.

Older self-report studies found males significantly more involved in status offenses and less serious delinquent behaviors (Gold and Reimer, 1975; Jensen and Eve, 1976), with African-American males reporting the most offenses, followed by white males, African-American females, and white females, respectively (Jensen and Eve, 1976). Another older self-report study, however, found that while boys were more likely than girls to report delinquent activity and to commit offenses more frequently, "the activities most frequently engaged in by the males, are, by and large, the activities most frequently engaged in by the females" (Hindelang, 1971, 526). Moreover, although girls were less likely to report delinquency than boys, girl delinquents were "generalists," committing a variety of offenses (Hindelang, 1971).

Some more recent self-report studies indicate a similarity in female and male offending rates for status, drug, and less serious offenses, although male offending remains considerably higher for more serious property and all violent offenses (Canter, 1982; Chesney-Lind, 1987; Feyerherm, 1981; Figueira-McDonough et al., 1981; Richards, 1981). An analysis of over 1,500 youth in a self-report study using the National Youth Survey, for the 22 offenses listed under the categories of "status offenses," "vandalism," "theft," and "assault," boys were more likely to report *every* crime except running away and hitting a parent, for which boys and girls reported similar rates (about 5 percent of each ran away from home and about 4 percent of each hit a parent) (Triplett and Myers, 1995). Similar to other research, this study also found that the more serious the offense, the greater the gender gap in committing it. When this study examined the *number of times* (incidence) of the commission of the 22 offenses for those youth who had committed the offense at least once, there were very few gender differences. Notably, for these few gender differences, girls reported higher frequencies than boys for all three offenses: running away, damaging school property, and carrying a hidden weapon. Finally, this study attempted to determine gender differences in the *context* of juvenile offending. Overall, for status, property and theft offenses there were few gender differences in the context of committing the crimes. The exceptions for this regarded the destination when youth ran away, the form of assaults, the extent of injury in assaults, whether the youth was on drugs during the assault, the purpose of force in assaults, and whether victims were hurt in the assault (ibid.). More specifically, girls were more likely than boys to report (1) running to a friend's house when they ran away,

(2) hurting their assault victims when the victims were students, and (3) using force for reasons other than to get money. Regarding the context of committing assaults, boys were more likely than girls to report (1) being on drugs during the assault, (2) hurting their victims if their victims were not students, (3) beating their victims or attacking them with a weapon, and (4) having their victims cut or hospitalized. Thus, there were few gender differences in the context of offending for status, vandalism (property), or theft offenses, and the context of offending results in gender gaps more often in the commission of violent offenses.

Where race and sex were controlled, studies on juvenile offending found no strong gender-racial differences (Canter, 1982; Cernkovich and Giordano, 1979; Datesman and Aickin, 1984; Jensen and Thompson, 1990), except occasionally Black males tended to be more delinquent than the remaining gender—racial categories (Black females, white females, and white males), which clustered together (Hindelang, 1981; Laub and McDermott, 1985; Young, 1980).

When categorizing offending patterns by gender—racial differences, age should also be considered, as there is a likelihood that patterns may vary between junior high, high school, and older populations (Chilton and Datesman, 1987; Hindelang, 1981; Richards, 1981). Also, future research needs to use a variety of means in addition to official statistics and self-report surveys to assess gender differences in delinquency. For example, interviews with teenage prostitutes in Miami found numerous and extreme gender differences. Five percent of males and 87 percent of females reported prostituting in the prior 12 months, with an average of 26 acts for the males and 431 for the females (both females and males had male clients) (Inciardi et al., 1991). For the females, there was a high correlation between drug use and sex work. Intravenous drug use was least prevalent among white males and most prevalent among African-American females. Finally, whereas only 3 percent of the males reported exchanging sex for crack cocaine, 71 percent of the females reported this (Inciardi et al., 1991).

In conclusion, regarding juvenile delinquency, there is a strong indication that for less serious crimes there are few differences in the commission rates of girls and boys, even when controlling for race. It has been stated that "the adolescent subculture of minor delinquency appears to now include both boys and girls, whereas it used to be a predominantly male domain" (Figueira-McDonough et al., 1981, 23). However, for the more serious offenses, gender differences appear to persist.

Girl and Women Gangs

Until recently, female participation in gangs has typically been viewed as an extension of male gang membership, with the female gang members viewed as sidekicks and sex objects for the male gang members (see Campbell, 1990; Chesney-Lind and Hagedorn, 1999). Another view, however, is that the girls' "auxiliary" gangs "are not simply composed of separate, identifiable groups, but, rather, reflect gendered boundaries based on power" (Messerschmidt, 1999, 121). Moreover, in the introduction to the first reader ever published on female gangs in the United States, Chesney-Lind and Hagedorn (1999, 6) stated: "One could argue that some (particularly the earliest accounts) are atheoretical, racist, or sexist, since they represent beginning attempts by white male social scientists, social workers, and journalists to describe a phenomenon in which they had little interest." Thus, beginning with Thrasher's 1927 publication of his book *The Gang,* with the only chapter devoted to females tellingly entitled "Sex in the Gang," a precedent was set for scholars and journalists to conduct their research on female gang members through a sexist and racist lens (see Chesney-Lind and Hagedorn, 1999).

More recent research suggests that "girls in gangs" are more dynamic, independent, and interesting than the criminologists from the 1950s and 1960s and earlier would have us believe (see Campbell, 1990; Chesney-Lind and Hagedorn, 1999; Wing and Willis, 1997). Chesney-Lind and Hagedorn (1999) highlight that in addition the sexist and racist lens through which girls in gangs have been viewed, the studies on girls and women in gangs have been too few and fraught with methodological weaknesses and have typically viewed the female gang members as afterthoughts in studies on male gang members.

Wing and Willis's (1997) research on gangs, race, and gender notes the racism and sexism of "gangs" being perceived as synonymous with Black male criminality. Additionally, they are troubled by the invisibility of Black women's roles in gang life. Wing and Willis (1997, 244) identify six "frequently overlapping" roles of African American women's gang involvement: (1) full-fledged members of their own, female-only gangs; (2) auxiliaries to male gangs; (3) gangsters in coed gangs; (4) girlfriends and wives of male gang members; (5) mothers of male gang members' children; and (6) mothers, sisters, and daughters of male gang members. Thus, they conclude that Black women "have the capacity to affect gang members on profoundly intimate levels." Therefore, Black women must play a pivotal role in providing solutions to the gang problem (Ibid, 243).

Studies vary in what they report as girls' representation in gang membership. A Los Angeles study reported that females were 9 percent of gang members there (Felkenes and Becker, 1995), but another study reported that females and males are equally likely to belong to a gang (Bjerregaard and Smith, 1993), and an extensive survey found that girls constitute 38 percent of gang members (Esbensen and Winfree, 1998). Chesney-Lind and Hagedorn's (1999, 7) writings on the historical invisibility of female gang members ask whether there really were so few female gangs in the past, or "did the sexist researchers just not see them?" Further, they cite documentation that girls have been a part of the gang scene for years and that "their behavior has always been more complex and diverse than the incessant focus on girls' sexuality in the literature would permit" (ibid., 6). Ironically, the historical writings on girls in gangs have presented their consensual sexual experiences, pregnancies, and motherhood as indicators of their delinquency and deviance, while glossing over and minimizing the sexual victimizations (including gang rapes) that many of these young women report.

A frequently asked question regarding girls in gangs is, "Why would a girl want to join a gang?" Laura T. Fishman's (1999, 71) study using data collected on African-American gangs in the early 1960s in Chicago reported that the membership in the Vice Queens, a female auxiliary gang of the Vice Kings, represented for its members "a collective solution" to the "harsh milieu" in which they lived. "Not only did the gang provide friendship, easy access to boys, and a means of achieving status, it provided girls with protection against undesirable men in the neighborhood" (1999, 71). Campbell (1999a, 252) states that females' gang membership "offers solutions to their two most fundamental needs: acceptance and safety." Messerschmidt (1999, 120) describes gangs as a place for both female and male, lower-class, youth of color, to "develop strong 'family ties' with members of their neighborhood," with youth "like themselves," in an environment where they can find "companionship, safety, and a sense of belongingness." A study of largely Hispanic youth gangs in Los Angeles found that while over 90 percent of the youth reported pride in their Hispanic culture, about two-fifths of both the girls and boys reported that they believed they were discriminated against for being members of a Hispanic gang, and the authors indicated this race-based discrimination was related to their high school drop out rate (about two-fifths of both sexes dropped out of high school) (Felkenes and Becker, 1995). Similarly, Joe and Chesney-Lind's (1999, 229) study of Hawaiian gang members found that for both girls and boys, the gang provides a "social outlet and tonic" for growing up in communities "racked by poverty, racism, and rapid population growth" and lives fraught with boredom due to limited recreational outlets. In addition, for both sexes, gang membership provides a sense of family for those youth whose parents are forced (due to the economy) to work numerous hours, or worse, for those youth whose home lives are abusive (ibid.).

A study of Los Angeles Hispanic gang members reported that the youths reported marginal satisfaction or happiness levels with their families, and girls' were generally less satisfied than boys' (Felkenes and Becker, 1995). A study of an African-American girl gang in San Francisco reported their reasons for joining the gang included stature, a sense of belonging, and "family" (Lauderback, Hansen, and Waldorf, 1992). Simlarly, Moore's (1999) study of female and male gang members and their families in East Los Angeles reported that, while gang membership serves as a "family" for both sexes, given that female gang members are more likely than their male counterparts to report incest histories, more troubled families, living with a chronically sick relative, living with a relative who died, living with a relative who was a heroin addict, and living with a relative who was arrested, gang membership may represent a different peer group outlet and be more of a refuge from family for female than male gang members. "Paradoxically, the sense of solidarity achieved from sharing everyday life with similarly situated others has the unintended effect of drawing many gang youth—both girls and boys—into behaviors that ultimately create new problems for them" (Joe and Chesney-Lind, 1999, 229).

In a survey of over 3,000 girls across the United States, Deschenes and Esbensen (1999) attempted to distinguish girls and gangs from their counterparts not in gangs. They found that these two groups of girls "differ in background, behavior, and attitudes" (ibid., 292). This study found that girls' social isolation in their homes was a greater predictor of gang membership than were social isolation in schools or with friends. Gang girls held much lower levels of attachment to their mothers and their fathers and reported far less parental monitoring of their activities.

In addition to motivations for joining gangs, another important issue for girls in gangs is the types of delinquencies and offenses in which they engage and whether the offending of gang members is gendered. That is, do females and males in gangs commit similar or different offenses? Peggy Giordano's (1999) important work on this topic drawing on data from over 100 girls incarcerated in the 1970s focuses on the importance of *peer influence*. More specifically, she found that the more time girls spent with delinquent girls, particularly girl gang members, the more likely they were to commit delinquent acts. She emphasizes that, while male/boys' peer influence plays a role in girls' delinquency, the approval of their *female peers* is also very important.

> Therefore, the girls who *do* become involved in delinquency would
> be likely to first feel that girls in general and themselves in particular
> are capable of committing certain behaviors, that others like *them*
> (girls) also probably engage in it, and that these girls are not likely
> to regard them with disdain if they were to engage in the behavior
> themselves. . . . . [I]t is likely that *other girls* are the most important
> reference group, or at least the group to which they compare themselves.
> (ibid., 98–99)

Another recent and extensive survey of youth found that girls in gangs report lower levels of all types of offending than boys with one exception: male and female gang members are equally likely to report drug use (Esbensen and Winfre, 1998). Moreover, this study found that gang girls are considerably more delinquent than nongang boys. Other research on gangs has also found that peer influence/pressure is the major reason provided by both girls and boys for their criminal activities (Joe and Chesney-Lind, 1999) and that both experiencing and committing violence are associated with girls' gang membership. In other words, girls in gangs are more likely than their counterparts who are not in gangs to both experience and commit violence (Artz, 1998; Deschenes and Esbensen, 1999). Furthermore, and not surprisingly, other research supports the idea that girls in gangs are more likely than their peers not in gangs to report high levels of commitment to their delinquent peers (Deschenes and Esbensen, 1999). Other research suggests that although gang membership increases both males' and females' delinquent activities, male gang members report significantly more delinquent activity and substance use than female gang members (Bjerregaard and Smith, 1993; Morash, 1983).

Joe and Chesney-Lind's (1999) study of female and male gang members in Hawaii in the early 1990s reported that in addition to the boys' gangs being larger in size, delinquency is more prevalent in male than female gangs. About 90 percent of the boys had been arrested compared to 75 percent of the girls. Moreover, boys committed a wider range of offenses than girls. Although girls were as likely to report status offenses as they were criminal offenses, about a third of the girls had arrests for a violent crime. Thus, although the girls committed more offenses, particularly violent offenses, than they have historically been portrayed, they were still significantly less involved in this behavior than boys (ibid.). In addition, in this study of gang members in Hawaii, the girls were far less likely than the boys to sell drugs and rob; however, the girl members were more likely than the boy members to report arrests for running away from home, status offense problems, problems on the streets, and both parents and society at large holding a double standard of what is acceptable behavior for girls versus boys.

Paramount in this discussion of female gang members' offending is establishing their use of violence. One study reported that when female gang members fight, it is often over threats to their personal integrity, such as attacks on their sexual reputations, whereas boys are more likely to fight over a gang than over an individual challenge (Campbell, 1984). Fishman's (1999) analysis of the Vice Queens in Chicago in the 1960s reported that although the members would accompany the Vice Kings to their fights and subsequently fight the Vice Kings' enemy's auxiliary female gang members, the Vice Queens were far more likely to participate in their own fights with other female gangs, independently of what was going on with the Vice Kings. Most of the fights the Vice Queens engaged in had to do with issues of loyalty and integrity, with integrity involving a "threat to or attack on their public reputation" (ibid., 75). Notably, "fighting a male, and especially winning, carried a particular status among the girls" (ibid.). Campbell's (1999b, 115) study of Puerto Rican girls gang members in New York City from 1979 to 1981 found that the gang girls "took pride in their ability to fight" and "stress their aggressiveness and work hard at developing a reputation as a fighter." Campbell (ibid., 116) concluded: "More than winning a fight, it was important to be ready to enter one." A study of Los Angeles gangs reported that girls in gangs "do indeed engage in violent and/or criminal behavior" and found that twice as many male (24 percent) as female (13 percent) gang members reported they would kill someone if asked to do so by the gang (Felkenes and Becker, 1995, 8).

Messerschmidt's (1999, 127) attempt to understand how female and male gang members "do gender" in the context of violence reports that participating in group violence is likely "the most positively sanctioned site for displaying one's 'badness.' " Messerschmidt is convinced that girl gang members' use of violence is conducted in a manner of "doing femininity" or accommodating their "proper" gender roles and masculine dominance. "For girls in the gang, doing femininity means occasionally, and in appropriate circumstances, doing violence" (ibid., 129). The girl gang members "doing violence," then, is not an attempt to "pass as males" but rather to construct "a specific type of femininity, race, and class" where "femininity is assessed both in terms of willingness to defend the 'hood' and on doing difference" (ibid., 130).

Hagedorn and Devitt's (1999) extensive study of primarily Latina female gangs in Milwaukee in 1995 included eight gangs. One quarter of their sample was African-American female gang members. They reported that their sample was fairly even divided between the female gang members who "liked to fight" and those who fought to maintain solidarity with their gang members. The small number of women who reported that they were "not fighters" were frowned upon by their gang peers for violating the gang norms. Notably, the women who "liked to fight" had less of a male-centered outlook on life (e.g., were less likely to agree that all women "need" a man to order their lives), whereas the women who fought for gang solidarity were more likely to be in a current intimate relationship with a man. Latina gangs were most likely to fight because of turf battles or a rival gang "representing," whereas fights with other gangs constituted less than half of African-American women gang members' fights. African-American women gang members' fights were more likely over "respect" and also "jealousy" issues than were the Latina women's gang fights.

Fishman (1999) also examined sex work (prostitution) as a form of girl gang members' delinquency. She states that virtually every girl in the Vice Queens had participated in sex work and described sex work as "the strongest indication of the Vice Queens' acceptance of female-oriented, illegitimate hustles" (ibid., 76). Campbell's (1999b) analysis of Puerto Rican female gang members in New York City in the late 1970s and early 1980s described their frustration with the public perception of them as "whores" or "ho's." In this gang, the girls "exerted a good deal of social control over one another's sexual behavior," where "serial monogamy was the norm and sexual promiscuity was frowned upon" (ibid., 113). At the same time, they were quite aware of and frustrated with the double-standard where males' infidelity in intimate relationships was accepted and even expected.

In sum, the earliest research on girls in gangs, when the gang research bothered to include females, presented them in highly sexist manners. They were most frequently viewed as extensions, sidekicks, and sexual outlets for the important gang members: male gang members. More current analyses not only report far more dynamic and independent girls in gangs but document that these earlier depictions, in addition to being racist and sexist, were inaccurate. Thus, girls in gangs, despite their often difficult childhoods of sexism, racism, and poverty, show a significant amount of agency, and gang membership, as for boys, allows them an important sense of belonging and "family." At the same time, the research in recent years on females in gangs notes the heterogeneity of female gang membership. That is, there is considerable difference in the amount of violence used and what female gang membership means depending on the time/era, the location in the city, and the race/ethnicity of the gang. In short, female gang membership is far more complex and dynamic than the early studies implied.

Theft

Property offenses of a minor nature have often been attributed as female gender-related. Although larceny and thefts (for example, forgery, counterfeiting, fraud, and embezzlement) constitute a considerable amount of female arrests and convictions, males still account for the vast majority of these arrests and convictions (Eaton, 1986; Leonard, 1982). A study comparing changes in the imprisonment rates of women, however, indicated that while women's violent crime rates decreased by 8 percent between 1979 and 1986, the largest increase in women's imprisonment rate was due to an increase in larceny/theft convictions (Kline, 1993). Similarly, a study of men's and women's arrests from 1960 to 1980 found overall genderstability, except for larceny. While the majority of larceny arrests were still of men, women's arrests showed significant growth, particularly for Black women (Chilton and Datesman, 1987). Thus, it has been concluded that while men still dominate larceny crimes, the women's rate is growing. This is likely due to women's deteriorating economic situation—the "feminization of poverty."

Shoplifting has frequently been assumed to be female gender-related. Stereotypes link women with shopping and portray them as being tempted by clothes, jewelry, and makeup. A closer examination suggests that shoplifting may be gender-neutral or male gender-related. Two studies found no significant differences between males' and females' shoplifting rates (Hudson, 1989; Smart, 1976). Other studies, however, report that males are more likely to shoplift than females (Buckle and Farrington, 1984; Chesney-Lind and Shelden, 1992; Mawby, 1980) and steal more items and items of greater value than the food and clothing typically shoplifted by females (Buckle and Farrington, 1984; Gibbens and Prince, 1962; Hoffman-Bustamante, 1973).

Robbery and Burglary

One of the few studies on female robbers examined imprisoned women and found that one-third acted alone or with another woman, and the major motivators were financial (often to purchase drugs) or peer pressure (often from a boyfriend). Two-fifths were arrested as juveniles, many were from single-parent homes, and most used a firearm in committing the offense (Fortune et al., 1980). The sample was evenly divided between two typologies: *situational* and *career* robbers. *Situational robbers* were motivated by external sources such as peer pressure or economic crises and had no commitment to robbery, while *career criminals* incorporated robbing as part of a continuing pattern of criminal activities (ibid.).

Sommers and Baskin's (1993) study of 65 violent females charged with robberies and aggravated assaults, claimed the women varied significantly in the number of robberies they had committed (ranging from 1 to 16), although one-quarter had committed more than ten robberies. Two-thirds of the women reported the robbery occurring in the course of and subsequent to other crimes such as prostitution, drug dealing, nonviolent theft, and fraud. Most of the robberies were not planned but were more spontaneous, or spur-of-the-moment. Regarding motivations to rob, 89 percent reported committing the robbery to obtain money, with four-fifths of those committing it for money stating that it was money for drugs, with the remaining fifth wanting the money for clothes, jewelry, and electronic equipment. About 10 percent reported their motivation was the excitement, loyalty to friends, or vengeance.

Notably, however, for many of these women their early robberies were not motivated by financial desires, but their subsequent robberies were financial, usually to buy drugs. Now turning to the victims of these women's robberies, almost three-quarters were strangers, equally likely to be other women as men. However, when they robbed without a weapon, their victims were more likely to be other women. They reported choosing stranger victims who looked weak and vulnerable. About two-thirds of the robberies were committed with accomplices, and of these, 60 percent were committed with other women.

> From early on in their criminal careers, women in the robbery sample reported that they acted out of self-determination and not in concert with or for boyfriends. Although the women sometimes were involved in criminal activities that involved men or activities that at times were controlled by men, they did so most often as equal partners." (Sommers and Baskin, 1993, 149)

Miller's (1998) ethnographic study of 14 women and 23 men robbers found overall gender similarities in motivation for robbing: Robbers of both sexes rob to get money and primarily to get money for status or material goods (e.g., jewelry) and to a lesser degree to support a drug addiction. To a lesser extent, both males and females are motivated to rob by the "psychological thrill" it entails or for revenge. The only gender difference in motivation to rob was that young men were more likely to report the pressure to have their own money and to own status goods. The gender differences in Miller's (ibid.) study of robbers, then, had less to do with *motivations* to rob and more to do with how the robberies are carried out. The men used primarily one method to rob: "using physical violence and/or a gun placed on or at close proximity to the victim in a confrontational manner" (ibid., 47). Women, on the other hand, are more eclectic in their enactments of robbery, reporting three strategies. The most frequently reported strategy is *targeting female victims,* reported by 71 percent of the women robbers. Half of the women robbers reported two other strategies: (1) promising men sexual favors for money, where they don't "deliver" the sexual favors, and (2) working with men (friends, relatives, or boyfriends) to rob men.

Although little effort has been made to study gender differences in burglary, in a notable exception, numerous gender differences were found: (1) Males were more likely than females to admit to crimes in addition to the burglary; (2) females were more likely than males to work with others in committing the burglary; (3) females were more likely than males to report being drug addicts; (4) males started their burglary "careers" at an earlier age than the females; (5) males reported committing more burglaries than the females; (6) females reported less contact with the crime-processing system than the males; and (8) females and males were equally likely to use drugs (Decker et al., 1993). Maher's (1997) research on sex workers identified a type of robbery, "viccing," specific to this group, where sex workers rob their clients. Maher and Curtis (1992) view "viccing" as motivated by sex workers' frustration with the devaluation of their work and their bodies and their extreme vulnerability to victimization.

White-Collar Crime

The "liberation" hypothesis implies that as women become more equal to men, their offending rates will converge with men's. Given that the slow movement toward gender equality has benefitted middle-class women the most, we might expect to see a similarity in men's and women's offenses most clearly in white-collar jobs. The limited research on this topic, however, has found significant gender differences. A study of white-collar convictions in U.S. federal courts found major differences between convicted men and women: (1) Women were usually employed as clerical workers, and men were usually employed as managers and administrators; (2) 60 percent of convicted female embezzlers were bank tellers, whereas only 14 percent of male embezzlers were tellers; (3) men's financial gains were much larger than women's; (4) women tended to work alone in committing the crime, whereas men were more likely to work with others; (5) women were more likely than men to report "family need" as motivating their offense; (6) women's crimes were more petty than men's; (7) women's share of corporate crime was low; and (8) men were more likely than women to be influenced by other white-collar workers to commit the crime (Daly, 1989). In fact, the gender differences in these white-collar offenders were so extreme and the nature of the differences were such to make one wonder whether the crimes of most of these women should really be classified under white-collar offenses.

Drug Use and Selling

Before reviewing the research on women and girls as drug users and drug sellers, it is useful to examine the political nature of women and drugs. Chesney-Lind (1997, 147) makes a convincing argument that "without any fanfare, the 'war on drugs' has become a war on women and has contributed to the explosion in women's prison populations." She reports this has been significantly affected by the implementation of urinalysis and other technologies that are used on paroled women to send them back to prison at unprecedented rates for drug use. Diaz-Cotto (1996) makes the important and rarely recognized point that women's drug selling is often a better indication of the feminization of poverty than of women's increased drug use. More specifically, she points out that not all women drug sellers are drug users, but rather, as stated in other parts of this book regarding drug selling and other crimes, it is one of the few options they have to make money.

> [W]hile a distinction has been made here between economic and drug-related crimes, it is widely accepted among criminal justice personnel that many of the drug-related crimes committed by Latinas were, in fact, economically motivated. That is, many were not using drugs but engaging in the importation and distribution of illegal drugs to meet economic needs within a deteriorating national and international economy. (ibid., 274)

A review of the research on gender comparisons in illicit drug use reported interesting differences (Inciardi et al., 1993). First, young women are more likely to be introduced to drugs by husbands and boyfriends than young men are to be introduced by intimate female companions. (In fact, women are more likely to be in a position to have to exchange sex and companionship for drugs from a dealer.) Second, while both females and males often begin using drugs out of curiosity and a desire to experiment, there are gender differences in the motivations for continued drug use. Women are less likely than men to use illegal drugs for pleasure or thrill seeking and from peer pressure and are more likely than men to use drugs as "self-medication" to "treat" existing depression. Thus, women are more likely than men to continue drug use in responses to crises and psychological stresses (and may be more likely to have crises and psychological stresses) and are more likely than men to have been depressed before developing a drug problem (see Inciardi et al., 1993).

Although little research exists examining gender differences in selling drugs, one study of crack dealers that included 6 women in the sample of 40 addressed gender differences once and in this instance reported that women and men crack dealers "hang together" in groups for protection (the police are less likely to confront a group of suspects than individuals) and that this works to women crack dealers' advantage because they are viewed as just hanging out with the male dealers, not dealing themselves (Jacobs, 1996). An ethnographic study of the marijuana industry in rural Kentucky reported gender-distinguished roles, dependent on social class membership (Hafley and Teweksbury, 1996). The three distinct roles for women in the rural marijuana industry community were "strumpets," "decent women," and "women-in-between." "Strumpets" were typically young, uneducated, and unmarried and often have one or more children out of wedlock. Her role is to emotionally, sexually, and domestically support male marijuana growers. She is expendable to these men and knows it, thus, despite strong loyalty to men of the marijuana industry, if he goes to prison, moves or drops her, she seeks the next man to take his place. Needless to say, she is looked down upon within her community. The "decent woman," then, is far more respected and typically a female relative of an active male in the marijuana industry (e.g., mother, sister, wife, grandmother, daughter, etc.). Although they are aware of the illegal activities of "their men" in the marijuana industry, they rarely participate themselves. "However, Decent Women's expressed disapproval does not lead the men to curtail their activities, for after all, they are 'just women' " (ibid., 88). Finally, the in-between-women fall between the strumpets and decent women and are unique in that they play active roles in growing and distributing the marijuana. They are less respected than "decent women" but more respected and hold more power than "strumpets." "Across the board, women's roles are predominantly passive, although within the last decade women-in-between have begun to play more active roles. For the male marijuana grower, women fulfill essential, but subservient roles" (ibid., 91).

An important focus of the research on drug use and abuse is attempting to determine how it is related to other types of criminal acts and behavior. The previous chapter discussed how girls who run away from home often use drugs to numb their pain (especially if they are survivors of violent childhoods) and/or may turn to sex work. In this way, then, different forms of offending are inextricably linked: running away (a status offense), drug use, and sex work. Notably, a certain amount of research indicates that drug users are sometimes "forced" into sex work to support their habits. A study of white and Chicana women drug abusers found that, like male drug users, theft is the most popular crime they commit and that using sex work to support the drug habit was relatively rare, especially among the Chicanas. While the women were more likely to turn to crime after (rather than before) the drug addiction, white women reported less crime than Chicana women (Anglin and Hser, 1987). Another study examined two cohorts of women drug users in Miami, reporting that the first cohort (1977–1978) was more heavily involved with drugs in general, while the second cohort (1983–1984) was more heavily involved with cocaine and narcotics (Inciardi and Pottieger, 1986). Although both cohorts reported committing their first crimes at age 15 or 16 and that both were heavily involved in property crimes and rarely involved in violent crimes, the younger cohort was more involved in drug sales and sex work. Finally, a study of female violent street criminals found differences between women who had become criminals as girls (about age 11) and those who had turned to crime as young adults. Females initiated into crime as girls were more involved with drugs than females who became violent offenders as young adults. Moreover, addiction to drugs appeared to be related to an increase in violent offending for the group that became offenders as young adults (Baskin and Sommers, 1993).

One study on women and crack cocaine found extremely high regularity of women performing oral sex (in particular) on men in crack houses in exchange for occasional hits of crack during the sexual act, an obvious form of sex work:

> [I]t is also not unusual for a man to approach a woman for the purpose of having a sex partner throughout a smoking encounter. Some men will enter a crack house, purchase enough rocks for two people for several hours, and then make it clear to every woman in the house what he has in mind. . . . [T]here seems to be an expectation [in the crack house] that if a man wants to have sex with a woman, she will not oppose the offer. The expectations are implicit. Everyone involved—the house owner, the male user/customer, and the female user/prostitute are all aware of what is expected. Because the rules and the roles are known to all parties, there is little negotiating. (Inciardi et al., 1993, 74–75)

Although studies have not agreed on the link between sex-work and drugs, there is, undoubtedly, an important connection. Maher's (1997) ethnographic fieldwork with women crack users in the early 1990s in three Brooklyn (New York City) neighborhoods reports that income generation within the street-level economy falls into three overlapping and interdependent options: drug-business hustles, nondrug hustles, and sex work. Maher (ibid., 130) reports that "sex work was the only income-generating activity consistently available to women drug users." And given the risks of "death, rape, and disfigurement" that the sex work entailed, "suggests that overall these women had few [income-generating] choices indeed" (ibid., 189).

Maher (1995), however, challenges the research presentation of female drug users as "innocent" and "hapless victims," often lured into both drug use and sex work. "Such accounts perpetuate stereotypical images of women as weak and submissive; as incapable of exercising agency and unable to make any kind of choice in relation to drug use" (ibid., 132). She reports the gendered use of crack as far more complex than previous gender analyses of drug use. First, she is resistant to the existing paradigm of female drug using that denies women agency: "Women, like me, choose to use drugs. Not one of the women in this study was forced to stick a needle in her arm or coerced into taking a blast off a crack stem" (ibid., 160). (However, Maher describes one woman user whose boyfriend "exerted considerable pressure," including "blowing the smoke in her mouth" [ibid., 141]). Regarding initiation into crack use, unlike previous research, Maher found that few of the women were initiated by boyfriends or husbands: "Rather, women's experiences of initiation were mediated by many factors including the influence of same-sex peers, previous drug use experience, availability and cost of the drug, patterns of consumption and the reciprocal relationship with popular cultural images" (ibid., 133). In fact, some women felt pressured by other *women* to try crack. Maher's overall description of "the street-level drug users in one of the poorest neighborhoods in New York City" follows:

> The majority used a combination of crack cocaine and heroin on a daily basis. Most were members of racial/ethnic minorities. Nearly all were homeless. Many were mothers and a significant proportion were HIV positive. These women were both the perpetrators and victims of violence and all engaged in law-breaking, principally street-level sex-work, as a means of supporting their drug consumption. (1997, 29)

Maher notes, however, that while the initiation into crack use is less gendered than women's drug use is typically viewed in research, once immersed in the consumption of crack, their experiences and options are likely gendered. For example, women disproportionately suffer the economic marginalization and social stigma associated with crack use (Maher and Curtis, 1992), and the structure of the drug economy does not provide "equal opportunity employment," working to women's disadvantage (Maher, 1995, 161). Moreover, she notes the gendered nature of homelessness for crack users, in that men were more able to shelter themselves from the worst aspects of street life, particularly in terms of the risk of harassment, violence, and victimization (Maher, 1997). "By virtue of their economic position, many elderly males were able to accommodate their own demands for sexual activity and drug use by providing shelter to homeless women drug users" (ibid., 54). Interestingly, a study of an African-American girl gang reported that the inception of crack sales in the mid-1980s by their boyfriends resulted in the formation of this female gang (Lauderback, Hansen, and Waldorf, 1992). More specifically, after continued dissatisfaction with the division of labor and profits from crack-selling ventures with their boyfriends, these young women entered into the crack-selling business themselves. At the same time as noting the gendered nature of crack use and selling crack, Maher (1997, is perhaps most effective in presenting these drug users more powerfully and with more agency than existing research: "As it turns out, the women I studied were remarkable in many ways, but perhaps most of all for their resilience, their capacity for the hardest of labors, and the sheer tenacity of the struggles to survive."

Friedman and Alicea's (1995) research is a departure from the vast majority of drug research in that their sample is composed of 30 white middle- and upper-class women heroin and methadone users. (Most research has been on men, and the research on both men and women has focused on the most economically and socially disenfranchised.) This study found that many of these class- and race-privileged women reported their initial heroin use was a means to reject the patriarchy and the restrictive gender roles they perceived and experienced. These women, then, reported using heroin precisely because it "did not fit the traditional image of good girls" and "it felt empowering and gave them a sense of control because it required some degree of autonomy and assertiveness" (ibid., 437). Moreover, in addition to the "in-your-face" aspect of societal rejection by becoming heroin users, heroin use provided these women with feelings of pleasure and happiness and offered them "strength, self-confidence, and feelings of invincibility" (ibid., 438). However, over time, the drug stopped working as a "liberating mechanism," and they frequently reached a point of crisis where they redefined heroin as "the villain" instead of "the hero" (ibid., 439). Thus, while these wealthy white women's motivations for using the drug are likely different from those typically studied (the most marginalized of the population), their addictions resulted in both the positive and negative aspects that drug addiction does for everyone else. Also, while they had started using heroin as a rebellion against patriarchy and although it initially helped their self-esteem, addiction resulted in quite the opposite:

> They could not reconcile a perspective of being "in control" when they witnessed the horrible things they saw themselves doing for their men and their drug. They began to see the heroin world as a mirror of the dominant culture, which both relegated women to low status and devalued them as individuals. Heroin was no longer a vehicle for rejecting patriarchy. (ibid., 442)

The women in this sample described prostituting themselves to get more drugs for themselves and often their male partners/lovers or offering physicians "blow jobs" to get drugs. This was hardly the picture they had of themselves as independent women flaunting the patriarchy. Thus, distrust of men became another theme in their "epiphany" of realizing that heroin was "the villain." Unfortunately, they found the methadone clinics they went to in order to get off heroin were often sexist and difficult to work with. The authors report: "At the point that women choose to use methadone, they believe that they have no resources (social and economic) and no other alternatives for survival" (ibid., 443). However, they also reported the treatment as unbearably sexist as well.

In addition to the gendered nature of sex work associated with drug use and addiction, one of the most gendered aspects of illegal drug use is the threat, perpetrated largely by the media, of drug-using pregnant women and mothers, particularly "crack mothers" (Humphries, 1999). A scholar in this area, Drew Humphries (ibid., 15) asks: "How and with what consequences did an unusually powerless category of women emerge as a threatening symbol of disorder, the unenviable enemy in the domestic war on drugs?" Humphries's (ibid.) focus is to merge the existing scientific data on rates of crack and cocaine use over time and research on the health of babies from women on crack with her careful research on how these rates and babies' health were represented in the television media between 1983 and 1994. The image presented in the media, and likely adopted by the general public, is of poor women of color in inner cities who use crack and who don't care that they're pregnant and what effect their crack use will have on the developing fetus. Through her careful examination of both research on the topic of drug-using women and content analysis of television news portrayal of these women, Humphries (ibid.) provides a powerful presentation of the four stages of the social construction of crack mothers by the media (see Figure 3.3). She states:

> The networks distorted the record on crack babies, representing the worst possible outcomes as the norm. . . . The prevailing wisdom, then, held that the prenatal cocaine exposure risked the life or health of the newborn, that crack-addicted women who used drugs during pregnancy should be prevented from inflicting avoidable harm to the fetus and newborn, and that someone should take action. (ibid., 66)

Similar to Humpries (ibid.), Boyd's (1999) extensive literature review of research on the effects of illicit drug use on mothering reports that although it "is viewed as inconsistent with good mothering, many researchers have demonstrated that women who use illicit drugs can be adequate parents." Boyd cites research that found that drug-addicted mothers are no more likely to be child abusers and indeed are less likely to use physical forms of violence than nonaddicted mothers (Colten, 1982) and generally hold the same parenting values as nondrug-abusing mothers (Rosenbaum et al., 1990). Boyd (1999) notes that the only specific effect of pregnant women's use of drugs is the chance that their babies will experience drug withdrawal and that not all such babies experience withdrawal, also known as neonatal abstinence syndrome (NAS). Further, Boyd (ibid., 36) identifies NAS as appearing to be a "cultural fabrication" consistent with Humphries's (1999) identification of the social fabrication in "creating" a mythical image of "crack mother." Indeed, it appears that alcohol (via Fetal Alcohol Syndrome) likely has a greater impact than drugs, although few of the pregnant woman drug studies have included alcohol intake as a variable in addition to drug intake (Boyd, 1999). Thus Boyd (ibid., 25) concludes her review of the literature with the need to question the legal, medical, and social service assumption that "illicit drug use equals poor

Stage 1: Recreational Cocaine Use (1983–1985)—Characterized by affluent, white, remorseful women formerly addicted to cocaine, interviewed about their addictions from their own homes or a treatment facility. They were treated sympathetically by the news media as "vulnerable" to the "myth of recreational drugs." Discovery of pregnancy was not sufficient to stop the use. They tended to have healthy babies, however, although physicians had concerns about these babies' long-term health. These women were not subjected to punishment.

Stage 2: The Discovery of Crack (1985–1987)—Characterized by inner-city street corner Blacks and Hispanics after crack, a highly addictive, cheaper form of cocaine hit the drug market in 1985. Crack news stories overshadowed cocaine ones, except emotionally charged stories of white cocaine-using pregnant women and their af-flicted babies.

Stage 3: The Crusade against Crack Mothers (1988–1990)—Characterized by inner-city, largely African-American pregnant women, or such women with recently born "crack babies," filmed on the streets or in hospitals shortly after the births. The ba-bies in the coverage had serious defects. The sensationalist news coverage led to highly publicized cases of these women charged with manslaughter, injecting a minor with drugs, and child endangerment.

Stage 4: Recovering Mothers and Resilient Children (1991–1994)—News stories and researchers began questioning the reality and severity of trauma experienced by "crack babies" and documented that the prenatal transference of crack-cocaine was not as harmful as originally portrayed. "Crack mothers" were portrayed as "survivors" and interviewed in treatment. However, crack mothers were still vilified by the legal system with approaches and policies that made crack-addicted pregnant women, especially those of color or poor, reluctant to pursue treatment for fear of landing in jail or prison.

FIGURE 3.3 Humphries's Stages in the Social Construction of Crack
Mothers as Presented on Television News Stories

SOURCE: Humphries, Drew. 1999. *Crack Mothers: Pregnancy, Drugs, and the Media.* Columbus, OH: Ohio State University Press, based on content analysis of television media representation from 1983–1994, using mostly ABC, CBS, and NBC news presentations (*N* = 84).

parenting, which places children at risk." Also consistent with Humphries's (1999) speculation, Boyd (1999) found that the 28 illicit-drug–using women in her study were afraid to contact medical professionals for help when they found they were pregnant for fear of being stigmatized and jailed in their attempts to get "clean" and/or receive prenatal care. Boyd (ibid.) goes on to report not only horror stories about the medical community's treatment of drug–using women when their babies were born but also the truly deplorable conditions that their babies labeled with NAS were subject to at birth (e.g., lit-tle or no human touch, light, inability to bond with any human including a parent, and so on, for days at a time).

It is vital in the assessment of the crackdown on drug–using women to acknowledge the racist and racialized nature of the phenomenon and response to it. Robert's (1997, 127) overview on the phenomenon of charging women who give birth to babies testing positive for drugs notes that most of these women are poor, Black, and addicted to crack:

> The prosecution of drug-addicted mothers is part of an alarming trend
> toward greater state intervention into the lives of pregnant women under

the rationale of protecting the fetus from harm. Such government intrusion is particularly harsh for poor women of color. They are the least likely to obtain adequate prenatal care, the most vulnerable to government monitoring, and the least able to conform to the white middle-class standard of motherhood. They are therefore the primary targets of government control.

General Aggression

Although other sections in this chapter have addressed or will address gender differences in aggression in terms of juvenile delinquency, gangs, child abuse, and homicide, it is also useful to devote a section simply to aggression. Chapter 1 included a discussion on the role of biology versus social learning as explanations for the consistent finding that males are more aggressive than females, concluding that this is primarily a *gender,* not a *sex,* difference. More specifically, males are generally more aggressive than females due to prescribed and gendered social roles. Mary B. Harris has conducted a significant amount of research, on-going since the 1970s, addressing gender differences in aggression, accounting for race/ethnicity and context (see, for example, Harris 1973, 1974a, 1974b, 1976, 1992, 1996). She has used both experimental and survey research designs on large populations of college students and concludes some of the following:

- men generally report more aggressive behavior than women, particularly at the more serious levels of aggression
- when women are the aggressors, men are more likely to be slapped or called unethical or cruel
- men generally report being the target/victim of aggressive behavior, with the exception of rape, more than women
- when the target/victim is a female, males are more likely than females to report teasing her or making obscene gestures toward her
- men and women are more likely to report *receiving* aggressive behavior from men than women, with the exception of being slapped
- men and women are more likely to report *directing* their aggressive behavior at men than at women
- men are more likely than women to report inciting others to act aggressively
- men are more likely than women to report yelling at, committing property damage, and harming the target/victim when they are aggressive
- women are more likely than men to report feeling guilty about, tell others, and cry about their aggressive behaviors
- both women and men are more likely to cry about the aggression they perpetrated if it was against the opposite sex

- both men and women are more likely to report threatening men than women

- men are more likely than women to report physical injuries and legal problems resulting from the aggression they initiated, whereas women are more likely than men to report interpersonal difficulties resulting from the aggression

- almost all men and women identified at least some positive effect of their own use of aggression

- men are more likely than women to report being angered by a man hurting another person or a woman using physical aggression

- women were more likely than men to report (1) condescending or insensitive behavior from either sex, (2) verbal aggression from a woman, or (3) physical aggression from a man, as highly anger-provoking

- being called "promiscuous" was reported as more insulting for women than men

- being called a "coward" or "wimp" by either sex or being called an obscene term (including implying someone was sexually inadequate) by a woman, was reported as more insulting for men than women

- African-Americans, especially African-American women, were more likely than whites to report physical aggression from men as highly anger-provoking

- African-American women were more likely than white women to report physical aggression from a woman as the most anger-provoking (Harris, 1996)

Harris's research indicates the importance of examining many factors in attempting to address gender differences in aggressive behavior, including not only gender differences in the use of aggression but also differences in how aggression is used depending on the sex of the victim, gender differences in what "provokes" one to use aggression, differences in people's perceptions about the adequacy of using aggression based on whether the aggressor is female or male, and racial/ethnic differences in perceptions and use of aggression. These studies indicate that both personal use and assessment of others' use of aggression are highly gendered. The use and assessment of others' use of aggression is less affected by race/ethnicity, yet there were some differences indicating that "the use of verbal and physical aggression may be different for members of different ethnic groups" (Harris, 1996, 128).

A study of 65 violent women offenders examined the context of *assaults* committed by these women and reported that the motivations were often aggressive response to aggression from those designated as their victims (Sommers and Baskin, 1993). "These women are not roaming willy-nilly through the streets engaging in 'unprovoked' violence. They are frequently thrust in violence-prone situations in which the victim enters into it as an active participant, shares the actor's role, and becomes functionally responsible for it" (ibid., 154). However, the respondents' aggression was typically more aggressive than that of their victims. The authors describe these women as primarily associated with others involved in crime, who become increasingly socially and psychologically alienated from conventional life (ibid., 156). These women's assaults were described as "often impulsive and unorganized," frequently involving weapons and occurring when they were intoxicated (ibid., 152). One-fifth of the assaults were planned, and these usually involved vengeance, "either related to money or false accusations" (ibid.). Fourteen percent of the assaults were related to drug dealing.

Nonlethal and Lethal Child Abuse

Other female gender-related offenses are the nonsexual offenses against children and infants (Smart, 1976), such as neglect, cruelty, and abandonment. Whether these crimes are actually committed more by women than men is debatable, especially if the amount of contact a parent has with her or his child is taken into consideration. Women probably abuse children much less often per hour spent with them than men do. If women are indeed more likely than men to be reported for cruelty to children, it is likely due to the fact that they shoulder most of the responsibility for child care (ibid.). However, Dougherty (1993) is concerned that existing analyses of mothers who abuse their children ignore the influence of patriarchy within the family and how females' own past and present experiences of victimization, especially of male violence, may be related to the abuse they perpetrate. She suggests that future analysis should consider how both women's power (over their children) and powerlessness (in regard to their husbands) might influence the likelihood that they will abuse their children. Specifically, she notes research that states parents' stress is positively related to their likelihood to abuse their children, commenting on the high stress women battered by their husbands experience and how this might increase the chances that they will abuse their children.

The previous chapter discussed how addressing female criminality is impossible to dislocate from the issue of women and girls "violating" socially prescribed gender roles. Probably nowhere is the violation of culturally bound gender roles (including sex work and female-initiated sexuality and "freedom") more sensationalized and symbolic than women who harm their own children. Although men and women appear to be equally likely to kill their children and stepchildren (Greenfeld and Snell, 1999), when women do so it receives massive media attention.[1] An example of this was when Susan Smith admitted to strapping her young children into their car seats and setting the car in motion into a lake, resulting in their drowning. As the case unfolded, the gendered nature of it was difficult to ignore. First, how would this crime have been viewed if it had been the children's father instead of their mother? Second, Ms. Smith's father, high up in the "Christian Right," had molested her

---

[1]"Between 1976 and 1997, parents and stepparents murdered nearly 11,000 children" (Greenfeld and Snell, 1999, 4).

as a child. Should this be considered relevant? Although Susan Smith was convicted of killing her children, to many people's surprise, she was not given the death penalty. I like to think it was because when our "peers" (jurors) are able to actually hear the context and consequences of a person's life, they are more understanding of how these criminal behaviors and acts result. The goal, then, is not to excuse Susan Smith but rather to understand what places someone at risk for offending. As stated in the last chapter, childhood sexual abuse, particularly incest, is a strong predecessor to delinquency and offending.

When abortion and birth control are illegal or simply difficult or impossible to obtain, a likely consequence both historically and currently is the occurrence of maternal infant-killings. Whether this was acted out in the past by house-maids or factory workers raped by their male employers and who could not afford raising children and resisted the labels of "bastard" for their children (and worse for themselves) or more recently by such high-profile cases as the girl who delivered her baby in the bathroom at her senior prom and left him there to die, it is clear that women's and girls' infanticide acts are not simply a historical phenomenon. What is clear is that both historically and presently, girls and women have often been faced with inadequate or no birth control and inadequate or no access to abortion where female sexuality outside of marriage and "unmarried motherhood" is still stigmatized.

At the same time that we live in a highly sexualized culture (e.g., MTV, television commercials, films, and billboards) and a culture where sexual victimization, especially of young women and girls, occurs at epidemic levels (see Chapters 6 and 7), girls and young women are told not to have sex, and most schools are resistant to providing birth control or even lecturing on the need for it if one chooses to be sexually active. When women commit infanticide, the focus on them is usually "mad" (insane) or "bad" (evil and criminal) (Frigon, 1995), with little focus on the males who impregnated them (including when the pregnancy is a result of rape) and often aid in the actual killing of the infant. Notably, analysis of women and men in the United States who killed their children or step-children found mothers commit more of these killings of children during infancy, "while fathers were more likely to have been responsible for the murders of children age 8 or older" (Greenfeld and Snell, 1999).

A study conducted on 20 men and 28 women who killed their own children in Wales and England examined the gender differences and similarities (Wilczynski, 1995). It is important to note that, similar to findings from other such studies of parents killing their own children, most of these killings "were not instrumental or premeditated—they were usually sudden and impulsive" (ibid., 168). Wilczynski (ibid.) divided the motivations for killing the children into 10 categories, ranging from *retaliating* to *altruistic* killings (see Figure 3.4). (There is also an eleventh category called "motive unknown.") Although Wilczynski's (ibid.) is far from "the final answer" on the issue of gender and parent killings, particularly given the small sample size, it is certainly an important first step in examining the relationship between parents' gender and their motivations for killing their own children.

Figure 3.4 below summarizes the seven motivations Wilczynski (ibid) estimates as likely gender related. In summary, fathers are more likely than mothers to commit retaliating, jealousy/rejection, and discipline killings of their
children, while mothers are more likely than fathers to commit altruistic, psychotic, Munchausen syndrome by proxy killings, and killing their children
(usually infants) because they were unplanned and not wanted. Again it is
important to remember that Wilczynski's (ibid.) sample is small and future
research is necessary on this topic. There were three other types of child
killings by parents Wilczynski (ibid.) found in the literature that she did not
locate in her sample. First is the *secondary to sexual or ritual (or organized) abuse,*
where a child is killed (usually inadvertently) during sexual or ritual abuse, or
the child is killed purposely because the parent is afraid the child will inform
others of the abuse. Another motivation for child killings by parents not noted
in this sample is *self-defense* killing, where a parent kills a child in self-defense
(because the child is assaulting the parent). The final category of child-killing
parent motivation (also not found in Wilczynski's sample) is the *no intent to kill
or injure the child killing.* This category includes parents who batter their children but don't intend the physical abuse to result in the children's death, or
parents whose neglect of their children results in their children's deaths. Given
that Wilczynski (ibid.) did not find these final three categories in her sample,
she was unable to estimate whether gender was related.

Male-Dominated Child-Killings by Parents

- *Retaliating killings*—anger toward another person, usually the person's spouse, is displaced onto the child.
- *Jealousy of, or rejection by, the victim*—e.g., cases where the parent believes the child is not biologically his, resents the other parent's attention given to the child, feels rejected by the child (often because he has abused the child in the past)
- *Discipline killings*—children killed during the course of being disciplined or punished

Female-Dominated Child-Killings by Parents

1. *Unwanted child killings*—children unwanted or unplanned; usually involved killings of children less than 24 hours old
2. *Altruistic killings*—The parent believes it is in the child's best interest to be killed because the child is suffering from an illness ("mercy killing") or because the parent believes her or his own depression or situation results in an unacceptable situation for the child.
3. *Psychotic killings*—parents diagnosed as psychotic at the time of the killing, often killing under some delusion
4. *Munchausen Syndrome by Proxy*—A parent induces an illness in a child or fakes one, often presenting the child repeatedly to medical authorities.

FIGURE 3.4 Wilczynski's Gender Analysis of Child-Killings by Parents

SOURCE: Wilczynski, Ania. 1995. "Child-Killing by Parents." Pp. 167–180 in *Gender and Crime,* edited by R. E. Dobash, R. P. Dobash, and L. Noaks. Cardiff: University of Wales Press.

Homicide

Researchers estimate that 10 to 20 percent of all homicides in the United States are committed by women, but evidence suggests that women's "share" of homicides has been decreasing in recent years. The percentage of female homicide arrests decreased from 17 percent in 1960 (Steffensmeier, 1993) to 10 percent in 1990 (Gauthier and Bankston, 1997; Steffensmeier, 1993). Indeed, the per-capita rate at which women commit murder has declined steadily since 1980, and it was the lowest in 1998 that it has been since 1976, when these statistics were first collected (males' murder rate peaked in 1991) (Greenfeld and Snell, 1999). The only group of women for which the rate of murder has not decreased is those aged 18 to 24 (ibid.).

Thus, men commit the vast majority of homicides, and their already large proportion of homicide offenses may be increasing. Although in the United States men commit far more homicides than women *overall,* when women kill, their victims are typically their male partners (boyfriends, husbands, ex-husbands, etc.) (Browne and Williams, 1989; Gauthier and Bankston, 1997; Greenfeld and Snell, 1999). Moreover, a study of murders in the United States between 1976 and 1997 reported that although men kill their current and former wives and girlfriends more often than women kill their current or former husbands or boyfriends, a much higher percent of female than male-perpetrated homicides involve intimate partners (see Figure 3.5).

Gauthier and Bankston's (1997) study of homicides in U.S. cities in 1990 where the populations were 100,000 or greater reported the importance of examining the type of homicide (intimate partner or not) and the role of gendered economic equality (see Figure 3.6). Consistent with findings from similar studies, Gauthier and Bankston (ibid.) found that while women make up a tiny minority of arrests for nonintimate homicides, the gender gap narrows for intimate-partner homicides. Moreover, this gender gap is mediated by the

Victim	Female-Perpetrated Murders		Male-Perpetrated Murders	
	%	(n)	%	(n)
Spouse	28.3	(16,978)	6.8	(26,890)
Ex-spouse	1.5	(900)	0.5	(1,977)
Boyfriend/girlfriend	14.0	(8,399)	3.9	(15,422)
Child/step-child	10.4	(6,240)	2.2	(8,700)
Other family	6.7	(4,020)	6.9	(27,286)
Acquaintance	31.9	(19,139)	54.6	(215,913)
Stranger	7.2	(4,320)	25.1	(99,257)
Total	13.2	(59,996)	86.8	(395,446)

FIGURE 3.5 Victim-Offender-Relationships in Male- vs. Female-Perpetrated U.S. Murders, 1976–1997

SOURCE: Calculated from Greenfeld, Lawrence A., and Tracy L. Snell. 1999. *Women Offenders.* Bureau of Justice Statistics: Special Report. U.S. Department of Justice, December, p. 4.

Overall Homicides

—Men were arrested for 10 percent of all homicides.

Nonintimate Homicides

—For every 100 nonintimates killed by men, women kill 6 nonintimates.

Intimate-Partner Homicides

—Intimate-partner homicide arrests constitute 6 percent of all homicide arrests (and 10 percent of all homicide arrests where the victim and offender know each other)

—On average, 62 women kill their intimate male partners for every 100 men that kill their intimate female partners.

—Men's proportion of intimate-partner homicides is greater in cities where women's economic advantage is relatively high, and this is particularly true in cities in the southern United States (where, arguably, the gender roles are more restricted).

FIGURE 3.6 Gauthier and Bankston's Gender Analysis of 1990 U.S. Homicides

SOURCE: Gauthier, DeAnn K., and William B. Bankston. 1997. "Gender Equality and the Sex Ratio of Intimate Killing." *Criminology* 35(4):577–600.

gender equality in the economic structure for the city in which the homicide arrest occurs. Contrary to what the "liberation" or "emancipation" hypothesis suggests (Adler, 1975), women constitute a lower proportion of intimate-partner homicide arrests in cities where they are doing better economically, and this is particularly true in southern states of the United States (Gauthier and Bankston, 1997). These authors conclude: "Again, we find a consistent explanation in suggesting males are increasingly exercising violence to maintain control over women in a context in which male status dominance is most threatened" (ibid., 594).

Careful analysis of these homicides points out the importance of women's ability to protect themselves from male aggression. Women who kill their male intimates are often acting in self-defense after a long history of abuse (Browne and Williams, 1989; Goetting, 1988; Jones, 1994; Jurik and Winn, 1990). Incidentally, the most popular murder weapon of female homicide offenders is a firearm (Goetting, 1988; Jurik and Winn, 1990; Weisheit, 1984), which is often the firearm that the batterer used to threaten them with in the past.

A number of studies have been conducted recently on female homicide offenders, many of whom killed men who battered them (which is discussed in more detail in Chapter 8). Three studies conducted to describe female homicide offenders found them to be mostly African-American, acting alone, poorly educated, and unemployed. They were most likely to kill someone of their own race, in the home, with a gun, and the victim was usually an intimate male partner (and very rarely a stranger) (Goetting, 1988; Mann, 1987; Weisheit, 1984). In 4 to 9 percent of the cases, the victim was a child (Goetting, 1988; Weisheit, 1984). Probably due at least in part to the increased attention and prejudice Blacks receive from the police, Black women homicide offenders are more likely to have experienced contact with the crime-processing system than their white counterparts (Mann, 1987).

Again, it is useful to examine the gendered aspect of intimate-partner homicides. More specifically, how do female-committed intimate-partner homicides relate to male-committed ones? It appears that in both the legal system and the media, it is "worse" for a woman to kill her former or current boyfriend or husband (even if he abused her) than it is for a man to kill a current or former intimate partner (see Wykes, 1995). In fact, how many of us have seen cases on a routine basis in the newspaper or television news where a woman either "disappears" or is brutally murdered and we see pictures of her "grieving" male partner, only to find out it wasn't a dangerous stranger but rather her intimate partner who murdered her? Wykes (ibid.) provides a powerful portrait of how women who kill their intimate male partners who have seriously battered them are often viewed as serious criminals or insane in the media and in court. At the same time, men (including those with a long history of battering) who kill their former or current wives or girlfriends are often viewed as having been "pushed" into it by these women's "nagging," "drunkenness," or "wanton sexual behavior" (see Wykes, 1995).

Notably, one study showed that female homicides of male partners decreased between 1976 and 1984, and these crimes were significantly lower in states with more domestic violence legislation and more resources for battered women (Browne and Williams, 1989). Also, when audiences were present during the offense, they were more likely to encourage the violence of male offenders and to discourage the violence of female offenders (Jurik and Winn, 1990). These studies show that although women rarely kill, when they do it is often their abusive male partners that they kill; thus, the roles of domestic violence and self-defense are vital to understanding the majority of female-perpetrated homicides.

SUMMARY

In the studies of female offending, particularly those examining gender differences and patterns over time, the findings are inconsistent; however, some patterns have emerged. First, if there is any support for gender-convergence in offending, it appears to be for less serious offenses and drug use. This is particularly apparent in self-report data. Second, the reliability of studies finding gender-convergence for more serious crimes often suffered because of fluctuations in offending patterns over time; many fluctuations could be attributed to changes in the economy and in law enforcement practices. Third, analyses controlling for race and age are essential to understanding the true nature of female criminality and criminality in general.

Women's offending rates appear to be "catching up" to men's in the area of larceny/theft. This is probably due more to the feminization of poverty than to any liberating effects of the women's movement. Furthermore, although there is evidence that women's involvement in larceny/theft is increasing relative to men's, women still commit far fewer of these offenses. Although more recent data need to be analyzed, the most recent research suggests gender-convergence between white males and African-American females for some crimes, especially larceny. What used to be a fairly stable offending hierarchy represented by research, with African-American males at the top, followed by white males, African-American females, and white females, respectively, is appearing to collapse, although some studies find African-American males distinctly ahead of other gender-race groups' offending rates. This may, however, be at least partially due to increased police surveillance of these youth. Future research needs to continue to follow these patterns and to study other races in addition to Black and white (such as Hispanics, Native Americans, and Asian Americans). In the meantime, it appears that regarding most offenses, especially serious and violent crimes, it is still a "man's world."

REFERENCES

Adler, Freda. 1975. *Sisters in Crime: The Rise of the New Female Criminal.* New York: McGraw-Hill.

Ageton, Suzanne S. 1983. "The Dynamics of Female Delinquency, 1976–1980." *Criminology* 21:555–584.

Alarid, Leane Fiftal, James W. Marquart, Vlemer S. Burton, Francis T. Cullen, and Steven J. Cuvelier. 1996. "Women's Roles in Serious Offenses." *Justice Quarterly* 13(3):431–454.

Alder, Christine M. 1998. " 'Passionate and Willful' Girls: Confronting Practices." *Women and Criminal Justice* 9(4):81–101.

Andersson, Jan. 1990. "Continuity in Crime: Sex and Age Differences." *Journal of Quantitative Criminology* 6:85–100.

Anglin, M. Douglas, and Yih-Ing Hser. 1987. "Addicted Women and Crime." *Criminology* 25:359–397.

Artz, Sibylle. 1998. *Sex, Power, and the Violent School Girl.* New York: Teachers College.

Baskin, Deborah R., and Ira Sommers. 1993. "Females' Initiation into Violent Street Crime." *Justice Quarterly* 10:559–581.

Belknap, Joanne, and Kristi Holsinger. 1998. "An Overview of Delinquent Girls." pp 31–64 in *Female Crime and Delinquency,* edited by Ruth T. Zaplin. Gaithersburg, MD: Aspen Publishing.

Bjerregaard, Beth, and Carolyn Smith. 1993. "Gender Differences in Gang Participation, Delinquency, and Substance Use." *Journal of Quantitative Criminology* 9:329–355.

Boritch, Helen, and John Hagan. 1990. "A Century of Crime in Toronto: Gender, Class, and Patterns of Social Control, 1859 to 1955." *Criminology* 28:567–599.

Boyd, Susan C. 1999. *Mothers and Illicit Drugs: Transcending the Myths.* Toronto: University of Toronto Press.

Browne, Angela, and Kirk R. Williams. 1989. "Exploring the Effect of Resource Availability and the Likelihood of Female-Perpetrated Homicides." *Law and Society Review* 23:75–94.

Buckle, Abigail, and David P. Farrington. 1984. "An Observational Study of Shoplifting." *British Journal of Criminology* 24:63–73.

Bunch, Barbara J., Linda A. Foley, and Susana P. Urbina. 1983. "The Psychology of Violent Female Offenders: A Sex-Role Perspective." *The Prison Journal* 63:66–79.

Cain, Maureen (Ed.). 1989. *Growing Up Good: Policing the Behavior of Girls in Europe.* London: Sage.

Campbell, Anne. 1984. "GIRLS' TALK: The Social Representation of Aggression by Female Gang Members." *Criminal Justice and Behavior* 11:139–156.

———. 1990. "Female Participation in Gangs." Pp. 163–182 in *Gangs in America,* edited by G. R. Huff. Newbury Park, CA: Sage.

———. 1999a. "Female Gang Members' Social Construction of Female Gangs." Pp. 248–255 in *Female Gangs in America: Essays on Girls, Gangs and Gender,* edited by M. Chesney-Lind and J. M. Hagedorn. Chicago: Lakeview Press.

———. 1999b. "Self-Definition by Rejection: The Case of Gang Girls." Pp. 100–117 in *Female Gangs in America: Essays on Girls, Gangs and Gender,* edited by M. Chesney-Lind and J. M. Hagedorn. Chicago: Lakeview Press.

Campbell, Gayle. 1990. "Women and Crime." *Juristat* 10:1–8.

Canter, Rachelle J. 1982. "Sex Differences in Self-Report Delinquency." *Criminology* 20:373–393.

Cernkovich, Stephen, and Peggy Giordano. 1979. "A Comparative Analysis of Male and Female Delinquency." *The Sociological Quarterly* 20:131–145.

Chesney-Lind, Meda. 1974. "Juvenile Delinquency: The Sexualization of Female Crime." *Psychology Today* (July):43–46.

———. 1986. "Women and Crime: The Female Offender." *Signs* 12:78–96.

———. 1987. "Girls and Violence: An Exploration of the Gender Gap in Serious Delinquent Behavior." Pp. 207–230 in *Childhood Aggression and Violence,* edited by D. Crowell, I. Evans, and C. O'Donnell. New York: Plenum.

———. 1997. *The Female Offender: Girls, Women, and Crime.* Thousand Oaks, CA: Sage.

Chesney-Lind, Meda, and John M. Hagedorn, Eds. 1999. *Female Gangs in America: Essays on Girls, Gangs and Gender.* Chicago: Lakeview Press.

Chesney-Lind, Meda, and Randall G. Shelden. 1992. *Girls, Delinquency, and Juvenile Justice.* Pacific Grove, CA: Brooks/Cole.

Chilton, Ronald, and Susan K. Datesman. 1987. "Gender, Race, and Crime: An Analysis of Urban Trends, 1960–1980." *Gender and Society* 1:152–171.

Colten, M. 1982. "Attitudes Experiences, and Self-Perceptions of Heroin-Addicted Mothers." *Journal of Social Issues* 38(2):77–92.

Daly, Kathleen. 1989. "Gender and Varieties of White-Collar Crime." *Criminology* 27:769–794.

Datesman, Susan K., and Mikel Aickin. 1984. "Offense Specialization and Escalation among Status Offenders." *Journal of Criminal Law and Criminology* 75:1246–1274.

Decker, Scott, Richard Wright, Allison Redfern, and Dietrich Smith. 1993. "A Woman's Place Is in the Home: Females and Residential Burglary." *Justice Quarterly* 10:143–162.

Deschenes, Elizabeth P., and Finn-Aage Esbensen. 1999. "Violence among Girls: Does Gang Membership Make a Difference?" Pp. 277–294 in *Female Gangs in America: Essays on Girls, Gangs and Gender,* edited by M. Chesney-Lind and J. M. Hagedorn. Chicago: Lakeview Press.

Diaz-Cotto, Juanita. 1996. *Gender, Ethnicity, and the State: Latina and Latino Prison Politics.* Albany, NY: State University of New York.

Dougherty, Joyce. 1993. "Women's Violence against Their Children: A Feminist Perspective." *Women and Criminal Justice* 4:91–114.

Eaton, Mary. 1986. *Justice for Women? Family, Court and Social Control.* Philadelphia: Open University Press.

Erez, Edna. 1988. "The Myth of the New Female Offender: Some Evidence from Attitudes toward Law and Justice." *Journal of Criminal Justice* 16:499–509.

Esbensen, Finn-Aage, and L. Thomas Winfree. 1998. "Race and Gender Differences between Gang and Non-gang Youths: Results from a Multisite Survey." *Justice Quarterly* 15(3):505–526.

Farnworth, Margaret. 1984. "Male-Female Differences in Delinquency in a Minority-Group Sample." *Research in Crime and Delinquency* 21:191–212.

Farnworth, Margaret, M. Joan McDer-mott, and Sherwood E. Zimmerman. 1988. "Aggregation Effects on Male-to-Female Arrest Rate Ratios in New York State, 1972 to 1984." *Journal of Quantitative Criminology* 4:121–135.

Felkenes, George T., and Harold K. Becker. 1995. "Female Gang Mem-bers: A Growing Issue for Policy Makers." *Journal of Gang Research* 2(4):1–10.

Feyerherm, William. 1981. "Gender Differences in Delinquency: Quantity and Quality." Pp. 82–93 in *Women and Crime in America,* edited by L. H. Bowker. New York: Macmillan.

Figueira-McDonough, Josephine, William H. Barton, and Rosemary C. Sarri. 1981. "Normal Deviance: Gender Similarities in Adolescent Subcul-tures." Pp. 17–45 in *Comparing Female and Male Offenders,* edited by M. Q. Warren. Beverly Hills, CA: Sage.

Fishman, Laura T. 1999. "Black Female Gang Behavior: A Historical and Ethnographic Perspective." Pp. 64–84 in *Female Gangs in America: Essays on Girls, Gangs and Gender,* edited by M. Chesney-Lind and J. M. Hagedorn. Chicago: Lakeview Press.

Fortune, E. P., M. Vega, and I. J. Silver-man. 1980. "A Study of Female Robbers in a Southern Correctional Institution." *Journal of Criminal Justice* 8:317–326.

Friedman, Jennifer, and Marisa Alicea. 1995. "Women and Heroin: The Path of Resistance and Its Consequences." *Gender and Society* 9(4):432–449.

Frigon, Sylvie. 1995. "A Genealogy of Women's Madness." Pp. 20–48 in *Gender and Crime,* edited by R. E. Dobash, R. P. Dobash, and L. Noaks. Cardiff: University of Wales Press.

Gauthier, DeAnn K., and William B. Bankston. 1997. "Gender Equality and the Sex Ratio of Intimate Killing." *Criminology* 35(4):577–600.

Gibbens, T. C. N., and J. Prince. 1962. *Shoplifting.* London: ISTD.

Giordano, Peggy C. 1978. "Girls, Guys, and Gangs: The Changing Social Context of Female Delinquency." *Journal of Criminal Law and Criminol-ogy* 69:126–132.

———. 1999. "The Changing Social Context of Female Delinquency." Pp. 90–99 in *Female Gangs in America: Essays on Girls, Gangs and Gender,* edited by M. Chesney-Lind and J. M. Hagedorn. Chicago: Lakeview Press.

Giordano, Peggy C., Sandra Kerbel, and Sandra Dudley. 1981. "The Econom-ics of Female Criminality: An Analy-sis of Police Blotters, 1890–1976." Pp. 65–82 in *Women and Crime in America,* edited by L. H. Bowker. New York: Macmillan.

Goetting, Ann. 1988. "Patterns of Homi-cide among Women." *Journal of Inter-personal Violence* 3:3–19.

Gold, Martin, and David J. Reimer. 1975. "Changing Patterns of Delinquent Behavior among Americans 13 through 16 Years Old: 1967–72." *Crime and Delinquency Literature* 7:483–517.

Greenfeld, Lawrence A., and Tracy L. Snell. 1999. *Women Offenders.* Bureau of Justice Statistics: Special Report. U.S. Department of Justice, Decem-ber, 14 pp.

Hafley, Sandra R., and Richard Tewks-bury. 1996. "Reefer Madness in Bluegrass County: Community Struc-ture and Roles in the Rural Kentucky Marijuana Industry." *Journal of Crimi-nal Justice* 29(1):75–94.

Hagedorn, John M., and Mary L. Devitt. 1999. "Fighting Female: The Social Construction of Female Gangs." Pp. 256–276 in *Female Gangs in America: Essays on Girls, Gangs and Gender,* edited by M. Chesney-Lind and J. M. Hagedorn. Chicago: Lakeview Press.

Harris, Mary B. 1973. Field Studies of Modeled Aggression in a Field Experiment." *Psychological Reports* 69:1–2.

———. 1974a. "Aggressive Reactions to a Frustrating Phone Call." *Journal of Social Psychology* 92:193–198.

———. 1974b. "Mediators between Frustration and Aggression in a Field Experiment." *Journal of Experimental Social Psychology* 10:561–571.

———. 1976. "Instigators and Inhibitors of Aggression in a Field Experiment." *Journal of Social Psychology* 98:27–38.

———. 1992. "Sex, Race, and Experiences of Aggression." *Aggressive Behavior* 18:201–217.

———. 1996. "Aggression, Gender, and Ethnicity." *Aggression and Violent Behavior* 1(2):123–146.

Hill, Gary D., and Elizabeth M. Crawford. 1990. "Women, Race, and Crime." *Criminology* 28:601–626.

Hindelang, Michael J. 1971. "Age, Sex, and the Versatility of Delinquent Involvements." *Social Problems* 18:522–535.

———. 1979. "Sex Differences in Criminal Activity." *Social Problems* 27:143–156.

———. 1981. "Variations in Sex-Race-Age Specific Incidence Rates of Offending." *American Sociological Review* 46:461–474.

Hoffman-Bustamante, Dale. 1973. "The Nature of Female Criminality." *Issues in Criminology* 8:117–136.

Hudson, Barbara. 1989. "Justice or Welfare? English and French Systems." Pp. 96–113 in *Growing Up Good,* edited by M. Cain. London: Sage.

Humphries, Drew. 1999. *Crack Mothers: Pregnancy, Drugs, and the Media.* Columbus, OH: Ohio State University Press.

Inciardi, James, Dorothy Lockwood, and Anne E. Pottieger. 1993. *Women and Crack-Cocaine.* New York: Macmillan.

Inciardi, James, and Anne E. Pottieger. 1986. "Drug Use and Crime among Two Cohorts of Women Narcotics Users: An Empirical Assessment." *Journal of Drug Issues* 16:91–106.

Inciardi, James, Anne E. Pottieger, Mary Ann Forney, Dale Chitwood, and Duane C. McBride. 1991. "Prostitution, IV Drug Use, and Sex-for-Crack Exchanges among Serious Delinquents: Risks for HIV Infection." *Criminology* 29:221–235.

Jacobs, Bruce A. 1996. "Crack Dealers' Apprehension Avoidance Techniques." *Justice Quarterly* 13(3):359–382.

Jensen, Gary J., and Raymond Eve. 1976. "Sex Differences in Delinquency." *Criminology* 13:427–448.

Jensen, Gary F., and Kevin Thompson. 1990. "What's Class Got to Do with It: A Further Examination of Power Control Theory." *American Journal of Sociology* 95:1009–1023.

Joe, Karen, and Meda Chesney-Lind. 1999. "Just Every Mother's Angel: An Analysis of Gender and Ethnic Variations in Youth Gang Membership." Pp. 210–222 in *Female Gangs in America: Essays on Girls, Gangs and Gender,* edited by M. Chesney-Lind and J. M. Hagedorn. Chicago: Lakeview Press.

Jones, Ann. (1994). *Next Time, She'll Be Dead: Battering and How to Stop It.* Boston: Beacon Press.

Jurik, Nancy C., and Russ Winn. 1990. "Gender and Homicide: A Comparison of Men and Women Who Kill." *Violence and Victims* 5:227–242.

Kline, Sue. 1993. "A Profile of Female Offenders in State and Federal Prisons." Pp. 1–6 in *Female Offenders: Meeting the Needs of a Neglected Population.* Laurel, MD: American Correctional Association.

Kruttschnitt, Candace. 1996. "Contributions of Quantitative Methods to the Study of Gender and Crime, or Bootstrapping Our Way into the Theoretical Thicket." *Journal of Quantitative Criminology* 12(2):135–161.

Laub, John H., and M. Joan McDermott. 1985. "An Analysis of Serious Crime by Young Black Women." *Criminology* 23:81–98.

Lauderback, David, Joy Hansen, and Dan Waldorf. 1992. *Gang Journal* 1 (1): 57–72.

Leonard, Eileen B. 1982. *Women, Crime, and Society: A Critique of Criminology Theory.* New York: Longman.

Lewis, Diane K. 1981. "Black Women Offenders and Criminal Justice: Some Theoretical Considerations." Pp. 89–105 in *Comparing Female and Male Offenders,* edited by M. Q. Warren. Beverly Hills, CA: Sage.

Maher, Lisa. 1995. "Women and the Initiation to Illicit Drugs." Pp. 132–166 in *Gender and Crime,* edited by R. E. Dobash, R. P. Dobash, and L. Noaks. Cardiff: University of Wales Press.

———. 1997. *Sexed Work: Gender, Race and Resistance in a Brooklyn Drug Market.* Oxford: Clarendon Press.

Maher, Lisa, and R. Curtis. 1992. "Women on the Edge of Crime: Crack Cocaine and the Changing Contexts of Street-Level Sex Work in New York City." *Crime, Law and Social Change* 18 (3):221–258.

Mann, Coramae Richey. 1984. *Female Crime and Delinquency.* Montgomery: University of Alabama Press.

———. 1987. "Black Women Who Kill." Pp. 157–186 in *Violence in the Black Family,* edited by R. L. Hampton. Lexington, MA: Lexington Books.

Mawby, Rob. 1980. "Sex and Crime: The Results of a Self-Report Study." *British Journal of Sociology* 31:525–541.

McCormack, Arlene, Mark-David Janus, and Ann W. Burgess. 1986. "Runaway Youths and Sexual Victimization: Gender Differences in an Adolescent Runaway Population." *Child Abuse and Neglect* 10:387–395.

Messerschmidt, James. 1999. "Feminist Theory, Criminology, and the Challenge of Diversity." Pp. 118–132 in *Female Gangs in America: Essays on Girls, Gangs and Gender,* edited by M. Chesney-Lind and J. M. Hagedorn. Chicago: Lakeview Press.

Miller, Brenda, William R. Downs, and Dawn M. Gondoli. 1989. "Delinquency, Childhood Violence, and the Development of Alcoholism in Women." *Crime and Delinquency* 35:94–108.

Miller, Jody. 1998. "Up it Up: Gender and the Accomplishment of Street Robbery." *Criminology* 36(1):37–66.

Moon, Dreama G., Ruby J. Thompson, and Regina Bennett. 1993. "Patterns of Substance Use among Women in Prison." Pp. 45–54 in *Women Prisoners: A Forgotten Population,* edited by Beverly R. Fletcher, Lynda D. Shaver, and Dreama G. Moon. Westport, CT: Praeger.

Moore, Joan W. 1999. "Gang Members' Families." Pp. 159–176 in *Female Gangs in America: Essays on Girls, Gangs and Gender,* edited by M. Chesney-Lind and J. M. Hagedorn. Chicago: Lakeview Press.

Moore, Joan W., and John M. Hagedorn. 1999. "What Happens to Girls in the Gang?" Pp. 177–186 in *Female Gangs in America: Essays on Girls, Gangs and Gender,* edited by M. Chesney-Lind and J. M. Hagedorn. Chicago: Lakeview Press.

Morash, Merry. 1983. "Gangs, Groups, and Delinquency." *British Journal of Criminology* 23:309–335.

Morris, Allison. 1987. *Women, Crime and Criminal Justice.* Oxford: Basil Blackwell.

Naffine, Ngaire. 1987. *Female Crime: The Construction of Women in Criminology.* Sydney, Australia: Allen and Unwin.

Nagel, Ilene, and John Hagan. 1983. "Gender and Crime: Offense Patterns and Criminal Court Sanctions." Pp. 91–144 in *Crime and Justice: An Annual Review of Research,* Vol. 4, edited by M. Tonry and N. Morris. Chicago: University of Chicago Press.

O'Brien, Robert M. 1988. "Exploring the Intersexual Nature of Violent Crimes." *Criminology* 26:151–170.

Richards, Pamela. 1981. "Quantitative and Qualitative Sex Differences in Middle-Class Delinquency." *Criminology* 18:453–470.

Roberts, Dorothy E. 1997. "Punishing Drug Addicts Who Have Babies: Women of Color, Equality, and the Rights of Privacy." Pp. 127–135 in *Critical Race Feminism,* edited by Adrien K. Wing. New York: New York University Press.

Rosenbaum et al. 1990. Cited in Boyd (1999)

Rosenbaum, M., S. Murphy, J. Irwin, and L. Watson. 1990. "Women and Crack: What's the Real Story?" *The Drug Policy letter* 11(2): 2–6.

Sampson, Robert J. 1985. "Sex Differences in Self-Reported Delinquency and Official Records: A Multiple-Group Structural Modeling Approach." *Journal of Quantitative Criminology* 1:345–367.

Sarri, Rosemary C. 1987. "Unequal Protection under the Law." Pp. 375–393 in *The Trapped Woman,* edited by J. Figueira-McDonough and R. Sarri. Newbury Park, CA: Sage.

Simon, Rita. (1975). *Women and Crime.* Lexington, MA: D. C. Heath.

Simpson, Sally S. 1991. "Caste, Class, and Violent Crime: Explaining Difference in Female Offending." *Criminology* 29:115–135

Smart, Carol. 1976. *Women, Crime and Criminology: A Feminist Critique.* London: Routledge and Kegan Paul.

———. 1982. "The New Female Offender: Reality or Myth?" Pp. 105–116 in *The Criminal Justice System and Women,* edited by B. R. Price and N. J. Sokoloff. New York: Clark Boardman.

Smith, Douglas A., and Christy A. Visher. 1980. "Sex and Involvement in Deviance/Crime: A Quantitative Review of the Empirical Literature." *American Sociological Review* 45:691–701.

Sommers, Ira, and Deborah R. Baskin. 1993. "The Situational Context of Violent Female Offending." *Journal of Research in Crime and Delinquency* 30(2):136–162.

Steffensmeier, Darrell J. 1980. "Sex Dif-ferences in Patterns of Adult Crime, 1965–1977: A Review and Assessment." *Social Forces* 58:1080–1108.

———. 1981. "Crime and the Contemporary Woman: An Analysis of Changing Levels of Female Property Crime," 1960–1975. Pp. 39–59 in *Women and Crime in America,* edited by L. H. Bowker. New York: Macmillan.

———. 1982. "Trends in Female Crime: It's Still a Man's World." Pp. 118–130 in *The Criminal Justice System and Women,* edited by B. R. Price and N. J. Sokoloff. New York: Clark Boardman.

———. 1993. "National Trends in Female Arrests, 1960–1990: Assessment and Recommendations for Research." *Journal of Quantitative Criminology* 9:411–441.

Steffensmeier, Darrell J., and Emilie A. Allan. 1988. "Sex Disparities in Arrests by Residence, Race, and Age: An Assessment of the Gender Convergence/Crime Hypothesis." *Justice Quarterly* 5:53–80.

Steffensmeier, Darrell J., and Michael J. Cobb. 1981. "Sex Differences in Urban Arrest Patterns, 1934–1979." *Social Problems* 29:37–50.

Steffensmeier, Darrell J., and R. H. Steffensmeier. 1980. "Trends in Female Delinquency." *Criminology* 18:62–85.

Steffensmeier, Darrell J., and Cathy Streifel. 1992. "Time-Series Analysis of the Female Percentage of Arrests for Property Crimes, 1960–1985: A Test of Alternative Explanation." *Justice Quarterly* 9:77–104.

Suh, Alexandra. 2000. "Military Prostitution in Asia and the United States." Pp. 144–158 in *States of Confinement: Policing, Detention, And Prisons,* edited by Joy James. New York: St. Martin's Press.

Thrasher, Frederic M. 1927. *The Gang.* Chicago: University of Chicago Press.

Tolman, Deborah L. 1994. "Doing Desire: Adolescent Girls' Struggles for/with Sexuality." *Gender and Society* 8(3):324–342.

Triplett, Ruth, and Laura B. Myers. 1995.

"Evaluating Contextual Patterns of Delinquency: Gender-Based Differences." *Justice Quarterly* 12(1):59–84.

Tyson, James L. 1993. "Mandatory Sentences Lead to Surge of Women in Prison." *The Christian Science Monitor* (November 19):1, 18.

U.S. Department of Health and Human Services. 1991. *Annual Report to the Congress on the Runaway and Homeless Youth Program, Fiscal Year 1990.* Washington, DC: Office of Human Development Services.

Walker, Lenore E. 1993. "Battered Women as Defendants." Pp. 233–257 in *Legal Responses to Wife Assault,* edited by N. Z. Hilton. Newbury Park, CA: Sage.

Warren, Margaurite Q., and Jill L. Rosenbaum. 1986. "Criminal Careers of Female Offenders." *Criminal Justice and Behavior* 13:393–418.

Weisheit, Ralph A. 1984. "Female Homicide Offenders: Trends over Time in an Institutionalized Population." *Justice Quarterly* 1:471–490.

Wilczynski, Ania. 1995. "Child-Killing by Parents." Pp. 167–180 in *Gender and Crime,* edited by R. E. Dobash, R. P. Dobash, and L. Noaks. Cardiff: University of Wales Press.

Wing, Adrien K., and Christine A. Willis. 1997. "Sisters in the Hood: Beyond Bloods and Crips." Pp. 243–254 in *Critical Race Feminism,* edited by Adrien K. Wing. New York: New York University Press.

Wolfe, Nancy T., Francis T. Cullen, and John B. Cullen. 1984. "Describing the Female Offender: A Note on the Demographics of Arrests." *Journal of Criminal Justice* 12:483–492.

Wykes, Maggie. 1995. "Passion, Marriage, and Murder." Pp. 49–76 in *Gender and Crime,* edited by R. E. Dobash, R. P. Dobash, and L. Noaks. Cardiff: University of Wales Press.

Young, Vernetta D. 1980. "Women, Race, and Crime." *Criminology* 18:26–34.

4

✳

Processing Women
and Girls in the System

> But men have indeed molded our legal system, which echoes the
> contradictions felt toward women: at times regarding them as evil
> and deceptive, at times treating them as childlike and defenseless.
>
> (LEONARD, 1982, 44)

U ntil the 1970s it was unusual for anyone to question whether males and
females were differently treated and processed by the police, prosecutors, judges, jurors, probation officers, prison guards, and parole boards.
Although mainstream criminologists have agreed for some time that a defendant's race is inappropriate as a classification for processing in the system, the
question of whether a person's sex is an equally inappropriate consideration has
been unresolved. This is likely because "unlike claims of racism in the application of laws and sanctions, there is no general presumption that women have
historically been subjected to a consistent pattern of discrimination" in crime
processing (Nagel and Hagan, 1983, 92).

Regardless of the historical lack of documentation of sexism in the official
decision making of alleged offenders, it has long been the case that the official
agents at every level of the system are "overwhelmingly male" (Schur, 1984,
224). Unfortunately, increased interest in female offenders since the 1970s has
focused more on questioning whether the feminist movement increased female
offending than on stimulating awareness of the paucity of scholarly attention
and programmatic change directed at female offenders (Chesney-Lind, 1987).

Crime processing refers to responses by the juvenile and crime-processing decision makers, from the police to parole boards, regarding the handling of alleged offenders. (For simplicity, the term crime processing will include the processing of status offenses, although technically these are not crimes.) Research on crime processing has been conducted at many different stages of decision making in the system (such as arrest, pretrial, conviction versus acquittal, and sentencing) and in many jurisdictions. Since the 1970s, increased attention has been given to exploring whether sex discrimination in crime processing exists. Unfortunately, this endeavor is hampered by the fact that there are no routinely collected statistics for court decision making (for example, sentencing length and conviction rates) in various states and jurisdictions, comparable to the statistics the Uniform Crime Reports provide for police decision making (for example, arrest rates) (Schur, 1984).

This chapter discusses how sex discrimination has surfaced in both criminal and sentencing laws and also describes current gender differences in crime processing in various jurisdictions and stages of the system. In addition, the processing of juveniles is discussed as well as the ways age, race, and class have affected how females are handled by the crime-processing system. Finally, the adherence of females to gender stereotypes is examined to see how this influences the likelihood of leniency or increased harshness toward female offenders.

CRIMINAL LAWS AND SEX DISCRIMINATION

The drafters of criminal law have been accused of attempting to perpetuate women's dependency (Scutt, 1981), and the criminal laws themselves have been described as a measure of the gender inequality in society (Leonard, 1982). This section discusses how criminal laws and their applications are often gendered.

Gender-neutral laws are written so that no differentiation is made regarding applicability to females and males. Gender-specific laws, on the other hand, specify in writing that they apply to only one sex or specify that they apply differently to the sexes. (Gender-neutral and gender-specific may also be used to describe noncriminal laws, which are evaluated more closely in Chapter 9.) There are three general forms of sex discrimination in criminal laws: (1) implementing and applying gender-specific laws, (2) applying gender-neutral laws differently to female and male defendants, and (3) applying gender-neutral laws in a manner that values males' victimizations more seriously than females' victimizations.

Historically, most laws have been gender-neutral, and with the exception of affirmative action laws, gender-specific laws have increasingly become gender-neutral over time. For example, until recently, most rape laws defined the offender as male, and most prostitution laws defined the offender as female. In addition, the infanticide law, even as recently as the 1970s in England and Australia, applied only to women (Scutt, 1981; Smart, 1976). A review of Australian criminal law by Scutt (1981, 17) is equally applicable to U.S. and English criminal laws, as well as to those of other countries:

> As with many of our other institutions of power, the law has functioned to maintain the status quo. Where women are concerned, the law has been drawn with reference to the way in which men define women—as dependent wives with no ability to make their own decisions; or as wretched whores responsible for their "ability" to lead men into committing offenses against them. (Scutt, 1981, 17)

An important aspect of U.S. history in terms of gender-specific laws surrounds the efforts in the latter part of the 1800s and the early part of the 1900s to raise the age of statutory rape (Odem, 1995). Odem (ibid.) documents how during this period white middle- and upper-class women engaged in formal efforts to raise the age from as young as age 7 (and usually age 10) to which a girl could legally consent to sex in 1885. This movement was successful in terms of raising the age; by 1920 most states had raised the age of consent to 16 or 18 years old. Clearly, this was a sex-specific law because it did not address at what age a male was able to consent to sex. The reformers who brought about the law change, however, were far more concerned with white girls well-being than that of girls of color, particularly African-American girls' (ibid.). That is, the white women reformers were motivated by efforts to save poor white girls from lecherous older men. However, African-American women reformers were concerned about African-American girls' vulnerability to lecherous older men as well and thus were motivated to have the statutory rape age raised as well. The history of this movement is useful to examine not only in terms of examining racism within this "feminist" movement to raise the statutory rape law but also to examine ways the law backfired for these women advocating for (white) girls. Specifically, while successful in raising the age in statutory rape law, in practice the law most direly affected girls and young African-American men. White men processed in adult courts for violating the statutory rape laws were rarely punished, whereas African-American men charged with having sex with "underage" girls, no matter how consensual, were far more likely to be punished (ibid.). Moreover, girls who had sex with men, either by consent or via force (raped), were processed harshly in the juvenile courts and punished for being sexually active (ibid.). Thus, the history of the statutory rape law not only symbolizes the important intersection between racism and sexism, but it also exemplifies how a law designed to protect girls can backfire and result in more harm.

Over time, particularly during the 1970s and 1980s, many gender-specific laws were revised to make them gender-neutral, consistent with the majority of the laws. Writing laws as gender-neutral, however, does not ensure that their application will be gender-neutral. That is, some laws that were intended to be gender-neutral have treated males and females differently in their applications. Smart (1976) discusses gender-neutral British laws whose applications have been influenced by the defendant's sex and marital status; for example, women who commit crimes with their husbands may be viewed as less culpable.

Numerous authors cite prostitution as an example of institutionalized sex discrimination in criminal laws and crime processing (Edwards, 1984; Leonard, 1982; Schur, 1984; Smart, 1976). The Contagious Diseases Acts passed during the 1860s in England were designed to guarantee sailors and soldiers a "clean" supply of prostitutes by incarcerating prostitutes with venereal diseases. The police had free reign to arrest any "suspicious" women (Windschuttle, 1981).

Even today, prostitutes are singled out for "routine and perfunctory harassment" while the customers usually go free (Schur, 1984, 225). A 1966 court ruling in Australia concluded that a man soliciting a woman to act as a prostitute was not "engaged in a sexual purpose," but a woman prostitute soliciting a customer was engaged in such a purpose. The man—unlike the woman—was thus undeserving of arrest (Scutt, 1981). The huge gender discrepancy between the sanctioning of female prostitutes and male customers is further compounded when one accounts for race and class: The customers are typically white, employed, middle-class, middle-aged men, living in the suburbs, while those penalized for this crime are usually poor women of color (Bernat, 1984; Leonard, 1982).

Prostitutes not only report being harassed by the police for their offenses, but they are rarely taken seriously by the police when they are victims, particularly when they are raped and murdered (Morris, 1987). Ironically, the 1910 White Slave Traffic Act (also known as the Mann Act)

> was to be directed at the elimination of the business of securing women and girls and selling them outright or exploiting them for immoral purposes. Instead, it was used to prosecute the voluntary and ordinary immoralities of people and to punish the women "victims" whom the law was designed to protect. (Beckman, 1985, 86)

In 1978 the implementation of a gender-neutral New York state statute to make prostitution and patronization of prostitute crimes of equal severity did not result in gender-neutral application. The police continued their nonenforcement of patrons, and women were still discriminated against (Bernat, 1985).

The third manner in which criminal laws may result in sex discrimination is not concerned with how male and female defendants are differently treated, but rather how the laws' enactments may judge the harshness of the crime based on whether the victim was male or female. Chapters 6 through 8 discuss this in more detail regarding female victims of rape and battering. Another example of this, however, is in the enactment of the gender-neutral death penalty laws, where women's and children's lives are generally less valued than men's. An in-depth analysis found that killing strangers for gain is much more likely to result in receiving the death penalty than killing a spouse (usually a woman) or child in anger (Rapaport, 1991). Thus, it is hardly surprising that the crimes most likely to receive the death penalty are committed by men against men or by men who killed women and children in another man's family (ibid., 1991). Moreover, the death penalty is given in such a manner that male and parental dominance is supported because crimes in the home, of which women and children are disproportionately victims, are seen as less deserving of the death penalty than violence against (usually male) strangers, such as the "luckless clerk on night duty at a convenience store" (ibid., 379).

Rapaport (ibid.) does not aim either to weigh the moral grounds of the death penalty or to minimize the murder of night clerks. Rather, she shows how the murder of women and children by men they know is ranked far less seriously than the murder of men by strangers (usually for financial gain) when examining who receives the death penalty. Another study found that decisions to try a case (rather than plea bargain) are based on the strength of evidence and the credibility and blamelessness of the victim. This study also found that cases where the victims were male were more likely to go to trial than be plea bargained, suggesting gender differences in credibility and blamelessness of victims (Myers and Hagan, 1979).

In conclusion, with the exception of rape and prostitution laws, most laws are gender-neutral, written to apply equally to both sexes. In the 1970s and 1980s, most of the few gender-specific laws were changed to gender-neutral laws. Unfortunately, the practice of enforcing laws does not always follow the gender-neutrality written in most law codes. The next section of this chapter discusses how gender-specific legislation on sentencing has worked to the disadvantage of female offenders. The final section of this chapter discusses empirical research findings on gender differences in crime processing at various stages of the system.

SENTENCING LAWS
AND SEX DISCRIMINATION

Many of the efforts to improve the lot of women in the crime-processing system have backfired, resulting in worse treatment or stricter guidelines for females. Examples of this include the first sex-segregated penal institutions and sex-specific sentencing laws. This section shows how the history of sex-segregated prisons is related to discriminatory sex-specific sentencing laws. Chapter 5 discusses in more depth how sex-segregated prisons often increase incarcerated women's oppression.

The first women-only prisons in England and the United States were designed to help women. They were labeled "reformatories" and "industrial homes" in an effort to distinguish them from the harsher "penitentiaries" housing male offenders. Women's prisons were designed to rehabilitate, whereas men's penitentiaries had punishment as the primary goal (Temin, 1980). The assumption was that women were more malleable and amenable to rehabilitation than men.

The result of this supposed better rehabilitative treatment of female offenders was that judges' sentences for women became indeterminate (uncertain) and longer than males' determinate (fixed) sentences for the same crimes. The justification was that women should stay in prison until they were rehabilitated.

Although most states had a limit on the maximum sentence for each crime, women were actually serving more time than men for the same crimes.

This patronizing "helping" of women offenders is analogous to the effects of the juvenile and family courts created for children in the late 1800s. The supposed increased care of minors through *parens patriae* (where the court is assigned to act in a protective parental role toward children) did more to restrict than to liberate children (see Chesney-Lind, 1982; Naffine, 1989). This is consistent with the contention that "the deprivation of rights of women as a group has been historically justified by their definition as inferior human beings" (Figueira-McDonough and Sarri, 1987, 13–14), including treating them as children. The fact that both women and children have been subjected to this denial of rights in the name of "help" should not be lost. (The "infantalization" of women offenders is discussed further in Chapter 5.)

The 1913 Muncy Act of Pennsylvania is the most famous example of sex discrimination in sentencing. The act required judges to sentence women age 17 and older who were convicted of an offense punishable by more than one year to an indeterminate sentence in the Muncy State Industrial Home for Women. The act gave judges much less discretion for sentencing female than male offenders, particularly with regard to shortening women's sentences. The effect of this act was that women were not eligible for parole as early as men convicted of the same offenses. As recently as the 1970s, Arkansas, Connecticut, Iowa, Kansas, Maine, Maryland, Massachusetts, New Jersey, and Ohio had laws similar to the Muncy Act, which permitted longer sentences for females than males convicted of the same offense (Temin, 1980).

The first attack on the Muncy Act occurred in 1966. Jane Daniel, a convicted robber, was originally sentenced to one to four years. One month later, her sentence was extended to three and one-half to ten years, as stipulated by the Muncy Act. Had Jane Daniel been a male, the judge would have been allowed to give "him" the one- to four-year sentence. The Superior Court of Pennsylvania denied that this was an infringement of her rights, stating that men's and women's inherent physical and psychological differences justified differential treatment. Therefore, it was deemed reasonable for women to receive longer sentences, especially because they supposedly received more effective rehabilitation while incarcerated.

The one judge who dissented in this opinion was sufficiently convincing for the Supreme Court of Pennsylvania to hear the appeal. Daniel's appeal was joined by the case of Daisy Douglas, a woman convicted of aggravated robbery with a male codefendant. Douglas's record consisted only of prostitution arrests, whereas her paramour and codefendant had six prior convictions for burglary. Following the Muncy Act, Douglas received the maximum allowable sentence—twenty years—while her codefendant received a three- to ten-year sentence. The appeal centered on denial of the Fourteenth Amendment's equal protection clause. The Douglas case was crucial in overturning Muncy because it could actually show that a woman and a man were treated differently in the same case. The court could find no reason why women should receive longer sentences and ruled in favor of Douglas and Daniel. Connecticut followed suit shortly afterward, striking down their equivalent of the Muncy Act.

Unfortunately, two weeks after the Daniel decision, the Pennsylvania legislature passed the Muncy Act Amendment, which ordered the court not to fix a minimum sentence for a woman convicted of a crime; only a maximum sentence not to exceed the maximum term specified in the law could be given. Thus, women were still denied equal treatment, making the Daniel decision practically moot. Sex discrimination was further institutionalized because a man was entitled to have a minimum sentence set by a judge in an open hearing with mandated counsel, whereas women's sentences were decided in closed sessions by parole boards. "Arguably, this constitutes as much a denial of equal protection as the imposition of mandatory maximum sentences" (Temin, 1980, 267).

Feinman (1992) traced a similar sentencing practice in New Jersey (State v. Costello, 1971). A 1973 State Supreme Court ruling struck down indeterminate sentencing of women when men received minimum–maximum term sentences on the grounds that such decision making violated the equal protection clause of the Fourteenth Amendment (State v. Chambers, 1973). However, this practice ended only when a state code was implemented in 1979 (Feinman, 1992).

In summary, during the 1960s and 1970s, there was a concerted effort to challenge many of the gender-specific laws requiring different sentencing practices for women and men. Observers of the implementation of these laws recognized that they resulted in *de jure* discrimination against women, who were receiving significantly longer sentences than men convicted of the same crimes. Challenges to these laws were resisted, but eventually most sexist laws were overturned in favor of gender-neutral sentencing laws.

THREE HYPOTHESES OF SEX DISCRIMINATION IN CRIME PROCESSING

Three hypotheses can be tested to establish whether there is sex discrimination in crime processing and if so, whether it is against females or males: the equal treatment hypothesis, the chivalry (or paternalism) hypothesis, and the "evil" woman hypothesis. The equal treatment (or the null) hypothesis states that there is no sex discrimination in crime processing: Males and females are treated identically. An example of equal treatment would be minor males and females receiving similar sentences if caught drinking beer by a police officer. The chivalry or paternalism thesis hypothesizes that there is sex discrimination against male offenders; that is, females are treated or processed more leniently than males. This belief was first suggested by Thomas (1907) and then by Pollak (1950), who were discussed in Chapter 2. For example, a girl caught drinking beer would be told to pour her beer out and go home, whereas a boy caught drinking beer would be arrested and brought before juvenile court. The third category, the evil woman hypothesis, purports that sex discrimination against females exists in crime processing: Females are treated more harshly than males for similar offenses. The reasoning behind this belief is that offending females have violated gender roles as well as laws; thus, "female defendants will be sanctioned not only for their offenses, but also for their inappropriate sex role behavior" (Nagel and Hagan, 1983, 116). The evil woman hypothesis is often viewed as the counter thesis to the chivalry or paternalism thesis. In this case, the beer-drinking boy would be sent home with no record, while the beer-drinking girl would be sanctioned and sent to juvenile court.

Farnsworth and Teske (1995) identified three corollaries to the *chivalry hypothesis:* The *typicality hypotheses,* the *selectivity hypothesis,* and the *differential discretion hypothesis.* The typicality hypothesis "proposes that women are treated with chivalry in criminal processing, but only when their charges are consistent with stereotypes of female offenders" (1995, 23). The selectivity hypothesis, on the other hand, states that decision makers extend chivalrous treatment disproportionately to white females. Finally, the differential discretion hypothesis suggests that the stage in the system matters, specifically that chivalrous decision making is more likely in informal decision making, such as charge reduction decisions (Farnworth and Teske, 1995).

CHIVALRY AND PATERNALISM

It has been noted that criminologists and lay people frequently assume that chivalry is the most common practice of the three options (Curran, 1983; Leonard, 1982; Morris, 1987; Visher, 1983). Therefore, much of the research on sex discrimination in crime processing has focused on the idea of chivalrous treatment as an example of "reverse discrimination." Where it exists, however, chivalrous treatment is far more complex than the simple preferential treatment of females. Rather, chivalrous treatment is usually a bartering system in which women in general are viewed as being less equal. This bartering system is extended to only certain kinds of females, according to their race, class, age, sexual orientation, demeanor, and adherence to "proper" gender roles. Chivalrous treatment may be viewed as an exchange or bargain, where the interaction between the usually male official and the female violator "is transformed into an exchange between a man and a woman" (Visher, 1983, 6). The chivalrous treatment is likely extended, then, only to females who conform to traditional gender stereotypes (ibid.).

To understand the current costs and complexities of chivalrous treatment, it is necessary to be aware of the historical underpinnings of chivalry and paternalism.

> The term chivalry emerged in Europe during the Middle Ages. It described an institution of service rendered by the crusading order to the feudal lords, to the divine sovereign, and to woman kind. "Ladies" were special beneficiaries of the practice of chivalry—knights were sworn to

protect their female weakness against dragons and devils. After the disappearance of chivalry as a formal institution, however, a number of chivalrous practices regarding women continued to exist in the world of social convention. (Moulds, 1980, 279)

Some believe that it is important to distinguish between chivalry and paternalism (Moulds, 1980; Nagel and Hagan, 1983). Chivalry is associated with placing an individual on a pedestal and behaving gallantly toward that person, whereas paternalism involves taking care of the powerless and dependent. Both chivalry and paternalism, however, imply weakness and a need to protect another person or group, which can have dangerous repercussions when "protect" becomes "control." It is often difficult to tell whether preferential treatment of female defendants, when it occurs, is due to chivalry or paternalism, some combination of the two, or other factors.

A cursory look at the chivalrous treatment of women and girls may indicate that females inevitably benefit, often at the expense of males. This form of human interaction, however, is more in tune with "political paternalism," for which there may be a cost. "If the gentle treatment women are said to enjoy is based on this political inferiority, we should be aware of the high price paid for the so-called benefits of chivalry" (Moulds, 1980, 278). On the other hand, some question whether equal treatment is necessarily the right objective because it ignores the fact that men and women have different access to power in society and often experience different roles and responsibilities (such as in child rearing) (Daly, 1989a; Morris, 1987). These issues resurface later in this chapter and again in Chapter 9, when we examine laws that have been used to "protect" women from "men's" employment, often restricting women to the unpaid and devalued work in the home. In short, there is often a high price to pay for chivalrous/paternalistic treatment: Women are viewed as children in "need" of additional attention and control.

EMPIRICAL FINDINGS ON GENDER
DIFFERENCES IN CRIME PROCESSING

It is difficult to evaluate the validity of the equal treatment, chivalry, or evil woman hypotheses without accounting for the type of offense, the stage in the crime-processing system, the demographic characteristics of the alleged offender, and the degree to which defendants fit gender stereotypes. In their review of research that tests the chivalry and evil woman hypotheses, Nagel and Hagan (1983, 135–136) suggest that the evil woman hypothesis is not the opposite of the chivalry hypothesis but rather its corollary. Women may receive chivalrous treatment as long as they commit less serious crimes, exhibit the "appropriate" passive demeanor, and have little evidence against them.

Thus it may be that women are preferentially treated, compared with men, until such time as the basis for that preferential treatment—chivalry or paternalism—is rendered inappropriate. Then, by virtue of the seriousness of the offense charged, the lessening of the presumption of innocence, and the evidence of deviation from traditional female patterns of behavior, the woman is moved into the evil woman category, and preferential treatment ceases. (Nagel and Hagan, 1983, 135–136)

The earliest research on gender differences in crime processing found strong support for the chivalry hypothesis rather than the equal treatment or evil woman hypotheses. For the most part, however, these findings supporting the preferential treatment of females could be explained by the studies' failure to account or control for two important legal variables: the defendant's prior record and the type of offense the defendant was accused of committing. If the crime-processing system is indeed just, then we expect the decision making to be related to legal variables about the case and not extralegal variables, such as the defendant's sex, race, and class.

Since the 1980s, studies evaluating gender bias in crime processing have been more likely to include the type of offense and prior record. Consequently, there is less support for the chivalry hypothesis and more for the equal treatment hypothesis. To understand how this works, consider a study that simply compares the raw percentages of males' and females' arrest, conviction, and sentencing severity and finds that males are far more likely than females to be arrested, convicted, and given lengthy sentences. These percentages imply chivalry, or the lenient treatment of females. Suppose, however, that after the analysis controls for the seriousness of the offense and the defendant's prior record, it finds that males and females with similarly serious offenses and similar prior records receive the same rates of arrest, conviction, and sentence length. Such findings (which are common) point to a more fundamental gender difference (already discussed in the last chapter) than how alleged offenders are processed: Males generally receive harsher sanctions than females in crime processing because they generally commit more serious crimes and have lengthier and more serious records.

Despite the increasing evidence that chivalrous treatment is less common than once thought, the picture of gender differences in crime processing is more complex than simple support for the equal treatment hypothesis. First, there is some evidence that chivalrous treatment still exists in some situations, even when controlling for the legal variables. Second, some studies have found support for the evil woman hypothesis when controlling for the legal variables. Most important, even when analyses find evidence for chivalrous treatment or equal treatment in crime-processing decisions, there is often additional evidence that different factors were used to determine males' and females' culpability and punishment. For example, one study found that what appeared on the surface to be chivalrous treatment was actually the result of extraordinarily harsh sanctioning of African-American males relative to everyone else (all females and white males), implying that the intersection of race and sex alone can have a huge impact (Spohn et al., 1985). Thus, regardless of which of the three hypotheses is supported by the overall findings, many studies find that different factors are used to make decisions about females' versus males' culpability.

The remainder of this chapter describes findings from empirical studies that tested the three hypotheses on gender discrimination in crime processing: the equal treatment, chivalry, and evil woman hypotheses. The factors that need to be considered to determine whether gender bias occurs in crime processing include (1) the race, class, and age of the alleged offender; (2) the importance of reforms in the processing of juveniles; (3) the stage in the crime-processing system; (4) the type of offense; and (5) how gender-role stereotypes affect gender bias in crime processing.

Differences among Females: Race, Class, and Age

The idea behind chivalry, that women are placed on a pedestal and need to be protected, is likely to be afforded more to white women than to women of color. Crime-processing decisions are often based on stereotypes that white women are more feminine, fragile, and deserving of protection than women of color (see Young, 1986). Similarly, with regard to social class, poorer women may be less likely to be treated as "ladies" than their wealthier sisters and thus be less likely to experience chivalrous crime-processing treatment. Regarding the age variable, there is evidence that the evil woman approach is more predominant for girls than for women (Nagel and Hagan, 1983, 115).

Any evaluation of crime processing must first recognize that there are different life experiences among females, depending on such factors as their race, class, and age. For example, interviews with African-American women prisoners confirmed that childhood incest was related to running away from home, which was related to the delinquent labeling of these young women and to their subsequent imprisonment (Arnold, 1990). The powerlessness of these women as girls had been compounded by class and "structural dislocation." (Structural dislocation, in this study, referred to ways that girls were marginalized within or forced to leave three primary socializing institutions: the family, education, and occupation. Such dislocation often increased the likelihood of turning to crime.) Many of the young women had been good students, but being a good student did not buy clothes and food. "Although school was a refuge for many women, it was not a sufficient counterbalancing force for the significant damage to personhood and self-esteem that occurred within an impoverished environment, and within the institution of the family" (ibid., 157). Not surprisingly, incest and other childhood victimizations were related to subsequent drug addiction. A less intensive study in Canada found not only that Native Americans were imprisoned disproportionately compared to whites but that this was particularly true for women (LaPrairie, 1989).

A considerable amount of research confirms that chivalrous treatment may be reserved for "certain kinds" of females, based on their personal characteristics. A number of crime-processing studies have found that African-American women and other women of color tend to receive more severe responses by the system than white women (Agozino, 1997; Chigwada-Bailey, 1997; Krohn et al., 1983; Kruttschnitt 1981; Spohn et al., 1987; Visher, 1983), poorer women receive more severe responses than wealthier women (Kruttschnitt, 1981), and younger women are discriminated against compared to older women (Farrington and Morris, 1983; Visher, 1983). The influence of age interacting with sex is somewhat difficult to determine, but some studies have found that younger women receive harsher treatment than older women (see Chesney-Lind and Shelden, 1992; Hiller and Hancock, 1981; Krohn et al., 1983). Regarding class and economic issues, one study found that welfare status had a more detrimental impact on sentencing severity than either race or income (Kruttschnitt, 1981). A study of British magistrates' (judges') processing of women offenders found clear class bias in the sentencing of women:

> Respectable, middle-class wives and mothers are assumed to be so sensitive that they will be reformed by a minimum of punishment (or no punishment at all). Working-class women are perceived to be tougher (more like men?) and therefore need to be treated more harshly if any impression is to be made on them, on the grounds that punishment is the only thing "people like that" understand. (Worrall, 1990, 88)

These findings confirm that not all females are treated similarly in the crime-processing system. As a rule, women of color, poor women, and younger women are afforded less leniency than other females.

Reforms in the Processing of Juveniles

The juvenile court has been accused of punishing the noncriminal (status) offenses of girls the same as or more harshly than the criminal offenses of boys (or girls) (Chesney-Lind, 1973, 1981, 1987; Conway and Bogdan, 1977; Datesman and Scarpitti, 1977; Schlossman and Wallach, 1982). Also, girls charged with promiscuity have historically been treated more harshly than girls committing other nonsexual offenses (Terry, 1970). Girls not only have been formally and informally punished for consensual sexual activities that boys are more likely to "commit," but girls additionally have had their sexual victimizations merged with their sexual "offenses":

> One of the most problematic aspects of the juvenile justice system is its failure to distinguish offenders from victims. Nowhere is this more true than in the case of sexual abuse and sexual behavior. Females are often identically handled for abuse and promiscuous behavior or prostitution. (Sarri, 1983, 382)

Perhaps the most disturbing aspect of the processing of females has been the historically pervasive forced submissions of juveniles to gynecological exams. The excuses given for these exams were to determine whether they had venereal diseases and whether they were virgins. (The courts were apparently unconcerned with venereal disease or virginity in boys.) The first study to document this practice was conducted on Honolulu juvenile court cases between 1929 and 1964 (Chesney-Lind, 1973). Only one-quarter of boys' but three-quarters of girls' arrests were for status offenses, and 70 to 80 percent of the girls were forced to have "physical exams," even for nonsexual charges such as larceny. The girls were more likely than the boys to be sent to pretrial deten-tion, and they spent three times as long there as their male counterparts.

> Besides the jail-like atmosphere that confronts young people held in de-tention facilities, young women in the past underwent an extra and sig-nificant violation of their civil rights: pelvic examinations and, more recently, vaginal searches. . . . The accounts suggest that blanket admin-istration of pelvic examinations occurred well into the 1970s in various parts of the United States. (Chesney-Lind and Shelden, 1992, 149–150)

Shelden's (1981) study of Memphis, Tennessee, court records between 1900 and 1917 found that nonconsensual sexual experiences (rape victimizations) as well as consensual sexual activity of girls resulted in harsh sanctions against them. Such sanctions were nonexistent for boys. Gynecological exams to determine whether girls were virgins (in order to assess their criminality) were commonplace. Even when controlling for race, class, and offense, girls were treated more harshly than boys. In a similar study of Honolulu juvenile court cases between 1929 and 1964, Chesney-Lind (1973) found not only that girls were more likely than boys to be referred to court and forced to have pelvic exams but also that three times as many girls as boys were institutionalized.

A more recent British study found that girls' sexual activity is still moni-tored more closely and punished more severely than boys,' and the harsh treat-ment of girl runaways is linked to their sexual "promiscuity" (Gelsthorpe, 1989). A study of U.S. family court records found that boys received harsher dispositions than girls for criminal offenses (felonies and misdemeanors), but girls received harsher dispositions than boys for status offenses. Half of the girls, but only one-fifth of the boys, had been referred to family court for status offenses (Datesman and Scarpitti, 1980). U.S. studies also report that the fam-ily courts are most likely to warrant official intervention of status offenders when they are white girls and least likely when they are African-American boys; this is consistent with race-gender stereotypes (Datesman and Aickin, 1984; Datesman and Scarpitti, 1980). An Australian court study on juveniles found that girls are more likely to be given such "rehabilitative" sentences as probation, supervision, and institutionalization, while boys are "treated" with more legalistic measures such as bonds, fines, and adjournment (Hiller and Hancock, 1981).

A study of France, England, and Wales found that girls were only one-sixth of the youth with criminal charges, yet they made up half of the juveniles removed from the home and placed in institutions (Hudson, 1989). Moreover, girls received special scrutiny and discrimination. They were judged by their "femininity" and were sanctioned for typical adolescent behavior, including immaturity in judgment and acting "silly." Boys who exhibited these same behaviors were less likely to be sanctioned for them. A study of youth recom-mended for supervision (a court punishment that requires checking in with a supervisor for two to three years) in England and Wales reported discrimination against girls, in that they were far more likely than boys to be recommended for supervision for trivial offenses (Webb, 1984). Similarly, a comparative analysis of ten European criminal courts found that girls are still more severely punished than boys for status offenses, especially for sexual activity, and are more likely to be incarcerated and for longer periods than boys (Cain, 1989, 232).

The role of parents in the offense processing of youths is particularly important, especially when the goal is to examine gender differences. There is ample evidence that parents play a crucial role in many juveniles' first formal contact with the crime-processing system and that girls are at much greater risk than boys of having their parents turn them into the police or juvenile courts (Chesney-Lind and Shelden, 1992; Hiller and Hancock, 1981; Sarri, 1983; Teilmann and Landry, 1981). Parents are often less tolerant of their daughters' than their sons' identical behaviors whether they are status offenses (for example, running away, breaking curfews, drinking alcohol, and being sexually active) or more traditional offenses (for example, larceny, and assaults). Moreover, parents are more likely to report problems with daughters than with sons, and they are more likely to physically and sexually abuse their daughters (Chesney-Lind and Shelden, 1992). (This victimization often causes juveniles to run away, to drink alcohol, and to engage in other "acting out" behaviors, as discussed in Chapter 3.) Finally, one study reported that almost one-third of families refused to take their children back after their release from court custody as "persons in need of supervision" (PINS) (Conway and Bogdan, 1977).

The establishment of the juvenile court in 1899 was the culmination of the "child-savers' " efforts to control youths' lives. This was particularly apparent for girls who were the "losers in the reform movement," which resulted in girls' high referral rates to juvenile courts and subsequently high institutionalization rates for "immorality" and "waywardness" (Chesney-Lind and Shelden, 1992, 120). The police and the juvenile courts have historically condoned more punitive reactions to female than male status offenders, reaffirming a double standard for male and female sexuality. Although this was more common in the early years of the juvenile court, "there is evidence that the pattern continues" (Chesney-Lind and Shelden, 1992, 115).

The Juvenile Justice and Delinquency Prevention (JJDP) Act of 1974 was designed to divert and deinstitutionalize status offenders from secure facilities. For states to receive federal funding for delinquency prevention programs, they had to discontinue institutionalizing status offenders in "training schools," detention centers, and adult jails and to develop plans to treat status offenders in places other than juvenile detention or correctional facilities. Because girls have been disproportionately sanctioned as status offenders, it was predicted that this would have a huge impact on the processing of girls. As expected, there was a decline in the admission of girls to detention facilities and "training schools" following the 1974 JJDP Act (Chesney-Lind, 1986, 1988; Sarri, 1983). Between 1975 and 1979, males' detention rate decreased by 20 percent, and females' rate decreased by 44 percent. These gender differences were largely due to the overrepresentation of girls in status offenses and to the policy's goal to divert status offenders from detention (Krisberg and Schwartz, 1983). Another study assessing the impact of the JJDPA on deinstitutionalization of delinquent youth found that girls are "transinstitutionalized" into mental health facilities for "inappropriate" behaviors, while African-American youth "warehoused in the public system of juvenile institutions," and thus, white males are the most likely to have benefitted from deinstitutionalization (Federle and Chesney-Lind, 1992).

The initial optimism that accompanied the deinstitutionalization of status offenders is tempered by the findings from (1) monitoring deinstitutionalization rates over time and (2) examining the private juvenile "correctional" system that replaced the traditional secure facilities. Regarding the first point, there is some concern that the decline of institutionalized status offenders leveled off between 1979 and 1982, and "the gains made against judicial sexism are very much in jeopardy" (Chesney-Lind, 1986, 90). In fact, between 1982 and 1986, arrests for both male and female runaways increased (Chesney-Lind, 1988). Moreover, while female admissions to "training schools" decreased 37 percent in the five years after the JJDP Act, male admissions increased by 9 percent (Krisberg and Schwartz, 1983).

Turning to the second point, it is not clear that the diversionary programs have resulted in any less stigmatizing of juvenile offenders than the detention facilities before the JJDP Act (Datesman and Aickin, 1984). More important, however, a study in Minnesota discovered that many of the status offenders who previously would have been institutionalized in the traditional secure facilities (such as "training schools") were institutionalized in increasing numbers in the "hidden" or private juvenile "correctional" system following the 1974 JJDP Act. This system includes mental health and chemical dependency programs (Schwartz et al., 1984). Although this study did not examine gender per se, case studies portray many of these youth as females whose parents disapproved of their (often sexual) behavior: "More often than not, these youth are referred by their parents . . . [and] many of the admissions are not as 'voluntary' as one might think" (ibid., 382). The authors describe the case of a 16-year-old girl with no history of serious delinquency or chronic status offending, whose parents had her repeatedly institutionalized in private mental hospitals for periods as long as nine months simply because her father, a prominent university administrator, was embarrassed by her "punk" attire and "punk" friends. The authors question what rights parents should have to institutionalize their children against their will in psychiatric or chemical-dependency programs. It is also important to examine how this "hidden" juvenile-processing system might be affecting girls differently from the way it affects boys.

Similarly, a study of girls institutionalized in delinquent "homes" in England found that many girls were not in these homes for delinquent offenses but because of emotional and family problems, such as their parents' fighting (Gelsthorpe, 1989). In comparison, South Australia implemented a policy in 1979 to abolish status offenses. This act has been far more successful than the JJDP Act in the United States and other countries' attempts to curb the criminalization of juveniles. South Australia's abolishment of status offenses appears to have resulted in equal treatment for boys and girls and a decreasing concern with girls' sexuality (Naffine, 1989).

The Presence of Gender Bias
in Different Stages of Processing

Many studies examine gender bias in various crime-processing decision points in the system: arrest, detention versus pretrial release, prosecution, dismissal of charges, negotiations and the guilty plea, conviction versus acquittal, incarceration, sentence severity, parole, and reconviction. It is often difficult to compare these studies because they are conducted in numerous and varied jurisdictions, at various stages or decision points in the system, and in different time periods. It is necessary, however, to attempt to determine the overall findings from these studies.

As stated in Chapter 3, women are generally far less serious offenders than men and have less extensive prior records. Thus, they are less likely to have their cases reach the final stages of the crime-processing system. Therefore, analyses that focus only on the latter stages may not adequately represent the processing of female offenders.

The first evaluation of studies on gender bias in crime processing stated that chivalry was most likely in the beginning stages and least likely in the later stages (Nagel and Hagen, 1983). A more recent review, however, found the opposite: Chivalry is least likely in the beginning and most prominent in the later stages of crime processing (Chesney-Lind, 1987). These opposing findings are likely due to the fact that the more recent evaluation was able to include more studies on the original contact with the system (the police) and the more recent studies have been more likely to control for legal variables. The overall findings regarding studies evaluated for this section of the chapter are consistent with the more recent (ibid.) review: Chivalry is least common in the beginning stages of crime processing and most common in the latter stages.

As explained in detail in the following paragraph, the most support for the evil woman hypothesis is at the earliest stages of decision making (the police); support for the equal treatment hypothesis is most evident in the middle decision-making stages (the decisions to prosecute, dismiss charges, and convict); and support for the chivalry hypothesis is most evident in the final decision-making stages (the decision to incarcerate, the severity of the sentence, and the likelihood of reconviction). Most studies did not find sex to be a strong predictor, as the legal variables usually are. Many researchers found that evidence for chivalry in the original analyses of their data disappeared (or gender differences became negligible) when they controlled for other, usually legal, variables (Farrington and Morris, 1983; Fisher and Mawby, 1982; Landau, 1981; Landau and Nathan, 1983; Spohn et al., 1985).

Police Decision Making Decision making by police is the stage that has the most support for the evil woman hypothesis. Even here, however, this support is not consistent and can be explained by the unusually harsh police treatment of female status offenders. Two studies found that women were discriminated against in police decision making (Ghali and Chesney-Lind, 1986; Wilbanks,

1986), three found lenient or chivalrous treatment by the police (DeFleur, 1975; Krohn et al., 1983; Mastrofski et al., 1995), and one found equal treatment (Visher, 1983). Notably, the strongest and most consistent support for the evil woman hypothesis in police decision making was found in research on police responses to status offenders (Chesney-Lind and Shelden, 1992; Hiller and Hancock, 1981; Sarri, 1983; Teilmann and Landry, 1981).

In the past it was common for the police, when looking into nonsexual offenses of juveniles, to question girls—but not boys—about their sexual experiences and then to add the sexual offense charges to the original offense (Chesney-Lind, 1974). Most young women, then, enter the crime-processing system as status offenders, for running away from home, incorrigibility, waywardness, curfew violations, and so on. Although females constitute a small proportion of the system, when they are in the system, it is most often for status offenses (Chesney-Lind, 1981). Most empirical research, then, dispels the notion that females are treated chivalrously at the beginning stages of the crime-processing system. Indeed, this is where most practices consistent with the "evil woman" occur. An area of processing women that has received little research attention, and yet impacts many women, is the intersection of racism and anti-immigrant sentiment with sexism where non–citizen Black women are disproportionally detained by airport authorities because of the mythical assumption that "Black immigrant equals [drug] courier, unless otherwise proven" (Agozino, 1997, 142).

An area of the police "processing" of women and girls that has received little research could also be included in the victimization section of this book. More specifically, Kraska and Kappeler (1995) researched the sexual exploitation and abuse of females perpetrated by police officers. They label this phenomenon *police sexual violence* (PSV) and report how it occurs on a continuum ranging from invasions of privacy to using force to rape (see Figure 4.1) The various unethical, unprofessional, violating, and exploitative behaviors are perpetrated against a variety of women and girls, including female victims and female defendants. An example of police PSV against female victims was a woman whose business partner, without her consent and knowledge, had videotaped them having sex and was using this illegally taped sex to extort insurance money from her by threatening to show the tape to her family. The police convinced the woman that they needed the tape to process the case, assuring her that it would be handled discreetly and confidentially (Kraska and Kappeler, 1995). Instead it was widely viewed by members of the police department, including the chief of police. An example of the sexual exploitation of female defendants/offenders was what Kraska and Kappeler (ibid.) reported as a seemingly common practice among some officers to wait outside bars for women exiting alone and following them, stopping them for drinking under the influence, and either coercing them to have sex in order to get out of tickets or outright raping them with force. (Notably, not all of these women were drunk.) Finally, Kraska and Kappeler (ibid.) suggest that the most marginalized women in society may be those most at risk of PSV, particularly poorer women, young women, and women of color. They also offer considerable

Unobtrusive Behavior	**Obtrusive Behavior**	**Criminal Behavior**
Viewing victims, photographs, and sexually explicit videos.	Custodial strip searches, body cavity searches, warrant-based searches, illegal detentions, deceptions to gain sexual favors.	Sexual harassment, sexual contact, sexual assault, rape.
Invasions of privacy, secondary victimization.	Provision of services for sexual favors, sexual harassment.	

FIGURE 4.1 Kraska and Kappeler's Continuum of Police Sexual Violence (PSV)

From Kraska and Kappeler (1995, 94). Adapted for permission.

support for how PSV is a part of the policing tradition, both in the institution of police department and in the media and films that portray women as flirting with police officers and eager participants with police they have never met (ibid.) Although more research needs to be done on this extreme violation by the police, the secret nature of these events and the code of covering up for fellow officers make such research difficult.

Pretrial Court Decisions Most of the research on sexism in courtroom decision making focuses on judge, jury, and trial decisions, although fewer than one in ten cases go to a full trial (Figueira-McDonough, 1985). Not only are pretrial decisions more common, but much of the pretrial decision making is not subject to the due process requirements of formal trials, leaving more room for discrimination.

An important stage in crime processing is the detention versus pretrial release decision, which "refers to the terms under which a defendant may be allowed to remain free in the interim between arrest and case disposition" (Kruttschnitt and McCarthy, 1985). This decision not only is important regarding a defendant's immediate freedom but can also have implications on the subsequent processing of the case: A defendant who has been detained may be more likely to be viewed as a confirmed offender or "inmate" (see Frazier and Cochran, 1986). Research on gender bias at the detention/pretrial release decision suggests that chivalrous treatment may be reserved for adult women who are not prostitutes (Bernat, 1985; Frazier and Cochran, 1986; Kruttschnitt, 1984; Kruttschnitt and Green, 1984; Teilmann and Landry, 1981). The treatment of juveniles and prostitutes at the detention/release stage, on the other hand, was more consistent with the evil woman hypothesis.

Research examining gender bias in the decision to prosecute or dismiss charges largely supports the equal treatment hypothesis (Curran, 1983; Ghali and Chesney-Lind, 1986; McCarthy, 1987; Nagel et al., 1982; Steffensmeier et al., 1993; Teilmann and Landry, 1981), although there is also some support for chivalry (*Albonetti, 1986; Gruhl et al., 1984; Spohn et al., 1987;

Wilbanks, 1986). A study of California felony theft and assault cases found an important interaction between court defendants' race and sex in the decision to reduce charges. Specifically, controlling for prior record and the type and severity of the offense, 72 to 76 percent of females of all races and white males received reduced charges, while African-American males (66 percent) were the least likely group to receive reduced charges (Farnworth and Teske, 1995). Moreover, this study found that the charge reduction decision significantly affected the final sentence in a gendered manner: Females with no charge reduction were less likely (22 percent) than males with no charge reduction (37 percent) to be sent to prison.

A study examining the likelihood of referring juveniles to juvenile court found chivalry in court referrals for youth charged with delinquent acts but support for the evil woman hypothesis for youth charged with status offenses (Datesman and Aickin, 1984). One study on juveniles, however, found that the sex of the offender had a significant interaction with her or his race regarding charge dismissal: white boys had the best chance for dismissal, white girls for diversion, African-American girls for probation, and African-American boys for formal processing (Sarri, 1983). Another study of a juvenile district court in Iowa from 1980 to 1989 reported no gender differences in the processing of the youthful offenders at the various stages of court processing (from intake through disposition); however, African-Americans and Native Americans fared worse than whites at every decision-making point (Leiber, 1994).

Regarding the likelihood of pleading guilty or negotiating a plea, two studies found equal treatment of the sexes (Curran, 1983; Gruhl et al., 1984), while two found support for the evil woman hypothesis (Ghali and Chesney-Lind, 1986; Figueira-McDonough, 1985). Figueira-McDonough's (1985) is perhaps the most important of these studies because it was the most carefully conducted. She found that although women and men were equally likely to plead innocent, men were nearly twice as likely to plead guilty to a lesser charge. Furthermore, the use or possession of a gun added seriousness to women's but not men's offenses, and the presence of a witness was more likely to influence women than men to plead guilty. Women were less able to bargain and more willing to plead guilty, which may have been due to their limited access to attorneys, education, and experience (or power in general). Men were also more likely to receive both charge reductions and sentence reductions. Finally, only men were rewarded for their guilty pleas.

Trial and Posttrial Decision Making Research on the conviction stage of decision making is most consistent with the equal treatment hypothesis (Curran, 1983; Ghali and Chesney-Lind, 1986; Gruhl et al., 1984; Steffensmeier et al., 1993), except for one study that supported the chivalry hypothesis (Wilbanks, 1986). The research on gender bias at the incarceration decision generally supports the chivalry hypothesis (Farnworth and Teske, 1995; Gruhl et al., 1984; Nagel et al., 1982; Nobiling et al., 1998; Steffensmeier et al., 1993) more often than the equal treatment hypothesis (Ghali and Chesney-Lind, 1986; Kruttschnitt and Green, 1984). One study that reported support for the chivalry hypothesis found it was important to understand the interactions between sex and race/ethnicity. Specifically, Farnworth and Teske's (1995) analysis of California felons found, as stated earlier, that African-American males were least likely to have charges reduced and that charge reduction significantly affected later decisions. For example, for those without charge reductions, males were more likely than females to be sentenced to prison (the females were more likely than the males to be sentenced to jail and receive probation). For those with reduced charges, males were more likely to be sent to jail, and females were more likely to receive probation. White women were about twice as likely to have assault charges reduced to nonassault charges, while white men were about one-and-one-half times as likely as African-American men to have such charge reduction. Finally, "females with no prior record were more likely than similar males to receive charge reductions, and this enhanced females' chances for probation" (Farnworth and Teske, 1995, 23). An Urban Reform Era study in Ontario, Canada, supported the evil woman hypothesis (Boritch, 1992).

Research findings fairly consistently support the chivalry hypothesis in the sentencing severity stage of decision making (Curran, 1983; Farrington and Morris, 1983; Kruttschnitt, 1984; Nagel et al., 1982; Steffensmeier et al., 1993; Wilbanks, 1986). Exceptions included two studies reporting "equal treatment" of the sexes at the sentencing phase (Nobiling et al., 1998; Zatz, 1984). (Again, the Urban Reform Era study in Ontario supported the evil woman hypothesis regarding sentence severity [Boritch, 1992].) One study was conducted using fifty data sets on gender and court sentencing, mostly collected during the 1970s (but some from the 1980s and 1990s), and reported (1) half of these cases were cases were consistent with the chivalry hypothesis, and one-quarter showed mixed or no effects; (2) chivalrous sentencing in the courts was most likely in felony offenses, cases prosecuted in felony courts, and in courts in urban areas; and (3) chivalry was more likely in the decision to incarcerate (women were less likely to be sentenced to prison) and less likely in the length of the sentence (which evidenced more "equal treatment" processing than the decision to incarcerate) (Daly and Bordt, 1995).

Similarly, studies on gender bias in reconviction (Farrington and Morris, 1983) and probation (Ghali and Chesney-Lind, 1986; Nagel et al., 1982) decision making consistently supported the chivalry hypothesis, except for one study that found equal treatment of the sexes in probation decisions (Kruttschnitt, 1984).

A final area of gender differences in court processing, one that has received little attention, is death penalty sentencing. Between 1976 and 1987, 14 percent of those charged with murder or nonnegligent manslaughter were women; however, only 2 percent of the prisoners on death row are female (Rapaport, 1991). This appears to be chivalrous treatment of female offenders, but a closer examination by Rapaport (ibid.) suggests otherwise. First, felony murders are rarely committed by women (4 to 6 percent), and women are more likely to kill intimates in anger or defense than to kill strangers for a predatory purpose (such as economic or sexual gain) (ibid.). Second, male murder defendants are four times more likely than female murder defendants to have a prior conviction for a violent felony. Third, females are far less likely than males to be accused of murdering multiple victims (ibid.). Given these gender differences in murders and murderers, it is "logical" that women constitute only 2 percent of death row prisoners.

Gender Differences in Crime Processing Based on the Type of Offense

In addition to determining the validity of the equal treatment, chivalry, and evil woman hypotheses based on personal characteristics of the offender and the stage in the crime-processing system, it is important to control for the type of offense. It is likely that the direction of sex discrimination (whether it is against males or females) may be closely linked with the nature of the offense. In fact, Naffine (1987, 2) states: "The agents of the law are clearly inconsistent, even in their paternalism." Her review of gender and crime-processing studies concluded that chivalry is more likely when women commit less serious crimes but that women are treated more harshly than men when they commit more serious crimes. The less serious and more serious offenses, however, are closely linked with gender-role stereotypes. It has been stated that women whose offenses more closely fit traditional gender stereotypes (for example, shoplifting) will fare better than their less traditional counterparts who commit robberies, assaults, and so on (Nagel and Hagan, 1983, 116). Therefore, women who commit traditionally "masculine crimes" are expected to be treated more harshly than men (Chesney-Lind, 1987).

Some studies, however, have found that women are treated more chivalrously for felony or violent crimes and less chivalrously for minor and property offenses (Hepburn, 1978; Steffensmeier et al., 1993; Visher, 1983). A study of juveniles found that girls were treated chivalrously for property crimes but as "evil women" for status offenses (Hiller and Hancock, 1981).

Sarri (1987) states that examining the interaction between the offense type and the gender likelihood of committing the offense is necessary to determine gender disparities in crime processing. For some crimes, females and males are equally likely to be involved, and yet females are sanctioned more harshly (for example, running away and prostitution); for other crimes, males and females are equally likely to be involved and are treated equally (for example, larceny); and for yet others, females are much less likely to commit the crimes but are more severely sanctioned when they do (for example, sexually abusing children) (Sarri, 1983). Similarly, a study on the abduction and fondling of children found that women are treated more harshly than men throughout the crime-processing system, while for charges of fraud, men are treated more harshly than women (Wilbanks, 1986). A California study on males' and females' felony theft and felony assault cases found no indication of gender discrimination based on the type of offense at the court level (Farnworth and Teske, 1995).

In summary, there are no consistent findings regarding the relationship between the type of offense and the presence of chivalry. This investigation merits further inquiry.

Gender Stereotypes and Crime Processing

Early studies on sex discrimination in crime processing recognized that chivalrous treatment was often reserved for females who displayed "appropriate" feminine behavior. A study of drug arrests found that females were less likely than males to be arrested if they cried, expressed concern for their children, or claimed to have been "led" by men (DeFleur, 1975). Similarly, another study found that women whose demeanor represented antagonism toward the police were often discriminated against (Visher 1983), and a study on sentencing concluded that women generally fare better than men unless they are nontraditional women (Nagel et al., 1982).

In the late 1980s, an important addition to the understanding of gender bias in crime processing was the recognition that chivalrous treatment in the processing of adult offenders may not be the direct result of sexist behavior on the decision-makers' parts alone but could also be the indirect effects of sexism and the very real gender differences in the responsibilities of women's and men's lives. That is, the specified gender roles in society likely influence differences in the processing of female and male defendants. Moreover, "women are more likely than men to be processed according to an assessment of their personal circumstances, rather than their offense" (Worrall, 1981, 90).

For example, rightly or wrongly, persons in charge of dependent children and with little access to legitimate means may be given special consideration by crime-processing decision makers. In most cultures, such persons are usually women. Thus, evidence of chivalrous treatment in crime processing might in fact be a manifestation of institutionalized gender roles in society at large. If women are fulfilling their "natural" roles as mothers and to some extent wives, they may be given more lenient sanctions. This important addition to understanding gender differences in crime processing is attributed to Kathleen Daly, Candace Kruttschnitt, and Mary Eaton. Daly (1989a) points out that "protecting" women in so-called chivalrous sentencing might actually be an attempt to protect children and families.

Eaton's (1986) analysis of court cases in a London suburb found that while men and women were treated similarly when they were in similar circumstances, women and men were rarely in similar circumstances. Although the court did not overtly discriminate based on sex, it endorsed separate and unequal roles for men and women, particularly with respect to traditional families. Men were expected to provide financially for families, while women's roles included emotional support and child care. Thus, when a probation officer conducted a home visit, a description of the home was more common with a female defendant than with a male defendant (ibid., 67). Eaton's study found some evidence of surface chivalry, such as women being more likely to get probation and less likely to be given prison or jail sentences; however, women also tended to have less serious crimes and records than men. Thus, chivalrous processing may be due more to an inherently unequal society than to an inherently biased crime-processing system. Moreover, the judges are not necessarily ignorant of women's status in the economic structure:

Family circumstances and disposable income were rarely similar for men and women and this affected the sentences. . . . [M]any magistrates commented in interviews on the difficulty of fining a woman with no disposable income. The women before them were usually responsible for the care and maintenance of children, supported either by social security benefits or by such small housekeeping allowances that to deduct any amount to pay a fine would be to deprive the children. (Eaton, 1986, 39)

Similarly, Daly's (1987) interviews with crime-processing court officials (judges, prosecutors, probation officers, and defense attorneys) found that they regularly described work and family roles to explain defendants' deserved leniency. Defendants described as "familied" provided care or economic support for others and were provided more leniency than their "nonfamilied" counterparts, who had no such responsibilities. In a study of state criminal court judges, Daly (1989a) found the judges' primary motive in sentencing was to protect children (not women) and women's and men's economic support for families. The defendants' work–family relations influenced the sentencing of both men and women, but there were differences in sentencing of the sexes based on what they "did" for families. "Living with families, contributing to the support of families, or doing something for the welfare of others were positive qualities cited by these judges for men defendants" (ibid., 16). The "good family woman" cares for children or other dependents, and ideally she works or obtains welfare to provide economic support; the "bad family woman," on the other hand, does not care or provide for young children (ibid., 17). Thus, judges found it harder to sentence "good family men" and "good family women"—those perceived as contributing to the well-being of their families in a manner consistent with gender stereotypes—to prison or jail.

"Family men" and "family women," however, are not evenly represented in either society or the offender population: More familied women than familied men exist in society at large and are processed in the courts (Daly, 1987, 1989a, 1989b). Therefore, women's chivalrous treatment may in fact be a result of a response to their increased likelihood to be "familied." "Even if a family woman provides economically for her family, the fact that she cares for dependents (almost always meaning children) while a family man usually does not explain why judges find it more difficult to jail the family woman than the family man" (Daly, 1989a, 19). Notably, the judges ranked caring for children as more important than providing economic support; thus, familied women tended to fare better than familied men, especially among black defendants (Daly, 1987, 1989a). Similarly, a study of British magistrates (judges) found that they favored giving women probation because it least disrupted their domestic duties (Worrall, 1990). Conversely, another study found that men, but not women, who provided significant emotional support for dependents were less likely to receive prison sentences, and men who provided significant economic support for their children were not granted a break in sentencing (Bickle and Peterson, 1991). This led the authors to conclude that taking care of familial dependents is rewarded "only when it is not a part of traditional gender–based role expectations" (ibid. 385).

The marital status of a defendant appears in crime processing, similar to society at large, to be a more relevant factor for women than for men. Some studies found that being married helped women but not men in crime-processing outcomes (Erez, 1992; Nagel et al., 1982). (Stated alternatively, being unmarried hurt women but not men in crime-processing outcomes) Similarly, being divorced or separated hurt women more than men in sentencing (Farrington and Morris, 1983). Although another study found that being married decreased the chances of both sexes being held in detention, this was afforded to men only when they had dependents as well as being married (Daly, 1989b). Unexpectedly, another study found that marital status was unrelated to the sentencing of women, whereas men were treated more harshly if they were married than if they were not (Bickle and Peterson, 1991).

Overall, the recent research on dependent children suggests that chivalrous sanctioning may be a result of women's increased likelihood (over men) to have dependent children (see Daly, 1989a, 1989b; Eaton, 1986; Steffensmeier et al., 1993; Worrall, 1990). One of these studies found that pregnant women as well as women with children received more lenient sentencing from judges, but this was partly due to some judges' belief that the bad conditions in women's prisons resulted in extra harsh punishment for women (Steffensmeier et al., 1993). The advantages afforded to women with dependents in their sanctioning may be a more recent phenomenon. A study of the Urban Reform Era (1871 to 1920) in Ontario, Canada, concluded that "judges appeared to view women's criminality as prima facie evidence of their inadequacy as mothers and showed little hesitancy in removing them from their child-care roles" (Boritch, 1992, 319).

Some research has focused on the influence of employment status and economic dependence on the crime processing of women (and men). Generally, women have been sanctioned more harshly for working outside of the home than for being homemakers (Boritch, 1992; Kruttschnitt, 1981, 1982). One study found that being employed decreased men's sentences, while being unemployed decreased women's sentences (Crew, 1991). Another study found that unemployed women generally received harsher sentences than employed women, but unemployed students and full-time homemakers received more lenient sentences than women employed outside of the home (Kruttschnitt, 1981). One study, however, found employment status related equally to women's and men's sentencing (Kruttschnitt, 1984). Probation and parole officers in other studies were more concerned with men's than women's employment problems, although women reported equal or more severe employment problems (Erez, 1989, 1992). Similarly, employment status affected men's more than women's pretrial release likelihood (Kruttschnitt and McCarthy, 1985).

In addition to the variables typically associated with gender differences (such as marital and employment status, child dependents, and demeanor), studies have found other variables that differently affect male and female sanctioning. Some studies found that legal variables (for example, prior record and offense seriousness) tend to influence men's sanctions more than women's (Boritch, 1992; Kruttschnitt and McCarthy, 1985; Nagel et al., 1982; Steffensmeier et al., 1993). One of these studies of court outcomes in Ontario, Canada, from 1871 to 1920 concluded that "judges appeared to adopt the attitude that the form a woman's criminality took was secondary to the fact a woman appeared before the court on any charge" (Boritch, 1992, 317). On the other hand, another study found that both being from a "broken home" and acting with another offender influenced women's sanctioning more than men's (Farrington and Morris, 1983). There is some evidence, although this needs to be further explored, that characteristics about the victim may influence females' and males' sanctions differently (See Jamieson and Blowers, 1993; Kruttschnitt, 1992; Visher, 1983). For example, in one study, the victim–offender relationship did not influence police decisions to arrest female suspects, but police were less likely to arrest male subjects who knew their victims (as friends or relatives) than those males who were unacquainted with their victims (Visher, 1983).

In conclusion, despite which of the three sanctioning hypotheses is supported (equal treatment, chivalry, or evil woman), studies that have provided in-depth analysis find other variables often interact with sex in a manner that provides a different pattern for crime-processing male and female offenders. Most studies confirm that being married, caring for dependent children, and being a homemaker increase a woman's chance of chivalrous sanctioning. For men, having stable employment and providing for families appear to effect leniency in their sanctioning. Overall, because women are more likely than men to be "familied" and because "familied" women generally fare better than "familied" men, much of the chivalry in crime processing, at least at the sentencing stage, may be explained by these gender differences in responsibilities. Consistent with gender stereotypes, such factors as employment and legal variables appear to influence men's sentences more than women's. It should be noted that there is a built-in discrimination against lesbians and gays, people who are not married, and people who are childless, with regard to the preceding factors.

SUMMARY

This chapter covered the numerous factors likely to affect the crime processing of male and female offenders. Criminal laws and sentencing laws have historically included legal codes that specified different treatment of the sexes. Even when these laws are gender-neutral, however, this does not guarantee that male and female defendants will be treated equally. To determine support for the three sanctioning hypotheses on gender differences (equal treatment, chivalry, and evil woman), it is first necessary to acknowledge that the treatment of females may vary based on such characteristics as their race, class, and age and that the treatment of female offenders may vary based on the types of offenses they commit. Moreover, the stage in the crime-processing system appears to influence gender patterns in crime processing: The evil woman hypothesis is supported most at the beginning stages, equal treatment at the middle stages, and chivalry during the latter stages. Finally, this chapter discussed the extraordinarily harsh treatment of female status offenders as well as the impact of gender stereotyping in crime processing concerning the marital, dependent child, and employment status of women.

REFERENCES

Agozino, Biko. 1997, *Black Women and the Criminal Justice System*. Aldershot, England: Ashgate Publishing Company.

Albonetti, Celesta A. 1986. "Criminality, Prosecutorial Screening, and Uncertainty: Toward a Theory of Discretionary Decision Making in Felony Case Processing." *Criminology* 24(4):623–45.

Armstrong, Gail. 1982. "Females under the Law: 'Protected' but Unequal." Pp. 61–76 in *The Criminal Justice System and Women*, edited by B. R. Price and N. J. Sokoloff. New York: Clark Boardman.

Arnold, Regina A. 1990. "Processes of Victimization and Criminalization of Black Women." *Social Justice* 17:153–166.

Beckman, Marlene D. 1985. "The White Slave Traffic Act: Historical Impact of a Federal Crime Policy on Women." Pp. 85–102 in *Criminal Justice, Politics, and Women*, edited by C. Schweber and C. Feinman. New York: Haworth Press.

Bernat, Frances P. 1984. "Gender Disparity in the Setting of Bail: Prostitution Offenses in Buffalo, NY, 1977–1979." Pp. 21–48 in *Gender Issues, Sex Offenses, and Criminal Justice: Current Trends*, edited by S. Chaneles. New York: Haworth Press.

———. 1985. "New York State's Prostitution Statute: Case Study of the Discriminatory Application of a Gender Neutral Law. Pp. 103–120 in *Criminal Justice Politics and Women*, edited by C. Schweber and C. Feinman. New York: Haworth Press.

Bickle, Gayle S., and Ruth D. Peterson. 1991. "The Impact of Gender-Based Family Roles in Criminal Sentencing." *Social Problems* 38:372–394.

Boritch, Helen. 1992. "Gender and Criminal Court Outcomes: A Historical Analysis." *Criminology* 30:293–326.

Cain, Maureen (Ed.). 1989. *Growing Up Good: Policing the Behavior of Girls in Europe*. London: Sage.

Chesney-Lind, Meda. 1973. "Judicial Enforcement of the Female Sex Role." *Issues in Criminology* 8:51–70.

———. 1974. "Juvenile Delinquency: The Sexualization of Female Crime." *Psychology Today* (July):43–46.

———. 1981. "Judicial Paternalism and the Female Status Offender: Training Women to Know Their Place." Pp. 354–366 in *Women and Crime in America*, edited by L. H. Bowker. New York: Macmillan.

———. 1982. "Guilty by Reason of Sex: Young Women and the Juvenile Justice System." Pp. 77–104 in *The Criminal Justice System and Women*, edited by B. R. Price and N. J. Sokoloff. New York: Clark Boardman.

———. 1986. "Women and Crime: The Female Offender." *Signs* 12:78–96.

———. 1987. "Female Offenders: Paternalism Reexamined." Pp. 114–140 in *Women, the Courts, and Equality*, edited by L. L. Crites and W. L. Hepperle. Newbury Park, CA: Sage.

———. 1988. "Girls and Status Offenses: Is Juvenile Justice Still Sexist?" *Criminal Justice Abstracts* 20:145–165.

Chesney-Lind, Meda, and Randall G. Shelden. 1992. *Girls, Delinquency, and Juvenile Justice.* Pacific Grove, CA: Brooks/Cole.

Chigwada-Bailey, Ruth, 1997. *Black Women's Experiences of Criminal Justice.* Winchester, England: Waterside Press.

Cohn, Y. 1970. "Criteria for the Probation Officer's Recommendation to the Juvenile Court." In *Becoming Delinquent,* edited by P. G. Garabedian and D. C. Gibbons. Chicago: Aldine.

Conway, Allan, and Carol Bogdan. 1977. "Sexual Delinquency: The Persistence of a Double Standard." *Crime and Delinquency* 23:131–135.

Crew, Keith B. 1991. "Sex Differences in Criminal Sentencing: Chivalry or Patriarchy?" *Justice Quarterly* 8:59–84.

Curran, Deborah. 1983. "Judicial Discretion and Defendant's Sex." *Criminology* 21:41–58.

Daly, Kathleen. 1987. "Structure and Practice of Familial-Based Justice in a Criminal Court." *Law and Society Review* 21:267–290.

———. 1989a. "Rethinking Judicial Paternalism: Gender, Work-Family Relations, and Sentencing." *Gender and Society* 3:9–36.

———. 1989b. "Neither Conflict nor Labeling nor Paternalism Will Suffice: Intersections of Race, Ethnicity, Gender, and Family in Criminal Court Decisions." *Crime and Delinquency* 35:136–168.

Daly, Kathleen, and Rebecca L. Bordt. 1995. "Sex Effects and Sentencing: An Analysis of the Statistical Literature." *Justice Quarterly* 12(1):141–176.

Datesman, Susan K., and Mikel Aickin. 1984. "Offense Specialization and Escalation among Status Offenders." *Journal of Criminal Law and Criminology* 75:1246–1275.

Datesman, Susan K., and Frank R. Scarpitti. 1977. "Unequal Protection for Males and Females in the Juvenile Court." In *Juvenile Delinquency,* edited by T. N. Ferdinand. Newbury Park, CA: Sage.

———. 1980. "Unequal Protection for Males and Females in the Juvenile Court." Pp. 300–319 in *Women, Crime, and Justice,* edited by S. K. Datesman and F. R. Scarpitti. New York: Oxford University Press.

DeFleur, Lois B. 1975. "Biasing Influences on Drug Arrest Records: Implications for Deviance Research." *American Sociological Review* 40:88–103.

Eaton, Mary. 1986. *Justice for Women? Family, Court and Social Control.* Philadelphia: Open University Press.

Edwards, Susan. 1984. *Women on Trial: A Study of the Female Suspect, Defendant and Offender in the Criminal Law and Criminal Justice System.* Manchester, England: Manchester University Press.

Erez, Edna. 1989. "Gender, Rehabilitation, and Probation Decisions." *Criminology* 27:307–327.

———. 1992. "Dangerous Men, Evil Women: Gender and Parole Decision-Making." *Justice Quarterly* 9:105–126.

Farnworth, Margaret, and Raymond H. C. Teske. 1995. "Gender Differences in Felony Court Processing." *Women and Criminal Justice* 6(2):23–44.

Farrington, David P., and Allison M. Morris. 1983. "Sex, Sentencing and Reconviction." *British Journal of Criminology* 23:229–248.

Federle, K. H. and Meda Chesney-Lind. 1992. "Special Issues in Juvenile Justice: Gender, Race, and Ethnicity." Pp. 165–195 in I. M. Schwartz (Ed.), *Juvenile Justice and Public Policy: Toward a National Agenda* (pp. 165–95). New York: Macmillian.

Feinman, Clarice. 1992. "Criminal Codes, Criminal Justice and Female Offenders: New Jersey as a Case Study." Pp. 57–68 in *The Changing Roles of Women in the Criminal Justice System,* 2nd ed., edited by I. L. Moyer. Prospect Heights, IL: Waveland Press.

Figueira-McDonough, Josefina. 1985. "Gender Differences in Informal Processing: A Look at Charge Bargaining and Sentence Reduction in

Washington, D.C." *Journal of Research in Crime and Delinquency* 22:101–133.

Figueira-McDonough, Josefina, and Rosemary C. Sarri. 1987. "Catch-22 Strategies of Control and the Deprivation of Women's Rights." Pp. 11–33 in *The Trapped Woman: Catch-22 in Deviance and Control,* edited by J. Figueira-McDonough and R. Sarri. Newbury Park, CA: Sage.

Fisher, C. J., and R. I. Mawby. 1982. "Juvenile Delinquency and Police Discretion in an Inner City Area." *British Journal of Criminology* 22:63–75.

Frazier, Charles E., Wilbur E. Block, and John C. Henretta. 1983. "The Role of Probation Officers in Determining Gender Differences in Sentencing Severity." *Sociological Quarterly* 24:305–318.

Frazier, Charles E., and John C. Cochran. 1986. "Detention of Juveniles: Its Effects on Subsequent Juvenile Court Processing Decisions." *Youth and Society* 17:286–305.

Gelsthorpe, Loraine. 1989. *Sexism and the Female Offender.* Aldershot, England: Gower.

Ghali, Moheb, and Meda Chesney-Lind. 1986. "Gender Bias and the Criminal Justice System: An Empirical Investigation." *Sociology and Social Research* 70:164–171.

Gruhl, John, Susan Welch, and Cassia Spohn. 1984. "Women as Criminal Defendants: A Test for Paternalism." *Western Political Quarterly* 37:456–467.

Hepburn, John R. 1978. "Race and the Decision to Arrest: An Analysis of Warrants Issued." *Journal of Research in Crime and Delinquency* 15:54–73.

Hiller, Anne Edwards, and Linda Hancock. 1981. "The Processing of Juveniles in Victoria." Pp. 92–126 in *Women and Crime,* edited by S. K. Mukherjee and J. A. Scutt. North Sydney, Australia: Allen and Unwin.

Hudson, Barbara. 1989. "Justice or Welfare? A Comparison of Recent Developments in the English and French Juvenile Justice System." Pp. 96–113 in *Growing Up Good: Policing the Behavior of Girls in Europe,* edited by M. Cain. London: Sage.

Hutton, Chris, Frank Pommersheim, and Steve Feimer. 1989. " 'I Fought the Law and the Law Won' ": A Report on Women and Disparate Sentencing in South Dakota." *New England Journal on Criminal and Civil Confinement* 15:177–202.

Jamieson, Katherine M., and Anita Blowers. 1993. "A Structural Examination of Court Disposition Patterns." *Criminology* 31:243–262.

Kraska, Peter B., and Victor E. Kappeler. 1995. To Serve and Pursue: Exploring Police Sexual Violence against Women." *Justice Quarterly* 12(1):85–112.

Kratcoski, P. 1974. "Delinquent Boys and Girls." *Child Welfare* 53:16–21.

Krisberg, Barry, and Ira Schwartz. 1983. "Rethinking Juvenile Justice." *Crime and Delinquency* 29:333–365.

Krohn, Marvin, James P. Curry, and Shirley Nelson-Kilger. 1983. "Is Chivalry Dead? An Analysis of Changes in Police Dispositions of Males and Females." *Criminology* 21:417–437.

Kruttschnitt, Candace. 1981. "Social Status and Sentences of Female Offenders." *Law and Society Review* 15:247–265.

———. 1982. "Women, Crime, and Dependency." *Criminology* 19:495–513.

———. 1984. "Sex and Criminal Court Dispositions: The Unresolved Controversy." *Research in Crime and Delinquency* 21:213–232.

———. 1992. " 'Female Crimes' or Legal Labels? Are Statistics about Women Offenders Representative of Their Crimes?" Pp. 81–98 in *The Changing Roles of Women in the Criminal Justice System,* edited by I. L. Moyer. Prospect Heights, IL: Waveland Press.

Kruttschnitt, Candace, and Donald E. Green. 1984. "The Sex-Sanctioning Issue: Is It History?" *American Sociological Review* 49:541–551.

Kruttschnitt, Candace, and Daniel Mc-Carthy. 1985. "Familial Social Control and Pretrial Sanctions: Does Sex Really Matter?" *Journal of Criminal Law and Criminology* 76:151–175.

Landau, Simha. 1981. "Juveniles and the Police." *British Journal of Criminology* 21:27–46.

Landau, Simha, and Gad Nathan. 1983. "Selecting Delinquents for Cautioning in the London Metropolitan Area." *British Journal of Criminology* 23:128–149.

LaPrairie, Carol P. 1989. "Some Issues in Aboriginal Justice Research: The Case of Aboriginal Women in Canada." *Women and Criminal Justice* 1:81–92.

Leiber, Michael J. 1994. A Comparison of Juvenile Court Outcomes for Native Americans, African Americans, and Whites." *Justice Quarterly* 11(2):257–279.

Leonard, Eileen B. 1982. *Women, Crime and Society.* New York: Longman.

Mann, Coramae R. 1990. "Female Homicide and Substance Use: Is There a Connection?" *Women and Criminal Justice* 1:87–110.

Mastrofski, Stephen D., Robert E. Worden, and Jeffrey B. Snipes. 1995. "Law Enforcement in a Time of Community Policing." *Criminology* 33(4):539–563.

McCarthy, Belinda R. 1987. "Preventive Detention and Pretrial Custody in the Juvenile Court." *Journal of Criminal Justice* 15:185–200.

Morris, Allison. 1987. *Women, Crime and Criminal Justice.* Oxford: Basil Blackwell.

Moulds, Elizabeth F. 1980. "Chivalry and Paternalism: Disparities of Treatment in the Criminal Justice System." Pp. 277–299 in *Women, Crime, and Justice,* edited by S. K. Datesman and F. R. Scarpitti. New York: Oxford University Press.

Myers, Martha A., and John Hagan. 1979. "Private and Public Trouble: Prosecutors and the Allocation of Court Resources." *Social Problems* 26:439–451.

Naffine, Ngaire. 1987. *Female Crime.* Sydney, Australia: Allen and Unwin.

———. 1989. "Towards Justice for Girls: Rhetoric and Practice in the Treatment of Status Offenders." *Women and Criminal Justice* 1:3–20.

Nagel, Ilene H., John Cardascia, and Catherine E. Ross. 1982. "Sex Differences in the Processing of Criminal Defendants." Pp. 259–282 in *Women and the Law,* Vol. I, edited by D. K. Weisberg. Cambridge, MA: Schenkman.

Nagel, Ilene H., and John Hagan. 1983. "Gender and Crime: Offense Patterns and Criminal Court Sanctions." Pp. 91–144 in *Crime and Justice,* Vol. 4, edited by M. Tonry and N. Morris. Chicago: University of Chicago Press.

Nagel, Stuart S., and Lenore J. Weitzman. 1971. "Women as Litigants." *Hastings Law Journal* 23:171–198.

Nobiling, Tracy, Cassia Spohn, and Miriam DeLone. 1998. "A Tale of Two Counties: Unemployment and Sentencing Severity." *Justice Quarterly* 15(3):459–486.

Odem, Mary E. 1995. *Delinquent Daughters: Protecting and Policing Adolescent Female Sexuality in the United States, 1885–1920.* Chapel Hill: The University of North Carolina Press.

Pollak, Otto. 1950. *The Criminality of Women.* Westport, CT: Greenwood Press.

Rapaport, Elizabeth. 1991. "The Death Penalty and Gender Discrimination." *Law and Society Review* 25:368–383.

Sarri, Rosemary C. 1983. "Gender Issues in Juvenile Justice." *Crime and Delinquency* 29:381–398.

———. 1987. "Unequal Protection under the Law: Women and the Criminal Justice System." Pp. 394–427 in *The Trapped Woman: Catch-22 in Deviance and Control,* edited by J. Figueira-McDonough and R. Sarri. Newbury Park, CA: Sage.

Schlossman, Steven, and Stephanie Wallach. 1982. "The Crime of Precocious Sexuality: Female Juvenile Delinquency in the Progressive Era."

Pp. 45–84 in *Women and the Law,* Vol. I, edited by D. K. Weisberg. Cambridge, MA: Schenkman.

Schur, Edwin M. 1984. *Labeling Women Deviant.* New York: McGraw Hill.

Schwartz, Ira, Marilyn Jackson-Beeck, and Roger Anderson. 1984. "The Hidden System of Juvenile Control." *Crime and Delinquency* 30:371–385.

Scutt, Jocelynne A. 1981. "Sexism in Criminal Law." Pp. 1–21 in *Women and Crime,* edited by S. K. Mukherjee and J. A. Scutt. Sydney, Australia: Allen and Unwin.

Shelden, Randall G. 1981. "Sex Discrimination in the Juvenile Justice System: Memphis, Tennessee, 1900–1917." Pp. 55–72 in *Comparing Female and Male Offenders,* edited by M. Q. Warren. Beverly Hills, CA: Sage.

Smart, Carol. 1976. *Women, Crime and Criminology.* London: Routledge and Kegan Paul.

Sokoloff, Natalie, and Barbara R. Price. 1982. "The Criminal Law and Women." Pp. 9–34 in *The Criminal Justice System and Women,* edited by B. R. Price and N. J. Sokoloff. New York: Clark Boardman.

Spohn, Cassia, John Gruhl, and Susan Welch. 1987. "The Impact of the Ethnicity and Gender of Defendants on the Decision to Reject or Dismiss Felony Charges." *Criminology* 25:175–191.

Spohn, Cassia, Susan Welch, and John Gruhl. 1985. "Women Defendants in Court: The Interaction between Sex and Race in Convicting and Sentencing." *Social Science Quarterly* 66:178–185.

Steffensmeier, Darrell, John Kramer, and Cathy Streifel. 1993. "Gender and Imprisonment Decisions." *Criminology* 31:411–446.

Teilmann, Katherine S., and Pierre H. Landry. 1981. "Gender Bias in Juvenile Justice." *Journal of Research in Crime and Delinquency* 18:47–80.

Temin, Carolyn E. 1980. "Discriminatory Sentencing of Women Offenders:

The Argument for ERA in a Nutshell." Pp. 255–276 in *Women, Crime, and Justice,* edited by S. K. Datesman and F. R. Scarpitti. New York: Oxford University Press.

Terry, Robert M. 1970. "Discrimination in the Handling of Juvenile Offenders by Social Control Agencies." In *Becoming Delinquent,* edited by P. G. Garabedian and D. C. Gibbons. Chicago: Aldine Press.

Thomas, W. I. 1907. *Sex and Society.* Boston: Little, Brown.

Tjaden, Patricia G., and Claus D. Tjaden. 1981. "Differential Treatment of the Female Felon: Myth or Reality?" Pp. 73–88 in *Comparing Female and Male Offenders,* edited by M. Q. Warren. Beverly Hills, CA: Sage.

Visher, Christy A. 1983. "Gender, Police Arrest Decisions, and Notions of Chivalry." *Criminology* 21:5–28.

Webb, David. 1984. "More on Gender and Justice: Girl Offenders on Supervision." *Sociology* 18:367–381.

Wilbanks, William. 1986. "Are Females Treated More Leniently by the Criminal Justice System?" *Justice Quarterly* 3:517–529.

Windschuttle, Elizabeth. 1981. "Women, Crime, and Punishment." Pp. 31–50 in *Women and Crime,* edited by S. K. Mukherjee and J. A. Scutt. North Sydney: Allen and Unwin.

Worrall, Anne. 1981. "Out of Place: Female Offenders in Court." *Probation Journal* 28:90–93.

———. 1990. *Offending Women: Female Lawbreakers and the Criminal Justice System.* London: Routledge and Kegan Paul.

Young, Vernetta D. 1986. "Gender Expectations and Their Impact on Black Female Offenders and Victims." *Justice Quarterly* 3:305–328.

Zatz, Marjorie. 1984. "Race, Ethnicity, and Determinate Sentencing." *Criminology* 22:147–171.

5

✳

Incarcerating, Punishing, and "Treating" Offending Women and Girls

What I had *not* anticipated when I began going to Rikers Island [Correctional Facility] was the extent to which physical assaults, emotional degradation, marginalized/tenuous status and overt racism formed a seemingly impermeable web of despair around the African American battered women in the jail. Nor did I expect to find such stories of resistance, resolve and respectability. For despite the seemingly overwhelming circumstances, the lives of the African American battered women I met at Rikers Island Correctional Facility reflected a complex dualism; they are at once victims and survivors, inspiring and overwhelmed, courageous and terrified, sometimes engaged social actors and other times passive witnesses to the oppressive chaos around them.

(RICHIE, 1996, 3–4)

This chapter presents the many issues surrounding incarcerated females. Like males, females are incarcerated in juvenile institutions, such as "training" schools; in the short-term facilities known as jails; or in prisons, which are usually reserved for adults with sentences of a year or more. The first major studies on women prisoners were not conducted until the 1960s (Heidensohn, 1985), and female offenders were not even mentioned in the huge 1967 report, a national study of crime, by the President's Commission on Law Enforcement and the Administration of Justice. In contrast to the vast and extensive research on men's prisons since the 1940s, little was known about the isolated and inaccessible women's prisons until the 1970s (Pollock-Byrne, 1990; Sarri, 1987). Furthermore, the earliest books on women's prisons have been noted more for their focus on the female prison subculture, especially homosexuality, than for their examination of the deplorable conditions of women's incarceration (see Giallombardo, 1966; Ward and Kassebaum 1965). Like homeless and mentally ill women, women prisoners are among the most neglected and oppressed groups in society.

Three reasons have been offered for the invisibility of incarcerated women (relative to incarcerated men): (1) Women have constituted a small proportion (typically 5 percent) of the total prison and jail population, (2) generally women are incarcerated for less dangerous and serious crimes than men, and (3) incarcerated women are less likely than incarcerated men to "riot, destroy property and make reform demands" (Mann, 1984, 190). Women prisoners, who have suffered the dual stigmas of "woman" and "prisoner," have been neglected even within the women's rights and prisoners' rights movements (Haft, 1980). In fact, the first decade of U.S. federal court prisoners' rights cases, the 1960s, failed to benefit women prisoners (Leonard, 1983). Moreover, in the 1970s, when males prisoners in North America were filing case after case to address inhumane institutional conditions, the few cases women prisoners brought were to obtain parity with the inhumane and unfair conditions and opportunities in men's prisons (Faith, 1992). Even today, despite significantly worse prison conditions and opportunities, females are far less apt than males to file lawsuits against prisons and jails (Aylward and Thomas, 1984; Barry, 1991; Rafter, 1989; Schupak, 1986; Van Ochten, 1993; Wheeler et al., 1989).

HISTORY OF INSTITUTIONALIZING FEMALES

Women and men were subject to the same penalties in preindustrial societies, most of which were noncustodial and included burnings at the stake, whippings, hangings, and public ridicule (Dobash et al., 1986; Heidensohn, 1985; Morris, 1987). Although confinement in castles, monasteries, and nunneries existed during the Middle Ages, confining women and men for prolonged periods was unusual until the late sixteenth century and was not accepted as the most appropriate response to criminals and deviants until the nineteenth century (Dobash et al., 1986).

Historians have noted that although the overall punishments of women and men were similar, the exceptions were largely to women's disadvantage and involved punishing them for crimes against their husbands, violating the standards for sexuality, or both. For example, during the Middle Ages, it was not uncommon for women to be burned to death for committing adultery or murdering a spouse, while male adulterers and wife killers were rarely considered offenders (ibid.). Similarly, during colonial times in the United States

(1620 to the 1760s), women were punished far more harshly than men for adultery, and they could be punished by the church as well as the state (Feinman, 1983). Public humiliation was also more common in the punishing of women than men, such as forcing female convicts to give confessions before they were hanged (Dobash et al., 1986; Feinman, 1983). The strength of these antiwoman and antisex (for women) values carried over into the twentieth century. In 1923, half of the women in U.S. prisons were convicted of sex offenses (prostitution, fornication, and adultery) (Lekkerkerker, 1931), and until 1950, women in Massachusetts convicted of having sex outside of marriage were charged with fornication and sentenced to prison (Janusz, 1991).

In the early 1700s in England, a new alternative for a commuted death sentence was to transport convicts to the American colonies and Australia with various work sentences. Women were one in eight of those sent to Australia. They were usually young (in their teens or twenties) and typically were transported for a first offense such as a petty theft (Dobash et al., 1986). The conditions of the transported women were far worse than those of the transported men, and the women's "sentences" usually included being forced into prostitution in Australia (Dobash et al., 1986).

With the exception of a few private and often religious experiments, men and women prisoners were housed in the same institutions until the 1850s in England and the 1870s in the United States. Usually these prisons provided separate rooms for women and men, but both sexes were under the supervision of exclusively male wardens and guards. A similar regime was used for both male and female prisoners because the system was designed to respond to the majority of prisoners—the male prisoners (Heidensohn, 1985; Morris, 1987).

Although most historical accounts of imprisoning women and men together emphasize their similar treatment, the differences that existed were significant, particularly women's high risk of rape. Moreover, incarcerated women were often blamed for the "sexual disturbances"—their rapes (Rafter, 1985, 12). There existed a policy of calculated neglect of women in the "men's" prisons, where the sexual abuse often resulted in pregnancy and the floggings sometimes caused death (Feinman, 1981, 1983).

In addition to their high risk of rape, services for incarcerated women were substantially limited relative to those for incarcerated men, and the authorities were unwilling to hire female guards to supervise them because of their small numbers.

> These prisoners were thus often left entirely on their own, vulnerable to attacks by one another and male guards. Secluded from the main population, women had less access than men to the physician and chaplain.
> Unlike men, they were not marched to workshops, mess halls, or exercise yards. Food and needlework were brought to their quarters, where the women remained day in and day out, for the years of their sentences. (Rafter, 1985, xx).

Thus, while women and men imprisoned in the same institutions were treated similarly overall, the few differences were largely to the gross disadvantage of women.

The movement for reform in women's prisons has occurred in fits and starts, without consistent progress. The most active reform in the imprisonment of women began in the nineteenth century and was conducted by wealthy white women who often held stereotypical views of women's roles in society. On the one hand, they recognized that women offenders were often not deviant per se but rather victims in a male economic and crime-processing system. On the other hand, these same women reformers generally strove to "purify" and control the "fallen women," whom they viewed as a threat to society (Feinman, 1983). In both the United States and England, the women's prison reformers were particularly concerned with the sexual abuse of incarcerated women by male officials in institutions housing both sexes.

The reformers' solution was to help these women rather than to punish them. The first penal reformer to focus exclusively on women was Elizabeth Fry, who established the Ladies Society for Promoting the Reformation of Female Prisoners in England. A Quaker, Fry developed reforms based on the Society of Friends when she began her work in 1816. Her approach was to convince the authorities that women and men had different needs, women's specific needs being "useful" labor, which included needlework and personal hygiene, and religious instruction, requiring the hiring of "decidedly religious" female guards (Dobash et al., 1986, 52). Elizabeth Fry promoted the idea that female offenders were not dangerous criminals but rather "fallen women" who needed a helping hand. Fry and her committee of "ladies" experimented on the women at London's Newgate Gaol in 1818, with their program of resocializing the prisoners. The experiment was claimed a success by most (Windschuttle, 1981).

Despite Fry's experimental success, only three of her requests in 1818 were passed by Parliament before 1948 (Morris, 1987), and most of her ideas were quite unpopular by the time of her death (Windschuttle, 1981). The three changes Fry was instrumental in effecting, however, were significant: (1) segregating prisons by sex; (2) hiring women to supervise women prisoners; and (3) decreasing the hard labor required of women prisoners (Morris, 1987). With the exception of the sex of the employees and the requirement for hard labor, however, men's and women's institutions were still similar in their harsh regimens. Some reformers continued to believe after Fry's death that there should be more differences between men's and women's prisons, given that men were usually incarcerated for serious crimes, while women were typically imprisoned for drunkenness, prostitution, and petty thefts. Suffragists imprisoned between 1905 and 1914 in England provided the public with graphic descriptions of the deplorable conditions for these mostly petty offenders (ibid.).

The reform movement for incarcerated women in the United States began somewhat later than in England and was also led by middle- and upper-class white women. Similar to Fry's experiment, a group of these women established the Magdalen Home in 1830 to reform prostitutes through religious instruction and motivational instruction. The reform goal was to remold rather than punish women by encouraging "proper" gender roles (Feinman, 1981; Rafter 1985). The deaths of hundreds of thousands of soldier "breadwinners" in the Civil War resulted in a new class of poor women who filled the jails as prostitutes, vagrants, and thieves during the 1860s (Freedman, 1974). After the Civil War, U.S. society was obsessed with controlling social disorder and credited restoring "women's inherent purity" as one means of doing so. Therefore, female offenders were considered deserving of harsher punishment than male criminals and thus experienced worse aspects of the prisons (ibid.).

In the 1860s, women activists in the United States heightened public awareness of the significant increase in the rate of women's imprisonment, the horrendous conditions for incarcerated women, and the sexual abuse of women prisoners by male guards. The reformers of this time started questioning the "fallen woman" label and pointed out that "fallen men" were aiding and abetting women and girls into prostitution. Moreover, once confined in prison, it was not unusual for incarcerated women to be lashed until they would have sex with male prison officials. This is similar to the situation of the female offenders transported from England to Australia, who were forced into prostitution as part of their sentence. (Unfortunately, even today, high-ranking prison administrators solicit women prisoners for sexual "favors" [Aylward and Thomas, 1984].) As in England, the U.S. reform movement called for single-sex prisons where women prisoners would be administered by women (Freedman, 1982).

The reformers of the 1870s and 1880s in the United States were from the northern states, and they were Quakers, charity workers, and feminists. They viewed women prisoners as victims of male judges, wardens, and prison guards (Freedman, 1982, 142). Rafter (1985, 1989) distinguishes between custodial institutions and reformatories. Custodial institutions were the traditional prisons that were usually designed for men but also housed women, where the goal was not rehabilitation but rather to "confine inmates at the lowest cost (a profit, if possible) until their sentences expired" (Rafter, 1989, 91). Initially, most custodial women's institutions were attached to men's prisons, where the women received less in structures designed to address incarcerated males (ibid.). Women felons were routinely housed in these men's prisons in the late eighteenth and early nineteenth centuries, where they were increasingly isolated and negelected (ibid.). In addition to having little privacy from either male guards or male prisoners, the mortality rate of infants born to incarcerated women was very high (ibid., 92).

> The custodial model, although eventually supplemented by women's institutions of the reformatory type, did not disappear. Most of the states that established a separate reformatory for women continued to operate a custodial unit, in or nearby their central prison, for female offenders convicted of the most serious crimes and those transferred out of reformatories for misbehavior. Other states—particularly those in the South and West—never created a women's reformatory. (ibid.)

Reformatories, as noted in Chapter 4, were designed specifically to house women offenders. Their structure reflects gender stereotypes, often entailing a cottage-style architectural design. To this day, many women's prisons are called reformatories. (Some facilities incarcerating juveniles are also referred to as reformatories.)

Rafter (ibid.) states that the reformatory model began to evolve in the United States in the Northeast and Midwest after the Civil War, organized by women's groups and run by women, based on the view of women as innately different from men and on a rehabilitation approach (ibid.). The first women's reformatory in England was constructed in London in 1853, and the first women's reformatory in the United States was opened in 1874 in Indiana. Shortly afterward, women's reformatories were built in Massachusetts and New York. The female staff in the first U.S. reformatories practiced Elizabeth Fry's correctional theories (Freedman, 1974). Despite resistance and hostility from the male authorities who supervised the first sex-segregated and woman-managed reformatories, they were claimed a success. Thus, they were allowed to move from housing a small number of young, white, and native-born female offenders to a larger and more diverse group of convicted women.

Similar to some of the disparate laws based on gender, these institutions were in theory designed to protect women and based on a view of women as more like children than like men: "[T]hey discouraged inmates from acting as independent adults—from competing with men in the industrial job market and participating in the activities (meeting men in dance halls, smoking cigarettes, traveling alone) of other working-class women" (Rafter, 1989, 93). Men's reformatories, though rare, were established in the late nineteenth and early twentieth centuries and were limited to felons, while the misdemeanants were housed in jails and state institutions (Rafter, 1989, 93). Many of the women sent to reformatories were women convicted of minor sex offenses such as prostitution, lewdness, and pregnancy out of wedlock—offenses for which men were not prosecuted, much less convicted (Rafter, 1989). The loose sentencing available to judges with the perceived view of reformatories as light sentences encouraged a double standard in sentencing and punishing, given that the differential sentencing and institutions resulted in harsher punishment for female than male prisoners (ibid., 93).

The founders of the U.S. reformatories saw their goals as reform and refuge; their aim was to train the prisoners in the "important" female role of domesticity (Feinman, 1981, 1983; Freedman, 1982). Thus, an important part of the reform movement in women's prisons was to encourage and ingrain "appropriate" gender roles, such as vocational training in cooking, sewing, and cleaning. To accommodate these goals, the reformatory cottages were usually designed with kitchens, living rooms, and even some nurseries for prisoners with infants. Despite their relatively gentle appearances, these institutions were run with "firmness, authority, and strict discipline" (Freedman, 1982, 145). Moreover, parole frequently involved being released to a "good" Christian home as a domestic servant (Feinman, 1983; Rafter, 1985). This indentured servant format was new in the United States but not in Europe and was supported by the middle class who could afford/exploit these inexpensive yet hard-working laborers (Janusz, 1991).

The Progressive era, the first two decades of the 1900s, brought in a new generation of reformers. The two characteristics distinguishing this era's reformatories were the increased professionalism of the female prison administrators and the incorporation of a medical model (Rafter, 1985). For the first time, the reformatories were managed by educated and experienced women professionals, who put more distance between themselves and the prisoners than their predecessors had. The Progressive era was also distinguished by the establishment of physicians,' psychiatrists,' and psychologists' roles in classifying offenders and an obsession with identifying and responding to incarcerated women's venereal diseases.

Their approach was more feminist than that of the first wave of reformers. Although they continued to support a sex-segregated prison system, they questioned the treatment of women that encouraged them to stay in traditional roles, as these reformers had rejected such roles in their own lives (Freedman, 1982). The second wave of reformers were less likely than their foremothers to base their beliefs on religious and biological underpinnings. They were less concerned with the "moral uplifting" valued by the first wave of reformers, and they targeted what they viewed as the cause of women's crime: low wages and limited opportunities for women in work and education (ibid.). The reformers during the twentieth century were also invested in the suffrage movement, partly because they believed that the conditions for incarcerated women would improve with women's right to vote. But the success of the women's prisons soon resulted in their overcrowding, and legislators were unwilling to fund the needed expansion of vocational, recreational, and educational programs (ibid.). Moreover, overcrowding resulted in disciplinary problems (Rafter, 1985). Ironically, in 1915, just as the reformers started realizing that sex segregation meant reduced opportunities for incarcerated women (relative to incarcerated men), state officials were finally supporting the legitimacy of the sex-segregated facilities (Freedman, 1982).

After 1915, the population of incarcerated women began to change, with a huge influx of incarcerated prostitutes and drug users and an increase in African–American women prisoners due to the northern migration of southern blacks (ibid.). African–American women and drug users were perceived as dangerous and in need of being controlled, and racially segregated housing was used in the cottages (ibid.). In the 1920s, the training of the women prisoners in "homemaking" became popular again. The women prisoners' "rights," therefore, were changed to include less rigid clothing rules and more freedom to decorate their walls. The vocational training, however, continued to support gender stereotypes (ibid.).

The custodial and reformatory models of women's incarceration merged about 1930, "pooling their respective disadvantages to create the women's prison system as we know it today" (Rafter, 1989, 93). Any vestiges of progressive features in women's reformatories were lost by 1930; sex segregation and the gender stratification of male and female institutional regimes had become standard throughout the United States (Freedman, 1982). After the

Great Depression, many custodial institutions were closed, and most women were imprisoned in the reformatories, which lost many of the reformatory ideals and took on more of the custodial regimes (Rafter, 1985). The 1940s and 1950s have been characterized as a time in which the reformatories switched the goal from turning women prisoners into good housemaids to making them good housewives (Carlen, 1983; Morris, 1987; Windschuttle, 1981). Either way, valuing women as domestic servants, in their own or others' homes, was commonplace in the women's penal reform movement. After this period, the reform movement for incarcerated women temporarily died down, and there was little change in women's imprisonment in the middle of the twentieth century (Heidensohn, 1985).

Three occurrences in the 1960s and 1970s renewed interest in women's penal reform: (1) the rise of modern feminism and reappraisal of women's roles in society as deviants and as victims; (2) concern that women's crime rates were growing faster than men's; and (3) in England, a 1968 policy that claimed women offenders should be treated uniquely given their special physical and psychological problems (Heidensohn, 1985). With the reemergence of feminism in the 1970s, U.S. reformers began to question the value of sex-segregated prisons. Although these segregated facilities had significantly decreased the abuse (especially sexual) of women prisoners, they had also served to promote damaging gender stereotypes and restricted incarcerated women's opportunities (Freedman, 1982).

It is also useful to examine the establishment of juvenile institutions and how strongly this process, like the women's prisons, was racist in nature. Vernetta D. Young (1994) offers a comprehensive historical accounting of this, beginning with the refuge movement for juveniles out of adult facilities in the Southern United States. This began prior to the Civil War, although an impactful demand did not occur for another three decades, the end of the 1890s. Young (ibid.) argues that the development of institutions for youth was predicated on the need to control different segments of the population in the South, tracing how the development of incarceration varied among youth depending on their sex and race. More specifically, white male youth were separated from white male adults in adult prisons, while Black male youth prior to the Civil War were controlled by slavery and the adult penal system. After abolition, Black male youth remained in the adult prison system and were processed through the convict lease system (ibid.). Juvenile institutions for Black male youth were introduced only to maintain social control, once the mechanisms of the convict lease system failed, and the "new" method of maintaining social control was by using these youth as needed laborers. The institutions designed for white female delinquents were motivated by the desire to save these girls from sexual immorality by providing them with instruction in "women's" work. Special institutions for Black female youth were not implemented until it became practically or fiscally prohibitive to remand them to adult institutions or "ship" them out of state (ibid.).

WOMEN'S PRISONS TODAY

Despite the discrimination and inequities that exist among police, judges, and prosecutors, the most serious problems for female offenders exist in residential facilities: jails, reformatories, lockups, and prisons.

(SARRI, 1987, 415)

A mong prison experts, there is agreement that women's prisons changed relatively little from the beginning of the twentieth century and into the 1980s (Feinman, 1981; Sarri, 1987). Unfortunately, the gender stereotypes that influenced the first women's reformatories continue to affect the treatment, conditions, and opportunities for the postprison success of incarcerated women today (Feinman, 1981).

Currently, women's prisons are smaller, fewer in number, and different from men's prisons (Pollock-Byrne, 1990). In both the United States and England, women make up a small proportion of prisoners (about 5 to 9 percent); thus, there are relatively few women's prisons (usually one per state in the United States), and most jails simply throw all of the female offenders into one unit. This has resulted in institutionalized sexism:

1. Women's prisons are generally a farther distance from friends and families because of their sporadic and isolated locations, making visits from children, other family, and friends more difficult, particularly for the poor.

2. The relatively small number of women in prison and jail is used to "justify" the lack of diverse educational, vocational, and other programs available to incarcerated women.

3. The relatively small number of women in prison and jail is used to "justify" low levels of specialization in treatment and failure to segregate the more serious and mentally ill offenders from the less serious offenders (as is done in male prisons and jails).

Structures built specifically to be used as women's reformatories in the United States usually have a cottage-style design and are often compared to college campuses. In addition to their "tamer" architectural appearance, these women's prisons were less likely to have gun towers, armed guards, high concrete walls, and other intimidating, prisonlike features. However, in the United States there has been a growing tendency to place high fences with rolls of barbed wire around these "campuses" over the past decade. Despite the less threatening appearance of women's reformatories, the conditions for women prisoners are usually significantly worse than those for male prisoners (Morris, 1987; Rafter, 1989). For example, women prisoners have more restricted access to legal libraries, medical and dental care, and vocational and educational opportunities and are subjected to higher levels of security and discipline (see Morris, 1987; Rafter, 1989). These issues are discussed in more detail in the following sections, but in the meantime it is important to understand that most of the law suits brought by incarcerated women since the mid-1970s have compared women's access to job assignments, pay for job assignments, work furlough, vocational opportunities, outdoor recreation, contact visits from family and friends, living conditions, cell sizes, and other "equal protection" gendered issues relative to incarcerated men (Rafter, 1989). Unfortunately, these suits are most effective as threats, and most that resulted in legal action or consent decrees were followed by little official action (ibid.).

Feminists who have worked toward establishing gender equality in the treatment of prisoners are mounting growing concerns about the response of prison administrators and policy-makers (Chesney-Lind, 1991; Hannah-Moffat, 1994; Wheeler et al., 1989). "Gender equality" has resulted in (1) a building "binge" to imprison more women (Chesney-Lind, 1991) and (2) an assumption that female prisoners can simply "fit into" male prisoners' building structures and programs (Chesney-Lind, 1991; Hannah-Moffat, 1994).

The lack of adequate women's prisons concerned feminists in the 1970s because women prisoners were often sent out of state if there were no institutions to house them in their own state (Chesney-Lind, 1991; Rafter, 1989). Since then, in both the United States and England, more women's prisons have been built, and "holding tanks" for convicted women have been created by converting buildings designed for other purposes (for example, men's and juveniles' facilities) (Chesney-Lind, 1991). In fact, two out of three facilities used as women's prisons in 1990 were not designed to house females (American Correctional Association, 1990). Whether built or created to hold convicted women, women's prisons have appeared at exponential rates. Only 2 or 3 women's prisons were built or created per decade between 1930 and 1950, but there were an additional 7 in the 1960s, 17 in the 1970s, and 34 in the 1980s (Chesney-Lind, 1991). Similarly, women's prison programs are designed along the same lines as those for men, with no consideration of the special needs of women, many of whom have survived rape and battering (Hannah-Moffat, 1994). Thus, feminists have increasingly questioned why women's prisons should be expanded when they appear to harm more than help the women they so severely punish (Chesney-Lind, 1991; Hannah-Moffat, 1994; Rafter, 1989).

The regime of women's prisons has been described as "discipline, infantalize, feminize, medicalize, and domesticize" (Carlen and Tchaikovsky, 1985). Discipline for incarcerated women is overly harsh, especially relative to that for incarcerated men. A recent study of Texan prisoners found that women were far more likely to be cited for rule infractions, particularly minor ones, and far more severely punished for them (McClellan, 1994). The women received citations for drying their underwear, talking while waiting in lines, displaying too many family photographs, and failing to eat all of the food on their plates. "Contraband" included having an extra bra or pillowcase, a borrowed comb or hat, and candy. Sharing shampoo in the shower and lighting another prisoner's cigarette were classified as "trafficking." Such minor everyday occurrences never resulted in citations or punishment in men's prisons (ibid.). Thus, in addition to reinforcing gender stereotypes such as domesticity and femininity, women's prison policies and supervision treat women like children (Carlen, 1983; Fox, 1975; Leonard, 1983; Moyer, 1984).

The medicalization of incarcerated women is also evident (Carlen and Tchaikovsky, 1985; Dobash et al., 1986). For example, even women returning from such permitted leaves as court appearances, furloughs, and giving birth in hospitals are often subjected to vaginal searches for contraband (and the searches are typically by security, not medical, staff). These searches are not only humiliating but often painful and dangerous, resulting in bleeding and infection (Holt, 1982; Mann, 1984; McHugh, 1980). "What is ironic about this procedure is that these vaginal examinations are frequent, yet the preventive pap test for cervical cancer is not often given" (Mann, 1984, 213). Furthermore, despite a change of policy in England and Scotland in the 1960s and 1970s that assumed an inherent mental instability and illness of women prisoners, treatment is difficult to obtain and when obtained is rarely helpful (Dobash et al., 1986).

Women defendants, as noted in Chapter 4, face a number of restrictions in the legal system en route to prison. One study found that 50 percent of incarcerated women saw their public defenders for 15 minutes or less, most didn't even know the names of their public defenders, and those who saw public defenders for more than 15 minutes were charged with a capital crime, and even then met with their defenders for only about an hour (Pendergrass, 1975). Incarcerated women's legal battles begin well before incarceration and extend well into their incarceration. Legal cases in the 1980s challenged why women prisoners had to have their lights out earlier than male prisoners and why they received vocational training only in sewing prison clothes while male prisoners in the same state received training in a variety of vocational skills (such as electronics or carpentry) (Leonard, 1983). Limitations for current-day incarcerated women include disadvantages (relative to incarcerated men) in access to law libraries, jailhouse lawyers, and, consequently, the courts (Alpert, 1982; Carlen, 1983; Haft, 1980; Wheeler et al., 1989). In fact, only about half of U.S. women's prisons have law libraries available for prisoner use (American Correctional Association, 1990). One study found a lack of legitimate channels for incarcerated women to report abuses or seek effective help for their problems, reinforcing their belief that they are not taken seriously (Carlen and Tchaikovsky, 1985).

One of the worst legal problems incarcerated women and girls have faced historically involves reproductive freedom. Not only have many imprisoned and institutionalized women and girls had abortions against their will (Holt, 1982; Leonard, 1983; McHugh, 1980), but those who want abortions, particularly indigents, are not necessarily guaranteed access to them (Haft, 1980; Holt, 1982; Knight, 1992; McHugh, 1980; Resnick and Shaw, 1980; Vitale, 1980; Vukson, 1988). Additionally, girls in juvenile institutions and women prisoners are encouraged and sometimes forced to give up their babies for adoption (Baunach, 1992; Haft, 1980; Haley, 1980; Mann, 1984; Ross and Fabiano, 1986), even if they became pregnant while incarcerated (Mann,

984). A more recent assessment of imprisoned women's access to reproduc-
ve health care reports: "There are no consistently applied policies regarding
contraception, abortion, and general reproductive education and counseling
for incarcerated women. When these services are available, they are rarely provided in a comprehensive or consistent manner" (Acoca, 1998, 56).

Incarcerated pregnant women and girls often face considerable hostility,
resentment for their special medical and physical needs, and discrimination by
the staff (Holt, 1982; McHugh, 1980). Although pregnancy tests do not appear
to be routine in the intake of women prisoners, research suggest that between
5 and 6 percent of U.S. women are pregnant at intake into jails or prisons
(American Correctional Association, 1990; Greenfeld and Snell, 1999).
Another study estimated that 9 percent of all incarcerated women are pregnant
(Bloom and Steinhart, 1993). Other researchers estimate that one-quarter of
women prisoners either were pregnant at intake or gave birth during the previous year (Church, 1990). Given the large and growing number of incarcerated females, this is not an insignificant number.

Finally, current research on the incarceration of women and girls rarely
mentions sexual abuse by the male staff. Although sexual abuse likely has
decreased from earlier times, there has been no systematic research to determine the extent to which it still exists. Research published as recently as the
1970s, however, documented the high risk of women in southern U.S. jails
being sexually assaulted by male sheriffs and jail trustees (Sims, 1976). In addition to outright rape, it was not unusual for male staff to coerce or force
women and girls into doing sexual "favors" in order to get their basic needs
met (for example, food and family contact). Sexual assault of jailed females in
the South was overlooked until 1974, when Joan Little, an African American
in jail appealing a larceny conviction, struggled with an white male jailer who
was trying to orally rape her. During the struggle, the jailer fell on the ice pick
he was using to assault her and died. Little's case received national recognition
when she claimed she couldn't get a fair trial in Beaufort County, North Carolina, and she was acquitted after a change of venue (Feinman, 1986).

There have been recent allegations of women prisoners being sexually
assaulted and sexually harassed by male staff (Van Ochten, 1993). Despite the
fact that female prisoners are far more likely to be sexually abused by male
guards than male prisoners are to be abused by female guards, there is more sex
integration of workers in women's than men's prisons (Goetting, 1987). This
is due to the unfounded belief that women workers pose a security risk in
men's prisons.

RATES OF IMPRISONMENT

The media, academics, and prison reformers have noted the surge in incarceration rates in recent years. Although women's recent incarceration rates are
growing at a faster pace than men's, the discussions on the rates frequently fail

to account for women or simply lump them in with the men. Increases in women's incarceration rates have exceeded men's every year since 1981 (Kline, 1993; Pollock-Byrne, 1990). The number of women in U.S. prisons tripled during the 1980s (Church, 1990; Fletcher and Moon, 1993a; Immarigeon and Chesney-Lind, 1992; Kline, 1993), while the number of incarcerated men about doubled (Kline, 1993). Similar incarceration-rate explosions for women have occurred in England (Morris, 1987). Between 1980 and 1994, men's rates of incarceration in the United States sky-rocketed by doubling (increasing 214 percent), but women's corresponding rates were almost twice the rate of the men's, almost quadrupling (increased 386 percent) (Acoca and Austin, 1996).

There are a number of interesting points regarding women's disproportionately high increases in incarceration rates. First, there does not appear to be a corresponding increase in women's criminality overall (Immarigeon, 1987a; Morris, 1987). Second, the proportion of women imprisoned for violent crimes has actually decreased (Immarigeon and Chesney-Lind, 1992). In fact, most of the increase in women's imprisonment can be accounted for by minor property crimes (mostly larceny/theft) and drug and public order offenses (Chesney-Lind, 1991; Immarigeon 1987a; Immarigeon and Chesney-Lind, 1992; Kline, 1993; Mann, 1984; Sarri, 1987). Two-thirds of women are in prison for such minor offenses as larceny, theft, prostitution, and disturbing the peace (Immarigeon, 1987a). There is some indication in England, however, that younger women are committing more serious offenses today than three or four decades ago (Morris, 1987).

A third important point is that the growth in the building of women's prisons and the addition of female units in existing prisons are unprecedented (Immarigeon, 1987a; Immarigeon and Chesney-Lind, 1992; Sarri, 1987), although "nearly all imprisoned women are nondangerous, property offenders, drug abusers and/or victims of domestic violence" (Immarigeon, 1987a, 4). Some reports say sentence lengths have not increased (Immarigeon, 1987a), while others say that women's sentence lengths have increased along with their increased likelihood of incarceration (Sarri, 1987). Overall, there appears to be an increasing willingness to incarcerate women (Immarigeon and Chesney-Lind, 1992).

Fourth, women's increased incarceration rates can be traced to implicit policy changes. Chesney-Lind (1991) believes the "war on drugs" has been translated into a "war on women," given the extreme growth of women's incarcerations for drug crimes. She attributes the increase in women's imprisonment to this war on drugs/women and to changes in decision making in the crime-processing system (such as the implementation of new sentencing guidelines).

Finally, despite the huge increase in women's incarceration, women constituted only about 6 percent of incarcerated persons in the United States in 1990 (U.S. Department of Justice, 1992). Given the even greater increase in women's than men's incarceration in the United States, by 1996 "women accounted for about 9% of all state prison admissions" (Greenfeld and Snell, 1999, 10). Indeed, in 1996, the number of women in U.S. state or federal prisons increased 9.1 percent (from 68,494 to 74,730), while men's increased "only" 4.7 percent (from 1,057,799 to 1,107,439) over 1996 (Mumola and Beck, 1997, 5). Texas led the nation with a 25.2 percent increase (from 7,935 female inmates in 1995 to 9,933 in 1996) (ibid.). States vary considerably in the percent of the prison population constituted by women, with Maine (2.6 percent) and Vermont (2.8 percent) as the lowest and Oklahoma (9.9 percent), Hawaii (9.6 percent), and New Mexico (8.0 percent) the highest in 1996 (ibid., 6). Oklahoma holds the "distinction" of incarcerating the highest number of women per 100,000 women in the population, at 122, followed by Texas at 102 (Greenfeld and Snell, 1999, 9).

Because the overall proportion of women prisoners is still small relative to the total prison population, the special problems of women prisoners continue to be minimized, and their rising incarceration growth rate is overlooked. However, it's important to remember that although women make up less than 10 percent of the prison population, there are huge numbers of women in prison: By the end of 1998 over 75,000 women were in state prisons, and over 9,000 women were in federal prisons in the United States (ibid).

WHO IS IN WOMEN'S PRISONS
AND DELINQUENT GIRLS' INSTITUTIONS?

Until recently, little effort has been made to describe female prisoners. This section briefly summarizes research describing incarcerated females. But first it is useful to understand which women and girls are in these institutions. Figures 5.1 and 5.2 provide generalized descriptions of these individuals.

The most obvious characteristic distinguishing women and girls who have been incarcerated from those who have not is race. The women's prisons, like the men's, have a long history of racism. Even prior to 1865, African-

- on average, 14 to 15 years old (though may have started acting out a few years earlier)
- poor and grown up in a neighborhood with a high crime rate
- belong to an ethnic minority (50 percent of female juveniles in detention are African-American, 34 percent white, and 13 percent Hispanic)
- a history of poor academic performance and may be a high school drop-out
- a victim of physical, sexual, and/or emotional abuse or exploitation
- used and abused drugs and/or alcohol
- gone without medical and mental health needs addressed
- feel that life is oppressive and lack hope for the future

FIGURE 5.1 A Profile of Delinquent Girls in the United States

Source: Greene, Peters, and Associates, 1998. *Guiding Principles for Promising Female Programming.* Office of Juvenile Justice and Delinquency Prevention, October, p. 2.

American women were disproportionately incarcerated, and after the Civil War the rate of imprisoned African–American women swelled even more (Rafter, 1985). It has been pointed out that the recent media and academic recognition of the highly disproportionate incarceration of African-Americans has focused almost exclusively on males, although some researchers report that there have often been higher rates of blacks in women's prisons than in men's prisons (Binkley-Jackson et al., 1993; Goetting and Howsen, 1983; Rafter, 1985) and that the rate of women of color in prison is increasing over time (Sarri, 1987). However, a recent governmental report on persons in the United States sentenced to prison under state or federal jurisdictions between 1985

- Approximately 950,000 women were under the care, custody, or control of "correctional" agencies in 1998, with probation or parole agencies supervising 85 percent of these offenders in the community. (This equals a rate of 1 of every 109 adult women in the U.S. population involved with the criminal-processing system.)
- About 84,000 women were confined in prisons in 1998.
- The average sentence and time served were shorter for women than men with equivalent offenses in 1996.
- Women "in custody" of the criminal-processing system in 1998 were the mothers of approximately 1.3 million minor children.
- Of women incarcerated in state prisons, about 6 in 10 report past physical or sexual abuse, over one-third report abuse by an intimate partner, and just under one-fourth report prior abuse by a family member.
- In 1997, an estimated 1 in 40 children in the United States had an incarcerated father and 1 in 359 children had an incarcerated mother. Almost 3 percent of children under 18 in the United States have at least one parent in jail, or in a state or federal prison.
- Women incarcerated in state prisons (65 percent) are less likely than men in state prisons (77 percent) to have a prior conviction record, particularly a juvenile record (38 percent of males compared with 19 percent of females).
- About one in three women prisoners were on probation when their offense occurred compared to one in five men.
- In 1996, new court commitments to state prisons report that men's commitments were equally likely (about 30 percent each) to be for violent, property, and drug offenses, whereas women (about two-fifth) were mostly likely to be committed to prison for drug offenses with slightly fewer (36 percent) for property offenses, and 17 percent for violent offenses. (All other offenses constituted 8 percent of women's and 12 percent of men's prison commitments.)
- Research on the estimates of one's chances of being sent to prison indicate that 5 out of every 1,000 white women, 15 out of every 1,000 Hispanic women, and 35 out of every 1,000 African-American women will be subjected to prison during their lifetime.
- In 1997, the 44 women (30 white women and 14 Black women) sentenced to death made up 1.3 percent of those persons on death row.

FIGURE 5.2 A Profile of Adult Incarcerated and "In Custody"[a] Women in the United States

[a]"In custody" refers to women under the care, custody, or control of any "correctional" agencies, ranging from probation and parole to jail and prison.

Source: Greenfeld, Lawrence A., and Tracy L. Snell. 1999. *Women Offenders.* Bureau of Justice Statistics: Special Report. U.S. Department of Justice, December, p. 4.

and 1995 indicates that African-Americans constitute between about 46 and 51 percent of male prisoners during this period and about 48 to 52 percent of women prisoners. The same report indicates that the rate of Hispanic females incarcerated has increased more rapidly than the rate of Hispanic males incarcerated between 1985 to 1995 (Mumola and Beck, 1997). A little-addressed form of racism in prisons is the representation of Native Americans. Luana Ross (1998) points out that although Native Americans constituted 6 percent of Montana's population in 1995, Native men were 17 percent of the men's prison population and Native women were 25 percent of the women's prison population in Montana. It is painfully apparent that poor women of all races are vastly overrepresented in women's prisons (Morris, 1987) and men of color are vastly overrepresented in men's prisons. A recent British study reported that in 1994, 25 percent of the female prison population were ethnic minorities, with the vast majority Black (21 percent) (Chigwada-Bailey, 1977, 13). Notably, 16 percent of the British male prisoners were ethnic minority members.

Although collecting data on class is more difficult than gathering data on race, a recent government report indicated that incarcerated women are significantly more economically disadvantaged than incarcerated men (a largely poor group) (Greenfeld and Snell, 1999). For example, in this study comparing incarcerated men's and women's financial status prior to the arrest for the offense that led them to a U.S. state prison: (1) 40 percent of women and 60 percent of men had been employed full-time prior; (2) 37 percent of women and 28 percent of men had incomes of less than $600 per month; and (3) almost 30 percent of women and less than 8 percent of men were receiving welfare prior to their arrests.

In addition to race and class, a distinguishing characteristic of incarcerated females is their significantly increased likelihood of having survived sexual and/or physical violence, particularly by a male relative or intimate partner (American Correctional Association, 1990; Arnold, 1990; Bunch et al., 1983; Carlen, 1983; Chesney-Lind and Rodriguez, 1983; Coker et al., 1998; Fletcher et al., 1993; Gilfus, 1992; Gray, Mays, and Stohr, 1995; Greenfeld and Snell, 1999; Immarigeon, 1987a, 1987b; Sargent et al., 1993). Research also shows that women in prison have experienced unusually high rates of extremely abusive "discipline" from parents, involvement in drugs, and prostitution, whether they were imprisoned for these crimes or not (Bunch et al., 1983; Chesney-Lind and Rodriguez, 1983). Many of the incarcerated women and girls report that they believe their offending/incarceration, sexual victimization, drug abuse, and prostitution are all interrelated (Chesney-Lind and Rodriguez, 1983; Gilfus, 1992; Sargent et al., 1993).

One study was conducted to try to determine how chronic female offenders in prison differed from nonchronic incarcerated females (Danner, Bount, Silverman, and Vega, 1995). The greatest differences between the chronic and nonchronic females, reported in order of most to least predictive, were age of first arrest, substance abuse, offense seriousness, and racial/ethnic group status. Specifically, the chronic group was about 4 years younger than the nonchronic females at age of first arrest, the chronic group reported more drug-use problems than the nonchronic group, the chronic group tended to be serving time for a less serious offense, and chronic offenders were more likely to be African-American. The surprising finding that the nonchronic were in for more serious offenses, the authors explain by the possibility of battered women who kill their batterers but have no offense history as "skewing" the findings (ibid). It is also likely that the finding of African-American females as overrepresented is related to the racist processing of females (and males) and that Black girls are more harshly processed and labeled by the system than white girls.

A recent study of women incarcerated in Oklahoma reported that 30 percent are married, almost 30 percent never married, almost 20 percent divorced, and the rest separated, divorced, or something else (Holley and Brewster, 1996). Over 40 percent of the prison population was Black, 7 percent Native American, and 43 percent white. Five percent were white-Hispanic and 8 percent were Black-Hispanic (biracial). Three-quarters reported having at least one child, with 60 percent giving birth to their first child when they were 18 or younger. Over 70 percent had used drugs at age 19 or younger, over 25 percent at age 14 or younger. Over one-third experienced sexual abuse as a child or adult and almost half experienced physical abuse, usually by current or former boyfriends or husbands (ibid.). Over half had another family member incarcerated, usually a brother. Over one-third had run away from home at some time, and over one-third had experienced drug treatment prior to their incarceration. Sixty percent reported needing more education. Most were serving time for an economic or drug crime, and most were in prison for the first time (ibid.).

GIRLS' "CORRECTIONAL" INSTITUTIONS

Although separate penal institutions were developed for adult women in the mid-1800s, separate facilities for girls date from the early 1900s (Sarri, 1987). To date, women and girls in jails are usually placed in what are essentially male facilities. For the arrested girl, this usually amounts to solitary confinement in jail, which places youths at high risk for suicide, particularly given girls' high rates of prior sexual and physical victimizations (Chesney-Lind and Shelden, 1992). Not only are girls more likely than boys to be placed in jail for trivial (status) offenses, but the conditions for girls in jail is worse than those for boys. In addition to experiencing high rates of solitary confinement, they appear to be at risk of being sexually assaulted by the male staff and other jail inmates (Chesney-Lind and Rodriguez, 1983). One study comparing institutionalized delinquent girls' and boys' victimizations prior to their incarceration found that 61 percent of the girls and 25 percent of the boys reported prior sexual victimization (Dembo, Williams, and Schmeidler, 1993). This suggests that although childhood sexual abuse is gendered, delinquent boys still experience it at epidemic levels, thus boys' *and* girls' delinquency prevention and treatment programs should provide programming for childhood sexual abuse.

One study of adolescent offenders found that girls (65 percent) were more than twice as likely as boys (26 percent) to report that they had *thought about suicide,* and girls (56 percent) were more than twice as likely as boys (26 percent) to attempt suicide (Miller, 1994). Although for both boys and girls the most frequently given reason for thinking about suicide (80 percent) was due to feelings of "hopelessness," girls who attempted suicide were far more likely (92 percent) than boys who attempted suicide (60 percent) to report "hopelessness" as a reason they attempted suicide (ibid.). Notably, boys (20 percent) were more likely than girls (0 percent) to report a family member dying as a rationale for attempting suicide. Wells (1994, 5) suggests that girls have nowhere to turn for help after they've been victimized, and they are more frequently victimized than boys: "[I]t may be that the invisible delinquent and troubled girls who actually experience earlier and more serious damage." A study on juvenile delinquents' emotional disorders did not separate the boys' from the girls' responses but found that for a large population of delinquent youth in Ohio, the delinquent youths' psychometric profiles were more similar than dissimilar to a clinical, mentally ill population (Davis et al., 1991). About one-fifth of the youth had made suicide threats, and 13 percent had attempted it. Although the authors only briefly discussed gender differences in the sample, they found "striking" findings regarding a comparison between the department of youth services (delinquent) girls and the profiles of girls in psychiatric facilities. Specifically, the delinquent girls had "both greater behavioral and emotional difficulties," reporting greater emotional distress and social immaturity than the psychiatric sample (ibid., 8). The authors conclude this study highlighting the need to respond to youth exhibiting mental illness problems so that they don't become delinquents or aren't processed and labeled as delinquents when the correct diagnosis and treatment would be for mental health needs (Davis et al., 1991).

Like women's prisons, juvenile girls' institutions often reinforce gender stereotypes and roles (Gelsthorpe, 1989; Kersten, 1989; Smart, 1976). The girls are subject to greater rule rigidity and control and offered fewer vocational and other programs than the boys (Kersten, 1989; Mann, 1984). A British study comparing incarcerated boys and girls found that despite no set gender differences in policies, the gender differences practiced in treatment and activities were quite severe (Gelsthorpe, 1989). The girls were rewarded for feminine behavior such as acting maternal, being affectionate, showing sensitivity, and crying. Moreover, even the activities were sex-prescribed: Boys swam, jogged, and played ping-pong, darts, soccer, and volleyball, while girls watched from the sidelines. If girls attempted to join in the "boys' " activities, they were negatively labeled "tomboys" or "unladylike." Conversely, the girls' activities included exercises to keep slim, sewing, and cooking because the staff viewed the girls as "destined for marriage and family life" (ibid., 114).

Ruth Wells (1994) powerfully illustrates how girls have been lost in the shuffle of budgeting for and responding to delinquency. She believes that one reason boys receive so many more resources and attention is that they are more likely than girls to leave behind a victim. She points out that "downsizing" in juvenile corrections, while a gender-neutral term, is gendered in practice: Girls' programs are often the last funded and the first cut. Wells (ibid., 4) states that "all we offer to America's delinquent and troubled girls [is] fragments of services."

At worst, like the jails, delinquent girls' institutions have proven to be dangerous for female juvenile offenders. "Studies of the conditions in the nation's detention centers and training schools indicate that rather than protecting girls, many neglect their needs and, in some instances, further victimize the girls" (Chesney-Lind and Shelden, 1992, 164). This is particularly disturbing given that in 1989, 22 percent of girls and 3 percent of boys held in public juvenile facilities were there for nondelinquent reasons (for example, status offenses, abuse and neglect, and voluntary commitment) (U.S. Department of Justice, 1991a). An important area of penal reform, then, is changing the institutionalization and treatment of female youth offenders. Given the vastly growing number of women prisoners, this could be an important preventive effort.

PSYCHOLOGICAL ASPECTS
OF WOMEN'S IMPRISONMENT

One of the most serious problems incarcerated females face is the institutional reinforcement of many of the early criminologists' (for example, Lombroso's) assumptions about their nature, "namely that women and girls who commit offenses are abnormal either biologically or psychologically" (Smart, 1976, 144). Many of the treatment policies in women's prisons have been grounded in the assumption that convicted female offenders are "sick" individuals.

> Apparently policy-makers, like many criminologists, perceive female criminality as irrational, irresponsible and largely unintentional behavior, as an individual maladjustment to a well-ordered and consensual society. (Smart, 1976, 145)

Such assumptions ignore the sexist implication that it is abnormal or "sick" for women—but not men—to commit crimes. The assumption of female offenders as "sick" also ignores the growing amount of research cited earlier of their high rates of violent victimization (usually by males), poverty, and other hardships (see also Carlen, 1983).

A disturbing aspect of women's and girls' confinement is the relatively high rate of self-mutilation. Some speculate that incarcerated women's disproportionately high suicide attempts (e.g., Miller, 1994), cell destruction, and self-mutilation are a result of women's tendency to internalize anger, while incarcerated men are more likely to externalize anger by assaulting other prisoners or prison staff (see Dobash et al., 1986; Fox, 1975). One reason offered for the self-mutilation is that it is a way for incarcerated females to feel *something,* particularly for those who in their efforts to survive traumatic pasts have effectively trained themselves to cut off all emotions (see Morris, 1987). Indeed,

Faith (1993, 230) views incarcerated women's and girls' self-mutilation related to two phenomena. First, women and girls are often "unable to direct their anger at more appropriate targets" (than themselves). Second, women and girls who injure themselves are disproportionately survivors of childhood sexual abuse (ibid.). Addressing the high rates of tattoos (which some view as self-mutilation), Faith (ibid., 239) states: "Traditionally, they have been a key means by which Western 'deviants' in general, and prisoners in particular, could lay claim to their own bodies, as well as signify their identification with the outcast culture."

Without reporting male prisoners' rates of receiving medication for emotional disorders, a recent governmental report stated that 17 percent of women in jails and 23 percent of women in state prisons in the United States receive such drugs (Greenfeld and Snell, 1999). There is, however, considerable evidence that psychotropic drug prescriptions are far more common in women's than men's prisons (Heidensohn, 1985; Mann, 1984; Morris, 1987; Ross and Fabiano, 1986). Incarcerated women's and girls' increased levels of psychotropic and tranquilizer drug prescriptions may be due to (1) females experiencing imprisonment more severely than males (Morris, 1987); (2) women experiencing more pain due to separation from children (Morris, 1987); and/or (3) an increased likelihood of prison staff to value or justify the social control of females relative to males (Fletcher and Moon, 1993b; Sarri, 1987). Unfortunately, there is some indication that the medical staff frequently prescribe these drugs without checking to determine whether the woman is pregnant, although these drugs can be quite harmful to fetuses (McHugh, 1980). Another important point has been made by Luana Ross concerning prison prescriptions of psychotropic drugs for Native American women:

> Many Native women at the WCC [Montana's Women's Correctional Center] responded to the harsh prison environment by being detached, by observing how things were conducted. Prison counseling staff misinterpreted their behavioral reaction as a suppression of anger, which led to the overprescribing of a variety of mind-altering drugs. The women believed that because the counseling staff did not know how to relate to them as Native Americans, they tried to control them with drugs, which they were forced to take. (2000, 134)

Women's rate of incarceration for drug offenses has grown (Immarigeon and Chesney-Lind, 1992; Moon et al., 1993; Morris, 1987). "Roughly twice as likely as men to be imprisoned for drug-related offenses, women inmates are more likely to have entrenched alcohol and other drug dependencies" (Acoca, 1998, 51–52). Additionally, many women incarcerated for nondrug offenses report drug and alcohol addiction problems (Chesney-Lind and Rodriguez, 1983). Notably, a recent governmental report states that for every measure of drug use in the month prior to incarceration and used during the commission of the offense that "landed" them in prison, women in state prisons reported higher usages than similarly situated men (Greenfeld and Snell, 1999). (In contrast, every measure of alcohol use prior to and during the offense was higher for incarcerated men than incarcerated women.) In fact, in a 1989 survey of jail inmates, women were significantly more likely than men to report drug use in general, as well as more frequent use and use of more serious drugs, such as LSD, heroine, crack cocaine, and methadone (U.S. Department of Justice, 1991b). Given these statistics, it is not surprising that a study of Connecticut prisons in 1995 found that women (45 percent) were more than twice as likely as men (22 percent) in prison to require treatment for chronic substance abuse (Greenfeld and Snell, 1999). Unfortunately, little research has been conducted to examine the effectiveness of various chemical dependency programs for incarcerated females (Ross and Fabiano, 1986).

Incarcerated women commonly worry about how they will stay off drugs after completing their prison sentences. Unfortunately, the programs to aid in confronting alcohol and drug addiction (including the twelve-step programs) have been sorely lacking in women's prisons and sections relative to males' institutions (see, for example, Belknap, 2000; Gray et al., 1995; Moon et al., 1993; Prendergrast et al., 1995; Wellisch et al., 1996). This is particularly disturbing for two reasons: (1) The extensive physical and sexual abuse women prisoners have survived may require special consideration in chemical dependency treatment, and (2) drug-abusing convicts have a high rate of reoffending and returning to prison (Moon et al., 1993).

Another source of psychological stress that is dealt with in more detail in the next section is guilt and worry about separation from their families, especially their children. As stated earlier, a form of institutionalized sexism in incarceration is that given the fewer number of women's prisons, women prisoners are generally incarcerated farther away from their family members and support systems *and their children* than are men (Farrell, 1998). Women prisoners are more likely than men to feel guilty about their incarceration because of the lack of contact with their children. Women prisoners are more likely to worry that grandparents, foster parents, and others given temporary custody of their children may not adequately supervise the children (see Baunach, 1992). Women who believe that their convictions were unjust are likely to feel doubly traumatized by the separation from their children. Thus, policies need to be developed that recognize not only the pain incarcerated women experience through the separation from their children, but the pain the children, particularly young, dependent children, experience in their separation from their mother (see Bloom and Steinhart, 1993; Farrell, 1998).

Finally, the geographic isolation of women's prisons is not the only reason women prisoners get so few visits. The different values families place on the male members (husbands, fathers, sons, and brothers) as opposed to the female members (wives, mothers, daughters, and sisters) is evident in that incarcerated females receive fewer visits from family members than men receive. "Even while women are still at the county jail level (before being sent off to the remote prisons), they are not visited and stuck by with the same loyalty as men are by families, partners, and friends" (Swain, 1994).

PARENTHOOD: A GENDER DIFFERENCE
AMONG PRISONERS

Incarcerated women are far more likely than incarcerated men to be the emotional and financial providers for children. Although four out of five women and three out of five men entering prison are parents, research indicates that almost all incarcerated women have custody of their children prior to imprisonment, while fewer than half of the men do (Church, 1990; Koban, 1983). A recent study found that 65 percent of incarcerated women with minor children and 47 percent of incarcerated men with minor children reported that their children lived with them prior to incarceration (Schafer and Dellinger, 1999). Thus, one of the greatest differences in stresses for women and men serving time is that the separation from children is generally a much greater hardship for women than for men. "Unlike men sentenced to prison, women seldom have been able to rely on a spouse to care for their children; therefore they have suffered more anxiety about the welfare of their families" (Rafter, 1985, 179). Indeed, one study found that 90 percent of men who are incarcerated report that the other parent had custody of their children once they were incarcerated (Schafer and Dellinger, 1999). Another study found that only 10 percent of incarcerated women's children are taken care of by the children's fathers (Glick and Neto, 1982), while a more recent study indicated 23 percent of incarcerated women report the children's fathers had custody once they were institutionalized (Schafer and Dellinger, 1999). Testimony to incarcerated women's increased dedication to be reunited with their children relative to incarcerated men is evidenced in a recent study that found women prisoners are significantly more amenable to sentencing alternatives to prison (and are willing to endure them for longer periods) than are incarcerated men, particularly when they are primary caregivers (Wood and Grasmick, 1999). In her study of almost 300 women prisoners, Owen (1998, 101) describes most women's relationships with their children as "sacred," providing "a basis for attachment to the outside world not always found among male prisoners."

Not only do women prisoners exhibit more concern than men about their children, but children are far more likely to be affected by an incarcerated mother than an incarcerated father. The general acceptance that children whose parents go to prison are likely to be far more affected by their mothers' than their fathers' incarceration is apparent from the titles of the first books on this topic: *Unfit Mothers* (Mahan, 1982), *When Mothers Go to Jail* (Stanton, 1980), and *Why Punish the Children? A Study of Children of Women Prisoners* (McGowan and Blumenthal, 1978). In fact, it is difficult to find studies on parenting issues with regard to incarcerated fathers.

The most likely caregiver for a child whose mother has been incarcerated is a grandparent, and this is usually the maternal grandmother (Belknap, 2000; Bloom and Steinhart, 1993; Farrell, 1998; Owen, 1998; Schafer and Dellinger, 1999). Most women prisoners want to take an active role in determining where their children will stay while they are incarcerated, and when given a

choice, they most frequently request their own mothers (or the children's maternal grandmothers) This is largely because the maternal grandmothers often play a large role in the children's lives, and the incarcerated mothers will have fewer difficulties regaining custody after release (Baunach, 1992). After their maternal grandmothers, the children of incarcerated women are most likely to be cared for by another relative of the mother's (e.g., an aunt) (Owen, 1998). The children of incarcerated women run a high risk of having to change schools (as well as caretakers) and are less well off financially after their mothers' incarceration (Stanton, 1980). There is also no guarantee that the initial placement of a child, say with a family member, will last the duration of the mother's incarceration (McCarthy, 1980). Some incarcerated women report fearing to apply for financial help for the relatives caring for their children while they are imprisoned because it may lead to institutionalizing the children rather than letting them live with their relatives (Carlen, 1983).

The average number of dependent children per incarcerated woman is between two and three (American Correctional Association, 1990; Baunach, 1985; Fletcher, et al. 1993; McGowan and Blumenthal, 1976, 1978), and the percent of incarcerated women with children is growing (Sarri, 1987). In addition to acknowledging the pain that incarcerated women suffer from being separated from their children, *it is of utmost importance to acknowledge the suffering most children experience when their mothers are incarcerated* (Bloom and Steinhart, 1993; Henriques, 1996; Owen, 1998). It is likely that children's separation from their mothers due to their mothers' imprisonment increases these youths' chances of going to prison (American Correctional Association, 1990; Bloom and Steinhart, 1993). Given that most incarcerated mothers want to be reunited with their children upon their release and that most children of incarcerated mothers want to be reunited with their mothers, it is important and necessary to examine these occurrences and dynamics. "Positive reunion is often the result of opportunities for continued contact between mothers and their children during a mother's incarceration" (Henriques, 1996, 85). Thus, it is necessary not only that prisons have such visitation programs and possibilities in place but also that it is recognized that incarcerating women, particularly poor women (most of the women in prison), at great distances from their children not only hinders a woman's incarceration experience but it likely has devastating and lasting effects on her children as well (Henriques, 1996).

One of the most controversial debates surrounding the imprisonment of women is whether they should be allowed to keep infants and small children with them in prison. On the one hand, some argue that innocent children shouldn't be raised in prisons. On the other hand, others claim that it is unfair for innocent children to be separated from their mothers. A comprehensive book on children of prisoners states: "Often they are removed abruptly from their homes, schools, and communities, shuttled from one caretaker to another, deprived of seeing their parents or siblings, teased and avoided by their peers, and left to comprehend on their own what is happening" (McGowan and Blumenthal, 1978). It is not surprising that these children's school performance and behavioral problems begin or get worse after their mothers' incarceration (Stanton, 1980). Although a small number of women are imprisoned specifically for neglecting, abusing, or killing their children, a far greater number are in prison for stealing or prostituting in order to provide for themselves and their children. Notably, those few women in prison for harming or killing their children face more ostracism from the other prisoners than anyone else (Kaplan, 1988; Mahan, 1984).

Prisons and jails have varying policies regarding visitation with children and placement of babies born to incarcerated women. Many of the early women's reformatories allowed babies and young children to stay in the prisons with their mothers until they were 2 years old (Lekkerkerker, 1931). A reformatory in Massachusetts built a nursery in 1880 and encouraged all of the women to visit and care for the babies. "This 'communal' maternal care proved to be, in many ways, the most effective therapy" (Janusz, 1991, 11). More recently, social workers have decided whether babies born to pregnant prisoners would be cared for by relatives or put up for adoption (Baunach and Murton, 1973). Overall, flexibility to allow contact and maintain the mother–child relationship appears to be limited in the United States. Only two out of five prisons allow extended visits between mothers and children (American Correctional Association, 1990). A few U.S. women's prisons still allow infants to live in the prisons, sometimes up to the age of 2 (Baunach, 1982, 1992; Haft, 1980; Haley, 1980; Heidensohn, 1985; Holt, 1982; McCarthy, 1980; Schupak, 1986).

The preceding policies also hold true for Denmark, England, Russia, Taiwan, and Jamaica. Peru, India, and Canada allow women to keep children up to 5 or 6 years old (Henriques, 1994; Vachon, 1994; Weintraub, 1987). A comparative study of women's prisons reported that children forbidden from living with their incarcerated mothers frequently ended up on the streets (Weintraub 1987).

Most U.S. women's prisons with nurseries house the babies only temporarily, until placement with foster parents or other caregivers is determined (Boudouris, 1985). Fewer than half of the jails allow women contact visitation (where they can touch, hold, and move freely) with children, but all U.S. women's prisons allow mothers contact visitation with their children (American Correctional Association, 1990). Over half of incarcerated women in a recent study reported that their children had never visited them in prison, with the most-cited reason being the great distance between the children's home and the prison (Bloom, 1993). It can be disconcerting to children, especially young children, to have limited communications with their mothers, especially if they are feeling abandoned. Moreover, it is not uncommon for U.S. prisoners to be allowed only one 15-minute (collect) phone call per month.

Most incarcerated women's children are cared for by relatives, state foster homes, or other institutions. "One of the most painful problems confronting mothers in prison is the possibility of gradual loss of their children. . . . There is also the feeling of helplessness arising from concern for the welfare of children" (Fox, 1975, 192). Many women justifiably worry that it will be difficult or impossible to retain custody from a foster parent or relative when they are released from prison. There are also cases of fathers who "disappear" with the children during the mothers' incarceration. Child welfare laws allow "termination of parental rights if the parent has failed to maintain an adequate relationship with a child who is in foster care. Imprisonment, by its very nature, poses serious obstacles to the maintenance of the mother–child relationships" (Bloom, 1993, 66). Prison sentences alone have been used as reasons to negate parental rights for women (Haley, 1980; Knight, 1992; Pollock-Byrne, 1990). Incarcerated women are more likely than incarcerated men to have their parental rights revoked (Fletcher and Moon, 1993b). Furthermore, it is usually difficult for incarcerated women to respond to legal custody hearings:

> Obviously, if the mother is in prison she will not be able to appear at a hearing concerning the child's welfare and defend herself. Legal help is often nonexistent and consequently no one is there to represent the woman's interests. It is possible in some states for the woman to lose all rights and to lose the child completely to adoption proceedings, despite her objections. (Pollock-Byrne, 1990, 67)

Consequently, one of the first goals of many women released from prison is to reestablish custody of their children. They may first be required to prove that they have stable housing and employment, which is difficult for anyone leaving prison. Even getting back on welfare can be time consuming because of the enormous amounts of "red tape." Often the woman is placed in a position of having to borrow from loan sharks or friends and family (Stanton, 1980). Moreover, a number of jailed mothers report desertion or divorce by their male partners or husbands while they were incarcerated (ibid.).

In conclusion, it is ironic that prisons have unabashedly programmed female offenders into their "proper" gender roles as wives and mothers but simultaneously make few or no provisions for them to maintain contact with even their youngest children (Haft, 1980; Knight, 1992; Sarri, 1987).

EDUCATIONAL, VOCATIONAL, AND RECREATIONAL PROGRAMS

Women prisoners have typically been viewed as unworthy or incapable of training or education, thus confirming their dependent status in and out of prison. "In general, treatment and training programs for female offenders are distinctively poorer in quantity, quality, and variety, and considerably different in nature from those for male offenders" (Ross and Fabiano, 1986). Moreover, frequently women have less access to or are simply excluded from educational and vocational opportunities, work release programs, halfway houses, furloughs, and other programs available to incarcerated men in the United States (Janusz, 1991; Rafter, 1989). (This is not to imply that education and training programs in men's prisons are adequate or should be the model.) Indeed, most of the law suits brought by incarcerated women in the past few decades have to do with sex discrimination in access to equal treatment, for example, regarding disparity in recreational facilities, the size of their cells, and so on (Rafter, 1989): "All [sex discrimination law suits brought by incarcerated women] contrast the conditions of male and female prisoners; conclude that women's conditions are poorer; and argue that the differences constitute sex discrimination in violation of the Fourteenth Amendment's Equal Protection Clause" (ibid., 90).

Historically, the justifications offered for discrimination against women prisoners include that they are not major "breadwinners" or in need of remunerative employment (Smart, 1976). Although this situation has improved somewhat, there is still a theme in prison programming for women to reflect society's bias that the most acceptable role for women is that of mother and wife (Carlen, 1983; Diaz-Cotto, 1996; Feinman, 1983; Natalizia, 1991). The focus on women as domestic servants or wives and mothers clearly belies the vast and growing number of single women who are heads of households. Furthermore, assumptions about who "deserves" jobs and programs are often sexist. Other excuses offered for the lack of women's prison programs are that women constitute a small portion of prisoners and that they are in prison for relatively short time periods compared to men. Few work assignments are available to women incarcerated in the United States; those that exist "are not considered prison industries with marketable job skills" (American Correctional Association, 1990, 38). It should be noted that programs in jails are even more limited for incarcerated women than in the prisons (Glick and Neto, 1982; Gray et al., 1995) and that work-release programs are far more available to incarcerated men than to incarcerated women (Diaz-Cotto, 1996; Ross and Fabiano, 1986). Indeed, few changes have been made in the programs and opportunities offered to women prisoners since the beginning of this century:

> Far less than half of women inmates are enrolled in educational programs, although most are educationally disadvantaged; there are few non-traditional jobs in the limited prison industries which exist. Most spend their days in idleness subjected to monotonous control and discipline. (Sarri, 1987, 416)

Most women's prisons have programs in cosmetology, office skills, typing, sewing, hairdressing, and homemaking, but few train women in skills to help them become legitimately independent on their release. This is particularly troubling when examining the gender differences in educational and vocational programs in prisons:

> [T]he vocational and educational programs available to males far exceed those available to females. Typically, women's programs are small in number and usually sex stereotyped. Thus, whereas men may have access to programs in welding, electronics, construction, tailoring, computers, and plumbing, and to college programs, women may have cosmetology, and child-care, keypunch, and nurse's aide programs, and often high school is the only education available to women. (Pollock-Byrne, 1990, 168–169)

Diaz-Cotto's (1996, 284) study of New Bedford Prison in Massachusetts reported that vocational classes offered in the 1970s were data processing and cosmetology, but during the 1980s the programming broadened to also include electronics, general business education, building maintenance, computer programming, commercial art, food service, and printing. She reports that in the 1980s occasionally vocational training in nontraditional ("men's") jobs were implemented (e.g., auto mechanics), but they never lasted long due to factors such as the inability to place women in these jobs upon release, staff resistance to them, and competing with support for programs in men's prisons.

Furthermore, women prisoners who have questioned policies and attempted to change their restricted educational and vocational opportunities are often punished—sometimes with long periods in solitary confinement (Sarri, 1987). While some legal cases have successfully challenged the sex discrimination in prison vocational programs and educational opportunities, the decisions of the federal courts "have had little impact because of prison overcrowding, the dominance and resistance of male administrators, the punitive attitudes of legislators and court officials, and the fact that many social action organizations have ignored the plight of these offenders" (ibid., 417).

Both the prisoners and the staff rank education as the most valuable resource for women during incarceration (Glick and Neto, 1982; Mawby, 1982). This is not surprising given that less than one-third of all incarcerated females hold a high-school degree at intake (American Correctional Association, 1990). A study on coed prisons found that the women were more likely than the men to request academic programs, while women and men were equally likely to request vocational programs (Wilson, 1980). One study found, however, that the women with more education prior to incarceration were the most likely to participate in prison educational programs (Mawby, 1982).

Research has also found sex discrimination in the availability of activities for incarcerated men and women. A study in Scotland found that male prisoners were allowed to play darts, cards, ping-pong, dominoes, and so on, whereas these activities were unavailable to imprisoned women (Carlen, 1983). Another study reported, as if this were perfectly normal and acceptable, that an activity called the "Hen House" provided an opportunity for the women in a coed prison to get together with the staff wives, to make Christmas cookies and spend the evening sewing, knitting, and talking (Campbell, 1980). Men's prisons have vastly better recreational facilities and programs, based on the myth that men need more physical exertion than women (Goetting, 1987). Apparently there is a related assumption that men are more in need of heterosexual contact than women, given that some states allow male prisoners conjugal visits, while providing no such opportunity for female prisoners (Boudouris, 1985).

Little research addresses gender differences among prisoners and access to religious and spiritual opportunities. An exception to this is Luana Ross's (2000) description of how the American Indian Religious Freedom Act of 1978 affected incarcerated Native men more than Native women. This act states that "imprisoned Natives have the right to fully practice their Native traditions" (ibid., 141). In her study of Montana, Ross reports that white women and men have "full access" to their Judeo–Christian based religions, Native men have access to the sweat lodge, but Native women do not have access to a sweat lodge, which Ross points out is a violation of the 1978 act.

Although little research exists examining women incarcerated in jails, two such studies indicate that the gender discrimination in jails is similar to that in prisons, although likely even worse (Gray et al., 1995; Prendergast et al., 1995). One of these studies reported that the major finding was that, with the exception of treatment programs provided by community groups, such as Alcoholics Anonymous and Narcotics Anonymous, "the programming in women's jails is woefully inadequate" (Gray et al., 1995). Only 12 percent of the women received any educational, vocational, or work training or programming, despite the sample of women reporting these as their top-priority program desires. The jail administrators claimed they were constrained by their budget to provide better programming for these jailed women. Despite high rates of the incarcerated women's reports of sexual victimization, only about 4 percent of the women had access to programs on this topic (ibid.).

Scholars have suggested that for both prisons and jails, one partial solution to provide better programming and treatment is to expand the utilization of community volunteer and private resources (Gray et al., 1995; Rafter, 1989). These could include violence against women organizations, drug programs, and so on.

HEALTH CARE SERVICES

Incarcerated women may have more serious health problems than women outside of prison because of their increased likelihood of living in poverty, limited access to preventive medical care, poor nutrition, chemical dependency, and limited education on health matters (see Ross and Fabiano, 1986). One of the major problems in women's prisons is the lack of skilled and available medical care (Fletcher and Moon, 1993a; Pollock-Byrne, 1990; Resnick and Shaw, 1980). In fact, most lawsuits filed by or on behalf of incarcerated women are for problems in receiving medical services (American Correctional Association, 1990; Aylward and Thomas, 1984). Access to medical care is difficult for women prisoners, and the staff often patronize and minimize their requests for medical care (Dobash et al., 1986). One study found that women prisoners claimed it was easy to get illegal drugs while in prison but very difficult to get needed prescribed medications. Furthermore, transportation and scheduling limit the women's access to physicians (Mahan, 1984). For emergency situations, women frequently must be transported from rural prisons to city hospitals (Pollock-Byrne, 1990). Again, the small number of women prisoners relative to men prisoners is the justification used for not having extensive medical services on prison grounds.

A study comparing incarcerated women's and men's medical care at Riker's Island Correctional Complex in New York City found that while men and women had similar reasons for requesting medical care (with the exception of obstetrics and gynecological problems for women), incarcerated males were four times as likely as female prisoners to see a physician (instead of a nurse), more likely to receive treatment, and half as likely to be given psychotropic drugs (Shaw et al., 1982). Moreover, the medical staff held the general perceptions that female prisoners were "mostly healthy complainers," while male prisoners were viewed as "stoic sufferers more in need of services" (ibid., 6).

The shortage of medical care for women is further exacerbated when one acknowledges women's greater medical needs. Given that most of women's increased needs for medical attention are related to gynecological issues, it is problematic that one in five U.S. women's prisons do not have gynecological/obstetrical services available at least once a week (American Correctional Association, 1990). In addition to standard medical treatment, some of the concerns include "the detection and treatment of sexually transmitted infections; cancer examinations (breast and pelvic); general gynecological care; prenatal, childbirth, and postpartum care; abortion; menstrual problems; and problems associated with poor nutrition and the abuse of drugs" (Ross and Fabiano, 1986, 52). The epidemic of women with AIDS is apparent in women's prisons, particularly given the prostitution and drug abuse backgrounds of many of these women. In fact, female prisoners are more likely than male prisoners to test HIV positive (Greenfeld and Snell, 1999; Hankins et al., 1994; Lawson and Fawkes, 1993). In 1997 about 2,200, or 3.5 percent, of women in state prisons in the United States tested positive for HIV, while 2.2 percent of the male prison population was HIV-positive (Greenfeld and Snell, 1999). "The percentage of the female inmate population that was HIV-positive peaked in 1993 at 4.2 percent" (ibid.). A Canadian study reported that 6.9 percent of the incarcerated women tested HIV-positive and that 13 percent of those with drug injection histories and 13 percent of those reporting prostitution as their primary income source prior to incarceration tested HIV-positive (Hankins et al., 1994). Notably, a warden at one Northeastern women's prison reported that between 25 and 30 percent tested HIV-positive in their routine testing for this AIDS virus, a much higher rate than other studies indicate (Acoca, 1998). Moreover, HIV-medication and care taking is yet another area where the medical facilities are sorely lacking in responding to incarcerated women (see Acoca, 1998; Clark and Boudin, 1990; Hankins et al., 1994; Lawson and Fawkes, 1993). (Another study highlights the strong correlation between childhood rape experiences and the likelihood of cervical displasia (precancerous cervical lesions that can lead to ovarian cancer) among incarcerated women (Coker et al., 1998). Specifically, incarcerated women reporting forced sex before the age of 17 were six times as likely as those who didn't to exhibit cervical displasia, and the younger the age that the forced sex occurred, the greater the risk of cervical displasia.

Especially poignant are the medical needs of incarcerated pregnant women who often receive little or no prenatal care or even appropriate nutrition, such as milk (Barry, 1991; Mann, 1984; McHugh, 1980; Resnick and Shaw, 1980). There is also some indication that women with gynecological complaints are too frequently given unnecessary hysterectomies (McHugh, 1980). Ironically, while the prison system seems to be intolerant of offending women procreating and has a history of forced abortions and adoptions, there appears to be little effort to educate incarcerated women and girls on birth control and their gynecological health. Additionally, there is little evidence that health care is provided either for pregnant incarcerated women addicted to drugs or for their infants (ibid.), and recent research attests to horrific conditions that pregnant women face in prisons and jails, particularly when they go into labor (Vaughn and Smith, 1999).

A survey of U.S. women's prisons found that (1) less than half provided prenatal care; (2) only 15 percent provided special diets and nutritional programs for pregnant women; (3) only 15 percent provided counseling to help mothers find suitable placement for the infant after birth; and (4) only 11 percent provided postnatal counseling (Wooldredge and Masters, 1993). Additionally, the wardens listed the following as problems not addressed in the survey: (1) inadequate resources for false labors, premature births, and miscarriages; (2) a lack of maternity clothes; (3) a requirement for prisoners in labor to wear belly chains on the way to the hospital; and (4) the housing of minimum security pregnant women in maximum security prisons (ibid.). Another recent study reported that incarcerated women, after delivering their babies and being forced to give them up, suffered from not being given medication to dry up their breast milk, which not only often resulted in breast infections but also increased their sense of loss and depression (Acoca and Austin, 1996). Research has established that the conditions for pregnant women housed in jails are equally deplorable (Barry, 1991). A recent governmental report indicated that about half of those pregnant when jailed and four-fifths of those pregnant when admitted to state prisons receive prenatal care. This report did not indicate the quality of this care (Greenfeld and Snell, 1999).

The psychological strain of being a pregnant prisoner is also evident. Owen (1998) found that pregnant women's presence alone was hard on women separated from their dependent children outside of prison. She also reported "pains of pregnancy" for prisoners. "First, many women report that being pregnant in prison was an 'ugly feeling.' Second, not having a place to send one's child was very painful. . . . Third, many women said that returning to prison after giving birth was extremely difficult" (ibid., 101–102).

"Mental illness often results in behavior that the state criminalizes, and incarceration generally adds stress to the lives of mentally ill prisoners, exacerbating their illnesses" (Suh, 2000, 155). In a recent study on incarcerated women, more than one in five reported attempting suicide in the past (Holley and Brewster, 1996). Another recent study reported that 45 percent of incarcerated women in the United States need mental health treatment (Acoca and Austin, 1996). Perhaps not surprisingly, then, one study of women's prisons found that social workers were more accessible than the medical personnel. (Of course, they are much less costly than physicians, too.) Unfortunately, the social workers' time was consumed with responding to the women's practical concerns (such as contact with children, legal and court problems, and securing employment and housing on release), limiting their abilities to provide counseling (Dobash et al., 1986). The psychiatrists available to the prisoners were more concerned with the women's criminal and mental health histories than with the stresses of incarceration, and the women requesting psychiatric help were often labeled mentally unstable. Therapy, consistent with other programs in women's reformatories, was considered "successful" when gender stereotypes, such as dependence and compliance, were reestablished (Dobash et al., 1986).

But worse than deficiency, some studies have found the medical "care" in women's prisons to be abusive, with the psychiatrists among the "worst offenders" (Faith, 1993, 257). Faith (ibid.) recounts stories of imprisoned women coerced into being guinea pigs to test ineffective medications, psychiatrists who viewed and treated all incarcerated women's problems as "penis envy," and hysterectomies given indiscriminately to large numbers of women by unaccredited medical establishments and retired general practitioners with no gynecology experiences. In my own research, incarcerated women reported horrific practices by the dentist, including not changing gloves between patients, talking on the phone while removing teeth, and ignoring *all* dental needs (including cleaning and filling teeth) *except* pulling teeth (Belknap, 2000). Although the physicians appeared to be less abusive, the women reported waiting so long to see a doctor that by the time they saw one, sometimes weeks later, they no longer had the condition (Belknap, 2000).

In addition to recognizing that medical needs for prisoners may be gendered, it is important to recognize varied needs *among* women. One study found that the two biggest predictors of the types of programs incarcerated women requested were whether they reported drug/alcohol dependency and their race/ethnicity (ibid.). As expected, women reporting drug/alcohol dependency were more likely than those not reporting this to want more drug/alcohol treatment programs. In particular, they wanted a greater variety than the currently offered 12-step programs. This study found that African-American women were more likely than their white counterparts to participate in G.E.D. and high school programs, non-12-step drug programs, and to request vocational programs (ibid.). Only white women reported participating in arts and crafts programs.

One little-addressed aspect of incarcerated women is the topic of women prisoners with learning and physical disabilities. One of the few studies to do so was a large survey of incarcerated women in Oklahoma. Two-fifths of the women reported impaired vision, over 5 percent reported a hearing impairment, and one-fifth indicated they had a physical disability (Holley and Brewster, 1996). Owen (1998) briefly discusses issues for incarcerated women in wheelchairs in her study of a California women's prison. She discusses how these women are more restricted in the prison, largely given their greater reliance on staff. She states: "Women in wheelchairs have specific problems in the prison world such as mobility, obtaining specialized care, developing a satisfactory program, and establishing satisfactory relationships with other prisoners" (ibid., 102). A study of delinquent youth in Ohio reported severe learning problems, including speech and language disorders, in almost one-fifth of the sample, far exceeding the general population (Davis et al., 1991). Acoca (1998) begins an article on incarcerated women's health with a prisoner in a wheel-chair left out in the yard who is badly sunburned. In conclusion, the few stud-ies that address women prisoners who are physically disabled suggest quite dire implications. More research is needed in this area.

THE PRISON SUBCULTURE

The information reported to this point suggests that just about everything that is bad in men's prisons is worse in women's prisons (e.g., the increase in incar-ceration rates, HIV rates, the disproportionate number of prisoners of color, proximity to friends and family, and access to educational, vocational, medical, and recreational programs and professionals). However, one important distinc-tion between the prison subculture in women's and men's institutions is how the prisoners treat each other and the general prison subculture. The prison subculture has to do with prisoners' norms and values and the adjustment and coping prisoners do to counterbalance the negative aspects of confinement (Hart, 1995, 71). Owen (1998, 63) states: "In the simplest sense, a study of prison is about doing time." She reports that in a practical sense, "the major-ity of women shape the day around a job, vocational training, or a school assignment" (ibid., 103).

There is speculation that males adapt to incarceration by isolating them-selves, while females, conversely, adjust to imprisonment by forming close relationships with other prisoners (Fox, 1975). The friendships and networks women prisoners form are based on a variety of characteristics. Diaz–Cotto (1996, 295) describes this best: "Women prisoners generally formed informal groups based on housing assignments, race and ethnicity, homegirl networks, social and recreational activities, prison family/kinship networks, and political underground reform–oriented activities. . . . Latinas further subdivided according to nationality and language spoken."

Gender differences in the prison/jail subculture is evidenced by a study reporting the implementation of a state-of-the-art "new generation" jail that was experienced very differently by incarcerated men and women with men reporting far higher satisfaction than women (Jackson and Stearns, 1995). This gender difference was largely explained by a changed "guarding" style of a direct supervision structure designed to "undermine negative peer relation-ships" through dismantling power hierarchies (ibid., 216). The overall male evaluation was strong support, and the overall female reaction was one of dis-satisfaction. The authors report that the new style "may not necessarily be well-suited to handle more dependent, cooperative, family-like relationships that exist among female inmates" (ibid.). The study concluded that the "new generation" design assumed a male prisoner and thus focused on what would overcome the problems in *men's* jails, wrongly assuming that what worked for males would work for females, despite very different peer relations (Jackson and Stearns, 1995).

In contrast to the gendered nature of women prisoners' tighter relationships with each other relative to men prisoners, some research suggests that male prisoners "stick together" in adherence to the "convict code" more so than female prisoners (Kruttschnitt, 1983; Owen, 1998). The women in Owen's (1998, 73) study report that this is because the women prisoners are more afraid than the men prisoners of losing days (due to rule violations) because they are more stressed out about their families outside of prison. "[F]or many women, reuniting with their children becomes a primary goal and acts as a form of informal social control during the days in prison" (ibid., 120). Similarly, Diaz–Cotto's (1996, 271) analysis of women prisoners in the 1960s and 1970s points out that the women tended to prioritize "family matters over other concerns," such as engaging in work strikes, riots, or widespread litigation. A result of this was that they were seen as "apolitical" relative to incarcerated men who were active, and women's "apolitical" practices deemed them as unworthy by the media, Department of Corrections administrators, and others of the reform and support offered to some of the more political and active male prisoners at that time. Thus, women prisoners tend to focus more on how they are going to get out as quickly as they can to be reunited with family, while the male prisoners appear to feel more empowered to fight the oppressions in the prisons. Further, Owen (1998, 120) claims that the primacy of incarcerated women's relationships with their children "has an impact on the values shaping prison culture in several ways, such as making conversations about children sacred, acknowledging the intensity and grief attached to these relationships, sanctioning those with histories of hurting children, and other child-specific cultural beliefs or behaviors." However, Diaz–Cotto (1996, 298) reports that the pseudofamilies (which she refers to as prison family/kinship networks) "were created to address a wide range of prisoner concerns. While the politicizing capability of such groups has generally been denied or ignored by social scientists, their structure included the potential for contributing to prisoner politicization and reform-oriented organizing."

Turning to prisoner-on-prisoner violence, although some research reports that incarcerated females and males are equally violent toward each other, Faith (1993, 232) explains how this biased presentation occurs: "If men in prison beat up and rape each other it receives little attention because it is so commonplace. Exaggerated perceptions of female violence are formed because when two women get into a serious physical fight it is a noteworthy event."

Despite the consistent findings that imprisoned women and girls are far kinder to each other than institutionalized males, the focus on gender differences in the prison subculture has been almost exclusively on how incarcerated women (and girls) are far more likely than incarcerated men (and boys) to form close emotional and sexual bonds with each other. Some rather dated (and often homophobic) research suggests that females' socialization to be caring and to value family relationships has resulted in the structuring of "pseudofamilies" in women's prisons and girls' juvenile institutions (see Carter, 1981; Ford, 1929; Giallombardo, 1966, 1974). Despite the homophobic context in which these early studies presented the pseudofamilies and lesbian relationships, more recent research also identifies the existence of the pseudo-families but not through a homophobic lens (e.g., Bowker, 1981; Owen, 1998). Rather, these studies suggest that pseudofamilies are a logical extension for incarcerated women, who like most women have "been socialized to concentrate their energies on family relationships, women presumably miss these relationships more than men do and therefore create pseudo families to replace lost familial relationships" (Bowker, 1981, 415). Both heterosexual and lesbian girls and women are in these "family" systems (Mann, 1984), although not all incarcerated females are in a "family."

> Kinship relationships vary in size dependent upon the family network and the number of "relatives" in the family. The basic dyad, of course, consists of the parents. Then there are children, aunts, uncles, grandparents, cousins, in-laws, and the like. The second major variable requisite in the understanding of this social system is the male role played by the female inmate—for example, husband, brother, uncle, or grandfather. (Mann, 1984, 188)

Some research from the 1980s suggests that the pseudofamilies were either exaggerated in earlier studies or became less common in women's prisons (Bowker, 1981; Mahan, 1984; Mawby, 1982). However, given that women are raised to value others and friendship more than men are, it should not be surprising that incarcerated women form closer and more intimate bonds than incarcerated men. An example of this is a recent study assessing gender differences in prisons of prisoners' reported levels of *social support* (Hart, 1995). "Social support refers to interpersonal ties that are rewarding to and protective of an individual" (ibid., 68). Similar to studies on nonincarcerated populations, Hart (ibid.) found that women prisoners report higher levels of social support than men prisoners and that in women's prison there was a relationship between social support and psychological well-being, whereas no such relationship existed in men's prisons.

The partnerships in these prison families are not necessarily sexual. In fact, many of the lesbian relationships reported in prison are based more on affection with a sexual connotation than actual sexual activity (Pollock-Byrne, 1990). Furthermore, while some women and girls arrive at prison or juvenile institutions already identifying themselves as lesbians, others assume a lesbian status only while incarcerated, and others "come out" as lesbians while institutionalized and maintain this status after their release (see, for example, Diaz-Cotto, 1996). As in the world outside of prison, this confirms a high degree of both lesbianism and bisexuality. Owen's (1998, 138) study of almost 300 women in a California prison reported that some women come into prison "straight" and stay that way, while others come in lesbian and stay that way, and still others while identifying as lesbian before coming to prison "avoid any sexual or emotional entanglements while in prison." Faith's (1993) thoughtful research on this topic provides insight. First, she states that not all incarcerated women who love another woman prisoner are "lesbian" (1993, 214). Second, she notes that some incarcerated women who "learn to love" another woman in prison learn to love themselves in the process. Specifically, she addresses, often through incarcerated women's own words, how these first experiences of loving another woman were the first times they had someone who knew a lot about them still love them and how they came to feel better about themselves and their bodies through this love of another woman (ibid.). Faith (ibid.) does not view these woman-loving-woman relationships as simply a replacement because they have no men available to love but rather observes many of the women who have their first lesbian experience in prison as women who "discover they are attracted to women in their own right." Moreover, Faith states:

> Prisons tend to intensify every emotion, and when women fall in love it can become a consuming passion even if the circumstances prevent sexual contact. As is the case with many lesbians in the "free" world, for women in prison sexual passion is often subordinate to the shared emotional comfort, social comradery, spiritual communion and political connectedness that can be achieved in balanced relationships. (1993, 215)

Owen (1998, 146) reports that the same-sex relationships are sometimes the source of fights in the prison, given their intensity, "jealousy seems to be at the base of many of the [prison] conflicts."

Research from the 1970s and 1980s indicates that approximately one in four incarcerated women report involvement in a lesbian relationship (Mawby, 1982; Moyer, 1978). More recent research states that no reliable means are available to identify the number of women in prisons in intimate sexual relationships but that conservative estimates are that between 30 and 60 percent of incarcerated women are in lesbian relationships in prison (Owen, 1998, 138). According to one study, the prisoner lesbian relationships typically end when one of the partners is released from prison or the staff separate the women (Moyer, 1978). Notably, one study found that a strict policy against homosexuality in women's prisons is more likely to foster than discourage homosexuality (Mahan, 1984). Moreover, the staff's obsession with deterring homosexuality often results in women being penalized simply for forming friendship bonds with other prisoners. Subsequently, many women report a fear of developing emotional ties with other prisoners, which exacerbates their feelings of isolation and loneliness and their inability to cope with imprisonment (Moyer, 1980).

Due to the intensity of homophobia, there is a troubling tendency by prison experts/researchers, prison administrators and workers, and lay people alike to mistakenly lump consensual homosexuality and same-sex rape together. This alarming practice is most prevalent when discussing prisons. *It is important to distinguish consensual homosexual sex from homosexual rape, just as it is important to distinguish consensual heterosexual sex from heterosexual rape.* Given the gender roles and misogyny in the outside world, it is hardly surprising that the subculture in men's prisons views homosexual rape as acceptable, while consensual gay relationships are considered taboo (see Bowker, 1980; Wooden and Parker, 1982). The opposite is true in women's prisons; consensual lesbian relationships are more common and less taboo. The rape of women in prison by other prisoners is rare. However, sexual abuse perpetrated by prison admin-istrators and guards, much of it extremely violent and all of it inherently coer-cive and ironic, occurs far too commonly. Thus, while male prisoners are more likely to be raped by fellow prisoners than are female prisoners, female pris-oners are more likely than their male counterparts to be raped by prison guards or administrators.

A powerful documentation of this is a 1996 book by the Human Rights Watch Women's Rights Project entitled *All Too Familiar: Sexual Abuse of Women in U.S. State Prisons.* This book describes not only violent rapes of incarcerated women by male guards but also the vulnerability of many incar-cerated women to sexual "relationships" with guards (and other prison staff), that appear consensual at first. For example, the book describes how the sheer loneliness of prison life places women at risk of "falling for" an unprofessional and unethical guard who pursues romantic and sexual relationships. Reading about these exploitative guards reminded me of some of the research on lech-erous college professors who develop reputations for "hitting on" female stu-dents and forming romantic and sexual relationships with them (e.g., Glaser and Thorpe, 1986). In both instances, the incarcerated women as well as the women college students realize too late the seriousness of the power difference and how these men have a cadre of women they have (ab)used similarly, often at the same time. To compound the trauma of these exploitative and abusive experiences, the study of sexual abuse of women in U.S. prisons found that the women who reported the abuses were frequently retaliated upon by the per-petrator himself, other guards, or the entire system (Human Rights Watch, 1996). Moreover, women who became pregnant from the sexual encounters with guards were sometimes forced to have abortions they did not want, one reporting being dragged through abortion protesters at an abortion clinic (ibid., 1445). The "punishment" of the sexual abusers and exploiters in the prison system is similar to findings about sexual harassers: They were simply transferred to other (usually male) prisons (1996).

One study points out that another distinctive gender issue for prisoners is the different way that incarcerated men and women may experience cross-gender searches (Farkas and Rand, 1999). It does this by describing a 1993 court case, *Jordan v. Gardner* (986 F2d. 1521 Ninth Circuit), where the court "appropriately recognized that because of their histories of abuse, female pris-oners are more likely to be psychologically harmed by cross-gender [body] searches in prison" (Farkas and Rand, 1999, 33). That is, given the extraordi-narily high incidence of abuse in incarcerated women's lives, particularly sex-ual abuse perpetrated by males, having strip searches performed by males can be extremely traumatic. Farkas and Rand (1999) point out that cross-gender searches for survivors of these abuses is likely counter to any treatment that may be provided by the prison regarding healing from these abuses.

Finally, future research needs to compare and contrast the supportive bonds that both women and men prisoners form that help them survive prison. It is possible that male prisoners' bonds have been overlooked by researchers with stereotypical views of gender, emotions, and friendship. One woman who was

incarcerated in a federal prison and now works with female and male prisoners states:

> I think there are some differences between the way women bond with
> each other in prison and the way men bond to each other in prison, but
> I know that it happens in both populations. And I believe it is what al-
> lows both men and women to survive prison with at least a little bit of
> our emotional beings intact. (Swain, 1994)

An important distinction between incarcerated women and incarcerated
men reported in some research is the degree to which race is emphasized
(Owen, 1998). That is, race is much less of a social organizing factor in
women's than men's prisons. This does not mean that racism is never an issue
and does not come up in women's prisons, but it seems most likely to be a factor in terms of some types of resources, particularly unfair access to prisoners'
jobs (ibid., 154). Ross's (2000) research on incarcerated Native American women
reported strained relationships between them and white women in prison:
"[R]acism spilled over into their interactions," and this was largely due to
racism regarding Native women's culture, such as ridiculing religion. Diaz-
Cotto (1996, 296) reports that although personal and sexual relationships
among the women were often interracial and interethnic, "divisions based on
race and ethnicity were entrenched enough to make the formation of coali-
tions among large numbers of prisoners difficult." She describes the unique
problem for monolingual Spanish-speaking prisoners, who were forbidden to
speak Spanish to *anyone*. Thus, they were not only penalized when they spoke
Spanish, but their inability to understand the prison rules, provided only in
English, made them more prone to rule infractions they were unaware existed
(Diaz-Cotto, 1996, 2000). Diaz-Cotto concludes:

> While the literature on imprisoned women seldom mentions how pris-
> oners have sought to reform prison conditions, my study found that
> when outside sources of support were available, for example, in the form
> of prisoners' rights attorneys, prisoners were more than willing to join
> together to engage in litigation efforts against the facility. (2000, 129)

CO-CORRECTIONS

It is important to remember that the first prisons were "co-ed" or "co-
corrections," although the few women prisoners were typically housed in
"special" sections of what were basically men's prisons (Faith, 1993, 135).
While the original and primary goal of women's prison reformers was sex-
segregated prisons (as discussed previously in this chapter), in the early 1970s
sex-segregated prisons were offered as the major reason for gender inequality
in prisons. The first attempt in almost a hundred years to reestablish co-ed
prisons occurred in 1971 in Fort Worth, Texas. Although men and women are
still housed in separate buildings or cottages, they share some or all prison

programs and services in co-corrections (Schweber, 1985). Five federal co-correctional institutions opened in the 1970s, and fifteen state co-correctional facilities operated in 1977. By 1984, however, only six states had co-correctional facilities (Ryan, 1984). Long-term policies toward co-corrections in both state and federal prisons appear to have fizzled out by 1989 (Mahan, 1989), although two federal co-correctional institutions remained as recently as 1994 (Smykla and Williams, 1996).

A recent 1990 survey by the American Correctional Association reported that 45 percent of "correctional" facilities currently house both males and females. The availability of programs for women in co-corrections and the degree of interaction allowed between the male and female prisoners vary among institutions (Schweber, 1985). Only about one-third of these facilities allow interactions between females and males during such activities as recreation/leisure, prison programs, dining, and work crews, and 13 percent allow men and women to work together in prison industry (American Correctional Association, 1990, 95). These percentages suggest that the programs and opportunities probably remain separate and unequal. In a more recent comprehensive review of the impact of co-corrections, the general finding was that "co-corrections offers women prisoners few, if any, economic, educational, vocational, and social advantages. Co-corrections benefits male prisoners and system maintenance" (Smykla and Williams, 1996, 61).

An examination of the early literature on co-corrections suggests that prison administrators and feminists perceived very different potential advantages of co-corrections. Prison administrators who implemented co-corrections in the 1970s hoped that sex integration would normalize the prison experience, making reintegration of ex-prisoners into society easier. To these administrators, an added benefit of co-corrections would be a supposed decrease in homosexual activity. To feminists, the two potential advantages of co-corrections were (1) reducing sex discrimination in prison experiences and increasing women's access to educational, vocational, work, social, and medical programs and activities; and (2) decreasing the chances that women will be detained at a great geographic distance from their children, other family, and friends.

While there is little information to support or refute that co-corrections has increased incarcerated women's likelihood of being near friends and family members, the remaining perceived potential advantages of co-corrections have not been realized. It is difficult, however, to assess most of the research on co-corrections because the research itself is often based on sexist and homophobic assumptions. It is apparent, however, that co-corrections has done little to make things better for imprisoned women (and they may in fact be worse).

The traditional gender roles continue to be encouraged in co-corrections (see Campbell, 1980; Heffernan and Krippel, 1980). For example, women are likely to be given positions subservient to men, who dominate the high-status positions in the prison community (Schweber, 1985); co-corrections men are more likely than co-corrections women to rank the furlough and work/

education programs as positive and fairly distributed (Almy et al., 1980); co-corrections men have more freedom to move around the facility than co-corrections women (Chesney-Lind and Rodriguez, 1983); co-corrections women are more likely than co-corrections men to be disciplined (ibid.; Wilson 1980); co-corrections rarely decreases the traditional women's programs; when men prisoners are "added" to women's prisons to make them co-correctional, the men get many of the best prisoner jobs (Ross and Heffernan, 1980). One study in a co-correctional facility found that women were routinely denied access "to virtually all programs at the facility" (Chesney-Lind and Rodriguez, 1983). Thus, women frequently are the "losers" when co-corrections is implemented (see Rafter, 1989).

> Critics have noted that co-corrections "normalizes" in another way—it places women in a minority situation in which their needs are subordinated in a male-dominated environment. There is nothing about a co-correctional institution which prohibits management from deciding in allotting programs and services to focus on the needs of the majority—the men. (Ross and Fabiano, 1986, 66–67)

Nowhere in co-corrections is sex discrimination more obvious than in sexual control. Both homosexual and heterosexual activity are against institutional regulations; however, both homosexual and heterosexual activity still occur. In fact, there is evidence not only of pregnancies occurring during incarceration in co-correctional facilities but also of prostitution, where women are coerced or agree to do sexual favors in return for cigarettes or contraband (Chesney-Lind and Rodriguez, 1983; Heffernan and Krippel, 1980; Ruback, 1980). There has been some variation in what heterosexual romantic activity is allowed, although no homosexual romantic behaviors are allowed. For example, some institutions don't allow any physical contact between heterosexuals, others allow hand holding, and still others allow hand holding and putting arms around each other as long as the couple isn't lying down (Anderson, 1978). Notably, co-corrections does not appear to have decreased the rate of homosexuality in the prisons for either women or men (Campbell, 1980; Ross and Fabiano, 1986).

Women in the co-correctional facilities who are "caught" having heterosexual sex are more likely than men to receive punishment. The burden of upholding the "no sexual contact" policy in co-correctional facilities falls more heavily on the women, which has resulted in closer observation of the women than the men in these facilities (and closer observation of the women in co-corrections than in women-only prisons) (Schweber, 1985). One study reported that while 29 men and 29 women were written up for being in a "compromising sexual situation," 29 women and only 7 men were written up for having sexual intercourse. This discrepancy was attributed to the fact that women who get pregnant are automatically "caught" and that even when caught "in the act," men are somehow better able to avoid identification (Anderson, 1978). In a similar study, a staff member reported: "When a female gets pregnant by another inmate in here, it's all hers. There are no attempts to make the father take responsibility for the child after the initial disciplinary hearings are over" (Mahan, 1984, 235).

Finally, the obsession with keeping the women and men prisoners separated in the co-correctional facilities does not prevent the male staff from sexually harassing and exerting pressure for sexual favors on the women prisoners (Chesney-Lind and Rodriguez, 1983). One study confirmed reports of staff–prisoner sexual relations in co-corrections but did not discuss its exploitative nature (Mahan, 1989). Thus, co-corrections appears to be one of those "nice-in-theory-not-so-great-in-practice" institutions. Perhaps co-corrections institutions *could* provide the best possibility of gender equity in imprisonment regarding the costs (e.g., distance the prison is from family) and opportunities (e.g., educational, vocational, medical, and recreational access). Unfortunately, to date, that does not appear to be the case. Notably, Faith (1993) reviews a Canadian survey of convicted women law breakers that reports that incarcerated women who have *not* been in a prison that also holds men tend to believe that they would prefer being held with men; however, those who *have* experienced co-corrections report being doubly exploited in terms of being treated and perceived as both sex objects and nurturers (Shaw et al., 1990). Faith (1993, 136) concludes her discussion of co-corrections with the observation that in both the United States and Canada, women continue to be held with men despite the poor evaluations of co-corrections, in places "where there are too few women to justify the cost of building separate prisons."

In a recent overview of co-correctional prison facilities in the United States Smykla and Williams (1996, 74) conclude: "It is disconcerting to find that co-corrections is still beset with divergent policies, wide ranges in the level of policy implementation, inconsistent modes of action, and heated debates about the actual and ideal policies, programs, and objectives." These authors state that co-corrections have been implemented in a manner to "meet the system needs" and by failing to alter standard prison operations in the process when the prison begins to house both males and females, it inevitably fails. They suggest that a key component to making the implementation of co-corrections successful is through the assigned roles and training of the guards in these institutions, who should offer a guidance as well as a security role (Smykla and Williams, 1996).

WOMEN AND THE DEATH PENALTY

Relatively little research has been conducted on women receiving the death penalty/execution for their offenses. A notable is exception is a study by Baker (1999) on executions of females in the United States between 1632 and 1997. Baker (1999, 82–83) establishes how the executions of these 357 women had a considerable amount to do with their race and the political climate. For example, most women who received the death penalty did so for murder convictions, African-American women constitute all of the females "executed for robbery, arson, poisoning and unspecified felonies," and white women constitute all of the females executed for "witchcraft, spying/espionage, adultery, and concealing the birth or death of an infant." Three-fifths (59 percent) of U.S. women receiving the death penalty were African-American, two-fifths (39 percent) were white, 1.5 percent were Native American, and 0.9 percent were Latinas (Baker, 1999). Baker (ibid., 83) states that the "preponderance of Black female executions during slavery" was a result of these women "who spurned white male sexual exploitation." Thus, once again, the processing of alleged female offenders has everything to do with race.

SUMMARY

This chapter traced the beginnings of the punishment of women and the treatment of incarcerated women historically to current responses to convicted females. The development of women's reformatories during the nineteenth and early twentieth centuries has had long-term effects on the institutionalization of female offenders. While the reformatories were important in providing safety from sexual abuse, they were built on a foundation that stereotyped women and girls into roles of homemakers and maids. To this day, women's prisons are fraught with programs and activities that reaffirm women's "appropriate" role as homemakers. Gender differences in women's and men's prison experiences and access to services and activities generally show discrimination against incarcerated females. Although the implementation of co-corrections was perceived as a means to decrease gender discrimination in prison opportunities, this appears not to have happened. One thing that becomes apparent from comparing the gender differences in incarceration in the United States, regarding most factors, the conditions of women's prisons are worse than the deplorable conditions of men's prisons. Whether we measure this as proximity to family and loved ones or access to health care, recreation, education, or disproportionate rates of people of color, HIV-status, or distribution of psychotropic drugs, or likelihood of being raped by a guard, women in prison appear to be far worse off than most men in prison. The only way that women appear to be better off—and it is a significant one—is that incarcerated women appear to be far less likely than their male counterparts to be raped by fellow prisoners. Finally, the issues of pregnancy and parenting for incarcerated women are some of the most difficult and heartrending in the prison system today.

REFERENCES

Acoca, Leslie. 1998. "Defusing the Time Bomb: Understanding and Meeting the Growing Health Care Needs of Incarcerated Women in America. *Crime and Delinquency* 44(1):32–48.

Acoca, Leslie, and James Austin. 1996. *The Crisis Women in Prison*. San Francisco, CA: The National Council on Crime and Delinquency, February.

Alder, Christine M. 1998. " 'Passionate and Willful' Girls: Confronting Practices." *Women and Criminal Justice* 9(4):81–101.

Almy, Linda, Vikki Bravo, Leslie Burd, Patricia Chin, Linda Cohan, Frank Gallo, Anthony Giorgianni, Jeffrey Gold, Mark Jose, and John Noyes. 1980. "A Study of a Co-Educational Correctional Facility." Pp. 120–149 in *Co-Ed Prison,* edited by J. O. Smykla. New York: Human Services Press.

Alpert, Geoffrey P. 1982. "Women Prisoners and the Law: Which Way Will the Pendulum Swing?" Pp. 171–182 in *The Criminal Justice System and Women,* edited by B. R. Price and N. J. Sokoloff. New York: Clark and Boardman.

American Correctional Association. 1990. *The Female Offender: What Does the Future Hold?* Arlington, VA: Kirby Lithographic Company.

Anderson, David C. 1978. "Co-corrections." *Corrections Magazine* Sep. 4:33–41.

Arnold, Regina. 1990. "Processes of Victimization and Criminalization of Black Women." *Social Justice* 17:153–166.

Aylward, Anna, and Jim Thomas. 1984. "Quiescence in Women's Prison Litigation." *Justice Quarterly* 1:253–276.

Baker, David V. 1999. "A Descriptive Profile and Socio-Historical Analysis of Female Executions in the United States: 1632–1997. *Women and Criminal Justice* 10(3):57–94.

Barry, Ellen M. 1991. "Jail Litigation concerning Women Prisoners." *The Prison Journal* 71:44–50.

Baunach, Phyllis Jo. 1982. "You Can't Be a Mother and Be in Prison . . . Can You? Impacts of the Mother–Child Separation." Pp. 155–170 in *The Criminal Justice System and Women,* edited by B. R. Price and N. J. Sokoloff. New York: Clark and Boardman.

———. 1985. *Mothers in Prison.* New Brunswick, NJ: Transaction Books.

———. 1992. "Critical Problems of Women in Prison." Pp. 99–112 in *The Changing Roles of Women in the Criminal Justice System,* edited by I. L. Moyer. Prospect Heights, IL: Waveland Press.

Baunach, Phyllis Jo, and Thomas O. Murton. 1973. "Women in Prison: An Awakening Minority." *Crime and Corrections* 1:4–12.

Belknap, Joanne. 2000. "Programming and Health Care Responsibility for Incarcerated Women." Pp. 109–123 in *States of Confinement: Policing, Detention, and Prisons,* edited by Joy James. New York: St. Martin's Press.

Binkley-Jackson, Deborah, Vivian L. Carter, and Garry L. Rolison. 1993. "African-American Women in Prison." Pp. 65–74 in *Women Prisoners: A Forgotten Population,* edited by Beverly R. Fletcher, Lynda D. Shaver, and Dreama G. Moon. Westport, CT: Praeger.

Bloom, Barbara. 1993. "Incarcerated Mothers and Their Children: Maintaining Family Ties." Pp. 60–68 in *Female Offenders: Meeting the Needs of a Neglected Population.* Laurel, MD: American Correctional Association.

Bloom, Barbara, and D. Steinhart. 1993. *Why Punish the Children?* San Francisco: National Council on Crime and Delinquency.

Boudouris, James. 1985. *Prisons and Kids.* College Park, MD: American Correctional Association.

Bowker, Lee. 1980. *Victimization in Prisons.* New York: Elsevier.

———. 1981. "Gender Differences in Prisoner Subcultures." Pp. 409–419 in *Women and Crime in America,* edited by L. H. Bowker. New York: Macmillan.

Bunch, Barbara J., Linda A. Foley, and Susana P. Urbina. 1983. "The Psychology of Violent Female Offenders: A Sex-Role Perspective." *The Prison Journal* 63:66–79.

Campbell, Charles F. 1980. "Co-Corrections—FCI Fort Worth after Three Years." Pp. 83–109 in *Co-ed*

Prison, edited by J. O. Smykla. New York: Human Services Press.

Carlen, Pat. 1983. *Women's Imprisonment: A Study in Social Control.* London: Routledge and Kegan Paul.

Carlen, Pat, and Chris Tchaikovsky. 1985. "Women in Prison." Pp. 182–186 in *Criminal Women,* edited by P. Carlen, J. Hicks, J. O'Dwyer, and D. Christina. Cambridge: Polity Press.

Carter, Barbara. 1981. "Reform School Families." Pp. 419–431 in *Women and Crime in America,* edited by L. H. Bowker. New York: Macmillan.

Chesney-Lind, Meda. 1991. "Patriarchy, Prisons, and Jails: A Critical Look at Trends in Women's Incarceration." *The Prison Journal* 71:51–67.

Chesney-Lind, Meda, and Noelie Rodriguez. 1983. "Women under Lock and Key." *Prison Journal* 63:47–65.

Chesney-Lind, Meda, and Randall G. Shelden. 1992. *Girls, Delinquency, and Juvenile Justice.* Pacific Grove, CA: Brooks/Cole.

Chigwada-Bailey, Ruth. 1997 *Black Women's Experiences of Criminal Justice,* Winchester, England: Waterside Press.

Church, George. 1990. "The View from behind Bars." *Time Magazine* (Fall) 135:20–22.

Clark, Judy, and Kathy Boudin. 1990. "Community of Women Organize Themselves to Cope with the AIDS Crisis: A Case Study from Bedford Hills Correctional Facility." *Social Justice* 17:90–109.

Coker, Ann L., Nilam J. Patel, Shanthi Krishnaswami, Wendy Schmidt, and Donna l. Richter. 1998. "Childhood Forced Sex and Cervical Dysplasia among Women Prison Inmates." *Violence against Women* 4(5):595–608.

Danner, Terry A., William R. Blount, Ira J. Silverman, and Manual Vega. 1995. "The Female Chronic Offender: Exploring Life Contingency and Offense History Dimensions for Incarcerated Female Offenders." *Women and Criminal Justice* 6(2):45–66.

Davis, Daniel L., Gerald J. Bean, Joseph E. Schumacher, and Terry Lee Stringer. 1991. "Prevalence of Emotional Disorders in a Juvenile Justice Institutional Population." *American Journal of Forensic Psychology* 9(1):5–17.

Dembo, Richard, Linda Williams, and James Schmeidler. 1993. Gender Differences in Mental Health Service Needs among Youths Entering a Juvenile Detention Center. *Journal of Prison and Jail Health* 12(2):73–101.

Diaz-Cotto, Juanita. 1996. *Gender, Ethnicity, and the State: Latina and Latino Prison Politics.* Albany, NY: State University of New York.

————. 2000. "Race, Ethnicity, and Gender in Studies of Incarceration." Pp. 123–131 in *States of Confinement: Policing, Detention, and Prisons,* edited by Joy James. New York: St. Martin's Press.

Dobash, Russell P., R. Emerson Dobash, and Sue Gutteridge. 1986. *The Imprisonment of Women.* Oxford: Basil Blackwell.

Faith, Karlene. 1993. *Unruly Women: The Politics of Confinement and Resistance.* Vancouver: Press Gang Publishers.

Farkas, Mary Ann, and Kathryn R. L. Rand. 1999. "Sex Matters: A Gender-Specific Standard for Cross-Gender Searches of Inmates." *Women and Criminal Justice* 10(3):31–56.

Farrell, Ann. 1998. "Mothers Offending against Their Role: An Australian Experience." *Women and Criminal Justice* 9(4):47–69.

Feinman, Clarice. 1981. "Sex-Role Stereotypes and Justice for Women." Pp. 383–391 in *Women and Crime in America,* edited by L. H. Bowker. New York: Macmillan.

————. 1983. "A Historical Overview of the Treatment of Incarcerated Women: Myths and Realities of Rehabilitation." *Prison Journal* 63:12–26.

————. 1986. *Women in the Criminal Justice System,* 2nd ed. New York: Praeger.

Fletcher, Beverly R., and Dreama G. Moon. 1993a. "Introduction." Pp. 5–14 in *Women Prisoners: A Forgotten Population,* edited by Beverly R. Fletcher, Lynda D. Shaver, and Dreama G. Moon. Westport, CT: Praeger.

———. 1993b. "Conclusions." Pp. 5–14 in *Women Prisoners: A Forgotten Population,* edited by Beverly R. Fletcher, Lynda D. Shaver, and Dreama G. Moon. Westport, CT: Praeger.

Fletcher, Beverly R., Garry L. Rolison, and Dreama G. Moon. 1993. "The Woman Prisoner." Pp. 15–26 in *Women Prisoners: A Forgotten Population,* edited by Beverly R. Fletcher, Lynda D. Shaver, and Dreama G. Moon. Westport, CT: Praeger.

Ford, C. 1929. "Homosexual Practices of Institutionalized Females." *Journal of Abnormal and Social Psychology* 23:442–448.

Fox, James G. 1975. "Women in Crisis." Pp. 181–205 in *Man in Crisis,* edited by H. Toch. Chicago: Aldine-Atherton.

Freedman, Estelle. 1974. "Their Sisters' Keepers: A Historical Perspective on Female Correctional Institutions in the United States, 1870–1900." *Feminist Studies* 2:77–95.

———. 1982. "Nineteenth-Century Women's Prison Reform and Its Legacy." Pp. 141–157 in *Women and the Law: A Social Historical Perspective,* Vol. I, edited by D. Kelly Weisberg. Cambridge, MA: Schenkman Publishing.

Gelsthorpe, Loraine. 1989. *Sexism and the Female Offender.* Aldershot, England: Gower.

Giallombardo, Rose. 1966. *Society of Women: A Study of a Women's Prison.* New York: John Wiley.

———. 1974. *The Social World of Imprisoned Girls.* New York: Wiley.

Gilfus, Mary E. 1992. "From Victims to Survivors to Offenders: Women's Routes of Entry and Immersion into Street Crime." *Women and Criminal Justice* 4:63–90.

Glaser, R. D., and J. S. Thorpe. 1986. "Unethical Intimacy: A Survey of Sexual Contact and Advances between Psychology Educators and Female Graduate Students." *American Psychologist* 41(1):43–51.

Glick, Ruth M., and Virginia V. Neto. 1982. "National Study of Women's Correctional Programs." Pp. 141–154 in *The Criminal Justice System and Women,* edited by B. R. Price and N. J. Sokoloff. New York: Clark and Boardman.

Goetting, Ann. 1987. "Racism, Sexism, and Ageism in the Prison Community." *Federal Probation* 49:10–22.

Goetting, Ann, and Roy M. Howsen. 1983. "Women in Prison: A Profile." *The Prison Journal* 63:27–46.

Gray, Tara, G. Larry Mays, and Mary K. Stohr. 1995. "Inmate Needs and Programming in Exclusively Women's Jails." *The Prison Journal* 75(2): 186–202.

Greene, Peters, & Associates. 1998. *Guiding Principles for Promising Female Programming.* The Office of Juvenile Justice and Delinquency Prevention, October, 94 pp.

Greenfeld, Lawrence A., and Tracy L. Snell. 1999. *Women Offenders.* Bureau of Justice Statistics: Special Report. U.S. Department of Justice, December, 14 pp.

Haft, Marilyn G. 1980. "Women in Prison: Discriminatory Practices and Some Legal Solutions." Pp. 320–338 in *Women, Crime, and Justice,* edited by S. K. Datesman and F. R. Scarpitti. New York: Oxford Press.

Haley, Kathleen. 1980. "Mothers behind Bars." Pp. 339–354 in *Women, Crime, and Justice,* edited by S. K. Datesman and F. R. Scarpitti. New York: Oxford Press.

Hancock, Linda. 1986. "Economic Pragmatism and the Ideology of Sexism: Prison Policy and Women." *Women's Studies International Forum* 9:101–107.

Hankins, Catherine A., Sylvie Gendron, Margaret A. Handley, Christiane Richard, Marie Therese Lai Tung, and Michael O'Shaughnessy. "HIV Infection among Women in Prison." *American Journal of Public Health* 84(10):1637–1640.

Hannah-Moffat, Kelly. 1994. "Unintended Consequences of Feminism and Prison Reform." Forum on Corrections Research 6:7–10.

Hart, Cynthia B. 1995. Gender Differences in Social Support among Inmates." *Women and Criminal Justice* 6(2):67–88.

Heffernan, Esther, and Elizabeth Krippel. 1980. "A Co-ed Prison." Pp. 110–119 in *Co-ed Prison,* edited by J. O. Smykla. New York: Human Services Press.

Heidensohn, Frances M. 1985. *Women and Crime: The Life of the Female Offender.* New York: New York University Press.

Henriques, Zelma W. 1994. "Imprisoned Mothers and Their Children: A Cross-Cultural Perspective." Paper presented at "Prisons 2000," an International Conference on the Present and Future State of Prisons. Leicester, England, April.

———. 1996. "Imprisoned Mothers and Their Children: Separation-Reunion Syndrome Dual Impact." *Women and Criminal Justice* 8(1):77–96.

Holley, Philip D., and Dennis Brewster. 1996. "The Women at Eddie Warrior Correctional Center: Descriptions from a Data Set." *Journal of the Oklahoma Criminal Justice Research Consortium.* 3:107–114.

Holt, Karen E. 1982. "Nine Months to Life: The Law and the Pregnant Inmate." *Journal of Family Law* 20:523–543.

Human Rights Watch Women Rights Project. 1996. *All Too Familiar: Sexual Abuse of Women in U.S. State Prisons.* New York: Human Rights Watch.

Immarigeon, Russ. 1987a. "Women in Prison." *Journal of the National Prison Project* 11:1–5.

———. 1987b. "Few Diversion Programs Are Offered Female Offenders." *Journal of the National Prison Project* 12:9–11.

Immarigeon, Russ, and Meda Chesney-Lind. 1992. *Women's Prisons: Overcrowded and Overused.* San Francisco: National Council on Crime and Delinquency.

Jackson, Patrick G., and Cindy A Stearns. 1995. "Gender Issues in the New Generation Jail." *The Prison Journal* 75(2):203–221.

Janusz, Luke. 1991. "Separate but Unequal: Women behind Bars in Massachusetts." *Odyssey* (Fall):6–17.

Kaplan, Mildred F. 1988. "A Peer Support Group for Women in Prison for the Death of a Child." *Journal of Offender Counseling, Services, and Rehabilitation* 13:5–13.

Kersten, Joachim. 1989. "The Institutional Control of Girls and Boys." Pp. 129–144 in *Growing Up Good: Policing the Behavior of Girls in Europe,* edited by M. Cain. London: Sage.

Kline, Sue. 1993. "A Profile of Female Offenders in State and Federal Prisons." Pp. 1–6 in *Female Offenders: Meeting the Needs of a Neglected Population.* Laurel, MD: American Correctional Association.

Knight, Barbara. 1992. "Women in Prison as Litigants: Prospects for Post Prison Futures." *Women and Criminal Justice* 4:91–116.

Koban, Linda A. 1983. "Parent in Prison: A Comparative Analysis of the Effects of Incarceration on the Families of Men and Women." *Research in Law, Deviance and Social Control* 5:171–183.

Lawson, W. Travis, and Lena Sue Fawkes. 1993. "HIV, AIDS, and the Female Offender." Pp. 43–48 in *Female Offenders: Meeting the Needs of a Neglected Population.* Laurel, MD: American Correctional Association.

Lekkerkerker, Eugenia C. 1931. *Reformatories for Women in the United States.* J. B. Wolters' Groningen-The Hague: Batavia.

Leonard, Eileen B. 1983. "Judicial Decisions and Prison Reform: The Impact of Litigation on Women Prisoners." *Social Problems* 31:45–58.

Mahan, Sue. 1982. *Unfit Mothers.* Palo Alto, CA: R and E Associates.

———. 1984. "Imposition of Despair: An Ethnography of Women in Prison." *Justice Quarterly* 1:357–384.

———. 1989. "The Needs and Experiences of Women in Sexually Integrated Prisons." *American Journal of Criminal Justice* 13:228–239.

Mann, Coramae Richey. 1984. *Female Crime and Delinquency.* University of Alabama Press.

Mawby, R. I. 1982. "Women in Prison: A British Study." *Crime and Delinquency* 28:24–39.

McCarthy, Belinda R. 1980. "Inmate Mothers: The Problems of Separation and Reintegration." *Journal of Offender Counseling, Services and Rehabilitation* 4:199–212.

McClellan, Dorothy S. 1994. "Disparity in the Discipline of Male and Female Inmates in Texas Prisons." *Women and Criminal Justice* 5:71–97.

McGowan, Brenda, and Karen L. Blumenthal. 1976. "Children of Women Prisoners: A Forgotten Minority." Pp. 121–136 in *The Female Offender,* edited by L. Crites. Lexington, MA: D. C. Heath.

———. 1978. *Why Punish the Children? A Study of Children of Women Prisoners.* Hackensack, NJ: National Council on Crime and Delinquency.

McHugh, Gerald A. 1980. "Protection of the Rights of Pregnant Women in Prisons and Detention Facilities." *New England Journal on Prison Law* 6:231–263.

Miller, Darcy. 1994. "Exploring Gender Differences in Suicidal Behavior among Adolescent Offenders." *Journal of Correctional Education* 45(3):134–138.

Moon, Dreama G., Ruby J. Thompson, and Regina Bennett. 1993. "Patterns of Substance Use among Women in Prison." Pp. 45–54 in *Women Prisoners: A Forgotten Population,* edited by Beverly R. Fletcher, Lynda D. Shaver, and Dreama G. Moon. Westport, CT: Praeger.

Morris, Allison. 1987. *Women, Crime and Criminal Justice.* Oxford: Basil Blackwell.

Moyer, Imogene L. 1978. "Differential Social Structures and Homosexuality among Women in Prison." *Virginia Social Science Journal* 13:13–19.

———. 1980. "Leadership in a Women's Prison." *Journal of Criminal Justice* 8:233–241.

———. 1984. "Deceptions and Realities of Life in Women's Prisons." *Prison Journal* 64:45–56.

Mumola, Christopher J., and Allen J. Beck. 1997. *Prisoners in 1996.* Bureau of Justice Statistics. U.S. Department of Justice, June, 15 pp.

Natalizia, Elana. 1991. "Feminism and Criminal Justice Reform." *Odyssey* (Fall):19–20.

Owen, Barbara. 1998. *In the Mix: Struggle and Survival in a Women's Prison.* Albany, NY: State University of New York Press.

Prendergast, Michael L., Jean Wellisch, and Gregory P. Falkin, 1995. "Assessment of and Services for Substance-Abusing Women in Community and Correctional Settings. *Prison Journal* 75(2):240, 256.

Pendergrass, Virginia E. 1975. "Innovative Programs for Women in Jail and Prisons." Pp. 67–81 in *The Female Offender,* edited by A. M. Brodsky. Beverly Hills, CA: Sage.

Pollock-Byrne, Joycelyn M. 1990. *Women, Prison, and Crime,* Pacific Grove, CA: Brooks/Cole.

Rafter, Nicole Hahn. 1985. *Partial Justice: Women in State Prisons, 1800–1935.* Boston: Northeastern University Press.

———. 1989. "Gender and Justice: The Equal Protection Issues." Pp. 89–109 in *The American Prison,* edited by Lynne Goodstein and Doris MacKenzie. New York: Plenum Press.

Resnick, Judith, and Nancy Shaw. 1980. "Prisoners of Their Sex: Health Problems of Incarcerated Women." Pp. 319–413 in *Prisoners' Rights Sourcebook,* Vol. 2, edited by Ira P. Robbins. New York: Clark Boardman.

Richie, Beth E. 1996. *Compelled to Crime.* New York: Routledge.

Ross, James, and Esther Heffernan. 1980. "Women in a Co-ed Joint." Pp. 248–261 in *Co-ed Prison,* edited by J. O. Smykla. New York: Human Services Press.

Ross, Luana. 1998. *Inventing the Savage: The Social Construction of Native American Criminality.* Austin: University of Texas Press.

———. 2000. "Imprisoned Native Women and the Importance of Native Traditions." Pp. 132–144 in *States of Confinement: Policing, Detention, and Prisons,* edited by Joy James. New York: St. Martin's Press.

Ross, Robert R., and Elizabeth A. Fabiano. 1986. *Female Offenders: Correctional Afterthoughts.* Jefferson, NC: McFarland.

Ruback, Barry. 1980. "The Sexuality Integrated Prison." Pp. 33–60 in *Co-ed Prison,* edited by J. O. Smykla. New York: Human Services Press.

Ryan, T. A. 1984. *Adult Female Offenders and Institutional Programs: A State of the Art Analysis.* Washington, DC: U.S. Department of Justice.

Sargent, Elizabeth, Susan Marcus-Mendoza, and Chong Ho Yu. 1993. "Abuse and the Woman Prisoner." Pp. 55–64 in *Women Prisoners: A Forgotten Population,* edited by Beverly R. Fletcher, Lynda D. Shaver, and Dreama G. Moon. Westport, CT: Praeger.

Sarri, Rosemary. 1987. "Unequal Protection under the Law: Women and the Criminal Justice System." Pp. 394–426 in *The Trapped Woman: Catch-22 in Deviance and Control,* edited by J. Figueira-McDonough and R. Sarri. Newbury Park, CA: Sage.

Schafer, N. E., and A. B. Dellinger. 1999. "Jailed Parents: An Assessment." *Women and Criminal Justice* 10(4):73–91.

Schupak, Terri L. 1986. "Comments: Women and Children First: An Examination of the Unique Needs of Women in Prison." *Golden Gate University Law Review* 16:455–474.

Schweber, Claudine. 1985. "Beauty Marks and Blemishes: The Co-ed Prison." *Prison Journal* 64:3–15.

Shaw, Margaret, with Karen Rodgers, Johanne Blanchette, Lee Seto Thomas, Tina Hattem, and Lada Tamarack. 1990. *Survey of Federally Sentenced Women.* Ottawa: Ministry of the Solicitor General, Corrections Branch.

Shaw, Nancy S., Irene Browne, and Peter Meyer. 1982. "Sexism and Medical Care in a Jail Setting." *Women and Health* 6:5–24.

Sims, Patsy. 1976. "Women in Southern Jails." Pp. 137–148 in *The Female Offender,* edited by L. Crites. Lexington, MA: D. C. Heath.

Smart, Carol. 1976. *Women, Crime and Criminology: A Feminist Critique.* London: Routledge and Kegan Paul.

Smykla, John O., and Jimmy J. Williams. 1996. "Co-Corrections in the United States of America, 1970–1990: Two Decades of Disadvantages for Women Prisoners." *Women and Criminal Justice* 8(1):61–76.

Stanton, Ann M. 1980. *When Mothers Go to Jail.* Lexington, MA: Lexington Books.

Suh, Alexandra. 2000. "Military Prostitution in Asia and the United States." Pp. 144–158 in *States of Confinement: Policing, Detention, and Prisons,* edited by Joy James. New York: St. Martin's Press.

Swain, Lorry. Personal correspondence, May 19, 1994.

U.S. Department of Justice. 1991a. *Children in Custody, 1989.* Office of Juvenile Justice and Delinquency Prevention. NCJ-127189. Washington, DC, January.

———. 1991b. *Drugs and Jail Inmates, 1989.* Special Report NCJ-130836. Bureau of Justice Statistics. Washington, DC, August.

———. 1992. *Census of State and Federal Correctional Facilities, 1990.* NCJ-137003. Bureau of Justice Statistics. Washington, DC: Government Printing Office.

Vachon, Marla M. 1994. "It's about Time: The Legal Context of Policy Changes for Female Offenders." *Forum on Corrections Research* 6:3–6.

Van Ochten, Marjorie. 1993. "Legal Issues and the Female Offender." Pp. 31–36 in *Female Offenders: Meeting the Needs of a Neglected Population.* Laurel, MD: American Correctional Association.

Vaughn, Michael S., and Linda G. Smith. 1999. "Practical Penal Harm Medicine in the United States." *Justice Quarterly* 16(1):175–232.

Vitale, Anne T. 1980. "Inmate Abortions: The Right to Government Funding behind the Prison Gates." *Fordham Law Review* 48:550–567.

Vukson, Todd M. 1988. "Inmate Abortion Funding in California." *California Western Law Review* 24:107–126.

Ward, David A., and Gene G. Kassebaum. 1965. *Women's Prison: Sex and Social Structure.* Chicago: Aldine.

Weintraub, Judith F. 1987. "Mothers and Children in Prison." *Corrections Compendium* 11:1, 5.

Weisheit, Ralph A. 1985. "Trends in Programs for Female Offenders: The Use of Private Agencies as Service Providers." *International Journal of Offender Therapy and Comparative Criminology* 29:35–42.

Wellisch, Jean, Michael L. Prendergast, and M. Douglas Anglin. 1996. "Needs Assessment and Services for Drug-Abusing Women Offenders: Results from a National Survey of Community-Based Treatment Programs." *Women and Criminal Justice* 8(1):27–60.

Wells, Ruth Herman. 1994. "America's Delinquent Daughters Have Nowhere to Turn for Help." *Corrections Compendium* (November):4–6.

Wheeler, Patricia A., Rebecca Trammell, Jim Thomas, and Jennifer Findlay. 1989. "Persephone Chained: Parity of Equality in Women's Prisons." *The Prison Journal* 69:88–102.

Wilson, Nancy K. 1980. "Styles of Doing Time in a Co-ed Prison: Masculine and Feminine Alternatives." Pp. 150–171 in *Co-ed Prison,* edited by J. O. Smykla. New York: Human Services Press.

Windschuttle, Elizabeth. 1981. "Women, Crime, and Punishment." Pp. 31–50 in *Women and Crime,* edited by S. K. Mukherjee and J. A. Scutt. North Sydney, Australia: Allen and Unwin.

Wood, Peter B., and Harold G. Grasmick. 1999. "Toward the Deveopment of Punishment Equivalencies: Male and Female Inmates Rate the Severity of Alternative Sanctions Compared to Prison." *Justice Quarterly* 16(1):19–50.

Wooden, Wayne S., and Jay Parker. 1982. *Men behind Bars: Sexual Exploitation in Prison.* New York: Plenum.

Wooldredge, John D., and Kimberly Masters. 1993. "Confronting Problems Faced by Pregnant Inmates in State Prisons." *Crime and Delinquency* 39:195–203.

Young, Vernetta D. 1994. "Race and Gender in the Establishment of Juvenile Institutions: The Case of the South." *Prison Journal* 73(2):244–265.

✳

Female Victims
of Male Violence

6

✳

The Image
of the Female Victim

There is widespread violence against women around the world,
based on considerations of their sex alone . . . . Violence against
women is an ancient story recounted in art, literature,
and personal accounts, but not in history books.

(CHAPMAN 1990, 54)

The image of the female victim has changed considerably in recent years.
Until the 1970s, female victims were relatively invisible. Since then, not
only has awareness of the frequency of male violence against women and
girls grown significantly, but "new" types of these victimizations have been
identified and studied. All of the types of victimizations that are discussed in
this section have always occurred, yet they have been recognized as significant
social and legal problems only since the 1970s. For example, the term *battered
woman* did not exist until 1974 (Schechter, 1982, 16), *sexual harassment* was not
a labeled behavior until 1975 (Evans 1978), and *date rape* was first identified as
a problem in the early 1980s (Warshaw 1988). Most recently, *stalking* has been
defined as the "crime of the nineties" (Wallace 1995).

Today we all have some idea of what these words (woman battering, date
rape, sexual harassment, and stalking) mean, although we may not agree on the
behaviors that constitute each. For example, some people still believe a woman
or girl wasn't raped if she drank or used drugs, invited the man or boy on
the date, wore certain types of clothes, had a "bad" reputation, or initiated

intimacy. Some people believe it is justifiable for a man to abuse his wife or girlfriend if she "talks back," gets a job, flirts with someone else, or breaks up with him. Although many people still believe the stereotypes surrounding female victimization, the frequency and facts about the sexual, physical, and emotional/psychological (e.g., stalking) victimization of women and girls have been increasingly documented. In addition to the types of violence against women and girls already listed, Chapman's (1990) list of forms of violence against women includes suttee, foot binding, infibulation, clitoridectomy, dowry death, selective malnourishment, bride burning, female infanticide, daughter neglect, forced prostitution, international sexual trafficking and slavery, homicide, human sacrifice, and pornography. This chapter looks at how women victims of male violence have been viewed historically and how awareness of their victimization has changed over time.

The focus of the next few chapters is on the victimizations most frequently associated with women and girls: sexual victimization and battering, which were labeled in 1979 as the "most underreported crimes against persons in the criminal justice system" (Gelles, 1979, 121). Unfortunately, it is beyond the scope of this book to address some of the other victimizations associated with women, particularly those involving reproductive freedom. There is substantial evidence not only of "botched" legal and illegal abortions but also of coerced and forced sterilization of women, especially poor women and women of color (see Davis, 1981; Gordon, 1977).

Both the physical and sexual victimization of women and girls have been shrouded in beliefs that these occurrences are rare, the victim's fault, and shameful for the victim. The understanding of sexual victimization has been muddled because of puritanical views of rape as an "unmentionable" crime (Sanders, 1980). Historically, battered women have been thought of as deserving victims, "nags," and inadequate wives. Although the stereotype of the "real" rape victim usually assumed the victim to be white and middle- or upper-class (Estrich 1987), the stereotype of a battered woman was of a woman involved in a "family disturbance" in a working-class or poor neighborhood. Research has shown that these stereotypes are myths: All women and girls are at risk of male violence, regardless of race, age, or ethnicity.

Although male violence against women and girls has been a historical constant, recognition of the epidemic proportions of these crimes has been relatively recent. Russell (1984) traced the recognition of various phenomena as identified social problems. Social problems are phenomena that have often occurred for centuries but were not labeled as problematic or common until data were collected and a critical mass of society accepted them as problematic. Russell (ibid., 20) identifies, in order of their appearance from the 1960s to the early 1980s, the following social problems that came to the public's attention: (1) nonsexual child abuse, (2) the rape of women by strangers and other nonintimates, (3) nonsexual wife abuse, and (4) the sexual abuse of children (particularly incest). The identification of each of these social problems helped set the stage for the others to follow. Since the publication of Russell's (ibid.) book, the threats and reality of physical and sexual dating violence, marital rape, sexual harassment, stalking, and satanic cult victimization of women and girls have been increasingly documented. It appears that for all types of "family" or "domestic" violence, girls and women are the "losers." For example, studies on *elder abuse* committed by family members highlights this as yet another area where women are the most frequent targets (Anetzberger, 1997).

Sexual abuse, battering, and stalking are not always distinct victimizations. Homes where woman battering occurs are often homes where children are physically and sexually abused as well (Edleson, 1999). Additionally, physical and sexual violence in dating or courtship relationships often go hand in hand. Many men who batter their wives or girlfriends also sexually victimize these women (Finkelhor and Yllo, 1985; Meyer, Vivian, and O'Leary, 1998; Russell, 1990, 1984; Schechter, 1982). More recent research has identified the significant role that stalking plays in woman battering, such as women and girls being followed and threatened by current or former male partners (Lowney and Best, 1995).

THE LINK BETWEEN
ACTUAL VICTIMIZATIONS
AND THE FEAR OF CRIME

A number of (male) researchers have claimed that males are far more likely to be victims of crime in general than are females (for example, Cohen and Felson, 1979; Gottfredson, 1986; Miethe et al., 1987). Other research has consistently shown that females have higher fear of crime than males (Braungart et al., 1980; Clemente and Kleiman, 1976; LaGrange and Ferraro, 1989; Ortega and Myles, 1987). One study stated that "women think they are more likely [than men] to be the victim of a personal crime" (LaGrange and Ferraro, 1989). Certainly for the crimes we typically associate with "female victims"—rape and battering—most people and researchers agree these are gendered in that males are usually the perpetrators and females are usually the victims. However, even looking at overall 1998 violent crime rates (except murder) collected across the United States through the National Crime Victimization Survey (NCVS), females constitute 30 percent of these victimizations (Rennison, 1999). Another study using National Crime Victimization Survey data to study "workplace violence" between 1992 and 1996 in the United States indicates that 83 percent of the perpetrators of violence in the workplace is committed by men, and one-third of the victims are women (Warchol, 1998). Thus, even using more traditional measures, the NCVS—which often fails to adequately measure sexual victimization (see Belknap et al., 1999)—women still constitute about one-third of violent victimizations.

Given the lower rates of female victimization reported in most statistics, some criminologists have suggested that women's higher fear of crime is irrational, and indeed women's and the elderly's low victimization rates compounded with their high fear of crime has been labeled the "paradox of fear" (by Warr, 1984, as cited in Madriz, 1997). The major problems with this rationale—that women and girls are unduly afraid of crime—are that (1) awareness of the extent and frequency with which females are victimized is relatively recent and often ignored, (2) the nature of the victimization is different for crimes associated with female victims (rape and battering), and (3) the way the culture *encourages* women and girls to be afraid of crime. Regarding the first point, the extent and frequency of females' victimizations are not clearly known because sexual victimization and battering are the least likely offenses to be reported to the police (Young, 1992). The earliest comprehensive, valid study of rape victimization not relying on police reported rapes found that 44 percent of women reported being the victims of rape or attempted rape at least once, and only 8 percent of those victimized reported it to the police (Russell, 1984). Other researchers estimate that 40 to 50 percent of women in the United States experience battering at the hands of intimate male partners (Smith, 1994; Walker, 1979).

If crimes such as rape and battering were reported to the police (or even the National Crime Survey) as consistently as the types of crimes males tend to experience, statistics would likely begin to define females as significantly more at risk of violence than males. Females' high levels of fear and low reported victimizations are likely due to researchers' unwillingness to accept fear levels as realistic assessments of risk (Young, 1992). Other research found that most women rarely tell anyone about physical and sexual intrusions because of fear, humiliation, and self-blame. Moreover, when they do tell someone, a decision is usually made to keep the incident "private" (Stanko, 1992). A number of reasons have been offered as to why women don't report physical and sexual abuse to researchers or to the police: too personal to discuss, embarrassment or shame, fear of reprisal by the abuser, or repression due to the trauma (Smith, 1994).

Although improved statistics would likely show the high risk of female victimization compared to male victimization (and some of these newer studies are reported in the next chapter), quantity alone is not sufficient to address gender differences in these crimes. It is vital to address the nature of crimes regularly perpetrated against females (Riger, 1981). With the exception of murder, rape is the most fear-inducing crime (Brodyaga et al., 1975). The severity and threat of rape cannot be overemphasized. A recent study of two major universities in Greece reported that women college students are significantly more afraid of rape than their male counterparts, they view it as a more serious crime, and they consider themselves far more likely to raped (Softas-Nall et al., 1995), which is hardly surprising but confirms how not just actual rape victimization, but the fear of rape is an important gendered aspect of our lives. Similarly, not only is battering violent, but it is additionally disturbing for the victim to receive abuse from a person who is supposed to love and care for her and on whom she and her children may be economically dependent.

The third problem (noted earlier) with perceiving women and girls as "irrational" in their fear of crime is that most women and girls are raised and conditioned to be afraid of male violence—particularly rape. Madriz (1997) provides convincing documentation of this conditioning, starting with child-hood fairy tales, such as *Little Red Riding Hood,* which teach us to constantly fear predatory males but to rely on "good males" to save us from the preda-tory ones. Women's and girls' conditioning to fear male violence comes from all around us: our parents, our siblings, and the numerous media depictions instilling fear. The media depictions range from television news "magazines" that often sensationalize rapists, stalkers, and batterers to MTV videos and "slasher" films that eroticize male violence against women or at least use it as entertainment "value." To compound this problem of raising girls to be afraid—addressed more thoroughly in the sections on the effects of culture on gender roles and victim blaming—is that when women and girls "fail" to fol-low the socially prescribed roles, such as going out alone, drinking alcohol, or wearing certain clothes—then they are often blamed by their families, the police, the courts, and others for their victimizations.

> The fear of crime, and specifically the fear of male violence, not only perpetuates the image that women are powerless, weak, and more vul-nerable than men but also feeds into the notion that women and men are not entitled to the same rights: women should not and cannot go places where men can go; women cannot engage in activities which are open to men; women should wear "proper" attire so that they are not molested by men; and since women must protect themselves and their children from criminal victimization, they had better stay home and be "good girls." Further, the fear of crime reinforces the subordinate role of women [and heterosexism]: if a woman wants to be safe and protected, she had better be accompanied by a man. (Madriz, 1997, 15–16).

Stanko (1990) views fear of danger as so commonplace in women's lives that they simply learn to manage it. In fact, fear is so routine that it is almost unrecognizable. A 63-year-old widow whom Stanko interviewed about safety was sure that she would have nothing to contribute:

> When the interview was complete, she recalled being fondled by a shop owner when she was 8, feeling physically threatened by her brother as an adult, being attacked as a nurse while working at night in a hospital and being hassled by men for sexual favors after the death of her husband. (1990, 11)

Madriz (1997) also addresses this "everyday" management of the threat of male violence in girls' and women's lives, adding significant understanding to the problem. First, she notes that fear and concern aren't the only responses women and girls have to this threat, many also report *anger.* Second, Madriz (ibid.) documents significant race/ethnicity and class differences in females' fears about and experiences with crime. More specifically, she found that white women report the highest fears of rape, which she attributes partly to the media, which most often "cast" white women or reports on white women as rape victims. Madriz (ibid.) effectively documents the important intersection between racism and sexism in the lives of women and girls of color, not only in their risks of victimization but also how the police and courts respond to them. But Madriz (ibid.) also points out the unique and significantly additional types of violence that poorer women and girls experience, such as being mugged, robbed, or even murdered in their neighborhoods, and higher levels of school violence.

Websdale (1996) points out how the social construction of who women are most threatened by is consistent with patriarchal ideology. To make his case, he examines Washington state's 1990 law and the media coverage leading up to this law on "sexual predators." He argues that the law and media focused on "predators as sick strangers," ignoring the far greater sexual predator threat to children and women *by men in their own families.* Websdale (ibid.) does not believe the passage of the act was conspiratorial in terms of legislators trying to let the most threatening men, marital rapists, and incest-perpetrating males off the hook. Rather, he states that the legislators reasoned that it would be difficult, primarily for financial reasons, for women to turn their abusive mates in if this law covered husbands and other relatives. "Nevertheless, because of the definitional imperatives of the predator law and the media sensationalization of rare one-on-one stranger violence, everyday sexual violence against women and children remains marginalized" (ibid., 49).

EFFECT OF CULTURE ON GENDER ROLES

Sex-role stereotyping begins even before birth. Not only do the names parents choose for their children often differ depending on the child's sex, but frequently parents' expectations of that child depend on the child's sex. The societal image of women as weaker, less intelligent, and less valued influences the likelihood of victimization. Women and girls have frequently been objectified and perceived "to be almost wholly passive, devoid of both judgment and decision" (Sanders, 1980, 22). Historically, men have been viewed as people, whereas women have been viewed as property (Sanders, 1980). Laws historically defined rape as theft, and rape laws were designed to protect upper- and middle-class white men in the case of their "property" (daughters and wives) being devalued by rape.

In a sense, then, many women and girls have been socialized to be victims of male violence. Girls are rewarded for passivity and "feminine" behavior, whereas boys are rewarded for aggressiveness and "masculine" behavior. These stereotypes are often reaffirmed in the media, where strong, independent female characters are rare, whereas violent, controlling male characters are abundant. Moreover, these images affect both males' and females' perceptions of males' dominance and females' (in)ability to resist male dominance. A woman or girl resisting an attacker is in need of resistance techniques that she has often been conditioned or instructed not to use (Estrich, 1987).

Our culture often suggests that women need men for protection and financial security. For example, a social expectation is that women on dates usually assume their dates will take care of them. This expectation leaves women vulnerable to date rapists who often plan situations where the woman has little control (Ehrhart and Sandler, 1985; Kanin, 1985; Martin and Hummer, 1989; Medea and Thompson, 1974; Sanday, 1990; Schwartz and De Keseredy, 1997). To compound this, men who perpetrate physical and sexual violence against women they know, or are even intimately involved with, often receive peer support from male friends who may encourage the abuse (DeKeseredy, 1988; Gwartney-Gibbs and Stockard, 1989; Martin and Hummer, 1989).

There is a tendency to view instances of male aggressiveness (violence) against women and girls as somehow "natural," just as females are supposedly inherently passive. Explanations of women experiencing male violence often center around whether male aggression was "natural" in relation to the woman's behavior (Stanko, 1985, 10). This implies that there are particular behavioral patterns and roles inherent biologically in both males and females that encourage and justify the victimization of females by males. Furthermore, it implies that women are the precipitators of men's violence and that in some cases men are justified in their violent behavior. In 1993 a judge in Ohio released a man with a criminal record to shock probation who had severely beaten his estranged wife and her daughter (from another relationship) with a crow bar. The judge blamed the woman because she had allegedly been in bed with another man when her estranged husband barged into her home. Such an image of male and female roles and behavior clearly deters the correct assignment of blame and the inhibition of male violence. A recent study of college students found that women were less likely than men to hold false beliefs inherent in rape myths. Those who believed rape myths (mostly males) were also more likely to blame the victims and support conservative gender roles (Fonow et al., 1992).

Gender stereotyping perpetuates mythical perceptions of both sexual assault offenders and victims. There is a tendency to think that only certain types of women and girls are sexually victimized and battered and that certain types of men are batterers and rapists. Raped women are often stigmatized for being "provocative" and sexually uncontrolled and for not knowing where to draw the line (Stanko, 1985). These stereotypes are frequently associated with racist and classist assumptions, such as that poor, African-American women are more likely to be battered women, and young, white, middle-class women are more likely to be sexual assault victims. Similarly, rapists and batterers are frequently assumed to be poor, black men, often mentally ill or drug addicted. Such perceptions are not based on reality and inhibit our ability to understand and protect ourselves from sexual victimizations. In the United States, most rapists are white, and 90 percent of rapes are intraracial (within race); yet African-American men are disproportionately convicted of rape (Fonow et al., 1992).

GENDER DISPARITIES IN POWER

Susan Brownmiller's book *Against Our Will: Men, Women and Rape* (1975) received a great deal of attention. As well as enlightening its many readers on the history and terror of rape, *Against Our Will* exposed the anger many women feel about living in a culture where rape is minimized, ignored, or joked about. *Against Our Will* was a path-breaking book and the first widely read feminist analysis of rape. Unfortunately, despite the power of this book in raising awareness about rape, it has also been criticized for reinforcing myths about black rapists (Davis, 1981; Tong, 1984; Williams, 1981). However, Brownmiller addresses how lynchings of blacks in the United States were racially motivated, targeting black men for fabricated rapes of white women. Overall, *Against Our Will* has had a significant impact on the discourse of rape.

A controversial contention in *Against Our Will* is the statement that rape "is nothing more or less than a conscious process of intimidation by which all men keep all women in a state of fear" (Brownmiller, 1975, 5). Brownmiller, then, views rape as a conscious means by which men control women. Russell (1984, 153), on the other hand, views rape and other male violence against women as "a consequence of the power disparity between the sexes that has existed as long as recorded history." Brownmiller sees rape as causing the disparity between women and men, whereas Russell views the power disparity between the sexes as causing rape. Consistent with Russell's (1984) belief, a cross-cultural study found that rape levels were related to the levels of society's adherence to patriarchal roles. Rape-prone societies were associated with lower levels of female power and authority, including women's lack of participation in public decision making (Sanday, 1981). Similarly, studies on Serbia (Mrsevic and Hughes, 1997) and the former Yugoslavia (Nikolic-Ristanovic, 1999) exemplify how wars often enhance not only the militarism, nationalism, and poverty within a country but also often increase adherence to tradition and patriarchy in manners that ultimately result in increased violence toward women both inside and outside the home.

A more accurate depiction of the preceding debate is that female victimization and gender-power disparity reinforce each other (see Figure 6.1). More specifically, victimization and the threat of victimization of females decrease the power of women and girls. Simultaneously, inequalities in power between males and females make females more likely to be victims and males more likely to be aggressors/offenders. There are many ways in which society, culture, and the crime-processing system contribute to this cycle of female victimization and gender-power disparity, such as advertisements linking sex and violence, images of women as passive, and police and court officials who blame victims. Thus we need to simultaneously construct the empowerment of women and girls as equal to that of men and boys in the minds of both females and males.

This power disparity is not limited to physical power but pervades most facets of our lives—men also tend to have higher economic, political, and social status than women. A study of fifty U.S. cities found that as the eco-

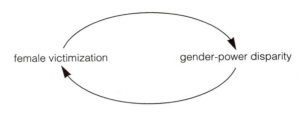

FIGURE 6.1 Cycle of Female Victimization and Gender Disparity

nomic, political, and legal status of women decreased, the rape rate increased (Baron and Straus, 1987). These more obvious power differences result in less obvious social and psychological power disparities between men and women. The aggregated gender status differences are equally obvious at the individual level. The verbal and psychological abuses of battered women exemplify this:

> Battered women consistently complain of degrading verbal abuse: "You can't do anything right"; "How could I have ever married a pig like you!" Verbal assaults, like physical ones, may go on for hours in a relentless attack on a woman's sense of dignity and self-worth and almost always include threats: "I'll cut your throat from one end to another"; "If you try to leave me, you're dead." (Schechter, 1982, 17)

Thus, power may be asserted in many forms: physically (battering), sexually, economically, and verbally. Male power, perceived and real, limits the freedom and rights of women and girls.

Sexual victimization, like woman battering, is an act of power. Sexual offenders are motivated by a desire to dominate, not simply to achieve sexual gratification. The forced sexual submission is clearly a manner of controlling and humiliating a victim; it is a way for a victim to experience that she does not have control over her own body, whereas the rapist does.

THREAT OF VIOLENCE

Although both male and female children lead lives that are restricted because they are vulnerable and need protection, such limitations often follow females for the rest of their lives. Women are constantly reminded of their vulnerability by messages from friends, family, and the media. "Such fear can induce a continuing state of stress in women and can lead to the adoption of safety precautions that severely restrict women's freedom, such as not going out alone at night or staying out of certain parts of town" (Riger and Gordon, 1981, 73). Similarly, the threat of rape may deny women employment, keep them off the streets at night, and influence them to be "passive and modest for fear that they will be thought provocative" (Griffen, 1971, 35). This myth is not confirmed by recent research reports that unemployed women are more at risk of rape than employed women (Avakame, 1999). However, the message of the vulnerability of women and girls is deeply and culturally embedded: Females should restrict their behavior, actions, and clothing, or something dreadful will happen. Women are reminded of their vulnerability and male violence every time they read or hear of another woman being raped. Moreover, women are rarely able to predict when a threatening or intimidating form of male behavior will escalate to violence. As a result, many women are frequently on guard to the possibility of men's violence, particularly if they have already been victimized (Stanko, 1985, 1990).

The battering of women by their husbands or boyfriends, similar to their sexual victimization, keeps women under the control of men. The belief that a man is the "king of his castle" is still accepted by many people in society. Battering, both actual and threatened, reduces the control the battered woman has over her life, while increasing the batterer's control. Just as sexual assault is more likely in a culture with large power disparities between the sexes, the same can be expected of the battering of women. The more authority men are perceived to hold over women, the more likely that battering will occur. The implications of woman battering are significant:

> Violence signifies crossing a boundary in which violation and degradation, previously unacceptable in a loving relationship, are now used as tools of power and coercion. Battering is far more than a single event, even for the woman who is hit once, because it teaches a profound lesson about who controls a relationship and how that control will be exercised. . . . Self-consciously exercised, violence temporarily brings a man what he wants— his wife acquiesces, placates him, or stops her demands. As a form of terrifying intimidation, violence signifies that the man's way will prevail even when the woman struggles against this imposition. Leaving her in a constantly vigilant state, violence forces a woman to worry about the time, place, or reason for the next attack. (Schechter 1982, 17)

The threatened and actual victimization of women and girls (whether it is sexual, physical, or verbal) serves to define the "place" of females in the culture. It restricts the freedom and quality of life of women and girls. Brownmiller's (1975) assertion that all men benefit from rape is more understandable when one recognizes that it is not necessary for all men to victimize all women in order for all women to be afraid of male violence. The fact that some men victimize some women serves to control most females' lives through at least some degree of fear.

This fear affects many aspects of women's lives, such as enrolling in day classes, deciding to walk on the opposite side of the street when they see an unknown male walking toward them, or deciding not to wear certain clothes for fear of being perceived as "fair game" to all men. "Women worry more than men do in the same situations: going to laundromats, using public transportation, or being downtown alone after dark" (Gordon and Riger, 1989, 14). Many women report that the fear of rape crosses their minds regularly (Gordon and Riger, 1989). Compounding the fear of victimization by strangers is the growing awareness that women and girls are more likely to be victimized by males they know.

VICTIM BLAMING

Women and girls who don't follow society's unwritten rules are often blamed if they are raped. Persons who believe that women and girls should lead restrictive lives also tend to believe that a woman or girl who "violates" these "rules" is at least partially responsible if she is victimized. Thus, many people believe that girls or women who drink alcohol, especially to the point of getting drunk, are at least partly at fault for their victimization (e.g., Bromley and Territo, 1990). Notably, while research supports the contention that alcohol (and drug) use increases the risk of sexual victimization (e.g., Schwartz and Pitts, 1995; Ward et al., 1991; Warshaw, 1988), research also indicates that women and girls are most at risk of rapes committed by current or former boyfriends and husbands (e.g., Russell, 1984). It is not a coincidence that cultural norms dictate that women should not drink, but they *should* date and marry men. One study of college women found that in addition to greater alcohol consumption being related to a greater likelihood of being raped, women who are friends with men who get women drunk in order to have sex with them are at a greater risk of sexual victimization (Schwartz and Pitts, 1995). Notably, although a recent study of college students evaluating rape scenarios found little relative victim-blaming overall, alcohol-consuming victims were viewed by *female* raters as more careless and more culpable for their victimizations (Scronce and Corcoran, 1995).

Victims of rape and battering are more likely to be blamed than victims of any other crimes. Both battered women and sexual assault victims are frequently accused of having provoked the abusive behavior. In fact, "battered wives and rape victims are often accused of 'asking for,' 'deserving,' or 'enjoying' their victimization" (Gelles, 1979, 121). If a batterer tells the police he hit his wife because she wasn't home when he got home from work, the police officer may ask the battered woman, "Why weren't you home when your husband got home from work?" Similarly, the police officer investigating a sexual assault may ask the victim why she left her door unlocked.

Rape victims are blamed for wearing certain clothing, failing to lock doors or windows, drinking alcohol, waiting for buses late at night, or hitchhiking. It is important for potential victims to know what situations increase their risk of victimization, but it is also important to remember that women don't always have access to their own transportation and that offenders, not victims, are responsible for violence. Again, although reliable statistics inform us that women are most at risk of being raped by husbands and boyfriends (see Russell, 1984), few people are prepared to tell women and girls not to date and marry.

It is not only the "person on the street" who often has preconceived ideas of what "kinds" of people get victimized. Persons responsible for the treatment of victims and punishment of offenders also are frequently misinformed. One study on the perception of sexual assault victims' reputations in court found that divorced women, women of color, and women out alone at night are stereotyped as more readily consenting to more men in more situations (Burt and Albin, 1981). "Having assumed a generalized propensity to consent and attached it to whole classes of women, this line of reasoning then particularizes the argument to this woman (victim) in this situation (alleged rape) and infers consent to this man (alleged assailant). Therefore, following this reasoning, this situation is not a rape" (ibid., 214). A review and meta-analysis of existing studies on attributions of rape victims' "responsibility" in their own victimizations indicated that the victim's *"clothing revealingness"* and *character* (e.g., sexual reputation) are most likely to result in blaming the victim, whereas the *victim-offender relationship* and her *physical attractiveness* were less important (Whatley, 1996). The implication is that certain women are "fair game" to be sexually victimized, and therefore they cannot be assessed as legitimate rape victims. Such women have supposedly lost their rights to determine with whom they are sexual. Moreover, women and girls are expected to be "sexy, but modest; attractive, but not provocative" (Gordon and Riger, 1989, 53). Obviously, these are absurd notions.

Similar to females who are sexually victimized, battered women are frequently blamed for the abuse they receive. "When activists speak about battered women, even sympathetic audiences continually scrutinize the victim's behavior, moral 'failings,' or 'stupid' reactions, returning repeatedly to the question, 'Why do these women stay?' " (Schechter, 1982, 16). One myth is that violence is a "way of life" for some people; therefore, women who are members of these "violence-prone" groups will not be as traumatized by rape or battering as other women. There are inherently classist and racist overtones in this assertion. Victimization hurts regardless of who it happens to, and violence is appropriate only when used in self-defense. The following is an excerpt from a 1984 journal article in *Victimology* depicting the abused wife's "responsibility" in her own victimization:

> The husband, perhaps burdened with a childhood in which violence was a fact of life, strikes the wife; she insults him, perhaps assaulting his masculinity or dredging up an incident from the past, or cringes, begging him to please stop, or runs away with him in hot pursuit, or laughs, or returns the blow. Any of these responses—it's a no-win game—leads to further blows, followed by further counters, etc. In a few weeks or months, the couple is locked into the twisted sequence of regenerative feedback, with no easy way out, rather like two super-powers maniacally escalating an arms race. (Erchak, 1984, 251)

This is not only an example of relieving the offender of responsibility (he was abused as a child) and blaming the victim (she insults him, insults his masculinity, and laughs at him) but is a clear example of ignoring gender-power disparity. It is unrealistic to refer to the husband and wife as "two super-powers." This is not a situation of two equals "battling it out." In analyses of why some men are violent, a common problem is claiming they are violent because of the violence that has occurred to them. Why then aren't most females violent, since they have experienced so much more victimization?

Why are some victims blamed for their victimization? One explanation is Lerner's (1965) "just world" hypothesis, which states that most people want to believe that we get what we deserve (Karmen, 1984). Therefore, when we hear of bad things happening to people, we often question behaviors that put them more at risk. In this way, we comfort ourselves by thinking "This won't happen to me because I didn't do . . . . " For instance, often when we hear that someone has cancer, one of our first thoughts is "Did she (or he) smoke?" This makes some sense because we know smoking may lead to cancer (but it is certainly not a very sensitive question!). In cases of rape, people often ask "What was she wearing?" This denies that violence is random and rarely predictable. "Assuming that women can predict their rapists' behavior sets up a situation where sexually assaulted women are blamed for not avoiding what these advisors suggest could have been avoided" (Stanko, 1985, 39).

The "just world" approach not only results in the assumption that only certain types of people can be victimized but also serves as a way for people to deceive themselves that they are free from victimization because of who they are and how they behave. Unfortunately, this is not the case—anyone can be a victim. Studies of rape victims and battered women have a difficult time determining who is most at risk because the focus of research has often been on what is unusual about the victims rather than what it is about offenders that makes them likely to rape or batter. Much of the research on woman battering has been sexist, where "aberrant behavior" is more likely to be attributed to the victim than to the offender (Wardell et al., 1983).

In line with having to accept that violence is random, it is also necessary to acknowledge that the battering and sexual victimizations of most women and girls are committed by persons known to them. Research suggests that about four in five rape victims know their assailants (National Victim Center, 1992; Russell, 1984). Estrich (1987, 10) explains how the "simple" rape cases, "the cases where a woman is forced to have sex without consent by only one man, whom she knows, who does not beat her or attack her with a gun" are far more common than the "aggravated" rape cases, characterized by extrinsic violence, multiple assailants, or no prior relationship between the victim and the offender. The issue of victim blaming is exemplified by Wolfgang's (1958) coining of the term victim *precipitation,* which focuses on the "role" victims play in their own victimization. This approach implies that victims are at least partially responsible. In 1975 a psychiatrist published the following statement in the respected *British Journal of Criminology:* "Apparently, some pedophilia offenses never lead to prosecution and consequently are not recorded by courts. Obviously, this is the case in particular when the offense is a minor one and the victim's precipitation very strong" (Virkkunen, 1975, 178).

Victim blaming for the battered woman usually comes in the form of the question "Why does she stay with him?" The implication is that if she doesn't want to be battered, she should leave her partner. This view ignores the fact that many women do leave, we just don't often hear about them. Blaming battered women for staying also ignores the economic dependence many women and their children have on the batterers and the fear many battered women have developed of being either financially destitute and/or further victimized—even killed by their abusers—if they leave. There are also the issues of family, friends, and the crime-processing system workers who often ignore the offense or encourage the victim to try to work things out. Again, victim blaming often includes asking the woman what she did to precipitate the violence. She is often blamed for starting the violence and for staying in the battering relationship. This diverts the focus from the real problem: the offender.

THE VICTIMIZATION OF WOMEN
AND GIRLS OF COLOR

The diversity of the U.S. population is such that cultural differences and the effects of racism and classism often provide vastly different life experiences. Williams (1981, 18–19) claims that Third-World women in the United States (in which she includes African-Americans) are disproportionately victims of rape, battering, and sterilization abuse. A recent study of homeless women found that women of color were more victimized overall—and raped in particular—than white women (Costin, 1992). Using NCVS data for the United States, one study reported that between 1993 and 1998 African-American women experienced the highest rates of intimate partner violence, 35 percent higher than white women's rates and about 2.5 times the rate of women of all other races (Rennison and Welchans, 2000). In this same study, regarding Hispanic ethnicity, there were no significant differences in intimate partner violence rates between Hispanics and non-Hispanics. A U.S. survey reported that Native American/Alsakan Native women had the highest lifetime rates of being raped (34 percent), followed by mixed-race women (24 percent), African-American women (19 percent), white women (18 percent), and Asian/Pacific Islander women (7 percent) (Tjaden and Thoennes, 1998). Finally, an Australian study found that Black/Aboriginal women were at increased risk of male violence, yet they are silenced, and their victimizations are too often invisible (Lucashenko 1996).

Black women have been particularly vulnerable to sexual assault historically, in slavery, and currently because of the negative images associated with them, such as being "hot-natured" and morally "loose" (Davis, 1997; Giddings, 1984, 31). DeFour (1990) and Cho (1997) effectively documents the intersection between sexism and racism regarding the risk of sexual harassment for women-of-color students on college campuses. In a discussion of racist stereotypes of African American, Latina, Asian American, and Native American women, DeFour (ibid., 48) describes how "[t]hese images either portray the women as weak and thus unlikely to fight back if harassed, or they are perceived as very sexual and thus desiring sexual attention." Ontiveros (1997, 188) carefully portrays the gender and race dynamics in sexual harassment in the workplace:

> Since workplace harassment is a power dynamic, women of color serve as likely targets because they are the least powerful participants in the workplace. Unlike white women, they are not privileged by their race. Unlike men of color, they are not privileged by gender. Although a white man might harass any woman, a man of color is not likely to feel that he has the prerogative to harass a white woman. He may feel that he is not able to harass her because of his lack of racial status or because he knows he could be subject to disproportionate reaction stemming from society's deep-seated, historical fears of attacks on white women by nonwhite men. Harassers may also prefer those women of color, such as Latinas and Asian American women, whom they view as more passive and less likely to complain.

Compounding this is the fact that it is not unusual for society or for crime-processing workers to treat women of color as if they aren't really victims. Thus, women of color appear to have disproportionately high victimization rates, yet they are much less likely to have their victimizations acknowledged. This limited and racist legal response is even more profound for immigrant women of color, particularly when they are not legal immigrants (Ontiveros, 1997).

"Racism and the rape laws are unquestionably inseparable" (Schwendinger and Schwendinger, 1983, 110). Even the laws well into the twentieth century "stated that women who worked outside the home, or whose race had a history of sexual exploitation, were outside the realm of 'womanhood' and its prerogative" (Giddings, 1984, 49). Thus, the law implied that women of color weren't legally capable of being raped. In fact, rape laws were originally mandated to protect upper-class white men whose wives and daughters could be assaulted (Davis, 1981). Thus, in addition to the rape laws emerging because of a view of women as men's property, there were significant racist and classist components in the development of these laws.

The crime-processing system and society as a whole, then, tend to minimize female victims of male violence, and this is particularly true if the victims are of color and/or poor. The incongruity between high victimization rates and low validation rates for persons of color in this society serves to further victimize and oppress this group. The lack of response by the crime-processing system may lead victims to take matters into their own hands to protect themselves. However, any female victim of sexual assault or battering who uses self-defense runs the risk of being charged with a crime herself. This is most evident for women of color, as Williams (1981) exemplifies through a large number of cases of women of color who were incarcerated for protecting themselves against violent men. These women failed to be taken seriously as victims but were taken extremely seriously as so-called offenders in their efforts to protect themselves and their children.

Chapter 1 discusses the dichotomy of women into madonnas or whores (Feinman, 1986). Women more consistent with the madonna image (for example, virgins and white women) are more likely to be viewed as legitimate victims than women in the "whore" category. None of Young's (1986) categories of black women portrays a woman who could be perceived as a legitimate victim: Amazons are viewed as capable of protecting themselves; sinister sapphires are viewed as vindictive or as precipitating the violence against them; and seductresses receive no validation as credible victims. Similarly, Tong (1984, 155) discusses how the view of black women as "less sexually puritanical than white women" is objectionable and racist, and it furthermore implies that black women do not want or need protection against male violence. Clearly, these mythical and racist views of women and girls of color affect how they are treated (or not treated) by the crime-processing system.

The black community and feminists need to join forces in fighting both racism and violence against women (Matthews, 1993; Tong, 1984; Williams, 1981). Historically, there has been a cleavage between white and African-American women fighting male violence because the black women have also had to fight the stereotype of black male offenders. In the late 1800s, black activist Ida B. Wells publicly stated that there was a focus on accusing black males of raping white females, whereas the rape of black girls and women by white males was overlooked (Giddings, 1984). "While slave masters and other white men raped black women freely, death was the punishment for a black man convicted of raping a white woman" (Schwendinger and Schwendinger, 1983, 108). The abolishment of slavery did not abolish capital punishment for black men who raped white women. Black males, "the guilty and innocent alike," are still indiscriminately brought to "justice" for rape (Davis, 1981). More recent research confirms the disproportionately harsh treatment of African-American males charged with rape compared to the treatment of white males (Walsh, 1987). Davis (1981) discusses how it has been difficult for African-American women to be active in the anti-rape movement, given the treatment of black men (particularly innocent black men) charged with rape. The anti-rape movement in the United States began at the same time as black feminism and as African-American women began feeling distrustful of white feminists (Matthews, 1993). In more recent years, however, rape-crisis centers and battered-women's shelters have become more integrated and more dedicated to combating racism as well as sexism and male violence.

THE VICTIMIZATION OF WOMEN
AND GIRLS WITH DISABILITIES

Many people assume that women and girls with physical or mental disabilities are less at risk for victimization of any kind. This erroneous assumption is based largely on two faulty beliefs. First is the belief that no one would want to harm someone who is already "harmed" or vulnerable. The second faulty belief, which is most pronounced for sexual victimizations, is that no one would find such women or girls sexually attractive. The reality is that disabled women and girls are at an *increased* risk of victimization, but the silence surrounding this violence makes their victimizations "invisible and unknown" (Chenoweth, 1996, 391). One study reported that children with disabilities in the United States are almost twice as likely as children without disabilities to be sexually victimized (Cross, Kaye, and Ratnofsky, 1995, as cited in Chenoweth, 1996). A group of mentally and/or physically disabled women and girls who is at particularly high risk of sexual victimization is those who are institutionalized (Chenoweth, 1996). Chenoweth (ibid., 405) also states that disabled women and girls are in a paradox of being perceived as *both* asexual *and* sexually promiscuous and depraved. "Once a woman's identity is constructed as asexual, the license to commit many abuses usually follows" (ibid.).

Elman's (1997, 257) research on "disability pornography," the pornography made of disabled girls and women, reports that these media "both sexualize and ridicule women and girls whose health and relative immobility make them especially vulnerable to sexual abuse." Although some of these portrayals, such as in *Playboy,* claim to liberate women with disabilities from the "stigma of sexual unattractiveness," Elman (ibid., 258) claims that pornography has never promoted sexual liberation for any women, and for disabled women and girls, their disabilities are used to sexualize their passivity and immobility, fetishizing their disabilities. Indeed, one adolescent "humor" magazine, *Slam,* "told how to rape mentally retarded girls and advised that [the boys readers] will probably get away with it" (ibid., 259). Elman compares the pornography of disabled women and girls to that of Black women, where the woman is "portrayed as a sexual object who delights in her brutal subordination" (ibid., 262). Finally, Elman (ibid., 265) describes how the sadomasochistic representations of disabled women and girls includes tying women to wheelchairs and where "orthopedic bandages replace the leather and rope" in the sadomasochistic pornography.

SUMMARY

The foremost image of the female victim has been invisibility. Battering and sexual victimization are the most underreported crimes against persons in the crime-processing system. Information on the victimization of females is becoming more widespread, including knowledge that it happens more frequently than once thought and the nature of these victimizations is more threatening and violent than once acknowledged. Moreover, culture and society tend to support gender roles that encourage the likelihood of male violence against females. Women and girls are encouraged to be passive and "ladylike," whereas men and boys are encouraged to be aggressive.

Determination of the causes of the victimization of females is grounded in the acceptance of gender disparities in power. This chapter discussed the victimization of females as both a result and a reinforcement of gender-power disparity. That is, the threat and existence of the victimization of females decreases the power of women and girls; simultaneously, this power disparity encourages victimization. Furthermore, the threat of violence against females restricts the freedom of women and girls. Fear of sexual victimization influences where, when, and how women will work, take classes, socialize, and live. Women learn they are not safe alone, at night, in certain areas of town, and with certain types of people. Compounding these restrictions is the more recent acknowledgment of the high degree of sexual victimization perpetrated by persons known, often well known, to the victim. Awareness of the prevalence and controlling nature of woman battering has also grown.

Stereotypical images in society imply that some women "ask for" rape through their clothing, behavior, and even race or class. Therefore, this view perpetuates the myth that the "real" rape victims are white, wealthy, virgins who resisted the attack. Similarly, stereotypical images imply that women who "nag," who commit adultery, or who engage in other "demasculizing" or "obnoxious" behavior precipitate their battering victimizations. Victim blaming not only holds victims responsible for the violence and exploitation against them but also mistakenly assures persons that violence is not random.

REFERENCES

Anetzberger, Georgia J. 1997. "Elderly Adult Survivors of Family Violence." *Violence against Women* 3(5):499–514.

Avakame, Edem F. 1999. "Females' Labor Force Participation." *Violence against Women* 5(8):926–949.

Baron, Larry, and Murray A. Straus. 1987. "Four Theories of Rape: A Macrosociological Analysis." *Social Problems* 34:467–489.

Belknap, Joanne, Bonnie Fisher, and Francis Cullen. 1999. "The Development of a Comprehensive Measure of the Sexual Victimization of College Women." *Violence against Women* 5(2):185–214.

Bowker, Lee. 1981. *Women and Crime in America.* New York: Macmillan.

Braungart, Margaret M., Richard G. Braungart, and William J. Hoyer. 1980. "Age, Sex, and Social Factors in Fear of Crime." *Sociological Forces* 13:55–66.

Brodyaga, A. L., M. Gates, S. Singer, M. Tucker, and R. White. 1975. *Rape and Its Victims: A Report for Citizens, Health Facilities and Criminal Justice*

Agencies. Washington, DC: Government Printing Office.

Bromley, M. L. and L. Territo. 1990. *College Crime Prevention and Personal Safety Awareness.* Springfield, IL: Charles C. Thomas.

Brownmiller, Susan. 1975. *Against Our Will: Men, Women and Rape.* New York: Simon and Schuster.

Burt, Martha R., and Rochelle S. Albin. 1981. "Rape Myths, Rape Definitions, and Probability of Conviction." *Journal of Applied Social Psychology* 11:212–230.

Chapman, Jane Roberts. 1990. "Violence against Women as a Violation of Human Rights." *Social Justice* 17(2):54–70.

Chenoweth, Lesley. 1996. "Violence and Women with Disabilities." *Violence against Women* 2(4):391–411.

Cho, Sumi K. 1997. "Converging Stereotypes in Racialized Sexual Harassment: Where the Model Minority Meets Suzie Wong." Pp. 203–220 in *Critical Race Feminism,* edited by A. K. Wing, New York: New York University Press.

Clark, Anne. 1987. *Women's Silence, Men's Violence.* London: Pandora Press.

Clemente, Frank, and Michael B. Kleiman. 1976. "Fear of Crime among the Aged." *Gerontologist* 16:211–219.

Cohen, L. E., and M. Felson. 1979. "Social Change and Crime Rate Trends: A Routine Activity Approach." *American Sociological Review* 44:588–608.

Costin, Charisse T. M. 1992. "The Influence of Race in Urban Homeless Females' Fear of Crime." *Justice Quarterly* 9:721–730.

Cross, S. B., E. Kaye, and A. C. A. Ratnofsky. 1995. *A Report on the Maltreatment of Children with Disabilities.* Washington, DC: National Center on Child Abuse and Neglect.

Davis, Angela Y. 1981. *Women, Race, and Class.* New York: Vintage Press.

Davis, Deidre E. 1997. "The Harm That has No Name: Street Harassment, Embodiment, and African American Women." Pp. 192–202 in *Critical Race Feminism,* edited by A. K. Wing, New York: New York University Press.

DeFour, Darlene C. 1990. "The Interface of Racism and Sexism on College Campuses." Pp. 45–52 in *Ivory Power: Sexual Harassment on Campus,* edited by M. A. Paludi. Albany, NY: State University of New York Press.

DeKeseredy, Walter S. 1988. *Woman Abuse in Dating Relationships: The Role of Male Peer Support.* Toronto: Canadian Scholars Press.

Edleson, Jeffrey L. 1999. "The Overlap between Child Maltreatment and Woman Battering." *Violence against Women* 5(2):134–154.

Ehrhart, Julie K., and Bernice R. Sandler. 1985. *Campus Gang Rape: Party Games?* Washington DC: Project on the Status and Eduction of Women, Association of American Colleges.

Elman, R. Amy. 1997. "Disability Pornography: The Fetishization of Women's Vulnerabilities." *Violence against Women* 3(3):257–270.

Erchak, G. M. 1984. "The Escalation and Maintenance of Spouse Abuse: A Cybernetic Model." *Victimology* 9:247–253.

Estrich, Susan. 1987. *Real Rape.* Cambridge, MA: Harvard University Press.

Evans, Laura J. 1978. "Sexual Harassment: Women's Hidden Occupational Hazard." Pp. 202–223 in *The Victimization of Women,* edited by J. Roberts-Chapman and M. Gates. Beverly Hills, CA: Sage.

Feinman, Clarice. 1986. *Women in the Criminal Justice System.* New York: Praeger.

Finkelhor, David, and Kersti Yllo. 1985. *License to Rape: Sexual Abuse of Wives.* New York: Free Press.

Fonow, Mary Margaret, Laurel Richardson, and Virginia Wemmerus. 1992. "Feminist Rape Education: Does It Work?" *Gender and Society* 6:108–121.

Frohmann, Lisa. 1991. "Discrediting Victims' Allegations of Sexual Assault: Prosecutorial Accounts of Case Rejection." *Social Problems* 38:213–226.

Gelles, Richard J. 1979. *Family Violence.* Beverly Hills, CA: Sage.

———. 1983. "An Exchange/Social Control Theory." Pp. 151–165 in *The Dark Side of Families,* edited by D. Finkelhor, R. J. Gelles, G. T. Hotaling, and M. A. Straus. Beverly Hills, CA: Sage.

Giddings, Paula S. 1984. *When and Where I Enter: The Impact of Black Women on Race and Sex in America.* Toronto: Bantam Books.

Gordon, Linda. 1977. *Women's Body, Women's Right: A Social History of Birth Control in America.* New York: Penguin Books.

Gordon, Margaret, and Stephanie Riger. 1989. *The Female Fear.* New York: Free Press.

Gottfredson, Michael R. 1986. "Substantive Contributions of Victimization Surveys." In *Crime and Justice: An Annual Review of Research.* Chicago: University of Chicago.

Griffen, Susan. 1971. "Rape: The All-American Crime." *Ramparts* (September): 26–35.

———. 1981. *Pornography and Silence.* New York: Harper Colophon Books.

Gwartney-Gibbs, Patricia, and Jean Stockard. 1989. "Courtship Aggression and Mixed-Sex Peer Groups." Pp. 185–204 in *Violence in Dating Relationships,* edited by M. Pirog-Good and J. E. Stets. New York: Praeger.

Kanin, Eugene J. 1985. "Date Rapists." *Archives of Sexual Behavior* 6(1):67–76.

Karmen, A. 1984. *Crime Victims: An Introduction to Victimology.* Monterey, CA: Brooks/Cole.

Krulewitz, J. E., and J. E. Nash. 1979. "Effects of Rape Victim Resistance, Assault Outcome, and Sex of Observer on Attributions about Rape." *Journal of Personality* 47:557–574.

LaGrange, Randy L., and Kenneth F. Ferraro. 1989. "Assessing Age and Gender Differences in Perceived Risk and Fear of Crime." *Criminology* 27:697–718.

Lerner, M. 1965. "Evaluation of Performance as a Function of Performer's Reward and Attractiveness." *Journal of Personality and Social Psychology* 1:355–360.

Lowney, Kathleen S., and Joel Best. 1995. "Stalking Strangers and Lovers: Changing Media Typifications of New Crime Problem." In *Images of Issues: Typifying Contemporary Social Problems,* 2nd ed. Joel Best (Ed.). New York: Aldine De Gruyter.

Lucashenko, Melissa. 1996. "Violence against Indigenous Women." *Violence against Women* 2(4):378–390.

Madriz, Esther. 1997. *Nothing Bad Happens to Good Girls: Fear of Crime in Women's Lives.* Berkeley: University of California Press.

Martin, Patricia Y., and Robert A. Hummer. 1989. "Fraternities and Rape on Campus." *Gender and Society* 3:457–473.

Matthews, Nancy A. 1993. "Surmounting a Legacy: The Expansion of Racial Diversity in a Local Anti-Rape Movement." Pp. 177–192 in *Violence against Women: The Bloody Footprints,* edited by P. B. Bart and E. G. Moran. Newbury Park, CA: Sage.

Medea, Andra, and Kathleen Thompson. 1974. *Against Rape.* New York: Farrar, Straus and Giroux.

Meyer, Shannon-Lee, Dina Vivian, K. Daneil O'Leary. 1998. "Men's Sexual Aggression in Marriage." *Violence against Women* 4(4):415–435.

Miethe, T. D., M. C. Stafford, and J. S. Long. 1987. "Social Differentiation in Criminal Victimization: A Test of Routine Activities/Lifestyle Theories." *American Sociological Review* 52:184–194.

Mrsevic, Zorica, and Donna M. Hughes. 1997. "Violence against Women in Belgrade, Serbia." *Violence against Women* 3(2):101–128.

National Victim Center. 1992. *Rape in America.* Arlington, VA, 18pp.

Nikolic-Ristanovic, Vesna. 1999. "Living without Democracy and Peace: Violence against Women in the Former Yugoslavia." *Violence against Women* 5(1):63–80.

Ontiveros, Maria L. 1997. "Three Perspectives on Workplace Harassment of Women of Color." Pp. 188–192 in *Critical Race Feminism,* edited by A. K. Wing. New York: New York University Press.

Ortega, Suzanne T., and Jessie L. Myles. 1987. "Race and Gender Effects on Fear of Crime: An Interactive Model with Age." *Criminology* 25:133–152.

Rennison, Callie Marie. 1999. "Criminal Victimization 1998." Bureau of Justice Statistics. U.S. Department of Justice, July, 12 pp.

Rennison, Callie Marie, and Sarah Welchans. 2000. "Intimate Partner Violence." Bureau of Justice Statistics. Department of Justice. Special Report, May, 11 pp.

Riger, Stephanie. 1981. "On Women." Pp. 47–66 in *Reactions to Crime,* edited by D. A. Lewis. Beverly Hills, CA: Sage.

Riger, Stephanie, and Margaret T. Gordon. 1981. "The Fear of Rape: A Study in Social Control." *Journal of Social Issues* 37:71–92.

Riger, Stephanie, Margaret T. Gordon, and R. K. LeBailly. 1978. "Women's Fear of Crime: From Blaming to Restricting the Victim." *Victimology* 3:274–284.

Rush, Florence. 1980. *The Best Kept Secret: Sexual Abuse of Children.* New York: McGraw-Hill.

———. 1983. "Foreword." In *I Never Told Anyone,* edited by E. Bass and F. Rush. New York: Harper and Row.

Russell, Diana E. H. 1984. *Sexual Exploitation: Rape, Child Sexual Abuse, and Workplace Harassment.* Beverly Hills, CA: Sage.

———. 1990. *Rape in Marriage.* Bloomington, Indiana: Indiana University Press.

Sanday, Peggy R. 1981. "The Socio-Cultural Context of Rape: A Cross-Cultural Study." *Journal of Social Issues* 37:5–27.

Sanday, Peggy R. 1990. *Fraternity Gang Rape.* New York: New York University Press.

Sanders, William B. 1980. *Rape and Woman's Identity.* Beverly Hills, CA: Sage.

Schechter, Susan. 1982. *Women and Male Violence.* Boston: South End Press.

Schwartz, Martin D., and Walter S. DeKeseredy. 1997. *Sexual Assault on the College Campus.* Thousand Oaks, CA: Sage

Schwartz, Martin D., and Victoria L. Pitts. 1995. "Exploring A Feminist Routine Activities Approach to Explaining Sexual Assault." *Justice Quarterly* 12:9–31.

Schwendinger, Julia R., and Herman Schwendinger. 1983. *Rape and Inequality.* Beverly Hills, CA: Sage.

Scronce, Christine A., and Kevin J. Corcoran. 1995. "The Influence of the Victim's Consumption of Alcohol on Perceptions of Stranger and Acquaintance Rape." *Violence against Women* 1(3):241–253.

Smith, Michael D. 1994. "Enhancing the Quality of Survey Data on Violence against Women: A Feminist Approach." *Gender and Society* 8:109–127.

Softas-Nall, Basilia, Achilles Bardos, and Michael Fakinos. 1995. "Fear of Rape." *Violence against Women* 1(2): 174–186. Spencer, Cassie C. 1987. "Sexual Assault: The Second Victimization." Pp. 54–73 in *Women, Courts, and Equality,* edited by L. L. Crites and W. L. Hepperle. Newbury Park, CA: Sage.

Stanko, Elizabeth A. 1985. *Intimate Intrusions: Women's Experience of Male Violence.* London: Routledge and Kegan Paul.

———. 1990. *Everyday Violence: How Women and Men Experience Sexual and Physical Danger.* London: Pandora.

———. 1992. "The Case of Fearful Women: Gender, Personal Safety and Fear." *Women and Criminal Justice* 4:117–135.

Tjaden, Patricia, and Nancy Thoennes. 1998. Prevalence, Incidence, and Consequences of Violence against Women." U.S. Department of Justice. Research in Brief. November, 16pp.

Tong, Rosemarie. 1984. *Women, Sex, and the Law.* Totawa, NJ: Rowman and Allanheld.

Virkkunen, M. 1975. "Victim-Precipitated Pedophilia Offenses." *British Journal of Criminology,* 15:175–180.

Wallace, Harvey. 1995. "A Prosecutor's Guide to Stalking." *Prosecutor.* February 29, Vol 26.

Walker, Lenore E. 1979. *The Battered Woman.* New York: Harper and Row.

Walsh, Anthony. 1987. "The Sexual Stratification Hypothesis and Sexual Assault in Light of the Changing Conceptions of Race." *Criminology* 25:153–174.

Warchol, Greg. 1998. "Workplace Violence, 1992–1996." Bureau of Justice Statistics. U.S. Department of Justice, July, 8 pp.

Ward, S.K., K. Chapman, S. White and K. Williams. 1991. "Acquaintance Rape and the College Social Scene." *Family Relations* 40:65–71.

Wardell, Laurie, Dair L. Gillespie, and Ann Leffler. 1983. "Science and Violence against Wives." Pp. 69–84 in *The Dark Side of Families,* edited by D. Finkelhor, R. J. Gelles, G. T. Hotaling, and M. A. Straus. Beverly Hills, CA: Sage.

Warr, Mark. 1984. "Fear of Victimization: Why Are Women and the Elderly More Afraid?" *Social Science Quarterly* 65:681–702.

Warshaw, Robin. 1988. *I Never Called It Rape.* New York: Harper and Row.

Websdale, Neil S. 1996. "Predators: The Social Construction of ` Stranger-Danger' in Washington State as a Form of Patriarchal Ideology." *Women and Criminal Justice* 7(2):43–68.

Whatley, Mark A. 1996. "Victim Characteristics Influencing Attributions of Responsibility to Rape Victims: A Meta-Analysis." *Aggression and Violent Behavior* 1(2):81–96.

Williams, Lynora. 1981. "Violence against Women." *The Black Scholar* (January/February):18–24.

Wolfgang, Marvin. 1958. *Patterns in Criminal Homicide.* Philadelphia: University of Pennsylvania Press.

Young, Vernetta D. 1986. "Gender Expectations and Their Impact on Black Female Offenders and Victims." *Justice Quarterly* 3:305–328.

———. 1992. "Fear of Victimization and Victimization Rates among Women: A Paradox?" *Justice Quarterly* 9:419–442.

7

✳

Sexual Victimization

DEFINING SEXUAL VICTIMIZATION

Problems arise from the limitations implied when defining the word *rape*. From 1770 to 1845 in England, rape was defined as penetration of the vagina by the penis, where ejaculation had taken place (Clark, 1987, 8–9). This was extremely difficult to prove in court. The traditional, common-law definition of rape states: "A man commits rape when he engages in intercourse . . . with a woman not his wife; by force or threat of force; against her will and without her consent" (Estrich, 1987, 8). Rape, then, has most commonly been defined as forced penile–vaginal intercourse, committed by an adult male stranger against an adult female.

There is growing awareness, however, that the majority of sexual victimizations do not fit this definition. Nevertheless, there is a tendency to minimize or redefine situations that do not meet the criteria of the traditional definition of rape. In fact, "many rape situations might be misconstrued as traditional heterosexual behavior rather than as rape. This would be especially likely when the victim offers less than extraordinary resistance" (Krulewitz and Nash, 1979, 558).

It is necessary to broaden the definition of rape. In reality, rape can occur between a variety of persons (female and male, young or old) and in many forms. Although most states have worked to expand the legal definition of rape or "sexual conduct," there still tends to be a focus on penile–vaginal penetration, as well as on violence and brutality as "proof." This definition excludes all sexual victimization of males as well as molestation, attempted rape, oral and anal rape, and sexual assaults using foreign objects. In fact, in a study of 100 women who reported rape to University Hospital in Cincinnati, Ohio, in 1985, there were 87 penile–vaginal rapes, 24 oral rapes, and 9 anal rapes.[1] Clearly, it is vital to recognize the existence and devastating effects of oral, anal, and other forms of sexual victimization. For instance, attempted rapes are often minimized as "near misses" by society, by the crime-processing system, and by the victims themselves. However, victims of attempted rapes frequently experience the psychological trauma associated with "completed" rapes.

For these reasons, it is necessary to redefine rape. Russell (1984, 21) believes that the term *sexual assault* is too restrictive because some forms of sexual conduct (in particular some instances of child sexual abuse and sexual harassment) are violating rather than violent. Russell (1984) prefers the term *sexual exploitation* over sexual assault because rape, child sexual assault, and sexual harassment all include abuse of power by the offender over the victim, whether that power is economic, physical, and/or status in nature. Similarly, Medea and Thompson (1974, 12) define rape as "any sexual intimacy forced on one person by another."

Restricting the definition of sexual victimization (or rape) decreases understanding of the problem and overlooks many cases of sexual victimization. It is important to recognize that sexual victimization consists of a variety of forms and occurs between a wide variety of persons. Because the term *rape* is associated with such a restrictive definition, the term *sexual victimization* will be used in this book in order to include the various forms of sexual violations discussed. Thus, sexual victimization will include penile–vaginal rape, anal and oral rape, molestation, sexual harassment, attempted rape, and sexual assault with foreign objects. For the purposes of this book, sexual victimization is any forced or coerced sexual intimacy.

HISTORICAL ISSUES IN DEFINING SEXUAL VICTIMIZATION

Few words in the English language have as powerful an impact as the word *rape*. Historically, children have not been educated about the meaning of rape. In spite of ignorance of its meaning, girls are raised to know that rape restricts them and is something to fear. Stanko (1985, 2) claims that "female children are even taught to be on guard for male strangers who wish to offer them candy or money to do something unspeakable (unspeakable, because, of course, few of us were ever told why male strangers might wish to offer us goodies)." The lifestyles of girls and women are affected by the specter of potential rape. They learn that their vulnerability restricts their options: where and how they live, and where and when they work and go out. They learn the conflicting messages that men are to be both feared and depended on for protection. The fine line between victimization and protection regarding women,

men, and rape has been compared to the victimization and "protection" in the Mafia; the Mafia is often feared by the very people who depend on it for protection (Griffen, 1971). Similarly, women are frequently victimized by men and yet are socialized to view men as their protectors. It is assumed that "known men will protect women from aberrant strange men's violence" (Stanko, 1992), yet women are more likely to be victimized by known men.

Turning to ancient history, *lex talionis,* better known as "an eye for an eye" system of crime processing, viewed women and girls as men's (fathers' and husbands') property. A "rape for a rape" meant that the father of a raped daughter was permitted to rape the rapist's wife (Brownmiller, 1975). "Bride capture," where a male staked a claim to a woman by raping her, was the earliest form of permanent mating relationships (ibid.). Brownmiller (ibid.) points out that rape has been so ingrained and accepted as part of society that Hebrew law did not include "Thou shalt not rape" in the Ten Commandments (although, significantly, the Ten Commandments warn against committing adultery).

Throughout history, rape laws were aimed mostly at protecting virginal daughters in wealthy families (ibid.). In the late eighteenth century, rape was used to "justify" women's "place" in the home (Clark, 1987). The system went from trivializing rape, then, to using it as an excuse to restrict women from working or traveling outside the home.

In eighteenth-century England, sexually victimized women were in a double bind if they wished to involve the court system to receive justice (ibid.). Being raped itself caused a woman to lose her credibility. Any woman charging rape had by admittance had sex (although forced) with a man not her husband. By raping a woman, a man not only victimized her but also stripped her of her credibility as a victim. Subsequently, conviction was extremely rare unless (1) the woman that proved her chastity was preserved by being "only" the victim of an attempted rape (it was much more difficult to obtain convictions for completed rapes because they implied the victim's culpability), or (2) a husband or father of a raped woman went to court to challenge his loss of property value (ibid., 47). Unfortunately, some men still view women as their property. This is addressed more thoroughly in the next chapter.

In the 1970s, when sexual victimization was first becoming defined as a social problem, the focus was on adult–stranger rapes. The effort to acknowledge two broad categories of sexual victimizations based on the victim–offender relationship has been more recent. Stranger rapes are those sexual victimizations where the victim and offender had no prior relationship. Acquaintance rapes are forced or coerced sexual intimacy by someone the victim knows. Their prior relationship could be as distant as "a friend of a friend," a neighbor, or a fellow student or as intimate as a boyfriend, husband, or father.

Sexual victimization runs on a continuum from coercion to force. Force is a physical method to obtain power, such as hitting or stabbing. Coercion is a psychological method to obtain power. Using coercion, a rapist may achieve sexual intimacy through various threats. For instance, a man may threaten a girl with telling her mother that she was smoking if she doesn't comply sexually.

A boyfriend may tell his girlfriend he will break up with her if she won't have sex with him. A foster father may threaten a girl with removal of support if she does not submit to his sexual demands. These examples of coercion show how physical force is not always necessary in order to sexually victimize.

STATISTICS ON SEXUAL VICTIMIZATION

Determining the rates of sexual victimization has been problematic for a number of reasons. First, it has been difficult to gather sexual victimization statistics. Until the National Crime Survey (NCS) was implemented in 1973, the Uniform Crime Reports (UCR) provided most of the victimization data in the United States. The UCR data are limited for any crime because they include only crimes reported to the police. This is particularly problematic for sexual victimizations because these are the most underreported of the index crimes. The humiliation and intimate violation involved in sexual victimizations make them difficult to report to strangers, be they researchers or police officers. Because many victims/survivors do not report rapes to the police or even to interviewers, the statistics on sexual victimization are often invalid.

A second limitation of sexual victimization statistics is that some victimization cases are disproportionately reported to the police depending on characteristics of the victim and the assailant. Sexual victimizations that the culture and the crime-processing system view as "real" rapes—those occurring between strangers, those where the victim is white, those where the offender is black, those where the victim has a "good reputation," and so on—are disproportionately reported to the police. Acquaintance rapes are underreported to the police because they are often more difficult to prove and the victim is more likely to feel some responsibility. "Pressure not to involve the police, fear of causing an embarrassing situation for themselves in a relatively closed community, and fear that their names will not be kept confidential often prevents victims from reporting" acquaintance rape (Parrot, 1986, 2). Similarly, although many prostitutes experience sexual victimization, these assaults are rarely reported to the police because they usually are not taken seriously. Notably, one study found that rape victims who know their attackers are not just less likely to report to the police, they are more likely to delay telling *anyone* about the rape than do stranger rape victims (Sudderth, 1998).

Sexual victimization is particularly troublesome when the victims are children. Children and youth typically are less informed of their rights, and access to crime-processing authorities is more limited. Furthermore, they are usually in less powerful positions than adults to report, particularly if the rapist is related to them.

Another significant problem concerns acquaintance rapes in which the victim and the offender had a consensual sexual relationship prior to the rape. Victims of date and marital rape sometimes fail to define their experiences as rapes or sexual victimizations. Even if they do, they believe (often correctly) that the police and the courts will not define them as rapes, so they do not report them. One study found that younger women and women who were raped by men they knew were the least likely to define the assaults as rapes (ibid.).

Just as characteristics of the victim and the offender influence reporting to the police, characteristics of the sexual victimization itself also influence the validity of rape statistics. For instance, anal and oral sexual assaults, as well as sexual victimizations with a foreign object, are less likely to be reported to the police because of the additional humiliation sometimes associated with these experiences. Also, many rape statistics don't "count" these as "real" rapes. Another reason that sexual victimization statistics are difficult to collect accurately is that there is a tendency among some victims (especially victims of attempted rape) to believe that their victimizations are not "important enough" to report to the police. Finally, many times rape victims fail to label their own victimizations as rapes (e.g., Russell, 1984; Schwartz and Leggett, 1999; Sudderth, 1998). They may not consider it rape because it is confusing and doesn't fit the "stranger-in-the-bushes-or-alley" image they've been told, or they don't want to admit that a man they would go out with is a rapist, or they blame themselves. (For a review of measuring sexual victimization, see Belknap et al., 1999.)

As mentioned in Chapter 6, Russell's (1984) San Francisco study found that 44 percent of the 930 randomly sampled women age 18 and older had been victims of completed or attempted rape (defined as completed or attempted forced penile–vaginal penetration) at some point in their lives, and 24 percent had experienced completed rapes. We refer to these rates over a person's lifetime as *prevalence* rates. Similarly, 53 percent of women in a study in Charleston County, South Carolina, reported experiencing sexual assault at least once in their lives (Murphy et al. 1988). A study by Gail E. Wyatt (1993) and her colleagues involved in-depth interviews about both consensual and nonconsensual (sexually abuse) sex with 122 white women and 126 African-American women in Los Angeles (Wyatt et al. restricted their definition of nonconsensual sex to vaginal and anal, excluding oral, rapes.) Wyatt et al. (ibid.) found that 22 percent of the women experienced rape or attempted rape as adults, and the only racial/ethnic difference was that the African-American women were more likely to delay disclosing their rape victimization to *anyone* until years later. (However, a more recent study on African-American rape survivors did *not* find a delayed reporting of the rape to others [Neville and Pugh, 1997].)

A study, termed the National Women's Study, conducted a national probability sample of over 4,000 women in the United States (National Victim Center, 1992). Rape was defined as force or threat of force to penetrate the victim's vagina, mouth, or rectum. The researchers projected that over 12 million U.S. women (or 1 in 8) have been the victims of rape at some point in their lives. A more recent national telephone survey on violence against women conducted in 1995 and 1996, the National Violence against Women (NVAW) Survey, sampled 8,000 women and 8,000 men. The NVAW survey results indicated that 18 percent of women and 3 percent of men experienced a completed or attempted rape at some point in their life, with rape defined as forced oral, anal, or vaginal intercourse (Tjaden and Thoennes, 1998). This translates into 1 in 6 women and 1 in 33 men in the United States reporting an attempted or completed rape as a child and/or as an adult.

Incidence rates, on the other hand, are measured as rates within some period, usually a year, prior to the interview or survey. The NCS/NCVS and UCR statistics are incidence rates. Russell (1984) compared her 1974 incidence rates with the 1974 UCR and NCS incidence rates because all of these methods measured rape and attempted rape in the traditional method (penile–vaginal). Russell (ibid.) found that the incidence rate in her study (3 percent in the prior year) was 13 times greater than the UCR incidence rate and over 7 times greater than the NCS incidence rate.[2] Although NCS techniques, unlike those of the UCR, capture some rapes not reported to the police, even the NCS questionnaire design is fraught with problems, bringing into question the validity of this rape measure (see Eigenberg, 1990). The NCS interviewers never directly ask respondents whether they have been raped or sexually victimized. This information is assumed to be volunteered when the respondents are asked if they have been assaulted. Nonetheless, it was recently suggested that NCS data are a likely approximation of trends in rape frequencies, while the UCR statistics better reflect police organizations' management of rape cases (Jensen and Karpos, 1993). The NCS in its now revised form, the National Crime Victimization Survey (NCVS), addressed some of the problems in the NCS with measuring rape (Bachman and Taylor, 1994). However, even this new improved measure is still fraught with problems in defining rape (see Belknap et al., 1999 and Koss, 1996).

The various studies indicate quite varied estimates of the prevalence and incidence of rape. This is likely due to the varied measures (do they include anal and oral rapes?), the sampling plans (are they phone interviews, written surveys, or in-person interviews?), and the wording. Although Russell's (1984) research design is often held up as the ideal, even it is limited because of her restricted definition of rape as penile–vaginal and because her sample excluded such high-risk women as those confined in prison and mental institutions. What is clear from the studies is that rape is a serious social and legal problem and it is highly gendered in both its perpetration and victimization.

WHO ARE THE VICTIMS?

Traditionally, "real" rape has tended to be viewed as something that happens in alleys to young, white women who are alone late at night. The offenders are often viewed as insane perverts, usually black. Chapter 6 dealt with many of these stereotypes. These misleading portrayals have been largely perpetuated by the media. Research, on the other hand, portrays all women at risk, regardless of age, race, or class. Anyone can be a victim.

Females are much more likely to be victims of sexual assault than males. Statistics from the NCS covering a 10 year period between 1973 and 1982 reported that 762 females were victims of rape or attempted rape. (Information on other sexual victimizations was not collected.) For this same time period, only 36 males reported rape or attempted rape.[3] Because of gender-power inequalities (see Chapter 6) and the societal view of women and girls, it is not surprising that females are more likely to be sexually victimized than males.

Research has also pointed out some commonalities regarding who is most at risk of rape. It is important to remember, however, that official statistics on sexual victimization overrepresent stranger assaults (because they are disproportionately reported); most sexual victimizations occur between non-strangers. The statistics imply that rape tends to occur to women between the ages of 16 and 24 (Amir, 1971; Belknap, 1987; Russell, 1984; Skogan, 1976). Black females appear to be more at risk of rape than white females (Amir, 1971; Costin, 1992; Schram, 1978; Skogan, 1976). Russell (1984) found that black females were more at risk of stranger rapes, while white females were more at risk of acquaintance rapes. Women and girls have a high risk of being raped in their own homes—even by strangers (Belknap, 1987; Sanders, 1980; Schram, 1978). Research focusing on stranger rapes also finds that rapes are more likely to occur at night and in the summer months (Amir, 1971; Belknap, 1987; Sanders, 1980).

WHO ARE THE OFFENDERS?

Groth's (1979) research on convicted sex offenders warns against describing rapists as simply "oversexed." In fact, one-third of the rapists in his study were sexually active with their wives at the time of the rapes. Similarly, many mothers of incest victims are shocked on discovering that their husbands sexually abused their daughter(s), given that their own sex lives with the perpetrator were very active (Russell, 1986). Sexual victimization is fundamentally a power issue—a need to dominate. Groth (1979, 13) describes rape as "sexual behavior in the primary service of non-sexual needs." Thus, domination is the goal, and sex is the means through which domination is achieved.

Groth's (1979) attempts to categorize types of rapists have been somewhat limited because of his focus on convicted rapists. Because only a small percentage of rapists are convicted, it is highly unlikely that convicted rapists are representative of rapists at large. Nonetheless, his three categories are useful to examine. Anger rapes are characterized by physical brutality, where sex is used to express rage and anger. Excessive force is used to dominate the victim. The second pattern, power rapes, are characterized not by the rapist wishing to harm his victim but rather by the rapist wanting to "possess her sexually" (ibid., 25). The goal is sexual conquest, and only the amount of force necessary to achieve this is used. The final pattern, the sadistic rape, fuses sexuality and aggression so that aggression itself becomes eroticized (Groth, 1979, 44).

This type of rapist finds the victim's suffering sexually gratifying. Groth's (ibid., 58) study found that 55 percent of the cases were power rapes, 40 percent were anger rapes, and about 5 percent were sadistic rapes. He contends that if his sample weren't restricted to convicted rapists, he would have seen more power rapists and fewer anger and sadistic rapists, given that anger rapes are more likely than power rapes to include corroborating evidence, and sadistic rapes are more likely to provide evidence of force—both of which increase conviction rates.

Another study of convicted rapists' perceptions of themselves and their victims found that most of the men experienced no guilt or shame regarding their behavior (Scully, 1988). Furthermore, their inability to empathize influenced their self-control, or lack thereof. Scully (ibid., 211) identified two groups of rapists: "Some of the men viewed women as opponents to be reduced to abject powerlessness. Others, adopting the cultural view of women as sexual commodities, reduced their victims to meaningless objects."

Although the crime statistics tend to show black males overrepresented as sexual offenders, Tong (1984, 166) suggests that this is because black offenders are more likely to be reported to and taken seriously by the crime-processing system. Despite the fact that the vast majority of rapes are intraracial (white on white, black on black, and so on), the U.S. legal system has followed a legacy from slavery to the present day that treats the rape of white women by black men "with more harshness than any other kind of rape" (Wriggins, 1983, 116). Wriggins (ibid.) argues that this is a result of patriarchal values (controlling both white women and African-American men). Moreover, she points out the numerous consequences of focusing on black-on-white rapes: (1) It denies all sexual victimizations of African-American women; (2) it denies the majority of sexual victimizations of white women (those perpetrated by white men); and (3) it falsely depicts rape as largely black on white and stranger oriented (given the highly segregated U.S. society). This focus on black-on-white rapes discriminates against black men and leaves out victims who are other women of color in addition to African American. As Wriggins (ibid., 117) states, "[R]ape is painful and degrading . . . regardless of the attacker's race."

The "typical rapist" has frequently been portrayed as "crazy," "sexually starved," or "psychotic." However, empirical research is unable to confirm these beliefs, and rapists are no more likely than nonrapists to be mentally ill (see Bart and O'Brien, 1985; Russell, 1984; Scully, 1990). Interviews with men who confessed to raping, as well as with men who hadn't raped, represented how many men who aren't rapists often (1) blame women for "turning them on," (2) link sex and violence, and (3) report wanting to be violent toward women they perceive as trying to "tease" them (Beneke, 1982). Just as with sexual-assault victims, rapists come from every racial, ethnic, and economic group. They include doctors, lawyers, ministers, priests, professors, politicians, and many others. Thus, just as anyone can be a rape victim, so too, can anyone be a rapist.

Why, then, do we have the common image of rapists as abnormal, African American, and oversexed? First, the media often portrays them as such. Second, women are socialized to be wary of strangers, especially strange men and there pose strong racist implications regarding which men are "strange" and threatening. And third, akin to the previously discussed "just world" hypothesis, it is probably another attempt to feel control over one's environment. We feel safer if we think we can determine whether someone is a rapist by his appearance. Unfortunately, this is not the case.

THE VICTIM–OFFENDER RELATIONSHIP

Research reports vary in the stranger-versus-acquaintance rates of sexual victimizations. This is largely a result of how the studies were conducted. For example, in a classic study from the book *Forcible Rape,* using police UCR data, 42 percent of the rapes in a study of police reports were committed by strangers (Amir, 1971), whereas 50 percent of the single-offender and 58 percent of the multiple-offender ("gang") attempted and completed rapes were committed by strangers in an NCS study (Belknap, 1987). Russell's (1984, 59) random study of women found that only 16 percent of completed and attempted rapes were committed by strangers.

Russell's (ibid.) study no doubt has the highest rates of nonstranger rapes because of her data-collection method (a process that did not rely on cases reported to the police, as did UCR statistics) and because she used a random sample where the respondents were directly asked whether they were raped (unlike NCS statistics). In any sexual victimization situation, it is difficult for the victim to report it to the police or even to an interviewer. This is particularly the case if the offender is known to the victim. First, the victim is likely to feel ashamed to admit that a friend or loved one sexually victimized her. Second, she may fear retaliation if the offender finds out that she reported him (particularly to the police but also to an interviewer or a friend). Finally, the victim of acquaintance rape may not define the situation as rape or sexual victimization.

> Many acquaintance rape victims feel that they were forced to have intercourse, but deny that they were raped. This discrepancy in terms stems from our socialization and cultural standards, which leads to the common notion that rape only happens when a stranger jumps out of the bushes. (Parrot, 1986, 4)

CHILD SEXUAL VICTIMIZATION

One of the most disturbing aspects of sexual victimization is the high degree to which children are victims. This was once thought to be a rare occurrence, particularly cases of incest. Child sexual abuse was reported to social service agencies during the 1800s, but it was not labeled as a "social problem" until the early 1980s (Gordon and O'Keefe, 1984). A 1987 article in *Psychology*

Today claimed that 40 million Americans (about 1 in 6) may have been sexually victimized as children (Kohn, 1987, 54). "There is scarcely a study, report or investigation into aspects of human sexuality which does not indicate that child–adult sex is an active, prevalent pastime" (Rush, 1980, 5).

The National Women's Study found "the majority of rape cases occurring during childhood and adolescence. Twenty-nine percent of all forcible rapes occurred when the victim was less than 11 years old, while another 32 percent occurred between the ages of 11 and 17" (National Victim Center, 1992, 3). Similarly, the National Violence against Women Survey reported that of women who were raped, 22 percent reported their first rape was when they were under 12 years old, 32 percent were when they were 12 to 17 years old, 29 percent were when they were 18 to 24 years old, and 17 percent were when they were 25 years old and older (Tjaden and Thoennes, 1998). Gail Wyatt and her colleagues' (1993) in-depth interviews with 248 adult women in Los Angeles about their childhood sexual abuses reported that when *noncontact sexual victimization* (e.g., exposure, masturbating in front of a child, or asking the child to engage in sex) was combined with *contact child sexual abuse* (e.g., molesting, or attempted or completed rape), *almost two-thirds (62 percent) of the women reported such experiences.* When Wyatt et al. (ibid.) restricted the abuse to "only" contact child sexual abuse, *almost half (45 percent) of the women reported such childhood experiences.* In one-third of these cases, the child told no one, and 70 percent of the undisclosed cases were contact sexual abuse cases (ibid.). Regarding incest, Russell (1984) found that 12 percent of the women reported familial child sexual abuse occurring when they were under 14, and 16 percent reported it occurred when they were under 18. The offenders were most likely to be fathers or uncles. These are extremely high rates for a crime that we know has such devastating psychological, and often physical, effects. A review of empirical research on the prevalence of child sexual abuse states:

> [T]here is considerable variation in the prevalence rates for child sexual abuse derived from the various North American studies. Reported rates range from 6% to 62% for females and from 3% to 31% for males. Although even the lowest rates indicate that child sexual abuse is far from an uncommon experience, the higher reported rates would point to a problem of epidemic proportions. (Peters et al., 1986, 19)

Probably no other area of crime processing has remained so hidden and protected from the public eye as child sexual abuse, particularly incest. While statistics suggest that female children are more at risk of child sexual victimization (70 percent of cases) than boys (30 percent of cases), boys—unlike men—are under substantial risk (Finkelhor and Baron, 1986, 60–64). Ninety-five percent of the perpetrators of sexual abuse against girls and approximately 80 percent of the perpetrators of sexual abuse against boys are male (Finkelhor and Baron, 1986; Russell, 1984). Thus, the victims of child sexual abuse tend to be girls, and the abusers tend to be men.

As mentioned previously, child sexual victimization was not acknowledged as a social problem until the 1980s. Prior to this, it was viewed as a taboo that rarely occurred. Just as it has been extremely difficult for adult women to "speak out" about sexual victimization, this has also been the case for children. The power of children is even further minimized by their increased psychological, emotional, and financial dependencies, in addition to their small physical statures. Given these conditions, it is not surprising that the crime of child sexual victimization has remained so invisible, despite its wide occurrence. Most child sexual abuse victims do not report their victimizations until they are adult survivors. Even then, many choose to keep it a secret or even repress the memory.

> Why is it that children who have been molested, sexually abused, or even raped rarely or never tell? They never tell for the same reason that anyone who has been helplessly shamed and humiliated, and who is without protection or validation of personal integrity, prefers silence. Like the woman who has been raped, the violated child may not be believed (she fantasized or made up the story), her injury may be minimized (there's no harm done, so let's forget the whole thing), and she may even be held accountable for the crime (the kid really asked for it). (Rush, 1983, 13)

Psychiatrist and pioneer of psychoanalysis Sigmund Freud is partly to blame for the coverup of child sexual abuse. He was amazed at the large numbers of women who reported having experienced sexual victimization as children, most often naming their fathers as the offenders. Although he initially believed his clients, other psychologists doubted him. He then restructured his theories and proposed the Oedipus complex, which is "the theory of innate erotic attraction of children to parents" (Rush, 1980, 84).

Although it is unusual for a child to wish to be "seduced," as children do not understand sexuality and sexual feelings, it is apparent that sometimes children's behavior is sexual. Often this is a "natural" curiosity, customarily "acted out" by exploring their own and often their peers' bodies (for example, playing "doctor"). People who work with children who have been sexually abused note that these children have heightened and often troubling sexual behavior. This is hardly surprising given that they have learned that this is "appropriate." This sexual behavior might also make these children more at risk for revictimization. It is the adult's responsibility to make sure that he or she does not cross sexual boundaries with the child. Unfortunately, the child victim often feels guilty about the crime that was committed against her or him. One adult survivor claims the following about her victimization:

> I felt enormously guilty about my participation in the incest, as if I had been responsible. I know now I was not. It was my father's responsibility as an adult and as a parent to prevent sexual contact between us, but I didn't understand that at the time. (Forward and Buck, 1978, 1)

Similar to the other victimizations discussed previously, the sexual abuse of children occurs in all races, neighborhoods, and income levels, and it happens with alarming frequency. It is difficult to determine patterns and realistic statistics because child sexual abuse is a covered-up crime. However, researchers have uncovered some tendencies: Abusers are usually male and usually well known to the child, the abuse is often not limited to a single episode, and the abuser rarely uses force (Gomes-Schwartz et al., 1990; Kohn, 1987).

Why do some people sexually abuse children? Just like motivations for battering and the sexual victimization of adult women, the sexual victimization of children is strongly related to power and inequality. Children are particularly at risk: "With their naivete and their natural capacity for affection, children are far more capable of idolatry than any of the adults the abuser knows" (Crewdson, 1988, 63). Groth (1979, 154) discusses how perpetrators of child sexual abuse use sex as a weapon to discharge power and/or anger in order to control their victims. "Such offenders capitalize on the relative helplessness of a child to coerce her or him into the sexual activity" (ibid.). Children abused by parents, on whom they are economically and emotionally dependent, are in extremely powerless and vulnerable positions.

> Father–daughter incest is not only the type of incest most frequently reported but also represents a paradigm of female sexual victimization. The relationship between father and daughter, adult male and female child, is one of the most unequal relationships imaginable. It is no accident that incest occurs most often precisely in the relationship where the female is most powerless. The actual sexual encounter may be brutal or tender, painful or pleasurable; but it is always, inevitably, destructive to the child. The father, in effect, forces the daughter to pay with her body for affection and care which should be freely given. (Herman, 1981, 4)

Society has been blamed for encouraging child sexual abuse through advertisements, media, and pornography, which frequently blur distinctions between adult women and girl children—women are photographed to look childish, and girls are photographed to look sensuous (Bass, 1983). It is not unusual for pedophiles to photograph their victims and exchange the photographs with other pedophiles. *Playboy* published a cartoon of a lecherous worker in a doll factory assembly line who changed one doll's voice from "Momma" to "Wanna have a party, big boy?" (Crewdson, 1988, 249). Such forms of "entertainment" perpetuate the myth that children are willing participants and are not being assaulted, abused, exploited, and raped when they have sex with adults. In reality, children are not in a position to make decisions about sex with adults.

Similar to men who rape adult women, the child sexual abuser is indistinguishable in the population (ibid., 55). In fact, as evidence to contradict the myth that child sexual abusers are "dirty old men," one study found that 71 percent of child sexual abusers were under the age of 35 (Groth, 1979). One trait that seems to be prevalent among (although not exclusive to) child sexual abusers is a high propensity toward narcissism (Crewdson, 1988). The abusers may feel unworthy and powerless, but they attempt to portray an image of importance and superiority. They often have inflated views of their appearance, abilities, and intelligence (ibid., 61). Additionally, the narcissist is better able to overcome the taboos associated with child sexual abuse because "he secretly believes that rules and laws are meant for others" and thus is less concerned with the consequences of being apprehended (ibid., 64). In this view, the child sexual abuser is primarily focused on his own well-being and gratification and sees himself as above the law.

A further disturbing aspect of child sexual abusers is the movement among some to publicly encourage adult–child sex as "healthy" and "natural." There are a number of groups such as the Rene Guyon society, which was founded in 1962 and boasts thousands of members, who advocate legalizing sex with children (ibid., 97). Their slogan is "sex by year 8, or else it's too late." Child sexual abuse quadrupled between the early 1900s and the early 1970s (Russell, 1986, 82). Five explanations for this epidemic increase include (1) an increase in child pornography and the sexualization of children; (2) the sexual revolution with its "all-sex-is-okay" philosophy; (3) the backlash against sexual equality (men who can't cope with women as equals turn to girls); (4) the recycling of untreated child sexual abuse, in which victims grow up to become victimizers; and (5) the increase in stepfamilies, where girls are especially at risk of incest (Russell, 1986).

Research has shown that initial reactions to child sexual abuse include anxiety, depression, fear, anger and hostility, and inappropriate sexual behavior (Browne and Finkelhor, 1986). While some victims of child sexual abuse become quite withdrawn, many victims react by becoming very sexual; they have "learned" that their most important asset is to service others sexually. Other research on the immediate impact of child sexual abuse found differing ranges of the effects, ranging from very serious damage to apparently unaffected children (Conte and Schuerman, 1987). In the long term, most adults and children psychologically survive child sexual abuse, but its effects can be extremely painful.

In addition to the trauma and danger that victims of child sexual abuse experience during and immediately after abuse, they frequently also experience long-term effects. Adult survivors of child sexual abuse report depression, self-destruction, anxiety, isolation, stigma, negative feelings about men, fear, and mistrust (Browne and Finkelhor, 1986; Murphy et al., 1988; Russell, 1984). Long-term behaviors that are associated with adult survivors of child sexual abuse include drug and alcohol abuse and sexual dysfunction (Browne and Finkelhor, 1986). Research also shows that sexually abused children have an extremely high rate of rape revictimization (Browne and Finkelhor, 1986; Murphy, 1991; Murphy et al., 1988; Russell, 1986, 158). Revictimization may be associated with low rates of self-esteem and high rates of chemical dependency. Low self-esteem and chemical dependency are associated with surviving sexual victimization as well as being sexually victimized. That is, rapists often "pick" victims who look vulnerable, and vulnerability is often an effect of sexual victimization.

In summary, child sexual abuse can occur to anyone, and its effects are often devastating.

The sexual abuse of children spans all races, economic classes, and ethnic groups. Even babies are its victims—hospitals treat three-month old infants for venereal disease of the throat. Sexually abused children are not more precocious, pretty, or sexually curious than other children. They do not ask for it. They do not want it. Like rape of women, the rape and molestation of children are most basically acts of violation, power, and domination. (Bass, 1983, 24)

The frequency and prevalence with which child sexual abuse occurs is outrageous. Again, power plays a tremendous role, as it does in other forms of sexual assault and sexual harassment.

DATE RAPE

Date rape is forced or coerced sexual intimacy by someone with whom one has had a romantic or dating relationship but does not include someone with whom one has been living as a spouse. Thus, date rape is one type of acquaintance rape; the victim and the assailant have experienced a relationship including some kind of romantic involvement, however briefly. Sexual victimization may occur on the first date or years into a dating relationship. It is distinct from marital rape in that the victim and the offender are neither married nor living as spouses. Date rape is not a recent phenomenon, although it has only recently been made public. Clark (1987) traces sexual assault in England between 1770 and 1845 and found that rape in courtship was not particularly unusual. She examined why some men raped the women they dated and found it was not because the women had refused them sexually, but rather the men "refused to acknowledge women's right to desire or refuse themselves, and believed they had a right to women's bodies" (Clark 1987, 85). Some of the women raped during courtship felt pressured into marrying the rapist, because views were such that a woman should be sexual only with her husband. Unfortunately, more recent research has also found that some women who are raped by their boyfriends or fiancés feel an obligation to marry them because they have already been sexual with them, however forced (Russell, 1982, 1984).

In 1957 Kanin published an article in a well-known sociology journal claiming that 62 percent of first-year college women reported experiencing some level of "offensive erotic intimacy" in the 12 months prior to starting college. Nonetheless, date rape remained unrecognized publicly until Mary P. Koss's study in conjunction with *MS.* magazine, published early in the 1980s, for which she developed the Sexual Experiences Survey to measure acquaintance/date rape (Barrett, 1982). In studies of college women, 70 to 80 percent reported having a man misinterpret the degree of sexual intimacy they desired or having a man use sexual aggression (Koss and Oros, 1982; Muehlenhard and Linton, 1987). Furthermore, 15 percent of the women and 7 percent of the men reported being involved in sexual intercourse against the woman's will, or rape, as it is commonly defined. In a more recent and larger-scale study of over 6,000 students at 32 U.S. colleges and universities, 12 percent of the women had experienced attempted rape, and another 15 percent had experienced

completed rape. Six and one-half percent of the women reported experiencing completed rape in the 12 months prior to the study. Approximately 3 percent of men reported committing attempted rapes, and 4 percent admitted
committing completed rapes (Koss et al., 1987). A recent review of this
research states that most of the studies of college women's acquaintance rape
victimizations places these as occuring to between 15 and 25 percent of college women (Rubenzahl and Corcoran, 1998). Schwartz and DeKeseredy
(1997) report similar levels of sexual victimization using a slightly modified
version of Koss's Sexual Experiences Survey on almost 2,000 women and over
1,000 men in community colleges and universities in Canada. More specifically, regarding incidence levels, about 28 percent of the women reported sexual assaults in the previous year, and 11 percent of the men reported sexually
assaulting a female dating partner in the previous year. Regarding prevalence
levels, 45 percent of the women reported a sexual assault victimization since
leaving high school, and 20 percent of the men reported committing at least
one incident of sexual assault since leaving high school (ibid., 15).

It is apparent that roughly three-fourths of college women have experienced sexual victimization (excluding sexual harassment). Approximately one
in four has experienced completed or attempted rape since the age of 14.
Eighty-four percent of these rapes were acquaintance rapes, and "[f]ifty-seven
percent of the rapes happened on dates" (see Warshaw, 1988, 11).

College students may be particularly vulnerable "[s]ince the majority of
acquaintance rape victims are between the ages of 15 and 24," with the average age of 18 (Glavin, 1986). In fact, college women are less likely to be victims of acquaintance rape the longer they are in college: Freshmen women are
most at risk, and senior women are least at risk (Parrot, 1986). Culture and
society have been blamed for the high rates of date and acquaintance rapes.
Our dating scheme often sets up conditions where the woman is at risk. For
instance, if she is expected to have her date pick her up and bring her home,
she is somewhat dependent on him. There are additional unwritten assumptions adopted by some men (and women) that if he pays for dinner, movies,
and so on, then she "owes" him sex.

In addition to dating practices negatively affecting gender differences in
power, there are also the more fundamental beliefs regarding "masculinity" and
"femininity." Women are "supposed" to be passive, weak, dependent, and yet
in control of sexual encounters with men. They are in the double bind of having to appear attractive to men but not to be sexual. Men, on the other hand,
are expected to be aggressive, strong, and independent and to take control with
women (and other men). Despite recent awareness surrounding date rape,
there are still many people who believe women don't "mean it" when they say
"no" to sex with men.

Women who have been using drugs or alcohol, who wear "revealing"
clothing, who have a reputation for being sexually "free," or who have been
intimate with the rapist prior to the rape are even less likely to be viewed as
"legitimate" rape victims—that is, as women who had a legitimate right to
say "no." Men's and women's different socialization may result in different

interpretations of the same behaviors. Some behaviors that women interpret as friendly or showing some interest in a man, men interpret as an invitation to sex; such behaviors include a woman visiting a man's apartment or accepting a ride home from a party (Spencer, 1987).

Research also indicates that to truly understand and deter sexual assaults on campus (and likely elsewhere), it is necessary to understand the role of male peer support. In particular, Schwartz and Dekeseredy (1997) effectively document in their study of Canadian college students how male peer-support, particularly in terms of belonging to male friendship/peer groups where masculinity is narrowly and traditionally defined, where there is a high degree of group secrecy and loyalty, and where women are sexually objectified is a strong precursor to date rape. They convincingly demonstrate how the socialization of males in North America in a male-dominated/patriarchal society, replete with rape myths and pornography, prepare boys/men to rape. Certainly, anecdotal cases indicate that men who belong to high-profile sports teams and fraternities have a greater sense of entitlement to rape and abuse women and girls. For example, Benedict (1998, 93) reports that "demonstrated masculinity is an occupational necessity" for male athletes, and when you combine this with an abundance of "groupies" who willingly provide sex to the male athlete, he views women and girls as "a purely sexual function" that, in turn, "shortens the distance between socially irresponsible behavior and criminal sexual assault." Descriptions of rapes in fraternities provide a similar sense of the members viewing their sexual access to women and girls as a given (see Sanday, 1990, 1996).

Boeringer's (1996) study of almost 500 U.S. male college students found that fraternity members were significantly more likely than nonfraternity members to report using intoxicants and verbal coercion to obtain sex, but they were no more likely to use physical force than nonfraternity members. Male athletes reported the highest proclivity toward rape but not greater coercive or aggressive sexual behaviors than nonathlete males. In another study, Boeringer (ibid.) found that male athletes, followed by male fraternity members, and finally a control group of male students (who were neither fraternity nor athletic team members) reported the strongest adherence to rape myths. Another study of the judicial affairs offices in Division I universities reported that male student-athletes are overrepresented in reports of the sexual victimization and intimate-partner battering of women on college campuses (Crosset et al., 1996). Schwartz and Nogrady's (1996, 148) study of a large midwestern university found that while "there was strong evidence uncovered that male peer support for victimization of women exists and that it is related to extensive alcohol use, . . . there is no evidence that fraternity men are different on these factors from other men." In summarizing some of the diverse findings from these studies regarding differently situated male college students (e.g., athletes v. nonathletes and fraternity members v. "independents"), Koss and Cleveland (1996) suggest we interpret these studies with caution given some of the methodological and conceptual problems, supporting the need for more research addressing how the environment and culture affect fraternity members' and athletes' proclivity toward and attitudes about the victimization of women.

Date rapes on college and university campuses, then, particularly in the form of gang rapes, are related to the environment of fraternities and other campus parties (Boswell and Spade, 1996; Ehrhart and Sandler, 1985; Martin and Hummer, 1989; Sanday, 1990, 1996). These studies indicate that women are most at risk of rape in settings where there is general misogyny and devaluing of women. Although most male students do not gang rape, it is important to respond to those who do. The campus gang rape can take many forms; however, there is usually a pattern. They tend to take place during parties where there is a free flow of alcohol (and often drugs), the music is loud, and women can be easily controlled and isolated. Gang rapes are particularly humiliating in that these rapes are often watched by others, are photographed, and otherwise occur with a multitude of witnesses who either decide to participate or refuse to take action (Warshaw, 1988, 102). Most victims of such gang rapes transfer to another college or drop out.

> At one Maine school, fraternity members participated in ledging: That's where, in the words of one woman graduate, "a fraternity member invites all his brothers to watch his conquest of a naive freshman woman, and then she hears about it for months afterward." The name "ledging" for this practice refers to the woman's being driven to the point of suicide by the harassment. (Warshaw, 1988, 109)

Gang rapes exhibit a bonding between the rapists, where the participants feel a need to "perform" in front of their peers. Instigators of gang rape place pressure on onlookers to participate (Groth, 1979). This pressure is probably particularly apparent between fraternity brothers. Also, male athletes' disproportionately high rates of sexual assaults have been attributed to the intense bonding of living and playing with other male athletes (Eskenazi, 1990). A combination of high-status privilege (often attributed to male athletes) and a "pack mentality" likely influences male athletes' rape-prone behavior. It is also disturbing that these onlookers (whether they are fraternity brothers, friends, and so on) usually choose to join in or at least watch but rarely feel an obligation to stop the victimization.

> [I]n some gang rapes each offender in turn becomes more aggressive than his predecessor and forces more degrading acts onto his victim, in part to prove his toughness to his cohorts, but also because it seems that, in his eyes, the victim is a whore because she is having sex with all the men in the gang. The fact that she is submitting under duress seems irrelevant. (Groth, 1979, 114)

Frequently, the assailant will purposely work to create an environment that minimizes the victim's control. Two factors often associated with acquaintance rapes are (1) the consumption of alcohol/drugs prior to the victimization, and (2) the playing of loud music (Parrot, 1986, 10). One study of campus rape found that almost all campus gang rapes involved alcohol or drugs, and every one of the fraternity gang rapes they identified involved drugs or alcohol, which helped decrease men's inhibitions and weakened women's ability to determine threatening situations and resist sexual victimizations (Ehrhart and Sandler, 1985). A study using NCVS data found that a man's drinking alcohol decreases the chances that the attempt at rape will be completed but increases the likelihood of victim injury (Martin and Bachman, 1998). Thus, alcohol likely plays gendered roles, making women and girls who use it more vulnerable to victimization due to decreased resistance abilities; at the same time it may disinhibit men and boys to "allow" them to rape but ultimately make it more difficult to accomplish.

The playing of loud music is probably used in acquaintance rapes to "cover the victim's non-compliant sounds and increase the victim's feeling of helplessness" (Parrot, 1986, 10). Alcohol and drug use and the playing of loud music serve to further debilitate the woman's ability to resist sexual victimization. Many date rapists actually plan the situation in advance in order to maximize their advantages and limit their victims' resistance (Warshaw, 1988, 87). It is not unusual for these men to invite their dates to their own or a friend's apartment on the pretext of seeing the friend or picking something up. The victim later realizes her victimization was planned, often in collusion with the "friend" who vacated the apartment. Even more disturbing, 84 percent of the men in one study "who committed rape said that what they did was definitely not rape" (ibid., 90). Notably, there is an assumption that when intoxicated women have been raped without force, but through "taking advantage" of their intoxicated state, that this is *not traumatic,* and calling it "rape" is simply a way to get over the guilt for having sex with a "bad date" (Roiphe, 1993). However, research testing this assumption found it to be false: Women raped through an inability to give consent due to intoxication were just as likely as women raped through physical force to report emotional trauma resulting from the rape (Schwartz and Leggett, 1999).

To better understand date rape, it is important to study men as well as women. One study of college men found that over half thought it was somewhat justifiable to force kissing with tongue contact, and over one-fifth thought it was somewhat justifiable to touch the woman's genitals against her wishes (Muehlenhard et al., 1985). Thirty-five percent of college males in a study in the United States and Canada reported that they would commit rape if they knew they could get away with it (Malamuth, 1981). Still another study of male college students found that 15 percent reported forcing intercourse at least once, 28 percent reported using directly coercive methods at least once, and only 39 percent denied coercive sexual involvement. Consistent with the earlier contention that some men do not listen when a woman says "no" or "stop," over one-third of college men reported ignoring a woman's protests (Rapaport and Burkhart, 1984). The most recent study on this topic involved over 100 college men, with an average age of 23.5 years old, using Koss's Sexual Experiences Survey (Rubenzahl and Corcoran, 1998). This study found that using a more encompassing definition of sexual victimization, including engaging in sexual intercourse with a woman who didn't want it by overwhelming her with continual arguments and pressure, indicated that 24 percent of these college men responded affirmatively to at least one type of acquaintance rape. When the definition was restricted to a more traditional definition of acquaintance rape, such as threatening or actually using force to obtain sex from a woman who didn't want to give it, 10 percent of these college men reported such rape behavior (ibid.).

Miscommunication is often blamed for the occurrence of date rapes. While the woman may perceive her own flirtatious behavior as simply meaning "I may be interested in you" or even "I am interested in you," she likely does not mean it to be interpreted as "I will have sex with you under any conditions." He may believe (for reasons stated earlier) that he has the "license" to force sex with her. After a date rape, even though she knows she said "no" and didn't want sex with him, and he physically forced her, she may still not define the behavior as rape. Fear, shock, confusion, guilt, disbelief, degradation, and loss of control are some of the common reactions of acquaintance rape victims. Many women, so overcome with guilt, often don't realize that they have been raped. Some victims are so preoccupied with blaming themselves for wanting to be with their date that they view the entire episode as their fault. If there were any romantic exchanges prior to the attack, such as innocent hugging or kissing, the victim often feels that she went "too far" before she said "no" and therefore caused the rape to occur by pushing the man to the edge of sexual frustration (Glavin, 1986, 3).

Although it is important to address the role of miscommunication in the occurrence of date rapes, as well as the accompanying gender differences associated with this miscommunication, it is also important not to use miscommunication as *the* explanation of date rapes. Clearly, many date rapists proceed to rape despite significant communication from victims that they are not consenting, or when the victims are asleep or passed out and unable to consent. Nonetheless, perceptions about consent are at the crux of almost every rape trial, and nowhere is this more complex and significant than date rapes—especially if she invited him out, she let him pay for dinner, she invited him to her apartment, she let him kiss her, and so on. Research from the 1980s suggests that "a gender gap in sexual communication exists" (Weiner, 1983, 147) and that males are more likely than females to interpret various behaviors and verbal communications as sexual (Abbey, 1987; Miller and Marshall, 1987; Muehlenhard, 1989). However, a more recent study reports that there are *not* significant gender differences in what men and women report as indicators of sexual interest/consent, sexual refusal/nonconsent, and sexual coercion (McCaw and Senn, 1998):

> There was a striking similarity in the cues that men and women used, across all categories that were examined. . . . [M]ale participants did not overestimate women's interest in sex. . . . Men did not dismiss women's refusals as token, nor did they simply not perceive them. . . . Finally the results of the present study suggest that most men may be well aware of those behaviors that women experience as sexually

coercive, so that relatively few men may engage in sexual coercion without realizing, or being able to realize, that is what they are doing. (McCaw and Senn, 1998, 621–622)

Similarly, another study of college men comparing sexually aggressive with sexually nonaggressive men found that more in-depth qualitative data (unlike closed-ended quantitative survey data) indicate profound differences between these two groups of college men (Yescavage, 1999). More specifically, the sexually aggressive men were more accusatory of the *victims' responsibility* in "getting herself" raped, and the sexually aggressive men's comments implied "that forced sex is a woman's consequence for allowing some sexual activity to occur" (ibid., 809). Moreover, the sexually aggressive men's comments suggest that these men know that force is being used to inflict harm. Thus, this study concludes that college men rape out of a sense of *male entitlement* more than a sense of that the victim only offered *token resistance.*

Some studies show that women tend to be more at risk of date rape the longer they have been dating someone (Henton et al., 1983; Muehlenhard and Linton, 1987). However, date rape can also occur early on in the dating relationship, even on the first date. The reason for many date rapes occurring later in the dating relationship may be that men feel more entitled to sex in a long-term relationship (Weis and Borges, 1973).

Data in recent years have shown the extent to which date rape affects young women's lives. To date, most of this research has been carried out on college campuses. While a few date rape studies have been conducted in high schools, none have been conducted on older women or younger women not in college. Future research needs to address this class and institutionalized bias. Additionally, research on fraternity rapes and rapes committed by male athletic "stars" suggests that some fraternity members and sports stars perceive that their fraternity or "star" association allows them to have sex with whomever they desire, whether it is voluntarily, coercively, or forcefully. Future research must address these perceived "privileges" and how they are fostered.

MARITAL RAPE

I've heard from many different people that martial rape cannot possibly be as bad as being raped by a stranger. To me, it is worse. It was devastating to know that the one person I trusted and shared a part of my life with could violate and traumatize me in such a way.

(BURTON, 1999, 1084)

Many people still view "marital rape" as a "contradiction in terms," believing that husbands should have complete say on when, how, and how often they have sex with their wives. Persons who adhere to these beliefs, however, are often unaware of the extreme brutality in many marital rapes, as well as the effects of routinely having sex against one's will with someone who is supposed to be loving. Unfortunately, media images of marital rape as simply a "conflict over sex" or an "unpleasant, but not particularly serious, marital squabble" have resulted in a sanitary stereotype of marital rape (Finkelhor and Yllo, 1985, 13). Marital rape is either minimized as a petty conflict (Finkelhor and Yllo, 1985) or romanticized as highly erotic for the husband and the wife (for example, in movies such as *Gone with the Wind* and *The Thorn Birds*).

Although there is still a lot to learn, research in the 1980s first addressed the issues surrounding marital rape. Most research conducted on marital rape defines it as rape in a marital relationship, including common-law marriages and sometimes persons living together as spouses although not legally married. Rape by former spouses is also typically included under the label "marital rape." Rape occurs in marriage with alarming frequency (Finkelhor and Yllo, 1983, 1985; Russell, 1982, 1984; Shields and Hanneke, 1983). In fact, Russell's (1984, 62) random sample found that 12 percent of the married women had experienced sexual assault by a husband. Another study, examining marital sexual aggression in the previous year compared married couples seeking marital counseling with a community sample of married couples *not* seeking such counseling (Meyer et al., 1998). This study found that 5 percent of the women in the counseling group reported experiencing threatened forced or actual forced sex in the previous year, whereas about one-half of one percent (0.5 percent) of the noncounseled, community group reported such aggressive sexuality in their relationships in the previous year. However, turning to husbands' use of *sexual coercion* (the pressuring of wives for sex), over one-third (36 percent) of the women in the couples' counseling group reported sexual coercion, and almost one-quarter (23 percent) of women in the community (noncounseling group) reported sexual coercion in the previous year. Research is consistent in reporting a significant overlap between couples where the man is nonsexually physically aggressive and relationships where then man is sexually aggressive. That is, men who severely abuse their wives in nonsexual ways are also likely to sexually victimize their wives (e.g., Campbell and Soeken, 1999; Finkelhor and Yllo, 1983, 1985; Meyer et al., 1998; Russell, 1982, 1984). Moreover, women who reported that their husbands used psychological aggression/abuse against them were also more likely to report that their husbands were *sexually coercive,* pressuring for sex (Meyer et al., 1998).

Researchers have identified two typologies of marital rape. The first, by Finkelhor and Yllo (1985), categorizes marital rapes as *battering rapes, nonbattering rapes,* and *obsessive rapes.* In *battering rapes,* sexual violence occurs in addition to verbal and physical violence, or rather, as part of the battering. *Nonbattering* rapes are marital rapes in relationships where there is little nonsexual physical violence, but rape occurs (usually as a result of sexual conflicts). *Obsessive rapes* are marital rapes that involve "bizarre sexual obsessions," largely perpetrated by men who (consume) considerable amounts of pornography (Finkelhor and Yllo, 1983, 123–125).

The second typology of marital rapes, by Russell (1982), is a result of her belief that Finkelhor and Yllo's typology is too limiting and not exhaustive.

Russell is concerned that the Finkelhor and Yllo typology neglects the less extreme forms of wife rape. In fact, Russell (ibid., 145) believes that although many men who physically abuse their wives also sexually abuse them, "there are probably many more wives who are raped by their husbands but not [physically] battered" in extreme and repeated forms. Therefore, Russell (ibid., 133–143) proposes the following typology of husbands in relation to wife rape:

1. Husbands who prefer raping their wives to having consensual sex with them
2. Husbands who are able to enjoy both rape and consensual sex with their wives or who are indifferent to which it is
3. Husbands who prefer consensual sex with their wives but are willing to rape when their sexual advances are refused
4. Husbands who would like to rape their wives but don't act on these desires
5. Husbands who have no desire to rape their wives

Rape by intimates is difficult to uncover. The victims themselves often redefine what they experience, believing it cannot be rape if the offender is a husband, a boyfriend, or a relative. Marital rape victims often attempt to minimize or forget that they were sexually abused by their husbands (Basile, 1999; Bergen, 1995; Kelly, 1988). In fact, many times it is not until years later, looking back at a situation, that a woman recognizes that the forced sex she experienced with her husband was indeed rape (Basile, 1999; Kelly, 1988; Sheiner, 1987). It is important in any discussion on marital rape to understand that some of the most violent rapes are rapes that occur in marriage *and* that some of the marital rapes, while highly coercive in nature, are *not* violent per se. Regarding the former point, one study found that women *sexually assaulted* by their husbands are most at risk of being *killed* by their partners (Campbell and Soeken, 1999). Research on marital rape using the NCVS data reports that marital rapes involve not only more frequent sexual assaults than other acquaintance rapes and stranger rapes, *but* marital rape survivors are less likely than the survivors of acquaintance and stranger rapes to seek medical, police, or agency help (Mahoney, 1999). Regarding the latter point, that many marital rapes are more coercive than forceful, one study found five ways in which women "give in" to unwanted sex with their husbands, presented in Figure 7.1 (Basile, 1999). These five "types of acquiescence" ranged from less serious ("I don't feel like it, but maybe I can") to more serious ("If I don't do this 'voluntarily,' he's going to make/rape me"). Thus, in this and other studies many women reported that when they tried to resist marital rape, they were injured worse, thus nonresistance was a learned mechanism to minimize the level of injuries accompanying the rape (Basile, 1999; Bergen, 1995). These studies emphasize that even the less violent/more coercive marital rapes are often symbolic of the potential for rape, gender inequality, and the perceived and real consequences when women don't respond to their husbands' sexual demands. It is likely that these same behaviors are experienced by men and women in dating relationships.

1. **Unwanted turns to wanted:** The woman did not initially want to have sex but v able to enjoy it ultimately.
2. **It's my duty:** The woman has sex because she believes it is her marital obligation, not because she wants to have sex.
3. **Easier not to argue:** The woman has sex because she can't tolerate any more verbal or nonverbal behavior from her partner, and sex is the easiest way out of the situation.
4. **Don't know what might happen if I don't:** The woman has sex because she is afraid of a negative consequence if she doesn't.
5. **Know what will happen if I don't:** The woman knew from experience that, if she didn't comply, she would be raped and/or experience other serious forms of violence.

FIGURE 5.1 Basile's Five Types of Unwanted Marital Sex/Rape by Acquiescence

Notably, martial rape was made illegal in many other countries before it was made illegal in the United States (Laura X, 1999). In the mid 1970s in Michigan, a courageous judge, Judge Victor Baum, took the liberty of breaking with legal precedent "by insisting to the jury that Judy Hartwell had a right to defend herself" from her husband who was trying to rape her, even though marital rape was not illegal anywhere in the United States at that time (ibid.). Hartwell had been charged with murdering her husband. Despite considerable resistance, the United States has gone from having marital rape a crime in only 5 states in 1978 to the 1990s, where marital rape is legally a crime in all 50 states (ibid.).

SEXUAL HARASSMENT

- A woman is walking by a construction site, and one of the workers whistles at her.
- A student goes to her professor to discuss a paper she is writing for his class, and he asks her on a date.
- A woman's supervisor tells her she has "nice legs."
- A woman's pastor tells her he knows he shouldn't, but he has sexual fantasies about her.

These are all examples of sexual harassment. Sexual harassment is typically viewed as something that happens only in the workplace or on the street. However, sexual harassment can occur anywhere, including in a college classroom, in a doctor's office, and at social gatherings. Sexual harassment can gradually erode the victim's sense of self-respect and privacy, whether it's a junior executive looking down one's blouse, an obnoxious drunk at the next table making lewd comments, or a construction worker whistling and cat-calling (Medea and Thompson, 1974, 50). Similar to discussions on other victimizations of women and girls, power plays a huge role in sexual harassment. The unwanted, intrusive, and insulting behaviors included in sexual harassment have the effect of controlling, angering, and humiliating women and girls.

Most research on sexual harassment has focused on sexual harassment in the workplace. In fact, Stanko (1985, 60) defines sexual harassment as "many forms of unwanted sexual attention that occur in working situations: visual (leering) or verbal (sexual teasing, jokes, comments, or questions) behavior; unwanted pressure for sexual favors or dates; unwanted touching or pinching; unwanted pressure for sexual favors with implied threats of retaliation for non-cooperation." The most comprehensive study on sexual harassment in the workplace was conducted by the Merit Systems Protection Board and initiated by the Subcommittee on Investigations of the House Committee on Post Office and Civil Service. This 1981 report involved questionnaires completed by 20,000 randomly selected federal employees. They found that 15 percent of all male employees and 42 percent of all female employees reported sexual harassment on the job. A study conducted on almost 1,000 workers in Taiwan found that 36 percent of the women and 13 percent of the men reported sexual harassment at work (Luo 1996). The harassment typically took the form of unwanted sexual jokes and comments, followed by deliberate body touching, and requests and pressure for dates. Most of the harassment was by co-workers of the opposite sex and the victims attributed the harassment to the harrasers' insensitivity (ibid.).

Sexual harassment has been viewed as existing on a continuum of five levels: (1) *gender harassment* involves sexist remarks "putting down women" but not necessarily sexual in nature, (2) *seductive behavior* includes behaviors such as sexual advances or requests to discuss the victim's personal and sexual life, (3) *sexual bribery* is where sex is solicited with a promise of a reward, (4) *sexual coercion* involves threatening someone with punishment for failing to comply with a sexual demand, and (5) *sexual assaults, gross sexual imposition, and indecent exposures* constitute the last and most severe level (Till, 1980). For clarification, an example of sexual bribery is where a student is asked out on a date by her professor, indicating that it will help her grade, whereas sexual coercion would be a professor telling a student if she didn't go out with him, she would flunk the course. Thus, these five levels, as listed, imply the least to the most serious types of sexual harassment. It is evident that sexual harassment is often very confusing for the victims, who feel they "should be" flattered by the attention but aren't or are even afraid.

Legally, sexual harassment has been identified as potentially occurring in two manners. The first, *quid pro quo harassment* involves trading educational or work sustenance or advancement for sexual favors. That is, the victim is promised a grade, a job, a promotion, or some other educational or work "favor" for complying with a sexual request. The second way that sexual harassment has been legally defined as operating is called *hostile environment sexual harassment*. This type of sexual harassment involves behaviors, "decorations," and so on that make a person's work or educational environment intimidating or offensive.

The causes of sexual harassment are exemplified in a recent study of over 1,000 men and over 300 women serving in combat positions in the U.S. military (Rosen and Martin, 1998). This study found that the male officers' *tolerance of sexual harassment* was related to their reported levels of *hostility toward women, negative masculinity* (measured as characteristics believed to be socially undesirable for both sexes, but more prevalent in males, such as greed, arrogance, selfishness, cynicism, and boasfulness), *acceptance of women as equals,* and *race*. As expected, men reporting higher levels of tolerance for sexual harassment reported higher levels of hostility toward women and hypermasculinity and lower levels of acceptance of women as equals (ibid.). Notably, African-American male soldiers were significantly less tolerant of sexual harassment than were white soldiers, and African–American female soldiers were less tolerant of sexual harassment than white female soldiers.

The coercion involved in sexual harassment cannot be overstated. Just as a woman may decide to take a less convenient route to her destination to avoid sexual harassment on the street, women students or women workers may reasonably fear they will do poorly in a class or be fired or denied promotions at work if they refuse to put up with the sexual harassment. It has been suggested that such women keep their jobs at the expense of their self-respect (Farley, 1978). Women are increasingly deciding to confront their harassers, either informally or through university or job policies or laws. The 1991 U.S. Senate confirmation hearings regarding the appointment of Clarence Thomas helped advance awareness on sexual harassment more than anything to date. Thomas was confronted with accusations of sexually harassing Anita Hill, a former employee, at the Equal Employment Opportunity Center office. Although Thomas was confirmed, much of the country was moved by Hill's integrity, and many victims and survivors of sexual harassment came forward to tell their stories as well.

Many people view sexual harassment as harmless or even flattering. Besides having an effect that is often demeaning (making victims feel "cheap" or like a "piece of meat" or a "sexual object"), sexual harassment is yet one more manner in which women are controlled. One article on sexual harassment on the street states that "the message is not that you are attractive enough to make a man lose his self-control but that the public realm belongs to him and you are there by his permission as long as you follow his rules and as long as you remember your place" (Benard and Schlaffer, 1997, 396). The threat behind sexual harassment cannot be minimized. The victim is often unsure as to what degree the harasser will go to attempt to demean or control her. If she confronts the harasser for whistling, might she end up being physically sexually assaulted? The severity of sexual harassment is witnessed in a study where more than one in five women reported being sexually assaulted (that is, raped) by someone they knew from work (Schneider, 1991). One study involved the researchers asking street sexual harassers why they do it (Benard and Schlaffer, 1997). Most of these men minimized their behaviors and claimed it was a result of boredom or the camaraderie they felt with other men when they did it. Most had not given it any thought, but about 15 percent claimed that they purposely set out to humiliate and anger their victims (ibid.).

Fear of losing jobs or promotions or failing courses and so on if they stand up to sexual harassment at work and school keeps women and girls from pursuing their goals and careers. The threat of sexual harassment also serves to keep women from pursuing or maintaining jobs traditionally held by males, which are also the jobs that pay the most. This is not to imply that jobs traditionally held by women are free from sexual harassment.

> In such [traditionally female] jobs a woman is employed as a woman. She is also, apparently, treated like a woman, with one aspect of this being the explicitly sexual. Specifically, if part of the reason the woman is hired is to be pleasing to a male boss, whose notion of a qualified worker merges with a sexist notion of the proper role of women, it is hardly surprising that sexual intimacy, forced when necessary, would be considered part of her duties and his privileges. (MacKinnon, 1979, 18)

Clearly, sexual harassment is not harmless when it has such devastating effects. Yet, a study of prime-time television shows reported that sexual harassment on television is both highly visible *and* highly invisible. That is, 84 percent of the shows had at least one incident of sexual harassment, but they were presented as humorous, harmless, and easy for the "victims" to end (Grauerholz and King, 1997). Some research has been conducted at universities in order to determine levels of sexual harassment. A review of research on sexual harassment on college campuses reported that the most common perpetrators of sexual harassment on college campuses are professors and that approximately one-third of undergraduate and graduate women report sexual harassment victimizations by a faculty member over the course of their education (Belknap and Erez, 1997). A more recent study, comparing 1989 and 1993 rates of undergraduate women who were seniors at a northeastern public university in the United States, found that the incidents of sexual harassment decreased during this four-year period from 25 percent to 20 percent (McCormack, 1995). Although the rate decreased, still one in five of these women had experienced sexual harassment over the course of their undergraduate experience. Also, even though faculty members and to some extent university staff were identified as offenders, the most common perpetrator was fellow students (ibid.).

Sexual harassment is a problem that occurs on the job, on the street, in the classroom, in the library, and many other places. Some recent publications evaluate sexual harassment in religious settings (Majka, 1991; Whitson, 1997), also a place not covered by the work or education legal definition of where sexual harassment can be charged. Notably, a focus group study of African-American Methodist women found that, although they reported significant levels of sexual harassment in the male-dominated church setting, they were reluctant and unlikely to report it to their church community or leaders because they were afraid they would be blamed for it (Whitson, 1997).

In sum, sexual harassment can be as "mild" as leering and as extreme as a physical sexual assault. Sexual harassment demeans women; it poses a threat, thus serving as a control over women. It can limit women economically from pursuing certain careers or cause them to lose jobs, wages, or promotions. Sex-

ual harassment can dictate when and where women and girls feel safe to
and in which social communities they can even informally report it. In
sexual harassment occurs to many women in many environments.

SEXUAL VICTIMIZATION AND THE CRIME-PROCESSING SYSTEM

The sexual assault victim has frequently been referred to as being twice victimized: once by her assailant and once by the crime-processing system. But
not just police, judges, and juries have been reported to be ignorant about sexual victimization and hostile to the victims. Often times even family members
and friends respond with hostility toward rape victims, and this is particularly
true when the women or girls were raped by men they knew (Sudderth,
1998). There are also accounts of doctors, nurses, therapists, and administrators who behave insensitively to victims, often failing to take victimizations
seriously. An analysis of 100 years (from 1880 to 1980) of medical indexes
found a recurring theme, particularly in indexes prior to 1960, of advice to
view rape victims as liars and to "be extremely meticulous in your examination and history, as many women and girls falsely accuse men of sexual assault;
if you make erroneous hasty conclusions, you may be responsible for sending
an innocent man to his death" (Mills, 1982, 53). Fortunately, Mills (1982)
reports improvements by physicians and hospitals since then.

The sexual assault victim is likely not to have any witnesses to her assault.
If she decides not to inform anyone of her victimization, it is usually "easy"
for her to keep her victimization a secret. Unfortunately, this lack of witnesses
has served to further hurt her chances of being viewed as a victim if she decides
to report the incident. The victim may decide not to tell anyone, to tell only
a close friend or relative, to tell the police, and/or to tell a rape-crisis center.
Rape-crisis centers have proven helpful in providing the victim with a variety
of services. In addition to emotional support, they usually provide volunteers
to accompany the victim to the hospital, to the police department, and to
court if she opts to use any of these services.

Victims who formally report the assault will likely have to deal with
responses from a variety of persons, including physicians, counselors, family,
and friends, as well as the various actors of the crime-processing system.
Making their victimizations public, then, often requires survivors to deal
with various persons' views and beliefs, as well as myths associated with rape.
Regardless of responses by the police and courts, the community response is
important. If there are no community services for rape victims, or if the
community values sexist and rape-supportive myths, "then the victims' needs
will undoubtedly go unaddressed" (Koss and Harvey, 1991, 95). However, a
study of fraternity gang rapes found that people who publicly condemned
"the brothers" received obscene calls and death threats over the phone (Sanday, 1990).

The Police

Sexual victimization is particularly difficult for the victims to make public because of the shame involved, the fear of retaliation by the assailant, and the need to convince others (sometimes even themselves) that they did not "ask for" or deserve the assault. The first contact most victims have with the criminal justice system is the police. The police serve an important function, not only in that they are the first contact but also that victims are dependent on the police to "make" the case for them. Victims' fears of the way police view rape, rapists, and the rape victims themselves often inhibit them from formally reporting the crime (LeDoux and Hazelwood, 1985, 211). Rape victims, unlike other victims, must often prove nonconsent, with the assumption that most women lie when charging rape (Spencer, 1987, 56).

Consistent with this, researchers argue that rape is far more susceptible to unfounding than other crimes (Brownmiller, 1975; Russell, 1984). *Unfounding* refers to the practice by which police determine that a "victim" is making false charges. As a result, the case is dropped. Rape is more susceptible to unfounding because of the mistaken belief that women "cry" rape after consensual sex in order to protect their reputations. More recently, some departments have forbidden the unfounding of rape cases. It is likely that unfounding is less common today, but little effort has been made to document this.

One study in Indianapolis found that the police unfounded rape cases because of complaints about the victim's moral character or conduct (71 percent), lack of victim cooperation (20 percent), and technical reasons (such as the rape occurring outside of the departmental jurisdiction) (9 percent) (LaFree et al., 1985). Notably, "nonconforming" victims—women who hitchhiked, had sex outside of marriage, went to bars without male escorts, and willingly went to the defendant's apartment—were less likely to have their cases result in arrests (ibid.).

A study of over 2,000 police officers found that although police officers are not insensitive to rape victims overall, they "are suspicious of victims who meet certain criteria, such as previous and willing sex with the assailant, or who 'provoke' rape through their appearance or behavior" (LeDoux and Hazelwood, 1985, 219). Furthermore, some of these officers strongly agreed with statements such as "Nice women do not get raped," and "Most charges of rape are unfounded." Rapes that police determine to be unfounded never appear in official statistics of victimization (such as the UCR), thus increasing the invisibility of sexual victimization. Significantly, a study of police officers, counselors, rapists, and citizens found that both citizens and the police were more closely aligned with rapists' attitudes toward rape than they were to counselors' views of rape (Feild 1978).

Russell (1984) found that only 8 percent of attempted or completed rapes were reported to the police, and the National Victim Center (1992) found that 16 percent of forcible rapes were reported to the police. As expected, stranger rapes are far more likely than acquaintance rapes to be reported (ibid.). Furthermore, 86 percent of U.S. women reported they would be less likely to report a rape to the police if the media disclosed victims' names (National Victim Center, 1992). Other studies found that on the average, only 5 percent of the child sexual assault cases and 5 percent of date rape cases were reported to the police (Russell, 1984; Warshaw, 1988). Problems of credibility, insensitivity, and invisibility are not restricted to the adult sexual assault victim. The crime-processing system has been criticized for its inadequate treatment of and response to the victims of child sexual abuse, particularly incest victims. A 1979 journal published the following:

> Most police officers, however, use an adversary approach when conducting an interview with a child-victim because it is an approach with which they are familiar. The police officer also employs this approach because the child victim must convince the officer that an offense has been committed. Furthermore, the officer must determine the victim's potential effectiveness as a courtroom witness. (Kirkwood and Mihaila, 1979, 681)

Given the perceptions held by a significant portion of the population of the police being (1) insensitive to rape victims, and (2) racist in processing cases, it is hardly surprising that women and girls of color may feel some community pressure not to report rapes (or batterings), particularly when their abusers are also of color. One of the few studies to address this involved interviews and surveys of African-American women rape survivors (Neville and Pugh, 1997). The women in this study reported moderate support for the hypothesis that African-American women experience police officers' reputation for hostility and unfairness to African Americans as a barrier to reporting their rape victimizations to the police. Notably, however, a more significant barrier reported by the women in this study was the nonracial reputation police as a group have for their treatment of rape victims (ibid.).

The Court Process, or "Whose Trial Is It, Anyway?"

Assuming that her sexual assault case is not unfounded by the police and a suspect has been identified, the victim may choose to prosecute if there is an identifiable offender. However, the unfounding pattern may not have ended with the police. Now it is the prosecutor's turn to determine whether the accuser is "really a victim" and whether the case is worth the prosecutor's time (not taking the victim's wants or needs into account). Like police, prosecutors rely on gender stereotypes in their efforts to assess "credible" female victims (Stanko, 1982). Thus, the prosecutor's reliance on irrelevant characteristics about the victim and the prosecutor's acceptance of rape myths may result in the victim's not being able to prosecute. In short, prosecutors and judges have been accused of having the same limited attitudes about rape that many police hold (LaFree, 1989).

Less than 35 percent of arrests for rapes end up in convictions (Estrich, 1987, 17); the rest are dismissed or acquitted. Of the 670 attempted and completed rapes reported in Russell's (1984) study, only 2 percent resulted in arrests, and 1 percent resulted in convictions. LaFree (1989) found that 37 percent of rape cases reported to the police ended in arrests, 12 percent resulted in guilty pleas or verdicts, 6 percent went to trial, and less than 5 percent resulted in a prison sentence. A more recent study of over 1,000 court rape cases in Detroit reported that, in 18 percent of the cases, all charges were dismissed, and in 34 percent of the cases, the court cases ended in a conviction, two-thirds of the defendants were incarcerated, and the average maximum sentence in months for the convicted rapist was 167 (Spohn and Spears, 1996). Another study analyzed prosecutors' unfounding of rape cases and found that of victims who report to the police, rape victims are just as likely to want to take their cases to court as aggravated assault, robbery, and burglary victims. However, rape victims are more likely to be perceived as lying by prosecutors than are aggravated assault, robbery, and burglary victims. "[R]ape victims are as willing to undergo the ordeal of the court process as are other victims, despite the fact that it may be more grueling for them. However, they are less frequently believed than other victims" (Williams, 1981, 32). A more recent study found that judges still base their decisions on who they view as "genuine" or "real" rape victims, and women who are "risk takers"—women who hitchhike, walk alone late at night, go to a bar alone, or use alcohol or drugs—are less likely to have their court cases result in a conviction, particularly if the offender is black and the victim is white (Spohn and Spears, 1996).

Prosecutors' ignorance of the dynamics surrounding sexual victimization negatively affects victims who attempt to secure prosecution of their rapists. A study of prosecutors' screening of sexual assault cases found a centrality of victim discredibility in the prosecutors' decisions to reject many rape cases (Frohmann, 1991). This was done by looking for discrepancies in the victim's account or between the victim's account and the police report and trying to determine whether the victim had ulterior motives for filing a false report (for example, not wanting to tell her boyfriend she got a venereal disease from consensual sex with another man). These decisions were heavily based on the often incomplete and mistaken police reports and on the victim's criminal connections. "Rap" sheets chronicling a person's arrests and convictions were routinely run on victims who were homeless, who were involved in illegal activities, or who simply lived in African-American and Latino neighborhoods, but they were not run on women from the wealthier, "white" part of the city (ibid.). Typifications of the victim's behavior and knowledge of the victim's personal life also influenced prosecutors' decisions to reject rape cases. What prosecutors may think is "typical" rape behavior is likely inaccurate, yet it often affects their perceptions of victims' credibility. "Unless we are able to challenge the assumptions on which these typifications are based, many rape cases will never get beyond the filing process because of unconvictability" (ibid., 224).

A number of factors influence whether a rape charge results in a conviction. Estrich (1987, 18–19) identifies three such factors: (1) the victim–offender relationship, (2) the amount of force used by the defendant and the level of resistance offered by the victim, and (3) the quality of the evidence (that is, the perceived plausibility of the victim's testimony and whether her account can be corroborated).

Studies on the relationship between the victim and the offender in sexual assault cases consistently find that convictions are less likely in cases where the victim knows the offender than in "stranger rapes" (Estrich, 1987; Russell, 1984; Williams, 1981). Although victims are much more likely to be able to identify the assailant in acquaintance rapes, stranger rapes are much more likely to be taken seriously by the crime-processing system (and most of the public) and to result in convictions. This is particularly troubling given that most sexual assaults are perpetrated by men known to the victim. Similarly, evidence about the victim's lifestyle, such as drinking, drug use, or extramarital sexual activity, also affects the verdict (LaFree et al., 1985). In fact, rape trials often seem more concerned with the victims' than the offenders' accountability, responsibility, and personal characteristics. Ironically, one study found that while the defendant's criminal history did not affect the likelihood of his conviction, the victim's criminal history significantly affected whether the offender was convicted (Williams, 1981).

Research has also addressed how levels of both offender aggression and victim resistance influence perceptions that a rape actually occurred. Predictably, both influence impressions of rape culpability. The greater the level of force used by the offender, the more likely the behavior will be labeled rape (Burt and Albin, 1981; Goodchilds and Zeliman, 1984). Similarly, the more actively a woman resists, the better chance she has of being viewed as a legitimate victim (Deitz et al., 1984; Gilmartin-Zena, 1988).

Regarding the quality of the evidence in rape cases, Williams (1981) found that witnesses and traces of physical evidence (such as torn clothing and the presence of sperm) positively affected the likelihood of conviction. Similarly, a review of empirical research found that medical corroboration and corroboration by a witness significantly improved the chances of conviction in sexual victimization cases (Estrich, 1987, 17). Conditions for child sexual abuse victims also tend to lack adequate crime-processing system responses. One problem is that even when conclusive medical evidence exists, the child is frequently too young to testify. If the child does testify, she or he is not exempt from the typical abrasiveness and victim blaming of defense lawyers. Finally, given the alarming number of child sexual abusers, it is not unlikely that at least one will end up on a jury (Crewdson, 1988).

The process of making her victimization public is likely to be a painful process for the sexually assaulted victim. In addition to shame and depression, she is likely to experience frustration and anger toward persons who are supposed to be helping her bring the offender to justice. However, there are costs to not prosecuting. A victim may experience a sense of denial of her victimization if she doesn't prosecute, as well as inhibiting the possibility of punishing the rapist. The victim who does not report may also feel a sense of responsibility that the rapist is free to continue assaulting other victims. On the other hand, deciding to take the case through the crime-processing system may not necessarily result in a sense of vindication. As stated previously, many women who have experienced sexual victimization fear how the police, lawyers, judges, and juries will respond to them.

The sexual assault victim, then, may suffer not only at the hands of the rapist but also through her experiences with the police department and the court system. Both the movie *The Accused,* starring Jodie Foster, and the real-life rape trial of William Kennedy Smith portrayed how women who charge rape are often treated in court.

Konradi's (1996) study of rape survivors' preparation for court describes how these women are aware of how they must battle victim-blaming and sexist stereotypes in their efforts to have their rapists found guilty. She found that these survivors engaged in six kinds of activities to prepare for the witness stand. First, they did *appearance work* through their clothing and make-up in order to demonstrate respect, conservativism, and nonsexual images. Second, they used the strategy of *rehearsal* through repeatedly telling the events of the rape to supporters before the trial due to their fears that they would become too emotional and cry and/or incorrectly remember the sequencing of events. Third, the survivors used *emotion work* in efforts to obtain the "correct" court demeanor, one who was polite, composed, deferent to the court's authority, and *not* angry or in pain. Fourth, the survivors worked on *team building,* or the recruiting of the appropriate support system to be available and present during the trial. (This might involve asking certain people, such as parents, *not* to attend.) Fifth, the survivors conducted *role research* in order to educate themselves about the rape law, the legal process, and potential court occurrences. Finally, the survivors used *case enhancement,* by bringing documents supporting their case to the legal personnel or the court case itself (ibid.). Not surprisingly, in this study the survivors who were the most critical of the process heard irregularly from the legal personnel about their cases and felt that the prosecutors were not invested in their cases. In sum, it is evident that while many women in society are cognizant of the often sexist and victim-blaming court systems, many of the court practitioners are not.

Turning to sexual harassment, litigation of these cases did not occur until the mid-1970s. One review of the laws surrounding this victimization reported that sexual harassment in the workplace (via Title VII of the Civil Rights Act) and in educational settings (via Title IX of the Civil Rights Act) is illegal but that claiming sexual harassment outside of these environments is almost impossible legally (Belknap and Erez, 1997). "[S]exual harassment occurs in many other contexts in which unwelcome sexual remarks or advances may disadvantage their recipients, but there appears to be little legal recourse available to these victims" (ibid., 154).

SUMMARY

This chapter explained the limitations inherent in how the term *rape* has traditionally been defined. To fully understand and measure sexual victimization, it is necessary to acknowledge that people are sexually victimized in many ways in addition to forced penile–vaginal penetration between adult strangers. The rate of sexual victimization in this country is much higher than once thought, particularly between acquaintances. Increased awareness of the probability of stranger rapes of adult women occurred in the 1970s. Next, the uncovering of acquaintance rapes of adult women occurred. Finally, in the early 1980s, the sexual abuse of children, particularly incest, became defined as a social problem, if not a national epidemic. Awareness of date and marital rape followed shortly after the identification of child sexual abuse as a social problem.

Of the eight index crimes, rape is the least likely to be reported. In addition to the humiliation associated with sexual victimization, victims may fear the offenders' retaliation or lack of support by the crime-processing system, and/or they may blame themselves for the assault. In the case of child sexual abuse, the victim may not be in a situation to report the behavior or even to understand that she or he has been victimized. Thus, in spite of increased attention by the media and researchers, for many reasons sexual victimization remains a highly invisible crime.

Determination of rates of sexual victimization has been hampered by some of the following factors: (1) Rape is one of the crimes that victims are least likely to report to the police; (2) stereotypical characteristics of the victim and the offender (such as whether they are strangers, whether she has a "bad reputation") often are mistakenly used to determine whether the rape was "real"; (3) the nature of the sexual victimization (that is, the increased humiliation of having been anally or orally raped or raped by a husband) may deter the victim from reporting; and (4) the victims of attempted rapes may perceive their victimizations as "not important enough to report" because they weren't "really" raped.

Although the NCS data collection method provides a more accurate assessment than the UCR of the degree to which rapes occur in the United States, neither the NCS nor the UCR adequately assesses the frequency of sexual victimization because of their methods of questioning and, in the case of the UCR, data collection. (Specifically, the UCR relies on rapes reported to the police, which presents a skewed picture of the overall distribution of rapes.) Improved data-collection methods have uncovered the high likelihood of U.S. females being sexually victimized, particularly by their families, close friends, and dates.

It was not until the 1980s that child sexual abuse was labeled a social problem. In a relatively short period of time, we have become aware that it may occur to as many as 62 percent of female children and 31 percent of male children (Peters et al., 1986). Child sexual victimization has remained invisible for the same reasons that the sexual victimization of adult women has remained invisible. However, in most cases, children are even less empowered than adult women to physically resist sexual victimization and to be able to report their victimizations.

Young women who have recently left home (for college or work) are also a high-risk group for sexual victimization. Date rape has recently been identified as a sexual problem. Research has also highlighted gang rapes on college campuses, where the victim and rapists knew each other prior to the assault.

This appears to be particularly prevalent during fraternity and dormitory parties and by male athletes. These rapes are frequently planned, using alcohol, drugs, and loud music to debilitate the victim (Parrot, 1986).

Sexual harassment is a form of sexual victimization. It is behavior that is sexual in nature and empowers the harasser by demeaning the victim. Occurrence of this behavior is most frequently associated with the workplace, but more recently, it is recognized as occurring anywhere: in educational settings, at work, in social settings, and on the streets. Sexual harassment is one more method by which women are threatened and their lives are shaped.

Unfortunately, many persons experiencing sexual victimization are further victimized through their encounters with the crime-processing system. Police and courts have frequently been found to be suspicious of any women, and often children, who claim to have been sexually victimized. Disbelief and cynicism on the part of the crime-processing authorities is most prevalent in the cases that occur most frequently and in which the victim is most likely to be able to identify the offender: acquaintance rapes. It is necessary for police officers, judges, and lawyers to be educated about the realities of sexual victimization. This education is also necessary for the public, not only because they serve on juries, but also in order that they may stop their own rape-prone behaviors and/or be supportive when someone they know experiences sexual victimization. Rape awareness education may reduce women's and girls' sexual victimization by making them aware of what makes them most at risk, as well as educating males about what constitutes rape and why it is illegal and immoral.

NOTES

1. *Cincinnati* magazine, December, 1986. These do not add up to 100 because some women were victims of more than one category of sexual victimization.

2. Russell (1984) had to extrapolate her data to make the necessary comparisons with the UCR and NCS findings, based on differences in sampling and reporting techniques. For instance, Russell's data are for persons 18 years old and older, the NCS is for persons 12 and older, and the UCR includes persons of all ages.

3. This is from analysis by the author on 10 years of NCS data (1973–1982).

REFERENCES

Abbey, Antonia. 1987. "Misperceptions of Friendly Behavior as Sexual Interest." *Psychology of Women Quarterly* 11:173–194.

Amir, Manachem. 1971. Patterns in Forcible Rape. Chicago: University of Chicago Press.

Bachman, Ronet, and Taylor, B. M. 1994. "The Measurement of Family Violence and Rape by the Redesigned National Crime Victimization Survey." *Justice Quarterly* 11:499–512.

Barrett, Karen. 1982. "Date Rape: A Campus Epidemic?" *Ms. Magazine*

(September): 49–51, 130.

Bart, Pauline B., and Patricia H. O'Brien. 1985. *Stopping Rape: Successful Survival Strategies.* New York: Pergamon Press.

Basile, Kathleen C. 1999. "Rape by Acquiescence: The Ways in Which Women 'Give in' to Unwanted Sex with Their Husbands." *Violence against Women* 5(9):1017–1035.

Bass, Ellen. 1983. "Introduction: In the Truth Itself, There Is Healing." Pp. 23–61 in *I Never Told Anyone,* edited by E. Bass and L. Thornton. New York: Harper and Row.

Belknap, Joanne. 1987. "Routine Activity Theory and the Risk of Rape: Analyzing Ten Years of National Crime Survey Data." *Criminal Justice Policy Review* 2:337–356.

Belknap, Joanne, and Edna Erez. 1997. "Redefining Sexual Harassment." *Justice Professional* 10:143–159.

Belknap, Joanne, Bonnie Fisher, and Francis Cullen. 1999. "The Development of a Comprehensive Measure of the Sexual Victimization of College Women." *Violence against Women* 5(2):185–214.

Benard, Cheryl, and Edit Schlaffer. 1997. " 'The Man in the Street': Why He Harasses." Pp. 395–398 in *Feminist Frontiers IV,* edited by L. Richardson and V. Taylor. New York: McGraw-Hill.

Benedict, Jeffrey R. 1998. *Athletes and Acquaintance Rape.* Thousand Oaks, CA: Sage.

Beneke, Timothy. 1982. *Men on Rape: What They Have to Say about Sexual Violence.* New York: St. Martin's Press.

Bergen, Raquel Kennedy. 1995. "Surviving Wife Rape." *Violence against Women* 1(2):117–138.

Boeringer, Scot B. 1996. "Influences of Fraternity Membership, Athletics, and Male Living Arrangements on Sexual Aggression." *Violence against Women* 2(2):134–147.

———1999. "Associations of Rape-Supportive Attitudes with Fraternal and Athletic Participation." *Violence against Women* 5(1):81–90.

Boswell, A. Ayres, and Joan Z. Spade. 1996. "Fraternities and Collegiate Rape Culture." *Gender and Society* 10(2):133–147.

Browne, Angela, and David Finkelhor. 1986. "Impact of Child Sexual Abuse: A Review of the Research." *Psychological Bulletin* 99:66–77.

Brownmiller, Susan. 1975. *Against Our Will: Men, Women and Rape.* New York: Simon and Schuster.

Burt, Martha R., and R. S. Albin. 1981. "Rape Myths, Rape Definitions, and Probability of Conviction." *Journal of Applied Social Psychology* 11:212–230.

Burton, Davie. 1999. "My Struggle." *Violence against Women* 5(9):1084–1085.

Campbell, Jacquelyn C., and Karen L. Soeken. 1999. "Forced Sex and Intimate Partner Violence." *Violence against Women* 5(9):1017–1035.

Clark, Anne. 1987. *Women's Silence, Men's Violence: Sexual Assault in England, 1770–1845.* London: Pandora Press.

Cluss, Patricia A., Janice Broughton, Ellen Frank, Barbara Duffy Stewart, and Deborah West. 1983. "The Rape Victim: Psychological Correlates of Participation in the Legal Process." *Criminal Justice and Behavior* 10:342–357.

Conte, John R., and John R. Schuerman. 1987. "The Effects of Sexual Abuse of Children." *Journal of Interpersonal Violence* 2:380–390.

Costin, Charisse T. M. 1992. "The Influence of Race in Urban Homeless Females' Fear of Crime." *Justice Quarterly* 9:721–730.

Crewdson, John. 1988. *By Silence Betrayed: Sexual Abuse of Children in America.* Boston: Little, Brown.

Crosset, Todd W., James Ptacek, Mark A. McDonald, and Jeffrey R. Benedict. 1996. "Male Student-Athletes and Violence against Women." *Violence against Women* 2(2):163–179.

Deitz, Sheila R., Madeleine Littman, and Brenda J. Bentley. 1984. "Attribution of Responsibility for Rape: The

Influence of Observer Empathy, Victim Resistance, and Victim Attractiveness." *Sex Roles* 10:261–280.

Ehrhart, Julie K., and Bernice R. Sandler. 1985. *Campus Gang Rape: Party Games?* Washington, DC. Association of American Colleges.

Eigenberg, Helen M. 1990. "The National Crime Survey and Rape: The Case of the Missing Question." *Justice Quarterly* 7:655–672.

Eskenazi, Gerald. 1990. "The Male Athlete and Sexual Assault." *New York Times,* June 30, p. 27.

Estrich, Susan. 1987. *Real Rape.* Cambridge, MA: Harvard University Press.

Farley, L. 1978. *Sexual Shakedown: The Sexual Harassment of Women on the Job.* New York: Warner.

Feild, H. S. 1978. "Attitudes toward Rape: A Comparative Analysis of Police, Rapists, Crisis Counselors, and Citizens." *Journal of Personality* 36:156–179.

Finkelhor, David, and Larry Baron. 1986. "High Risk Children." Pp. 60–88 in *A Sourcebook on Child Sexual Abuse,* edited by D. Finkelhor. Beverly Hills, CA: Sage.

Finkelhor, David, and Kersti Yllo. 1983. "Rape in Marriage: A Sociological View." Pp. 119–131 in *The Dark Side of Families: Current Family Violence Research,* edited by D. Finkelhor, R. J. Gelles, G. T. Hotaling, and M. A. Straus. Beverly Hills, CA: Sage.

———. 1985. *License to Rape: Sexual Abuse of Wives.* New York: Free Press.

Forward, Susan, and Craig Buck. 1978. *Betrayal of Innocence: Incest and Its Devastation.* Middlesex, England: Penguin Books.

Frohmann, Lisa. 1991. "Discrediting Victims' Allegations of Sexual Assault: Prosecutorial Accounts of Case Rejection." *Social Problems* 38:213–226.

Gilmartin-Zena, Pat. 1988. "Gender Differences in Students' Attitudes toward Rape." *Sociological Focus* 21:279–292.

Glavin, A. P. 1986. *Acquaintance Rape: The Silent Epidemic.* Massachusetts Institute of Technology, Campus Police Department, March.

Gomes-Schwartz, Beverly, Jonathan M. Horowitz, and Albert P. Cardearelli. 1990. *Child Sexual Abuse: The Initial Effects.* Newbury Park, CA: Sage.

Goodchilds, Jacqueline D., and Gail L. Zellman. 1984. "Sexual Signaling and Sexual Aggression in Adolescent Relationships." Pp. 233–243 in *Pornography and Sexual Aggression,* edited by N. M. Malamuth and E. Donnerstein. Orlando, FL:Academic Press.

Gordon, Linda, and Paul O'Keefe. 1984. "Incest as a Form of Family Violence: Evidence from Historical Case Records." *Journal of Marriage and Family* 46:27–34.

Grauerholz, Elizabeth, and Amy King. 1997. "Prime Time Sexual Harassment." *Violence against Women* 3(2):129–148.

Griffen, Susan. 1971. "Rape: The All-American Crime." *Ramparts* (September):26–35.

Groth, A. Nicholas. 1979. *Men Who Rape: The Psychology of the Offender.* New York: Plenum Press.

Henton, J., R. Cate, J. Koval, S. Lloyd, and S. Christopher. 1983. "Romance and Violence in Dating Relationships." *Journal of Family Issues* 4:467–482.

Herman, Judith L. 1981. *Father–Daughter Incest.* Cambridge, MA: Harvard University Press.

Jensen, Gary F., and Mary Altani Karpos. 1993. "Managing Rape: Exploratory Research on the Behavior of Rape Statistics." *Criminology* 31:363–386.

Kanin, Eugene J. 1957. "Male Aggression in Dating–Courtship Relations." *American Journal of Sociology* 63:197–204.

Kelly, Liz. 1988. "How Women Define Their Experiences of Violence." Pp. 114–132 in *Feminist Perspectives on Wife Abuse,* edited by K. Yllo and M. Bograd. Newbury Park, CA: Sage.

Kirkwood, L. J., and M. E. Mihaila. 1979. "Incest and the Legal System: Inadequacies and Alternatives." *University of California–Davis Law Review* 12:673–699.

Kohn, Alfie. 1987. "Shattered Innocence." *Psychology Today* (February):54–58.

Konradi, Amanda. 1996. "Understanding Rape Survivors' Preparations for Court." *Violence against Women* 2(1):25–62.

Koss, Mary P. 1996. The Measurement of Rape Victimization in Crime Surveys. *Criminal Justice and Behavior* 23:5–69.

Koss, Mary P., and Hobart H. Cleveland III. 1996. "Athletic Participation, Fraternity Membership, and Date Rape." *Violence against Women* 2(2):180–1990.

Koss, Mary P., C. A. Gidycz, and N. Wisniewski. 1987. "The Scope of Rape: Incidence and Prevalence of Sexual Aggression and Victimization in a National Sample of Higher Education Students." *Journal of Consulting and Clinical Psychology* 55:162–170.

Koss, Mary P., and Mary R. Harvey. 1991. *The Rape Victim: Clinical and Community Interventions,* 2nd ed. Newbury Park, CA: Sage.

Koss, Mary P., and C. J. Oros 1982. "Sexual Experiences Survey: A Research Instrument Investigating Sexual Aggression and Victimization." *Journal of Consulting and Clinical Psychology* 50:455–457.

Krulewitz, J. E., and J. E. Nash. 1979. "Effects of Rape Victim Resistance, Assault Outcome, and Sex of Observer on Attributions about Rape." *Journal of Personality* 47:557–574.

LaFree, Gary D. 1989. *Rape and Criminal Justice: The Social Construction of Sexual Assault.* Belmont, CA: Wadsworth.

LaFree, Gary D., Barbara F. Reskin, and Christy A. Visher. 1985. "Jurors' Responses to Victims' Behavior and Legal Issues in Sexual Assault Trials." *Social Problems* 32:389–407.

LeDoux, J. C., and R. R. Hazelwood. 1985. "Police Attitudes and Beliefs toward Rape." *Journal of Police Science and Administration* 13:211–220.

Lott, B., M. E. Reilly, and D. R. Howard. 1982. "Sexual Assault and Harassment: A Campus Community Case Study." *Signs* 8:296–319.

Luo, Tsun-Yin. 1996. "Sexual Harassment in the Chinese Workplace." *Violence against Women* 2(3):284–301.

MacKinnon, Catherine A. 1979. *Sexual Harassment of Working Women.* New Haven, CT: Yale University Press.

Mahoney, Patricia. 1999. "High Rape Chronicity and Low Rates of Help-Seeking among Wife Rape Survivors in a Nonclinical Sample." *Violence against Women* 5(9):993–1016.

Majka, L. 1991. "Sexual Harassment in the Church." *Society* May/June:14–21.

Malamuth, Neil M. 1981. "Rape Proclivity among Males." *Journal of Social Issues* 37:138–157.

Martin, P. Y., and R. Hummer. 1989. "Fraternities and Rape on Campus." *Gender and Society* 3:457–473.

Martin, Susan E., and Ronet Bachman. 1998. "The Contribution of Alcohol to the Likelihood of Completion and Severity of Injury in Rape Incidents." *Violence against Women* 4(6):694–712.

McCarty, M. 1986. "Rape." *Cincinnati Magazine,* December, pp. 58–64.

McCaw, Jodee M., and Charlene Y. Senn. 1998. "Perception of Cues in Conflictual Dating Situations." *Violence against Women* 4(5):609–624.

McCormack, Arlene Smith. 1995. 'Revisiting Sexual Harassment of Undergraduate Women." *Violence against Women* 1(3):254–265.

Medea, Andra, and Kathleen Thompson. 1974. *Against Rape.* New York: Farrar, Straus and Giroux.

Merit Systems Protection Board. 1981. *Sexual Harassment in the Federal Workplace: Is It a Problem?* Office of Merit Systems Review and Studies. Washington DC. Government Printing Offices.

Meyer, Shannon-Lee, Dina Vivian, K. Daneil O'Leary. 1998. "Men's Sexual

Aggression in Marriage." *Violence against Women* 4(4):415–435.

Miller, Beverly, and Jon C. Marshall. 1987. "Coercive Sex on the University Campus." *Journal of College Student Personnel* 28:38–47.

Mills, Elizabeth A. 1982. "One Hundred Years of Fear: Rape and the Medical Profession." Pp. 29–62 in *Judge, Lawyer, Victim, Thief,* edited by N. H. Rafter and E. A. Stanko. Stoughton, MA: Northeastern University Press.

Muehlenhard, Charlene L. 1989. "Misinterpreted Dating Behaviors and Risk of Rape." Pp. 241–256 in *Violence and Dating Relationships,* edited by M. A. Pirog-Good and J. E. Stets. New York: Praeger.

Muehlenhard, Charlene L., D. E. Friedman, and C. M. Thomas. 1985. "Is Date Rape Justifiable? The Effects of Dating Activity, Who Initiated, Who Paid, and Men's Attitudes toward Women." *Psychology of Women Quarterly* 9:297–310.

Muehlenhard, Charlene L., and M. A. Linton. 1987. "Date Rape and Sexual Aggression in Dating Situations: Incidence and Risk Factors." *Journal of Counseling Psychology* 34:186–196.

Murphy, John E. 1991. "An Investigation of Child Sexual Abuse and Consequent Victimization: Some Implications of Telephone Surveys." Pp. 79–88 in *Abused and Battered: Social and Legal Responses to Family Violence,* edited by D. D. Knudsen and J. L. Miller. New York: Aldine De Gruyter.

Murphy, Shane M., Dean G. Kilpatrick, Angelynne Amick-McMullan, Lois J. Veronen, Janet Paduhovich, Connie L. Best, Lorenz A. Veilleponteaux, and Benjamin E. Saunders. 1988. "Current Psychological Functioning of Child Sexual Assault Survivors." *Journal of Interpersonal Violence* 3:55–79.

National Victim Center. 1992. *Rape in America.* Arlington, VA, 18 pp.

Neville, Helen A., and Aalece O. Pugh. 1997. "General and Culture-Specific Factors Influencing African American Women's Reporting Patterns and Perceived Social Support following Sexual Assault." *Violence against Women* 3(4):361–381.

Parrot, Andrea. 1986. *Acquaintance Rape and Sexual Assault Prevention Training Manual.* Department of Human Services Studies. Ithaca, NY: Cornell University.

Peters, Stefanie D., Gail E. Wyatt, and David Finkelhor. 1986. "Prevalence." Pp. 15–59 in *Sourcebook on Child Sexual Abuse,* edited by D. Finkelhor. Beverly Hills, CA: Sage.

Rapaport, K., and B. R. Burkhart. 1984. "Personality and Attitudinal Characteristics of Sexually Coercive Males." *Journal of Abnormal Psychology* 93:216–221.

Roiphe, Katie. 1993. *The Morning After.* Boston: Little, Brown.

Rosen, Leora N., and Lee Martin. 1998. "Predictors of Tolerance of Sexual Harassment among Male U.S. Army Soldiers." *Violence against Women* 4(4):491–504.

Rubenzahl, Samuel A., and Kevin J. Corcoran. 1998. "The Prevalence and Characteristics of Male Perpetrators of Acquaintance Rape." *Violence against Women* 4(6):713–725.

Rush, Florence. 1980. *The Best Kept Secret: Sexual Child Abuse of Children.* New York: McGraw-Hill.

———. 1983. "Foreword." Pp. 13–14 in *I Never Told Anyone,* edited by E. Bass and L. Thornton. New York: Harper and Row.

Russell, Diana E. H. 1982. *Rape in Marriage.* New York: Collier Books.

———. 1984. *Sexual Exploitation: Rape, Child Sexual Abuse, and Workplace Harassment.* Beverly Hills, CA: Sage.

———. 1986. *The Secret Trauma: Incest in the Lives of Girls and Women.* New York: Basic Books.

Sanday, Peggy Reeves. 1990. *Fraternity Gang Rape: Sex, Brotherhood, and Privilege on Campus.* New York: New York University Press.

————. 1996. *A Woman Scorned: Acquaintance Rape on Trial*. New York: Doubleday Press.

Sanders, William B. 1980. *Rape and Woman's Identity*. Beverly Hills, CA: Sage.

Schneider, Beth E. 1991. "Put Up and Shut Up: Workplace Sexual Assault." *Gender and Society* 5:533–548.

Schram, Donna D. 1978. "Rape." Pp. 53–80 in *The Victimization of Women*, edited by J. R. Chapman and M. Gates. Beverly Hills, CA: Sage.

Schwartz, Martin D., and Walter S. DeKeseredy. 1997. *Sexual Assault on the College Campus*. Thousand Oaks: Sage.

Schwartz, Martin D., and Molly S. Leggett. 1999. "Bad Dates or Emotional Trauma? The Aftermath of Campus Sexual Assault." *Violence against Women* 5(3):251–271.

Schwartz, Martin D., and Carol A. Nogrady. 1996. "Fraternity Membership, Rape Myths, and Sexual Aggression on a College Campus." *Violence against Women* 2(2):148–162.

Scully, Diana. 1988. "Convicted Rapists' Perceptions of Self and Victim: Role Taking and Emotions." *Gender and Society* 2:200–213.

Scully, Diana. 1990. *Understanding Sexual Violence*. Boston: Unwin Hyman.

Sheiner, Marcy. 1987. "Battered Women: Scenes from a Shelter." *Mother Jones* (November): Pp. 15–19, 43–44.

Shields, Nancy M., and Christine R. Hanneke. 1983. "Battered Wives' Reactions to Marital Rape." Pp. 132–148 in *The Dark Side of Families: Current Family Violence Research*, edited by D. Finkelhor, R. J. Gelles, G. T. Hotaling, and M. A. Straus. Beverly Hills, CA: Sage.

Skogan, Wesley G. 1976. "The Victims of Crime: Some National Survey Findings." In *Criminal Behavior in Social Systems*, edited by A. L. Guenther. Chicago: Rand-McNally.

Spencer, Cassie C. 1987. "Sexual Assault: The Second Victimization."

Pp. 54–73 in *Women, Courts, and Equality*, edited by L. L. Crites and W. L. Hepperle. Newbury Park, CA: Sage.

Spohn, Cassia, and Jeffrey Spears. 1996. "The Effect of Offender and Victim Characteristics on Sexual Assault Case Processing Decisions." *Justice Quarterly* 13(4):649–680.

Stanko, Elizabeth A. 1982. "Would You Believe This Woman? Prosecutorial Screening for 'Credible' Witnesses and a Problem of Justice." Pp. 63–82 in *Judge, Lawyer, Victim, Thief*, edited by N. H. Rafter and E. A. Stanko. Stoughton, MA: Northeastern University Press.

————. 1985. *Intimate Intrusions: Women's Experience of Male Violence*. London: Routledge and Kegan Paul.

————. 1992. "The Case of Fearful Women: Gender, Personal Safety and Fear of Crime." *Women and Criminal Justice* 4:117–135.

Sudderth, Lori K. 1998. " 'It'll Come Right Back at Me': The Interactional Context of Discussing Rape with Others." *Violence against Women* 4(5):559–571.

Till, F. J. 1980. Sexual Harassment: A Report on the Sexual Harassment of Students. *Report of the National Advisory Council on Women's Educational Programs*. Washington, D.C.

Tjaden, Patricia, and Nancy Thoennes. 1998. "Prevalence, Incidence, and Consequences of Violence against Women." U.S. Department of Justice. *Research in Brief*. November, 16 pp.

Tong, Rosemarie. 1984. *Women, Sex, and the Law*. Totowa, NJ: Rowman and Allanheld.

Warshaw, Robin. 1988. *I Never Called It Rape*. New York: Harper and Row.

Weiner, Robin D. 1983. "Shifting the Communication Burden: A Meaningful Consent Standard in Rape." *Harvard Women's Law Journal* 6:145–161.

Weis, K., and S. S. Borges. 1973. "Victimology and Rape: The Case of the Legitimate Victim." *Issues in Criminology* 8:71–115.

Whitson, Marian. 1997. "Sexism and Sexual Harassment: Concerns of African-American Women of the Christian Methodist Episcopal Church." *Violence against Women* 3(4):382–400.

Williams, Kirk R. 1981. "Few Convictions in Rape Cases." *Journal of Criminal Justice* 9:29–40.

Wise, Sue, and Liz Stanley. 1987. *Georgie Porgie: Sexual Harassment in Everyday Life*. London: Pandora Press.

Wriggins, Jennifer. 1983. "Rape, Racism, and the Law." *Harvard Women's Law Journal* 6:103–141.

Wyatt, Gail Elizabeth, Michael D. Newcomb, and Monika H. Riederle.

1993. *Sexual Abuse and Consensual Sex*. Newbury Park, CA: Sage.

X, Laura. 1999. "Accomplishing the Impossible: An Advocate's Notes from the Successful Campaign to Make Marital and Date Rape a Crime in All 50 States and Other Countries." *Violence against Women* 5(9):1064–1081.

Yescavagae, Karen. 1999. "Teaching Women a Lesson: Sexually Aggressive and Sexually Nonaggressive Men's Perceptions of Acquaintance and Date Rape." *Violence against Women* 5(7):796–812.

8

✳

Woman Battering and Stalking

[W]ives are much more likely to be slain by their husbands
when separated from them than when co-residing. . . . .
One implication is that threats which begin 'If you ever leave
me . . .' must be taken seriously. Women who stay with
their abusive husbands because they are afraid to leave may
correctly apprehend that departure would elevate or spread
the risk of lethal assault. As one Chicago wife, a victim
of numerous beatings by her husband, explained to a friend
who asked why she didn't leave her husband, 'I can't because
he'll kill us all, and he's going to kill me.' He did.

(WILSON AND DALY, 1993, 9–10).

DEFINING BATTERING AND STALKING

Naming the phenomenon of males who abuse their current or former intimate
female partners has been problematic. Defining it as domestic violence con-
fuses the issue of separating child abuse, "elder" abuse,[1] and sibling abuse from
woman battering. Defining the phenomenon as spouse abuse hides the fact
that women are the victims and men are the perpetrators approximately 95
percent of the time (Berk et al., 1983; see Browne, 1987; Dobash et al., 1992).
Defining this phenomenon as wife abuse or wife battering ignores the fact that

many of the couples are dating or cohabiting and are not married (even if we include common-law marriages). Thus, the label *woman battering* is most appropriate to refer to the violence between heterosexual intimates.[2] Increasingly in recent years, in order to include same-sex partner abuse and to recognize that much of the violence occurs in dating or "broken up" relationships, the term *intimate partner violence* is used to describe current or former intimate partners where one or both are violent toward the other. Although this label is appealing on many levels, it does not recognize the gendered nature of this serious and prevalent form of victimization.

One force that keeps woman battering invisible is that the victims themselves are often reluctant to define themselves as victims or battered (Walker, 1979). They may believe that since it happens "only" once or twice a year, they aren't really victims. As was stated in Chapter 6, once the woman has been abused, she knows that potential is always there, and the threat of violence frequently serves to guide her relationship from then on. Furthermore, research has found that battered women usually understate the degree of violence or injury they incur (Browne, 1987, 15).

The tendency of battered women to minimize their victimization is further exacerbated by batterers' tendencies to minimize the frequency and seriousness of their violence. Studies of batterers found that batterers use excuses and *justifications* when confronted with their culpability (Dutton, 1988; Ptacek, 1988). Batterers use *excuses* in order to deny responsibility (Ptacek, 1988). Excuses are related to situational characteristics of the assault (Dutton, 1988). Batterers' excuses may include being drunk, being frustrated, or losing control. Justifications, on the other hand, are used to deny wrongness (Ptacek, 1988) and tend to include characteristics about the victim (Dutton, 1988). Justifications for battering include blaming the victim for "causing" the battering because she is a bad cook, is not sufficiently sexually responsive, is not deferential to the batterer, is not "faithful," and does not know when to "shut up" (Ptacek, 1988). Clearly, none of these excuses and justifications legitimizes abuse. Notably, batterers are more likely to use justifications than excuses. That is, batterers are more likely to blame their victims for "making" them violent than they are to offer situations to explain their violence (Dutton, 1988).

The issue of *control* is certainly an important one in intimate partner violence. Notably, in-depth interviews with battered women identified *control* as the overwhelming theme in these women's discussions of the battering (Eisikovits and Buchbinder, 1999). In the women's interview responses, control was divided into two main groups: (1) the battered women's discussions of the *batterers' self-control,* and (2) the battered women's discussions of *their own self-control.* Regarding the victims' discussions of the *batterers' self-control,* the women described their batterers as "being in a constant struggle for self-control," the unpredictability of his "explosions" in his "heroic efforts" to control himself, and his two faces: the stranger who is violent and the man she lives with. These perceptions of him help her to stay with him but also clearly let him "off the hook." So do the ways that she views her own self-control in the abusive relationship. In this case, she views herself as responsible for trying to control his explosions of violence (e.g., by keeping her mouth shut), for viewing self-control as gendered where men are unable to verbalize and thus are more physical and where the batterer "pushes" her to the point where she loses self-control and feels helpless. Obviously, the batterer's abuse is the batterer's fault. However, Eisikovits and Buchbinder (ibid., 860) believe the victim's perception in these cases works to make her view herself and her abuser "in similar positions of lack of control. Her sense of survival is based on her sense of control over her and his violence." Clearly these perceptions do not fit all battered women; some very distinctly view the batterer as entirely responsible for the abuse. However, in terms of responding to intimate partner violence, it is important to understand the varied ways that victims as well as offenders view control in their relationships.

Four categories of battering have been developed (see Tong, 1984, 125–126). It is not uncommon for more than one of these to occur within the same battering relationship. The first category is *physical battering,* which consists of slapping, hitting, burning, kicking, shooting, stabbing, or any other form of nonsexual physical violence. This is battering as it has been traditionally viewed. The second category, *sexual battering,* occurs when there is a sexual nature to the violence, such as beatings on the breasts or genitals, and oral, anal, or vaginal rape. Marital rape is discussed in more detail in Chapter 7.

The third category of battering, *psychological battering,* is often minimized but is potentially extremely harmful. Many battered women report psychological battering as the most damaging type of abuse. This exists where the offender threatens, demeans, and otherwise discredits the victim. The final category is the *destruction of pets and property.* It is not unusual for batterers to destroy the woman's property (anything from minor clothing to automobiles or even their houses) and abuse or kill animals belonging to the woman. Underlying the clear loss of a beloved animal or cherished property is the message that the victim and her/their children are also capable of being cruelly destroyed. One of the most disturbing aspects for the jury in listening to Francine Hughes's defense for killing her abusive husband (the famous *"Burning Bed"* case) was when her husband would not allow the pregnant family dog into the house during a cold snap in Michigan, and the dog and her puppies died (McNulty, 1980).

There are three commonalities among the four categories of battering: They all result in harm to the victim, all are manifestations of domination and control, and all occur in an intimate relationship (Tong, 1984, 126). Nonetheless, there is not complete agreement on what qualifies as battering. Researchers have suggested disagreement over such issues as to whether "only" psychological battering makes a woman battered. There is also disagreement as to whether a woman who is hit "only" once is battered. Some researchers' definitions of battering require a systematic occurrence where battering is an ongoing aspect of the relationship. In most cases, it appears that the violence and threat of violence are ongoing and that the different categories of violence operate simultaneously within battering relationships. That is, it is not uncommon for a battered woman to be physically, sexually, and psychologically abused as well as to experience destruction of property or pets.

Tjaden and Thoennes (1998b, 1) define stalking as "harassing or threatening behavior that an individual engages in repeatedly, such as following a person, appearing at a person's home or place of business, making harassing phone calls, leaving written messages or objects, or vandalizing a person's property." A stalker has also been described as "someone who persistently pursues another individual in a way that instills fear in the target" (Mustaine and Tewksbury 1999, 44), and as "obsessional following" (Meloy, 1996). Although stalking first became identified as a social problem regarding high-profile celebrity stalking cases, it has increasingly become identified as a phenomenon highly correlated with intimate partner abuse. Thus, the high-profile celebrity cases of the 1980s and 1990s, which included President Ronald Regan's and actor Jody Foster's stalker, comedian David Letterman's stalker, and actor Rebecca Schaeffer's (from the television show *My Sister Sam*) stalker and murderer, received unprecedented attention to this behavior that has existed for centuries. Increasingly researchers and the general public are aware that not only are noncelebrities also at risk of being stalked but that the vast majority of stalking is perpetrated in the context of intimate partner relationships and often those that already exhibit other forms of victimization and abuse.

THE HISTORY OF IDENTIFYING BATTERING AS A SOCIAL PROBLEM

Chapter 6 stated that the nonsexual physical abuse of women was not identified as a social problem until the 1970s. However, attempts had been made prior to the 1970s to bring attention to the problem of battering. Physical abuse by men toward their wives not only has been recorded for hundreds of years but often has been portrayed as acceptable, even expected, behavior (Martin, 1976). Although there were a few laws criminalizing wife beating in the United States in the 1600s and 1700s, formal complaints numbered only one or two per decade (Pleck, 1989). In 1776 Abigail Smith Adams wrote a letter to her husband, John Adams, requesting the freedom of women by restricting the power men held in marriages (Dobash and Dobash, 1979, 4). This plea apparently was ignored.

During the struggle for women's suffrage during the latter part of the nineteenth century, liberal feminists Elizabeth Cady Stanton and Susan B. Anthony spent considerable time attempting to bring the plight of battered women into the public eye (Pleck, 1983). However, their efforts were less effective than those of conservative feminists Lucy Stone and her husband, Henry Blackwell. Unlike Stanton and Anthony, Stone and Blackwell did not advocate divorce as a necessary solution; rather, they simply advocated suffrage and protective legislation. The second time that wife beating was addressed was as a part of the platform by British and U.S. suffragists during the beginning of this century (Dobash and Dobash, 1979).

The most recent and successful movement questioning the violence against wives began in 1971 in a small English town (ibid.). A group of over 500 women and children and one cow marched to protest rising food costs and the reduction of free milk for children. Although the march was not deemed a success regarding the problems it set out to address, it was a success and a historical event in that it led to solidarity among the women marching. This solidarity resulted in a community gathering place for local women, the Chiswick's Women's Aid. During discussions at Chiswick's Women's Aid, women began revealing and discussing the systematic violence they had experienced from their husbands. Woman battering and its frequency, then, were accidentally discovered, changing the focus of Chiswick's Women's Aid to woman battering (ibid.).

Feminists in the United States followed the lead set by British feminists. Public information on battering increased with Chiswick's Women's Aid founder, Erin Pizzey's publication (1974) in England of *Scream Quietly or the Neighbors Will Hear* and Del Martin's publication (1976) in the United States of *Battered Wives*. Since the mid-1970s, shelters for battered women have been established all over the United States, England, Canada, and many European and other countries. These early shelters were very basic, starting as grassroots, community-based efforts by feminists. Often the shelters were individual women's homes, which they volunteered as sanctuaries for battered women. Such make-do shelters still operate in some rural communities. Thus, the first step in the current battered women's movement was the setting up of emergency shelters by women within each community. "Since 1975, the movement has made substantial headway in three areas, besides emergency shelter: legislation, government policy and programs, and research and public information" (Tierney, 1983, 208). However, even today woman battering remains invisible to a large degree, and shelters are regularly underfunded and overpopulated, turning women and children away in large numbers.

Since the 1980s, literature has emerged portraying the widespread existence of what is labeled *courtship violence*. Courtship violence is sexual or other physical violence or threats of violence (emotional violence) that occur in dating relationships. A study that compared battering in premarital, marital, and ex-spousal relationships reported to the police found that unmarried couples resort to physical violence and use weapons somewhat more frequently than the other types of couples (Erez, 1986). While the premarital relationships have a higher percentage of assaults than the other two categories, the marital, and particularly postmarital (ex-spousal), relationships have the most serious assaults and injuries (Erez, 1986; Mahoney 1991). Indeed, research in recent years identifies leaving a violent relationship as one of the most dangerous times for battered women (Campbell, 1992; Ellis, 1987; Ellis and DeKeseredy, 1989; Mahoney, 1991; Pagelow, 1993; Sev'er, 1997; Wilson and Daly, 1993). Studies on the rates of courtship violence suggest that between one–fifth and one-third of college students report experiencing nonsexual, physical courtship violence (Bogal-Allbritten and Allbritten, 1985; Cate et al., 1982;

Knutson and Mehm, 1986; Lane and Gwartney-Gibbs, 1985; Makepeace, 1981, 1986; Matthews, 1984; Stets and Pirog-Good, 1987).

Davies et al., (1998) and Kanuha (1996) describe the social and public construction of "the battered woman" that activists and researchers devised. They call this depiction the "pure victim," who is characterized by a battered woman where (1) she is not herself violent unless in self-defense, (2) she has "experienced extreme physical violence separated by periods of emotional abuse," (3) the abuse against her is in a pattern in which it escalates in severity and frequency over time unless someone intervenes, and (4) she is terrified by the abuse (Davies et al., 1998, 15). While this image was useful in garnering public support and in accurately portraying many battered women, it failed in terms of classifying all battered women in this same venue. The pro-arrest laws (discussed later in this chapter) were geared toward these "pure victims," who did not hit back, wanted the police to arrest, and experienced the same violence in the same ways. Thus, women who did not fit this "pure victim" image were treated with disdain by the police and some advocates (Davies et al., 1998; Kanuha, 1996).

THE FREQUENCY OF BATTERING
AND STALKING

The gendered nature of intimate partner violence is hotly debated and quite clearly rests on how the studies sampled their participants and the questions they used to identify battering. A considerable amount of research suggests that men tend to batter women in approximately 95 percent of the battering situations (Berk et al., 1983; see Browne, 1987, 8; Dobash et al., 1992). A recent study using NCVS data from the United States reported that about 85 percent of intimate partner violence cases in 1998 were women victims (Rennison and Welchans, 2000). Dobash and Dobash (1988, 69) claim that "25 percent of all violent crimes are wife assaults." The National Violence against Women survey discussed in the last chapter, which interviewed 8,000 women and 8,000 men in the United States by telephone, found that 22 percent of women and 7 percent of men reported ever experiencing intimate partner violence as victims (Tjaden and Thoennes, 1998a). A recent national study in Canada stated that 29 percent of the women who were ever married or lived as common-law spouses with a man reported at least one incident of intimate partner abuse (Johnson, 1995). Notably, 15 percent of women reported that their current partner had abused them; when asked about previous married or cohabitating relationships with men, 45 percent of the women reported intimate partner abuse (ibid.). Others believe that as many as half of all women will be victims of battering by a husband or boyfriend (Mills and McNamar, 1981; Slote and Cuthbert, 1997; Walker, 1979; Yoshihama, 1999).

Determining the prevalence of battering (similar to rape rates) is difficult, as is evident from the range these statistics present. Problems inherent in determining the prevalence of battering are exemplified by researchers' frustrations in trying to find a control group of nonbattered women to compare with a group of battered women; they often find battered women in their "control group" (Browne, 1987, 5). One of the questions most often asked about battering is "What about men who are battered by women?" Some research views men and women as "mutually combative" or inflicting fairly equal amounts of violence on each other in intimate relationships (Steinmetz, 1977/1978; Straus, 1990, 1991; Straus and Gelles, 1986; Straus et al., 1980). However, it is important to emphasize that the wide range of study reports on women's versus men's proportion of offending and victimization in intimate partner violence depends on the sample and the measurement instruments used. Greater gender similarity is found typically at the more minor levels of violence, such as slapping, and the greatest gender disparities in victimization and offending are at the more serious battering levels, such as punching.

Much of the criticism regarding the findings reporting that women and men are "mutually combative" has centered around the Conflict Tactic Scale (CTS), a measurement instrument criticized by many as an incomplete and inadequate test to measure battering (Berk et al., 1983; DeKeseredy, 1995; Dobash and Dobash, 1988; Kurz, 1993; Schwartz, 1987; Stark and Flitcraft, 1983; Yllo, 1988). Specifically, the CTS oversimplifies the complexities of battering, focusing solely on behaviors and ignoring consequences of the social contexts in which the behaviors occur and their meanings to the victim and the offender (Ferraro and Johnson, 1983; Smith, 1994; Yoshihama, 1999). For example, the CTS fails to take into account the difference between a 250-pound man slamming a 100-pound woman into a wall and her shoving him back forcefully. Notably, in a public-opinion poll, respondents tended to blame women for battering whether they were the ones who hit or the ones who got hit (Greenblat, 1983). Finally, DeKeseredy (1995, 162) criticizes the CTS for ignoring "many injurious acts, such as suffocating, squeezing, sexual assault, stalking, and scratching" and for not providing "additional opportunities to disclose abusive experiences."

Thus, researchers and nonresearchers alike have had a tendency to blame women as equally responsible, if not more so, for battering. A more recent study interviewing both men and women about the violence in their relationships found that compared to women, men underestimate (1) the types/number of violence forms they use against their intimate female partners, (2) how often they use these forms of violence, (3) the likelihood of the abuse resulting in injuries, and (4) the types/numbers the woman/victim has (Dobash et al., 1998). A study on marital rape and aggression found very low correlation between wives' and husbands' versions in the same couple reports of the husband's use of sexual aggression and coercion against the wife, with wives reporting far higher rates of sexual aggression and marital rape than did husbands (Meyer et al., 1998). This indicates that one will find very different rates of marital rape based on whether we ask women or men about rape in their marriages and on the strong tendency for men to lie about or discount marital rapes they commit. A study using the CTS to measure intimate partner

abuse among 94 U.S. military couples suggests that there is likely more violence in these than nonmilitary couples but also that men reported higher rates
of their abuse against their wives than the wives reported these husbands perpetrated against them (Bohannon et al., 1995).

Another important point is that the violence husbands direct at wives is not
comparable to the violence wives direct at husbands: Battering damages
women's self-esteem, whereas men's self-esteem often appears unaffected by
violence from their wives (Mills, 1984). Not surprisingly, then, a study of college students revealed that females are more likely than males to report seeking an end to the relationship, informal controls, or formal controls if assaulted
by an intimate partner (Miller and Simpson, 1991). Notably, a study of dating
intimate partner violence among high school students found that girls who
experienced abuse at the hands of their boyfriends most commonly reported
fear and then *emotional hurt* as the effect. Boys reporting violence by their girlfriends, however, mostly commonly reported that they *thought it was funny* and
then *anger* as their responses (O'Keefe and Treister, 1998). Furthermore,
women usually resort to violence out of *self-defense or retaliation or to escape* situations where the man initiated and escalated the violence (Barnett et al.,
1997; Hamberger et al., 1997; Molidor and Tolman, 1998; Saunders, 1988;
Schwartz, 1987). Men, on the other hand, typically resort to violence against
their intimate female partners to *control* them (Barnett et al., 1997; Edleson
et al., 1991; Hamberger et al., 1997). Significantly, women are more likely
to incur serious injury than men in battering incidents (Berk et al. 1983;
Holtzworth-Munroe et al., 1997; Loving, 1980; Molidor and Tolman, 1998;
Oppenlander, 1982; Stets and Straus, 1990). Finally, men's greater economic
resources decrease their need for shelters (Straus, 1991), as do their lower levels of serious violence and fear.

The degree and frequency of violence differ among relationships where
battering occurs, but it often begins early on in marriages (Dobash and
Dobash, 1979, 124) or even during the courtship stage (Dobash and Dobash,
1979, 84; Erez, 1986; Flynn, 1990; Makepeace, 1981; Pirog-Good and Stets,
1989; Schwartz and DeKeseredy, 1997; Stets and Pirog-Good, 1987). Indeed,
a recent governmental report using NCVS data reported that women/girls
aged 16 to 24 years old experienced the highest per-capita rates of intimate
partner violence in the United States (Rennison and Welchans, 2000). An
extensive review of the research on the gendered nature of intimate partner
violence summarized that important gender distinctions exist: male-
perpetrated-against-female-victim intimate partner abuse (1) results in more
injury, fear, and psychological trauma (e.g., higher depression and lower self-
esteem) and (2) differs in motivation from female-perpetrated intimate partner
violence against male intimates (Holtzworth-Munroe et al., 1997). Regarding
the latter point, Holtzworth-Munroe et al. (ibid.) state that males use intimate
partner violence (IPV) to control their partners, whereas women use IPV to
excape violence or for self-defense. Moreover, husband-initiated IPV was "in
response to a wide variety of wife behaviors, and once husband violence
began, there were no wife behaviors that successfully suppressed husband vio-

lence. In contrast, wife violence escalated only in reaction to husband violence or emotional abuse" (ibid., 303).

Although stalking research is relatively new, indeed the labeling of stalking is new, research indicates that this behavior is also highly gendered. Tjaden and Thoennes's (1998b) National Violence against Women (NVAW) survey study found that of the 8,000 men and 8,000 women in the United States interviewed by phone, 8 percent of women and 2 percent of men reported stalking that involved high levels of fear. When they employed a broader definition of stalking, where the stalking also included "somewhat" or a "little" fear reported by the study participants, 12 percent of women and 4 percent of men reported stalking victimizations. Thus 6 percent of women and 1.5 percent of men in the United States reported experiencing stalking victimization. Similar to the studies on rape, American Indians/Alaskan Natives reported the highest rates of stalking victimization (5 percent of men, 17 percent of women), followed by individuals of mixed races (4 percent of men, 11 percent of women), whites (2 percent of men, 8 percent of women), African Americans (2 percent of men, 7 percent of women), and Asians/Pacific Islanders (2 percent of men, 5 percent of women) (ibid., 5).

The gender differences reported in stalking are even greater when one looks at perpetration rather than at victimization. More specifically, the NVAW survey findings were that 78 percent of stalking victims are women (thus 22 percent are men), and 87 percent of the stalkers (according to the victims) are males (thus 13 percent of the stalkers are females (Tjaden and Thoennes, 1998b). When one breaks this down further by sex, "94 percent of the stalkers identified by female victims and 60 percent of the stalkers identified by male victims were male" (ibid., 5). Tjaden and Thoennes (1998, 6) found some evidence that gay men are more at risk than straight men of being stalked and speculate that this is due three factors: the stalking of gay men by homophobic/"hate crime" stalkers, men stalking men based on sexual attraction, and males stalked in the context of gang membership/rivalries. A review of 10 studies on stalking published between 1978 and 1995 reported that about three-fourths of these "obsessional followers" were male, and these males were typically in their thirties with prior psychiatric backgrounds and a history of failed heterosexual relationships and tended to be more intelligent than other criminal offenders (Meloy, 1996). Although half of these stalkers threatened their victims with violence, the frequency of actual violence ranged from 3 to 36 percent, with less than 2 percent resulting in a homicide. Meloy (ibid., 147) states that their preoccupation with their victims is "fueled by a disturbance in their narcissistic fantasy linking them to their victims. Such disruption is usually caused by an acute or chronic rejection that stimulates rage as a defense against shame." On the other hand, some of the more recent research on stalkers suggests they stalk their current or former girlfriends and wives because they are jealous, because they feel they "own" them, and because they can—no one challenges their infringement on these women's autonomy and often safety.

WALKER'S CYCLE THEORY OF VIOLENCE

Psychologist Lenore E. Walker (1979) is credited with developing the "cycle theory of violence," which describes the pattern of battering over time. She identified three phases in the continuous cycle of battering. Phase one is the tension-building stage. This is a sort of "calm before the storm." The victim feels that the pressure is mounting and that a violent explosion is inevitable. While "minor" battering incidents may occur during this time (for example, shaking or slapping), a major abusive assault is what she most fears. She may try to calm her partner down with something that worked in the past, such as cooking his favorite meal or keeping the children quiet.

Phase two of Walker's (1979) battering cycle is the acute battering incident. Phase two is when the major battering actually occurs and is usually the briefest of the three phases in the cycle. If the police are notified at all (only 10 percent of Walker's sample had done so), it is usually during this phase. However, by the time the police arrive, the cycle has usually moved on to phase three.

Phase three is characterized by kindness and contrite loving behavior from the batterer. "He begs her forgiveness and promises her that he will never do it again" (Walker, 1979, 65). Usually, both the man and the woman want to believe that this violence was some fluke and that it will not occur again. It is easier for them to believe this when the battering first starts, as opposed to after years of battering. The batterer often appears very sincere in his apology and in his commitment to change. He may lavish the woman with gifts, quit drinking, or do other things to convince her that he really loves her and that the battering will never happen again. "It is during this phase that the woman gets a glimpse of her original dream of how wonderful love is. . . . The traditional notion that two people who love each other surmount overwhelming odds against them prevails" (ibid., 67–68). This phase is usually longer than phase two but shorter than phase one. At the beginning of a battering relationship, women are often confused, shocked, depressed, and in need of reassurance, making them vulnerable to the batterers' promises to stop the abuse (Browne, 1987, 62–63).

As phase three ends, phase one begins again, and the cycle continues. Other researchers have noted that over time the violence tends to increase in frequency, severity, and injuries, and thus more formal social agency assistance becomes necessary (Dobash and Dobash, 1979, 179). "Each successive violent episode leaves the woman with less hope, less self-esteem, and more fear" (ibid., 140). In more recent research, Walker (1983a, 44) has found that the length of the three phases in battering relationships changes over time. As the battering relationship progresses, tension building (phase one) is longer and more evident, and loving and contrition (phase three) decline. Batterers are less likely to apologize for their violence over time and more likely to blame the victims for "making" them violent (ibid., 117–123). This implies that once the batterer has established his power over the victim, he feels less of a need to apologize to keep her. Thus, hopefulness (the belief that he may change) may be replaced with fear (that he will kill or severely harm her and/or her/their children if she leaves) as the motivation for staying in the relationship.[3]

Although Walker's cycle appears to fit some battered women's experiences, it is important to note that it has not been extensively studied, and it is clear that it does not fit all battered women's and batterers' actions, responses, and experiences. More research is necessary in this area.

WHY DO (SOME) MEN BATTER?

Many men do not batter women regardless of how angry they may feel toward them. So why do some men batter? Most researchers focus on the family structure in attempts to explain battering. For instance, Goode (1971) stresses the importance of viewing the family as a power system, where power is unequally distributed. He points out that such characteristics as being male, being older, and having control over property, money, and gifts serve to enhance the power of the father/husband in the family system. Additionally, there are fewer restraints against aggression in the family than exist in other social settings because fights between family members are viewed as more socially acceptable (Sebastian, 1983). Furthermore, the dependency of some family members on others requires that they tolerate the abuse. This is particularly apparent regarding child abuse.

It is necessary to assess the battering of women and the family structure within a sociohistorical context. Gender disparities in the culture, the economy, and political environment have an inherent impact on the family (Bograd, 1988; Breines and Gordon, 1983, 508; Dobash and Dobash, 1979; O'Neill, 1998; Stark and Flitcraft, 1983; Yllo, 1983, 1988). Focusing on family inequality independent from the political context leads to an image of battered women dominated by rotten husbands. This removes the focus from such issues as inadequate governmental policies (such as welfare and child care) that encourage female subordination and patriarchal dependency (Stark and Flitcraft, 1983, 336). Similarly, Bograd (1988, 14) claims: "The reality of domination at the social level is the most crucial factor contributing to and maintaining wife abuse at the personal level." The family cannot be analyzed independently from the social, political, and economic structure of a society. These outside forces serve to reinforce the power disparity and dependence of women in marriage.

Stereotypical gender differences discussed earlier in this book are related to the expectations by some that men should be aggressive and women passive; these expectations have an impact on woman battering. While aggression may have many aims, "one of the aggressor's objectives is the injury of the target" (Berkowitz, 1983, 179). Men's violent and aggressive behavior is often viewed as "typical" and therefore goes unquestioned (Stanko, 1985). Similarly, there is a tendency to view both sexism and violence as an inevitable part of culture (Klein, 1981). Male violence, then, is more conforming than aberrant behavior (Bograd, 1988, 17). Men are socialized to dominate women, and male aggression is not only encouraged but often glorified. This can be seen in male sports such as football, hockey, and boxing, as well as in the media, with movies such as *True Lies, Lethal Weapon, Rambo, Robocop, Terminator,* and basically most of Arnold Schwartzenneger's and Sylvester Stallone's movies and James Bond movies. Stalking is glorified and minimized in the movie *Something about Mary.* Woman abuse, then, has not occurred as an event isolated from the community or against the general principles of acceptable behavior; rather, it is an institution in its own right (Dobash and Dobash, 1981, 565). Not only is male violence in general often tolerated by the media and culture, but male violence directed against females, specifically, is frequently tolerated and even glorified. In addition to some men, there are women who believe that woman battering is justified under certain situations (Haj-Yahia, 1998).

What benefits do batterers obtain? It is clear that violence or the threat of violence results in a strong sense of power and dominance for the batterer. Batterers may not always be conscious of their desire to control, but intimate partner violence is typically a result of *male entitlement*—batterers are angry and feel justified to abuse when they don't have the control they have been socialized to believe they deserve (see Schechter, 1982, 219). Batterers may have a sense that their behavior is justified—their victims "needed" to be punished or "taught a lesson." Batterers often view their victims as their property or as children who need discipline. These men usually feel threatened by any indication of their victims' autonomy—even time these women spend with their families or other women friends. It is not unusual for batterers to inflict violence when the victims are pregnant or when they feel jealous of attention the victims have given to their children. There is some belief that batterers act out of their own insecurities and become abusive to counteract feelings of powerlessness (Finkelhor, 1983).

Goolkasian (1986) claims that there are two reasons why woman battering continues to exist. First, "violence is a highly effective means of control" (ibid., 2). Thus, men batter in order to gain and maintain control over women. Second, "men batter because they can; that is because in most cases no one has told batterers that they must stop" (ibid.). Although the victim and her/their children may make attempts to communicate to the batterer that his behavior is unacceptable, the batterer often gets messages from many others that he is the "king of his castle" and can treat "his woman" in whatever manner he pleases. These messages often come from the media, friends, family and even the crime-processing system.

WHO ARE THE BATTERERS
AND STALKERS?

Who are the batterers? The stereotype of the unemployed, alcoholic, lower-class abuser is not necessarily accurate. Batterers as well as battering victims come from a range of backgrounds and experiences. Research in the 1970s attempted to refute the myth that batterers were all mentally ill or had a psychological disorder (Gelles, 1980, 876). Numerous researchers have pointed out that battering occurs in all socioeconomic and educational levels (Brisson, 1981; Flynn, 1977; Goolkasian, 1986; Holtzworth-Monroe et al., 1997). However, some research suggests that arrest works as a deterrent for employed batterers but *increases* the likelihood of subsequent violence for *unemployed* batterers (Pate and Hamilton, 1992; Sherman et al., 1992). The reasoning is that arrest has the intended impact on employed batterers because they have more to lose (e.g, their jobs).

The greatest risk factor for being a batterer is being male. A study of a phone hotline for women and children in Belgrade, Serbia, in the early 1990s found that 94 percent of the calls involved abuse by male family members (Mrsevic and Hughes, 1997). Of the 770 calls to the hotline over three years, 83 percent involved abusive husbands (65 percent), former husbands (13 percent), or boyfriends (5 percent). Two percent of the abuse perpetrators were fathers of the victims, and 8 percent were sons of the victims (ibid.). Research suggests that it isn't so much "being male" but rather being socialized as masculine that places a person at risk of battering. More specifically, at least for white men, men who score higher on femininity are less likely to be abusive to their girlfriends than are those men who score lower on femininity (Boye-Beaman, et al., 1993).

While a batterer may come from any background, the description of batterers by battered women suggests that batterers "all went to the same training school" (Walker, 1983a). Although this study found no "victim-prone women" (or types of women who were likely to become battering victims), "violence-prone" personalities for men were identified, including adherence to traditional views of women, possessiveness, and abuse of alcohol (ibid.). As stressed in Chapter 6, no nonabusive behavior of the victim's, perceived or real, justifies violent behavior from the batterer. However, it is still useful to examine how batterers perceive their own behavior. Researchers have found batterers strongly motivated by *jealousy* (Barnett et al., 1995; Brisson, 1981; Browne, 1987; Dobash and Dobash, 1979; Molidor and Tolman, 1998; O'Keefe and Treister, 1998; Straus et al., 1980; Walker, 1979, 1983a). This relates to the batterers' belief that their wives or girlfriends "belong" to them, and this "justifies" their violent behavior. Regarding alcohol abuse, most researchers agree that violence is not caused by substance abuse but that such use and abuse may disinhibit violence. Most men who beat their wives when they are drunk also beat them when they are sober. One study on battering found that "alcohol use at the time of violence is far from a necessary or sufficient cause for wife abuse despite the stereotype that all drunks hit their wives or all wife hitting involves drunks" (Kantor and Straus, 1987, 224).

One attitude about battering that is increasingly disputed is that it is a result of loss of control on the part of the batterer. In fact, groups who have organized to try to help batterers end their violent behavior concentrate on teaching batterers that battering is a choice, and they may choose not to batter. Others have pointed out that battering is indeed controllable if we assess battering via the "targets" of the battering (where the offenders place their blows) and the locations in which battering occurs (whether the assault takes place in public or at home). For instance, a batterer may attempt to excuse his abuse of his intimate partner because he was angry at something his boss did that day. It is important to note, however, that the target of his violence was not his boss but rather his wife or girlfriend. Thus, if it is a matter of simply losing control, how is it that he is able to control himself from hitting his boss, who provoked his anger? Also, batterers are often controlled enough to restrict their blows to places on the body that are least likely to be visible to other people, such as the stomach, breasts, and thighs.

Marital rape is also viewed as an effective "tool of control" by the batterer because the damage is not visible, and the victim is likely to be too ashamed to report it even to friends or family and particularly to law-enforcement officials. The fact that most batterers refrain from abusive behavior in public places also indicates a degree of control on the batterer's part in determining his own violent behavior.

> It seems reasonable to conclude that the men know their behavior is inappropriate, because they keep battering such a private affair. According to reports from the battered women, only the batterers can end the second phase. The woman's only option is to find a safe place to hide. Why he stops is also unclear. He may simply have become exhausted and emotionally depleted. It is not uncommon for the batterer to wake the woman out of a deep sleep to begin his assault. If she answers his verbal harangue, he becomes angrier with what she says. If she remains quiet, her withdrawal enrages him. She gets the beating no matter what her response is. (Walker, 1979, 61–62)

A number of researchers have focused on a hypothesized intergenerational transmission of violence in an attempt to explain why men batter (Dutton and Painter, 1981; Fagan et al., 1983). This theory contends that children who witness violence learn that violence is an acceptable way to resolve conflict (Dutton and Painter, 1981, 142). The intergenerational transmission of violence theory, then, views battering as a learned behavior that is passed down from one generation to another within the family system. In applying this theory, it is important to acknowledge that the experiential learning is likely to be different for males and females. While both males and females may learn that physical conflict is a legitimate response to family or interpersonal conflict, males may learn to be the oppressors, whereas females learn to be the victims. One study found that adult male survivors of child abuse by their parents, or adult males who had watched their fathers abuse their mothers, were more likely than adult males from nonabusive homes to view violence as an adequate response to family conflict and to abuse their own wives or girlfriends later in life (Fagan et al., 1983).

However, the theory of intergenerational transmission of violence has received criticism, too. For instance, it is possible that living in a violent home may result in an adult survivor's strong commitment to disallow violence in her or his own home. Adult survivors of homes where woman battering occurred may not all behave uniformly. Although witnessing parental violence increases the likelihood of a boy growing up to be a batterer, "the majority of wife assaulters have never witnessed parental violence" (Dutton, 1988, 47). The studies testing the intergenerational transmission of violence have been accused of committing "clinical fallacy" by examining only adult batterers and failing to include the effects of childhood violence on nonviolent adults (Breines and Gordon, 1983). An exception to this is a study that found that persons (male and female) raised in homes with "spousal violence" were at risk of being victims, not offenders, of battering as adults; it also found that "vulnerability to aggression was transmitted more than the learned role of perpetrator" (Cappell and Heiner, 1990, 135). In conclusion, while there are likely some implications for condoning violence if one grows up with it, overall the impact on later violent behavior is unclear.

Now turning to the question, "Who are stalkers?" once again it is clear that this behavior is highly gendered. As stated earlier, the NVAW survey findings indicate that women are 78 percent of the stalking victims and men are 87 percent of the stalking perpetrators (Tjaden and Thoennes, 1998b). Similar to previous research, the NVAW survey findings confirm that most stalking victims know their stalkers: "Only 23 percent of female stalking victims and 36 percent of male stalking victims were stalked by strangers" (ibid., 5). *Another significant manner in which stalking is gendered is that women are far more likely than men to be stalked by current or former intimate partners:*

> Thirty-eight percent of female stalking victims were stalked by current or former husbands, 10 percent by current or former cohabiting partners, and 14 percent by current or former dates or boyfriends. Overall, 59 percent of female victims, compared with 30 percent of male victims, were stalked by some type of intimate partner (Tjaden and Thoennes, 1998b, 6).

There is widespread belief that stalking in the context of intimate partner violence is a result of the woman leaving the relationship, thus, that stalking in the context of woman battering starts when women leave abusive or potentially abusive male partners/boyfriends. The NVAW study found that although 43 percent of the stalking experienced by women stalked by current husbands or partners occurred as speculated, that is, *after* the relationship ended. However, 21 percent stated that the stalking occurred before the relationship ended, and 36 percent reported that the stalking occurred both before *and* after the relationship ended. "Thus, contrary to popular opinion, women are often stalked by intimate partners while the relationship is still intact" (ibid.).

INHIBITORS TO LEAVING
A VIOLENT RELATIONSHIP

Battered women stay because they rarely have escape routes related to educational or employment opportunities, relatives were critical of plans to leave the relationship, parenting responsibilities impeded escape, and abusive situations contributed to low self-esteem and negative emotions—especially anxiety and depression (Forte et al., 1996, 69).

Much of the writing on battering, and even responses by the public as well as by the crime-processing system, have focused on asking why a woman stays in a battering relationship. This response tends to be victim blaming in that it implies she would leave if she really didn't like to be battered. Battering is a complex phenomenon, and it is important to understand why some women stay in or return to battering relationships.

First, we must ask why the focus is on "Why does she stay?" rather than on "Why does he batter?" Focusing on why battered women stay has resulted in the labeling of such women as "deviant" (Loseke and Cahill, 1984). Perhaps it would be more fruitful to ask questions such as "Why are men violent?" "Why are women so easily victimized?" "Why are violent men allowed to stay?" and "Why should the victims rather than the assailants be expected to leave?" (Hoff, 1990).

Second, it is rarely acknowledged that many women do leave battering relationships. There is a tendency to hear only about women who stay in battering relationships. Many women have left battering relationships, even after the first violent episode. However, shame and the tendency of others to discount their victimizations keep these survivors from identifying themselves as ex-battered women. In fact, 70 percent of 251 battered women who had contacted a counseling unit associated with the county attorney's office decided to leave their abusive partners (Strube and Barbour, 1984). Nonetheless, many women do stay for a period of time or indefinitely. Thus, it is important to understand the numerous obstacles these women face.

Third, some women stay in battering relationships because they face overwhelming restrictions in their attempts to leave. The previous section discussed the importance of looking at aggregate political and social realities that maintain men's power over women, particularly within the institutions of marriage and the family. Economic and psychological factors also help to explain why women stay. Forces restricting women's autonomy, then, function at aggregate levels in the political and social structure, as well as at individual economic and psychological levels.

Economic Restrictions

Frequently, it is simply not economically feasible for a woman to leave the man who batters her. This is particularly problematic for women who have children. It is not uncommon for a battering man to control all of the money they both earn and to place the woman on a minuscule allowance for which she must justify all spending. Furthermore, many women do not possess the skills or education necessary to support themselves and their children. Some research has shown that unemployed women are less likely to leave the battering relationship than employed women (Gelles, 1976; Strube and Barbour, 1984), while other research reports no difference in the employment status of battered women and their likelihood to leave/stay (Herbert et al., 1991). In a study of women in a low-income area of Chicago, "women who experienced [intimate partner] male violence were as likely to be currently employed as those who did not, [but] they were more likely to have been unemployed in the past, to suffer from health problems, and to have higher rates of welfare receipt" (Lloyd and Taluc, 1999). This study also pointed out the complexity of the role of battered women in the labor force: "Employed women may be less likely to enter, tolerate, or stay in abusive relationships, and others may be employed because they are compelled by their partners to work and to contribute income to the household" (ibid., 386). A study of Vietnamese immigrant women in the United States reported that women's economic participation was not related to the intimate partner abuse they experienced; however, "economic hardship could prevent women from leaving an abusive relationship to avoid further violence" (Bui and Morash, 1999, 789). A study of women's calls to a hotline in Belgrade, Serbia (discussed earlier in this chapter), found that the victims "were often forced to live with perpetrators because of the lack of available housing, which worsened due to privitization, economic sanctions against Serbia, and the influx of refugees. . . . Most refugees were housed in private homes, resulting in increased violence against women refugees and women hosts" (Mrsevic and Hughes, 1997, 101). Moreover, the study classified 6 percent of the calls to the hotline as reports of "economic violence," which included property damage, controlling women's wages and property, and restricting her "allowance" to a level that made it impossible to buy food for the family.

Although batterers and battered women come from "all walks of life," there is some indication in recent research that poor women may be at significantly increased risk of intimate partner violence (Browne et al., 1999; Craven, 1996; Forte et al., 1996; Kaplan, 1997; Pearson et al., 1999) and that leaving a batterer decreases a woman's income (Herbert et al., 1991). A longitudinal study of women living in extreme poverty in Worcester, Massachusetts, reported that women who experienced physical aggression/violence by a male partner in the previous 12 months were less likely/able to maintain employment in the subsequent year (Browne et al., 1999). Their mental health was also related to their capacity to maintain work (in the predicted direction), but job training, job placement services, and previous employment history enhanced the likelihood (as expected) of their subsequent work history. The authors conclude that the significant impact that recent intimate partner violence has on subsequent employment is problematic in terms of the work-to-welfare policies now popular in the United States (ibid.). A relevant issue in addressing battered women's economic concerns is that of child support. Legislation in 1996 in the United States, known as the Personal Responsibility and Work Opportunity Reconciliation Act (PRWORA), includes a "good-cause" exemption allowing a different process in filing for child support for cases where battered women are fearful that applying for child support could enable garner a current or former intimate partner abuser to locate and renew violence against them and their children (Pearson et al., 1999). Notably, a study of this found that while few women request this exemption, those who do appear to be in significantly dangerous circumstances (as are their children), and two-thirds are denied this request (ibid.).

Many batterers are so jealous and possessive that they do not want their wives or girlfriends to work outside the home for fear that they will start having affairs. However, even batterers who confine their victims to the home frequently accuse the victims of having extramarital affairs. Some experts believe that battered women not only need access to shelters and adequate police and court protection but they also need to be able to learn skills and obtain financial resources in order to be free of the batterers (Tong, 1984).

Sociological Restrictions

Women are confined to battering relationships in a number of cultural ways. First, people seem to have a need to believe that battering isn't happening, or if it is happening, that the victims deserve it. (This parallels Lerner's "just world" hypothesis discussed in Chapter 6.) Second, attitudes about marriage negatively affect a woman's ability to leave a battering relationship. Battered women frequently claim that their relatives, neighbors, and friends deny the battering and, if confronted with it, imply to the victim that she is somehow responsible and that she must work harder on her marriage. This is also true of many women who turn to religious guidance, such as priests, ministers, or rabbis. To some clergy, marriage is viewed as sacred, to be held together at all costs, however dangerous doing so may be to women and children. The children not only witness their mother's victimization (a form of emotional child abuse) but may be physically abused themselves (Bowker et al., 1988; Jaffe et al., 1986; Jaffe et al., 1990; Walker, 1989). A study of Asian Indian immigrant battered women in the United States found that these women's childhood socialization into "the ideals of 'good' wife and mother that include sacrifice of personal freedom and autonomy" placed them at risk, even when they had economic independence (Dasgupta and Warrier 1996, 238). Moreover, they feared dishonoring their family by divorce and felt responsible for their families' reputations in India. Similarly, a study of Palestinian women from the West Bank and Gaza strip found that those women who adhered to a patriarchal ideology were more likely to support "understanding" of batterers and not to blame them solely for their abusive behavior (Haj-Yahia 1998).

Battered women frequently report a feeling of "no escape" (see Browne 1987; Forte et al. 1996; Jones 1994) They may have exhausted every resource in order to leave a battering relationship. Many battering survivors have discussed attempts to gain help from their own relatives, the batterer's relatives, the police, and the courts (such as through divorces or restraining orders). Batterers continue to threaten and violate many of these victims, and sometimes their children (see Pagelow 1993). One study of battered women reported:

> Almost all [of the battered women] have sought help from a variety of sources. Most have, at some time, called the police for physical protection. Over two-thirds had received counseling from marriage counselors or clergy at some point. Few women, however, reported that their hus-

> bands were willing to cooperate with counseling. Over one-half had
> consulted with attorneys and almost half turned to divorce for resolution
> of the problem. However, divorce was not always found to be the suc-
> cessful resolution, as occasionally the assaulter continued to seek out his
> former wife to assault her or assaults occurred at the time of visitation
> with the children. (Flynn, 1977, 18)

In fact, some studies have shown that batterers' violence often escalates when
the victims attempt to leave the abusive relationship (Campbell, 1992; Ellis,
1987; Ellis and DeKeseredy, 1989; Mahoney, 1991; Pagelow, 1993; Sev'er,
1997; Wilson and Daly, 1993). Instead of asking "Why do (some) battered
women stay?" perhaps we should be asking, "What happened to you when
you left? What support did you get?" (Mahoney, 1991).

A specific area of sociological research that has only recently addressed intimate partner violence is the social experience of *environmental disasters.* Specifically, this area of research examines the sociology of communities experiencing
floods, earthquakes, and so on, as well as how prepared communities are for these
natural disasters. The sparse research in domestic violence in the context of disasters suggests that intimate partner violence increases in the wake of natural disasters and is particularly problematic in the area of housing for the battered
women and her children (see Enarson, 1999; Fothergill, 1999). "Living through
fear and intimidation on a daily basis, battered women are already in emotional
crisis before disaster. Attending to preparedness or evacuation warnings, stabiliz-
ing their lives in a disaster-stricken neighborhood, or accessing recovery
resources may be impossible tasks" (Enarson, 1999, 748). Women's safety and
well-being are likely to be additionally stressful if they are living in a shelter
requiring their second "evacuation" (the first being from their home with the
abuser), and "[r]elief funds may be more available to the abuser at home than to
women living in shelter" (ibid., 749). These problems are especially acute for
battered women who are poor and/or disabled (Fothergill, 1999).

While historical research documents that woman battering has occurred
over centuries, cross-cultural and comparative studies indicate that woman battering occurs cross-culturally and globally. A recent phenomenon in the
research on intimate partner violence focuses on issues of domestic violence
for immigrant women in the United States with the majority of these studies
on Asian immigrant women. Regarding the unique experiences of immigrant
women, Bui and Morash state:

> On one hand, immigrant women have brought their traditional cultures
> and their experience with legal norms and social structure of their coun-
> tries of origin to America. On the other hand, they have also internal-
> ized to some degree American culture as a result of resettlement and
> adaptation to a new life, and they and their families often experience
> stress related to relocation and a change in social status. (1999, 770)

A study of Vietnamese immigrant women in the United States reported that
"class, culture, gender, and immigration status could simultaneously affect

women's experience of violence by husbands" (ibid., 769). A study of South Asian immigrant women in the United States reported their susceptibility to marital rape, sexual control through manipulation of reproductive rights (e.g., not allowing birth control and causing continual pregnancies or denying the woman the right to have a child by abusing her when she's pregnant to the point of "losing" the pregnancy), sexual abuse by flaunting an "other" (e.g., "If you don't have sex when and how I want it, I'll take a lover"), and sexual abuse by others (e.g., raped by a brother-in-law) (Abraham, 1999).

Psychological Restrictions

Many psychologists have suggested various explanations for staying in a battering relationship. The victims themselves sometimes describe the psychological effects of abuse and exploitation as "brainwashing" (Finkelhor, 1983, 20). Efforts to determine which women are "victim-prone"—or likely to become battered women—not only are victim blaming but have proven fruitless. Researchers have been unable to establish what types of women are battered (Walker, 1983a). This informs us that *any woman could become a battered woman*—a frightening thought and counter to those who want to believe a "just world" exists.

Walker (1979) uses the social learning theory called *learned helplessness* to explain the battered woman's behavior. She bases this on (ethically questionable) studies of animals where all options of escape are closed off. The animals in these tests experience uncontrollable pain or harm on a random, unpredictable basis. Learned helplessness is characterized by persons (or animals) who have learned through repeated failure that they cannot control their destiny. Because they have no control over their environments, there is no point in trying. Therefore, even when faced with what outsiders may view as viable escapes, the person or animal with learned helplessness cannot identify these alternatives as escapes. In a later study, Walker (1983a) claimed that this learned helplessness may occur early or later in life. For instance, it may be a result of women growing up in a violent family and viewing battering as a coping strategy for family conflict. Or learned helplessness may occur later in life within the confines of a battering relationship. "Thus, learned helplessness has equal potential to develop at either time in the battered woman's life" (ibid., 35).

Walker's (1979, 1983a) learned helplessness theory has been criticized by some feminists (Dobash and Dobash, 1988; Gondolf and Fisher, 1988; Wardell et al., 1983). These critics believe that the learned helplessness approach suggests too strongly that battered women have wrongly assumed they cannot leave a battering relationship. The battered woman's recognition of a lack of alternatives is often rational, not simply a poor self-image, after she has sought help repeatedly from friends, family, the police, and the courts and is still in a threatening position (Wardell et al., 1983). Social learning theory focuses on battered women overlooking some of the alternatives available to them. Even if such such alternatives exist, (1) people under conditions of high anxiety or terror may not see them; and (2) people often make decisions that appear illogical to others, such as keeping their houses although their neighbors have been burglarized twice or getting a Ph.D. when universities are not hiring (ibid., 1983).

The theory of learned helplessness diverts attention from the abuse to the victim by labeling her response as "unreasonable" (ibid., 76). The focus is on what the victim is doing wrong rather than on the batterer's behavior and the woman's lack of alternatives. For these reasons, it has been suggested (tongue-in-cheek) that the police and judges who do nothing to help battered women may be the ones with learned helplessness (Gondolf and Fisher, 1988). Certainly, a vast amount of research documents ways that battered women have depended on, or even reached out to, the criminal-processing system and been disappointed with a lack of response, or even ones that support their batterers more than they do the victims (e.g., Browne, 1987; Cahn, 1992; Erez and Belknap, 1998; Jones, 1994; Rosewater, 1988).

Another psychological theory used to explain deterrents to women leaving battering relationships is that of *traumatic bonding*. Dutton and Painter (1981, 146–147) define this as "the development and course of strong emotional ties between two persons where one person intermittently harasses, beats, threatens, abuses or intimidates the other." This approach has been used to explain why hostage victims, children abused by their parents, or members of malevolent cults frequently bond with their aggressors. If viewed within this context, the relationship between battered women and their abusers may not be an isolated phenomenon but rather is an example of traumatic bonding (ibid., 146). The two common features of the various forms of traumatic bonding are (1) power imbalance and (2) intermittent abuse. It is not uncommon for the power imbalance to grow as a relationship becomes increasingly violent: The violent person feels more powerful and the victim less powerful as the violence progresses. The intermittent nature of the abuse may be exemplified in battering if we examine Walker's cycle, where violence is intermittently dispersed among expressions of sorrow, love, and affection (ibid., 150).

Closely related to the traumatic bonding approach, the *Stockholm syndrome* has been used as an explanation of battered women's reluctance to leave violent relationships: "In particular, when threatened with death by a captor who is also kind in some ways, hostages develop a fondness for the captor and an antipathy toward authorities working for their release. The captor may also develop a fondness for the hostages" (Graham et al., 1988, 218). The Stockholm syndrome was developed to describe the behavior of hostages, specifically bank robbery kidnap victims. This behavior includes bonding with one's captor (or abuser), often to the degree of wanting to protect the captor or abuser from punishment. The Stockholm syndrome is seen as a survival strategy. Indeed, hostages who develop it are more likely to survive captivity. It is hypothesized that four conditions allow the Stockholm syndrome to develop (ibid., 218–219):

1. A person threatens to kill another and is perceived as having the capability to do so.

2. The other cannot escape, so her or his life depends on the threatening person.

3. The threatened person is isolated from outsiders so that the only other perspective available to her or him is that of the threatening person.

4. The threatening person is perceived as showing some degree of kindness to the one being threatened.

Others claim that the experts on battered women have created a new problem in labeling battered women who stay as deviant: "It is typically marital stability, 'staying,' which is normatively expected and marital instability, 'leaving,' which requires an account. However, as far as the experts on battered women are concerned, once wife assault occurs, it is marital stability which requires explanation" (Loseke and Cahill, 1984, 297). Battering relationships, then, are not unlike nonbattering relationships in that marital stability is often accorded higher priority than marital quality. Men and women in long-term but low-quality relationships (low quality in other ways than violence) often stay together because an attachment exists, and they believe their mate is truly the only one for them (ibid., 1984). Given this attitude, battered women who stay are not so unusual; rather, they are typical. One study found, not surprisingly, that battered women who stay (thus far) in the relationship are distinguished from those who have left in that those who stay perceive more positive aspects of the relationship, such as little or no increase in the severity and frequency of the abuse (Herbert et al., 1991).

Scholarly publications often focus on the battered woman as inadequate and somehow deserving of her abuse because this "supports the conclusion that wife battering can be managed by offering social and psychological services to the victim, rather than through law enforcement efforts or socioeconomic changes in the status of women" (Morash, 1986, 258). However, in tracing the various theoretical and historical perspectives on what causes battering, it is clear that confronting battering must occur in many contexts. These include adequate divorce laws, services available to battered women and their children to help them leave and start over again, adequate legislation, and appropriate responses by the crime-processing system. Additionally, similar to the contention in Chapter 7 that sexual victimization and gender inequality reinforce each other, battering and gender inequality do so as well. As men and women become more equal, we should expect women to have more economic, psychological, and societal resources to leave battering relationships.

The Process of Victimization

In an interesting study of over 100 battered women in a shelter, Ferraro and Johnson (1983) identified six rationalizations battered women use to explain to themselves why they stay in violent relationships:

1. Appeal to the salvation of an ethic: The woman overidentifies with a nurturing gender role and wants to "save" the batterer from some internal problem (for example, chemical dependence).

2. Denial of the victimizer: Battering is viewed as a result of some force external to the relationship (for example, his job stress).

3. Denial of injury: Battering pain is viewed as normal or tolerable, and the woman focuses on everyday rituals (such as work and child care) to ignore the memory of the abuse.

4. Denial of victimization: The woman doesn't believe the violence against her was justified, but she blames herself for not avoiding it by being more conciliatory or passive.

5. Denial of options: Practical options (such as alternative housing or economic independence) and emotional options (such as outside supportive relationships) exist, but the woman doesn't believe that she can make it on her own (the abuser often ingrains this in her).

6. Appeal to higher loyalties: The woman endures the violence because of a religious or traditional commitment (such as a belief that divorce is wrong or children should live with both their mothers and fathers).

These categories are not mutually exclusive; a battered woman could adhere to one or more of the rationalizations at the same time. To leave a battering relationship, the woman must reject these rationalizations and view herself as a victim of abuse.

Ferraro and Johnson (1983) further identified six catalysts that help battered women redefine their experiences and view themselves as victims:

1. An increase in the level of violence: They realize the abuse is serious and may be fatal.

2. A change in resources: They find employment, housing, or a shelter.

3. A change in the relationship: Walker's (1979) loving and remorseful phase no longer occurs, and they see no positive aspects of the relationship.

4. Despair: They lose hope that things could ever improve.

5. A change in the visibility of the violence: The violence is more apparent to family, friends, or even strangers.

6. External definitions of the relationship: Friends, relatives, police officers, or others condemn the violence and tell her she is a victim.

These six catalysts not only help battered women redefine their experiences and relationships with batterers but also motivate women to leave the relationships. These catalysts—especially numbers 2 and 6—also emphasize the importance of shelters for battered women.

In summary, the dynamics of the reasons men batter and the limitations women face in attempting to escape violent relationships are complex. We cannot just use economic explanations, nor can we simply settle on sociological or psychological explanations; rather, we must consider a variety of factors.

THE CONSTANT THREAT OF DANGER

All of the inhibitors (economic, sociological, and psychological) addressed in the preceding section are influenced by a constant threat of danger and fear once the violence has begun for many battered women. If the batterer threatens to assault or actually does assault the victim, they both become aware of his potential to harm her. One study found that almost all battered women report a fear that their batterers may completely "lose control" and kill them during a beating (Star et al., 1979). Even if none of the other negative conditions, such as those suggested earlier (economic, sociological, and psychological), exists for the victim, the danger is still present. For instance, if a woman is beaten by her husband and decides to leave him, she may feel assured in doing this on many levels—she may hold a good job, his family and her family and friends may support her leaving him, and she may not have fallen victim to some of the psychological syndromes previously addressed. Even if her parents and friends do not support her breakup with him, she may have access to a battered women's shelter. However, he may still pose a powerful threat of danger. He may tell her he will kill her, her/their children, and/or her parents if she does not return to him. She has learned he is capable of violence, and she likely has reason to believe he may follow through on his threats. Even if she is not completely convinced he will carry out his threats, the risk of destruction to loved ones is logically perceived as too great to gamble.

If she is staying in a shelter or hotel or hiding out with friends or relatives, she may have to quit her job because he could locate her at work. It is not unusual for women who have left batterers to have the batterers show up at their places of employment or trace their new residences through friends, family, co-workers, or private detectives. When the victim is staying with her family to escape from the batterer, he will often use sufficient threats and pressure that one or more members of her own family might begin to advise her to "work it out" with him. Although a victim may have received a restraining order from the court, not allowing the husband on her property, he may still have rights to child visitation, so avoiding him is almost impossible (McCann, 1985; Walker, 1989). Many battered women survivors have had to move to a new city or state and change their names in order to be free of the violence. Clearly, such women often lose their family and friends, in addition to their possessions, which is often some batterers' goal.

Evidence shows that batterers' promises to kill their victims are not merely idle threats—some batterers do eventually kill the women they have battered. In fact, much of the worst violence battered women experience occurs after they have separated from or divorced their husbands (Campbell, 1992; Ellis, 1987; Ellis and DeKeseredy, 1989; Erez, 1986; Mahoney, 1991; Pagelow, 1993; Sev'er, 1997; Wilson and Daly, 1993). This may be most dangerous for unmarried battered women, whose rates of being murdered by their batterers increased from 1976 to 1987 (Browne and Williams, 1993).

A study of divorced women with children from a variety of backgrounds found that intimate partner battering is (a) what caused many of the women to file for a divorce *and* (b) played an important and threatening role in their efforts to negotiate for assets after they left (Kurz, 1996). This was most evident in negotiating for child support, a critical issue in setting divorced women above the poverty line. Across women from different classes and races/ethnicities, 30 percent of the women reported fears in negotiating chld support, and the more serious and frequent the violence they experienced in the marriage, the more fearful they were about child-support negotiations (ibid.).

WOMAN BATTERING AND THE CRIME-PROCESSING SYSTEM

A historical account of community-wide and crime-processing system responses to the battering of women leads one to believe that men were more likely to be punished for not dominating their wives than for beating them. A portrayal of community regulations of domestic authority since the fifteenth century states:

> Men could be subjected to ritualized rebukes if they were thought to be doing "women's work," were "henpecked," cuckolded, or believed to have been beaten by their wives—that is, when there was a perceived inversion of patriarchal authority and domination. . . . In addition to being ridiculed by the community for failing to maintain authority, men thought to have domineering or wayward wives were supported in their attempts to regain or retain dominance by ridiculing and shaming the woman publicly and/or by punishing her physically. (Dobash and Dobash, 1981, 566)

Thus, it was not acceptable for men and women to have any semblance of an equal relationship and certainly not one where women exhibited any sense of power. Woman battering was viewed as acceptable behavior, particularly in cases where women "needed" to be disciplined (by men) in order to understand their "rightful" place.

To challenge the accepted public beliefs and laws regarding battered women, we must challenge the contention that wives (women) belong to husbands (men). It was not until the latter half of the nineteenth century that such challenges began to appear in the legal code.

The public and systemic response to battered women, consistent with the focus on "why does she stay?" often gets in a rut of viewing battered women as "uncooperative" or "reluctant." This brings us back to the earlier discussion about "learned helplessness": Do battered women have this, or does the system that has historically failed to protect battered women asking for arrests and convictions have it? More recent research suggests that battered women, rather than being "uncooperative," are more likely extremely frustrated with a system that fails to address their victimizations (see Browne, 1987; Erez and Belknap, 1998; Jones, 1994). For example, despite the widely held belief that all battered women are upset when their abusers are arrested, even to the point of attacking the police themselves, a considerable body of research reports that police are often unwilling to make arrests even when the battered woman requests it (Bowker, 1982; Brown, 1984; Buzawa and Austin, 1993; Dolon et al., 1986; Ferraro, 1989b; Oppenlander, 1982; Pagelow, 1981; Websdale, 1995; Websdale and Johnson, 1997; Zoomer, 1989), even though battered women may be more likely than other assault victims to make such a request (Eigenberg et al., 1996; Oppenlander, 1982). Some research found that victim injury has no bearing on a police officer's likelihood of arresting a violent intimate partner (Berk and Loseke, 1981; Eigenberg et al., 1996; Hatty, 1989; Smith and Klein, 1984; Worden and Pollitz, 1984). Moreover, although police are more likely to arrest intimate partner abusers when a weapon is present or used, the levels of arrest even when a weapon is present have historically been quite low (Bachman and Coker, 1995; Buzawa and Austin, 1993; Eigenberg et al., 1996).

The Police

The police are usually the first, and often the only, contact battering victims and offenders face. Most research in the area of battering has criticized the police for their failure to respond adequately to battered women's calls for help. These calls are often viewed as frustrating and unimportant to police officers. Because most persons who aspire to become police officers do so with the idea that they are going to "fight crime," the aspects of their job that are viewed as more mundane, or "peace keeping," are often resented. Most assaults are viewed as a crime by the police; historically, however, woman battering has not been defined as criminal in the context of policing but rather is viewed as a "mild disturbance." Ironically, the police simultaneously perceive these as the most dangerous calls for them. A 1980s analysis of FBI statistics showed that estimates of police deaths during "domestic disturbances" were inflated by about 200 percent (Garner and Clemmer, 1986). This study laid to rest the belief that domestic violence calls were the most dangerous calls to which police respond. The error in prior studies was the manner in which "domestic disturbances" were operationalized. In addition to "family violence," domestic disturbance calls also included "bar fights, gang calls, general disturbances . . . , and incidents where a citizen is brandishing a firearm" (ibid., 2). In fact, if more accurate measures are used, analysis shows that between 1973 and 1984, more officers were killed accidentally as a result of their own or other police officers' actions (65 officers) than were killed in "domestic disturbances" (56 officers) (ibid.).

The potential for danger in responding to battering, however, is uncontested. First, the police are responding to a man who has already proven he is capable of violence. Second, the offender also probably believes that nobody, including the police, has any right to tell him how to treat his wife or girlfriend. Most batterers resent anyone telling them what do or coming to their victims' aid. Clearly, these are potentially explosive situations. Given that responding to violent calls is part of the job, police training needs to address the importance of responding to all calls, including battering, in a professional and effective manner.

Historically, the problem with law enforcement tended to start even prior to the police officers' arrival on the scene. Police dispatchers often downplay woman-battering calls, even when the assault is reported as "in progress"

(Oppenlander, 1982). When dispatchers describe the call as an "assault" rather than a "disturbance," officers' response is more immediate because the call is seen as a potential arrest (Stanko, 1985, 108–109). Moreover, the implementation of the 911 number and computer-aided dispatching may increase the likelihood that calls are screened out and that the individual needs of victims are ignored (Manning, 1992). Officers often justify slower response times to woman-battering cases because of their own personal (not departmental) policies and hope that the offender will have left and/or the dispute will be resolved by the time they arrive (Oppenlander, 1982).

Before the 1960s, police training in domestic violence was rare, and few departments had policies on how the police should respond to these calls. In the 1960s, mediation training and policies were implemented in many departments. Mediation policies and training encouraged police officers to treat woman battering as merely a breech of the public peace and to calm the parties down. However, a mediation response communicates to everyone involved—the victim, the offender, the children, witnesses, and the police—that a serious crime has not occurred. The batterer's violence goes unpunished and in some respects is actually sanctioned by the police department because they know what has occurred and still fail to restrict or punish the offender.

Evidence that mediation does not deter battering is apparent from the vast number of repeat calls police receive to return to relationships where they previously used mediation. Furthermore, research suggests that mediation is not even a temporary solution. One study found that "[e]ven when the patrol officer leaves the scene of conflict, nearly a fourth of the domestic assault victims remain in a state of distress" (ibid., 455). At the same time, National Crime Survey data analysis reports that 37 percent of the battered women who call the police do so to prevent an incident from happening (Langan and Innes, 1986). Also disturbing are research findings that the police tend to focus most concern on the offender rather than to adapt to the victim's needs (Oppenlander, 1982). In short, police response to woman battering, unlike other assaults, has traditionally included a formal or informal policy of arrest avoidance (Bell and Bell, 1991; Dobash and Dobash, 1979; Erez, 1986; Finesmith, 1983; Gondolf and Fisher, 1988; Hanmer et al., 1989; Oppenlander, 1982; Rowe, 1985; Schechter, 1982; Stanko, 1985; Tong, 1984; Zorza, 1992). Indeed, the only study conducted comparing police likelihood to arrest intimate partner versus other types of assaults found that police are significantly more likely (24 percent) to arrest assaults other than by intimate partner than they are to arrest for intimate partner assaults (17 percent) (Eigenberg et al., 1996).

Four factors helped to change the traditional police response of nonintervention (including mediation) in woman-battering calls. First, it was clear that mediation was as ineffective as nonintervention (Finesmith, 1983; Gee, 1983; Rowe, 1985; Stanko, 1985; Tong, 1984). Second, the feminist movement was gaining momentum and organizing around male violence against women, including the implementation of the first battered women's shelters and rape-crisis centers. This was related to the third factor—court cases aimed at police departments.

Battered women, often in class-action suits, began taking police departments to court for failing to arrest their batterers and leaving them in dangerous and life-threatening situations (see Eppler, 1986). The battered women were successful in the court outcomes, using the Fourteenth Amendment to contend that they were not treated equally by the police as persons assaulted by strangers. Probably the most famous of these is the 1984 *Thurman v. City of Torrington* case, where Tracey Thurman's repeated calls to the police and the restraining order she obtained were ineffective in acquiring police protection. During Thurman's final battering, the police not only delayed in responding to the call but watched for some time as her batterer severely assaulted her. Thurman suffered severe and permanent physical damage. However, Tracy Thurman not only won her lawsuit against the police department, but the aftermath of this lawsuit resulted in Connecticut's governor forming a state task force to examine responses to domestic violence (Davies et al., 1998).

The fourth and final factor influencing police policy changes in response to woman battering was research finding that arresting batterers "works." Sherman and Berk (1984) conducted the first of these studies in Minneapolis, Minnesota, where offenders were randomly assigned to three options: (1) arrest, (2) mediation, or (3) an order that the offender leave the premises. This research found that arrested batterers were the least likely to recidivate and stated that "an arrest should be made unless there are good, clear reasons why an arrest would be counterproductive" (ibid., 270).

Sherman and Berk's (ibid.) "Minneapolis experiment" was replicated, and their findings were confirmed throughout the 1980s (Berk and Newton, 1985; Jaffe et al., 1986). These four factors (mediation's ineffectiveness, feminists organizing against male violence, battered women's successful lawsuits against police departments, and research findings that arrest deters batterers) resulted in the adoption of pro-arrest (presumptive or mandatory arrest) policies in most large U.S. cities.

However, since the 1990s, a number of replications of the "Minneapolis experiment" (including ones conducted by the original researchers, Sherman and Berk) reported no differences in repeat violence by batterers who were and were not arrested (see Dunford, 1992; Dunford et al., 1990; Hirschel and Hutchison, 1992; Hirschel et al., 1991, 1992; Pate and Hamilton, 1992; Sherman et al., 1992). Thus, there is a current effort, seemingly led by Sherman, to withdraw the pro-arrest policies, given the more recent studies on their perceived ineffectiveness. This repeal effort is troubling to feminists for many reasons.

First, just because arresting batterers may not stop their battering does not in and of itself justify not arresting them. When many robbers keep robbing after being arrested, we don't throw our hands in the air and say, "Oh, we might as well not bother arresting them!" (robbery analogy made by Zorza [1992]). Second, arresting batterers gives battered women and their children an opportunity to escape, if the batterers spend at least a few hours being processed and in jail. Given this assumption, it is not surprising that an Oregon study found that the implementation of a state pro-arrest policy resulted in a significant decrease in the number of domestic homicides, women or men killing their spouses (Jolin, 1983). This study points out two important issues: (1) There is more than one way to measure the effectiveness of arrest, and (2) not only might pro-arrest policies save battered women's lives, but these policies are also likely to reduce the number of women forced into a situation where they kill their batterers in self-defense. (Interestingly, Jolin's research has received no attention by the same policing scholars who evaluated the pro-arrest policies.) A recent study using national U.S. data reported that there were about 3,000 intimate partner murders in 1976, and this has decreased over time to 1998, when there were about 1,830 such murders (Rennison and Welchans, 2000). Thus, these data indicate that the development of shelters and the implementation of pro-arrest policies have saved the lives of women *and men*. A fourth area of concern is that research evaluating pro-arrest policies has found that police often fail to comply with the policy; officers still tend not to arrest batterers even in jurisdictions with pro-arrest policies (Balos and Trotzky, 1988; Ferraro, 1989b; Lawrenz et al., 1988).

This does not mean that all feminists support pro-arrest policies. There is concern that these policies are implemented discriminantly—that batterers of color and from less wealthy neighborhoods are more likely to be arrested than their wealthier, white counterparts (Edwards, 1989; Hoff, 1990; Miller, 1989; Stanko, 1989). A second feminist concern with the pro-arrest policies is that they take decision making completely away from the victim, who may already feel powerless (Hoff, 1990; Rowe, 1985; Stanko, 1989). There is also evidence that the police arrest some victims who resist or fight back against their batterers (Martin, 1997; Stanko, 1989). While some feminists are also concerned that arresting batterers may increase violence toward the victim, there is too little research to verify this.

These feminist criticisms of pro-arrest policies do not necessarily mandate a withdrawal of the policies. Rather, they suggest that the policies need to be implemented fairly and that officers who fail to do so should be punished or held accountable in some way. Indeed, a recent study of Boulder County, Colorado, found high compliance rates with pro-arrest policies due to an "in-house" (within the government) agency responsible for following up on all dispatched domestic violence calls to determine whether there was an arrest, and if not, why (Jones and Belknap, 1999). Moreover, the crime-processing system should not avoid arresting batterers because of their potential to become more violent. Instead, police departments and the remainder of the crime-processing system must become more responsible for protecting battered women and their children. Unfortunately, the current efforts to repeal the pro-arrest policies have diverted attention from other important responses to woman battering, such as police use of referrals for victims, batterers, and their children; shelter funding and availability; and medical professionals' and court officials' responses to woman battering. Moreover, even in jurisdictions with pro-arrest policies, police compliance with these policies has been quite low, typically between only 15 and 30 percent of the dispatched calls (Balos and Trotzky, 1988; Bourg and Stock, 1994; Ferraro, 1989b; Lawrenz et al., 1988).

In addition to police officers frequently failing to arrest batterers, other options they make available to battered women have often been frustrating and ineffective. For instance, police officers are known to encourage battered women to obtain a peace bond or restraining order, although there is considerable evidence that police are often resistant to enforcing restraining orders (Erez and Belknap, 1998; Pagelow, 1993; Tong, 1984). Restraining orders were developed in order to reduce battering and to provide a remedy in addition to prosecution (Grau et al., 1985, 15). However, there are numerous limitations with the current structure of most restraining orders. Acquiring restraining orders normally places the burden on the victim. This is unrealistic in many battering situations in which a batterer leaves his victim with no access to transportation and the fear of getting "caught" trying to acquire the order overrides the desire to obtain it.

Temporary restraining orders (TROs) have been found to be more useful to fiscally independent women in less severe battering relationships but have not proven useful in more violent relationships with long histories of abuse (Chaudhuri and Daly, 1992; Grau et al., 1985). (TROs are court orders limiting a batterer's or stalker's access to any place that can be defined as the woman's "sphere of activity" [Ferraro, 1993, 173].) Although battered women's acquisitions of TROs may increase police responsiveness and empower women with more emotional and financial independence to leave abusive relationships, some women are at increased risk of violence by the batterer for retaliation for acquiring the TRO (Chaudhuri and Daly, 1992). There is also evidence that police are often reluctant to enforce restraining orders, making them useless and frustrating for the battered and stalked women who went to the efforts to get them (Erez and Belknap, 1998; Rigakos, 1997). However, research indicates that women pursue restraining orders when they have decided they've had "enough" (Fischer and Rose 1995), indicating that this may be the time that some women feel "ready" to leave the relationship. Although some criminal-processing system officials and victim advocates report frustration with battered women who obtain restraining orders and then drop them, Ford (1991) found that restraining orders are an important negotiating tool that battered women use to gain more power in their relationships with their abusers and to stop the abuse. Thus, regardless of whether some victims decide to drop restraining orders, police who routinely fail to enforce restraining orders when battered women report their violations are not only not doing their jobs but are likely reinforcing batterers' belief that it is their right to violate these women, and in doing so, these women are at risk of greater, even lethal, violence.

Finally, there is some indication that police officers are disproportionately likely, compared to the general population, to themselves be involved in intimate partner violence (see Neidig et al., 1992). Moreover, and not surprisingly, officers who themselves are abusive to their wives are more likely to take antivictim stances in responding to domestic violence calls (Stith, 1990). At the same time, it is important to note studies with positive findings about police responses. One study of over 300 pregnant Hispanic women who were abused by an intimate male partner found that of the 23 percent who had used the police, almost three-fourths rated the police as "somewhat" or "very" effective, and women who used the police reported less serious abuse than those who had not used the police (Wiist and McFarlane, 1998).

The Courts

The police are not the only actors in the crime-processing system who often fail to respond to the plight of battered women. A study in Minnesota and Illinois found that arrested batterers are convicted of felonies less than 10 percent of the time (Blodgett, 1987, 68). Furthermore, Barbara Hart, founder of the National Coalition against Domestic Violence, stated, "Judges don't usually do anything the first time a man violates an order of protection" (quoted in Blodgett, 1987).

The courts' condoning of woman battering is not a recent phenomenon. In fact, court responses have improved, although a great deal of change is still necessary to protect battered women adequately. Early British Common Law established the "rule of thumb," a ruling that allowed husbands to beat their wives with rods no larger than the thickness of their thumbs. In 1824, the Mississippi Supreme Court upheld this ruling. "Progress" was made in 1864 with North Carolina's "curtain rule": The law could interfere with a husband's chastisement of his wife (go beyond the curtain of the home) but only where the husband's violence resulted in permanent injury to the wife (Tong, 1984, 128). Thus, courts have historically defined some forms of wife abuse as legal.

A study of the abuse of women in San Deigo County in the late 1800s found that the "white male prosecutors, judges, juries, and police tended to respond with bipolar extremes: harness or leniency" (Parker, 1997, 294). More specifically, in those few cases where there was overwhelming evidence (particularly if the wife was murdered), serious action was taken against the male abuser. However, the more typical response was leniency, not wanting to compromise the husband's financial and social reputation. Similar to current day processing, men of color were most likely to have the harshest responses, as were poor men, and women's with "bad" reputations were rarely seen as worthy of the court's time.

With the implementation of pro-arrest policies, there has been a large increase in the number of battering cases that reach the court system (Goolkasian, 1986, 3). While battered women vary in what they want from prosecution, they have in common the experience of facing "significant barriers to safe and effective participation as victim-witnesses in the criminal justice process" (Hart, 1993, 625). Battered women frequently feel frustrated when they have made it to court, but the judge decides to take no action, to dismiss the case, or to acquit the batterer. This lets victims know that one more source of help has failed them. It is important to note that police officers also complain of the courts' failure to act. Understandably, police often wonder why they should bother trying to help the victim and make an arrest if the judge isn't going to sentence the batterer. Similarly, some battered women's shelter

workers have ambivalent feelings about encouraging victims to take the batterers to court, knowing the likelihood that nothing will be accomplished.
Unfortunately, the courts, as well as the police, have tended to favor mediation
as an appropriate response to battering (see Goolkasian, 1986).

A particularly vulnerable time for women who have decided to press
charges and follow through is the pretrial period. During this time, it is not
unusual for the batterer to attempt to "woo" his estranged victim back by
promising they can start over and that he won't be violent anymore. If this
doesn't work, he is likely to try to intimidate her with threats of what he will
do to her or to her loved ones if she goes to court. One study found that many
women who went in to drop battering charges were escorted by their batterers, and fear was the major reason battered women gave for dropping charges
against batterers (Quarm and Schwartz, 1985).

To address the lack of response to woman battering, many scholars and
activists have pushed for a more community-oriented and comprehensive
approach to handling this violence. Currently, the police, courts, and corrections often have conflicting goals. The police are often frustrated by judges'
dismissal of the often dangerous cases they diligently pursued. Judges sometimes fail to grant TROs in an effort to protect batterers' rights, and even
when they are granted they're often not enforced (McCann 1985). Therefore,
there is a need to coordinate the police, judiciary, and social services in order
to respond effectively to woman battering (Gamache et al., 1988). Battered
women who prosecute "frequently report that criminal justice system personnel appear to consider them 'unworthy victims' who are clogging up the
courts with unimportant family matters" (Hart, 1993, 626). There is evidence
that battered women are more likely to testify when they have support from
and access to community referrals and advocates assigned to their cases
(Goolkasian, 1986). In fact, social workers can serve as effective conduits of
information between the police, the prosecutor, and the victim, as well as help
establish trust between the victim and the crime-processing personnel (Martin, 1988; Mullarkey, 1988).

Just as police officers tend to focus on the offenders, judges also tend to
"side" with batterers (Crites, 1987). This is likely due to the judges' own sexist attitudes regarding a man's right to privacy, the desirability of keeping families intact, and even the husbands' justifications and excuses for abuse. Battered
women and their advocates hold realistic concerns that pursuing charges against
batterers may result in repeated and even escalated violence. Moreover, an
acquittal by the court likely empowers batterers to continue the abuse (ibid.).
In fact, battered women appear to be at an elevated risk for retaliatory violence
compared to other victim–witnesses who prosecute (Hart, 1993).

One development in the past decade has been the increased use of the battered women's syndrome (BWS) in court. This "diagnosis" is typically brought
in as a defense for women who killed their batterers and usually requires an
expert witness to verify that this particular woman suffers from BWS. Before
defining BWS, it is important to address the dynamics behind women killing
their batterers.

In some cases, the batterer may eventually become a victim of his own violence, particularly if the woman uses force to defend herself or others from his attacks. There are homes where the violence reaches lethal levels and it is difficult to predict who might ultimately die, although statistics suggest the victim will most likely be the woman. (Walker, 1983b, 102)

Men are more likely to kill battered women than women are to kill their batterers, even in self-defense (see, for example, Browne and Williams, 1993; Gauthier and Bankston, 1997; Greenfeld and Snell, 1999, and Chapter 3 in this book). Ironically, it has been noted that the same court system and judges who have refused to take the victims of battering seriously "appear to exercise little leniency toward women who kill their husbands in self-defense or after years of abuse" (Crites, 1987, 45). Women who are released from charges of killing their batterers have typically had to plead insanity or temporary insanity; however, the insanity plea is problematic. First, it could result in a stigma almost as harsh as criminality (Marcus, 1981, 1711). Second, the insanity plea is problematic in that most evidence shows these women were acting sanely, using the only means they had left to get themselves, and possibly their children, out of a lethal situation. Thus, the insanity plea negates the fact that women frequently have no other alternative but to kill their batterers.

In other words, the battered woman is a victim of battering and of the criminal justice system's seeming lack of responsibility in responding to and prosecuting wife abusers. In case after case, documentation exists which consistently shows that police were called more than one time (generally an average of ten times) to intervene in a domestic violence dispute. Documentation exists which graphically depicts the woman who is battered over a period of years and when she reaches out for help from friends, family, social service agencies and the police, the stance taken by those outsiders is one of nonintervention. (Kuhl, 1985, 202)

Frequently, women who have left (or divorced) their batterers experience even more severe battering after leaving (Mahoney, 1991). It is not unusual for the batterer to threaten the victim's life after she has left him or when he suspects or knows she is planning to leave (Browne, 1987, 66). When no one helps the victims keep the batterers away, the women often logically conclude that their lives will be less violent if they return to the batterers. This is frequently the case of women who eventually kill their batterers. Even divorcing the batterer and moving to a different state does not always stop the violence.

What factors influence the likelihood of a woman killing her batterer? Research comparing women who killed and women who haven't (yet) killed their batterers shows some characteristic distinctions between the two. First, battered women who kill are more likely to be involved with a batterer who physically and, often, sexually abuses her/their children (Browne, 1987; Ewing, 1987; Walker, 1989). Second, battered women who kill have perceived a more immediate sense of danger, usually involving violence that has increased in frequency, severity, and injury (Browne, 1987; Ewing, 1987;

Walker, 1989). Finally, battered women who kill are more likely to have received death threats and been terrorized with weapons (often firearms) (Browne, 1987; Ewing, 1987). It is useful to note that these findings suggest that the factors that "trigger" a battered woman to kill have more to do with actions of the batterer than actions of the victim.

While self-defense has been increasingly used as a defense in trials where women kill their batterers, it is also problematic with the courts. In three out of four cases where battered women kill, the homicide takes place during Walker's phase two, the battering incident, and often using the batterer's own weapons (Maguigan, 1991). However, one in five cases does not occur during confrontations. What occurs in the remaining 5 percent of cases is unknown (ibid.). If one accepts Walker's cycle of violence theory, it should not be surprising to find that one-fifth of the killings of batterers by victims takes place during nonconfrontations, probably the tension-building phase, in which the batterer often makes threats to kill the woman and/or her/their children. One study of battered women who kill found that 83 percent of these women's batterers had threatened to kill somebody. "Given their experience with the men's capacity for violence, the women took what they said quite seriously" (Browne, 1987, 65). Because she believes this threat, she may decide at the least to provide a defense and possibly to kill him. This is often after many requests to the police and others for help have not been granted. She realizes that for survival, she has to take matters into her own hands. Frequently, battered women who kill use weapons because they lack the physical strength to overpower their batterers. They may in fact simply be trying to stop the batterer temporarily (not to kill him); however, the use of weapons may lead to the batterer's death (Flynn, 1977, 17).

Although the victim realizes that a violent and possibly deadly interaction is probably inevitable in the near future, she does not know exactly when it will occur. She doesn't know if she'll come home from work, be wakened in the middle of the night, or be in the middle of a family reunion when he finally "blows." In some cases, a victim may take steps to defend herself prior to an attack, when she has more control over the situation. Pleading self-defense for a murder charge when the woman had clearly prepared for assault, and particularly where her violence did not occur during an incident where the batterer was actually hitting her, poses culpability problems to judges and jurors.

One battered woman in Browne's (1987) study was told by her husband that he was going to kill her if she did not find out what had happened to his current lover, whom he'd also abused and who had left him. This woman had no idea where her husband's other victim had fled, but she believed his threat. In this instance, she had prepared to defend herself by locating one of his guns. She did not shoot him even when he was shooting at her (with another one of his guns). She did not shoot him until he attempted to kill their child.

It is difficult to question a woman's rationality in the vast majority of these situations. Women who kill their batterers usually do so only after having exhausted alternatives, including leaving him and contacting the crime-processing system. These women have usually come to the conclusion that the batterer will never leave her alone—she can't stop him and the crime-processing system can't—or won't stop him. Thus, the victim might decide it is safer and more rational to kill the batterer before the violence escalates to Walker's phase two, when her chances of having any control in the confrontation are significantly diminished. The following experience of one woman who killed her batterer exemplifies how battered women who kill have frequently exhausted all "legitimate" resources:

> She had been shot by her husband six times, four bullets aimed at her, the last two at her young son, whose body she shielded with her own. The man was given six months in jail. She divorced him, had a restraining order, and had moved to another county. A few weeks before our interview she had seen her ex-husband on her property and called the police, who replied, "We can't help you. He hasn't done anything yet." When I asked the woman what she was going to do, she replied bitterly, "I bought a gun. Nobody's going to take care of me. If he comes back, I'm going to use my gun." (Rosewater, 1988, 205)

In some cases where women have killed their batterers, experts have been brought in to explain BWS. BWS has three components: Walker's cycle of violence, learned helplessness, and posttraumatic stress disorder (PTSD). The former two components were discussed earlier in this chapter. PTSD, developed to explain responses of U.S. Vietnam War veterans, claims that certain psychological symptoms result from experiencing severe and unexpected trauma or being unexpectedly and repeatedly exposed to abuse. Research suggests, as expected, that the likelihood of a battered woman being diagnosed with PTSD is related to the severity of the abuse and the types of abuse, as well as other life events and the availability of social support systems, in the predicted directions (see Astin et al. 1993; Kemp et al., 1995). However, there is some concern with using PTSD and defining battered women as psychotic or mentally ill. Also, we must approach the BWS with caution, in that it may define others as "experts," disallowing the woman's experience and reports of her own unique battering situation (Davies et al., 1998).

Expert witnesses have been employed since the 1980s to educate judges and juries about the dynamics behind battering (Attorney General's Task Force on Family Violence, 1984, 41). Testimony regarding BWS is usually used to provide evidence that the woman was indeed battered, as suggested by psychological indicators. Although feminists in part have supported the use of expert witnesses in cases where women have killed their batterers, the result is that battered women, particularly until more recently, have not had the chance to tell their own stories. The case of *People v. Eleuterio* (1975) portrays this:

> At the time of this killing she was 25 years of age, had an above average I.Q. and had attended college. She had been married to the decedent for five years and had two infant daughters. . . . [T]he decedent worked only irregularly and the support of the family was left largely to appellant. . . . [Her husband] had physically assaulted her frequently. She

tried on several occasions to leave him but he refused to permit it. Shortly before the killing she left the decedent, moved to Watertown and instituted divorce proceedings. Decedent followed her and insisted that she terminate the divorce action. Fearing injury to herself and her children she allowed him to move in with the family again. . . . On the night of the killing decedent and appellant argued again about separating. Decedent refused to do so, verbally abused her and struck her in the face. He then got his .22 caliber pistol, cleaned it and placed it on his pillow next to him before going to sleep. During the night appellant awoke and using her husband's gun fired two shots into his head. She then drove to the police station with the gun and turned herself in. (*People v. Eleuterio,* 1975, as cited by Marcus 1981, 1728)

The defendant in this case received an "indeterminate sentence of up to twelve years, despite medical testimony that appellant needed psychiatric treatment on an outpatient basis rather than institutionalization" (Marcus, 1981, 1728). In this case and many others where battered women have killed their abusers, they have little or no say in the trial. Their lawyers are often unlikely to let them take the stand to tell their own stories in spite of the fact that they wish to do so. Thus, the judge or jury may base the facts only on events recorded in the police reports, which do not identify a pattern of victimization against the accused victim. This is an effective way of silencing victimized women and appears to have resulted in extremely harsh sentences.

Many women survivors who have killed their batterers in self-defense have received life imprisonment in spite of an otherwise clean record. In fact, it is common for battered women who kill not only to admit that they killed but also to notify the police. Although usually in a state of shock, they often assume that it will be apparent to the police and courts that they acted in self-defense. This, unfortunately, is not often the case, as was discussed in Chapter 4. The heartbreak of these cases is further confounded by women who have killed in order to save their own and their children's lives, only to be in prison and have their children placed in foster homes or possibly with relatives of the batterer.

Most court cases of battered women who kill have resulted in convictions with no appeals (Gillespie, 1989). Some scholars believe that the BWS defense is necessary because the current interpretation of the self-defense law is largely patriarchal and fails to understand the threat of great bodily harm and death that victims experience (see Gillespie, 1989). However, a number of costs are associated with using BWS as a defense. Although it goes beyond insanity and self-defense claims to help women who kill their batterers, it perpetuates stereotypical images of women.

The aspect of BWS that has been most severely criticized by feminists is learned helplessness because it perpetuates images of women as passive and weak. An adoption of this view stereotypes women who kill their batterers as "abnormal," although their responses are quite normal compared to victims in similar situations (see Sheehy et al., 1991). Moreover, the guilt, low self-esteem, self-blame, and depression these women report might be a result of the failure of family, police, judges, and physicians to provide help (Gondolf and

Fisher, 1988). Some women's justifiable anger at being abused and not being protected by the crime-processing system at least partially explains why they kill their batterers. By definition, this anger fails to fit the "learned helplessness" model (see Allard, 1991; Mahoney, 1991). In fact, it has been noted that BWS is less likely to work for African-American women because they are more likely to be viewed as angry by judges and juries (Allard, 1991). Another cost of the BWS defense is that when women are viewed as abnormal, irrational, weak, mentally ill, or angry, they are at increased risk of losing custody of their children (Stark, 1992).

HEALTH PROFESSIONALS

Although health professionals are not direct operators in the crime-processing system, they have key interactions with victims. Women's health is very much related to intimate partner violence (for an excellent overview, see Stark and Flitcraft, 1996). Historically, the training on battering that physicians, welfare and mental health professionals, and the clergy traditionally received "reflects a bias toward keeping the family together at all costs" (Goolkasian, 1986, 3). Because of the severe injuries battered women frequently receive, it is not unusual for them to require help from their private physicians or emergency medical personnel. Although the potential for the medical field to deter battering is great, the response has been "slow and sporadic" (Kurz and Stark, 1988, 249). When workers in the health care professions—physicians, nurses, and social workers—fail to ask the cause of battered women's injuries, they perpetuate the invisibility of battering and contribute to the women's rationalization that they are not really victims (Campbell, 1991; Dobash and Dobash, 1979). Additionally, mental health clinicians and counselors frequently deal with battered women as their clients. It is important for all of these actors to label the act for what it is—violence.

Although physicians, particularly emergency room physicians, may be acutely aware that the woman they are treating is a battering victim, they are unlikely to address how the injury was caused (Star et al., 1979). Research in nursing journals claims a lack of sensitivity and appropriate action in treating battered women on the part of nurses as well as doctors (Drake, 1982). One study of emergency department staff workers found three responses to battered women: 11 percent had positive reactions, where they showed concern for the battered woman's safety as well as providing medical care; 49 percent provided a partial response where medical provisions were "brief" and "routine" and had low priority; and 40 percent of the staff did not respond to the battering aspect of the case (Kurz, 1987). This exemplifies how the invisibility of battered women is maintained among medical professionals. If one goal of medicine is prevention, then failure to address the cause is particularly problematic. Just as police officers should act professionally in response to battering calls, health care workers also have professional responsibilities to determine the cause of the injury and to plan for prevention of further injury. Responding similarly to many law enforcement officals, many health care workers lose their patience with victims who leave the hospitals with their batterers or have returned to the hospital with injuries, presumably from the same batterer. That health care professionals are "fed up" with battered women is not a legitimate excuse for ignoring their injuries.

Medicalization is a process by which medical professionals define an emerging social problem as belonging within their professional expertise (Kurz, 1987). Medical professionals are reluctant to medicalize woman battering and often view responding to battering as detracting from their proper role (ibid.). (This is similar to police officers who view the appropriate response to woman battering as "peace keeping" and who resent peace keeping because it is not considered "real" police work.) It is unusual for emergency room physicians to take detailed histories of women who are obviously victims of battering, even when serious wounds or injuries are present. These physicians rarely open up a discussion for such crucial questions as how the abuse occurred and who did it, often reinforcing some battered women's efforts to minimize the reality and severity of their abuse (Warshaw, 1993). One example of how negatively the emergency room professionals view battered women is that "battered women who attempted suicide were significantly more likely than nonbattered women to be sent home and/or to receive no referral of any kind after a suicide attempt" (Kurz and Stark, 1988, 253). More recent research reports that, not surprisingly, intimate partner violence, particularly marital rape, increases a woman' likelihood of severe depression (Campbell and Soeken, 1999; Campbell et al., 1997; Forte et al., 1996). Furthermore, one study found that battered women "who are able to retain a strong interest in their own welfare in spite of abuse will be more resistant to depression (Campbell et al, 1997, 288). This is an important finding in that the availability of resources and support for battered women likely increase their ability to retain an interest in their own welfare. Notably, leaving a battering relationship is not necessarily the end of the depression for the victim (Herbert et al., 1991), suggesting the impacts of intimate partner violence can be long term. One study found that upon immediate exit from a women's shelter, 83 percent of the battered women experienced depression, but 10 weeks later this proportion had decreased to one-half of the women (Campbell et al., 1995). Significantly, women who reported higher levels of social support in their lives were less likely to report depression, indicating the importance of adequate institutional responses to battered women (ibid.). Relative to the rest of the population, it is not uncommon for battered women or battering men to attempt suicide. Both the batterer and the victim in these cases believe (and it would seem logically so) that the violence is not going to stop until one of them dies.

In sum, both crime-processing and health professionals tend not only to keep woman battering hidden but to condone it through their own failure to respond adequately. Any other phenomenon that occurred as frequently and caused the degree of injury that woman battering does would likely result in a national outrage and an effort to treat the victim or control the cause (Star et al., 1979).

SUMMARY

Many of the myths and problems surrounding woman battering are discussed in this chapter. Battering may take place in many forms, but its results are always devastating. When exploring the causes of battering, it is not enough to simply examine batterers or the family system; rather, battering must be viewed in a sociohistorical context. Battering must be deterred not only by reacting to individuals but also by building a political, economic, and social system that is more equitable to women and a crime-processing and health system that is more responsive to battering. The current situation leaves battered women with little recourse to escape abusive relationships safely. Additionally, the culture provides an environment that accepts male violence as "normal." Not until gender equality and male violence are confronted on a more global and pervasive level will battering be viewed as unacceptable and indeed criminal.

NOTES

1. I placed elder in quotation marks because many advocates for older people find the term elder offensive, particularly when referring to persons in their sixties.

2. Battering in lesbian and gay relationships has been documented, although insufficient research exists to compare this to the rate of battering in heterosexual relationships. For more information on lesbian battering see Lobel (1986) and Renzetti (1992).

3. Consistently throughout this chapter I refer to the children as "her/their" since the batterer is not always the father of all or any of the children the battered woman is raising.

REFERENCES

Abraham, Margaret. 1999. "Sexual Abuse in South Asian Immigrant Marriages." *Violence Against Women* 5(6): 591–618.

Allard, Sharon A. 1991. "Rethinking Battered Woman Syndrome: A Black Feminist Perspective." *UCLA Women's Law Journal* 1:191–207.

Astin, Millie C., Kathy J. Lawrence, and David W. Foy. 1993. "Posttraumatic Stress Disorder among Battered Women." *Violence and Victims* 8(1):17–29.

Attorney General's Task Force on Family Violence. 1984. *Final Report,* September, 157 pp.

Bachman, Ronet, and Ann L. Coker. 1995. "Police Involvment in Domestic Violence." *Violence and Victims* 10:98–106.

Balos, Beverly, and Katie Trotzky. 1988. "Enforcement of the Domestic Abuse Act in Minnesota: A Preliminary Study." *Law and Inequality* 6:83–125.

Barnett, Ola W., Cheok Y. Lee, and Rose E. Thelen. 1997. "Gender Differences in Attributions of Self-Defense and Control in Interpartner Aggression." *Violence Against Women* 3(5):462–481.

Barnett, Ola W., Tomas E. Martinez, and Brendon W. Bluestein. 1995. "Jealousy and Romantic Attachment in Maritally Violent and Nonviolent Men." *Journal of Interpersonal Violence* 10(4):473–486.

Belknap, Joanne, and K. Douglas McCall. 1994. "Woman Battering and Police Referrals." *Journal of Criminal Justice* 22:195–208.

Bell, Daniel J., and Sandra L. Bell. 1991. "The Victim-Offender Relationship as a Determinant Factor in Police Dispositions of Family Violence Incidents." *Policing and Society* 1:225–234.

Berk, Sarah F., and Donileen R. Loseke. 1981. " 'Handling' Family Violence: Situational Determinants of Police Arrest in Domestic Disturbance." *Law and Society* 15:317–346.

Berk, Richard A., Sarah F. Berk, Donileen R. Loseke, and David Rauma. 1983. "Combat and Other Family Violence Myths." Pp. 197–212 in *The Dark Side of Families: Current Family Violence Research,* edited by D. Finkelhor, R. J. Gelles, G. T. Hotaling, and M. A. Straus. Beverly Hills, CA: Sage.

Berk, Richard A., Alec Campbell, Ruth Klap, and Bruce Western. 1992. "The Deterrent Effect of Arrest in Incidents of Domestic Violence: A Bayesian Analysis of the Colorado Springs Spouse Abuse Experiment." *Journal of Criminal Law and Criminology* 83:170–200.

Berk, Richard A., and Phyllis J. Newton. 1985. "Does Arrest Really Deter Wife Battery? An Effort to Replicate the Findings of the Minneapolis Spouse Abuse Experiment." *American Sociological Review* 50(2):253–262.

Berk, Richard A., David Rauma, and Donileen R. Loseke. 1982. "Throwing the Cops Back Out: The Decline of a Local Program to the Criminal Justice System More Responsive to Incidents of Domestic Violence." *Social Science Research* 11: 245–279.

Berkowitz, Leonard. 1983. "The Goals of Aggression." Pp. 166–181 in *The Dark Side of Families: Current Family Violence Research* edited by D. Finkelhor, R. J. Gelles, G. T. Hotaling, and M. A. Straus. Beverly Hills, CA: Sage.

Blodgett, Nancy. 1987. "Violence in the Home." *ABA Journal* (May, 1):66–69.

Bogal-Allbritten, Rosemarie, and William L. Allbritten. 1985. "The Hidden Victims: Courtship Violence among College Students." *Journal of College Student Personnel* 26:201–204.

Bograd, Michele. 1988. "Feminist Perspectives on Wife Abuse: An Introduction." Pp. 11–27 in *Feminist Perspectives on Wife Abuse,* edited by K. Yllo and M. Bograd. Newbury Park, CA: Sage.

Bohannon, Judy R., David A. Dosser, and S. Eugene Lindley. 1995. "Using Couple Data to Determine Domestic Violence Rates." *Violence and Victims* 10(2):133–141.

Bourg, S. and H. V. Stock. 1994. "A Review of Domestic Violence Arrest Statistics in a Police Department Using Pro-Arrest Policy." *Journal of Family Violence* 9:177–89.

Bowker, Lee H. 1982. "Police Services to Battered Women." *Criminal Justice and Behavior* 9:476–494.

Bowker, Lee H., Michelle Arbitell, and J. Richard McFerron. 1988. "On the Relationship between Wife Beating and Child Abuse." Pp. 158–174 in *Feminist Perspectives on Wife Abuse,* edited by K. Yllo and M. Bograd. Newbury Park, CA: Sage.

Boye-Beaman, Joni, Kenneth E. Leonard, and Marilyn Senchak. 1993. "Male Premarital Aggression and Gender Identity among Black and White Newlywed Couples." *Journal of Marriage and the Family* 55:303–313.

Breines, Wini, and Linda Gordon. 1983. "The New Scholarship on Family Violence." *Signs: Journal of Women in Culture and Society* 18:490–531.

Brisson, Norman J. 1981. "Battering Husbands: A Survey of Abusive Men." *Victimology* 6:338–344.

Brown, Stephen E. 1984. "Police Responses to Wife Beating." *Journal of Criminal Justice* 12:277–2.

Browne, Angela. 1987. *When Battered Women Kill.* New York: Free Press.

Browne, Angela, Amy Salomon, and Shari S. Bassuk. 1999. "The Impact of Recent Partner Violence on Poor Women's Capacity to Maintain Work." *Violence against Women* 5(4):393–426.

Browne, Angela, and Kirk R. Williams. 1993. "Gender, Intimacy, and Lethal Violence: Trends from 1976 through 1987." *Gender and Society* 7:78–98.

Bui, Hoan N., and Merry Morash. 1999. "Domestic Violence in the Vietnamese Immigrant Community." *Violence against Women* 5(7):769–795.

Burris, Carole Anne, and Peter Jaffe. 1983. "Wife Abuse as a Crime: The Impact of Police Laying Charges." *Canadian Journal* 25:309–318.

Buzawa, Eve S., and Austin, Thomas. 1993. "Determining Police Response to Domestic Violence Victims." *American Behavioral Scientist 36* (5):610–623.

Buzawa, Eve S., and Carl G. Buzawa. 1990. *Domestic Violence: The Criminal Justice Response.* Newbury Park, CA: Sage.

Cahn, N. R. 1992. "Innovative Approaches to the Prosecution of Domestic Crimes." Pp. 161–180 in *The Changing Criminal Justice Response,* edited by E. S. Buzawa and C. G. Buzawa Westport, CT: Auburn House.

Campbell, Jacquelyn C. 1991. "Public-Health Conceptions of Family Abuse." Pp. 35–48 in *Abused and Battered,* edited by D. D. Knudsen and J. L. Miller. New York: Aldine De Gruyter.

Campbell, Jacquelyn C. 1992. "If I Can't Have You, No One Can." Pp. 99–113 in *Femicide: The Politics of Woman Killing,* New York: Twayne Publishers.

Campbell, Jacquelyn C., Joan Kub, Ruth Ann Belknap, and Thomas N. Templin. 1997. "Predictors of Depression in Battered Women." *Violence against Women* 3(3):271–293.

Campbell, Jacquelyn C., and Karen L. Soeken. 1999. "Forced Sex and Intimate Partner Violence." *Violence against Women* 5(9):1017–1035.

Campbell, Rebecca, Cris M. Sullivan, and William S. Davidson. 1995. "Women Who Use Domestic Violence Shelters." *Psychology of Women Quarterly* 19:237–255.

Cappell, Charles, and R. Heiner. 1990. "The Intergenerational Transmission of Family Violence." *Journal of Family Violence* 5:135–152.

Cate, Rodney M., June M. Henton, James Koval, F. Scott Christopher, and Sally Lloyd. 1982. "Premarital Abuse: A Social Psychological Perspective." *Journal of Family Issues* 3:79–90.

Chaudhuri, Molly, and Kathleen Daly. 1992. "Do Restraining Orders Help? Battered Women's Experience with Male Violence and Legal Process." Pp. 227–252 in *Domestic Violence: The Changing Criminal Justice Response,* edited by Eve S. Buzawa and Carl G. Buzawa. Westport, CT: Auburn House.

Cohn, Ellen G., and Lawrence W. Sherman. 1987. "Police Policy on Domestic Violence, 1986: A National Survey." Crime Control Institute, *Crime Control Reports,* No. 5.

Craven, Diane. 1996. *Female Victims of Violent Crime.* Annapolis, MD: U.S. Department of Justice, Bureau of Justice Statistics.

Crites, Laura L. 1987. "Wife Abuse: The Judicial Record." Pp. 38–53 in *Women, the Courts, and Equality,* edited by L. L. Crites and W. L. Hepperle. Newbury Park, CA: Sage.

Dasgupta, Shamita, and Sujata Warrier. 1996. "In the Footsteps of 'Arundhati' ": Asian American Women's Experience of Domestic Violence in the U.S." *Violence against Women* 2(3):238–259.

Davidson, Terry. 1978. *Conjugal Crime: Understanding and Changing the Wife Beating Pattern.* New York: Hawthorne Books.

Davies, Jill, Eleanor Lyon, and Diane Monti-Catania. 1998. *Safety Planning with Battered Women.* Thousand Oaks, CA: Sage.

Davis, E. G. 1971. *The First Sex.* New York: Putnam.

Davis, P. W. 1981. "Structured Rationales for Non-Arrest: Police Stereotypes of the Domestic Disturbance." *Criminal Justice Review* 6(2):8–15.

DeKeseredy, Walter S. 1995. "Enhancing the Quality of Survey Data on Woman Abuse." *Violence against Women* 1(2):139–157.

Dobash, R. Emerson, and Russell Dobash. 1979. *Violence against Wives.* New York: Free Press.

————. 1988. "Research as Social Action: The Struggle for Battered Women." Pp. 51–74 in *Feminist Perspectives on Wife Abuse,* edited by K. Yllo and M. Bograd. Newbury Park, CA: Sage.

Dobash, Russell P., and Rebecca E. Dobash. 1981. "Community Response to Violence against Wives." *Social Problems* 28:563–581.

————. 1983. "The Context-Specific Approach." Pp. 261–276 in *The Dark Side of Families: Current Family Violence Research,* edited by D. Finkelhor, R. J. Gelles, G. T. Hotaling, and M. A. Straus. Beverly Hills, CA: Sage.

Dobash, Russell P., R. Emerson Dobash, Kate Cavanagh, and Ruth Lewis. 1998. "Separate and Intersecting Realities: A Comparison of Men's and Women's Accounts of Violence against Women." *Violence against Women* 4(4): 382–414.

Dobash, Russell P., R. Emerson Dobash, Margo Wilson, and Martin Daly. 1992. "The Myth of Sexual Symmetry in Marital Violence." *Social Problems* 39:71–91.

Dolon, Ronald, James Hendricks, and M. Steven Meagher. 1986. "Police Practices and Attitudes toward Domestic Violence." *Journal of Police Science and Administration* 14:187–192.

Drake, Virginia K. 1982. "Battered Women: A Health Care Problem in Disguise." *Image* 24:40–47.

Dunford, Franklyn W. 1992. "The Measurement of Recidivism in Cases of Spouse Assault." *Journal of Criminal Law and Criminology* 83:120–136.

Dunford, Franklyn W., David Huizinga, and Delbert S. Elliott. 1990. "The Role of Arrest in Domestic Assault: The Omaha Police Experiment." *Criminology* 28:183–206.

Dutton, Donald G. 1988. *The Domestic Assault of Women.* Boston: Allyn and Bacon.

Dutton, Donald G., and Susan L. Painter. 1981. "Traumatic Bonding: The Development of Emotional Attachments in Battered Women and Other Relationships of Intermittent Abuse." *Victimology* 6:139–155.

Edleson, Jeffrey L., A.C. Eisikovits, E. Guttman, and M. Sela-Amit, 1991. "Cognitive and Interpersonal Factors in Woman Abuse." *Journal of Family Violence* 6:167–182.

Edwards, Susan S. M. 1989. *Policing "Domestic" Violence: Women, the Law and the State.* London: Sage.

Eigenberg, Helen M., K. E. Scarborough, and Victor, E. Kappeler. 1996. "Contributory Factors Affecting Arrest in Domestic and Non-Domestic Assaults." *American Journal of Police* 15:27–54.

Eisikovits, Zvi, and Eli Buchbinder. 1999. "Talking Control: Metaphors Used by Battered Women." *Violence against Women* 5(8):845–868.

Ellis, Desmond. 1987. "Post-Separation Woman Abuse." *International Journal of Sociology of the Family* 19:67–87.

Ellis, Desmond, and Walter D. DeKeseredy. 1989. "Marital Status and Woman Abuse." *International Journal of Law and Psychiatry* 10:401–410.

Enarson, Elaine. 1999. "Violence against Women in Disasters." *Violence against Women* 5(7):742–768.

Eppler, Amy. 1986. "Battered Women and the Equal Protection Clause: Will the Constitution Help Them When the Police Won't?" *Yale Law Review* 95:788–809.

Erez, Edna. 1986. "Intimacy, Violence, and the Police." *Human Relations* 39(3):265–281.

Erez, Edna, and Joanne Belknap. 1998. "In Their Own Words: Battered Women's Assessment of Systemic Responses." *Violence and Victims* 13(3):3–20.

Ewing, Charles P. 1987. *Battered Women Who Kill.* Lexington, MA: Lexington Books.

Fagan, Jeffrey A., Douglas K. Stewart, and Karen V. Hansen. 1983. "Violent Men or Violent Husbands? Background Factors and Situational Correlates." Pp. 49–68 in *The Dark Side of Families: Current Family Violence Research,* edited by D. Finkelhor, R. J. Gelles, G. T. Hotaling, and M. A. Straus. Beverly Hills, CA: Sage.

Ferraro, Kathleen J. 1989a. "The Legal Response to Woman Battering in the United States." Pp. 155–184 in *Women, Policing, and Male Violence,* edited by J. Hanmer, J. Radford, and E. A. Stanko. London: Routledge.

Ferraro, Kathleen J. 1989b. "Policing Woman Battering." *Social Problems* 36(1):61–74.

———. 1993. "Cops, Courts, and Woman Battering." Pp. 165–176 in *Violence against Women: The Bloody Footprints,* edited by P. B. Bart and E. G. Moran. Newbury Park, CA: Sage.

Ferraro, Kathleen J., and John M. Johnson. 1983. "How Women Experience Battering." *Social Problems* 30:325–339.

Finesmith, Barbara K. 1983. "Police Responses to Battered Women: A Critique and Proposals for Reform." *Seton Hall Law Review* 14:74–109.

Finkelhor, David. 1983. "Common Features of Family Abuse." Pp. 17–28 in *The Dark Side of Families: Current Family Violence Research,* edited by D. Finkelhor, R. J. Gelles, G. T. Hotaling, and M. A. Straus. Beverly Hills, CA: Sage.

Fischer, Korla, and Mary Rose. 1995. "When 'Enough is Enough'". *Crime and Delinquency* 41(4):414–429.

Flynn, John P. 1977. "Recent Findings Related to Wife Abuse." *Social Casework* (January):13–20.

Flynn, Clifton P. 1990. "Sex Roles and Women's Response to Courtship Violence." *Journal of Family Violence* 5(1):83–94.

Ford, David A. 1991. "Prosecution as a Victim Power Resource: A Note on Empowering Women in Violent Conjugal Relationships." *Law and Society Review 25* (2): 313–334.

Forte, James A., David D. Franks, Janett A. Forte, and Daniel Rigsby. 1996. "Asymmetrical Role-Taking: Comparing Battered and Nonbattered Women." *Social Work* 41(1):59–73.

Fothergill, Alice. 1999. "An Exploratory Study of Woman Battering in the Grand Forks Flood Disaster." *International Journal of Mass Emergencies and Disasters* 17(1):79–98.

Gamache, D. J., J. L. Edleson, and M. D. Schock, 1988. "Coordinating Police, Judicial, and Social Service Response to Woman Battering." In *Coping with Family Violence,* edited by G. T. Hotaling, D. Finkelhor, J. T. Kirkpatrick, and M. A. Straus. Beverly Hills, CA: Sage.

Garner, Joel, and Elizabeth Clemmer. 1986. "Danger to Police in Domestic Disturbances—A New Look." National Institute of Justice, *Research in Brief Report* (November):1–8.

Gauthier, DeAnn K., and William B. Bankston. 1997. "Gender Equality and the Sex Ratio of Intimate Killing." *Criminology* 35(4):577–600.

Gee, Pauline W. 1983. "Ensuring Police Protection for Battered Women: The Scott v. Hart Suit." *Signs: Journal of Women in Culture and Society* 8(3):554–567.

Gelles, Richard J. 1976. "Abused Wives: Why Do They Stay?" *Journal of Marriage and the Family* (November): 659–668.

———. 1980. "Violence in the Family: A Review of Research in the Seventies." *Journal of Marriage and the Family* (November):873–885.

Gillespie, Cynthia K. 1989. *Justifiable Homicide: Battered Women, Self-Defense, and the Law.* Columbus, OH: Ohio State University Press.

Gondolf, Edward W., with Ellen R. Fisher. 1988. *Battered Women as Survivors.* New York: Lexington Books.

Goode, W. J. 1971. "Force and Violence in the Family." *Journal of Marriage and the Family* (November):624–636.

Goolkasian, Gail A. 1986. "Confronting Domestic Violence: The Role of Criminal Court Judges." National Institute in Justice/ *Research in Brief* (November):1–8.

Graham, Dee L. R., Edna Rawlings, and Nelly Rimini. 1988. "Survivors of Terror: Battered Women, Hostages and the Stockholm Syndrome." Pp. 217–233 in *Feminist Perspectives on Wife Abuse,* edited by K. Yllo and M. Bograd. Newbury Park, CA: Sage.

Grau, Janice, Jeffrey Fagan, and Sandra Wexler. 1985. "Restraining Orders for Battered Women: Issues of Access and Efficacy." Pp. 13–20 in *Criminal Justice Politics and Women: The Aftermath of Legally Mandated Change,* edited by C. Schweber and C. Feinman. New York: Haworth Press.

Greenblat, Cathy S. 1983. "A Hit Is a Hit Is a Hit . . . Or Is It?" Pp. 235–260 in *The Dark Side of Families: Current Family Violence Research,* edited by D. Finkelhor, R. J. Gelles, G. T. Hotaling, and M. A. Straus. Beverly Hills, CA: Sage.

Greenfeld, Lawrence A., and Tracy L. Snell. 1999. *Women Offenders.* Bureau of Justice Statistics: Special Report. U.S. Department of Justice, December, 14 pp.

Haj-Yahia, Muhammad M. 1998. "Beliefs about Wife Beating among Palestinian Women." *Violence against Women* 4(5):533–558.

Hamberger, L. Kevin, Jeffrey M. Lohr, Dennis Bonge, and David F. Tolin. 1997. "An Empirical Classification of Motivations for Domestic Violence." *Violence against Women* 3(4):401–423.

Hanmer, Jalna, Jill Radford, and Elizabeth A. Stanko. 1989. "Policing, Men's Violence: An Introduction." Pp. 1–12 in *Women, Policing, and Male Violence: International Perspectives,* edited by J. Hanmer, J. Radford, and E. A. Stanko. London: Routledge and Kegan Paul.

Hart, Barbara. 1993. "Battered Women and the Criminal Justice System." *American Behavioral Scientist* 36:624–638.

Hatty, Suzanne E. 1989. "Policing Male Violence in Australia." Pp. 70–89 *Women, Policing, and Male Violence,* edited by J. Hanmer, J. Radford, and E. A. Stanko. London: Routledge.

Herbert, Tracy B., Roxane C. Silver, and John H. Ellard. 1991. *Journal of Marriage and the Family* 53:311–325.

Hirschel, J. David, and Ira W. Hutchison III. 1992. "Female Spouse Abuse and the Police Response: The Charlotte, North Carolina, Experiment." *Journal of Criminal Law and Criminology* 83:73–119.

Hirschel, J. David, Ira W. Hutchison III, and Charles W. Dean. 1991. "The Charlotte Spouse Abuse Study." *Popular Government* (Summer):11–16.

Hirschel, J. David, Ira W. Hutchison III, and Charles W. Dean. 1992. "The Failure of Arrest to Deter Spouse Abuse." *Journal of Research in Crime and Delinquency* 29(1):7–33.

Hoff, Lee Ann. 1990. *Battered Women as Survivors.* London: Routledge and Kegan Paul.

Holtzworth-Munroe, Amy, Natalie Smutzler, and Leonard Bates. 1997. "A Brief Review of the Research on Husband Violence. Part III." *Aggression and Violent Behavior* 2(3):285–307.

Jaffe, Peter G., David A. Wolfe, Anne Telford, and Gary Austin. 1986. "The Impact of Police Charges in Incidents of Wife Abuse." *Journal of Family Violence* 1:37–49.

Jaffe, Peter G., David A. Wolfe, and Susan Kaye Wilson. 1990. *Children of Battered Women.* Newbury Park, CA: Sage.

Johnson, Holly. 1995. "Risk Factors Associated with Non-Lethal Violence against Women by Marital Partners." Pp. 151–168 in *Trends, Risks, and Interventions in Lethal Violence.* National Institute of Justice: Research Report.

Jolin, Annette. 1983. "Domestic Violence Legislation: An Impact Assessment." *Journal of Police Science and Administration* 11:451–456.

Jones, Ann. 1994. *Next Time, She'll Be Dead: Battering and How to Stop It.* Boston: Beacon Press.

Jones, Dana A., and Joanne Belknap. 1999. "Police Responses to Battering in a Pro-Arrest Jurisdiction." *Justice Quarterly* 16 (2):249–273.

Kantor, Glenda K., and Murray A. Straus. 1987. "The 'Drunken Bum' Theory of Wife Beating." *Social Problems* 3:213–230.

Kanuha, V. 1996. "Domestic Violence, Racism, and the Battered Women's Movement in the United States." Pp. 34–50 in *Future Interventions with Battered Women and their Families,* edited by J. Edleson and Z. Eisikovits. Thousand Oaks, CA: Sage.

Kaplan, A. 1997. Domestic Violence and Welfare Reform. *Welfare Information Network: Issue Notes* 1(8):1–9.

Kemp, Anita, Bonnie L. Green, Christine Hovanitz, and Edna I. Rawlings. 1995. "Incidence and Correlates of Postraumatic Stress Disorder in Battered Women." *Journal of Interpersonal Violence* 10(1):43–55.

Klein, Dorie. 1981. "Violence against Women: Some Considerations regarding Its Causes and Its Elimination." *Crime and Delinquency* 27:64–80.

Knutson, J. F., and J. G. Mehm. 1986. "Transgenerational Patterns of Coercion in Families and Intimate Relationships." Pp. 67–90 in *Violence in Intimate Relationships,* edited by G. Russell. New York: PMA Publishing Corporation.

Kuhl, Anna F. 1985. "Battered Women Who Murder: Victims of Offenders." Pp. 197–216 in *The Changing Roles of Women in the Criminal Justice System,* edited by I. L. Moyer. Prospect Heights, IL: Waveland Press.

Kurz, Demie. 1987. "Emergency Department Responses to Battered Women: Resistance to Medicalization." *Social Problems* 34:69–81.

———. 1993. "Social Science Perspectives on Wife Abuse: Current Debates and Future Directions." Pp. 252–269 in *Violence against Women,* edited by P. B. Bart and E. G. Moran. Newbury Park, CA: Sage.

———. 1996. "Separation, Divorce, and Woman Abuse." *Violence against Women* 2(1):63–81.

Kurz, Demie, and Evan Stark. 1988. "Not-So-Benign Neglect: The Medical Response to Battering." Pp. 249–268 in *Feminist Perspectives on Wife Abuse,* edited by K. Yllo and M. Bograd. Newbury Park, CA: Sage.

Lane, K. E., and P. A. Gwartney-Gibbs. 1985. "Violence in the Context of Dating and Sex." *Journal of Family Issues* 6:45–59.

Langan, Patrick A., and Christopher A. Innes. 1986. "Preventing Domestic Violence against Women." *Bureau of Justice Statistics Special Report,* August.

Lawrenz, Frances, James F. Lembo, and Thomas Schade. 1988. "Time Series Analysis of the Effect of a Domestic Violence Directive on the Number of Arrests per Day." *Journal of Criminal Justice* 16:493–498.

Lloyd, Susan, and Nina Taluc. 1999. "The Effects of Male Violence on Female Employment." *Violence against Women* 5(4):370–392.

Lobel, Kerry (Ed.). 1986. *Naming the Violence: Speaking Out about Lesbian Violence.* Seattle: Seal Press.

Loseke, Donileen R., and Spencer E. Cahill. 1984. "The Social Construction of Deviance: Experts on Battered Women." *Social Problems* 31:296–309.

Loving, N. 1980. *Responding to Spouse Abuse and Wife Beating: A Guide for Police.* Washington, DC: Police Executive Research Forum.

Maguigan, Holly. 1991. "Battered Women and Self-Defense: Myths and Misconceptions in Current Reform Proposals." *University of Pennsylvania Law Review* 140:379–486.

Mahoney, Martha. 1991. "Legal Images of Battered Women: Redefining the

Issue of Separation." *Michigan Law Review* 90:2–94.

Makepeace, J. M. 1981. "Courtship Violence among College Students." *Family Relations* 30:97–102.

———. 1986. "Gender Differences in Courtship Violence Victimization." *Family Relations* 35:383–388.

Manning, Peter K. 1992. "Screening Calls." Pp. 41–48 in *Domestic Violence: The Changing Criminal Justice Response,* edited by Eve S. Buzawa and Carl G. Buzawa. Westport, CT: Auburn House.

Marcus, M. L. 1981. "Conjugal Violence: The Law of Force and the Force of the Law." *California Law Review* 69:1657–1733.

Martin, Del. 1976. *Battered Wives.* San Francisco: Glide.

Martin, Margaret. 1988. "A Social Worker's Response." Pp. 53–61 in *The Violent Family,* edited by N. Hutchings. New York: Human Sciences Press.

Martin, Margaret E. 1997. "Double Your Trouble: Dual Arrest in Family Violence." *Journal of Family Violence* 12 (2):139–157.

Matthews, William J. 1984. "Violence in College Couples." *College Student Journal* 18:150–158.

McCann, Kathryn. 1985. "Battered Women and the Law: The Limits of Legislation." Pp. 71–96 in *Women-in-Law: Exploration in Law, Family and Sexuality,* edited by J. Brophy and C. Smart. London: Routledge and Kegan Paul.

McNulty, Faith. 1980. *The Burning Bed.* New York: Harcourt Brace Jovanovich.

Meloy, J. Reid. 1996. "Stalking (Obsessional Following): A Review of Some Preliminary Studies." *Aggression and Violent Behavior* 1(2):147–162.

Meyer, Shannon-Lee, Dina Vivian, K. Daneil O'Leary. 1998. "Men's Sexual Aggression in Marriage." *Violence against Women* 4(4):415–435.

Miller, Susan L. 1989. "Unintended Side Effects of Pro-Arrest Policies and Their Race and Class Implications for Battered Women: A Cautionary Note." *Criminal Justice Policy Review* 3:299–317.

Miller, Susan L., and Sally S. Simpson. 1991. "Courtship Violence and Social Control: Does Gender Matter?" *Law and Society Review* 25(2):335–365.

Mills, Billy G., and Mary L. McNamar. 1981. "California's Response to Domestic Violence." *Santa Clara Law Review* 21:1–19.

Mills, Trudy. 1984. "Victimization and Self-Esteem: On Equating Husband Abuse and Wife Abuse." *Victimology* 9:254–261.

Molidor, Christian, and Richard M. Tolman. 1998. "Gender and Contextual Factors in Adolescent Dating Violence." *Violence against Women* 4(2):180–194.

Morash, Merry. 1986. "Wife Battering." *Criminal Justice Abstracts* (June): 252–271.

Mrsevic, Zorica, and Donna M. Hughes. 1997. "Violence against Women in Belgrade, Serbia." *Violence against Women* 3(2):101–128.

Mullarkey, Edward. 1988. "The Legal System for Victims of Family Violence." Pp. 43–52 in *The Violent Family,* edited by N. Hutchings. New York: Human Sciences Press.

Mustaine, Elizabeth and Richard Tewksbury. 1999 "A Routine Activity Theory Explanation for Women's Stalking." *Violence Against Women* 5(1):43–62.

Neidig, Peter H., Harold E. Russell, and Albert F. Seng. 1992. "Interpersonal Aggression in Law Enforcement Families." *Police Studies* 15:30–38.

O'Keefe, Maura, and Laura Treister. 1998. "Victims of Dating Violence among High School Students." *Violence against Women* 4(2):195–223.

O'Neill, Damian. 1998. "A Post-Structuralist Review of the Theoretical Literature Surrounding Wife Abuse." *Violence Against Women* 4(4):457–490.

Oppenlander, Nan. 1982. "Coping or Copping Out." *Criminology* 20:449–465.

Pagelow, Mildred D. 1981. *Woman-Battering.* Beverly Hills: Sage.

Pagelow, Mildred D. 1993. "Justice for Victims of Spouse Abuse in Divorce and Child Custody Cases." *Violence and Victims* 8(1):69–83.

Parker, Linda S. 1997. "A 'Brutal Case' or (Only a Family Jar)?: Violence against women in San Diego County, 1880–1900." *Violence against Women* 3(3):294–318.

Pate, Antony M., and Edwin E. Hamilton. 1992. "Formal and Informal Deterrents to Domestic Violence: The Dade County Spouse Assault Experiment." *American Sociological Review* 57:691–697.

Pearson, Jessica, Nancy Thoennes, and Esther Ann Girswold. 1999. "Child Support and Domestic Violence." *Violence against Women* 5(4):427–448.

Pirog-Good, Maureen A., and Jan E. Stets. 1989. "The Help-Seeking Behavior of Physically and Sexually Abused College Students." Pp. 108–125 in *Violence And Dating Relationships.* New York: Praeger.

Pizzey, Erin. 1974. *Scream Quietly or the Neighbors Will Hear.* Middlesex, England: Penguin.

Pleck, Elizabeth. 1983. "Feminist Responses to 'Crimes against Women,' 1868–1896." *Signs: Journal of Women Culture and Society* 8:451–470.

———. 1989. "Criminal Approaches to Family Violence, 1640–1980." Pp. 19–58 in *Family Violence,* edited by L. Ohlin and M. Tonry. Chicago: University of Chicago Press.

Ptacek, James. 1988. "Why Do Men Batter Their Wives?" Pp. 133–75 in *Feminist Perspectives on Wife Abuse,* edited by K. Yllo and M. Bograd. Newbury Park, CA: Sage.

Quarm, Daisy, and Martin D. Schwartz. 1985. "Domestic Violence in Criminal Court: An Examination of New Legislation in Ohio." Pp. 29–46 in *Criminal Justice Politics and Women: The Aftermath of Legally Mandated Change,* edited by C. Schweber and C. Feinman. New York: Haworth Press.

Rennison, Callie Marie, and Sarah Welchans. 2000. "Intimate Partner Violence." Bureau of Justice Statistics. Department of Justice. *Special Report,* May, 11pp.

Renzetti, Claire M. 1992. *Violent Betrayal: Partner Abuse in Lesbian Relationships.* Newbury Park, CA: Sage.

Rigakos, George S. 1997. "Situational Determinants of Police Responses to Civil and Criminal Injunctions for Battered Women." *Violence against Women* 3(2):204–216.

Rosewater, Lynne B. 1988. "Battered or Schizophrenic? Psychological Tests Can't Tell." Pp. 200–216 in *Feminist Perspectives on Wife Abuse,* edited by K. Yllo and M. Bograd. Newbury Park, CA: Sage.

Rowe, Kelly. 1985. "The Limits of the Neighborhood Justice Center: Why Domestic Violence Cases Should Not Be Mediated." *Emory Law Journal* 34:855–910.

Saunders, Daniel B. 1988. "Wife Abuse, Husband Abuse, or Mutual Combat? A Feminist Perspective on the Empirical Findings." Pp. 90–113 in *Feminist Perspectives on Wife Abuse,* edited by K. Yllo and M. Bograd. Newbury Park, CA: Sage.

Schechter, Susan. 1982. *Women and Male Violence: The Visions and Struggles of the Battered Women's Movement* Boston: South End Press.

Schwartz, Martin D. 1987. "Gender and Injury in Spousal Assault." *Sociological Focus* 20:61–75.

Schwartz, Martin D., and Walter S. De Keseredy. 1997. *Sexual Assault on the College Campus.* Thousand Oaks, CA: Sage.

Sebastian, Richard J. 1983. "Social Psychological Determinants." Pp. 182–191 in *The Dark Side of Families: Current Family Violence*

Research, edited by D. Finkelhor, R. J. Gelles, G. T. Hotaling, and M. A. Straus. Beverly Hills, CA: Sage.

Sev'er, Aysan. 1997. "Recent or Imminent Separation and Intimate Violence against Women." *Violence against Women,* 3(6):566–589.

Sheehy, Lisa, Melissa Reinberg, and Deborah Krichway. 1991. *Commutation for Women Who Defended Themselves against Abusive Partners: An Advocacy Manual and Guide to Legal Issues.* Philidelphia: National Clearinghouse for the Defense of Battered Women.

Sherman, Lawrence W. 1992. *Policing Domestic Violence: Experiments and Dilemmas.* New York: Free Press.

Sherman, Lawrence W., and Richard A. Berk. 1984. "The Specific Deterrent Effects of Arrest for Domestic Assault." *American Sociological Review* 49:261–272.

Sherman, Lawrence W., Janell D. Schmidt, Dennis P. Rogan, Douglas A. Smith, Patrick R. Gartin, Ellen G. Cohn, Dean J. Collins, and Anthony R. Bacich. 1992. "The Variable Effects of Arrest on Criminal Careers: The Milwaukee Domestic Violence Experiment." *Journal of Criminal Law and Criminology* 83:137–169.

Slote, Kim, and Carrie Cuthbert. 1997. "Women's Rights Network (WRN)." Violence against Women 3(1):76–80.

Smith, Douglas A., and Jody R. Klein. 1984. "Police Control of Interpersonal Disputes." *Social Problems* 31:469–481.

Smith, Michael D. 1994. "Enhancing the Quality of Survey Data on Violence against Women." *Gender and Society* 8:109–127.

Stanko, Elizabeth A. 1985. *Intimate Intrusions.* London: Routledge and Kegan Paul.

———. 1989. "Missing the Mark? Policing Battering." Pp. 46–69 in *Women, Policing, and Male Violence: International Perspectives,* edited by J. Hanmer, J. Radford, and E. A. Stanko. London: Routledge and Kegan Paul.

Star, B., C. G. Clark, K. M. Goetz, and L. O'Malia. 1979. "Psychological Aspects of Wife Battering." *Social Casework: The Journal of Contemporary Social Work* (October):479–487.

Stark, Evan. 1992. "Framing and Reframing Battered Women." Pp. 271–292 in *Domestic Violence: The Changing Criminal Justice Response,* edited by Eve S. Buzawa and Carl G. Buzawa. Westport, CT: Auburn House.

Stark, Evan, and Anne Flitcraft. 1983. "Social Knowledge, Social Policy, and the Abuse of Women: The Case Against Patriarchal Benevolence." Pp. 330–348 in *The Dark Side of Families: Current Family Violence Research,* edited by D. Finkelhor, R. J. Gelles, G. T. Hotaling, and M. A. Straus. Beverly Hills, CA: Sage.

Stark, Evan, and Anne Flitcraft. 1996. *Women at Risk: Domestic Violence and Women's Health.* Thousand Oaks, CA: Sage.

Stark, Evan, Anne Flitcraft, and W. Frazier. 1979. "Medicine and Patriarchal Violence: The Social Construction of a 'Private' Event." *International Journal of Health Sciences* 9:461–493.

Steinmetz, Suzanne. 1977/1978. "The Battered Husband Syndrome." *Victimology* 2:499–509.

Stets, Jan E., and Maureen A. Pirog-Good. 1987. "Violence in Dating Relationships." *Social Psychology Quarterly* 50:237–246.

Stets, Jan E., and Murray A. Straus. 1990. "Gender Differences in Reporting Marital Violence and Its Medical and Psychological Consequences." In *Physical Violence in American Families,* edited by M. A. Straus and R. J. Gelles. New Brunswick, NJ: Transaction Press.

Stith, Sandra M. 1990. "Police Response to Domestic Violence." *Violence and Victims* 5(1):37–49.

Straus, Murray A. 1990. *Physical Violence in American Families.* New Brunswick, NJ: Transaction Publishers.

Straus, Murray A. 1991. "Physical Violence in American Families." Pp. 17–34 in *Abused and Battered,* edited by D. D. Knudsen and J. L. Miller. New York: Aldine De Gruyter.

Straus, Murray A., and Richard J. Gelles. 1986. "Societal Change and Change in Family Violence from 1975 to 1985 as Revealed by Two Surveys." *Journal of Marriage and the Family* 48:465–479.

Straus, Murray A., Richard J. Gelles, and Suzanne Steinmetz. 1980. *Behind Closed Doors: Violence in the American Family.* New York: Anchor Books.

Strube, M. J., and L. S. Barbour. 1984. "Factors Related to the Decision to Leave an Abusive Relationship." *Journal of Marriage and the Family* (November):837–844.

Tierney, K. J. 1983. "The Battered Women Movement and the Creation of the Wife Beating Problem." *Social Problems* 29:207–220.

Tjaden, Patricia, and Nancy Thoennes. 1998a. "Prevalence, Incidence, and Consequences of Violence against Women." U.S. Department of Justice. *Research in Brief.* November, 16pp.

———. 1998b. "Stalking in America." U.S. Department of Justice. *Research in Brief.* April, 20pp.

Tong, Rosemarie. 1984. *Women, Sex, and the Law.* Totowa, NJ: Rowman and Allanheld.

Walker, Lenore E. 1979. *The Battered Woman.* New York: Harper and Row.

———. 1983a. "The Battered Woman Syndrome Study." Pp. 31–49 in *The Dark Side of Families: Current Family Violence Research,* edited by D. Finkelhor, R. J. Gelles, G. T. Hotaling, and M. A. Straus. Beverly Hills, CA: Sage.

———. 1983b. "Victimology and the Psychological Perspectives of Battered Women." *Victimology* 1–2:82–104.

———. 1989. Terrifying Love: Why Battered Women Kill and How Society Responds. New York: Harper-Perennial.

Wardell, Laurie, Dair L. Gillespie, and Ann Leffler. 1983. "Science and Violence against Wives," Pp. 69–84 in *The Dark Side of Families: Current Family Violence Research,* edited by D. Finkelhor, R. J. Gelles, G. T. Hotaling, and M. A. Straus. Beverly Hills, CA: Sage.

Warshaw, Carole. 1993. "Limitations of the Medical Model in the Care of Battered Women." Pp. 134–146 in *Violence against Women: The Bloody Footprints,* edited by P. B. Bart and E. G. Moran. Newbury Park, CA: Sage.

Websdale, N. 1995. "Rural Woman Abuse: The Voices of Kentucky Women." *Violence against Women* 1:309–388.

Websdale, N., and B. Johnson. 1997. "The Policing of Domestic Violence in Rural and Urban Areas: The Voices of Battered Women." *Policing and Society* 6:297–317.

Wiist, William H., and Judith McFarlane. 1998. "Utilization of Police by Abused Pregnant Hispanic Women." *Violence against Women* 4(6):677–693.

Wilson, Margo, and Martin Daly. 1993. "Spousal Homicide Risk and Estrangement." *Violence and Victims* 8(1):3–15.

Worden, Robert E., and Alissa A. Pollitz. 1984. "Police Arrests in Domestic Disturbances: A Further Look." *Law and Society Review.* 18(1):105–119.

Yllo, Kersti. 1983. "Using a Feminist Approach in Quantitative Research: A Case Study." Pp. 277–288 in *The Dark Side of Families: Current Family Violence Research,* edited by D. Finkelhor, R. J. Gelles, G. T. Hotaling, and M. A. Straus. Beverly Hills, CA: Sage.

———. 1999. "Domestic Violence against Women of Japanese Descent in

Los Angeles." *Violence against Women* 5(8):869–897.

Yllo, Kersti. 1988. "Political and Methodological Debates in Wife Abuse Research." Pp. 28–50 in *Feminist Perspectives on Wife Abuse,* edited by K. Yllo and M. Bograd. Newbury Park, CA: Sage.

Zoomer, Olga J. 1989. "Policing Battered Women in the Netherlands"

Pp. 125–154 in *Women, Policing, and Male Violence,* edited by J. Hanmer, J. Redford, and E. A. Stanko; London: Routledge.

Zorza, Joan. 1992. "The Criminal Law of Misdemeanor Domestic Violence, 1970–1990." *Journal of Criminal Law and Criminology* 83:46–72.

Women Workers

9

✴

Working Women:
Breaking the Barriers

[F]or many years the legal profession was known for its guardedness,
and sometimes outright secrecy. This almost exclusively male
elite preserve not only excluded women but most of the rest
of society as well from knowledge of its workings.

(HAGAN AND KAY, 1995, 4)

Men have debated, legislated, taught and interpreted the law.
The virtual exclusion of women from lawmaking and legal
policy-making permitted, over time, the incorporation within
the law of values and perspectives belonging to men. This
inherently biased perspective, moreover, has been subtly masked
by the pervasive assumption that our system of justice,
together with its defining first principles and values,
is necessarily just and impartial.

(DURHAM, 1998, 217)

Part IV of this book examines the U.S. legal movement toward women's
equality and women professionals in the crime-processing system. This
chapter provides a historical account of how women have broken into the
nondomestic labor force and of changes in the labor market that have
occurred. It describes the movement of women from the private sphere (the

home) to the public sphere (society and the paid labor force). At first glance this may not seem appropriate for a book on women and crime; however, there are two reasons such a discussion is necessary. First, in many ways, women's attempt to hold paying jobs has itself been criminalized by the law, which is explained in this chapter. Second, restricting women's employment is usually most extreme in women's entrance into what have traditionally been considered "men's" jobs. Positions as prison guards, police officers, lawyers, judges, and even jury members have historically, and sometimes currently, been considered primarily "men's" jobs.

Given the significance of language in describing the world around us, there are a number of places in this book where frequently used words have been replaced with alternative, less common, terms. For example, I explained in the first chapter why I was using the term "criminal-processing system" instead of "criminal-justice system." In Chapter 5 I avoided the word "corrections" to discuss the jail and prison system, given that there is little evidence that the system emphasizes treatment to correct behavior and rehabilitate prisoners. Similarly, the term "correctional officer" is not used in this book to describe persons working with prisoners in prisons and jails (consistent with Zimmer [1986]). Given that U.S. prisons and jails do not train their employees in rehabilitation, nor do they hire significant numbers of employees with rehabilitative expertise, it seems inappropriate to call such workers "correctional officers." Therefore, the terms "prison and jail workers," "prison officers," and "guards" are used in place of the term "correctional officers" in this book. Additionally, I avoid the terms "policewoman" and "policewomen," opting for the bulkier "woman police officer" or "women police officers," given that regardless of sex, officers are today supposed to perform the same job. This is to deny neither the sexism still operating in job assignments and expectations in many departments nor the sexist treatment many women police officers experience on the job. Rather it is an effort not to imply in any way that women and men should have different responsibilities in policing jobs.

MOVEMENT FROM THE PRIVATE
TO THE PUBLIC SPHERE

To understand social and legal resistance to women's employment outside the home, it is necessary to examine sex discrimination in the historical context of women's and men's lives and rights. It is useful to examine how women's work outside the home has at times been criminalized or at least made "deviant" through legislation, policies, court decisions, and the culture because these forces have severely limited women's participation in the world outside of the home. It is also important to understand that sex discrimination does not occur in a vacuum; it often accompanies race, class, ethnicity, sexual preference, and other forms of discrimination. "Discrimination is the perpetration of unjustifiable inequality in consequence of bigotry" (Campbell, 1988, 16). Behavior does not have to be purposeful, conscious, or direct to classify as discrimination. *Sex discrimination* is when sex or gender specification is used to the disadvantage of one sex (definition adapted from Campbell, 1988, 22). Sex discrimination is overwhelmingly against women and girls.

There are political, economic, and social aspects to women's (and men's) lives in both the public (outside the home) and private (within the home) spheres (Bradley and Khor, 1993). This section of the chapter explores the public and private spheres of women's lives; however, the focus is on the economic aspects of the public domain, given that these make up most of the sex discrimination cases brought by both women and men regarding gender equality.

The History of Women's Movement into the Public Sphere

When the nation's founding fathers spoke of "We the People" they
were not using the term generically. Although subject to the
Constitution's mandates, women were unacknowledged in its text,
uninvited in its formulation, unsolicited in its ratification, and,
before the last quarter-century, largely uninvolved in its interpretation.

(RHODE, 1990, 121)

Women have traditionally been limited to the private sphere, while men have generally enjoyed more freedom in the public sphere. The private sphere includes the home and care of the family, while the public sphere includes life outside the home, such as in the paid labor force, the voting booth, and bars. Religiosity and sexuality were also tied to the separate spheres, where predictably, women were expected to be more religious, pure, and sexually chaste than men (see Welter, 1978). Separate spheres for women and men can be traced back to Aristotle, St. Paul, and Thomas Aquinas, who believed the only purpose for women was reproduction and marriage, while men were meant for loftier purposes (Harris, 1978). The precedent for separate spheres was set and remained for centuries, with the assumptions that (1) men are (and should be) "breadwinners," and (2) women (should and do) care for the home and children—for free (Atkins and Hoggett, 1984).

In addition to societal values, legal doctrine has "reflected and reinforced" men's dominance of the public sphere and women's confinement to the private sphere (Rhode, 1987, 13). Even leading feminists of the nineteenth century had difficulty arguing that women should *not* have the primary responsibility of the home and family. This was apparent in the 1873 U.S. Supreme Court case *Bradwell v. Illinois.* Justice Bradley had the following opinion about Myra Bradwell's (unsuccessful) request to overturn the law forbidding married women in Illinois to practice law:

> It is true that many women are unmarried and not affected by any of the
> duties, complications, and incapacities arising out of the married state,
> but these are exceptions to the general rule. The paramount destiny and
> mission of woman are [sic] to fulfill the noble and benign offices of wife

and mother. This is the law of the creator. And the rules of civil society must be adapted to the general constitution of things, and cannot be based upon exceptional cases. (*Bradwell v. Illinois,* 83 U.S. [16 Wall.] at 141–142 [1873])

Smart (1989, 85, 88) states that law is "grounded in patriarchy" and "defines how we think about women." The importance of laws, legal precedence, and legislation cannot be overemphasized. "Women were—and are—kept in place by laws" (Epstein, 1988, 121). While sex discrimination has been prevalent throughout history, sex discrimination as a legal concern is a recent phenomenon (Robinson, 1988). An analysis of laws affecting women's rights found that even in the 1960s, the view of women's primary function as homemakers was used as a basis for treating men and women differently under the law. The effect was the relegation of women to a service class: to serve man and the state (Eastwood, 1975, 327). Women and the laws affecting them have historically moved from the private sphere to the public sphere (Dahl, 1987). However, it was not until the 1970s, as a result of the women's movement, that the Supreme Court agenda included sex discrimination cases. It has been stated that the legal status of U.S. women changed more during the 1970s and 1980s than in the two centuries preceding the 1970s (Hoff, 1991, 229).

There are two important implications regarding women's work in the home: (1) the myth that all women have worked only in the home, and (2) the devaluation of women's work in the home. Although women have faced numerous restrictions to working outside of the home, many have done so; meanwhile their work inside the home often remains unrecognized and undervalued. Regarding the first point, women have worked outside of the home for many years, and many continue to do so, usually out of economic necessity. Frontier women, poor women, and slave women have always worked outside the home. "By 1930, one-quarter of all adult women and over half of all single women worked in the wage labor force" (Meyerowitz, 1988, 5). Women who worked outside the home have tended to be single, black, and poor; but married, white, and middle-class women have increasingly been employed outside of the home since the 1940s. It has been argued that the public/private distinction is relevant only for upper- and middle-class white women, given the government's historic interference in the public and private lives of the working class and the poor:

Welfare programs and policies have discouraged family life, sterilization programs have restricted reproduction rights, government has drafted and armed disproportionate numbers of people of Color to fight its wars overseas, and locally, police forces and the criminal justice system arrest and incarcerate disproportionate numbers of people of Color. There is no such thing as a private sphere for people of Color except that which they manage to create and protect in an otherwise hostile environment. (Hurtado, 1989, 849)

Now turning to the devaluation of women's work in the home, regardless of women's personal characteristics (marital status, race, and class), their work outside has rarely excused them from the onerous and devalued work inside the home. Domestic work in a woman's own home is unpaid, while domestic work in other people's homes is performed almost exclusively by women ("cleaning ladies") who are poorly paid (Burrows, 1988). There is no logical reason why women, and not men, perform these duties, and it is not a coincidence that they are severely underpaid. Moreover, the lack of acknowledgment of a person's or group's qualities and activities often results in a loss of dignity for the person or group (Dahl, 1987, 367). Women's work in the home lacks recognition and support—it is work that others expect of them, and it is rarely appreciated. Housework is not covered by the Social Security Act, often leaving divorced and widowed full-time homemakers without security for their labors (Thomas, 1991).

Meyerowitz (1988) accounts for "women adrift" between 1880 and 1930, when women's participation in the U.S. labor force increased from 2.6 million to 10.8 million. "Women adrift" were single, independent, wage-earning women who did not live with relatives or employers. "Women adrift" tended to be white, unmarried women from poor families who migrated to the cities, largely out of economic necessity, but also to escape abuse or stigma or to find adventure. However, "women adrift" were a heterogeneous group that also included Black women; separated, divorced, or widowed women; and women who deserted or had been deserted by their husbands. The wages of "women adrift" were extremely low—frequently below the poverty level—because women's wages were set for dependent wives and daughters who had access to additional (male) resources and income. These women challenged traditional views of women. "When they mingled freely with men in rooming houses, at work, and at places of recreation, they undermined the 'separation of spheres' that had segregated women from men by relegating them to the domestic world of the home" (ibid., *xix*). "Women adrift" represent a significant pattern of the movement of women from the private to the public sphere:

> The "women adrift," then, stand at a juncture in U.S. women's history. They moved from a female domestic world in predominantly rural societies to a sexually integrated, urban environment. Bereft of family support and confronted with poverty, they created new subcultures, challenged Victorian prescriptions, set patterns for contemporary sex roles, inspired social reformers, and influenced popular culture. Their history links together the history of women, work, sexuality, social reform, and popular culture in the late-nineteenth and early-twentieth century city. (Meyerowitz, 1988, xxiii)

Motivations for Restricting Women
to the Private Sphere

Various excuses have been given to restrict women from job opportunities and equality in general. These excuses often fall under the rubric of protection— protecting women "for their own good." Such a paternalistic attitude may "protect" women from certain physically grueling and dangerous jobs, but it often excludes women from many occupations and limits their ability to earn high wages and pursue career dreams. For instance, in 1948 the Supreme Court upheld a 1945 Michigan statute *(Goesaert v. Cleary)* that prohibited women from tending bars unless they were the daughters or wives of male bar owners. This was affirmed under the guise of protecting these women from unsafe patrons, despite evidence that showed that women had a civilizing influence on the patrons (Rhode, 1989).

Thus, the "protection" of women often results in excluding women from employment opportunities and basic rights. Almost every government report on women workers between 1918 and 1944 mentioned the concern that women workers might resist and undercut men's opportunities (Atkins and Hoggett, 1984, 20). Additionally, the policies and laws supposedly designed to protect women have not addressed health hazards in occupations traditionally occupied by women, such as brown lung disease in cotton mills (Epstein, 1988, 129). Even a recent study of policies and court decisions attempting to exclude women of "fertile ages" (which includes most working women) from employment found that employers are concerned only about potential harm to fetuses for women working in traditionally male occupations. Notably, excluding women of child-bearing ages from traditionally female jobs where harmful chemicals are abundant (such as beauty shops, nursing, cleaning, and garment industries) is unheard of (Draper, 1993).

Atkins and Hoggett (1984) discuss three ways the legal system has attempted to justify limiting women's job opportunities. First is a belief in *women's "natural" inferiority.* This view suggests that women are too emotionally, intellectually, and physically weak to endure certain jobs, most of which are outside the home and often relatively lucrative. Seen as the "weaker sex," women have been excluded, for example, from high-paying positions involving the use of machines and a full work week and have been relegated instead to low-paying and part-time employment. Particularly in the nineteenth century but also well into this century, judges upheld this "natural" inferiority to limit women's access to wages and job opportunities, including medicine (supposedly, women are too intellectually weak to be physicians). Women were traditionally barred from entering law schools and practicing law based on the assumption that females were inherently unable to perform the job and were best suited to their natural environment: the home.

Maternity is Atkins and Hoggett's (1984) second justification used to restrict women's work. This excuse was first posed in the 1847 House of Commons Factory Bill in England. The bill claimed that there was a danger to young infants whose mothers were working outside the home. If we combine the supposed inherent "weakness" of women with the idea that women are destined to stay home (since infants' well-being is supposedly dependent on their mothers not leaving the house), a bleak picture for women confronts us— women are trapped into staying home because society depends on them to do so. Until the mid-1970s, pregnant women workers were routinely "dismissed" (fired) and frequently were denied requests for reinstatement after giving birth.

Additionally, most state unemployment and insurance programs excluded pregnant women (Rhode, 1989). Ironically, as discussed later in this chapter, women's entry into working in policing was related to a maternal image of them, how they were ideally suited to help wayward and abused children and women (see Appier, 1998).

Much of the discussion about women's roles in the public and private spheres is bound up in societal expectations, perhaps wrongly believed by some to be a biological sex difference, regarding women's sense of responsibility to take care of others, particularly dependents. Petersen (1996) refers to this as "obligations to care and conflicts about care," noting that women are not only primarily responsible, whether they work outside the home or not, of taking care of healthy children but sick children as well. Thus, if a child is sick, it is often assumed that the mother rather than the father must miss work to tend to it. This could also be expanded to caring for the elderly, where women are primarily responsible to care not only for their own aging parents but often their husbands' parents as well. This example of the gendered nature of "obligations to care" illustrates how legal changes cannot necessarily shape the gendered imbalance in individuals' lives. Moreover, it is often seen as an expectation that women in criminal-processing jobs do the "emotional" work of dealing with a distraught victim. Finally, there is often a sense in all of this of women's caring as "natural" (relative to men) and as a weakness. Notably, despite the weakness assumed to be inherent in women, they are seen as potentially powerful enough to dismantle a seemingly healthy society by "shirking" their "womanly duties" and not staying home. Unfortunately, such a commitment to women's "rightful" place in the home is not simply a belief of the distant past. Criminologists published the following statement implying women's responsibility in the rising crime rate in 1983:

> [T]he changing economic status of women [through their increased participation in the job market] could contribute to higher crime rates in four distinct ways: each family's control over its own children is reduced; control over neighborhood children is reduced when women are not at home during the day; empty homes are targets for crime; and the women themselves are exposed to new opportunities to commit crimes in the workplace. (Chaiken and Chaiken, 1983, 21)

This statement suggests that a movement toward women's equality in the labor force will have a negative impact on society as a whole. "Women who seize their right to work outside the home, for instance, are being blamed for the break-down of the American family, when economic pressures are the true source of the problem" (Williams, 1981, 19). Even if a woman's family could survive on income from her spouse, it is unfair to suggest that women carry the burden of society falling apart simply because they pursue a career outside of the home. This implies that careers are only, or more important, for men. Given the high rates of female, single-head-of-household families, this argument is outdated as well as unfair. Furthermore, more recent research points out that family income and the supports available to working women mediate any spurious relationship between women's work and delinquency, and women with full-time employment may be less likely to have delinquent children (see Currie, 1985).

Marriage is Atkins and Hoggett's (1984, 18) third and final justification used to limit women's employment opportunities. This justification assumes that all women (should) marry and that the man's job should be in the public sphere and the woman should remain in the private sphere. William Blackstone's eighteenth-century legal treatise on wives was based on the *Bible,* where husband and wife were regarded as "one person in the law," where "the 'one' was the husband" (Rhode, 1989, 10). At the beginning of the nineteenth century in England, single women had more legal abilities than married women, especially regarding property ownership (Fergus, 1988). Similarly, in the United States, regardless of marital status, all women were barred from many professions and trades. However, married women fared much worse than unmarried women because they were viewed as their husbands' property (Kirp et al., 1986, 31). In fact, most nineteenth- and early twentieth-century women had to choose between marriage and employment in the paid labor force, which is probably why as late as 1920, four in five women in the paid work force were unmarried (Rhode, 1989, 13). Similar to the restrictions on married women lawyers previously referred to in this chapter, a commission on hiring women into policing in India, published in 1961, although favorable to hiring women, was opposed to enlisting *married* women onto the force (Natarajan, 1996).

Even today, although most women and men marry, marriage generally influences women's lives and life choices much more than men's (Okin, 1989). Some parties still propose that marriage is a justification for discriminating against women working outside of the home; they maintain that certain jobs should be left for men who have families to support. Not only does this discriminate against women seeking employment, but it ignores the contention that access to paid labor enables women to avoid being economically "forced" into marriage and gives them the means to leave bad marriages (Burrows, 1988). Consistent with a "no win" situation many marginalized people face, recent research in the field of law suggests ways that women in the legal profession are further stigmatized if they are *not* married. For example, a report on women judges states that women judges who are "single" are viewed as not only "odd" but as more "appropriate" for sexual harassment, including requests by male judges for sexual acts (Schafran and Wikler, 1989). Another study, comparing women and men of color lawyers found that women of color tend to advance more if they are married (while men of color do not); for example it increases their chances of obtaining a tenure-track faculty position in a law school (Merritt and Reskin, 1992).

The belief that women should marry and raise children and let men have careers results in obvious discrimination against women. If men can be married (and have children) and have careers, why can't women? Furthermore, the number of dependents should not be a criterion in assigning jobs. Even if the number of dependents were a legitimate criterion, there is a need to acknowledge the vast and growing number of single-parent mothers. Also, male workers vary by need and number of dependents. It is highly doubtful that males would want jobs assigned on the basis of the number of dependents.

These assumptions and explanations lead one to believe that separate spheres for women and men still exist. One study of professionals in an industrial corporation in the 1970s found that marriage and motherhood were used as excuses for not promoting women. Employers assumed that women would not want to go on business trips, which were a requirement for promotion (Kanter, 1977a). Even in the 1980s, the courts successfully used explanations of women's domestic roles to allow sex discrimination in terms of promoting only male teachers into administrative positions (*Gillespie v. Board of Education of North Little Rock* [1982]) and keeping women in lower paying, noncommissioned, dead-end sales jobs (*Equal Employment Opportunity Commission v. Sears, Roebuck, and Company* [1986]) (Eisenstein, 1988; Schultz, 1991).

MOVEMENT TOWARD GENDER EQUALITY

Women are discriminated against in a number of ways that perpetuate their lack of power in society. For women as a class to obtain political power, they must first obtain (1) equal treatment under the law, (2) protection from sex discrimination, and (3) physical self-determination (largely through reproductive freedom, such as access to birth control and abortion) (Eastwood, 1975). The history of women's equality encompasses a wide variety of issues. Central to these is the equal access to employment opportunities and the autonomy that such employment provides through financial independence. Regardless of whether women are married, they usually work because they need to support themselves and their families. However, a woman's average pay is two-thirds of a man's for comparable work, and the more an occupation is populated by women, the lower the pay (Thomas, 1991, 193).

Access versus Influence and the Necessity of Both

Women's right to vote (suffrage) and the movement for women's equality were in many ways two separate battles. Although earlier efforts toward feminist activist outcomes existed before the 1920s, it was a long struggle for women to receive the right to vote in 1920 (Berger, 1980). (However, in some individual states, women had the legal right to vote before 1920, just as some states had legal abortion statutes before *Roe v. Wade* [1973].) Why were they unsuccessful until 1920? One suggestion is that group consciousness, a prerequisite to effecting change for an oppressed group, was lacking until 1920. "Women first needed to recognize that they faced certain problems precisely because they were women in order for the feminist movement to emerge" (Klein, 1984, 3). Similarly, the wave of feminism in the 1960s has been attributed to "not only the increasing number of women in the work force who might experience discrimination, but also the increasing number of women who perceived it as such" (Rhode, 1989, 55).

Legislative and Supreme Court rulings have been important avenues for effecting social change. Virtually all of the movement of women into the areas of law enforcement, the courts, and prison and jail work has been because of lawsuits (initiated by women). The initial opportunities, as well as some current ones, were the result of court decisions, not genuine opportunity or good-will on the part of the dominant group (wealthy, white males). *Reed v. Reed* (1971) was the first successful major sex discrimination case (O'Connor, 1980). Sally Reed challenged an Idaho statute that favored males as estate administrators of the deceased. This case marked the first time that the equal protection clause of the Fourteenth Amendment was extended to women. Although this decision didn't directly tackle the separate spheres ideology, *Reed v. Reed* laid the groundwork for many other successful sex discrimination cases brought by women that explicitly condemned separate spheres. Nonetheless, the courts have been less understanding of "more subtle sex-based classifications that affect opportunities for and social views about women" (Bartlett, 1991, 372).

Unfortunately, although legal changes are usually necessary, they are not always sufficient to actually bring about change. Many citizens are unaware of their own legal rights, and some institutions who discriminate may be unaware that they are breaking the law (or even discriminating). However, even when some employers are aware of the laws they are breaking, they use various forms of direct or indirect coercion to override the law. For instance, even though a police department may have a policy against sexual harassment, a woman police officer may decide it is less costly emotionally and financially to "put up" with it or to change jobs than to take on the male-dominated police and court system. In the same vein, workers who know that they are being discriminated against may justifiably decide that to keep the job they have or even to maintain a good record for a future job, it is important not to "rock the boat." This is particularly crucial when the victims of discrimination or harassment have no other means of supporting themselves (and perhaps their dependents) during the time-consuming and costly experience of a trial. These are examples of how laws may be necessary but not sufficient in order to effect change.

Similarly, it is important to have both access and influence in order to achieve equality (Klein, 1984). Briefly, *access* involves acquiring recognition and rights, while *influence* is being in a position to use the rights and attain new advantages and power. For example, Title VII (a 1972 amendment to the 1964 Civil Rights Act) resulted in the hiring of many women on police patrol duties for the first time in U.S. history. However, because these women have remained in such small numbers overall (token status) and been in the lower strata of police departments (officers), it has been difficult for them to shape policing in a nonmale manner. Additionally, using the established law to fight discrimination can be "hazardous"; a backlash of countersuits and hostility— sometimes even violence—is often unleashed against oppressed groups and individuals who sue for basic rights (Smart, 1989, 138).

With regard to the access issue during the early part of this century, suffragists expected overnight political results once women achieved the right to vote. They believed women's votes would have a powerful influence on elections. Unfortunately, most women did not vote after initially acquiring the right, and of those women who did vote, there was no identifiable "gender gap" (differential candidate support between men and women) until the 1980 presidential election between Ronald Reagan and Jimmy Carter. (Women were more supportive of Carter, and men of Reagan.) This achievement of women's right to vote (access) with no apparent resulting effect (influence) is an example of achieving access without influence.

Overall, between 1920 and 1960, there appeared to be a lull in the fight for women's rights (Berger, 1980; Klein, 1984; Rhode, 1989). This is not to say that there was no feminist political activity between 1920 and 1960. The Equal Rights Amendment was first submitted to Congress in 1923 and every year after that until it was passed by the House and the Senate in 1972. (It was assumed that acquiring ratification by three-fourths of the states would be perfunctory, but a backlash against its ratification headed by antifeminist Phyllis Schlafly was extremely successful.) Thus, although there was some political activity to improve the equality of women, it lacked the widespread momentum and support the suffrage battle had acquired. In the 1960s, renewed political advocacy for women's rights was stimulated by the 1964 Civil Rights Act and the progress made by the political organizing for African Americans' rights.

Comparison of Racial and Gender Equality Activism

Comparisons and analogies are frequently made between political activism to promote racial equality and political activism to promote gender equality. Some people resist comparing gender to racial oppression, believing that because women do not constitute a minority in the population, they should not require special legislative appeals used by African Americans and other people of color. Nonetheless, women are a disadvantaged group despite their numerical dominance; they have limited access to rewards and opportunities in a system where the male is viewed as "normal" and the female is often viewed as deviant (Laws, 1975).

Comparing gender and racial oppression is complex. We need to keep in mind that the lynching of African Americans, the genocide of Native Americans, and the military conquest of Latinos are not identical to the physical abuse, discrimination, and cultural denigration experienced by women of all races and ethnicities (King, 1988, 15). However, both racial minority members and women experience "shared subordinate treatment on the basis of ascribed attributes and have internalized the social values that perpetuate such subordination" (Rhode, 1987, 20–21). While members of an oppressed group usually understand and are frustrated by this oppression, it is also evident that oppression can affect members' self-esteem, self-confidence, and sense of self-worth.

A major distinction between racism and sexism is that people of color do not tend to share the private sphere as intimately with the empowered (that is, white men), whereas white women often benefit, particularly financially, from the advantages accrued to their white fathers and white husbands.

Furthermore, racial and sex discrimination have been distinguished by motivation: Racial discrimination is more often motivated by the intent to degrade and disempower, while discrimination against women is more often motivated by paternalism (ibid, 21). Similarly, although the law has traditionally treated African Americans with "unremitting antagonism" and women as "frail" and "nobler" than men and thus in need of men's protection, the impact on women and African Americans has been the same: "a constraint on the choices open to individual blacks or individual women" (Kirp et al., 1986). Although the paternalism and protectionism supposedly guiding laws that restrict women are viewed more positively than the degrading laws restricting African Americans and other people of color, both paternalistic and degrading laws have extremely negative consequences. In some ways, the paternalistically motivated laws may be more difficult to fight because there is some element that is claiming to be helpful. Unfortunately, they usually serve to restrict women's rights (to employment, jury duty, and so on) and help to perpetuate stereotypes of women as weaker than or less than men.

In short, despite their proportion in the population, women have been considered "minorities" in some legislation and policies. This is a recognition of women's "deviant" status when they try to obtain rights ranging from educational and job opportunities to opportunities to play on athletic teams. Legislation and court decisions overturning sex discrimination acknowledge that society is not gender neutral, that boys and girls are raised with different attitudes about and access to rights and opportunities, and that males and females have different experiences. It is not surprising that one of the first successful sex discrimination cases in the United States, *Frontiero v. Richardson* (1973), compared the classification of sex to that of race. This case established sex as a "suspect class," similar to race, in that excuses unrelated to a group's abilities had been used historically to discriminate against members of the group (Hoff, 1991; Lucie, 1988). The Frontiero decision overturned regulations that denied female Air Force military officers the same dependents' rights as the male officers.

The impact of holding more than one stigmatized status at once can be more than cumulative. Occupying a subordinate status in both sex *and* race has been referred to as "double marginality," "double jeopardy," and "intersectionality." Similarly, poor women of color experience "triple jeopardy," based on sex, race, and class (King 1988). Examining the effects of racism *or* sexism fails to acknowledge that some individuals in society experience race discrimination *and* sex discrimination. For instance, the abysmally low wages earned by white "women adrift" in the early decades of this century were lower still for African-American "women adrift" (Meyerowitz, 1988). Black women who were leaders and key organizers in the civil rights movement remain, for the most part, unrecognized and invisible (Barnett, 1993). Even in the late 1980s, data from full-time workers indicate that the average white woman college graduate earned significantly less than the average man with a high school degree, and the average college-educated African-American woman earned about 90 percent of the average white woman's earnings, "a figure roughly equivalent to a white male high school dropout" (Rhode, 1989, 163).

The "intersectional experience" of being both black and female "is greater than the sum of racism and sexism" (Crenshaw, 1989, 140). The history of tension between the African-American and white feminist movements was discussed earlier. More recently, most white feminists have increased their attempts to acknowledge and address racism as well as sexism. Although many African-American women have traditionally viewed racism as a more powerful cause of their subordination than sexism, both black and white women are becoming more integrated in unified feminist and antiracist activities and goals (Lewis, 1977).

Impact of Movement to the Public
Sphere on Women's Equality

Surprisingly, many persons (including some women) who believed women had a right to vote did not believe men and women were equal. (This may not be too different from today. It is likely that the majority of people opposed to the Equal Rights Amendment believe women have a right to vote.) Thus, women's suffrage did not result in a movement for equality between the sexes. The catalysts for effecting a change in women's equality were the 1940s movement of women out of the home and the 1960s civil rights movement. The movement of women from the private sphere (the home) to the public sphere (society) has not simply been a result of feminist political activism. In fact, women's most successful movement to the public sphere was due more to economic conditions and technology than to feminist activism.

During World War II, when the labor supply was affected by "prime age" male workers who were fighting or being trained to fight, the U.S. government pursued a highly successful advertising campaign to attract women to "men's" jobs in factories, construction, and aviation. The government recruited women out of necessity because there were too few men left to perform the jobs. Thus, the women were recruited through the lure of helping their country. These women temporarily enjoyed improved wages and government-sponsored day care for their children while they worked and helped their country. (It is not clear why they weren't perceived as helping their country with their work inside the home, too.) Most of these privileges were reneged, however, when the war ended and the men returned. Nonetheless, once many of the women experienced working in the public sphere, they were no longer satisfied to return to the lack of wages and the isolation of life at home. This belief in their right to work outside the home helped bring about group consciousness of the oppression of women's rights (as previously discussed by Klein [1984]).

The 1960s were significant in the struggle for women's equality. Data from this era indicate that many U.S. women were dissatisfied with full-time domestic work. At the same time, "marriage and motherhood were becoming less stable foundations for an entire lifetime" as the divorce rate increased from one in six marriages in 1940 to one in two marriages in the 1980s (Rhode, 1989, 53). The number of women estimated never to marry increased to 10 percent in the late 1980s, while the percentage of single-parent families headed by a woman grew to almost twice that (ibid., 54). Rhode (ibid.) identifies *status deprivation* as another motivating force for a new wave of feminism in the 1960s: "a perception that women had less opportunity for social recognition than men with comparable talents and training." During the mid–1960s, many women were displeased with their treatment in the civil rights, antiwar, and other leftist organizations. *Consciousness-raising (CR) groups* became popular, where small groups of women met to discuss, among other issues, "the personal as political." This slogan represented a belief that patriarchy dominates all aspects of women's lives, their personal lives (for example, sexual activity and housework) as well as their public participation (for example, employment outside the home) (Hurtado, 1989; Jaggar, 1983). Consciousness-raising and similar groups helped organize the women's movement and push for women's equality.

Labor-market conditions for women have changed very slowly. For example, women were relegated to the lowest-paying jobs in the sex-segregated labor market during industrialization and development of the service economy in the late nineteenth and early twentieth centuries in the United States (Meyerowitz, 1988). By the 1970s, half of all female employees were concentrated in 17 occupations, while half of male employees were located in 63 occupations (Kanter, 1977a). Moreover, current working conditions for women in England may also be applied to the United States:

> As far as women's employment is concerned, the majority of women workers are to be found in a small number of occupations. They tend to be employed in the catering or service industries; they work as cleaners, hairdressers, shop assistants or clerical workers, or they are involved in repetitive assembly or packaging work. They are also over-represented within the education, welfare and health occupations. Within each occupation, they are heavily concentrated in the lower grades [with far lower wages]. (Gregory, 1987, 3)

A recent analysis of African Americans' progress toward economic equality notes that not only is employment outside the home necessary for single-women head of households (who are predominantly black), but such employment is also often necessary for women (and their families) who are married to African-American men, given their economic and social discrimination (Geschwender and Carroll-Seguin, 1990). African-American women's economic contributions to their families are relatively much greater than those of white women. The pressure of paid employment for married black women, then, is usually greater than for married white women, given the reduced earning capacity of black men. The decline in real income in recent years, combined with the lack of available educational and economic opportunities for African Americans, has not only loosened their precarious hold on the middle class acquired during the 1960s and 1970s but has also increased the proportion of blacks living in poverty (ibid.).

In conclusion, despite feminist attempts to widen women's working opportunities, there remains a stubborn adherence to sex-segregated jobs, with women's jobs being the lowest paid. This has the most severe impact on women of color and their families.

LEGAL IMPLICATIONS

Sex-Neutral Legislation

Although men and women hold different positions in society, the laws tend to be "unisex" in nature (Dahl, 1987, 361). In contrast with the sex-specific legislation discussed in the section following this one, most laws are sex neutral ("unisex"), even those created with hopes of rectifying gender equality. That is, most laws are *sex neutral* in that they do not even mention sex/gender, much less suggesting or requiring gendered applications. However, even laws attempting to address sex discrimination, which mention sex, simply state that a person should not be discriminated against based on her or his sex. Thus, even these sex–neutral laws that address/mention sex are "uni–sex" in nature. It is important to understand, however, that when the differing living conditions, needs, and potentials for men and women meet the unisex laws, the "legal rules will necessarily affect men and women differently" (ibid.). More simply, because men and women hold such different positions in society, unisex laws will have different results for women than for men. As Chamallas (1999, 18) points out, most institutions (be they governments or private businesses) "follow practices and policies saturated with implicit male bias. Simply to follow these 'neutral' rules and ignore gender reproduces patterns of exclusion and paradoxically assures that gender will continue to matter in the world." Alternatively stated, "Clearly the gender neutral terms of the federal constitution do not protect the rights of women to the same extent as they protect the rights of men" (Thomas, 1991, 116).

Title VII, a 1972 amendment of the 1964 Civil Rights Act, is an example of such sex-neutral legislation. Title VII states that is illegal to base any terms of employment (conditions, compensation, firing, hiring, and so on) on a person's sex, race, religion, or national origin. Ironically, although most employment sex-discrimination suits have been brought via Title VII, "sex" was added to the list of nondiscriminatory characteristics listed in the amendment (after race, religion, and natural origin) at the last minute before its passage, as an attempt to derail the entire Civil Rights Act; that is, antiwoman sentiment was used to try to deny racial equality (Deitch, 1993). In fact, when the inclusion of sex was read to Congress, it was met with laughter, and all but one of the men who had voted for including "sex" in the amendment voted against the whole bill (Deitch, 1993). This is another example of racism and sexism operating simultaneously.

Title VII allowed the Equal Employment Opportunity Commission (EEOC), a federal agency established in 1964, "the power to prosecute Title VII violators in the federal courts, a power it quickly utilized" (Zimmer, 1986, 4). In fact, most employment-discrimination suits have been brought pursuant to this amendment (Berger, 1980). However, it has also been stated that it took 10 years for Title VII to get some "teeth" and be effective (Hoff, 1991, 234).

Despite its positive influence, Title VII has important limitations. First, the *bona fide occupational qualification* (or BFOQ) defense was designed for exceptions where it would be considered rational to prefer the employment of one sex over the other. (Notably, race never qualifies as a BFOQ [Blankenship, 1993].) Some claim that the only rational BFOQs regarding sex are sperm donors and wet nurses. BFOQs, however, have been legally used to exclude women's employment from a variety of occupations, including prison chaplain, prison guard, and international oil executive (Epstein, 1988). Second, Title VII is problematic in that it is costly to litigate; the cost of discovery (proof of differential employee treatment) and the need for expensive experts prohibit most workers from charging these suits on their own (Berger, 1980, 39).

Third, even when female employees have had the resources to go to court, many of these decisions have been disappointing. In *Geduldig v. Aiello* (1974) and *General Electric Co. v. Gilbert* (1976), for example, the Supreme Court decided that a company's exclusion of pregnancy and pregnancy-related disorders from their disability plan "does not constitute a denial of equal protection . . . because no pregnant man is treated differently from any pregnant woman" (Berger, 1980, 22). Although the disability plan covered sports injuries, elective cosmetic surgery, vasectomies, and disabilities incurred while committing a crime, absences associated with pregnancy and childbirth were excluded. Justice Rehnquist, in fact, reportedly viewed the decision as *promoting* gender equality, given that women wouldn't be covered for anything men couldn't be covered for (Williams, 1991). This ruling not only reduced women's ability to move out of the private and into the public sphere, but it has an obvious class bias, given the additional burden for women (and their families) who are economically dependent on the job—they simply can't afford to have children.

Despite its unsuccessful outcome for the complainant, *General Electric Co. v. Gilbert,* was not a complete loss. The high visibility of the case prompted the American Civil Liberties Union (ACLU) to convince Congress to amend Title VII to include discrimination against pregnant women as a type of sex discrimination (Berger, 1980; Eisenstein, 1988; Minow, 1993; Williams, 1991). The 1978 *Pregnancy Discrimination Act* (PDA) required employers to treat pregnancy like any other temporary disability. Nonetheless, even 10 years after the inception of the PDA, one-third of working women did not have access to protected leaves during pregnancy, "and even those with such protection could not count on returning to their same position at the time they wished" (Rhode, 1989, 119).

The PDA also fails to protect women from pregnancy discrimination in situations other than employment. A 1990 ruling in *Pfeiffer v. Marion Center Area School District* found that it was acceptable for the high school's National Honor Society (NHS) to dismiss a pregnant student. It was decided that this was not sex discrimination because the basis for expulsion was premarital sex (obvious from her pregnant state), not the pregnancy itself. The testimony of a male NHS member who admitted to engaging in premarital sex and was not expelled was excluded. "Pregnant or not, it is unclear how premarital sex destroys one's academic achievement that warrants membership in the National Honor Society" (Thomas, 1991, 137).

Another problem with Title VII is that its bifurcation of race and sex has served to decrease the employment protection for women of color. The wording of Title VII separates race and sex, giving people of color, as a group, access to challenging employment discrimination that is different from what it provides for women as a group. In essence, the legislative history of Title VII suggests that women of color are not to be its beneficiaries (Blankenship, 1993). For example, *DeFraffenreid v. General Motors* (1976) was brought by five African-American women employees because of the hiring and laying-off practices of General Motors (GM). The court sided with GM because they showed that white women and black men had not been discriminated against in hiring and laying off. Thus, black women may be protected only insofar as their discrimination experiences coincide with those of black men or white women (Crenshaw, 1989).

Perhaps the greatest irony of the first 15 years of sex discrimination Supreme Court rulings is that males have been more successful than females both in their access to the courts and in obtaining favorable decisions (Rhode, 1987). The majority of cases recognizing sex discrimination overturned the few instances where the legal or social system favored women (the men in these cases claimed to have been the victim of "reverse discrimination"). "When one looks at the actual holdings [of Supreme Court triumphs on sex discrimination], the constant thread that runs through these 'women's rights' cases is that most of the winners have been men, and that women have won only when it was not at the expense of a man" (Berger, 1980, 19). Such legal cases granting men alimony eligibility (*Orr v. Orr,* 1979), social security benefits (Califano v. Goldfarb, 1977; Weinberger v. Weisenfeld, 1975), and access to all-female nursing schools (*Mississippi University for Women v. Hogan,* 1982) acknowledge what feminists have been arguing all along in their attempts to promote women's access: that persons should not be discriminated against because of their sex. Another example of "reverse discrimination" being overturned in court concerns airlines' policies against hiring male flight attendants in the 1970s and 1980s. While Pan American Airlines attempted to justify restricting flight attendant jobs to women because of their "maternal" role, Southwest Airlines built their case on the "sexy image" of female flight attendants in "hot pants" and high boots as a legitimate reason to exclude male workers. "In both cases, the courts reasoned that the 'essence' of the airline's business was safe transportation, and that other employment attributes were 'merely tangential' to that 'primary' function" (Rhode, 1989, 94). The subsequent switch in title from the gendered "stewardess" to nongendered "flight attendant," along with the substantial hiring of male flight attendants are likely results of the courts' rulings.

The 1963 Equal Pay Act has also been fraught with problems. Reportedly designed to rectify gender wage discrimination by prohibiting pay discrimination

for women and men performing the same job, it applies only where the jobs performed are substantiated as equal. Thus the Equal Pay Act can't be used to raise
the abysmally low wages for traditional women's work and thus is not applicable
to nearly half of all employed women and over two-thirds of employed women
of color (Berger, 1980; Blankenship, 1993).

In summary, although the courts are acknowledging discrimination based
on sex, the most successful cases in court are those that further advance males.
Or, put more simply, sex discrimination is more likely to be considered uncon-
stitutional in instances where males are discriminated against than in situations
where females are discriminated against. Unfortunately, of course, the vast
amount of sex discrimination is against females, and apparently that is the least
likely to be rectified. Additionally, two important legislative changes propos-
ing to help discrimination against working women, Title VII and the Equal
Pay Act, are written and applied in a manner that provides significantly less
coverage for women of color.

Sex-Specific Legislation

As stated earlier, most laws are "unisex" (or sex neutral). However, some laws
are *sex specific,* meaning that they identify the sex to which the laws apply and
restrict or give an advantage to one sex over the other. Historically, male
judges' and male legislators' sex-specific rulings were almost completely to the
disadvantage of women. A historical account of women's rights and the
Supreme Court states: "What is perhaps most striking is the utter unself-
consciousness with which an exclusively male judiciary interpreted statutes
adopted by exclusively male legislators to determine issues of male exclusivity"
(Rhode, 1987, 14). The year 1992 was called "the year of the woman" because
of record high numbers of women, especially African-American women, running for elected office and yet resulted in only six women in the U.S. Senate
and 47 in the U.S. House of Representatives. Furthermore, President Clinton's
efforts to appoint more women to high offices resulted in the intense scrutiny
of female nominees' child-care providers, an issue that had never been raised
for elected or appointed men in high-profile governmental positions. This so-
called "Nannygate" excluded many qualified women from offices if there were
any hint that nonlegal immigrants had been used as child-care workers or if
Social Security payments for the workers weren't appropriate. No one had ever
examined these issues for male nominees.

In 1908, the U.S. Supreme Court reinforced women's place as in the home
in *Muller v. Oregon* (cited in Rhode, 1987), which made maximum-hour work
weeks for women (but not men) constitutional. The motivation for this ruling
was paternalistic: to protect women from being overworked. The ruling, however, resulted in a limitation on women's hours at work outside of the home,
income, and jobs at which they could be employed. This decision made
women more expensive and less available for overtime and night shifts, limited
their occupational choices and bargaining power, and increased their unemployment rates (ibid., 17).

Historically, organized labor supported sex-specific laws denying or restricting women's employment opportunities, supposedly in attempts to secure better labor standards for all workers (Eastwood, 1975). Similarly, some current sex-specific legislation is labeled "benign discrimination" because the laws are supposedly designed to protect women. Predictably, this "protective" legislation has served to reinforce the separate spheres and stereotypical gender roles (Rhode, 1989). Thus, there may be a cost to sex-specific legislation where the goal is to compensate for women's lack of equality.

Formal Versus Compensating Equality Laws

Two distinct strategies exist for achieving equality through laws: (1) formal equality and (2) compensating equality (Gregory, 1987). *Formal equality laws* require that everyone be treated identically, regardless of sex or race. Thus, formal equality includes the sex-neutral legislation discussed earlier but is designed to enhance equality. An example of a formal equality law is the Equal Rights Amendment, which states, "Equality of rights under the law shall not be denied or abridged by the United States or by any state on account of sex." Title VII is another example of a formal equality law.

Compensating equality laws, on the other hand, are an attempt to overcome the limitations of formal equality laws "by compensating for the social equalities suffered by certain groups" (ibid., 5). Thus, compensating equality laws may be sex-specific in giving women an advantage over men in an attempt to address historical exclusion. An example of a compensating equality law would be affirmative action laws. While the Equal Rights Amendment simply requires that everyone be treated the same regardless of their sex, affirmative action legislation is more proactive and acknowledges that inequalities exist that need to be addressed and require compensation. The formal equality laws request no differential treatment (that is, men and women should be treated identically), whereas the compensating equality laws request preferential treatment in order to acknowledge that women and people of color are at a disadvantage. Notably, compensating equality laws also exist for groups that have not faced oppression, such as veterans (Glasser, 1988; Thomas, 1991). Programs for veterans have existed for over 100 years and provide a lifetime preference for civil-service jobs (Thomas, 1991). Interestingly, these laws have rarely been questioned or judged, while affirmative-action laws continue to be rigorously questioned and eroded.

Feminist scholars are not in agreement as to whether formal or compensating equality laws should be the preferred method to achieve women's equality. Some feminist scholars support compensating equality laws, believing that formal equality laws ignore the current gender differences in access and opportunity and thus serve to perpetuate gender inequality (Dahl, 1987; Finley, 1993; Gregory, 1987; Krieger and Cooney, 1993). Others support compensating equality laws because the progress on equality in women's employment has been slow due to court decisions being based on precedent that has a history of supporting sex discrimination (McLean, 1988; Mullen, 1988). Still others believe that formal equality can effect only limited change and, for example, can't ensure that job structures allow both females and males to work outside the home and parent (Becker, 1993). At the crux of this debate among feminists is the effect of how difference is perceived and treated. As stated earlier, applying all laws and policies equally to females and males has an inherent sexist result given the male–biased natures of our institutions. However, affirmative action and other compensating policies may backfire by stressing sex/gender differences and reinforcing stigmatization. Chamallas (1999, 18) refers to this struggle as *the dilemma of difference*, pointing out that "neither ignoring nor highlighting gender will necessarily translate into positive gains for women. Instead, feminists find themselves grappling with how fundamentally to alter the way people think about difference and how to resist the cultural tendency to equate difference with inferiority."

Nonetheless, other feminist scholars have concerns about compensating equality laws. For example, although the formal and compensating equality laws were constructed as mutually exclusive, it is difficult to justify using formal equality laws for some circumstances and compensating equality laws for others. By promoting one it is impossible not to undermine the other (Smart, 1989). Sex-specific compensating equality laws, then, often serve to affirm sex-based stereotypes, which in turn perpetuate sex-based inequality (Littleton, 1991; Lucie, 1988; Mezey, 1990; Rhode, 1989; Smart, 1989; Williams, 1991, 1993).

Feminist support for compensating versus formal equality laws has been dubbed the "equal treatment/special treatment debate," and this issue is especially apparent with regard to the rights of pregnant women (Williams, 1993). Women are distinguished from men by their ability to become pregnant, lactate, and give birth, but not all women can or choose to do so. Although some women never become pregnant, no men ever become pregnant. There is a fine line between beneficiary and victim when it comes to legal classifications surrounding pregnancy, such that women must not be "trapped by the argument that pregnancy is unique" (Lucie, 1988, 237). The federal PDA defines pregnancy as a "disability." Furthermore, the PDA can't stop states from mandating special maternity leaves, whether the woman wants one or not (Rhode, 1990).

The equal treatment/special treatment debate focuses on the following concern: Can we assert that men and women are equal and need to be treated equally and at the same time request special laws for women implying that women are different/special (not the same/equal)? This is particularly troubling when these "special" compensating equality laws reinforce gender stereotypes. Eisenstein concurs with the ACLU's fear that protective pregnancy legislation reinforces the myth that women belong in the private sphere:

> In the eyes of an employer, a woman is a potential mother whether or not she is pregnant. Pregnancy affects a woman's options in the labor force either by its absence (she is not pregnant now but she may become pregnant) or by its presence. Recognition of pregnancy through sex-specific legislation undermines discrimination at least as much as, if not more than, it enforced it. (1988, 204)

Recent research has documented how women's potential to bear children has negatively affected their employment opportunities and coerced some women to be sterilized in order to keep their traditionally "male" jobs (Draper, 1993). One solution offered to the equal treatment/special treatment debate is to implement formal equality laws overall and take account of biological differences (such as pregnancy) only when the differences are significant to the issue at hand. This approach views biological reproductive differences as "episodic and temporary" and thus should be relevant in legal cases only when they are relevant to the question at hand (Kay, 1993). Who will determine relevance and how it will be decided are problematic issues.

Feminist legal scholar, Martha Chamallas (1999) identified three separate stages of feminist legal theory pertaining to the last three decades of the twentieth century. First, Chamallas characterizes the 1970s as the *equality stage,* where the goal was to establish gender equality through eliminating sex-based classifications and by obtaining equal access to education and jobs and promoting equality in the family. Next, Chamallas labeled the 1980s the *difference stage,* where feminist legal scholarship and activism attempted to respond to the inadequacies of liberal feminism and to highlight how women's inclusion "into male-dominated sites was not the exclusive meaning of equality" (ibid., 47). That is, as is evident in the latter part of this chapter and in Chapter 10, simply hiring women into male-dominated jobs does not guarantee that they will be treated and paid as equals. The "difference" era of the 1980s was particularly motivated by the pregnancy discrimination rulings and ensuing debates. Finally, Chamallas identified the 1990s as the *diversity stage,* an attempt to redress the previous feminist activist and scholarship shortcoming of lumping all women together. More specifically, the goal of this stage was to be more inclusive of *all* women rather than to focus on middle-class and wealthy white women and their primary issues in sexism. For example, reproductive freedom was expanded from abortion rights to include women of color's violations in being involuntarily sterilized. Clearly, these stages coincide with the feminist theories discussed in the first chapter (liberal, radical, and postmodern feminism).

THE HISTORY OF WOMEN'S ENTRY
INTO DECISION-MAKING POSITIONS
IN THE CRIMINAL-PROCESSING SYSTEM

Women on Juries

Serving on juries is an area in which women have been short-changed historically and sometimes continue to experience discrimination. Although many people view jury duty as annoying or inconvenient, it is a fundamental form of citizenship. It has been argued that excluding women from jury duty and the military draft in fact excludes women from full citizenship and feeds stereotypes about women's weakness and dependency on men (Eastwood,

1975; Lucie, 1988). We are thus forced to ask, "When is an advantage discrimination?" (Lucie, 1988). For example, courts' restrictions of women from military service and some other occupations has "transformed biological distinctions into cultural imperatives" where biology becomes destiny (Rhode, 1990, 121). Jury duty is an important service, and jury selection should not systematically disallow members of the population. When laws or *voir dire* policies exclude women from jury duty, "they limit both the woman's right to participate in the judicial process and the plaintiff's and defendant's right to a representative jury" (Mahoney, 1987, 209).

An earlier portion of this chapter discussed the importance of achieving both access and influence in terms of power in order to create social, political, and economic change. Jury duty is an excellent example of how access was a hard-fought battle for women and a success that has not always included significant influence. Although at least some (propertied) women had the right to serve on juries in feudal England (Sommerlad and Sanderson, 1998, 59), it appears that this may have been a short-lived opportunity in a historical overview. In the United States, the 1957 Civil Rights Act permitted women to serve on federal court juries but had nothing to say about state courts (Mahoney, 1987, 210). It was fairly common during this period for states to have automatic exemptions for women. This meant that women could avoid jury duty simply because they were women (an example of sex-specific legislation). This automatic exemption may strike some people as an advantage for women, but it had two unfortunate results: (1) Juries were not representative (which may be unfair to complainants and defendants), and (2) in states where women had automatic exemption, clerks routinely and deliberately did not call women for jury duty because they assumed the women would want their exemption (Mahoney, 1987).

An all-male jury convicted Gwendolyn Hoyt of the second-degree murder of her husband. Her counsel appealed this decision to the U.S. Supreme Court, charging that requiring women to register for jury duty at the courthouse had denied Hoyt equal protection and a jury of her peers in *Hoyt v. Florida* (1961) (Thomas, 1991). The U.S. Supreme Court decided that despite the "advent of 'T.V.' dinners," women's domestic burdens were more important than their civil obligations; that is, women's "rightful" place in the home justified deterring them from jury duty. "The court found no suspicion of denial of equal protection when only 10 out of 10,000 jurors were women" (Mahoney, 1987, 211). It was not until *Taylor v. Louisiana* (1975) that women could no longer be exempt from jury service based simply on their sex. Interestingly, in this case with a male defendant accused of aggravated kidnaping and rape, the Supreme Court decided an all-male jury was not equal protection. Thus, sexism in jury selection was not considered problematic for a woman defendant (Hoyt), but it was viewed as unacceptable for a male defendant (Taylor).

Even though women have legally achieved the right to serve equally on juries, the process of voir dire—the questioning of the various possible jury members by lawyers prior to the trial—has resulted in discrimination. Lawyers often base their questions and attitudes on stereotypical views of women. This process was challenged in *Bobb v. Municipal Court* (1983), when attorney Carolyn Bobb was notified for jury duty and refused to answer questions regarding her marital status and spouse's occupation during the voir dire process. Bobb was annoyed because the lawyer was asking these questions only of the females in the jury pool. She was "held in contempt of court and taken into custody . . . sentenced to one day in jail with credit for time served" (Mahoney, 1987, 212).

A final example of access not being sufficient in jury duty to achieve women's equality is exemplified by the research finding that women serving on juries tend to be deferential to male jurists and more easily persuaded by other jury members' opinions (Constantini et al., 1983). Contrary to popular opinion, however, women jury members are not inherent enemies of or overly harsh to the women they are judging (Mahoney, 1987).

Women Lawyers and Judges

Although the status of attorney is much higher than that of police officer or jail or prison guard, women have been more successful at breaking into the occupation of law than policing or "corrections." Perhaps this is because in law there is less actual physical contact with male offenders than is likely with policing and prison jobs. Arresting, deterring, and guarding male offenders is perhaps the ultimate in machismo, while lawyers have more physical distance from offenders. At any rate, women have practiced law in the United States since colonial times, despite active efforts to keep them out of the law field. In fact, in efforts to keep women out of law, "bar associations claimed women lacked the physical strength to handle heavy case loads, and newspapers charged that attractive women would unfairly sway juries" (Morello, 1986, *xi*). Historical objections offered to restrict women from practicing law included accusations that women had inferior minds and bodies, an inability to be discreet, and a role conflict between career and wife and motherhood (Weisberg, 1982). (These are consistent with the images of women discussed in Chapter 1.)

The first woman to practice law in the United States arrived in the "New World" in 1638 and acquired considerable real estate holdings. She was addressed as "Gentleman Margaret Brent" in person and in court records (Morello, 1986). Brent was a highly successful attorney, particularly regarding land deals, and was consistently employed by the governor. Little is known about women practicing law from colonial times until the mid–1800s, except that they were denied acceptance to law schools and admission to the state bar. In the rare cases where women conducted litigation in court, they were usually there on their own behalf (Bernat, 1992). Although men could receive legal training either through clerkship with an attorney or by attending law school, both of these avenues were routinely closed to women unless a brother or husband "allowed" his sister or wife to clerk with him. "Males who oversaw the entrance of persons into law (judges, lawyers, law school professors and bar admission boards) argued that law was a hard-nosed, 'male' profession which could impugn the 'delicacy' of a female's biological character" (ibid, 310–311). Also, the case of *Bradwell v. Illinois* (1873), previously discussed, barred married women from practicing the law. Although at least some women were allowed to be lawyers *centuries* before they were allowed to work as police officers or as guards in men's prisons, it is interesting that similar to the pioneering women in policing and guard work, women lawyers' most significant resistors were their male colleagues. An assessment of women lawyers in the 1800s in the United States states: "Opposition to women lawyers came from male lawyers who perceived women as innately unsuited to practice law because of their emotional and sentimental nature" (Pollock-Byrne and Ramirez, 1995, 80).

Historical overviews of women becoming attorneys in many other countries suggests similar sentiments. An analysis of women breaking into the field of law in Canada states that the process was very similar to women's experiences in the United States, with the first woman "finally admitted as a barrister in [Ontario in] 1897" (Hagan and Kay, 1995, 7). In the United Kingdom, a successful challenge to women's exclusion from medical school in 1873 at the University of Edinburgh at least partially opened the door for women's entry into law school in the 1880s (Sommerlad and Sanderson, 1998, 60). Although a number of women consequently completed law degrees, their applications to the bar were denied with no stated reason. A bill to allow women to be barristers and solicitors first introduced in 1912, again in 1914, and again in 1917 failed after significant opposition citing the importance of "separate spheres" (ibid, 60–68). Finally, in 1919 obstacles to women's entry to the legal profession in England were removed. Carrie Morrison, in 1922, was the first woman admitted to the Law Society in England, and eight women followed the next year. Unfortunately, their attire was considered more significant than the remarkable academic characteristics of these women (Sommerlad and Sanderson, 1998). Also unfortunate was that likely due to the elite class of many of the first women in the legal profession in England, most were invested in maintaining and not challenging the male-dominated legal profession (ibid, 81–82).

Women lawyers were needed for the fight to acquire women's equality and particularly to combat the discrimination that was inherent for married women, as discussed in the last chapter. In the 1800s, married women were unable to receive professional educations, hold elective offices, enter into contracts, obtain custody of their children, and control their own money—even when they had earned it (Morello, 1986, 9). Ironically, women members of the legal profession "have used their expertise in courts and legislatures to gain the right to be admitted to law schools and state and federal bars, and to be permitted to plead cases before state and federal courts" (Feinman, 1986, 104).

Two historical events are related to legal training becoming accessible to women and the less wealthy in the 1830s and 1840s (Morello, 1986). First, as whites increasingly populated the western part of the United States, more women became lawyers. In fact, the first law schools open to women were in the West (Feinman, 1986). The westward movement of whites gave European-American women increasing amounts of freedom: The farther away women were from the staid northeastern society, the greater their independence (Morello, 1986). The corresponding decrease in the prestige of legal practice, predictably, opened the door to women. The second historical event that increased women's access to legal training was the Civil War. With men off fighting in the war, women had the opportunity to fill the vacant clerkship and law school positions.

The first woman formally admitted to the bar in the United States, Arabella Mansfield, passed the Iowa bar in 1869 (Feinman, 1986). Again, it was particularly difficult for married women to become lawyers unless they happened to be married to a lawyer who was willing to train them. In fact, more than one in six women lawyers in 1890 were married to lawyers (Weisberg, 1982). Still, even many married women who were legally permitted to practice law were often restricted by society and their own husbands and families who didn't believe women could have both marriages and careers (Drachman, 1989). In addition to the strong likelihood of having husbands and family members who were lawyers, another characteristic that the first women lawyers shared was their tendency to come from wealthy families (Weisberg, 1982).

Laws forbidding women to enter into contracts also stymied their ability to practice law. As might be expected, many of the first women practicing law in the United States were dedicated to fighting different aspects of discrimination, including women's issues (such as suffrage, birth control, and equal rights) and advocating for the poor, Native Americans, African Americans, and immigrants (Morello, 1986). In the late 1800s, the first woman lawyer to argue a case before the U.S. Supreme Court, Belva Lockwood, obtained a $5 million settlement for the Cherokee nation from the U.S. government (ibid.).

The Ivy League law schools were the last to accept women students. One letter directed to Yale Law School in 1872 suggested that perhaps "ugly women" should be allowed to enroll because they would not distract the male students (ibid.). Harvard Law School was one of the last law schools to accept women when it did so in 1950.

The link between women's right to vote (suffrage) and women's entry into legal professions is significant, as battling the law was necessary both for the right to vote and for women's greater equality. "The history of women's efforts to gain legal identity and citizenship status therefore reveals the interconnections between the common law as a crystallization of existing power relations, and the legal profession as both enforcers of those relations and a social nexus" (Sommerlad and Sanderson, 1998, 70). In England, between 1912 and 1919, the fight for women's suffrage was closely tied to women's fight to become barristers and solicitors (ibid., 1998).

Similarly, in the United States women lawyers weren't eligible for elective judgeships in most states until the Nineteenth Amendment (women's suffrage) was passed in 1920 (Cook, 1978; Flowers, 1987). Thus, women judges were a rarity prior to 1920 (Flowers, 1987). The first woman judge in the United States, Esther Morris, was appointed in 1870, and 50 years later, in 1922, Florence Allen was the first woman elected to a state supreme court (Abrahamson, 1998). The first women judges, however, did not preside over a criminal court (Feinman, 1985; Flowers, 1987). The first woman appointed to sit on the federal bench, Burnita Shelton Matthews, was appointed by President Truman in 1949. Few women, only 19 in fact, were on the federal bench by 1976, when Jimmy Carter was elected president. President Carter is credited with making "a concerted effort to diversify the bench by seeking out and appointing women and members of ethnic minorities" (Abrahamson, 1998, 197). Indeed, Carter appointed more women to the federal bench in his 4 years than Reagan and Bush did together in their 12 years (ibid., 198).

The first African-American women lawyers were caught in the double-marginalization discussed previously. Feminist activists had focused on white women's rights, and African-American activists focused on African-American men's rights, a problem that still exists to some extent. Thus, African-American women activists often felt ignored and forced to divide their loyalties (Morello, 1986). Even traditionally black Howard University resisted admitting women to the law school. In the 1880s, Charlotte E. Ray, the first African-American woman lawyer in the United States, gained entry to Howard Law School by using only her initials for her first and second names in her application. Nonetheless, being black and a woman, Ray was never permitted to join the ranks of practicing lawyers. She eventually resumed teaching in Brooklyn public schools and died in obscurity in 1911 (ibid.).

In the 1940s, Constance Baker Motley, the second African-American woman to attend Columbia University, was active in many important civil rights cases, working with Thurgood Marshall and serving as counsel to the Reverend Martin Luther King Jr. Ms. Motley served as a politician and a judge, as well. A brief biography of Motley states: "Three separate incidents of racial discrimination while in high school were probably the cause of her active participation in civil rights groups at an early age" (Alpha Kappa Alpha Sorority, 1968, 19). Her recently published autobiography is not only an important historical account of civil rights litigation, but is also a portrayal of the intersection of sexism with racism in Ms. Motley's personal and professional life. Further, it is and a carefully written account of the current state of racism, classism, and sexism in the United States (See Motley, 1998). A 1968 publication, *Negro Women in the Judiciary,* briefly highlights the contributions and lives of ten early African-American judges (including Motley) (Alpha Kappa Alpha Sorority, 1968). Similar to what has been written about Motley, many of these African-American women have experienced considerable economic hardship, racism, and sexism but have dedicated their lives to issues of justice and equality. Additionally, these publications on the first African-American women on the judiciary not only are a tribute to them but also underline the continuing need for attorneys who challenge the racist, sexist, and classist status quo.

Women Working as Prison and Jail Guards and Police

The first women working in the crime-processing system were white and predominantly social reformers from wealthier homes, and their work in the system tended to be volunteer (Appier, 1998; Feinman, 1986; Martin and Jurik,

1996; Morris, 1987; Schulz, 1995). There is a strong link between women's advancement into policing jobs and their advancement into prison and jail employment. Women prison reformers, however, "paved the way" for women to work in policing, as well as advancing women's roles from volunteer to paid/professional services (Schulz, 1989). The first woman hired as a jail matron was in 1822, and in 1832 the first women were hired as prison guards (Pollock-Byrne, 1995; Zupan, 1992). Significantly, these first women working in crime-processing professions "were admitted as women and not as professionals" (Morris, 1987, 139). As stated perviously, they were hired for their presumed maternal abilities. The separate institutions designed for women prisoners in the late nineteenth and early twentieth centuries not only provided women prisoners with more attention but also provided women with more opportunities to work with offenders (Zupan, 1992).

Black women's experiences working in prisons have mirrored the racism and sexism outside the prisons. Before the Supreme Court decision in *Brown v. the Board of Education* (1954), "racial segregation existed as institutional policy and practice, de jure in the South and de facto in the North" (Feinman, 1986, 141). Most superintendents and officers in the prisons were white, and when blacks were hired, it was usually to guard black prisoners, who were typically segregated and housed in the worst parts of prisons. Since the 1950s, African-American women's (and men's) employment in penal institutions has significantly increased. It has also been noted that as more nonprison jobs opened for white women, more African-American women moved into the vacuum created by their absence in prison employment (Feinman, 1986).

As previously stated, women prison reformers gained legitimacy for women professionals in public agencies caring for women, which "paved the way for the first police matrons and then policewomen to follow in establishing their own legitimacy in the criminal justice field" (Schulz, 1989, 117). The entrance of women into U.S. police work began in the late 1800s, spurred by increased problems with women and girls that male police officers seemed uninterested in or unable to confront, particularly prostitution (Appier, 1998; Feinman, 1986). Mrs. J. K. Barney, an executive officer of the Women's Christian Temperance Union (WCTU), "spent some 20 years agitating in New York City for the appointment of police matrons," whom she described as ideally middle-aged, "scrupulously clean in person and dress, with a face to commend her and a manner to compel respect; quiet, calm, observant, with faith in God and hope for humanity" (as cited in Segrave, 1995, 7). WCTU, "probably the most powerful women's group of the era," has been identified as spearheading the demand for police matrons in the United States for the last quarter of the 1800s (Schulz 1995, 12). Although New York State passed legislation in 1888 allowing New York City to appoint two such matrons to each station, they did not provide the funding for the positions, so no matrons were hired. Notably, the press played a significant role in the ensuing years, often arguing for the need of matrons in NYC (Segrave, 1995). "The first four matrons started work in New York City police stations on October 5, 1891, much later than in many other cities, and by 1899 the city employed 61 police matrons"

(Segrave, 1995, 10). In 1905, Lola Baldwin was hired as a "safety worker" in Portland, Oregon, to "protect" women and girls from "approaching" male miners, lumberjacks, and laborers (Feinman, 1986).

During World War I in England, women conducted voluntary police patrol work to control other women such as prostitutes (Morris, 1987). Drawing on Martin's working in distinguishing phases in the early history of women police in the United States, Heidensohn's comparison of British and U.S. policewomen's historical phases adds another phase, a preliminary one. Specifically, Heidensohn (1992, 41) describes the first phase of women's entry into policing as *moral reform, rescue, and matrons* (1840–1910 in the United States and 1915 in England), the second phase as *specialists and pioneers* (1910 in the United States and 1915–1930 in England), and the third phase as *latency and depression* (1930–1945 in both countries). Heidensohn (1992) has also noted an *expansion* phase as a fourth phase occurring in the late 1960s and 1970s, when both England and the United States saw an unprecedented number of women police officers hired. (Martin and Jurik [1996] report similar phases.)

Regarding the *moral reform, rescue, and matron phase* in policing, many of the first women police officers identified more as social workers than as "cops" and saw their role as helping women and children. Indeed, between 1880 and 1930 in the United States "many women activists devoted their entire careers in social work and social science to identifying the welfare needs of working-class women and children and pressing for the establishment of government programs and institutions to meet those needs" (Appier, 1998, 13). The first two decades of the 1900s in the United States were important in advancing women into police departments, albeit in stereotypical roles. Hence, the phase after the "preliminary" entrance phase for women (the moral reform, rescue, and matron phase) has been identified as the *specialist phase* (Heidensohn, 1992; Martin and Jurik, 1996). Between 1910 and 1930, women police officers largely worked in specialist roles within the police departments, usually confined to traditionally female skills (Martin, 1980). Martin and Jurik (1996, 49), however, state that the specialist phase in the United States lasted from the designation of the first policewoman in 1910 through Title VII in 1972. However, it appears that there were some unique characteristics about the 1910 to 1930 era as well. Although women were hired as "policewomen" in more cities from 1918 to 1929, "in absolute terms their number remained small" (Segrave, 1995, 44). "In 1930 there were reportedly 600 policewomen employed in 289 communities in the United States" (ibid., 85). Overall, policing itself didn't change much between 1920 and the 1940s, including the hiring and roles of women police officers (Schulz, 1993).

The first woman to hold the title "policewoman" was Alice Stebbins Wells, in Los Angeles, California, in 1910 (Feinman, 1986; Hale and Bennett, 1995; Segrave, 1995). The first African-American woman in the United States appointed to policing was Georgia Robinson, appointed as a matron to the Los Angeles Police department in 1916, and in 1919 she became a "policewoman" in this department (Schulz, 1995). In Toronto, two policewomen were appointed in 1913 (Segrave, 1995), and the first woman to be sworn in and given arrest powers in England occurred in 1915 in Grantham, England (Heidensohn, 1992, 29). It has been noted that England's struggle for policewomen, relative to the United States, required far more organizing and lobbying, and the battle to achieve the first hires were more prolonged (ibid.). However, in both of these countries, these initial hires did not guarantee the security of women in policing: instead, their entry was "every bit as precarious" as their initial hiring (ibid.). The phenomenon described in Heidensohn's (1992, 54) third phase in women's policing, latency and depression, where stagnation in hiring women occurred between 1930 and 1945, was partly due to the Depression, but even more so a result of women's "insecure" entry into policing which made "a poor basis for expansion." Evidence of this is that in 1925 the City Council in Los Angeles considered reclassifying women officers from members of the LAPD police force to civilian employees (Appier, 1998). After intensive lobbying, the women officers won the right to continue to be classified as "policewomen."

Making an international comparison of the "first" women police is difficult. Specifically, it is sometimes difficult to distinguish who qualifies as a "policewoman." Many of the early women gaining access to policing jobs across the globe, similar to those in the United States, were volunteers, or if paid, were still considered civilians. Thus, semantics makes it difficult to establish a clear time-line. In England, there was friction between different groups of women advocating for policewomen on the British police departments, particularly in London. In 1918 the Metropolitan Police Women Patrols was announced, but it was a blow to some organizers because these women had fewer powers, such as no power to arrest, that were available to the few policewomen elsewhere in the country (Douglas, 1999, 72). Natarajan (1996, 2) notes that women play more minor roles in policing in the more traditional societies, and "the willingness of various societies, and their criminal justice system to deploy women as line officers in their police forces varies with the stage of social and economic development in a given society and in relation to the strength of a resistive or supportive culture." Keeping in mind this disjuncture about what "counts" as a policewoman, Figure 9.1 is an attempt to identify the reported dates that various countries adopted some type of "policewoman" onto the police force.

Alice Stebbins Wells, the first "policewoman," was a social worker and theologian who believed that she could accomplish more to help women and girls through police work than through volunteer work (Feinman, 1986). When asked why she wanted to enter policing, she answered that women were more suited than men for some aspects of policing, such as comforting and guiding wayward or abused children, and preventing the victimization and offending of women and children (Appier, 1998). Although the press negatively characterized Wells as "unfeminine" and "muscular," she also received some support (Feinman, 1986). (This is an example of Rafter and Stanko's [1982] image of "the active woman as masculine," discussed in Chapter 1.) When she addressed the International Associate of Chiefs of Police in 1914, she was treated extremely rudely by the audience, including a heckler

Canada[a]	1913
China[a]	1933
England[c]	1915
Germany[a]	1903
India[b]	1939
Japan[a]	1946
Nigeria[a]	955
Poland[a]	1925
Sweden[a]	1949
United States[a]	1910

FIGURE 9.1 Different Countries' Adoption of Women
into Policing Roles

Compiled from data reported in the text in [a] Segrave (1995), [b] Natarajan (1996), (1995), [c] Heidensohn (1992).

who yelled, "Call the patrol wagon, another nut gone wrong" (Segrave, 1995, 15). It is unknown how long she stayed on the force, but it is evident she had retired at least by 1934. Soon after becoming the first "policewoman," Wells engaged in a heavy speaking tour across the United States and Canada and was influential mobilizing to bring about change in the hiring practices in many places (Appier, 1998).

There is considerable evidence of various women's groups in large cities across the United States advocating for the hiring of "matrons" and "police-women" around 1910, with many women willing to have these jobs. The pressure from these women's groups was significant regarding women's appointments to police departments in the United States between 1910 and 1970 (Segrave, 1995, 24). However, it is important to keep in mind that "[b]efore the 1970s, nearly all police officers in the United States were white men" (Martin and Jurik, 1996, 48).

Alice Stebbins Wells, along with other policewomen, is credited with help-ing to form the International Association of Policewomen (IAP). This profes-sional organization lasted from 1915 to 1932. Unfortunately, this and other women's groups declined along with other reformist and temperance groups (e.g., the WCTU), especially given the IAP leadership's lack of recognition from men's policing groups, particularly the International Association of Chiefs of Police (IACP) (Schulz, 1995). Schulz (ibid., 55) maintains that the demise of the IAP was partly due to the leaders' inability to anticipate societal shifts but that such a focus "fails to recognize that even though the early policewomen were greatly expanding women's sphere by entering the police environment, they continued to accept the view of different roles for men and women." Indeed, their approach helped fuel an extremely sexist approach to hiring police:

> In 1917 the U.S. Civil Service Commission established a minimum stan-dard for policewomen, consisting of a high school education and at least

two years' practical experience in social case work, or its equivalent in technical training and business experience. These standards were endorsed by the International Association of Chiefs of Police and by the International Association of Policewomen (IAP) and were then being implemented gradually in most areas. Male police had to meet a much lower standard, with high school graduation not being required in many areas until the 1960s [Segrave, 1995, 28].

Notably, the longevity of the sense of women as inherently nurturing and of the "appropriateness" of assigning women to specialized tasks commensurate with their nurturing is evidenced by the Los Angeles City Mothers' Bureau. This institution, a branch of the LAPD, lasted from 1914 to 1964 and was staffed completely by women police officers to work in crime prevention and give advice and aid on such matters as "disobedient children, spousal support, abusive husbands, alcoholism, immigration and citizenship, neighborhood quarrels, adultery, unemployment, and adoptions" (Appier, 1998, 73). During the postwar period of the 1950s and 1960s, the number of women police officers increased, but increased variation in roles was not commensurate (Schulz, 1993). Women police officers during this time, however, were actively attempting to broaden their roles. Title VII, therefore, did not create women police officers' desire for equality but rather provided legal support for changes that began in the 1950s (Schulz, 1993). Nonetheless, prior to 1968, "no women were assigned to the backbone of policing, patrol duty" (Martin, 1980, 48), and until 1972, women police officers' roles typically evolved around assisting male police officers (Hale, 1992).

> In 1968, when the Indianapolis Police Department assigned Betty Blankenship and Elizabeth Coffal to patrol, they became the first policewomen to wear uniforms, strap gun belts to their waists, drive a marked patrol car, and answer general purpose police calls on an equal basis with policemen. Although they eventually left patrol and returned to traditional policewomen's duties, they broke the link to the mothering concept that had been the basis of women's roles in policing. Once this link was severed, the stage was set for the modern women-on-patrol era to begin (Schulz, 1995, 5).

Thus, the culture of policing "remained virtually the same" for women from the late nineteenth-century to the 1960s (Hale and Bennett, 1995). Moreover, women were not appointed to the Secret Service and the Federal Bureau of Investigation as agents until 1972, and in 1993 almost 10 percent of the U.S. Secret Service agents were women (Segrave, 1995, 111–112). As Schulz (1995, 6) states, "exceedingly few women have reached the top of all but small police agencies." Penny E. Harrington served as the chief of the Portland (Oregon) police department between 1984 to 1986. "As of 1994, only two additional women had served as chiefs in major cities, and fewer than 100 of the more than 17,000 municipal law enforcement agencies were led by women" (ibid. 6).

Women's entry into policing, then, has been hard won and is certainly not over. A major part of women's roles in both policing and prison work is appearing to be "man enough" for the job. Segrave notes the following regarding the first woman police officer killed in the line of duty:

> The first policewoman killed in the line of duty was 24-year old Gail Cobb of the Washington, D.C., force, who was fatally shot in September 1974 while chasing a shotgun-toting fugitive. It was even suggested in some quarters that this incident would help ease the way for female entry into policing; that it would be a sort of baptism under fire and show that females were made of the right stuff. Needless to say, it had no such effect; discrimination and harassment continued apace. (1995, 115)

Similar to the serious limitations women police officers faced in their attempts to work the true crime-fighting role on patrol, women were not hired to work as officers with male prisoners until the 1970s. However, even when women worked in the "custodial institutions" for *women* prisoners (described in Chapter 5), they "tended to be subordinate to the *male* wardens at nearby *men's* prisons and were typically paid lower wages than their male counterparts" (Maschke, 1996, 34). Working in male prisons, however, provides important opportunities for women aspiring to a career in "corrections" for four reasons: There are better posts and shifts, there are more promotional opportunities, there are more locations to work in prisons, and working in a men's prison appears to be necessary for advancement into administration (Zimmer, 1986). The first three reasons are largely due to the fact that there are many more men's prisons than women's prisons (usually there is only one woman's prison per state), and the men's prisons are more highly populated, allowing for more positions in each rank, shift, and post. Significantly, the wardens of women's institutions have typically been men.

SUMMARY

This chapter addresses the successes and failures of attempts to achieve gender equality, particularly in the public sphere of employment. Women's movement from the private to the public sphere has occurred in fits and starts. First, women's suffrage in 1920 did not automatically enhance women's place in the public sphere, and the Equal Rights Amendment still remains unratified. During World War II, women's aspirations to equality were encouraged when they were "allowed" to participate in the labor market in wider numbers and in a greater variety of jobs—at increased pay. The 1960s spurred a third revival of attempts to bring women into the workplace, this time as equals.

Women have struggled with various legislation and court rulings in attempts to be active in the public sphere. This ranges from serving on juries to working in the same fields and on equal footing with men. Indeed, it has been noted that the concept "citizenship" is so fraught with male privilege and access that women are routinely excluded, and when included, they stand out as "gendered beings" (Jones, 1990). This has been especially problematic in employment in the crime-processing system. Ironically, while their female status and the presumed characteristics associated with it (e.g., weakness and deep emotions) were what kept women from access to policing and prison work, their initial entry into these fields was for their presumed "maternal" nature and strengths. Women's battle to overcome the barriers to work with male prisoners and serve as patrol officers in police departments has been grueling and continues to progress slowly. The resistance to change was not ended simply by "allowing" women to practice as lawyers, police officers, and correctional officers. It is a mistake to assume that legislation and communities committed to equality will in and of themselves remove all discrimination (McLean, 1988, 3). The next chapter examines women's employment in law enforcement, in prisons and jails, and in courts as attorneys and judges.

REFERENCES

Abrahamson, Shirley S. 1998. "Do Women Judges Really Make a Difference? The American Experience." Pp. 75–82 in *Women in Law,* edited by S. Shetreet. London: Kluwer Law International.

Alpha Kappa Alpha Sorority. 1968. *Negro Women in the Judiciary. Heritage Series Number 1,* August, 1968, 24 pp., Chigaco: IL.

Appier, Janis. 1998. *Policing Women: The Sexual Politics of Law Enforcement in the LAPD.* Philadelphia: Temple University Press.

Atkins, Susan, and Brenda Hoggett. 1984. *Women and the Law.* New York: Basil Blackwell.

Barnett, Bernice M. 1993. "Invisible Southern Black Women Leaders in the Civil Rights Movement." *Gender and Society* 7:16–82.

Bartlett, Katherine T. 1991. "Feminist Legal Methods." Pp. 370–403 in *Feminist Legal Theory: Readings in Law and Gender,* edited by K. T. Bartlett and R. Kennedy. Boulder, CO: Westview Press.

Becker, Mary E. 1993. "Prince Charming: Abstract Equality." Pp. 221–236 in *Feminist Legal Theory,* edited by

D. K. Weisberg. Philadelphia: Temple University Press.

Berger, Margaret A. 1980. *Litigation on Behalf of Women: A Review for the Ford Foundation.* New York: Ford Foundation Publication.

Bernat, Frances P. "Women in the Legal Profession," Pp. 307–322 in *The Changing Roles of Women in the Criminal Justice System,* 2nd ed., edited by Imogene L. Moyer. Prospect Heights, IL: Waveland Press.

Blankenship, Kim M. 1993. "Bringing Gender and Race In: U.S. Employment Discrimination Policy." *Gender and Society* 7:204–226.

Bobb v. Municipal Court, 143 Cal. App. 3d 849, 192 Cal. Rptr. 260 (1983).

Bradley, Karen, and Diana Khor. 1993. "Toward an Integration of Theory and Research on the Status of Women." *Gender and Society* 7:347–378.

Bradwell v. Illinois, 83. U.S. (16 Wall.) 130 (1873).

Burrows, Noreen. 1988. "Employment and Gender." Pp. 102–118 in *The Legal Relevance of Gender,* edited by S. McLean and N. Burrows. Atlantic Highlands, NJ: Humanities International.

Califano v. Goldfarb, 430 U.S. 199 (1977).

Campbell, Tom. 1988. "Sex Discrimination: Mistaking the Relevance of Gender." Pp. 16–39 in *The Legal Relevance of Gender,* edited by S. McLean and N. Burrows. Atlantic Highlands, NJ: Humanities International.

Chaiken, Jan M., and Marcia R. Chaiken. 1983. "Crime Rates and the Active Criminal." Pp. 11–30 in *Crime and Public Policy,* edited by J. Q. Wilson. San Francisco: ICS Press.

Chamallas, Martha. 1999. *Introduction to Feminist Legal Theory.* Gaithersburg, New York: Aspen Publishers.

Constantini, E. M., M. Mallery, and D. M. Yapundich. 1983. "Gender and Jury Partiality: Are Women More Likely to Prejudge Guilt?" *Judicature* 67:124.

Cook, Beverly B. 1978. "Women Judges: The End of Tokenism." Pp. 84–105 in *Women in the Courts,* edited by W. L. Hepperle and L. L. Crites. Williamsburg, VA: National Center for State Courts.

Crenshaw, Kimberle. 1989. "Demarginalizing the Intersection of Race and Sex: A Black Feminist Critique of Anti-Discrimination Doctrine, Feminist Theory and Anti-Racist Politics." *University of Chicago Legal Forum* 14:139–167.

Currie, Elliott. 1985. *Confronting Crime: An American Challenge.* New York: Pantheon Books.

Dahl, T. Stang. 1987. "Women's Law: Methods, Problems, and Values." *Contemporary Crises* 10:361–372.

DeFraffenreid v. General Motors, 413 F. Supp. (E. D. M. 1976).

Deitch, Cynthia. 1993. "Gender, Race, and Class Politics and the Inclusion of Women in Title VII of the 1964 Civil Rights Act." *Gender and Society* 7:183–203.

Douglas, R. M. 1999. *Feminist Freikorps: The British Voluntary Women Police, 1914–1940.* Westport, CT: Praeger.

Drachman, Virginia G. 1989. "My 'Partner' in Law and Life: Marriage in the Lives of Women Lawyers in the Late 19th and Early 20th Century America. *Law and Social Inquiry* 14:221–250.

Draper, Elaine. 1993. "Fetal Exclusion Policies and Gendered Constructions of Suitable Work." *Social Problems* 40:90–107.

Durham, Christine M. 1998. "Thoughtful and Worldly Women." Pp. 217–234 in *Women and Law,* edited by S. Shetreet. London: Kluwer Law International.

Eastwood, M. 1975. "Feminism and the Law." Pp. 325–334 in *Women: A Feminist Perspective,* edited by J. Freeman. Palo Alto, CA: Mayfield.

Eisenstein, Zillah R. 1988. *The Female Body and the Law.* Berkeley: University of California Press.

Epstein, Cynthia F. 1988. *Deceptive Distinctions: Sex, Gender, and Social Order.* New Haven, CT: Yale University Press.

Equal Employment Opportunity Commission v. Sears, Roebuck, and Company, 628 F. Supp. 1264 (N. D. Ill. 1986).

Feinman, Clarice. 1985. "Women Lawyers and Judges in the Criminal Courts." In *The Changing Roles of Women in the Criminal Justice System.* Prospect Heights, IL: Waveland Press.

Feinman, Clarice. 1986. *Women in the Criminal Justice System:* New York: Praeger.

Fergus, T. D. 1988. "Women and the Parliamentary Franchise in Great Britain." Pp. 80–101 in *The Legal Relevance of Gender,* edited by S. McLean and N. Burrows. Atlantic Highlands, NJ: Humanities International.

Finley, Lucinda M. 1993. "Transcending Equality Theory: A Way Out of the Maternity and the Workplace Debate." Pp. 190–210 in *Feminist Legal Theory,* edited by D. K. Weisberg. Philadelphia: Temple University Press.

Flowers, Ronald Barri. 1987. *Women and Criminality: The Woman as Victim, Offender, and Practitioner,* Westport, CT: Greenwood Press.

Frontiero v. Richardson, 411 U.S. 677 (1973).

Gates, Margaret J. 1976. "Occupational Segregation and the Law." Pp. 61–74 in *Women and the Workplace: The Implications of Occupational Segregation,* edited by M. Blaxall and B. Reagan. Chicago: University of Chicago Press.

Geduldig v. Aiello, 417 U.S. 484 (1974).

General Electric Co. v. Gilbert, 429 U.S. 125 (1976).

Geschwender, James A., and Rita Carroll-Seguin. 1990. "Exploding the Myth of African-American Progress." *Signs: Journal of Women in Culture and Society* 15:285–299.

Gillespie v. Board of Education of North Little Rock, 692 F. 2d 529 (8th Circ. 1982).

Glasser, Ira. 1988. "Affirmative Action and the Legacy of Racial Injustice." Pp. 341–358 in *Eliminating Racism: Profiles in Controversy,* edited by P. A. Katz and D. A. Taylor. New York: Plenum.

Goesaert v. Cleary, 335 U.S. 464 (1948).

Gregory, Jeanne. 1987. *Sex, Race and the Law: Legislating for Equality.* London: Sage.

Hagan, John, and Fiona Kay. 1995. *Gender in Practice: A Study of Lawyers' Lives.* New York: Oxford University Press.

Hale, Donna C., and C. Lee Bennett. 1995. "Realities of Women in Policing: An Organizational Cultural Perspective." Pp. 41–54 in *Women, Law, and Social Control,* edited by A. V. Merlo and J. M. Pollock. Boston: Allyn and Bacon.

Harris, Barbara. 1978. *Beyond Her Sphere.* Westport, CT: Greenwood.

Heidensohn, Frances. 1992. *Women in Control?: The Role of Women in Law Enforcement.* Oxford: Clarendon Press.

Hoff, Joan. 1991. *Law, Gender, and Injustice: A Legal History of U.S. Women.* New York: New York University Press.

Hoyt v. Florida, 368 U.S. 57 (1961).

Hurtado, Aida. 1989. "Relating to Privilege: Seduction and Rejection in the Subordination of White Women and Women of Color." *Signs: Journal of Women in Culture and Society* 14:833–855.

Jaggar, Alison M. 1983. *Feminist Politics and Human Nature.* Sussex, England: Rowman and Allanheld.

Jones, Kathleen B. 1990. "Citizenship in a Woman-Friendly Polity." *Signs: Journal of Women in Culture and Society* 15:781–812.

Kanter, Rosabeth M. 1977a. *Men and Women of the Corporation.* New York: Basic Books.

———. 1977b. "Some Effects of Proportions on Group Life: Skewed Sex Ratios and Responses to Token Women." *American Journal of Sociology* 82:965–990.

Kay, Herma H. 1993. "Equality and Difference: The Case of Pregnancy." Pp. 180–189 in *Feminist Legal Theory,* edited by D. K. Weisberg. Philadelphia: Temple University Press.

King, Deborah K. 1988. "Multiple Jeopardy, Multiple Consciousness: The Context of a Black Feminist Ideology." *Signs: Journal of Women in Culture and Society* 14:12–72.

Kirp, David L., Mark G. Yudof, and Marlene S. Franks. 1986. *Gender Justice.* Chicago: University of Chicago Press.

Klein, Ethel. 1984. *Gender Politics.* Cambridge, MA: Harvard University Press.

Krieger, Linda J., and Patricia N. Cooney. 1993. "The Miller-Wohl Controversy: Equal Treatment, Positive Action and the Meaning of Women's Equality." Pp. 156–179 in *Feminist Legal Theory,* edited by D. K. Weisberg. Philadelphia: Temple University Press.

Laws, Judith L. 1975. "The Psychology of Tokenism: An Analysis." *Sex Roles* 1:51–67.

Lewis, Diane. 1977. "A Response to Inequality: Black Women, Racism, and Sexism." *Signs: Journal of Women in Culture and Society* 3:339–361.

Littleton, Christine A. 1991. "Recon-
structing Sexual Equality." Pp. 35–56
in *Feminist Legal Theory: Readings in
Law and Gender*, edited by K. T.
Bartlett and R. Kennedy. Boulder,
CO: Westview Press.

Lucie, Patricia. 1988. "Discrimination
Against Males in the USA."
Pp. 216–243 in *The Legal Relevance of
Gender*, edited by S. McLean and N.
Burrows. Atlantic Highlands, NJ:
Humanities International.

Mahoney, Anne R. 1987. "Women Ju-
rors: Sexism in Jury Selection."
Pp. 208–224 in *Women, the Courts, and
Equality*, edited by L. L. Crites and
W. L. Hepperle. Newbury Park, CA:
Sage.

Martin, Susan E. 1980. *Breaking and Entering: Policewomen on Patrol*. Berkeley:
University of California Press.

Martin, Susan E., and Nancy C. Jurik.
1996. *Doing Justice, Doing Gender:
Women in Law and Criminal Justice
Occupations*. Thousand Oaks, CA:
Sage.

Maschke, Karen J. 1996. "Gender in the
Prison Setting: The Privacy-Equal
Employment Dilemma." *Women and
Criminal Justice* 7(2):23–42.

McLean, Sheila A. M. 1988. "The Legal
Relevance of Gender: Some Aspects
of Sex-Based Discrimination."
Pp. 1–15 in *The Legal Relevance of
Gender*, edited by S. McLean and N.
Burrows. Atlantic Highlands, NJ:
Humanities International.

Merrit, Deoborah J., and Barbara F. Re-
skin. 1992. "The Double Minority:
Empirical Evidence of a Double
Standard in Law School Hiring of
Minority Women." *Southern California
Law Review* 65:2299–2359.

Meyerowitz, Joanne J. 1988. *Women
Adrift: Independent Wage Earners in
Chicago, 1880–1930*. Chicago: Uni-
versity of Chicago Press.

Mezey, Susan B. 1990. "When Should
Difference Make a Difference: A New
Approach to the Constitutionality of
Gender-Based Laws." Pp. 105–120 in
Women, Politics and the Constitution,
edited by N. B. Lynn. New York:
Harrington Park Press.

Minow, Martha. 1993. "The Supreme
Court 1986 Term, Foreword."
Pp. 301–319 in *Feminist Legal Theory*,
edited by D. K. Weisberg. Philadelphia: Temple University Press.

Mississippi University for Women v. Hogan,
458 U.S. 718 (1982).

Morello, Karen B. 1986. *The Invisible
Bar: The Woman Lawyer in America, 1638
to the Present*. Boston: Beacon Press.

Morris, Allison. 1987. *Women, Crime, and
Criminal Justice*. Oxford, England:
Basil Blackwell.

Motley, Constance Baker. 1998. *Equal
Justice under Law*. New York: Farrar,
Straus and Giroux.

Mullen, Tom. 1988. "Affirmative Action."
Pp. 244–266 in *The Legal Relevance
of Gender*, edited by S. McLean
and N. Burrows. Atlantic Highlands,
NJ: Humanities International.

Natarajan, Mangai. 1996. "Towards
Equality: Women Police in India."
Women and Criminal Justice 8(2):1–18.

O'Connor, Karen. 1980. *Women's Organizations' Use of the Courts*. Lexington,
MA: Lexington Books.

Okin, Susan M. 1989. *Justice, Gender, and
the Family*. Basic Books.

Orr v. Orr, 440 U.S. 268 (1979).

Petersen, Hanne. 1996. *Home Knitted Law:
Norms and Values in Gendered Rule-
Making*. Aldershot, England: Dart-
mouth Publishing.

Pollock-Byrne, Joycelyn M. 1995.
"Women in Corrections: Custody and
the Caring Ethic." Pp. 97–116 in
Women, Law, and Social Control, edited
by A.V. Merlo and J. M. Pollock.
Boston: Allyn and Bacon.

Pollock-Byrne, Joycelyn M., and Barbara
Ramirez. 1995. "Women in the Legal
Profession." Pp. 79–95 in *Women,
Law, and Social Control*, edited by
A.V. Merlo and J. M. Pollock.
Boston: Allyn and Bacon.

Pfeiffer v. Marion Center Area School District,
917 F. 2d 779 (1990).

Reed v. Reed, 404 U.S. 71 (1971).

Rhode, Deborah L. 1987. "Justice, Gender, and the Justices." Pp. 13–34 in *Women, the Courts, and Equality,* edited by L. L. Crites and W. L. Hepperle. Newbury Park, CA: Sage.

———. 1989. *Justice and Gender: Sex Discrimination and the Law.* Cambridge, MA: Harvard University Press.

———. 1990. "Gender Difference and Gender Disadvantage." Pp. 121–136 in *Women, Politics and the Constitution,* edited by N. B. Lynn. New York: Harrington Park Press.

Robinson, O. F. 1988. "The Historical Background." Pp. 16–39 in *The Legal Relevance of Gender,* edited by S. McLean and N. Burrows. Atlantic Highlands, NJ: Humanities International.

Roe v. Wade, 410 U.S. 179 (1973).

Schafran, Lynn, and Winkler, Norma. 1989. "Integration of Women and Minority Judges into the American Judiciary." Pp. 43–56 in *The Judge's Book.* Chicago: American Bar Association.

Schulz, Dorothy M. 1989. "The Police Matron Movement," *Police Studies* 12:115–124.

Schulz, Dorothy M. 1993. "Policewomen in the 1950s," *Women and Criminal Justice* 4:5–30.

Schulz, Dorothy M. 1995. *From Social Worker to Crimefighter: Women in United States Municipal Policing.* Westport,CT: Praeger.

Schultz, Vicki. 1991. "Telling Stories about Women and Work: Judicial Interpretations of Sex Segregation in the Workplace in Title VII Cases Raising the Lack of Interest Argument." Pp. 124–155 in *Feminist Legal Theory: Readings in Law and Gender,* edited by K. T. Bartlett and R. Kennedy. Boulder, CO: Westview Press.

Segrave, Kerry. 1995. *Policewomen: A History.* Jefferson, NC: McFarland and Company.

Smart, Carol. 1989. *Feminism and the Power of Law.* London: Routledge and Kegan Paul.

Sommerlad, Hilary, and Peter Sanderson. 1998. *Gender, Choice and Commitment: Women Solicitors in England and Wales and the Struggle for Equal Status.* Aldershot, England: Ashgate Publishing Company.

Taylor v. Louisiana, 419 U.S. 522 (1975).

Thomas, Claire S. 1991. *Sex Discrimination in a Nutshell.* St. Paul, MN: West.

Weinberger v. Weisenfeld, 420 U.S. 636 (1975).

Weisberg, D. Kelly. 1982. "Barred from the Bar: Women and Legal Education in the U.S., 1870–1890." Pp. 231–258 in *Women and the Law,* Vol. 2, edited by D. Kelly Weisberg. New York: Schenkman.

Welter, Barbara. 1978. "The Cult of True Womanhood: 1820–1860." Pp. 224–250 in *The American Family in Social–Historical Perspective,* edited by M. Gordon. New York: St. Martin's Press.

Williams, Lynora. 1981. "Violence against Women." *The Black Scholar* 12:18–24.

Williams, Wendy W. 1991. "The Equality Crisis: Some Reflections on Culture, Courts, and Feminism." Pp. 15–34 in *Feminist Legal Theory: Readings in Law and Gender,* edited by K. T. Bartlett and R. Kennedy. Boulder, CO: Westview Press.

———. 1993. "Equality's Riddle: Pregnancy and the Equal Treatment/Special Treatment Debate." Pp. 128–155 in *Feminist Legal Theory,* edited by D. K. Weisberg. Philadelphia: Temple University Press.

Zimmer, Lynn. 1986. *Women Guarding Men.* Chicago: University of Chicago Press.

10

✳

Working Women:
On the Job

The question here is not simply whether there is room
in the law for women's voices, but whether the law allows
room for any voice that has not been woven into its fabric.

[BERNS, 1999, 13]

The preceding chapter examined women's historical struggle for equality both in general and with respect to the workplace. The latter half of the chapter focused on women's entry into various crime-processing jobs, including as jury members, police officers, prison and jail guards, and lawyers. This chapter addresses how women's entrance as professionals into three areas within the crime-processing system has taken hold. In particular, women's occupations in prisons and jails, policing, and the courts are discussed. This chapter explores the advances these "pioneer" women workers made in the crime-processing system. It analyzes the breakthroughs as well as the disappointing inhibitors for women workers' recognition and equality. Although laws discussed in Chapter 9 played a critical role in challenging policies that keep women from traditionally male jobs and offered important advancement for women's occupational opportunities in the prisons, policing, and the courts, "most occupations have remained highly gender-segregated or gender stratified" (Rhode, 1989, 161). This includes jobs in the crime-processing system.

Before addressing these issues, it is worth taking a moment to stop and think, "What difference could it have made to exclude women from these decision-making jobs in our justice system?" Might intimate partner violence and other forms of domestic violence and sexual victimizations have been taken more seriously by the police if women had been allowed to work as officers (and been promoted up into the ranks) and in the courts since the beginning of these institutions? Durham appropriately questions how judicial decisions may have been different had women been at the judicial helm earlier:

> It takes very little effort to identify countless ways in which the
> law . . . incorporates subtle and profound assumptions about the mean-
> ing of gender. What does it say about sex roles in marriage to enforce a
> rape statute that makes it legally impossible for a husband to rape his
> wife? What is going on when a divorce court assumes that a 53–year-old
> high-school graduate, wife and mother for 33 years is competent to sup-
> port herself and awards little or no spousal support? Why do girls experi-
> ence far more incarceration for juvenile-status offenses than do boys?
> Why do juries in civil suits award only a small percentage of the damages
> for loss of female life or services as opposed to male? (1998, 223)

LEGAL PRESSURE FOR WOMEN'S
EMPLOYMENT IN CRIME PROCESSING

As stated in the last chapter, there are significant parallels regarding women's entry into jobs as prison guards and those in policing. Both have long histo-ries of playing stereotypical roles (such as working in clerical roles or with juveniles or women offenders); both still represent small percentages of overall employees in their departments (particularly in administration), both attained their current status through court challenges and despite "strong male resis-tance"; and there is substantial evidence that both are as successful as their male counterparts (Pollock-Byrne, 1986, 5). Similar resistance to women tokens in law school is exemplified by the fact that women and men taking the bar exam in New York had to sit separately until 1971 because women would "excite the men" and distract them from taking their exams (DeCrow, 1974).

Legal pressure has been identified as the major impetus allowing equal entry of women into prison and jail employment (Jurik, 1985). In 1971 there were only seven women police officers on patrol in the United States (Gates, 1976), and the refusal to hire women to work in men's prisons was "unques-tioned and unchallenged" until 1972 (Zimmer, 1986, 1). Title VII, the 1972 legislation discussed previously, is viewed as the greatest motivation for hiring women into nongendered jobs in policing and prisons (see Morton, 1981). Title VII was also effective in a 1984 case, *Hishon v. King & Spalding,* in which Elizabeth Hishon brought a case against a prestigious law firm in Atlanta where she had been denied partnership after working there for seven years (Epstein, 1998). The court found that partnership decisions in law firms must be fair and are applicable to Title VII. Although Title VII's positive influence cannot be underestimated, there is concern that Justice Department and Supreme Court reinterpretations of Title VII in the 1980s had a "chilling effect on potential plaintiffs, making it more costly and difficult to win subsequent employment discrimination cases in the 1990s" (Martin, 1992, 285).

Unfortunately, although legislation has helped in many ways to improve women's opportunities, it has not provided clear guidelines allowing women equal opportunities. That is, while supporters of women working with male offenders have been somewhat successful in overturning height and weight requirements used to systematically deny women policing and prison employment, other blocks to women's equality in working with male offenders still exist. For example, although Equal Employment Opportunity Commission and affirmative action programs resulted in women being hired as police officers on patrol and to work with male prisoners, these programs do not guarantee women's employment in large numbers in these fields (Morton, 1981). Hiring women for police and prison work is still not the norm. Additionally, women police and prison workers have fallen victim to the last-hired, first-fired (or laid-off) practices. Presumably, the longevity of male workers' employment overrode the commitment to having female officers. Thus, while women have their foot in the proverbial door, they are frequently still only represented in token status in many criminal-processing institutions.

THE CURRENT RATES OF WOMEN'S EMPLOYMENT IN THE CRIMINAL-PROCESSING SYSTEM

In the 1996 edition of this book I reported that women constituted 11.5 percent of prison guards, 9 percent of sworn law-enforcement officers, and about 20 percent of practicing lawyers (Hagan et al., 1991; U.S. Federal Bureau of Investigation, 1993; U.S. Federal Bureau of Prisons, 1993). As of April 2000, the U.S. Federal Bureau of Prisons reported that 8,573, or 27.4 percent, of the U.S. prison staff are women, although it did not distinguish by rank or the sex of the staff at the institution (U.S. Federal Bureau of Prisons, 2000). Similarly, 1996 data from the U.S. Bureau of Justice Statistics indicates that of the custodial and security staff in U.S. prisons, women constitute 19 percent of the staff in both state and federal institutions, 14 percent of the staff in federal institutions, and 24 percent of the staff in state institutions (Bureau of Justice Statistics, 1997, 87). Unfortunately, these reports do not distinguish between male's and female's prisons, and it is likely that women's token status is far more drastic than these data indicate. The federal government reported that in 1998 10.5 percent of law enforcement/police officers in the United States were women (Uniform Crime Report, 1999). And, finally, the U.S. Census Bureau (1999) reported that women constituted 29 percent of both lawyers and judges in the United States in 1998. These changes indicate a significant rise in women in the United States working in crime-fighting jobs.

Information on the racial/ethnic breakdown of women working in the criminal-processing system is more difficult to identify. However, Martin and Jurik (1996) report that white men still constitute about three-quarters of law enforcement officers in the United States, and about 2 to 3 percent of law enforcement officers in the United States are African-American women, and about half of one percent are Hispanic women. A study of law-enforcement officers in Southern California reported similar findings. About two-thirds of the officers were white men, 2 percent were African-American women, 2 percent were Hispanic women, and 7 percent were white women (Schroedel et al. 1996).

Women and the Law: Women Attorneys, Judges, and Law Professors

The percent of women law students increased from 8.5 percent to 33.5 percent between 1970 and 1980, yet the percent of women lawyers increased only from 4.7 percent to 12.0 percent for the same time period (Epstein, 1983). Regarding law school attendees, Bernat (1992) stated that half of the law students in the United States are women. Women's representation in law schools and law firms, however, is more dismal. Pollock-Byrne and Ramirez (1995) report that women are only 8 percent of deans and about 16 percent of full professors in U.S. law schools. Consistent with other fields, in the field of law women are more predominant in the lower status, lower-paid positions (ibid.). Moreover, women faculty have more trouble getting tenure than their male counterparts, particularly when they specialize in feminist jurisprudence (see Pollock-Byrne and Ramirez, 1995).

A historical overview of women lawyers in the United States and Canada in the first half of the 1900s reported that in both countries (1) the number of lawyers about doubled in the first half of the 1900s; (2) the ratio of lawyers to the general population remained about the same from 1900 to 1961 (0.7 per 1,000 population in Canada and 1.25 per 1,000 in the United States); and (3) the ratio of men to women lawyers was declining (Hagan and Kay, 1995, 8). These authors report that "the addition of just a few women lawyers quickly reduced the size of the ratios"; however, "small but steady gains occurred for women in both countries through most of this century, with the most profound gains . . . since 1971" (ibid.). Similarly slow growth in the number of women lawyers was reported for the early years of women's admittance to this profession in England (Sommerlad and Sanderson, 1998, 80). In their review of Canada and the United States in the 1960s and 1970s, Hagan and Kay (1995, 10) report that the number of women increased from 3 to 14 percent of lawyers in the United States and from 3 to 15 percent in Canada. Similarly, in England, women represented less than 2 percent admitted to the profession in the 1920s, 3 percent in the 1940s, and 10 percent in 1971, and by the end of the 1980s were entering in equal proportions to men (Sommerlad and Sanderson, 1998, 89 and 106). "Although in 1911 there were only 7 women lawyers in all of Canada, by 1986 there were nearly 10,000" (Hagan and Kay, 1995, 11). Not surprisingly, women's advancement into judicial roles was far slower. Although the following overview is written in an upbeat and positive manner, it is somewhat distressing to think of this in terms that women constitute slightly over half of the population:

> In 1991, 25 of the 50 states had one woman on their highest court, and often she was the first woman to sit on that court; 21 states had no woman on the highest court. Four states and the District of Columbia had more than one Supreme Court justice who was a woman. In 1991 Minnesota became the first state with a female majority on its highest court, with four women among the seven justices of the court (Abrahamson, 1998, 196).

Abrahamson (ibid., 196–197), drawing on various publications, estimates that women constitute about 10 percent of federal district court judges and 13 percent of federal circuit court judges.

Women have fared much better with regard to their representation in law as compared to their representation in policing and guard work. However, most research on women and men attorneys reports that women continue to be overrepresented in family law and underrepresented in other types of law such as corporate, commercial, and civil litigation (e.g., Hagan, 1990; Hagan and Kay, 1995; Martin and Jurik, 1996; Sommerlad and Sanderson, 1998). On the other hand, women are making some advances in large firms in corporate settings (Hagan, 1990) and in the 1970s went from "virtual invisibility" in Wall Street corporate firms to "significant numbers" (Epstein, 1982). This is at least in part due to corporate firm members' fears of and experiences with sex-discrimination law suits, and a recent report on attorneys' income states that "women in the same kinds of practice as men, and at the same ranks, are now making 90 percent or more of male salaries" (Epstein 1998, 110). However, it is important to remember that men and women do not have equal access to the same practices and ranks; women and lawyers of color are more likely to end up in the lest prestigious lawyering jobs (Epstein, 1998). Furthermore, while experience increased the earnings for both women and men in a Canadian study, women gained "an annual average of about $3,000, compared to nearly $4,400 for men. The cumulative effect across careers is substantial" (Hagan, 1990, 845). This study concludes that, although there has been a "tremendous growth" in women entering the profession, "areas of law are still highly sex typed and gender cross-cuts other cleavages that stratify legal practice" (ibid., 849). Furthermore, a survey of women lawyers in large firms in the United States reported that while the women believed their salaries and bonuses were comparable to male lawyers, they also reported "they have fewer chances for top job assignments, litigation experience and promotions and that they are underrepresented in firm management" (Epstien, 1998, 114). Women lawyers are still less likely than their male colleagues to be made partners (Epstein, 1998; Graham, 1986; Hagan and Kay, 1995; Hagan et al., 1991; Sommerlad and Sanderson, 1998). In fact, a study on the effects of centralization and concentration of law partnerships found that the reduction of female partners was far greater than the corresponding decrease in male partners; this was most acute in small firms (Hagan et al., 1991).

Women are not as highly represented in judge positions as they are in the attorney pool as a whole. Predictably, when women are elected or appointed judges, it is frequently to judgeship roles consistent with stereotyped gender roles, especially "family law," divorce courts, juvenile courts, and the lower municipal courts. Women were first appointed to minor judicial positions in 1884, but only a "sprinkling" of women judges were appointed by various states in the following century (Epstein, 1983, 239). One study found that the higher a woman's income and the lower the birth rate in a state, the more women judges there were in the state (Cook, 1978). Women judges made up only 1 percent of federal judges until President Jimmy Carter made a concerted effort to appoint more women and people of color to the federal bench in the 1970s (Epstein, 1983). Sandra Day O'Connor, the first woman on the U.S. Supreme Court, was nominated by President Ronald Reagan in 1981. At that time, women made up about 5 percent of both state and federal court judges (Morello, 1986). Moreover, it was not until 1979 that all states had at least one woman serving in some judicial capacity (ibid.).

Women and Policing

Martin (1990, *xi*) notes that "[w]omen's representation in municipal police departments serving populations over 50,000 has grown from 4.2 percent of all officers in 1978 to nearly 9 percent of officers at the end of 1986." As stated previously, in 1998 women constituted 10.5 percent of law enforcement personnel in the United States. A study evaluating political factors related to hiring women police officers in urban departments found that departments experiencing budget reductions hired significantly fewer women police officers (Warner et al., 1989). Nonetheless, a growth in the number of available policing positions didn't result in a corresponding increase in the hiring of women. Notably, the more women on city council, the more women hired onto the police department. Furthermore, although verbal affirmative action commitments were unrelated to the rate of women police officers hired, court-imposed and formal voluntary programs were effective in increasing the number of women police officers (ibid.). These findings suggest the importance of having women in political leadership roles and for formal policies to increase the rate of women in policing. However, a Florida study examined the effect of the local labor market on women's representations in local law enforcement jobs and reported that "[n]either the degree of parity between men and women in local economic conditions nor the availability of a qualified female applicant pool" affected the percentage of women in individual departments (Poulos and Doerner, 1996, 19).

A study on the racial and gender make-up of law enforcement officers in Southern California reported that different factors are related to "who is hired" (Schroedel et al., 1996). Notably, while similar factors resulted in hiring both African-American women and African-American men, there were gender differences among the hiring of white officers and among the hiring of Hispanic officers. First, the percentage of the population in the jurisdiction served that is African American increases the likelihood of both African-American women and African-American men being hired as officers. Second, when the police chief is a person of color, there is a greater likelihood for both African-American women and African-American men to be hired. Third, affirmative action policies increased the likelihood of hiring African-American women but not African-American men. Fourth, the greater the Hispanic population, the greater the likelihood of Hispanic men but *not* Hispanic women being hired onto the police department. Fifth, when the police chief was a person of color, this increased the likelihood of Hispanic men but *not* Hispanic women hired. Sixth, the higher the violent crime rate, the less likely Hispanic men would be hired, but this variable was unrelated to the hiring of Hispanic women. Seventh, the greater the unemployment rate, the greater the likelihood of Hispanic women but not Hispanic men being hired. Eighth, affirmative action policies increased the likelihood of Hispanic women, but not Hispanic men, being hired. Ninth, the greater the white population, the more likelihood of white women but not white men being hired. Tenth, a police chief of color decreased the likelihood of hiring white women but had no effect on hiring white men. Eleventh, the higher the unemployment and the presence of affirmative action policies decreased white men's representation but had no effect on white women's. In sum, different factors appear to influence the likelihood of the hiring of various racial-gender groups (ibid.).

In 1973, Fanchon Blake, a twenty-five-year police force veteran, and some of her female co-workers brought a sex discrimination law suit against the city, chief, and police department in Los Angeles two years after the police chief, Ed Davis, announced that "women were no longer wanted or needed by the L.A.P.D." (Blake v. City of Los Angeles as cited in Felkenes et al., 1993). Davis reorganized the department not only to stop the hiring of women police officers but also to relegate the existing female officers into receptionist and secretarial roles. The plaintiffs won the suit in an appeals court in 1979, and in 1981 "a mutually agreed-upon 'Consent Decree' was signed" requiring better representation of women of all races as well as African-American and Hispanic men (Felkenes et al., 1993, 34). Although the decision resulted in an increase in the hiring of women, it was not within the required amount, and little was done to alleviate the daily hostility the women police officers experienced afterward.

WOMEN AS TOKENS IN THE WORKPLACE

Sociologist Robert K. Merton (1972) introduced the idea of viewing human behavior and organization through an insider-versus-outsider perspective. This perspective recognizes that some groups of people (insiders) have greater access to power and privilege than others (outsiders), and the distinctions between these groups is more likely based on ascribed rather than acquired characteristics. For example, a person may be more likely to receive a promotion because of race (an ascribed characteristic) than because of merit (an acquired characteristic). Being an insider (white, in this case) allows one more access to privilege (promotion in this case) than one's work record. The insider/outsider doctrine recognizes that powerful network memberships and decision making are often more heavily influenced by who you know and your ascribed characteristics than by who you are and what you have accomplished.

> Although programs such as affirmative action were developed to compensate for inequities, ascribed characteristics are still frequently the basis for hiring and promotional decisions. Additionally, outsiders hired into what have typically been insiders' jobs, whether or not their hiring was due to affirmative action policies, have often faced resistance. Women who break into male-dominated jobs are often viewed as "double deviants," first for being female and second for "aspiring to the attributes and privileges of the dominant class . . . [and] refusing the constraints of the ascribed status" (Laws, 1975, 53).

In 1944 Everett C. Hughes published an interesting analysis of a somewhat mobile society and its effects on status. He claimed that new groups acquiring employment status in professions from which they had previously been excluded could only hope to modify stereotypes; their hirings alone could not stop stereotypes. Tokens in the workplace may be compared to Merton's (1972) outsiders. Kanter (1977a) examines women in male-dominated jobs through a token/dominant perspective, where tokens are analogous to Merton's outsiders, and dominants are analogous to Merton's insiders.

> Tokens are not merely deviants or people who differ from other group members along any one dimension. They are people identified by ascribed characteristics (master statuses such as sex, race, religion, ethnic group, age, etc.) or other characteristics that carry with them a set of assumptions about culture, status, and behavior highly salient for majority category members. (Kanter, 1977a, 968)

Furthermore, Laws states:

> Tokenism is likely to be found wherever a dominant group is under pressure to share privilege, power, or other desirable commodities with a group which is excluded. Tokenism is the means by which the dominant group advertises a promise of mobility between the dominant and excluded classes. By definition, however, tokenism involves mobility which is severely restricted in quantity, and the quality of mobility is severely restricted as well. . . . The Token is a member of an under-represented group, who is operating on the turf of the dominant group, under license from it. (1975, 51)

The pressure of being a token within one's profession is heightened by the responsibility borne of representing every other person of one's token group.

For instance, a police department or law firm hiring its first woman may consciously or unconsciously base further hiring of women on this token's performance. In addition to standing out and being watched, this is a huge responsibility for a new token employee. The lack of logic should also be evident. Just as some white males are incompetent workers, so will some women and people of color be incompetent workers. However, most people do not use incompetent white male workers as a basis to form opinions on whether to hire other white males. It is recognized that even with affirmative action, some incompetent workers have been hired, but it is also necessary to recognize that many incompetent white males have been hired before and since affirmative action policies. Regardless of which hiring measures are used, some incompetent people of every racial, ethnic, sex, and class category will be hired. Unfortunately, there is a tendency to focus on the less competent employees of the outsider groups to "justify" discrimination in hiring.

Regarding crime-processing system employment, all "positions should be fully available to qualified women, just as they should be restricted to qualified men" (Morris, 1987, 159). Recent research evaluating gains and losses by African-American and white women and men from 1960 to 1980, however, found that while there were gains for African-American and white women and African-American men, these gains were "highly questionable" in the male-dominated (best paying) professions (Sokoloff, 1988).

A person's token status is heightened when (1) her or his social category is obvious (such as sex), and (2) her or his social category is new to the setting (Kanter, 1977a, 969). Both of these "heightening" characteristics exist for women breaking into the crime-processing system work force. These "pioneer" women did so mostly by maintaining a gender-specific role within these male-dominated jobs. For instance, the first women police, typically called "policematrons," worked with juveniles and "wayward women," the first female prison and jail workers were "matrons" for female offenders, and the first women lawyers and judges tended to work in juvenile courts and were often married to male lawyers. The term matron, lacking in a professional image, is certainly consistent with the nurturing and care-taking responsibilities these women were expected to perform. It is also consistent with the gendered expectations in physical and emotional care taking referred to earlier by Petersen (1996) as "obligations to care and conflicts about care." Indeed "matrons" are credited with bringing social service into police stations (Schulz, 1995, 17). Notably, the matrons in the prison work preceded the police matrons, and indeed the same group was responsible for the emergence of both police and prison matrons: prominent, upper-middle-class, well-connected, socially prominent women of native born families who were reformers (ibid., 2). For example, activists for women in policing "drew on middle-class gender stereotypes," claiming "that women's inherently compassionate nature would make them better than men at performing some police duties, such as preventing crime, handling female and juvenile cases, and protecting the moral and physical safety of women and girls in public" (Appier, 1998, 3). Undoubtedly, these token women were allowed to enter the male bastions of prison and policing work due not only to the work of these reformers, but also it is likely that "matron" was the least threatening role possible that a woman could hold in police and prison work. Pollock-Byrne (1995, 97–98) reports that "the attendant term of *matron* instead of *guard* or *correctional officer,* remained virtually unchanged until the 1960s, when women began to push for enlarged opportunities."

Hughes (1944, 358) claims that exceptions to jobs previously employing only white males (or only males, or only whites) do so through "some elaboration of social segregation. The woman lawyer may become a lawyer to women clients, or she may specialize in some kind of legal service in keeping with women's role as guardian of the home and morals." Another example is hiring women police officers to work solely with juveniles and sexual assault victims. Thus, sex segregation is maintained to some degree, which additionally provides excuses for gender pay discrimination and limited promotions. For example, in policing, promotions and advancement are directly tied to patrol, detective, and investigative work, yet women were historically barred from these jobs. One study on women police officers found that their token status affected their experiences on the job (Belknap and Shelley, 1993). For example, women from departments with 10 percent or fewer women police officers were more likely to report being seen as women first and police officers second.

Zimmer (1988) criticizes Kanter's (1977b) tokenism approach as overly simplified. She warns against perceiving male entrance into female-dominated jobs as identical to female entrance into male-dominated jobs. Tokenism alone will not account for problems women "pioneers" face as they advance into male jobs. For instance, Zimmer (1988) found that women integrated as guards in men's prisons faced substantial opposition from male co-workers. On the other hand, men recently hired in women's prisons reported no opposition from female staff or supervisors. In fact, the women's prison staff displayed appreciation for their addition. This may be because traditionally male jobs could be perceived as losing status by hiring more women, while traditionally female jobs may gain status by hiring more men (Yoder, 1991). Further evidence suggests that men more rigorously exclude token women from "their domain" in traditionally male jobs than women exclude token men in traditionally female jobs (Epstein, 1988). Given these hypotheses, it is not surprising that a study comparing male nurses and women police officers found that women police officers faced more sex stereotyping, were less accepted, experienced more sexual harassment, and felt more visible than the male nurses (Ott, 1989).

A related phenomenon is the "glass ceiling effect," which symbolizes a promotion block experienced by many women and people of color in jobs traditionally unavailable to them. Put another way, women and people of color may have gotten a foot in the door, but they are still unlikely to be police captains or prison wardens (especially in men's prisons) and less likely than men to become judges and partners in law firms. On the other hand, a study of men in the predominately female professions of nursing, elementary education teaching, librarianship, and social work found that unlike token women, most of the prejudice the token men faced was from people outside of their professions. Furthermore, instead of the "glass ceiling" that women tokens usually experience, this study found that token men in female-dominated jobs experienced a "glass escalator": Token men were given fair and often preferential treatment that enhanced their positions relative to their female co-workers (Williams, 1992).

Tokenism, then, must be examined in conjunction with sexism in order to understand women's experiences of entering male-dominated jobs. It is evident that it is not enough simply to increase women's proportions in male-dominated jobs—more important, gender-based attitudes on women's abilities and appropriateness in male-dominated jobs need to be changed. Clearly, this is not an easy feat. While increasing the number of women may help men to view women as competent, Zimmer (1988) fears a backlash with increased opposition to women and cites evidence where women are more intimidated and discriminated against when they enter in larger numbers. For whatever reasons, some males feel threatened to realize women can adequately perform jobs previously available to males only.

It is also important to recognize the additional token status burden and impact for those "new" workers who hold more than one token identity. More specifically, for women of color, women from a country other than the one they are working in, women with disabilities, lesbians, and so on, these women are often fighting oppression on more than one front, or stated another way, a wider range of forms of discrimination. Martin and Jurik (1996, 28) discuss how women breaking into criminal-processing jobs encounter gender as "an ongoing social production," where race and class interact with gender subordination, which also interact with "domination in other social institutions and sites (e.g., the state, family)." Greene's (1997) first hand account of being one of the pioneer African-American women law professors, starting in 1978, describes intense hostility she faced from students and colleagues alike. She states: "Tokenism masks racism and sexism by committing a small number of previously excluded individuals to institutions. At the same time, a system of tokenism maintains barriers of entry to others. Tokenism is therefore a symbolic equality (1997, 89).

WOMEN AS TOKENS IN CRIME-PROCESSING JOBS SINCE THE 1970s
Four Problem Areas for Women Professionals

Simply being "allowed," legally or otherwise, to have the opportunity to work in the crime-processing system was clearly not the last battle for women in these jobs. As this chapter testifies, since the 1970s, when women's presence and range of jobs has increased dramatically in the criminal-processing system professions, they have faced significant roadblocks, largely from male professionals, and to a lesser degree from their clients.

Baunach and Rafter (1982) identified four problem areas for women professionals in male-dominated crime-processing jobs. Although to some extent these apply more to the women hired shortly after Title VII, they still remain relevant, unfortunately. The first problem is the so-called "preferential" treatment women get when male co-workers and supervisors shield them from "real" work, such as female police officers and guards handling violent men (or even violent women), or women lawyers handling high-stress cases (including cases with violent men). Notably, similar to how studies reported (in Chapter 4) that chivalry and paternalism for offending women were more available to white women, a study on gender, race, and policing found that the preferential and protective treatment by co-workers and supervisors was more available to white women police officers than to African-American women officers (Martin 1990). A second problem area is that women tokens often face *higher expectations* than their male colleagues encounter, including the pressure of representing all women by any of their actions. For example, women lawyers and judges "have had to be smarter, work harder, and be better at what they do than their male colleagues" in order to succeed (Feinman, 1986, 126).

Lack of access to the "old boy" network, Baunach and Rafter's third problem area, presents the damned-if-you-do, damned-if-you-don't dilemma of "fraternizing" with male colleagues. If women socialize with male co-workers, they are often assumed to be having sex with them, which results in negative assessments about the woman's, but not the man's, professionalism. Women who don't socialize with their male colleagues risk not receiving important information about the job or promotions, as well as being labeled "cold" or "lesbians." Some male supervisors report consciously spending less time with female supervisees so that people won't think they are sexually involved. This is an obvious cost to women employees. Additionally, one study found that neither male nor female police officers tend to be very critical of male officers' taking advantage of the "informal 'buddy' relationships and insider status" and the other types of exchanged favors they received due solely to their male status; however, Black and white men and some Black and white women were highly critical of perceptions of women officers who "exchanged sexual favors for job-related benefits" (Martin, 1994, 388).

The final problem area identified by Baunach and Rafter (1982) is *sex stereotyping in the job assignment.* Women lawyers often report being assigned cases with women and children; women prison and jail workers are often restricted to working with juveniles and incarcerated women; and women police officers have historically been given "lighter" duties more commensurate with "feminine" ideals. For example, long before becoming a U.S. Supreme Court judge, Sandra Day O'Connor was unable to find a job other than working as a law clerk or secretary after graduating at the top of her class at Stanford Law School.

INSTITUTIONALIZED SEXISM

Institutionalized sexism has been instrumental in restricting women from crime-processing jobs. When a discriminatory behavior, policy, or law is institutionalized, it may not directly prohibit one group's rights but rather does so indirectly. Title VII itself may not protect women applicants or employees from institutionalized sexism. A number of examples of institutionalized sexism affecting women's employment in crime processing follow.

The first example of institutionalized sexism is height and weight requirements. Height and weight requirements not only effectively exclude the vast majority of women but also serve as institutionalized racism against Asian-American and Hispanic men who are generally proportionately smaller than their white counterparts. In 1975, in the Officers for Justice et al. v. the Civil Service Commission of the City and County of San Francisco, "a district court judge said that studies made by the police department failed to show any correlation between the height requirement and an officer's ability to perform police duties" (Gates, 1976, 71). Similarly, in 1977, the U.S. Supreme Court upheld in Dothard v. Rawlinson that the minimum height and weight requirement in a penal facility was not job related and thus could not be a condition for hiring. Similar court cases regarding denied access to women in policing based on their height and weight were settled in 1973, with the courts deciding that "these requirements had no relation to job duties" (Segrave, 1995, 112).

The second example of institutionalized sexism in hiring women police and prison officers is the physical agility test. Any criteria used to screen out potential employees should be relevant to performing the job in question. However, the Work Sample Test developed for the Houston Police Department in 1977 included a physical agility test in which a 7′6″ wall had to be scaled—although there were no 7-foot walls within the city limits (Townsey, 1982a). The focus on physical prowess in police and prison/jail recruiting tests ignores the importance of intelligence and communication skills, which are routinely necessary and probably more useful in policing and prison employment. Since the 1980s, more police departments have recognized this and developed physical agility tests that are less likely to discriminate against women. Indeed, a 1990 evaluation of women police officers reported that the litigation regarding physical fitness for women police has been successful. "Police executives are beginning to recognize the importance of departmental physical training programs as a way to improve the long-term physical fitness and health of both male and female officers through conditioning, diet, and stress reduction programs" (Martin, 1990, *xiii*).

The third example of institutionalized sexism is the veterans preference system—the "extra credit" for military service when making hiring and promotion decisions. Such a practice is far more likely to benefit males, given that women are neither expected nor encouraged to join the military, and should they enter the military, their jobs are more restricted than men's (Becraft, 1993a, 1993b; Berger, 1980).

The problem with establishing preferential treatment regarding military or some other status is deciding what factors should make one a preferential employee. For instance, a study of women working in a jail found that many women mentioned that one of the greatest assets women bring to the job is their experience raising children (Belknap, 1991). Child-rearing experience teaches patience, responsibility, and facility in dealing with crises. Unfortunately, this prior experience probably serves as more of a disadvantage than an advantage in hiring women in the crime-processing system. Indeed, many people are reluctant to hire women, but not men, with young children.

INSTITUTIONALIZED HETEROSEXISM

Another area of concern regarding women working in the criminal-processing system is the ongoing focus on these women's sexuality, particularly in terms of on-the-job harassment and discrimination. This homophobia and heterosexism is most evident for women working in prisons and policing, given that these women's desire to work in an arena where they potentially encounter physical interactions with male prisoners often results in labeling them as deviant. However, lawyering also entails a male-gendered norm, thus placing lesbians (and gay men) awaiting election or appointment to a judgeship under more intense scrutiny and a less likely chance of consideration for these posts in the first place. Robson (1998) discusses the problematic nature of "identity politics" in demanding that some judges be lesbians, while noting the concern that lesbian judges, if they exist, are invisible. Thus Robson is concerned with how lesbians are presented and represented in the criminal-processing system. She also asks: "What does it mean for a lesbian to prosecute other lesbians within the criminal justice system?" (Robson, 1998, 41).

GENDER SIMILARITIES AND DIFFERENCES
IN JOB PERFORMANCES

The vast majority of studies examining gender differences in crime-processing job performances have centered on policing. While a few exist concerning males and females working in prisons and jails, gender comparisons of job performances for attorneys are rare (perhaps because their actions are more difficult to follow and assess).

There have been a number of studies evaluating women police officers on patrol since 1972, and most report that women are as capable as men (Bartlett and Rosenblum, 1977; Bartol et al., 1992; Bloch and Anderson, 1974; Grennan, 1987; Sherman, 1975; Sichel, et al., 1978). This is particularly impressive given a study on the evaluations of women on patrol, which found that the studies themselves were sexist, valuing typically male traits and devaluing typically female traits—most of which were not shown to be meaningfully related to policing (Morash and Greene, 1986). In sum, then, most of the evaluations of women on patrol in some manner assumed that male police officers do the job right to see how well women police officers measure up. In fact, they "measured up" quite well. Progress in acceptance of women officers is evident in a 1990 study reporting :

> [T]he salience of the physical differences [between women and men officers] has decreased because women officers have proven their ability to defend themselves and their partners. In addition, defensive tactics courses have been developed to overcome many of the disadvantages of smaller stature, and departmental policies (often designed to avoid lawsuits) have curbed officers' physical aggressiveness. (Martin, 1990, *xiii*).

Researchers evaluating women police officers often report that, generally, they bring positive aspects to the policing role. For example, some research found that women police officers tend to have more support from and improved relations with citizens than do male police officers (Bloch and Anderson, 1974; Felkenes and Trostle, 1990; Marshall, 1973; Sichel et al., 1978). Other researchers suggest that women police officers and women prison and jail workers have a less aggressive style than male police officers and male penal workers and that the women are better at deescalating potentially violent situations (Belknap, 1991; Belknap and Shelley, 1993; Bell, 1982; Gates, 1976; Grennan, 1987; Kissel and Katsampes, 1980). Research has also indicated that women police officers may be more likely to have traits that should be associated with "good policing," such as having empathy for rape victims and battered women, and possessing a broader and more creative outlook on policing (Feinman, 1986; Homant and Kennedy, 1985; Kennedy and Homant, 1983; Price, 1974).

While there have been far fewer attempts to evaluate women prison officers and to compare them to male officers (as in policing), most of these evaluations portray these women favorably. Further, despite women officers' facing strong resistance from fellow officers, most male prisoners support women officers (Zimmer, 1986). "Overall, the presence of female officers in men's institutions seems to have normalized the environment, relaxed tension, and led to improvements in the inmates' behavior, dress and language" (Morris, 1987, 157). Perhaps instead of assessing how well women workers "measure up" to male workers, we should be asking how well male workers measure up to women workers.

Finally, one study comparing male and female trial judges in over 30,000 felony cases found that overall the only gender differences in judges' convicting and sentencing of male and female defendants were that women judges are less likely to find defendants guilty and more likely than male judges to send women defendants to prison (Gruhl et al., 1981). Perhaps women judges feel more pressure than male judges to appear to be not "siding" with defendants of their own sex.

ORGANIZATIONAL, SOCIAL, AND INDIVIDUAL RESISTANCE AND SUPPORT REGARDING WOMEN'S WORK IN CRIME-FIGHTING JOBS

Women's entry into policing, prison, and legal jobs has been fraught with sexism and barriers, evidenced particularly in the last chapter. Although women have made serious strides forward, particularly in terms of their sheer numerical representation in these criminal-processing jobs, there is some indication that mobility upward is limited and that women still face undue restraints and harassment because of their sex. As expected, the accounts of women of color's employment experiences in policing, prison work, and legal careers (including work as law professors and law students) suggest that the effects of racism and sexism are more than cumulative (Banks, 1997; Cho, 1997; Felkenes and Schroedel, 1993; Christopher et al., 1991; Dreifus, 1982; Greene, 1997; Hill, 1997; Martin, 1994; Moran, 1990–1991; Russell, 1997; Townsey, 1982b). That is, combining racism with sexism seems to result in more than twice the oppression. This section of Chapter 10 examines how the crime-fighting organizations in which women work in the fields of policing, prisons, and the law have responded to women workers, as well as women's experiences with individual co-workers, supervisors, administrators, and clients/civilians.

Women Working in Policing and in Prisons and Jails

Even legislation supporting women police and prison officers' rights to equal employment cannot guarantee male prisoners', offenders', fellow officers', supervisors', administrators', and citizens' acceptance of women as police officers and prison guards. Flynn (1982, 307) states that "legislative and judicial decree is neither the most expeditious nor the most efficient means for bringing about change. This is because most social change comes about incrementally, at a snail's pace, and largely as a result of multi-institutional and societal forces."

Despite the legal and societal advancements in women's entry into criminal-processing system jobs, many still face considerable resentment and resistance, and this is most typically at the hands of their male co-workers, supervisors, and administrators. It is likely that this is no more frequent or serious than in the form of sexual harassment experienced on the job (e.g., Bartol et al., 1992; Cho, 1997; Gratch, 1995; Greene, 1997; Hagan and Kay, 1995; Jurik, 1985; Martin, 1980; McMahon, 1999; Morash and Haarr, 1995; Pierce, 1995; Pogrebin and Poole, 1997; Pollock-Byrne, 1986; Pollock-Byrne and Ramirez, 1995; Rosenberg et al., 1993; Sommerlad and Sanderson, 1998; Stohr et al., 1998). For example, a recent study of women guards in Canada reported that in addition to the most extreme forms of sexual harassment, aggressive physically sexual attacks, the women reported sexual insults and teasing, offensive sexual comments, rumours about their sexuality, sexual propositions, and unwanted sexual touching by their male colleagues (McMahon, 1999).

The organizational structures of prisons and jails have also managed to restrict women's roles in numerous ways. Organizational barriers include gender differences (discrimination) in training, work assignments, and performance evaluations (Jurik, 1985). Women guards often face barriers of gender stereotyping in treatment and job assignments (e.g., Britton, 1997a; Flynn, 1982), in addition to bias from the veterans' preference system, physical requirements, safety considerations, and prisoners' privacy rights (Flynn, 1982). Indeed, in organizations such as policing and prisons, which are highly patriarchal, women are operating in repressive systems (Heidensohn, 1992, 26). A recent Canadian study of women working in a jail reported three major forms of gender discrimination that are organizational/structural in nature: limiting the work hours available to women guards, differential allocation of tasks to women guards, and exclusion of women guards from some assignments (McMahon, 1999).

The positive evaluations of women police officers on patrol have not sheltered them from considerable hostility from their fellow officers and sometimes from administration (e.g., Balkin, 1988; Belknap and Shelley, 1993; Bloch and Anderson, 1974; Christopher et al., 1991; Gratch, 1995; Heidensohn, 1992; Jacobs, 1987; Marshall, 1973; C. A. Martin, 1983; S. E. Martin, 1980, 1990, 1994; Martin and Jurik, 1996; Remmington, 1983; Rivlin, 1981; Segrave, 1995; Sherman, 1973; Timmins and Hainsworth, 1989; Wexler and Logan, 1983). Some male police officers believe many stereotypes about women in general and women police officers in particular. For example, research shows that some male police officers believe that women police officers are emotionally and physically weak, that they are more likely to use deadly force, and that they get sick every month when they menstruate (Balkin, 1988; Koenig, 1978). Furthermore, even citizens may balk at a woman officer's police authority, particularly if she is African American (Martin, 1994, 391).

A study of the first women police officers on patrol found that men's views of women police officers fell into three categories: traditionals, moderns, and moderates (Martin, 1980). *Traditionals* believe that women police officers don't belong on patrol and if present should be protected and treated as junior partners. *Moderns* are willing to work with women police officers as equals. Finally, *moderates* are neither supportive nor negative toward women police officers; they tend to be ambivalent. Consistent with other research on token women, African-American male co-workers were more supportive than white male co-workers of women police officers as equals (ibid.).

A study of some of the first women working in a men's prison found that male officers believed that (1) women workers impair prison security because they are both physically and emotionally weaker; (2) women officers need male officers' protection; (3) women officers can do only some of the job; and (4) it is unfair for women officers to be placed only in those parts of the jobs that they are "suited" for (Zimmer, 1986). Given this agenda, the only logical solution was to have no women working in the prison, according to many of the men (ibid.). Further, "rather than questioning the necessity of masculinity, most male guards question the ability of women to perform the job without it" (ibid., 57). If a woman can do the job, her "feminine" identity is questioned, and she is seen as abnormal or lesbian.

A recent assessment of gender differences in prison guards' perceptions of women officers indicated that while male guards are more accepting of their female co-workers than more dated research suggests, the women still face a considerable amount of sexism by these men (Lawrence and Mahan, 1998). For example, although most male guards believed that women should be hired as guards in men's prisons, one-fifth did not. Although the men typically reported that women could adequately perform various job requirements, the women rated themselves as significantly more able to perform the job tasks than the men did. The gender differences were greatest regarding officers' assessments of women's ability to use sufficient force to control prisoners, backing up a partner in a dangerous situation and during incidents and other emergencies. Thus, while the male guards' evaluations of the female guards abilities and job performance were generally favorable, the notable exceptions had to do with the men's assessments of the female guards' use of physical force (ibid.). Significantly, men with more years of experience on the job rated the women less favorably than they rated newer male employees. The authors conclude: "The resistance to women that persists among some men officers is likely to provide an obstacle for women seeking opportunities for advancement and promotion in male prisons" (ibid., 63).

Clearly these stereotypes are damaging for women who want to be taken seriously as police officers or guards. Given these reported attitudes, it is hardly surprising that some male police officers and male guards report that women as a group are unsuitable for employment in policing or guarding male prisoners (e.g., Pope and Pope, 1986; Poole and Pogrebin, 1997; Remmington, 1983; Zimmer, 1986). Thus, formal policies admitting women into policing or guarding male prisoners do not guarantee that they will be culturally or professionally integrated into their jobs if their male co-workers automatically view them as incapable of performing the job (e.g., Morris, 1987, 145). For example, a recent study evaluating the field-training evaluations of new police officers reported that women are rated significantly more harshly than men (Pelkey and DeGrange, 1996). Field training is the period when an officer has completed new recruit training and classes and is assigned to a field-training officer who does a sort of on-the-job training and evaluates the new officer's performance before she or he becomes "just another officer." Thus, bias in evaluations at this point in a new officer's career could have serious implications. However, despite these negative views that male supervisors and co-workers report of women police, it appears that their acceptance of and views toward women police and guards may have improved in more recent years (e.g., Lawrence and Mahan, 1998; Martin, 1990; Pogrebin and Pool, 1997). The token status is likely at issue. A recent study found that women guards employed in exclusively women's jails reported lower levels of sexual harassment than what was reported in studies where the institutions were solely for male prisoners (Stohr et al., 1998). Thus, as more women are hired into these traditionally male jobs, along with increased training and policies on harassment, it is hoped that women's work environment will be less hostile.

Although more recent research indicates greater tolerance and even acceptance of women police officers by administration and co-workers, a comparative study of the United States and England reported that the women officers had "varied and complex experiences" (Heidensohn, 1992, 129). More specifically, some reported more extreme experiences than others with sexism and sexual harassment. "Whatever their experience, however hard they had tried to be just 'one of the boys,' all had had to face questions about their role and status, simply because they were women" (ibid.).

In the same vein, a study of federal prison officers found that the security level of the prison predicts the acceptance of female officers more than any other variable—"as the level of security increases, personnel are less supportive of female officers. Moreover, the longer one has been employed in corrections, the less liberal his/her attitude toward women guards" (Simpson and White, 1985, 291). Similarly, in policing, male officers' understanding of police work is often culturally centered around the importance of physical strength and aggressiveness.

Research on both female prison guards and women police officers has found that their male co-workers often perceive the job as "macho" and are thus confused and threatened when they see women capably performing the job (Balkin, 1988; Martin, 1980; Martin and Jurik, 1996; Sherman, 1973; Wexler and Logan, 1983; Zimmer, 1986). The result of this "macho" confusion is a no-win situation for the female officer: Male officers may reject competent female officers because they are threatened by the fact that a woman can do "their" job; at the same time, they believe that incompetent women officers are "better women"—but unacceptable officers (Gross, 1984; Zimmer, 1986). Stated alternatively, Martin and Jurik (1996) report that the danger, power, and social control aspects of policing (which can be extrapolated to guarding male prisoners) make it a highly masculine job. "The men have opposed women's integration into their ranks as a threat to their definition of the work, occupational culture, social status, and self-image as men's men, which is a psychological fringe benefit of the job" (Martin and Jurik, 1996, 67). Martin and Jurik (ibid., 175) go on to state the result of this, suggesting how women's capabilities of doing these "male" jobs may increase the male hostility directed at them: "If women can do the job as well as men, the job is no longer a viable resource for constructing masculinity."

There are other forms of sex discrimination and gender stereotyping of women working in prisons and policing. For instance, an early study found that competent women police officers were rated more negatively than competent male police officers (Deaux and Taynor, 1973). A study of women prison officers found that their male co-workers frequently ignored them (acting as if they weren't present), assigned them the worst posts, and wrote them up for actions against prison policies that the male officers regularly violated and weren't sanctioned for (Zimmer, 1986). Considering their reported experiences of dealing with male co-workers' hostility, it is not surprising that most research reports that women police officers and women prison workers, particularly in the earlier studies after Title VII was passed, report higher stress levels than men in these professions (Martin, 1983; Rivlin, 1981; Van Voorhis et al., 1991; Wertsch, 1998; Wexler and Logan, 1983; Wright and Saylor, 1991). This stress may be largely due to dealing with male co-workers' hostility, but it may also be attributed to the constant pressure to prove competence (Martin, 1983; McMahon, 1999; Rivlin, 1981; Timmins and Hainsworth, 1989; Wertsch, 1998; Wexler and Logan, 1983). Recent studies of women police officers indicate that their work stress is highly related to the pressures related to their token status in a male-dominated institution (Bartol et al., 1992; Wertsch, 1998). This was manifested by decreasing their job satisfaction, motivation, and organizational commitment. However, the women still reported high levels of job commitment and a strong commitment to policing, although they reported a weak attachment to the police department (Wertsch, 1998).

Another recent study examined African-American and white police officers and their levels of reported stress and the ways they coped with job stress (Haarr and Morash, 1999). This study found that when men and women were compared overall, women reported slightly higher stress levels than men. However, when examining just white officers, there were no gender differences in reported stress levels, and when examining just African-American officers, the "African American women reported significantly higher stress levels than African American men" (ibid., 318). Although this study found numerous *racial* differences in how the officers coped with stress, the only significant gender difference in coping was that women reported higher levels of *escape* (e.g., avoiding superiors and co-workers and ignoring situations) than men. However, both men and women who reported high levels of job stress also reported significantly higher levels of using escape to cope with the job.

However, a more recent study attempts to examine guards' job stress and satisfaction in a multidimensional manner, by examining how the officers' race and sex intersect with each other, as well as with the number of years of experience on the job and the racial make-up of both the guards and the prisoners (Britton, 1997b). African-American officers of both sexes were generally less satisfied than their white counterparts with their work, regardless of the racial make-up of the prisoners or guards in the institution, and white women reported higher job satisfaction than white men. White women's higher rating of job satisfaction is associated with their higher evaluations of the supervision they experience on the job. African-American women reported low levels of job satisfaction compared with all other officers, and African-American males and females and Hispanic males report less job stress and more efficacy in working with prisoners, regardless of the prisoners' races/ethnicities (ibid.). Finally, the race and sex differences did not appear to change over time, that is, with longevity at the job.

A recent and comprehensive study on policing and stress, surveyed over 1,000 officers in 25 police departments in the United States (Morash and Haarr, 1995). Unlike previous studies, the findings from this more recent and extensive study suggest that, *although women reported higher levels of stress than men, as a whole, the difference was slight and the same factors that cause stress to men officers, generally cause stress to women officers.* In particular, for both female and male police officers, the greatest stressor is their sense of a lack of influence over day-to-day operations, or how "policing gets done" (ibid., 127). However, there were some predictors of stress for officers that were gendered. For example, sexist jokes and language harassment were significant predictors of women's but not men's stress. "An increase in women's stress is related to their spending time and energy dealing with sex, age, race, or ethnic group bias directed against others and themselves" (ibid., 132). Notably, being "set up" in dangerous situations and ridiculed by co-workers was a predictor of only men's stress, and this was particularly acute for Hispanic men. Comparing gender differences within races, there were no significant differences among whites and among Hispanics; however, African-American women reported significantly greater stress than did African-American men (Morash and Haarr, 1995).

Another study conducted on gender and police stress drew on small-town departments in Vermont (Bartol et al., 1992). The authors divided potential stressors into four categories. *External stressors* were primarily frustrations with the courts and the processing of their cases. *Organizational stressors* included departmental politics, lack of recognizing good work, insufficient personnel, and inadequate retirement plans. *Task-related stressors* were the day-to-day routines of policing, and *personal stressors* included their family lives. Similar to the findings by Morash and Haar (1995), this study found that *overall,* the stressors for the male and female officers were similar. Specifically, there were no gender differences in police officers' reported organizational, external, and personal stressors. However, also similar to Morash and Haarr (1995), those gender differences that existed were significant: (1) women officers reported the frequent exposure to tragedy as more stressful than did their male counterparts; (2) women officers reported the sense of constant danger to themselves and their co-workers as more stressful than their male counterparts; (3) women officers reported the responsibility of the lives and safety of others as more stressful than did the men; (4) consistent with other research, women officers reported the departmental rumors about themselves and their co-workers as more stressful than the men; and (5) women officers reported their relationships with their co-workers, the size of the department, and the lack of proper training, all as less stressful than did the male officers (Bartol et al., 1992).

Britton's (1997a, 802) study of women and men working in both men's and women's prisons as guards reports on "gendered organizational logic," or ways in which policies and practices within an organization are "explicitly and implicitly gendered." Britton (1997a) identified two ways in which the application of so-called gender-neutral policies and practices resulted in gender differences. First, the training for both the women and men guards presumed a male recruit. Second, the notions that administrators and the male and female officers themselves held about the "natures of male and female officers" superceded the gender-neutral policies. This was most apparent in the officers' assignments to various posts, which was strongly gendered by perceptions of women officers' (in)abilities to deal with violent prisoners, particularly in the men's (as opposed to the women's) prison (1997a, 808). Thus, Britton (ibid., 812, 814) concludes that the "organizational logic" is "deeply gendered" and that understanding it would likely be aided by applying a theory of "masculinized" organizations.

Martin (1994) conducted intensive interviews with police officers in an attempt to better understand the intersection of racism with sexism and some of the unique experiences of African-American women police. She found that although white women officers reported more sex discrimination than African-American women officers reported, the African-American women still reported serious levels of sex discrimination. Moreover, although many of the Black women reported experiencing both sexism and racism, (1) they reported experiencing racism at higher levels than they reported experiencing sexism, *and* (2) they reported higher levels of experiencing racism than the African-American male officers reported (ibid.). This study also found that court orders and affirmative action plans in particular departments worked to African-American women officers' disadvantage. Similar to discrimination highlighted in the first chapter of this book, Black women were left out of the decisions/promotions in terms that benefitted Black men and white women. Indeed, when the few coveted promotional places earmarked as for "women" *or* for "African Americans" became available, there was a sense that the former were for "white women" and the latter for "Black men." Thus some Black male officers were more hostile to Black women officers than white women officers with whom they had to compete with for the "Black" positions (ibid.). Martin (ibid., 396) concludes: "Men of each race control women's on-duty behavior by threatening them with social isolation."

Another form of organizational impact serving as institutionalized racism also concerned the racism in behaviors interacting with the racism in representation. Specifically, as noted about Martin's (1994) study, white male officers were protective of white, but not of Black, female officers. Although the Black male officers were generally protective of the Black female officers, they "were fewer in number and, therefore, less available when needed. In addition, they face pressures from the white men (or their shared resistance to women on patrol) not to back the women up" (ibid., 392). Another form of organizational impact regarding gender (and often, racism) was Martin's (ibid.) finding that as women (particularly Black women) advanced to some of the "station house" administrative jobs, their better clerical abilities (compared to the male administrators who worked there), actually "backfired." Martin (ibid.) found that these first women advancing to administration had far better typing skills and thus were able to more quickly and effectively complete paperwork. The result was that these jobs became organizationally redefined as "feminine," resulting in less prestige and authority. Finally, Martin (ibid.) documents the difficulty of women officers to unite against sexism across race. She notes that this is due not only to the effectiveness of white males' "divide and conquer" strategy but also to the fact that many of the Black women found the white female officers to be every bit as racist as the white male officers (ibid.).

On a more promising note, a review of policing and gender in the United States reported that formal organizational policy changes such as in seniority rules, the degree of civilianization, criteria for obtaining specialized assignment, and compliance with equal opportunity policies, has resulted in an improved integration of women into the policing jobs, serving a greater number of assignments, including in administration (Martin, 1990). Similarly, patterns of sexism on the job for women police, such as hostility, insufficient instruction, and alienation, were most visible for the first generation of women police (post–Title VII), suggesting that overall women's situation is improving (Martin, 1994). The improvement in women officers' situation is not only a result of organizational changes but is also due to the widening of individual women's preferences and skills and informal influence networks. Unfortunately, although the informal networks have improved for women police officers they are

> [O]ften excluded from the informal networks that are essential for success. They are less likely than their male counterparts to have mentors, are more likely than men to adopt a supervisory style that others regard as too unassertive or too bossy, and tend to be challenged by male subordinates who resent a woman telling them what to do (Martin, 1990, *xv*).

Women working in policing and prison/jails as guards are generally pessimistic about the likelihood of their own and other women's advancements and promotions (Belknap, 1991; Chapman et al. 1980; Martin and Jurik, 1996; McMahon, 1999; Nallin, 1981; Poole and Pogrebin, 1988). This is particularly acute for African-American women (Martin, 1994; Townsey, 1982b). Ironically, male police officers view women police officers as receiving unfair advantages in their promotional climbs and assignments; this view is at least partly due to the male police officers' negative attitudes about affirmative action (Weisheit, 1987). Despite the positive influence affirmative action has had on hiring and promoting women in the field of policing, women still have greater turnover rates and shorter policing careers than their male counterparts, which has been attributed to "an unrealistic view of police work when they enter policing, and rotating shifts and uncertain hours which are particularly problematic for women withe child care responsibilities" (Martin, 1990, *xvi*). Similarly, a Canadian study of women working in men's prisons and jails reported that the sexist climate of these institutions made these women employees' advancement unlikely and their turnover particular high (McMahon, 1999).

It is clear that while sex-stereotyping in policing and prison work for women professionals has improved over the past three decades, it is still in existence. However, some of the "war stories" from the pioneering women post–Title VII are valuable. Notably, as is evident in the classifications of women police officers (Martin, 1980) and of women guards (Zimmer, 1986) of these post–Title VII women, we cannot assume all these path-breaking workers were feminists. Indeed, their tenure with their male co-workers is likely much easier when they are not viewed as feminists. Consistent with research by Hunt

(1990) reported in the next section, for women police officers to "survive," they may need to balance extreme femininity and extreme masculinity. An autobiography of the first Los Angeles woman on police patrol, who served 20 years starting in 1969, suggests the ways that women officers are more accepted when they are able to both flirt and be "sexy" *and* act macho in terms of using foul language, catching criminals, and so on (Hays and Moloney, 1992). (Incidentally, her badge identified her as "Policewoman #1," an obvious way to distinguish her from the "real" officers, the "policemen.") This officer, Gayleen Hays, describes how she was asked in 1972 to enter a "Miss Fuzz" beauty contest for women officers in the L.A.P.D. in order to promote an (apparently sexist policing) film entitled *Fuzz* that was soon to be released.

> The day of the contest about twenty policewomen showed up to compete, everyone in hot pants and go-go boots. Unlike the Miss America pageant, the Miss Fuzz contest didn't have a 'talent' competition, and there was no one asking us questions to determine whether we were smart or had a good personality (however, I think they should have had a marskmanship competition). All we did was march slowly around a swimming pool and let the judges take a good look at us. Their decision would be final. (Hays and Moloney, 1992, 22)

For women to work as true equals, then, legislation must be far reaching, and even then it cannot guarantee that everyone's behavior will be open and nonsexist.

Women Attorneys and Judges

A 1998 publication reports that women make up 26 percent of lawyers and 11 percent of partners in the top 251 firms in the United States, reported as a significant improvement (Epstein, 1998, 109). Much of the research on the gendered nature of advancement in the legal profession contributes the lack of women's success in the legal profession to the gendered nature of mentoring by more senior attorneys. More specifically, male attorneys are mentored better than female attorneys (e.g., Hagan and Kay, 1995; Sommerlad and Sanderson, 1998). One study reported that sports talk and play was a way the men bonded, and sexist and racist banter by the white male attorneys not only undermined women and people of color in general but was a form of bonding and camaraderie for the white men regardless of age and rank (Sommerlad and Sanderson, 1998, 147).

A Canadian study found that "although women and men lawyers report working about the same number of hours overall, men report docketing and billing larger numbers of hours than women," and based on the number of hours billed, "[m]en gain nearly twice the return in earnings as women for each hour they work" (Hagan and Kay, 1995, 152). In one study women attorneys believed that if they were treated differently from men during the hiring process, it was to their own advantage. "In contrast, once the women lawyers were on the job, in salary, promotion, or task allocation, very few (from 1.5% to 10.2%) said they benefitted from different treatment based on gender"

(Rosenberg et al., 1993, 422). A study of gender trends in the upward mobility of lawyers during the last quarter of the 1900s in Canada reported, that while both women and men encountered a "ceiling" effect in upward mobility and a "shrinking partnership class" during this period, the impact was greater on women (Hagan and Kay, 1995). Legal scholar Cynthia Fuchs Epstein (1998, 106) identifies women as "one of the newest groups—and certainly the largest—whose talents, training and achievements qualify them to compete for places at the top of the [legal] profession." However, she also states that while ceilings exist in all fields, "they are strongest and most impenetrable in those in which wealth and power are located," where the dominant groups "typically defend their privileged access by obvious and subtle means, excluding contenders who hope to share their positions in society" (ibid.). However, Epstein (ibid., 109) also reports that women constitute a larger share of partners in large firms than they ever have, "although still at a slower rate than men," with women constituting 11 percent of partners in the top 251 firms in the United States.

The research on women lawyers' experience with sexism suggest that while it is "getting better," sexism, as well as racism, classism, anti–Semitism, and homophobia, are alive and well in most legal jobs (as well as in other jobs and in the private sphere). An important organizational aspect of sexism in lawyering is the distinction between governmental attorney jobs and private practice jobs. "In brief, women are proportionally underrepresented in private practice and overrepresented in government and corporate work; within each of these organizational hierarchies, they are concentrated on the bottom rungs of prestige and income" (Martin and Jurik, 1996, 115). Given the more stringent hiring, firing, and promotion guidelines in the public than the private sector, it is not surprising to find that sexism is more prevalent and in more manners in private law firms than in the public sector (see, for example, Katz, 1998; Rosenberg et al., 1993). Historically, public jobs were often the only lawyering jobs open to women, and they tend to be far better about issues such as maternity leave, child care, and flexible schedules (Katz, 1998). Notably, the public sector law jobs do not pay nearly as well as the private sector lawyering jobs (Beinish, 1998).

The limited research conducted on the experiences of women attorneys suggests that they also face a considerable amount of male hostility. This is most likely to be perpetrated by male lawyers, followed by clients, judges, and other legal staff, respectively (Rosenberg et al., 1993). Similar to women working in prisons and policing, *sexual harassment* by co-workers and supervisors is a major issue for many women attorneys (e.g., Hagan and Kay, 1995; Pierce, 1995; Pollock-Byrne and Ramirez, 1995; Rosenberg et al., 1993; Sommerlad and Sanderson, 1998). In one study, one in four of the women attorneys reported being sexually harassed in a professional situation, and this rate was significantly higher for women in private firms and in token positions in their practice (Rosenberg et al., 1993). Sexual harassment is effective in maintaining the gendered power differences: "Another means of [male lawyer's] heightening the boundaries between male and female attorneys is through sexual harassment. The sexualization of women is perhaps the most blatant way to exaggerate differences between the sexes" (Pierce, 1995, 108).

Women lawyers' careers are more governed than male attorneys' careers by decisions to have children (Epstein, 1998; Graham, 1986; Sommerlad and Sanderson, 1998), and women newly out of law school attempting to find jobs are more routinely questioned about and evaluated based on their plans to have children (see Hagan and Kay, 1995). Sommerlad and Sanderson (1998, 3), however, argue that the idea of lawyers' "commitment to work" is "itself gendered. It is predicated on a naturalized view of the independence of the public and private spheres, and the role of men and women in each. Thus studies of commitment . . . rarely if ever use the data to illuminate the question of men's commitment to their home lives, and the distinct work which is undertaken in the private sphere." Thus, Sommerlad and Sanderson (1998) call into question the whole focus and bias in the analysis of women's commitment to work versus family (focusing on attorneys), asking why we don't ask about men's commitments to their families when we ask about women's commitment to both work and family.

Given these assumptions about care taking and the differences between mothering and fathering, it is hardly surprising to find that women lawyers are less likely to be married than lawyers who are men (Epstein, 1998). A gender comparison of judges appointed by President Carter reported that although gender does not play a significant role in distinguishing judges' responses regarding a conflict between their careers and their roles as spouses, strong spousal support is "a major prerequisite to women's [but not men's] decisions to seek office" (E. Martin, 1990). A study comparing men and women lawyers of color beginning their first law school job found that while no gender differences existed in their likelihood of being married or having children, the women were far more likely than the men to be part of a "dual career" marriage (Merritt and Reskin, 1992). Furthermore, although both male and female judges report greater conflict balancing the parental roles with "judging" than balancing their spousal roles, male judges report far less conflict than female judges regarding balancing their career roles with their parenting roles (E. Martin, 1990).

Another recent study discusses the sex-segregation in most law firms in the United States, where most attorneys are still men, and most support staff (e.g., paralegals and legal secretaries) are still women (Pierce, 1995). The work is highly gendered, and the gendered nature of it is related to vast differences in men's and women's pay in the firms. Specifically, the women workers do the vast majority of the clerical work and most of the emotional work, particularly the "mothering" in the firm. Meanwhile, the men are primarily the trial lawyers, who exercise hypermasculinity and are what Pierce refers to as "Rambo litigators" (ibid.). Again, this is congruent with the work discussed earlier about women's expected role as emotional and physical care-takers (Petersen 1996). Gender is played out in other significant ways as well because "gender is not simply a social category but a signifier for power relations" (Pierce, 1995, 9). For example, Pierce's (ibid.) study found that men occupy more of the office space than women, the few males in paralegal positions have greater chances at upward mobility and are encouraged more by the male attorneys, and the male paralegals are given "more latitude to resist or ignore the feminized socio-emotional requirements" than are the female paralegals.

Women lawyers are also likely to struggle with whether they should appear "feminine" or "masculine" in order to be most effective (Blodgett, 1986; Sommerlad and Sanderson, 1998). This is similar to Martin's finding of women emphasizing the femininity in women police officers' roles and trying to negate femininity in the roles. One study of the legal profession in England found some women reporting that their sexuality was viewed as a commodity to advance in some firms, with more attractive women advanced to the top and used to "show off the firm" (Sommerlad and Sanderson, 1998, 176–177). Male judges are also known to have reinforced sexist stereotypes of women lawyers. In July 1986, Circuit Court judge Arthur Ceislik said to attorney Susan Tone Pierce in a pretrial conference on a rape case:

> "I am going to hear the young lady's case first. They say I'm a male chauvinist. I don't think that ladies should be lawyers. I believe that you belong at home raising a family. Ladies do not belong down here. Are you married?" (quoted in Blodgett 1986, 48)

Now turning to judges, research comparing female and male judges finds "that women judges tend to be younger, more liberal, less interested in politics, less wealthy . . . , and that they possess a higher degree of scholarship and academic talent on the average than the men" (Morello, 1986, 246). It has been noted that given the nature of the law and how it is structured, based very heavily on precedent (previous rulings), the Anglo-Saxon law is inevitably sexist, racist, and classist (e.g., Berns, 1999). Stated another way, elite white men were the designers of the Constitution and early laws, on which subsequent laws have been based, and historically attendees of law schools were almost exclusively wealthy white men. Subsequently, it is no easy task for a white male or a woman of any race or men of color who become judges to be able to buck the status quo, no matter how unfair, given that legal precedence drives judicial decision making in Anglo-Saxon culture.

Also of importance is that those not of the white male elite are likely to be better able to understand the variety of clients who come into their courtrooms than are the elite who have contact with a more restricted section of the population. In a gendered text, it has been noted that women judges are more likely than male judges to do their own housework and that Supreme Court Justice O'Connor's pushing her own cart in the grocery store might make her more in touch with the average citizen (Morello, 1986). Another study found in a comparison of female and male judges overall gender similarities in hiring someone else to do the actual housecleaning; however, women were more likely than men to be responsible for "running the house" (E. Martin, 1990).

Not surprisingly, this comparison between male and female judges found significant gender differences when the judges were asked to describe their major problems as "a woman or a man" in the law (ibid.). The problem most frequently listed by women (81 percent) was sex discrimination, while the most frequently listed problem of men was "professional challenges or time pressure" (ibid., 207). Given that the women in this study reported greater parenting and household running duties and stresses, it is likely that their "professional challenges and time pressures" were greater than the men's; however, compared to the other forms of sex discrimination they experienced, it was not ranked first. Notably, about one-fifth of these male, Carter-appointed judges reported racial or class discrimination as their major problem as men lawyers (E. Martin, 1990).

Surprisingly, a recent study of judges in Australia suggests that these "pioneering" women, the first of their kind appointed to the bench, face less sexism and discrimination than women attorneys who are *not* judges (Laster and Douglas, 1995). Laster and Douglas (ibid., 192) attribute women's acceptance into the judicial circle by their male colleagues, at least in part, to judges' isolation "from the mainstream of the profession" where they "cannot rely on assistance from the outside," and thus "organizational culture values mutual aid and tolerance." Additionally, women's relatively smooth acceptance to the bench by their male colleagues was also attributed to the more recent belief "that 'female' attributes are now consistent with the requirements of the job" for both women and men (ibid., 184). Thus, the authors conclude that women's entry to the bench "is a consequence rather than a cause of a significant paradigm shift already taking part in the courts" (ibid., 185), namely that more "feminine" qualities are needed in the legal culture. Finally, through their interviews with female and male judges, this study reported that they "do judging" similarly; they report weighing evidence and determining sentences the same. The one gender difference here was in the degree to which women were less comfortable with the adversarial approach. Upon closer examination, however, it appeared this was not a gender difference so much as a difference in longevity on the bench: Those with less experience on the bench, both women and men, were less comfortable with the adversarial approach (Laster and Douglas, 1995).

Although little has been written about women law professors, they too are still often represented in token status on law school faculties. Indeed, their barriers to faculty positions in law schools have been even greater than the barriers they faced in practicing law (Martin and Jurik, 1996). However, Martin and Jurik's (ibid., 122) review of various studies and data indicate that by the late 1980s women constituted about one-quarter of full-time law faculty. Unfortunately, they are still more predominant in the lower-paying, less prestigious and non-tenure-track faculty jobs. Driven by the finding that women of color face even more significant barriers than men of color in being hired and then retained on law school faculties, Merritt and Reskin (1992) attempted to understand the phenomenon through in-depth data collection. They found that the double marginalization of being a woman-of-color faculty member has resulted in what has been referred to as a "triple penalty" compared to men of color as faculty in law schools: Compared to men of color and law school faculties, women of color "enter teaching at lower ranks, teach at less prestigious schools, and are more likely to teach low-status courses" (ibid., 2322). This was despite controlling for differences in credentials and personal constraints (such as needing to stay in a particular geographical region). "These results suggest that law school, especially the most prestigious schools, *could* hire more minority women if they were willing to hire them on the same basis as they hire minority men" (ibid., 2356).

One African-American law professor notes that Black women need to be hired not just because they serve as role models for Black women law students, but because they hold the potential for a significant contribution to the study of law (Allen, 1997). Another Black woman law professor, however, points out how Black women professors' experiences as Black women in a white-male-dominated society provide a necessary perspective in law classes and legal academics (Banks, 1997). Yet another African-American woman describes the shock of acquiring an "honorary white pass" immediately after she began her job as a law professor:

> White students of the type who had been repulsed by me in law school (their own status threatened by the presence of blacks in their classes) now curried my favor. Secretaries who had once made me wait at the photocopying machine for hours now let me know I was too important to make a single copy myself. Restaurateurs wanted my business so badly that they shouted "Professor" as I came through the door (the better for the patrons to hear). Partners in law firms who made more in a year than my parents had made in their entire lifetimes sought me out at cocktail parties. (Moran, 1990–1991, 119)

This section noted a number of minor but mostly serious ways that women are discriminated against in "the bar." Given the breadth and seriousness of the hostility and discrimination women lawyers continue to face, perhaps it is not surprising that one study found that women are more than twice as likely to not practice law after passing the bar (Hagan and Kay, 1995, 115). Even an overview of women students in law school reports that although they typically constitute half of the class, they often face a highly gendered environment and report more dissatisfaction and alienation during their education (Martin and Jurik, 1996, 131). Moreover, law students who are women of color often report marginalization in their education and mentoring in terms of both their sex and race (e.g., Guinier, 1997).

PRISONER PRIVACY AND PRISON SAFETY: A ROADBLOCK FOR WOMEN GUARDS IN MALE PRISONS

The issue of prisoner privacy as a means to restrict women's employment in men's prisons easily fits under the previous heading regarding organizational barriers. However, the debate around this has been so significant that it deserves its own section in this chapter. Although some legislation has proven to be powerful in dismantling restrictions on women workers in men's prisons, other legislation has been instrumental in emphasizing why differential assignments of female and male officers should be considered bona fide occupational qualifications (BFOQs). (BFOQs are the "acceptable" sex discrimination employment practices provided for in Title VII, as discussed in Chapter 9.) Chapter 5 addressed the gendered nature of prisoners utilization of law suits for better and fairer conditions, reporting that male prisoners are far more likely to use the court system than their female counterparts. This holds true even regarding law suits about cross-sex prisoner supervision, even though female prisoners are far more likely than male prisoners to be leered at and sexually abused by opposite sex guards (Maschke, 1996). Maschke (ibid., 35) reports that when comparing the judges' processing of lawsuits brought by male as opposed to female prisoners' regarding cross-sex supervision privacy claims, the seriousness of the gender differences is profound: "Although male inmates may have objected to cross-gender supervision because they were unaccustomed to being objects of the 'female gaze,' female prisoners may have been resisting more than the gaze of male correctional officers," that is, physical sexual abuse.

There appear to be two major issues used in legislation defending women's restrictions in working with male prisoners: (1) male prisoners' rights to privacy, and (2) the impact of women officers on prison security. This section first addresses the issue of prisoners' rights to privacy and then briefly discusses the impact of women on prison security.

Over time, male prisoners' rights have been increasingly prioritized (over prison security) as a reason (or BFOQ) to exclude women from working in men's prisons (Morton, 1981). In fact, questions about whether guards of the opposite sex are invading a prisoner's right to privacy in showers and bathrooms never occurred until women were employed in men's prisons—when women moved into the dominant sphere. Subsequently, the concern for prisoner privacy in legislation appears to be far more prevalent regarding male prisoners with female guards than for female prisoners with male guards (ibid.). Moreover, state guidelines developed to protect prisoner privacy have resulted in women officers being excluded from posts that have high contact with male prisoners (Zimmer, 1986, 9).

However, two points are worth making here. First, reviews of 1970s and 1980s court cases on prisoners' rights to privacy from guards of the opposite sex shows that the courts have tended to favor the officers' right to employment over the prisoners' right to privacy, regardless of the sex of the prisoner or the officer (see Bernat and Zupan, 1989; Lawrence and Mahan, 1998; Martin and Jurik, 1996). Second, a 1993 court case found that while the use of male guards to perform body searches of female prisoners does not violate their right to privacy (the Fourth Amendment), such actions do violate women prisoners' rights to freedom from cruel and unusual punishment (the Eighth Amendment), given the high rate of women prisoners who have survived physical and sexual violence at the hands of men. It was found that such searches could exacerbate preexisting mental conditions resulting from prior victimizations (*Jordan v. Gardner* 986 F. 2d. 1521 U.S. App. 1993).

No set guidelines have been established to confront the problem of balancing prisoners' privacy with the employment of officers of either sex (Zimmer, 1986). It is significant that most of the focus on this problem has centered around women working in men's prisons, despite the history (including recent documentations) of the stronger likelihood for male officers to violate women prisoners' privacy than for women officers to violate men prisoners' privacy. Finally, research on women working in male penal facilities has found that the job is often structured to deny women and men equal assignments, to the disadvantage of women workers (Belknap, 1991; Zimmer, 1986).

In addressing prisoners' rights to privacy and balancing this with women's rights to work in men's prisons (where there are the most job, shift, and promotional opportunities), we must ask a few questions. First, how is this different from having a doctor or nurse of the opposite sex? The appropriateness and right to privacy of this "intimate" professional interaction is rarely questioned. Second, is it really different or more degrading for men to have women, rather than other men, see them shower, undress, and so on? Presumably, if a doctor, nurse, or prison guard acts professionally and discreetly, the sex combination of the prisoner/patient and the professional should be irrelevant. Third, it might be argued that when one is imprisoned, certain rights and privileges are lost, including the privilege to choose the sex of the prison staff. (Obviously, it is important that prisoners have access to grievance procedures that are seriously looked into and enforced when a staff person of either sex behaves inappropriately.) Despite all of the fuss made over male prisoners' rights to privacy, research reports that the majority of male prisoners do not report that women officers violate their privacy (Kissel and Katsampes, 1980; Zimmer, 1986).

Maschke's (1996, 37) careful legal analysis of the court cases prisoners have brought regarding privacy rights concludes that the court decisions have permitted prisoner employers "to discriminate against women without having to provide objective evidence of the need for the policies they had implemented." Moreover, given that there are far more male prisoners and men's prisons than female prisoners and women's prisons, to limit cross-sex supervising in any manner has a far greater impact on women's than men's potential prison guard jobs (Maschke, 1996). Denying women equal access to a career in "corrections" does not seem to be the answer to the prisoner privacy issue, especially given some of the advantages women officers might bring to these institutions (which is discussed later in this chapter). It has also been pointed out that opaque shower doors or partial barriers (where the prisoner's feet and head can be seen) could help balance prisoners' privacy with the employment of officers of either sex (Zimmer, 1986).

Regarding the security aspect of women working in men's prisons, although *Dothard* v. *Rawlinson* (1977) eliminated minimum height and weight requirements for officers in men's prisons, it upheld that under at least some circumstances, men's prisons qualified for a BFOQ exception. This exemption was given because of the belief that even one woman officer present might threaten the security of the prison, although there was no evidence to support this (Zimmer, 1986). In fact, recent research on men and women working in male prisons found that women guards perceive the prisons to be *less* dangerous than male guards do (Lawrence and Mahan, 1998; Wright and Saylor, 1991). Additionally, a study of guards in Minnesota found that male guards (37 percent) were more than twice as likely as women guards (16 percent) to believe that male guards' safety was endangered when they worked with women guards. Additionally, this same study, in reviewing the prisons' records on prisoner-on-guard assaults and injuries found that female guards were no more likely than male guards to be assaulted or injured by the prisoners (Lawrence and Mahan, 1998). Ironically, Dothard v. Rawlinson has not been successfully used in subsequent cases to deny women "guard" jobs (Bernat and Zupan, 1989; Zimmer, 1986). However, "[t]he privacy issue was raised again and left unresolved" in *Gunther* v. *Iowa,* which ruled that men's prisons must make the necessary arrangements so that women employees' right to promotion is not superceded by male prisoners' rights to privacy, but women guards should not be placed in direct confrontation with male prisoners' privacy (Flowers, 1987).

> In effect, these two cases [*Dothard* and *Gunther*], determined that although women will still be able to move up the promotional ladder based on seniority and capability, they have yet to achieve full equality with men in the prison system. Instead, Title VII's sexual integraption provisions has mandated a system of legally permitted 'near equality' among male and femal correctional officers. This has proved detrimental to women's momentum in corrections as well as their relationship with male guards with whom they have to compete and work at something less than full status while receiving full benefits. Equally affected are the prison administrators, whose job it is to implement and design integration policies effectively. (Flowers, 1987, 175)

Lawsuits about prison workers and sex discrimination in areas other than prisoners' rights to privacy and prison security have focused on discrimination in individual hiring, firing, and promotional decisions. These have routinely been decided in favor of men or against women (see Bernat and Zupan, 1989). It is hoped that in the future, prison security and prisoners' rights to privacy will not be misused to keep women from exploring careers working with offenders. Flynn (1982, 331) stresses that "[n]ot only should qualified women be given the opportunity to work in any potentially dangerous situation if they want to, but their work assignments should not differ, to any degree, from the assignments of their male counterparts."

CLASSIFICATIONS OF WOMEN
EMPLOYEES IN MALE-DOMINATED JOBS

Kanter's (1977b) research on women tokens in corporations found that the men tended to place women co-workers in female roles that were familiar to them since "female co-worker" was not a familiar role. The types of familiar female roles included "mother," "pet," "seductress," and "iron maiden." The "mother" is expected to attend to everyone's emotional needs in the office, and the "seductress" attends to the sexual stereotypes about women. The "pets" were the resident "cheerleaders," whose priority seemed to be to support male co-workers and build up their egos. The "iron maidens," on the other hand, were women who did not fit into any of the other categories, possibly resisting them by choice. A study of police officers found that the white male officers were often "protective" of the white women officers whom they could reduce to "pets," "mothers," and "seductresses," but when Black women acquiesced to these same roles, they did *not* receive the benefit of white male officers' protection and indeed were seen as "lazy" (Martin, 1994, 391).

Women Attorneys

Relative to the studies on women in policing and working in prisons and jails, little research effort has been conducted to determine categories of women lawyers. A notable exception, taking a somewhat different approach from those of the policing and guarding studies reported in the next section, is a study by Pierce (1995), who portrays the male attorneys as "Rambo litigators." Additionally, she carefully analyzes the gendered nature of the roles available to and expected of attorneys, describing them in terms of "gamesmanship":

> I described the two main components of the gamesmanship required of litigators—intimidation and strategic friendliness. Unlike male attorneys, women encounter a double bind in the aggressive component of the emotional labor. . . . [In her study] women attorneys were criticized for being 'too nice to the witnesses,' 'not forceful enough,' 'too bashful,' and 'unaggressive,' at the same time that they were admonished for being 'too aggressive.' Men, on the other hand, were sometimes criticized for being 'too aggressive' and not listening carefully to the witness but were more likely to be praised for their ruthlessness. This double bind emerged not only in the aggressive component of gamesmanship, but in its less confrontational—though equally manipulative—form, strategic friendliness. For example, when male attorneys used cajoling and placating strategies to achieve an instrumental end, they received support and encouragement from their colleagues. Women who adopted similar tactics were accused of using their "feminine wiles" to get their way with the witness or opposing counsel. (1995, 113)

Another study examining the experiences of women attorneys classified the women by professional role orientation into two groups (Rosenberg et al., 1993). *Feminists* displayed strong support for feminist positions, were members of women's organizations, and viewed the position of women in the legal system from a feminist base. *Careerists,* on the other hand, while supporting basic economic rights for women, rejected feminist labels. They were also less likely to conduct pro bono work for women's rights, support feminist candidates, or view the subordinate status of women lawyers as political. Instead they believed refining their legal skills was the best avenue for improving the position of women lawyers. Unexpectedly, the careerists were more likely than the feminists to report experiencing sexual harassment and gender-disparaging comments (ibid.).

Women in Policing

Consistent with some of Kanter's roles, a study on women police officers found that one-third of the women did not feel supported by male police officers, while the two-thirds who reported feeling close to male police officers expressed being viewed as "mothers," "sisters," and "women" but not as police officers (Jacobs, 1987). Similarly, another study found that male police officers uncomfortable with women police officers's presence resolve their own confusion by placing women into such stereotypical categories as "seductress," "mother," or "lesbian" (Hunt, 1990).

As noted earlier, some "macho" male police and prison officers are threatened by the idea that a woman can perform "their" job; they believe it is impossible that a person can be a woman and an officer. Thus, it is probably not surprising that the earliest research on women police officers on patrol found a tendency for these officers to emphasize either the police or the woman aspect of being a police officer, thus categorizing these officers as *police*women or police*women* (Martin, 1979). Martin classified those women who emphasized professionalism, assertiveness, occupational achievement, and departmental loyalty while downplaying their female status as *police*women. On the other hand, police*women* emphasized their female identity, often acquiescing to ascribed female roles (for example, "little girl"), and were isolated from "real" police work. Notably, the male police officers didn't appear to value either *police*women or police*women*. *Police*women were seen as strange women, while police*women* were viewed as incompetent officers. Thus, male police officers seemed threatened by evidence that women could do the job, as well as by evidence that they could not.

In a more recent study, working as a researcher in a police department, Jennifer Hunt (1984) found that her male co-workers frequently "tested" her (including showing her pornography and taking her to topless bars). She reports a tendency to dichotomize women police officers as "dykes" or "whores." She learned, like many other women police officers and women prison workers, to combine elements of both masculinity and femininity in order to gain acceptance:

> I was aggressive, tough, hard and corrupt like a "dyke" or a "whore." I was also sexually aloof, empathetic and vulnerable like a moral woman. As part man, I could be trusted to back up my partner and lie for the
> police. . . . My displays of masculinity, craziness and resistance were also important to the development of trust because they defined my opposition to the elite and identification with the rank and file. (Hunt, 1984, 293)

Martin (1994, 395), similar to Hunt (1984), found that many women police officers struggle "to negotiate an identity that allows them to maintain their femininity, succeed as officers, and gain individual acceptance as 'just me.'" In their attempts to do so, they are often critical of other women officers who they perceive as role-playing the other extremes by acting either too masculine or too feminine (e.g., "sluts," "clinging vines," or making their way around the department on "knee pads") (Martin, 1994, 395). They perceive these too masculine or too feminine women co-workers as confirming stereotypes that "rub off" on all women police, including those who have managed a compromise between masculine and feminine.

These categories of women officers are important concerning the various ways that women "do gender" (see Chapter 1). For some women (including in prison work), a manner of "coping" is maintaining a strong tie and image to the traditional gender role (e.g., Martin's police*woman*). Southgate (1981) collected surveys from almost 700 of the first women in England assigned to policing to do the same job as the male officers. In the survey, he distinguished three roles. The *traditional* role is characterized by women's specialized and gender "appropriate" and unique job assignments, such as working with minors and women as both victims and offenders. The *integrated role* is where women are expected to do the same job as the male officers. Finally, the *modified* role is characterized as a cross between the traditional and integrated roles, where women were provided with a wider range of duties than the traditional role but could "take account of differences between the sexes" (1981, 163). Almost half (49 percent) of these first women assigned to policing identical to their male counterparts preferred a "modified" role, while over one-third (36 percent) preferred the "integrated" role, and only 15 percent favored the specialized or "traditional" role (Southgate, 1981).

Natarajan's (1996) more recent survey of women in India similarly situated to those in Southgate's (1981) British study (because they were new to patrol work) found that a significant proportion of the women reported that men were better suited/more competent for the job of policing for a variety of policing activities, including foot patrol, traffic offenses and accidents, surveillance, motor patrol, lethal weapon situations, and crowds of males. However, many of the women officers believed they were more able than men to deal with some other situations, such as interviewing female suspects, writing reports, domestic violence calls, and juvenile situations. Clearly, the demarcation between these activities the women officers saw as men and women doing better/worse are very gendered. Drawing on Southgate's (1981) categories, Natarajan (1996, 9) asked the women which of the roles and styles of police departments they preferred. She found that almost half of the women officers (46 percent) preferred a traditional role, one-third (33 percent) an integrated role, and almost one-quarter (24 percent) a modified role. However, she also found that "only a minority of the women had experience in most of the listed duties" and that women who had experienced the wider range of policing duties, particularly the primary line functions such as patrol and crime prevention, were the most likely to favor nontraditional roles for women.

Women Prison Workers

Zimmer (1986) has identified three roles women working in men's prisons are likely to fall into, which she labels "adjustment strategies." The *institutional* role officers are similar to Martin's (1979) *police*women. They are rule and policy followers and tend to downplay their female status. They expect to do the same job as the male officers and are invested in maintaining professional relationships with everyone they work with in the prison. Zimmer's (1986) *modified* role is analogous to Martin's (1979) police*women*. These officers don't view themselves as being as capable as men of performing the job and prefer safe assignments where they have no contact with the prisoners. They often rely on male officers to back them up. Unlike Martin's (1979) women police officer roles, Zimmer has a third role for women prison workers: the *inventive* role. Women in this role don't view themselves as equal to or less capable than male officers, like the institutional and modified officers do. Instead, they see women officers as advantageous to the prison system. These women see their physical weakness (relative to men's) as overcompensated for by their communication skills and respect for prisoners. They believe in the importance of seeing the prisoners as individuals and count on backing from the prisoners. These officers receive the most hostility from male co-workers and are the most openly resentful of this hostility.

Prior research has also been concerned with how women prison workers develop strategies for coping with their often stressful jobs. Jurik (1988), drawing on Kanter's (1977b) categories of pet, mother, seductress, and iron maiden, found that women prison workers deal with negative stereotyping by "striking a balance" between these competing negative stereotypes. "Avoiding the role traps of incompetent pet and seductress often leaves female officers with a third iron-maiden-like stereotypic role. Female officers who work hard to demonstrate competence are alternatively described as 'climbers,' 'dykes,' or 'cold'; they are isolated and distrusted by their colleagues" (Jurik, 1988, 295). In fact, some of the strategies women officers developed to combat this oppression included emphasizing humor, professionalism, a team approach, and sponsorship (Jurik, 1988).

SUMMARY

This chapter traces the history of women in crime-processing jobs, which moved from being nonexistent, to volunteer and finally to paid work. The paid women workers in most current crime-processing employment, at least in theory, have the same responsibilities as their male co-workers. Nonetheless, this chapter points out how their experiences and opportunities often differ significantly from those of their male colleagues.

The history and experiences of women prison and police officers have been quite similar—generally sexist, hostile, and stressful, probably because of the belief that women aren't "macho" enough to control male offenders. Women's experiences in the field of law have also been stressful, but breaking into legal practice has not been as difficult as breaking into policing and prison work. Significant changes in women's employment in crime processing resulted from the 1972 Title VII amendment to the Civil Rights Act. While these legal changes were necessary and have effected change, alone they are not sufficient to change the culture and individual attitudes about women's access to crime-fighting jobs and how individual male co-workers, supervisors, administrators, clients, and citizens treat them.

REFERENCES

Abrahamson, Shirley S. 1998. "Do Women Judges Really Make a Difference? The American Experience." Pp. 75–82 in *Women in Law,* edited by S. Shetreet. London: Kluwer Law International.

Allen, Anita L. 1997. "On Being a Role Model." Pp. 81–87 in *Critical Race Feminism,* edited by A. K. Wing. New York: New York University Press.

Balkin, Joseph. 1988. "Why Policemen Don't Like Policewomen." *Journal of Police Science and Administration* 16:29–38.

Banks, Taunya Lovell. 1997. "Two Life Stories: Reflections of One Black Woman Law Professor." Pp. 96–100 in *Critical Race Feminism,* edited by A. K. Wing. New York: New York University Press.

Bartlett, Harold W., and Arthur Rosenblum. 1977. *Policewoman Effectiveness.* Denver: Civil Service Commission and Denver Police Department.

Bartol, Curt R., George T. Bergen, Julie Seager Volckens, and Kathleen M. Knoras. 1992. "Women in Small-Town Policing: Job Performance and Stress." *Criminal Justice and Behavior* 19 (3): 240–259.

Baunach, Phyllis J., and Nicole H. Rafter. 1982. "Sex-Role Operations: Strategies for Women Working in the Criminal Justice System." Pp. 341–358 in *Judge, Lawyer, Victim, Thief,* edited by N. H. Rafter and

E. A. Stanko. Stoughton, MA: Northeastern University Press.

Becraft, Carolyn. 1993a. "Women in the Military, 1980–1990." *Women and Criminal Justice* 4:137–154.

———. 1993b. "Women in the U.S. Armed Services: The War in the Persian Gulf." *Women and Criminal Justice* 4:155–164.

Beinish, Dorit. 1998. "Are Women More Successful in the Public Service than in Private Practice?" Pp. 99–104 in *Women in Law,* edited by S. Shetreet. London: Kluwer Law International.

Belknap, Joanne. 1991. "Women in Conflict: An Analysis of Women Correctional Officers." *Women and Criminal Justice* 2:89–115.

Belknap, Joanne, and Jill Kastens Shelley. 1993. "The New Lone Ranger: Policewomen on Patrol." *American Journal of Police* 12:47–75.

Bell, Daniel. 1982. "Policewomen: Myths and Reality." *Journal of Police Science and Administration* 10:112–120.

Berger, Margaret A. 1980, May. *Litigation on Behalf of Women: A Review for the Ford Foundation.* New York: Ford Foundation.

Bernat, Frances P. 1992. "Women in the Legal Profession." Pp. 307–322 in *The Changing Roles of Women in the Criminal Justice System,* 2nd ed., edited by I. L. Moyer. Prospect Heights, IL: Waveland Press.

Bernat, Frances P., and Linda Z. Zupan. 1989. "Assessment of Personnel Processes pertaining to Women in a Traditionally Male Dominated Occupation: Affirmative Action Policies and Practices in Prisons and Jails." *The Prison Journal* 9:64–72.

Berns, Sandra. 1999. *To Speak as a Judge.* Aldershot, England: Ashgate Publishing.

Bloch, Peter B., and Deborah Anderson. 1974. *Policewomen on Patrol.* Washington, DC: The Police Foundation.

Blodgett, Nancy. 1986. "I Don't Think that Ladies Should Be Lawyers." *ABA Journal* December 1:48–53.

Bradwell v. Illinois, 83. U.S. (16 Wall.) 130 (1873).

Britton, Dana M. 1997a. "Gendered Organizational Logic: Policy and Practice in Men's and Women's Prisons." *Gender and Society* 11(6):796–818.

———. 1997b. "Perceptions of the Work Environment among Correctional Officers: Do Race and Sex Matter?" *Criminology* 35(1):85–106.

Brown v. Board of Education, 347 U.S. 483 (1954).

Bureau of Justice Statistics. 1997. *Sourcebook of Criminal Justice Statistics 1996.* Washington, D.C.: US Government Printing Office.

Chapman, J. R., E. K. Minor, P. Ricker, T. L. Mills, and M. Bottum. 1980. *Women Employed in Corrections.* Washington, DC: Center for Women Policy Studies.

Cho, Sumi K. 1997. "Converging Stereotypes in Racialized Sexual Harassment." Pp. 203–220 in *Critical Race Feminism,* edited by A.K. Wing. New York: New York University Press.

Christopher, W., J. A. Arguelles, R. Anderson, W. R. Barnes, L. F. Estrada, M. Kantor, R. M. Mosk, A. S. Ordin, J. B. Slaughter, and R. E. Tranquada. 1991. "Report of the Independent Commission on the Los Angeles Police Department."

Cook, Beverly B. 1978. "Women Judges: The End of Tokenism." Pp. 84–105

in *Women in the Courts,* edited by W. L. Hepperle and L. L. Crites. Williamsburg, VA: National Center for State Courts.

Deaux, K., and J. Taynor. 1973. "Evaluation of Male and Female Ability: Bias Works Two Ways." *Psychological Reports* 32:261–262.

DeCrow, Karen. 1974. *Sexist Justice.* New York: Random House.

Dothard v. Rawlinson, 433 U.S. 321 (1977).

Drachman, Virginia G. 1989. "My 'Partner' in Law and Life: Marriage in the Lives of Women Lawyers in Late 19th and Early 20th Century America." *Law and Social Inquiry* 14:221–250.

Dreifus, Claudia. 1982. "Why Two Women Cops Were Convicted of Cowardice." Pp. 427–436 in *The Criminal Justice System and Women,* edited by B. R. Price and N. J. Sokoloff. New York: Clark Boardman

Durham, Christine M. 1998. "Thoughtful and Worldly Women: Women Judges and the Law." Pp. 217–234 in *Women in Law,* edited by S. Shetreet. London: Kluwer Law International.

Epstein, Cynthia F. 1982. "Women's Entry into Corporate Law Firms." Pp. 283–306 in *Women and the Law,* Vol. 2, edited by D. Kelly Weisberg. New York: Schenkman.

———. 1983. *Women in Law.* Garden City, New York: Anchor Books.

———. 1988. *Deceptive Distinctions: Sex, Gender, and the Social Order.* New Haven, CT: Yale University Press.

———. 1998. "Reaching for the Top: 'The Glass Ceiling' and Women in the Law. Pp. 105–130 in *Women in Law,* edited by S. Shetreet. London: Kluwer Law International.

Feinman, Clarice. 1986. *Women in the Criminal Justice System.* New York: Praeger.

Felkenes, George T., Paul Peretz, and Jean Reith Schroedel. 1993. "An Analysis of the Mandatory Hiring of Females: The Los Angeles Police Department Experience." *Women and Criminal Justice* 4:31–64.

Felkenes, George T., and Jean Reith Schroedel. 1993. "A Case Study of Minority Women in Policing." *Women and Criminal Justice* 4:65–90.

Felkenes, George T., and L. Trostle. 1990, July. *The Impact of Fanchon Blake v. City of Los Angeles.* The Claremont Graduate School.

Flowers, Ronald Barri. 1987. *Women and Criminality: The Woman as Victim, Offender, and Practitioner.* Westport, CT: Greenwood Press.

Flynn, Edith E. 1982. "Women as Criminal Justice Professionals: A Challenge to Tradition." Pp. 305–340 in *Judge, Lawyer, Victim, Thief,* edited by N. H. Rafter and E. A. Stanko. Stoughton, MA: Northeastern University Press.

Freedman, Estelle B. 1981. *Their Sisters' Keepers: Women's Prison Reform in America, 1830–1930.* Ann Arbor, MI: University of Michigan Press.

Gates, Margaret J. 1976. "Occupational Segregation and the Law." Pp. 61–74 in *Women and the Workplace,* edited by M. Blaxall and B. Reagan. Chicago: University of Chicago Press.

Graham, Deborah. 1986. "It's Getting Better, Slowly." *ABA Journal* December 1:54–58.

Gratch, Linda. 1995. "Sexual Harassment among Police Officers. Pp. 55–77 in *Women, Law, and Social Control,* edited by A.V. Merlo and J. M. Pollock. Boston: Allyn and Bacon.

Greene, Linda S. 1997. "Tokens, Role Models, and Pedagogical Politics: Lamentations of an African American." Pp. 88–95 in *Critical Race Feminism,* edited by A. K. Wing. New York: New York University Press.

Grennan, Sean A. 1987. "Findings on the Role of Officer Gender in Violent Encounters with Citizens." *Journal of Police Science and Administration* 15:78–85.

Gross, Sally. 1984. "Women Becoming Cops: Developmental Issues and Solutions." *Police Chief* (January): 32–35.

Gruhl, John, Cassia Spohn, and Susan Welch. 1981. "Women as Policymak-ers: The Case of Trial Judges." *American Journal of Political Science* 25:308–322.

Guinier, Lani, 1997. "Of Gentlemen and Role Models." Pp. 73–80 in *Critical Race Feminism,* edited by A. K. Wing. New York: New York University Press.

Haarr, Robin N., and Merry Morash. 1999. "Gender, Race, and Strategies of Coping with Occupational Stress in Policing." *Justice Quarterly* 16(2):303–336.

Hagan, John. 1990. "The Gender Stratification of Income Inequality among Lawyers." *Social Forces* 68:835–855.

Hagan, John, and Fiona Kay. 1995. *Gender in Practice: A Study of Lawyers' Lives.* New York: Oxford University Press.

Hagan, John., Marjorie Zatz, Bruce Arnold, and Fiona Kay. 1991. "Cultural, Capital, Gender, and the Structural Transformation of Legal Practice." *Law and Society Review* 25:239–262.

Hale, Donna C. 1992. "Women in Policing." Pp. 125–142 in What Works in Policing? *Operations and Administrations Examined,* edited by G. W. Cordner and D. C. Hale, Cincinnati: Anderson.

Hays, Gayleen, with Kathleen Moloney. 1992. *Policewoman One: My Twenty Years on the LAPD.* New York: Villard Books.

Heidensohn, Frances. 1992. *Women in Control? The Role of Women in Law Enforcement.* Oxford: Clarendon Press.

Hill, Anita F. 1997. "A Tribute to Thurgood Marshall." Pp. 118–122 in *Critical Race Feminism,* edited by A. K. Wing. New York: New York University Press.

Homant, Robert J., and Daniel B. Kennedy. 1985. "Police Perceptions of Spouse Abuse: A Comparison of Male and Female Officers." *Journal of Criminal Justice* 13:29–47.

Hughes, Everett C. 1944. "Dilemmas and Contradictions of Status." *American Journal of Sociology* 50:353–359.

Hunt, Jennifer C. 1984. "The Development of Rapport through the Negotiation of Gender in Field Work among Police." *Human Organization* 43:283–296.

———. 1990. "The Logic of Sexism Among Police." *Women and Criminal Justice* 1:3–30.

Jacobs, P. 1987. "How Female Police Officers Cope with a Traditionally Male Position." *Social Science Review* 72:4–6.

Jordan v. Gardner. 1986 F. 2d. 1521 U.S. App. 1993.

Jurik, Nancy C. 1985. "An Officer and a Lady: Organizational Barriers to Women Working as Correctional Officers in Men's Prisons." *Social Problems* 32:375–388.

———. 1988. "Striking a Balance: Female Correctional Officers, Gender Role Stereotypes, and Male Prisoners." *Sociological Inquiry* 58:291–304.

Kanter, Rosabeth M. 1977a. "Some Effects of Proportions in Group Life: Skewed Sex Ratios and Responses to Token Women." *American Journal of Sociology* 82:965–990.

———. 1977b. *Men and Women of the Corporation.* New York: Basic Books.

Katz, Deborah S. 1998. "Perspectives on Women in Public-Sector Law." Pp. 75–82 in *Women in Law,* edited by S. Shetreet. London: Kluwer Law International.

Kennedy, Daniel B., and Robert J. Homant. 1983. "Attitudes of Abused Women toward Male and Female Police Officers." *Criminal Justice and Behavior* 10:391–405.

Kissel, Peter J., and Paul L. Katsampes. 1980. "The Impact of Women Corrections Officers on the Functioning of Institutions Housing Male Inmates." *Journal of Offender Counseling, Services and Rehabilitation* 4:213–231.

Koenig, Esther J. 1978. "An Overview of Attitudes toward Women in Law Enforcement." *Public Administration Review* 38:267–275.

Laster, Kathy, and Roger Douglas. 1995. "Feminized Justice: The Impact of Women Decision-Makers in the Lower Courts in *Australian Justice Quarterly* 12(1):177–206.

Lawrence, Richard, and Sue Mahan. 1998. "Women Corrections Officers in Men's Prisons: Acceptance and Perceived Job Performance." *Women and Criminal Justice* 9(3):63–86.

Laws, Judith L. 1975. "The Psychology of Tokenism: An Analysis." *Sex Roles* 1:51–67.

Marshall, Patricia 1973. "Policewomen on Patrol." *Manpower* (October):15–20.

Martin, C. A. 1983. "Women Police and Stress." *Police Chief* 50:106–109.

Martin, Elaine. 1990. "Men and Women on the Bench: Vive La Difference?" *Judicature* 73 (4):204–208.

Martin, Susan E. 1979. "Policewomen and Policewomen: Occupational Role Dilemmas and Choices of Female Officers." *Journal of Police Science and Administration* 7:314–323.

———. 1980. *Breaking and Entering: Policewomen on Patrol.* Berkeley: University of California Press.

———. 1989, May. *Women on the Move? A Report on the Status of Women in Policing.* Washington, DC: The Police Foundation.

———. 1990. *On the Move: The Status of Women in Policing.* Washington, DC: The Police Foundation.

———. 1992. "The Changing Status of Women Officers." Pp. 281–305 in *The Changing Roles of Women in the Criminal Justice System,* 2nd ed., edited by I. L. Moyer. Prospect Heights, IL: Waveland Press.

———. 1994. " 'Outsider within' the Station House: The Impact of Race and Gender on Black Women Police." *Social Problems* 41(3):383–400.

Martin, Susan E., and Nancy C. Jurik. 1996. *Doing Justice, Doing Gender: Women in Law and Criminal Justice Occupations.* Thousand Oaks, CA: Sage.

Maschke, Karen J. 1996. "Gender in the Prison Setting: The Privacy-Equal

Employment Dilemma." *Women and Criminal Justice* 7(2):23–42.

McMahon, Maeve. 1999. *Women on Guard: Discrimination and Harassment in Corrections.* Toronto: University of Toronto Press.

Merrit, Deoborah J., and Barbara F. Reskin. 1992. "The Double Minority: Empirical Evidence of a Double Standard in Law School Hiring of Minority Women." *Southern California Law Review* 65:2299–2359.

Merton, Robert K. 1972. "Insiders and Outsiders: A Chapter in the Sociology of Knowledge." *American Journal of Sociology* 78:9–47.

Moran, Beverly I. 1990–1991. "Quantum Leap: A Black Woman Uses Legal Education to Obtain Her Honorary White Pass." *Berkeley Women's Law Journal* 6:118–121.

Morash, Merry, and Jack R. Greene. 1986. "Evaluating Women on Patrol: A Critique of Contemporary Wisdom." *Evaluation Review* 10:230–255.

Morash, Merry, and Robin N. Haarr. 1995. "Gender, Workplace Problems, and Stress in Policing." *Justice Quarterly* 12(1):113–140.

Morello, Karen B. 1986. *The Invisible Bar: The Woman Lawyer in America, 1638 to the Present.* Boston: Beacon Press.

Morris, Allison. 1987. *Women, Crime and Criminal Justice.* Oxford, England: Basil Blackwell.

Morton, Joann B. 1981. "Women in Correctional Employment: Where Are They Now and Where Are They Headed?" Pp. 7–16 in *Women in Corrections,* edited by B. H. Olsson. College Park, MD: American Correctional Association.

Nallin, J. A. 1981. "Female Correctional Administrators: Sugar and Spice Are Nice but a Backbone of Steel Is Essential." Pp. 17–26 in *Women in Corrections,* edited by B. H. Olsson. College Park, MD: American Correctional Association.

Natarajan, Mangai. 1996. "Towards Equality: Women Police in India." *Women and Criminal Justice* 8(2):1–18.

Officers for Justice et al. v. Civil Service Commission of the City and County of San Francisco, C-73-0657 RFP (N.D. Cal.) (1975).

Ott, E. M. 1989. "Effects of the Male–Female Ratio at Work: Police-women and Male Nurses." *Psychology of Women Quarterly* 13:41–58.

Pelkey, William L., and Michele L. DeGrange. 1996. "Gender Bias in Field Training Evaluation Programs: An Exploratory Analysis." *Women and Criminal Justice* 8(2):79–90.

Pierce, Jennifer L. 1995. *Gender Trials.* Berkeley: University of California Press.

Petersen, Hanne. 1996. *Home Knitted Law: Norms and Values in Gendered Rule-Making.* Aldershot, England: Dartmouth Publishing.

Pogrebin, Mark R., and Eric D. Poole. 1997. "The Sexualized Work Environment: A Look at Women Jail Officers." *The Prison Journal* 77(1):41–57.

Pollock-Byrne, Joycelyn M. 1986. *Sex and Supervision: Guarding Male and Female Inmates.* New York: Greenwood.

Pollock-Byrne, Joycelyn M. 1995. "Women in Corrections." Pp. 97–116 in *Women, Law, and Social Control,* edited by A. V. Merlo and J. M. Pollock. Boston: Allyn and Bacon.

Pollock-Byrne, Joycelyn M., and Barbara Ramirez. 1995. "Women in the Legal Profession." Pp. 79–95 in *Women, Law, and Social Control,* edited by A.V. Merlo and J. M. Pollock. Boston: Allyn and Bacon.

Poole, Eric D., and Mark R. Pogrebin. 1988. "Factors Affecting the Decision to Remain in Policing: A Study of Women Officers." *Journal of Police Science and Administration* 16:49–55.

Pope, K. E., and D. W. Pope. 1986. "Attitudes of Male Police Officers toward Their Female Counterparts." *The Police Journal* 59:242–250.

Poulos, Tammy Meredith, and William G. Doerner. 1996. "Women in Law Enforcement: The Distribution of Females in Florida Police Agencies." *Women and Criminal Justice* 8(2):19–33.

Price, Barbara R. 1974. "A Study of Leadership Strength of Female Police Executives." *Journal of Police Science and Administration* 2:219–226.

Rafter, Nicole H., and Elizabeth A. Stanko. 1982. "Introduction." Pp. 1–28 in *Judge, Lawyer, Victim, Thief: Women, Gender Roles and Criminal Justice,* edited by N. H. Rafter and E. A. Stanko. Stoughton, MA: Northeastern University Press.

Remmington, P. W. 1983. "Women in Police: Integration or Separation?" *Qualitative Sociology* 6:118–133.

Rhode, Deborah L. 1989. *Justice and Gender: Sex Discrimination and the Law.* Cambridge, MA: Harvard University Press.

Rivlin, G. 1981. "The Last Bastion of Macho: Policewomen." *Update on Law-Related Education* 5:22–24,65–67.

Robson, Ruthann. 1998. *Sappho Goes to Law School.* New York: Columbia University Press.

Rosenberg, Janet, Harry Perstadt, and William R. Phillips. 1993. "Now That We Are Here: Discrimination, Disparagement, and Harassment of Work and the Experience of Women Lawyers." *Gender and Society* 7:415–433.

Russell, Jennifer M. 1997. "On Being a Gorilla in Your Midst, or The Life of One Black Woman in the Legal Academy." Pp. 110–112 in *Critical Race Feminism,* edited by A. K. Wing. New York: New York University Press.

Schroedel, Jean Reith, Scott Frisch, Nancy Hallamore, Julie Peterson, and Nicole Vanderhost. 1996. "The Joint Impact of Race and Gender on Police Department Employment Practices." *Women and Criminal Justice* 8(2):59–77.

Schulz, Dorothy M. 1989. "The Police Matron Movement: Paving the Way for Policewomen." *Police Studies* 12:115–124.

———. 1993. "Policewomen in the 1950s: Paving the Way for Patrol." *Women and Criminal Justice* 4:5–30.

———. 1995. *From Social Worker to Crimefighter: Women in United States Municipal Policing.* Westport,CT: Praeger.

Segrave, Kerry. 1995. *Policewomen: A History.* Jefferson, NC: McFarland and Company.

Sherman, Lewis J. 1973. "A Psychological View of Women in Policing." *Journal of Police Science and Administration* 1:383–394.

———. 1975. "Evaluation of Policewomen on Patrol in a Suburban Police Department." *Journal of Police Science and Administration* 3:434–438.

Sichel, Joyce, Lucy Friedman, Janet Quint, and Michael Smith. 1978. *Women on Patrol: A Pilot Study of Police Performance in New York City.* Washington, DC: National Institute of Law Enforcement and Criminal Justice.

Simpson, Sally, and Mervin F. White. 1985. "The Female Guard in the All-Male Prison." Pp. 276–300 in *The Changing Roles of Women in the Criminal Justice System,* edited by I. L. Moyer. Prospect Heights, IL: Waveland Press.

Sokoloff, Natalie J. 1988. "Evaluating Gains and Losses by Black and White Women and Men in the Professions, 1960–1980." *Social Problems* 35:36–53.

Sommerlad, Hilary, and Peter Sanderson. 1998. *Gender, Choice and Commitment: Women Solicitors in England and Wales and the Struggle for Equal Status.* Aldershot, England: Ashgate Publishing Company.

Southgate, Peter. 1981. "Women in the Police." *The Police Journal* 54(2):157–167.

Stohr, Mary K., G. Larry Mays, Ann C. Beck, and Tammy Kelley. 1998. "Sexual Harassment in Women's Jails." *Journal of Contemporary Criminal Justice* 14(2):135–155.

Timmins, William M., and Brad E. Hainsworth. 1989. "Attracting and Retaining Females in Law Enforcement." *International Journal of Offender Therapy and Comparative Criminology* 33:197–205.

Townsey, Roi D. 1982a. "Female Patrol Officers: A Review of the Physical Capability Issue." Pp. 413–426 in *The Criminal Justice System and Women,* edited by B. R. Price and N. J. Sokoloff. New York: Clark Boardman.

————. 1982b. "Black Women in American Policing: An Advancement Display." *Journal of Criminal Justice* 10:455–468.

U.S. Census Bureau. 1999. *Statistical Abstract of the U.S. 1998.* Washington, DC: U.S. Government Printing Office.

U.S. Federal Bureau of Investigation. 1993. *Uniform Crime Reports for the U.S. 1992.* Washington, DC: U.S. Government Printing Office.

————. 1999. *Uniform Crime Reports for the U.S. 1998.* Washington, DC: U.S. Government Printing Office.

U.S. Federal Bureau of Prisons. 1993. *Federal Bureau of Prisons Annual Statistical Report Calendar Year 1992.* Washington, DC: U.S. Government Printing Office.

————. 2000. *Federal Bureau of Prisons Quick Facts, April 2000.* Washington, DC: U.S. Government Printing Office. Http://www.bop.gov/fact0598.html.

Van Voorhis, Patricia, Francis T. Cullen, Bruce G. Link, and Nancy T. Wolfe. 1991. "The Impact of Race and Gender on Correctional Officers' Orientation to the Integrated Environment." *Journal of Research in Crime and Delinquency* 28:472–500.

Warner, Rebecca L., Brent S. Steel, and Nicholas P. Lovrich. 1989. "Conditions Associated with the Advent of Representative Bureaucracy." *Social Science Quarterly* 70:562–578.

Weisberg, D. Kelly. 1982. "Barred from the Bar: Women and Legal Education in the U.S., 1870–1890." Pp. 231–258 in *Women and the Law,* Vol. 2, edited by D. Kelly Weisberg. New York: Schenkman.

Weisheit, Ralph A. 1987. "Women in the State Police: Concerns of Male and Female Officers." *Journal of Police Science and Administration* 15:137–143.

Wertsch, Teresa L. 1998. "Walking the Thin Blue Line: Policewomen and Tokenism Today." *Women and Criminal Justice* 9(3):52–61.

Wexler, Judi G., and D. D. Logan. 1983. "Sources of Stress among Women Police Officers." *Journal of Police Science and Administration* 11:46–53.

Williams, Christine L. 1992. "The Glass Escalator: Hidden Advantages for Men in the 'Female' Professions." *Social Problems,* 39:253–267.

Wright, Kevin N., and W. G. Saylor. 1991. "Male and Female Employees' Perceptions of Prison Work: Is There a Difference?" *Justice Quarterly* 8:505–524.

Yoder, Janice D. 1991. "Rethinking Tokenism: Looking beyond Numbers." *Gender and Society* 5(2):178–192.

Zimmer, Lynn E. 1986. *Women Guarding Men.* Chicago: University of Chicago Press.

————. 1987. "How Women Re-Shape the Prison Guard Role." *Gender and Society* 1:415–431.

————. 1988. "Tokenism and Women in the Workplace: The Limits of Gender-Neutral Theory." *Social Problems* 35:64–73.

————. 1989. "Solving Women's Employment Problems in Corrections: Shifting the Burden to Administrators." *Women and Criminal Justice* 1:55–80.

Zupan, Linda Z. 1992. "The Progress of Women Correctional Officers in All-Male Prisons." Pp. 232–244 in *The Changing Roles of Women in the Criminal Justice System,* 2nd ed., edited by I. L. Moyer. Prospect Heights, IL: Waveland Press.

PART V

✳

Conclusions

11

✳

Effecting Change

This book describes the state of women and girls as victims and offenders in the crime-processing system and the experiences of women crime-processing professionals. It also discusses how laws have differentially affected women, particularly in terms of employment outside of the home. Chapters 1–10 portray the invisibility and negative state of women and girls in crime processing, whether they are workers, offenders, or victims. This concluding chapter summarizes and describes recent advances in the visibility of females in criminological theories and the crime-processing system. Additionally, it offers some hope of solutions to the existing problems.

NEW THEORIES

Chapter 2 provides a discussion on various criminological theories and how women and girls were routinely excluded from most studies and theories, or if included, were done so in gender-stereotypical ways. Since the 1980s, feminist researchers have worked to make female offenders and victims visible (Morris and Gelsthorpe, 1991). Given that criminological theories are more interested in explaining offending, this section focuses on recent advances in theorizing about female (and male) offending.

Given that Chapter 2 provided a careful overview of the numerous feminist and pro-feminist research additions to the field of offending since the late

1970s, this chapter will not rehash these theories. *However, the most significant contribution to understanding why people offend in recent years are the "pathways" and similarly designed studies that incorporate a more inclusive "whole life" experience.* Feminists, in particular, have identified the importance of examining childhood traumas, such as various forms of abuse (e.g., physical and sexual) and neglect, and how these place youth at risk of offending. At the same time, feminists have identified ways that intimate partner abuse places women at risk of offending (e.g., Browne, 1987; Lake, 1993; Richie, 1996). Moreover, the feminist approach to include child and adult sexual and physical abuse, appears to also be useful for understanding *males'* risk of offending (e.g., Dembo et al., 1992; Dodge et al., 1990; Widom, 1989a, 1989b). Additionally, it is important to understand the roles of acute poverty, classism, and racism to understand risks for offending (e.g., Arnold, 1990; Richie, 1996; Sommers and Baskin, 1994). The gendered and "raced" nature of sexuality and masculinity/femininity are also paramount in understanding not only the commission of crimes, but like race and poverty, the differential (read: discriminatory) processing of offenses. This new approach to studying crime causation is appealing in that it accounts for both males and females, as well as the impact of gender, race, class, and sexuality. Furthermore, it explains crime and criminal processing within the important social structures that shape society and the individuals in it.

This new approach to studying crime causation is appealing in that it accounts for both males and females, as well as the impact of gender, race, and class. Furthermore, it explains crime and criminal processing within the important social structures that shape society and the individuals in it.

CHANGING THE TREATMENT
OF FEMALE OFFENDERS

Edwin Schur (1984, 235) states: "The persisting inclination to label women deviant is, quite simply, a deplorable fact of social life. It must be faced up to, if it is to be eliminated." Schur applies this deviance labeling of women to numerous aspects of women's lives but focuses, as this section does, on female offenders. Schur (ibid., 237) points out that men have been given the power to control labeling: "it usually has been men who have been in a position to define situations that might occasion the use of deviance labels." Furthermore, the mismatch between data from the experiences of women's lives and data from the legal definitions and assumptions about certain life situations reveals "whose power is being served by the law as it exists, what aspects of women's lives are legally visible, and how women's experience is distorted by the law" (Wishik, 1985, 74).

U.S. law has historically grouped women, children, and the mentally feeble as deficient in the qualities necessary to own property and vote (Wikler, 1987). The role of legal precedent and the isolation and insulation of judicial decision making serve to "allow" judges in the crime-processing system to maintain gender-role stereotyping in their rulings. As long as women were not part of the judicial "brotherhood," this was extremely difficult to challenge. Many women lawyers in the late 1960s and 1970s were concerned with how male judges' personal sexist biases and stereotypes strongly influenced their behavior and undermined legal reforms (ibid.).

A national judicial education program on gender bias was first conceived by Sylvia Roberts, a Title VII litigator and counsel for the NOW Legal Defense and Education Fund (NOW LDEF) in 1970. Because of a lack of financial support—a result of many people's unwillingness to believe that judges could make biased decisions—the idea for a program to educate judges on sexism was delayed until 1979, when the National Association of Women Judges was formed (ibid.). The role of these women judges as "insiders" helped launch NJEP—the National Judicial Education Program to Promote Equality for Women and Men in the Courts—in 1980. NJEP has been responsible for designing and implementing a number of educational programs on gender bias for judges, but its most significant impact has probably been the outgrowth of the Gender Bias Task Forces implemented in 35 states. At least 25 of these states have published reports (Van Voorhis et al., 1993). "Today the multiple efforts of NJEP, the state task forces, and the National Gender Bias Task Forces (created in 1985 by the National Association of Women Judges) continue the work of educating the judiciary on gender bias" (Wikler, 1987).

Chapter 4 includes a discussion of the "evil woman," "chivalrous," and "equal treatment" hypotheses on the processing of female offenders, as compared to the processing of male offenders. In an ideal world, it would seem that equal treatment should be the goal. Given that women and men have such varied experiences in terms of public, private, and criminal lives, however, "equal treatment" may have some detrimental effects for women offenders (Brodsky, 1975; Daly and Chesney-Lind, 1988). For example, laws proposed to create equality for women in the areas of divorce and child custody frequently worked to the disadvantage of women. No-fault divorces, supported by feminists to ease women's access to divorce, actually decreased divorcing women's "bargaining chips" and resulted in divorced women being significantly less well off economically than before these no-fault divorce procedures were implemented in the 1970s (Weitzman, 1985). Similarly, sentencing reforms designed to reduce class and race bias in men's sentencing may also negatively affect the sentencing of women by increasing their incarceration rates and the lengths of sentences (Daly and Chesney-Lind, 1988). Daly and Chesney-Lind (ibid., 526) conclude: "Criminologists, especially those involved in the formation of policy, should be aware that equal treatment is only one of several ways of redressing discrimination and of moving toward a more humane justice system." A refreshing approach to addressing prostitution/sex work is a court-ordered program designed by women *and men* called Sexual Exploitation Education Project (SEEP) in Portland, Oregon. Through cooperation with the district court, "men who are convicted of soliciting prostitution are required to participate in an intensive, 17-hour weekend workshop conducted by SEEP, in which they are educated about the realities of the sex industry and its exploitative nature" (Monto, 1998, 506).

In the early 1980s, Rafter and Natalizia (1981) made three recommendations regarding feminist research on crime processing: (1) Gather more data
on female criminality; (2) provide extensive research on the social contexts
of women's crime and the punishment of women; and (3) research the attitudes of crime-processing personnel toward female victims, offenders, and co-
workers. This book exemplifies that research on female offending has grown
exponentially since the 1960s. Indeed, it has grown significantly since the publication of the first edition of this book in 1996. Moreover, despite a backlash
against offenders in general and feminist research specifically, feminist criminologists have increasingly conducted this research. Nonetheless, research on
female offending, particularly the imprisonment of women, must be more rigorously addressed.

Sarri (1987) points out that women's prior victimizations place them at risk
for offending and also that our prisons are highly, disproportionately populated
with African-American women and other women of color. This may be due
to high unemployment rates, federal resistance to affirmative action, and the
many ways their "loser status" is reinforced. Society seems quite willing to
allow women

> to drift into crime in order to survive; then they end up in correctional
> facilities where the cost of their care exceeds any welfare benefit that
> they might have received by several hundred percent. Moreover, their
> children will be placed in foster care, which is both damaging and costly
> for them and for society. This is nearly the ultimate Catch-22. (Sarri,
> 1987, 418)

The numerous problems facing women in prison and jails are discussed at
length in Chapter 5. Not only do women experience worse conditions than
men, but they also have special concerns, such as pregnancy/medical needs and
the ability to maintain contact with and custody of their children. Given that
incarcerated women experience worse conditions and have fewer opportunities than men, efforts must be made to improve women's prisons.

A number of solutions to these problems have been offered in the form
of recommendations, some of which have been implemented. First, women's
prisons need to provide programs and opportunities to maintain contact
between incarcerated women and their children (American Correctional
Association, 1990; Baunach, 1992; Bloom, 1993; Bloom and Steinhart,
1993; McCarthy, 1980; McGowan and Blumenthal, 1981; Stanton, 1980).
Second, appropriate, adequate, and continuous child-care/temporary custody alternatives should be made for the children of incarcerated women
(Brodsky, 1975; McGowan and Blumenthal, 1981), including housing for
infants or even small children within the prison structure (American Correctional Association, 1990; Baunach, 1992; Bloom, 1993; Bloom and Steinhart, 1993; Haley, 1980; Knight, 1992; McCarthy, 1980; McGowan and
Blumenthal, 1981; Schupak, 1986).

Third, improved medical services should be provided, including the
needs of special populations such as HIV positive and pregnant women

(Acoca, 1998; American Correctional Association, 1990; Barry, 1991; Clark and Boudin, 1990; Knight, 1992; Greenfeld and Snell, 1999; Hankins et al., 1994; Lawson and Fawkes, 1993; McGowan and Blumenthal, 1981; McHugh, 1980; Ross and Fabiano, 1986; Schupak, 1986; Wooldredge and Masters, 1993). Many of the supporters of pregnant prisoners advocate that they should not be in prison for part or all of their pregnancy and for some period thereafter. (This recommendation is congruent with the following one.)

The fourth recommendation of women prisoner advocates is to stop the building of maximum-security prisons and provide alternative housing, particularly for the majority of women prisoners who are nonviolent, nonserious offenders with dependent children (American Correctional Association, 1990; Baunach, 1992; Chesney-Lind, 1991; Immarigeon, 1987a, 1987b; Immarigeon and Chesney-Lind, 1992; Owen, 1998; Rafter, 1985; Richie, 1996; Von Cleve and Weis, 1993). The fifth recommendation is to improve drug/alcohol treatment programs (American Correctional Association, 1990; Belknap, 2000; Greenfeld and Snell, 1999; McGowan and Blumenthal, 1981); the sixth is to improve legal services available to incarcerated women (McGowan and Blumenthal, 1981; Pendergrass, 1975); and the seventh is to improve vocational and educational programs, particularly literacy programs and training in traditionally male labor skills (American Correctional Association, 1990; Feinman, 1984; Knight, 1992; McGowan and Blumenthal, 1981; Ross and Fabiano, 1986; Stanton, 1980).

The next three recommendations regarding the incarceration of women are somewhat related. The eighth recommendation is to improve therapy and counseling (Acoca, 1998; Haley, 1980; McGowan and Blumenthal, 1981); the ninth recommendation is to provide empowerment programs (for example, participatory management in the prison system and peer counseling) (Baunach, 1992; Hardesty et al. 1993; Kendall, 1994; Pendergrass, 1975; Pollack, 1994); and the tenth recommendation is to provide postrelease services to help women incorporate themselves back into nonprison life (American Correctional Association, 1990; Belknap, 2000; McGowan and Blumenthal, 1981).

Most of these recommendations have been tried in some women's prisons in the United States. Unfortunately, budget constraints and the lack of power of incarcerated women often keep innovative programs from being funded or from being maintained once implemented. Also, there is little in the way of evaluative research and analysis to rate the effectiveness of these programs. Acoca (1998, 56) states: "There are no consistently applied policies regarding contraception, abortion, and general reproductive education and counseling for incarcerated women. When these services are available, they are rarely provided in a comprehensive or consistent manner" (ibid). Thus, for prison treatment to be effective, it needs to be of high quality, available, exhaustive, and comprehensive.

Notably, many of the preceding recommendations exist in a women's prison in Mexico. Jennifer Pearson (1993) studied Centro Feminil and reported positive, supportive conditions: Children can live inside the facilities with their mothers, a sense of respect and caring exists between the prisoners and the guards, visits and communication with family members are facilitated, and human rights are emphasized and based on the needs of the collective unit.

> The Mexican prison system I observed appeals to the strengths, rather than the weaknesses, of the inmates and their families. Imprisonment deprives a prisoner of her liberty. However, it seeks to do so as little as possible. Not only is it more humane, its costs—both social and economic—to society as a whole are far less. Deviants who can be rein-corporated back into the community through their primary networks are not incarcerated, a much less costly alternative. (Pearson 1993, 89–90)

Thus far, this chapter has focused on women's offending. More exciting changes have occurred regarding treating and responding to delinquent girls. Girls' are being processed through the system at alarming rates, particularly if one controls for how many of these girls are victims and *not* offenders or became offenders in response to their victimization. The bright light in all of this is that the Office of Juvenile Justice and Delinquency Prevention (OJJDP) has recently given unprecedented attention to research and evaluation of policies and treatment regarding delinquent girls.

In 1992 there was a reauthorization of the Juvenile Justice and Delinquency Prevention Act of 1974 (JJDPA) (the 1974 act was designed to deinstitutionalize status offenders). A significant aspect of this reauthorization was that the U.S. Congress heard and understood some of the concerns raised by some professionals who work with delinquent girls, that the existing program was insufficient for delinquent girls' needs. These professionals were convincing in their presentation of the existing programs as designed for boys, and even then, often unavailable for girls. Hence the 1992 Reauthorization of the 1974 JJDPA birthed the current focus on identifying and implementing the "gender-specific needs" of delinquent girls. The 1992 Reauthorization legislation provided that each state should (1) determine the need for and assessment of existing services and treatment for delinquent girls, (2) develop a plan to provide needed gender-specific services for the prevention and treatment of juvenile delinquency, and (3) provide assurance that youth in the juvenile system are treated fairly regarding their mental, physical, and emotional capabilities, as well as on the basis of their gender, race, and family income (Belknap et al., 1997). To this end, states across the United States have been receiving federal monies in attempts to attend to the three provisions outlined in the 1992 Reauthorization of the JJDPA. Most of this work is in progress, so it is too early to make conclusive statements.

Another significant outcome of this is that OJJDP funded Greene, Peters, and Associates (1998) to identify the most promising programming available for delinquent girls across the United States. This "inventory of best practices" not only highlights the best programs but also identifies what good program-

- *Need for physical safety and healthy physical development*
  —challenged by poverty, homelessness, violence, inadequate health care, inadequate nutrition, substance abuse
- *Need for trust, love, respect, validation from caring adults to foster healthy emotional development and form positive relationships*
  —challenged by abandonment, family dysfunction, poor communication
- *Need for positive female role models to develop healthy identity as a woman*
  —challenged by sexist, racist, homophobic messages, lack of community support
- *Need for safety to explore sexuality at own pace for healthy sexual development*
  —challenged by sexual abuse, exploitation, negative messages about female sexuality
- *Need to belong, to feel competent and worthy*
  —challenged by weakened family ties, negative peer influences, academic failure, low self-esteem

FIGURE 11.1 Girls' Needs for Healthy Development and the Challenges They Face to Obtain These Needs that Place Them at Risk for Delinquency

Cited verbatim from Greene, Peters, and Associates. 1998. *Guiding Principles for Promising Female Programming: An Inventory of Best Practices.* The Office of Juvenile Justice and Delinquency Prevention. Nashville, TN, p. 8.

ming for delinquent girls should look like. In order to further understanding of the challenges in girls' necessary pathways for healthy developmental, Greene, Peters, and Associates (1997, 8) identify not only the needs but also what may challenge these needs and place a girl at risk of becoming delinquent (see Figure 11.1).

Similar to Acoca's (1998) claim that programming for imprisoned women must be comprehensive, Greene, Peters, and Associate's make the same claim about delinquent girls' programming:

> [Gender-specific programming] represents a concentrated effort to assist all girls (not only those involved in the justice system) in positive female development. It takes into account the developmental needs of girls at adolescence, a critical stage for gender identity formation. It nurtures and reinforces "femaleness" as a positive identity with inherent strengths. (1998, 33)

Greene, Peters and Associates (1997, 36) also state that for a treatment to be truly comprehensive for delinquent girls, it must include addressing *all* of the following risks: poverty, ethnic membership, poor academic performance, teen pregnancy, substance abuse, victimization, health and mental health concerns, and gang membership. Figure 11.2 presents the elements identified by Greene, Peters, and Associates (1997) as most promising for effective programming for delinquent girls.

1. **Organization and Management:** Creating an environment of teamwork, where girls can make positive life choices, good communication within the environment, consistency in care.

2. **Staffing Pattern:** Charismatic and authentic staff, who have "been there" and "walk the talk." (All staff don't have to be female.)

3. **Staff Training:** Must include gender-specific training on adolescent female development, risks and resiliency of girls, cultural sensitivity, ability to assess a girl's needs.

4. **Intake Process:** Individualizing each girl's needs at intake, assessing her personal background and contact with the system.

5. **Education:** Addresses the needs of the whole person, including academic, life, and social skills. This includes education on and appreciation of women's history and ethnic histories, physical development, sexual behavior, and art, in addition to academic education in math and so on.

6. **Skills Training:** Designed to help girls discover their strengths and adopt pro-social skills (e.g., self-defense and physical training and self-esteem training).

7. **Promote Positive Development:** Teach girls that development is a life process, and even if they've gotten "off track," they can get back on.

8. **Relationship Building:** "Effective programs don't attempt to compete with girls' need for relationships. Instead, programs address girls' behavior in context by focusing on the choices they have made (both positive and negative) as a result of relationships" (1997, 49).

9. **Culturally Relevant Activities:** Programming must value diversity in race and culture to counteract the negative stereotypes the girls may have internalized about themselves and others.

10. **Career Opportunities:** Programming to help girls explore and prepare for careers.

11. **Health Services:** Effective programming includes comprehensive physical and mental health promotion and treatment.

12. **Recreational Activities:** Providing a variety of recreational activities including art, sports, volunteer and extracurricular activities.

13. **Responsive Services:** Programs may need access to outside services and support, particularly if a girl has a unique culture or health or family needs.

14. **Mentoring:** Allowing girls a chance to interact with capable women and girls who have "mastered life challenges of their own" (1997, p. 53).

15. **Peer Activities:** How to promote and have positive peer interactions and relationships in and out of treatment.

16. **Full Family Involvement:** Building positive family support for girls, includes involving parents in the treatment plan via home visits, discussion groups, etc.

17. **Community Involvement:** Involving girls in their communities in positive ways; girls see themselves as contributing members of their communities.

18. **Specific Treatment Concerns:** Based on an individual's needs, a girl may need treatment for a specific problem, such as substance abuse, prenatal or postpartum care, and well baby and day care.

19. **Re-entry into Community:** Assess and develop resources to assist girls with reentry so that they may best avoid behaviors that place them at risk of reoffending.

20. **Evaluation:** Evaluate through research various approaches to determine which are best for which types of girls.

FIGURE 11.2 Elements and Features of Promising Programs for Delinquent Girls

From Greene, Peters, and Associates. 1998. *Guiding Principles for Promising Female Programming: An Inventory of Best Practices.* The Office of Juvenile Justice and Delinquency Prevention. Nashville, TN, pp. 43–57.

CHANGING RESPONSES TO MALE
VIOLENCE AGAINST WOMEN

Abusive men have been structurally and psychologically accustomed to taking out their anger on women, and both sexism and violence against women are commonplace (Klein, 1981). Moreover, inequality between women and men fosters male violence against women (Russell, 1984; Sanday, 1981; Schwendinger and Schwendinger, 1983). Therefore, any discussion of effect-ing change regarding male violence against women must begin with the notion that abusive men and the societal factors that perpetuate male domi-nance and violence must change. Women and girls do not cause their sexual and battering victimizations. For abusive men to discontinue their violent and violating behaviors, the socialization of men and boys must change, as well as crime-processing system reactions to these abusers and the victims. Finally, we must also empower women and girls to resist these victimizations.

Sexual Victimization

During the 1970s and 1980s, every state repealed or modified traditional rape laws and enacted evidentiary reforms (Spohn and Horney, 1992).

> The most common changes were (1) redefining rape and replacing the single crime of rape with a series of graded offenses defined by the pres-ence or absence of aggravating conditions; (2) changing the consent stan-dard by eliminating the requirement that the victim physically resist her attacker; (3) eliminating the requirement that the victim's testimony be corroborated; and (4) placing restrictions on the introduction of evidence of the victim's prior sexual conduct. (Spohn and Horney, 1992, 21)

Many states have enacted rape law reforms to help victims prosecute, to broaden the definition of rape to include forms other than penile–vaginal, and to assert that rapes are actual assaults rather than crimes "of passion" (as they are commonly portrayed in the media and in rape trials). Unfortunately, at pre-sent, rape law reform appears to be more symbolic than productive. That is, although rape law reform is necessary to address the complex issues surround-ing sexual victimizations, the reforms are not sufficient to ensure that changes are actually practiced (Berger et al., 1988; Caringella-MacDonald, 1988; Hor-ney and Spohn, 1991; Spohn and Horney, 1991, 1992, 1993). Therefore, although the first step has been taken—to change the rape laws—it is now important that these laws be used to protect all rape victims, regardless of the victim–offender relationship, the victim's prior sexual history, and the form the abuse takes. (It should be noted that there are still major shortcomings to law reforms, including the fact that some states exempt marital rape.)

The following chart summarizes the changes that need to occur within communities in order to deter sexual victimization (Koss and Harvey, 1991). The remainder of this section discusses these issues.

- Challenge societal beliefs and cultural values that promote and condone sexual violence.
- Educate potential victims about risk, risk avoidance, and self-defense.
- Reduce the emotional and physical trauma of rape by early and appropriate attention to the needs of individual rape victims.
- Prevent recurrent instances of rape by offender incarceration and treatment.

Community Rape Prevention Strategies

Source: Koss, Mary P., and Mary R. Harvey. 1991. *The Rape Victim: Clinical and Community Intervention,* 2nd ed. Newbury Park, CA: Sage, p. 246.

Given that women can't count on rape law reform or individual violent men to stop raping, it is necessary to recognize and foster empowering behaviors and actions in women and girls. The research on sexual victimization points to the importance of instilling in women the confidence to identify and escape potentially threatening situations, as well as to physically fight back, where this is possible. Although sexually threatening situations may and often do develop to the point where it is impossible for the woman to escape, Parrot (1986) claims it is often possible to watch for danger signs in order to avoid sexual victimization. Specifically, women should trust their "gut feelings" when they feel that a situation or person is potentially dangerous. Women need to feel strong enough to say "no" or to leave situations in which they are uncomfortable (see Glavin, 1986; Parrot, 1986). Some women worry that they are "rude," "ungrateful," or even "prudish" if they don't go along with unwanted attention; however, men's offensive behavior is frequently a prelude to sexual victimizations.

Clearly, both women and men need to be educated that women and girls are to be respected, that women are to be believed when they say "no" or "stop," and that women should be able to leave potentially dangerous situations, however they are perceived, without feeling guilty about hurting someone's feelings. Research on both high school and college students has shown that rape awareness programs in the educational environment are effective in dispelling rape myths (Fonow et al., 1992; Proto–Campise et al., 1998). Therefore, such programs need to be implemented in all educational environments. This is particularly important given the wide range of positive and negative responses rape victims report they hear when they disclose their victimizations. Given the extremely negative reactions they receive, including from loved ones, the results of a study of rape survivors reported "the critical importance of the social context in which survivors discuss sexual victimization and why, at times, silence may be the most logical response" (Sudderth, 1998, 572).

Verbal, physical, and legal resistance to sexual victimization may all prove fruitful in deterrence. It is important to note that confronting sexual harassment has effectively raised awareness about it. Three years before the Anita Hill/Clarence Thomas hearings, it was pointed out that African–American women have been "at the forefront of the fight against sexual harassment," which has resulted in the legal definitions of sexual harassment, the identification of sexual harassment as sex discrimination, the Title VII prohibition

- Increased and improved training for police to promote sensitivity and reduce victim blaming
- Greater sensitivity from prosecutors
- Better treatment and better laws to protect victims in court
- Public education to increase awareness that rape is a crime and is not the victim's fault

Measures to Increase Sexual Assualt Victims' Willingness to Report to the Police

Source: National Victim Center. 1992, April 23. *Rape in America: A Report to the Nation,* p. 11.

against sexual harassment, and liability for employers who engage in sexual harassment (Eason, 1988, 140).

One study found that women college students base their decision to report sexual harassment on (1) severity of the harassment, (2) fear of being accused of lying, (3) perceived effectiveness of reporting, and (4) fear of the reporting procedure itself (Sullivan and Bybee, 1987). This implies the importance of universities and other institutions creating and maintaining policies and an environment that facilitate the reporting of and adequate response to sexual harassment charges. Another more recent study reported that most sexual harassment victims in college settings still don't report their victimizations to campus officials, largely due to their concerns about safety (Grauerholz et al. 1999). Thus, special networks must be implemented to create both a safer environment for sexual harassment victims to report and for those complaint-receivers to act on the reports (ibid.).

Research evaluating the best way to resist rape once an actual assault has begun consistently finds that in most cases it is best for victims to fight back. Victims who fight back are much less likely to experience "completed" rapes than those who do not resist (Bart and O'Brien, 1985; Kleck and Sayles, 1990; Ullman and Knight, 1992). Of utmost importance is to act immediately to the assault and to combine resistance strategies. The most effective combination of two strategies is physical force and yelling, the single most effective strategy is fleeing, and pleading and begging appear to have a negative effect, increasing the chance of a completed rape (Bart and O'Brien, 1985; Ullman and Knight, 1992). There is no evidence that resisting an attacker will lead to further injuries in addition to the rape in most cases—resistance rarely precedes injury (Bart and O'Brien, 1985; Kleck and Sayles, 1990; Ullman and Knight, 1992). Moreover, victims who fight back tend to have fewer psychological injuries after the attack, even if the rape was completed (Bart and O'Brien, 1985). It is also important to remember that not all rapes are escapable—some women (and men) are simply overpowered despite active resistance. Furthermore, victims who did not resist should not be blamed for their victimizations. As a whole, however, physical resistance appears to be the most powerful hindrance of sexual attacks.

Finally, the crime-processing system must become more responsive to both victims and offenders in an effort to stop sexual victimization. In Chapter 7, the numerous problems associated with crime-processing responses are discussed. The chart above summarizes factors that are important to enhance victims' likelihood to report sexual assaults to the police and follow through with the courts. Special care must also be taken in crime processing of child sexual abuse, not only to protect the child from further abuse but also to understand the victims' reluctance to answer police questions (Kirkwood and Mihaila, 1979).

Although most of the criticism of the crime-processing system is focused on the police, it is also important that the courts adequately address victims' needs and offenders' responsibility (see Klein, 1981; Smart, 1989; Spohn and Horney, 1992). Regarding legal reform for the processing of child sexual abuse cases, the following goals have been proposed: (1) Expedite the case; (2) provide advocates and guardians for the victims; (3) reduce unnecessary contact of the child with the crime-processing system; (4) institute "child-friendly" procedures; and (5) enhance case development through exceptions to hearsay rules and use of expert witnesses (Whitcomb, 1991).

In conclusion, important advances have been made in legal reforms and the general crime processing of sexual abuse cases. It is necessary, however, that the implementation of legal reforms occur, as well as evaluations and improvements of individual crime-processing professionals' responses to victims and offenders.

Woman Battering

Since the 1970s, the battered women's movement has increased public awareness of woman battering.

> For the first time, battered women have been singled out as a special population that needs a range of services. Funds and other material resources have been obtained by anti-wife beating groups. Government agencies and task forces have been established, new laws have been passed, and community organizations are making explicit efforts to aid battered women. (Tierney, 1982, 215)

A lack of shelters or available space in existing shelters and an often unresponsive crime-processing system continue to be problems. Nonetheless, progress has been made. For example, despite an effort since the early 1990s to withdraw support from pro-arrest policies for woman batterers (see Sherman, 1992), current research offers support for the crime-processing system's proactive responses against these offenders. Some scholars have criticized the current attempt to withdraw pro-arrest policies as a narrowly focused view of effectiveness—solely examining arrest and recidivism (Bowman, 1992; Frisch, 1992; Gondolf and Fisher, 1988; Lerman, 1992; Stanko, 1989). Such a focus ignores that arrest may provide positive outcomes unrelated to recidivism—such as an escape opportunity for victims and their children—and may communicate to all involved parties (the batterer, the victim, the children, and other witnesses) that battering is unacceptable and illegal behavior.

The focus on the arrest decision regarding the system's response to battering ignores the importance of court action (and inaction) in woman battering cases. For example, one study found that for cases where the prosecutor decided to proceed through the initial hearing, the batterer was less likely to recidivate (Ford and Regoli, 1992). In addition, two studies have shown how arrest empowers battered women. In one study batterers perceived arrest as increasing both the visibility and the risks of their behavior—including a greater likelihood of going to jail and having their abused partner leave them. The battered women perceived arrest as an opportunity to speak out to the authorities and others against the abuse and to exercise their power (Dutton et al., 1992). Moreover, results from another study (Ford 1991b) suggest that the dropping of charges by battered women does not necessarily negate the usefulness of filing the charges. Rather, battered women can use the threat of prosecution to influence the batterer to change (Ford 1991b). Perceived this way, dropping charges may be an indication that the system does work for some women.

Critics of pro-arrest policies also raise concerns that arresting batterers may place victims at increased risk of violence by retaliation of the offender. Research examining this issue, however, found the majority of battered women are not at risk of increased violence following the offender's arrest (Ford 1991a; Jaffe et al. 1986). For those few women who are more at risk of violence, the police should expand their protection (Stark, 1993). It is difficult to state definitively that jailing batterers is an effective deterrent due to insufficient research on this response, however, there are a variety of alternative sanctions that need to be evaluated that might also, or more effectively, hold batterers accountable and address victims' needs (e.g., Tolman, 1996). At any rate, it is important to allow individual battered women a voice in the decision making of their own cases through discussions with police and court officials (Davies et al., 1998; Ferraro and Pope, 1993). It may be necessary to allow the victim to unilaterally veto the arrest or prosecution decision, as she knows her situation and risks better than anyone. It is crucial for prosecution decision making to understand victim reluctance; such understanding increases the likelihood of victim cooperation and a successful disposition in court (Hart, 1993).

For effective and meaningful responses to battered women to exist, the many arms of the crime-processing system and other health and helping agencies must work together—from the police and the emergency room personnel to the social workers, prosecutors, and judges (see Belknap and McCall, 1994; Cahn, 1992; Gamache et al., 1988). For example, one study found that the most promising site for the "public health screening for victims of family or intimate assault and possibly for perpetrators" was the county hospital (Saltzman et al., 1997, 326). To date, most of the criminal-processing policy implementation geared at addressing woman battering focuses on changes in policing. In addition to police departments, *courts* must have stated policies and goals that recognize woman battering as a crime and force batterers to take responsibility for their behaviors. "They [courts] can then support police in their efforts, help break the cycle of violence, and control the abuser" (Cahn, 1992, 177).

It is not sufficient simply to have laws and policies in place to protect battered women—they must also be enforced (Ferraro, 1989; McCann, 1985). In fact, although policy reforms resulting from feminist activism finally criminalized woman battering, they also effectively moved control of this problem from feminists and battered women's advocates to crime-processing professionals, the press, mental health professionals, and academics who often fail to account for gender inequality in the family (Bush, 1993).

Therefore, programs in which battered women's groups are actively involved with the crime-processing professionals are the best hope for effective crime-processing responses to woman battering (Kurz, 1992; Pence and Shepard, 1988). Pro-arrest policies and other crime-processing actions against batterers may prove fruitless without a systems approach that includes a feminist perspective from battered women's groups (Kurz, 1992). Research shows that most battered women make "multiple efforts" to "seek help," and married women are those most likely to seek such help (Hutchison and Hirschel, 1998). Seeking help by identifying themselves and their needs provides the community and criminal-processing system an entry to helping them. Too often, these women report unfavorable responses from those from whom they've requested help. However, interaction between battered women's groups and the crime-processing system has provided productive models for change in the system in Denver, San Francisco, and Minneapolis (Kurz, 1992).

An important contribution to understanding the "best responses" to battered women is the recently published book *Safety Planning with Battered Women* (Davies et al., 1998). Two of the most important points of information in response about how best to be effective with responses to battered women are identical to what Greene, Peters, and Associates (1998) reported as "best practices" for delinquent girls. Specifically, battered women need a *comprehensive program* and they need an *individualized program*. Furthermore, Davies et al. (1998, 3) stress that the response be a *woman-defined advocacy*, defined as an "approach to advocacy that builds a partnership between advocates and battered women, and ultimately has each battered woman defining the advocacy and help she needs" (3). Too often, according to Davies et al. (ibid.) battered women are not consulted about their needs *and a service-defined program is used,* where women are simply expected to find and use available programming, regardless of whether it fits their needs. Needless to say, these practices often alienate battered women from the criminal-processing system, making them less likely to recontact shelters or the police or to seek assistance in the future.

Another important contribution that Davies et al. (ibid.) provide in *Safety Planning with Battered Women* is identifying the distinctions between *life-generated* and *batterer-generated risks* in a battered woman's life, given that both must be addressed. Life-generated risks are the environmental and social risks a woman must consider in her decisions to leave or report her abusive partner, including, financial limitations, racism, a woman's disability status, and sexual orientation (in same-sex battering cases). The batterer-generated risks involve the risks related to a batterer's control of the victim, such as physical and psychological harm and threats to the victim, her/their children, and her friends and family. Again, similar to what Greene, Peters, and Associates (1998) stressed about delinquent girls, Davies et al. (1988) stress about battered

women: Their lives are often complex, and these women vary on a wide variety of risk and life conditions (e.g., income, education, race/ethnicity, motherhood status, levels of abuse experienced, access to agencies and aid); thus it
is necessary that responses to them be individualized to meet each woman's
particular and varied needs. Davies et al. (1998) and others, such as Kanuha
(1996), highlight the racism that battered women of color encounter not only
in the police and courts but sometimes within victim advocacy agencies, such
as shelters. Vinton (1998) addresses the unique needs of older women (aged 60
and older) who are victims of intimate partner battering. Finally, Davies et al.
(1998) effectively show how many of the risks women face if they *stay* in abusive relationships are identical to those if they *leave* these relationships (e.g.,
increased abuse, loss of child custody, and so on), pointing out the problem
with blaming women for staying.

It is important in evaluating programs for battered women or individual survivors not to fall into the trap of measuring a successful outcome only in terms
of whether a woman leaves her abuser. Indeed, too much community chest and
other funding for shelters and victim advocacy agencies require this outcome
measure for continued funding. Many women, including women who've been
in shelters, return to their abusers. They still may eventually leave, but some stay
"forever." "In addition, a woman may have made critically important changes
without having left the abuser. Staying in the relationship does not mean the
battered woman is inactive or that an intervention has had no effect on her"
(Brown, 1997, 6). Brown (ibid.) states that for responses to battered women to
be effective, they must address the "stage of change" the woman is in. *Pre-
comtemplation phase* refers to a woman either being unaware of the abuse she's
subjected to or simply accepting it with no desire for change. The second stage,
contemplation, involves thinking about intentions to change. Next, in the *preparation stage* the woman actively plans change; this is followed by the *action stage,*
where she actually makes some changes. The final stage, the *maintenance stage,* is
where change is solidified and temptations to relapse are overcome. Brown
(ibid, 10) points out that progression through the stages "is not usually linear. It
is cyclical, with people progressing from precontemplation to contemplation
and then action, usually relapsing, and then recycling back to another stage
before moving forward again." Obviously, we must be careful in examining this
approach not to slip into the assumption that she stays because she isn't "self-
actualized" yet. As noted repeatedly in this book, many women don't have the
choice of leaving because it is too dangerous for them and/or their children.

One recent study examined the victims of batterers who were court-
ordered to treatment (Gondolf 1998). This study found that these women
were disproportionately from lower economic and educational levels than
women whose batterers were not court-ordered to treatment and that they
were more likely than other survivors of battering to seek help primarily
through the courts. Gondolf (ibid.) attempts to explain this court focus as
(1) it may be considered sufficient by these women; (2) they may be seeking
the short-term immediate results expected with treatment; (3) they may be
caught in the batterer–imposed isolation, not have ready access to services, or

may not believe the services will work. "Consequently, they may feel that they have to fend for themselves, as suggested in the high percentage of women who use informal strategies, such as threatening to leave the batterer or responding aggressively toward their batterer" (ibid., 673). Finally, although these women were optimistic about their batterers' discontinued use of abuse against them (which may be another reason that they are likely to limit their help-seeking to the courts and court-ordered treatment), only about half of the batterers completed the court-ordered treatment.

One of the more recent changes in responses to woman battering is the increasingly *globalized* response. Quite literally, advocates from across the world are working together not only to raise awareness about the problem and frequency of woman battering but also to unite in determining "best responses" (e.g., Edleson and Eisikovits, 1996; Heise, 1996; Roche et al., 1995; Slote and Cuthbert, 1997; Zabelina, 1995). From an international perspective, a key component of this is to get violence against women (e.g., rape and intimate partner abuse) acknowledged as a *human rights violation*. Regarding global issues at home, a significant contribution of the 1994 (the first) Violence against Women Act (in addition to funding research and programming on sexual harassment, rape, stalking and battering) is allowing "battered immigrant women to obtain lawful permanent resident status through self-petitioning or suspension of deportation" (Orloff and Kelly, 1995, 381). Although this is a huge step forward, abused women who are not legal immigrants to the United States still face incredible hardship in reporting their abuses and risking deportation. Similarly, a study of South Asian community-based responses to non-English speaking women in Toronto found that these feminist victim-advocacy organizations had to curb their criticisms of patriachal society to obtain state funding (Agnew 1998, 153): "Consequently, they give priority to ensuring access to social services for non-English speaking, working-class, immigrant women. But helping women with their problems does not expose the systemic power relations underlying wife abuse and, although some political and social change does occur, it is slow and moderate."

Chapter 8 includes a discussion of court problems for battered women who killed their batterers in self-defense. Current self-defense laws are insufficient to account for the resistance battered women must use to protect themselves (and often their children). Moreover, acquittal by reason of insanity has obvious negative repercussions for victims who were likely behaving quite sanely; for example, it may be difficult to find employment and retain custody of children. Therefore, some advocates for battered women who have killed abusive mates suggest that an entrapment defense be employed, including a psychological self-defense (Ewing, 1987; Stark, 1992). Such a defense proposes that women may have to use more force than men in similar situations and that battered women may be entrapped by a combination of social and psychological factors, making it impossible or seemingly impossible to escape (as discussed in Chapter 8).

Finally, the importance of battered women's shelters cannot be overemphasized. Shelters save the lives of battered women, their children, and even the batterers; an increase in shelters is correlated with a decrease in domestic homicides of both women and men (Browne, 1992; Steffensmeier, 1993; Walker, 1989). In addition to providing a safe haven for women and children and decreasing the likelihood of homicides, shelters advocate for and enable women to escape abusive relationships and to view themselves as worthy of respect (Ferraro and Johnson, 1983; Pence and Shepard, 1988). A recent evaluation of a shelter found that residents positively evaluated "the supportive nature of the staff, safety, relationships with other residents, and the child care. Residents expressed some concerns about the availability of counseling from busy staff and the appropriateness of some shelter residents. Generally, the women endorse the shelters as resources that save lives" (Tutty et al., 1999, 898).

CHANGES FOR WOMEN CRIME-
PROCESSING PROFESSIONALS

The experiences of women working in crime-processing jobs are described in Chapter 10. As a result of the women's movement, Title VII of the Civil Rights Act, and affirmative action, women have been accepted into law schools and employed in men's prisons and on police patrol in unprecedented numbers since the 1970s. For example, the percentage of women law students has grown from 4.2 percent in 1965 to 42.5 percent in 1991, and the percentage of women in the total lawyer population has grown from 2.5 percent in 1950 to 8.1 percent in 1980, 22 percent in 1990, and 27 percent in 1998 (American Bar Association, 1992; U.S. Census Bureau, 1999). Women have also been elected and appointed judges in larger numbers than ever before. While the rate of women as police officers and women working with prisoners (especially male prisoners) has not grown as significantly, there have been important advancements in terms of these women's promotions to sergeants, captains, lieutenants, and (rarely) chiefs and wardens (only in women's prisons).

Nonetheless, there is still considerable room for improvement. Many law school programs provide no training and coursework on feminist issues, such as representing battered women victims, battered women who've killed their batterers, rape victims, and women discriminated against in hirings, firings, and promotions. Women still make up about 10 percent of officers in most police departments and men's prisons. And the research summarized in Chapter 10 suggests that women in these nontraditional, male-dominated jobs continue to face considerable hostility from some of their male co-workers and supervisors. Although the research on gender comparisons of the stress levels of police officers and guards suggests that the gap is closing (women's higher rates of stress are less obvious), that where there are gender differences, they have to do with women's increased stress due to their token status (e.g. Bartol et al., 1992; Wertsch, 1998), sexist differences in job assignments (e.g., Britton, 1997), and the hostility and harassment from their male co-workers (e.g., Morash and Haarr, 1995; Pogrebin and Poole, 1997). Although women's representation in the field of law has increased significantly, women's representation as partners in law firms remains disappointingly low (Epstein, 1998; Hagan et al., 1991; Hagan and Kay, 1995; Sommerlad and Sanderson, 1998).

Research contributes the higher turnover rate in women's versus men's employment in policing as due to unpleasant working environments for women, problems mixing policing with family responsibilities (especially for single parents on rotating shifts), inadequate pregnancy leave and light–duty pregnancy policies, exaggerated views of police work portrayed on television and by police recruiters, and problems associated with being "tokens" (Martin, 1989; Martin and Jurik, 1996) These factors are probably equally applicable to women working in men's prisons. (Chapter 10 presents similar hostility and career blocks that women lawyers face.) Thus, policies must be implemented and followed to address conditions that make females' working environments more difficult than those of their male counterparts. To this end (Martin, 1990, *xvii*) identified a number of recommendations to "accelerate the integration of women into policing" (Figure 11.3).

1. Departments implement a voluntary affirmative action plan with women and people of color on the advisory group for its design and implementation.
2. Clear policies prohibiting sexual harassment should be adopted and vigorously enforced.
3. Recruit training should include physical fitness, self-defense, verbal and nonverbal communication, and gender and cultural differences training.
4. Outstanding women officers should be part of academy training to indicate women's effectiveness to officers.
5. Probationary officers' assignments should be monitored to ensure that all officers have similar opportunities in assignments needed for success and promotion.
6. Departments should periodically audit assignments to ensure that officers are tracked similarly (e.g., women aren't disproportionately tracked into clerical work).
7. Departments should create and maintain an open system of merit for promotion and encourage women to apply for promotions.
8. Soon-to-be-promoted-to-sergeant officers should spend some time apprenticing with an existing sergeant.
9. Women need to be given more responsibility for operations via increased promotions to command staff positions.
10. Departments need to implement ways to decrease family stresses, disproportionately experienced by women, in order to reduce burnout and high turnovers of women officers.
11. Departments should implement pregnancy policies that allow women officers to stay on the job in noncontact positions and improve opportunities for taking parental leaves for all parents (male and female) with newborn babies.
12. Equipment, facilities, uniforms, and language in the department should not be male-centered.
13. Specific job-related performance evaluations and measures need to be designed and routinely audited to ensure they don't stereotype women and aren't biased against them.
14. Research on the status of women in policing needs to be continued.

FIGURE 11.3 Policies and Practices to Accelerate the Integration of Women into Policing

From Martin, Susan E. 1990. *On the Move: The Status of Women in Policing*. Washington, DC: The Police Foundation.

Furthermore, the influence of tokenism is crucial. As long as women are hired as tokens—whether in policing, prison work, law firms, or as elected or appointed attorneys and judges—they are unlikely to be able to perform their duties as "just another professional" on the job. Research has shown that token status in these positions is likely to limit how much women can bring change to these jobs (see Belknap and Shelley, 1993). Additionally, the socialization in the training and on the job is so powerful that positive aspects women may bring to the job—such as empathy for rape victims—may be negated (see Spohn, 1990). For example, some women may be interested in becoming police officers or judges or lawyers because they want to change conditions for battered women or rape victims. However, they may be heavily inundated with victim-blaming messages during their "education" or formal and informal training. Thus, we must ask, can women change the way crime-processing jobs are done, or do these jobs change the women who are hired? The latter is far more likely as long as women continue to be hired in token status.

Crime-processing administrators, therefore, need to actively recruit more women and determine methods of keeping existing women employees in the field and promoting them. Regardless of whether women will, in fact, bring positive changes to these jobs, hiring, firing, and promotional decisions should not be made simply on the basis of sex.

SUMMARY

Considerable research is presented in this book, describing the invisibility of and injustices experienced by female victims, offenders, and workers in society and the crime-processing system. Important advances in terms of legal reforms and employment practices and policies have been made since the 1970s. Nonetheless, female victims of male violence, female offenders, and women working as crime-processing professionals continue to face damaging stereotypes and discrimination.

The feminist movement has advanced legal reforms and changes in hiring practices; however, further legal and policy reform is still necessary. Moreover, the implementation of policies and laws to improve the recognition and treatment of women and girls as victims, offenders, and workers must be carefully examined and evaluated to ensure gender equality and justice. However, women have made important strides in both their representation in sheer numbers and advancement in promotions. Although it isn't nearly to the point of being "equal," it is significant progress. Moreover, women's increased representation is likely having an effect on how they experience the job, given the more recent studies reported in this book indicating that women's stress as tokens and due to hostility from their male co-workers is decreasing. Thus, there appears to be growing acceptance of women as professionals in the criminal-processing system, and it is likely that they are more able to do their jobs in the manner they want to, rather than as merely token women, than ever before.

REFERENCES

Acoca, Leslie. 1998. "Defusing the Time Bomb: Understanding and Meeting the Growing Health Care Needs of Incarcerated Women in America." *Crime and Delinquency* 44(1):32–48.

Agnew, Vijay. 1998. "Tensions in Providing Services to South Asian Victims of Wife Abuse in Toronto." *Violence against Women* 4(2):153–179.

American Bar Association. 1992. *Legal Education and Professional Development and Education Continuum.* Chicago: Report of the Task Force on Law Schools and the Profession: Narrowing the Gender Gap.

American Correctional Association. 1990. *The Female Offender: What Does the Future Hold?* Arlington, VA: Kirby Lithographic Company.

Arnold, Regina. 1990. "Processes of Victimization and Criminalization of Black Women." *Social Justice* 17:153–166.

Barry, Ellen M. 1991. "Jail Litigation concerning Women Prisoners." *The Prison Journal* 71:44–50.

Bart, Pauline B., and Patricia H. O'Brien. 1985. *Stopping Rape: Successful Survival Strategies.* New York: Pergamon Press.

Bartol, Curt R., George T. Bergen, Julie Seager Volckens, and Kathleen M. Knoras. 1992. "Women in Small-Town Policing: Job Performance and Stress." *Criminal Justice and Behavior* 19(3):240–259.

Baunach, Phyllis Jo. 1992. "Critical Problems of Women in Prison." Pp. 99–112 in *The Changing Roles of Women in the Criminal Justice System,* 2nd ed., edited by I. L. Moyers. Prospect Heights, IL: Waveland Press.

Belknap, Joanne. 2000. "Programming and Health Care Responsibility for Incarcerated Women." Pp. 109–123 in *States of Confinement: Policing, Detention, and Prisons,* edited by Joy James. New York: St. Martin's Press.

Belknap, Joanne, Melissa Dunn, and Kristi Holsinger. 1997. *Moving toward Juve-*

nile Justice and Youth-Serving Systems that Address the Distinct Experience of the Adolescent Female. Gender Specific Services Work Group Report to the Governor. Office of Criminal Justice Services, Columbus, OH. February, 36 pp.

Belknap, Joanne, and Jill K. Shelley. 1993. "The New Lone Ranger: Policewomen on Patrol." *American Journal of Police* 12:47–75.

Belknap, Joanne, and K. Douglas McCall. 1994. "Woman Battering and Police Referrals." *Journal of Criminal Justice* 22:223–236.

Berger, Ronald J., Patricia Searles, and W. Lawrence Neuman. 1988. "The Dimensions of Rape Law Reform Legislation." *Law and Society Review* 22:329–357.

Bloom, Barbara. 1993. "Incarcerated Mothers and Their Children: Maintaining Family Ties." Pp. 60–68 in *Female Offenders: Meeting the Needs of a Neglected Population.* Laurel, MD: American Correctional Association.

Bloom, Barbara, and D. Steinhart. 1993. *Why Punish the Children?* San Francisco: National Council on Crime and Delinquency.

Bowman, Cynthia G. 1992. "The Arrest Experiments: A Feminist Critique." *Journal of Criminal Law and Criminology* 83:201–209.

Britton, Dana M. 1997a. "Gendered Organizational Logic: Policy and Practice in Men's and Women's Prisons." *Gender and Society* 11(6):796–818.

Brodsky, Annette M. 1975. "Planning for the Female Offender: Directions for the Future." Pp. 100–108 in *The Female Offender,* edited by A. M. Brodsky. Beverly Hills, CA: Sage.

Brown, Jody. 1997. "Working toward Freedom from Violence: The Process of Change in Battered Women." *Violence against Women* 3(1):5–26.

Browne, Angela. 1987. *When Battered*

Women Kill. New York: Free Press.

Browne, Angela. 1992. "Violence against Women: Relevance for Medical Practitioners." *JAMA* 267:3184–3189.

Bush, Diane M. 1993. "Women's Movements and State Policy Reform Aimed at Domestic Violence against Women." *Gender and Society* 6:587–608.

Cahn, Naomi R. 1992. "Innovative Approaches to the Prosecution of Domestic Crimes." Pp. 161–180 in *Domestic Violence: The Changing Criminal Justice Response,* edited by E. S. Buzawa and C. G. Buzawa. Westport, CT: Auburn House.

Caringella-MacDonald, Susan. 1988. "Marxist and Feminist Interpretations on the Aftermath of Rape Reforms." *Contemporary Crises* 12:125–144.

Chesney-Lind, Meda. 1991. "Patriarchy, Prisons, and Jails: A Critical Look at Trends in Women's Incarceration." *Prison Journal* 71:51–67.

Chesney-Lind, Meda., and Randall G. Shelden. 1992. *Girls, Delinquency and Juvenile Justice.* Pacific Grove, CA: Brooks/Cole.

Clark, Judy, and Kathy Boudin. 1990. "Community of Women Organize Themselves to Cope with the AIDS Crisis: A Case Study from Bedford Hills Correctional Facility." *Social Justice* 17:90–109.

Daly, Kathleen. 1992. "Women's Pathways to Felony Court: Feminist Theories of Lawbreaking and Problems of Representation." *Review of Law and Women's Studies* 2:11–52.

Daly, Kathleen, and Meda Chesney-Lind. 1988. "Feminism and Criminology." *Justice Quarterly* 5:497–538.

Davies, Jill, Eleanor Lyon, and Diane Monti-Catania. 1998. *Safety Planning with Battered Women.* Thousand Oaks, CA: Sage.

Davis, E. G. 1971. *The First Sex.* New York: Putnam.

Dembo, R., Williams, L., Wothke, W., Schmeidler, J. & Bronn, C.H. (1992). "The Role of Family Factors, Physical Abuse, and Sexual Victimization Experiences in High-risk Youths' Alcohol and Other Drug Use and Delinquency: a Longitudinal Model." *Violence and Victims,* 7(3), 245–266.

Dodge, Kenneth A., John E. Bates, and Gregory S. Pettit. 1990. "Mechanisms in the Cycle of Violence." *Science* 250:1678–1683.

Dutton, Donald G., Stephen D. Hart, Les W. Kennedy, and Kirk R. Williams. 1992. "Arrest and the Reduction of Repeat Wife Assault." Pp. 111–127 in *Domestic Violence: The Changing Criminal Justice Response,* edited by E. S. Buzawa and C. G. Buzawa. Westport, CT: Auburn House.

Eason, Yla. 1988. "When the Boss Wants Sex." Pp. 139–147 in *Racism and Sexism,* edited by P. S. Rothenberg. New York: St. Martin's Press.

Edleson, Jeffrey L., and Zvi C. Eisikovits. 1996. "Visions of Continued Change." Pp. 1–4 in *Future Interventions with Battered Women and Their Families,* edited by J. L. Edleson and Z. C. Eisikovits. Thousand Oaks, CA: Sage Publications.

Epstein, Cynthia F. 1982. "Women's Entry into Corporate Law Firms." Pp. 283–306 in *Women and the Law,* Vol. 2, edited by D. Kelly Weisberg. New York: Schenkman.

———. 1998. "Reaching for the Top: 'The Glass Ceiling' and Women in the Law. Pp. 105–130 in *Women in Law,* edited by S. Shetreet. London: Kluwer Law International.

Ewing, Charles P. 1987. *Battered Women Who Kill.* Lexington, MA: Lexington Books.

Feinman, Clarice. 1984. "A Historical Overview of the Treatment of Incarcerated Women: Myths and Realities of Rehabilitation." *The Prison Journal* 63:12–26.

Ferraro, Kathleen J. 1989. "Policing Woman Battering." *Social Problems* 36:61–74.

Ferraro, Kathleen J., and John M. Johnson. 1983. "How Women Experience

Battering: The Process of Victimization." *Social Problems* 30:325–339.

Ferraro, Kathleen J., and Lucille Pope. 1993. "Irreconcilable Differences: Battered Women, Police, and the Law." Pp. 96–126 in *Legal Responses to Wife Assault,* edited by N. Zoe Hilton. Newbury Park, CA: Sage.

Fonow, Mary M., Laurel Richardson, and Virginia A. Wemmerus. 1992. "Feminist Rape Education: Does It Work?" *Gender and Society* 6:108–122.

Ford, David A. 1991a. "Preventing and Provoking Wife Battery through Criminal Sanctioning: A Look at the Risks." Pp. 191–209 in *Abused and Battered: Social and Legal Responses to Family Violence,* edited by D. D. Knudsen and J. L. Miller. New York: Aldine De Gruyter.

———. 1991b. "Prosecution as a Victim Power Resource: A Note on Empowering Women in Violent Conjugal Relationships." *Law and Society Review* 25:313–334.

Ford, David A., and Mary Jean Regoli. 1992. "The Preventive Impacts of Policies for Prosecuting Wife Batterers." Pp. 181–207 in *Domestic Violence: The Changing Criminal Justice Response,* edited by E. S. Buzawa and C. G. Buzawa. Westport, CT: Auburn House.

Frisch, Lisa A. 1992. "Research That Succeeds, Policies That Fail." *Journal of Criminal Law and Criminology* 83:209–217.

Gamache, D. J., J. L. Edleson, and M. D. Schock. 1988. "Coordinated Police, Judicial, and Social Service Response to Woman Battering." In *Coping with Family Violence,* edited by G. T. Hotaling, D. Finkelhor, J. T. Kirkpatrick, and M. A. Straus. Beverly Hills, CA: Sage.

Glavin, Anne P. 1986. *Acquaintance Rape: The Silent Epidemic.* Massachusetts Institute of Technology: Campus Police Department.

Gondolf, Edward W. 1998. "The Victims of Court-Ordered Batterers." *Violence and Victims* 4(6):659–676.

Gondolf, Edward W., with Ellen R. Fisher. 1988. Battered Women as Survivors. New York: Lexington Books.

Grauerholz, Gottfried, Cynthia Stohl, and Nancy Gabin. 1999. "There's Safety in Numbers: Creating a Campus Advisers' Network to Help Complaints of Sexual Harassment and Complaint Receivers." *Violence against Women* 5(8):950–977.

Greene, Peters, and Associates. 1998. *Guiding Principles for Promising Female Programming: An Inventory of Best Practices.* The Office of Juvenile Justice and Delinquency Prevention. Nashville, TN, 93 pp.

Greenfeld, Lawrence A., and Tracy L. Snell. 1999. *Women Offenders.* Bureau of Justice Statistics: Special Report. U.S. Department of Justice, December, 14 pp.

Hagan, John, and Fiona Kay. 1995. *Gender in Practice: A Study of Lawyers' Lives.* New York: Oxford University Press.

Hagan, John., Marjorie Zatz, Bruce Arnold, and Fiona Kay. 1991. "Cultural, Capital, Gender, and the Structural Transformation of Legal Practice." *Law and Society Review* 25:239–262.

Haley, Kathleen. 1980. "Mothers behind Bars." Pp. 339–354 in *Women, Crime and Justice,* edited by S. K. Datesman and F. R. Scarpitti. New York: Oxford Press.

Hankins, Catherine A., Sylvie Gendron, Margaret A. Handley, Christiane Richard, Marie Therese Lai Tung, and Michael O'Shaughnessy. 1994. "HIV Infection Among Women in Prison." *American Journal of Public Health* 84(10):1637–1640.

Hardesty, Constance, Paula G. Hardwick, and Ruby J. Thompson. 1993. "Self-Esteem and the Woman Prisoner." Pp. 27–44 in *Women Prisoners: A Forgotten Population,* edited by B. R. Fletcher, L. D. Shaver, and D. G. Moon. Westport, CT: Praeger.

Hart, Barbara. 1993. "Battered Women and the Criminal Justice System." *American Behavioral Scientist* 36:624–638.

Heise, Lor L. 1996. "Violence against Women: Global Organizing for Change." Pp. 7–33 in *Future Interventions with Battered Women and Their Families,* edited by J. L. Edleson and Z. C. Eisikovits. Thousand Oaks, CA: Sage Publications.

Horney, Julie, and Cassia Spohn. 1991. "Rape Law Reform and Instrumental Change in Six Urban Jurisdictions." *Law and Society Review* 25:117–153.

Hutchison, Ira W., and J. David Hirschel. 1998. "Abused Women: Help-Seeking Strategies and Police Utilization." *Violence Against Women* 4(4):436–456.

Immarigeon, Russ., 1987a. "Few Diversion Programs Are Offered Female Offenders." *Journal of the National Prison Project* 12:9–11.

———. 1987b. "Women in Prison." *Journal of the National Prison Project* 11:1–5.

Immarigeon, Russ, and Meda Chesney-Lind. 1992. *Women's Prisons: Overcrowded and Overused.* San Francisco: National Council on Crime and Delinquency.

Jaffe, Peter, D. A. Wolfe, A. Telford, and G. Austin. 1986. "The Impact of Police Charges in Incidents of Wife Abuse." *Journal of Family Violence* 1:37–49.

Kanuha, Valli. 1996. "Domestic Violence, Racism, and the Battered Women's Movement in the United States." Pp. 34–52 in *Future Interventions with Battered Women and Their Families,* edited by J. L. Edleson and Z. C. Eisikovits. Thousand Oaks, CA: Sage Publications.

Kendall, Kathleen. 1994. "Creating Real Choices: A Program Evaluation of Therapeutic Services at the Prison for Women." *Forum on Corrections Research* 6:19–21.

Kirkwood, Laurie J., and Marcelle E. Mihaila. 1979. "Incest and the Legal System." *University of California, Davis Law Review* 12:673–699.

Kleck, Gary, and Susan Sayles. 1990. "Rape and Resistance." *Social Problems* 37:149–162.

Klein, Dorie. 1981. "Violence against Women: Some Considerations regarding Its Causes and Elimination." *Crime and Delinquency* (January):64–80.

Knight, Barbara B. 1992. "Women in Prison as Litigants: Prospects for Post Prison Futures." *Women and Criminal Justice* 4:91–116.

Koss, Mary P., and Mary R. Harvey. 1991. *The Rape Victim: Clinical and Community Interventions,* 2nd ed. Newbury Park, CA: Sage.

Kurz, Demie. 1992. "Battering and the Criminal Justice System: A Feminist View." Pp. 21–40 in *Domestic Violence: The Changing Criminal Justice Response,* edited by E. S. Buzawa and C. G. Buzawa. Westport, CT: Auburn House.

Lake, E. S. (1993). An exploration of the violent victim experiences of female offenders. *Violence and Victims,* 8(1), 41–51.

Lawson, W. Travis, and Lena Sue Fawkes. 1993. "HIV, AIDS, and the Female Offender." Pp. 43–48 in *Female Offenders.* Laurel, MD: American Correctional Association.

Lerman, Lisa G. 1992. "The Decontextualization of Domestic Violence." *Journal of Criminal Law and Criminology* 83:217–240.

Martin, Susan E. 1989. "Women on the Move? A Report on the Status of Women in Policing." *Police Foundation Reports* (May):1–7.

———. 1990. *On the Move: The Status of Women in Policing.* Washington, DC: The Police Foundation.

Martin, Susan E., and Nancy C. Jurik. 1996. *Doing Justice, Doing Gender: Women in Law and Criminal Justice Occupations.* Thousand Oaks, CA: Sage.

McCann, Kathryn. 1985. "Battered Women and the Law: The Limits of the Legislation." Pp. 71–96 in *Women-in-Law: Explorations in Law, Family and Sexuality,* edited by J. Brophy and C. Smart. London: Routledge and Kegan Paul.

McCarthy, Belinda R. 1980. "Inmate Mothers: The Problems of Separation and Reintegration." *Journal of Offender Counseling, Services and Rehabilitation* 4:199–212.

McGowan, Brenda G., and Karen L. Blumenthal. 1981. "Imprisoned Women and Their Children." Pp. 392–408 in *Women and Crime in America,* edited by L. H. Bowker. New York: Macmillan.

McHugh, Gerald A. 1980. "Protection of the Rights of Pregnant Women in Prisons and Detention Facilities." *New England Journal on Prison and Law* 6:231–263.

Messerschmidt, James W. 1993. *Masculinities and Crime: Critique and Reconceptualization of Theory.* Lanham, MD: Rowman and Littlefield.

Miller, Eleanor M. 1986. *Street Woman.* Philadelphia: Temple University Press.

Monto, Martin A. 1998. "Holding Men Accountable for Prostitution." *Violence against Women* 4(4):505–517.

Morash, Merry, and Robin N. Haarr. 1995. "Gender, Workplace problems, and Stress in Policing." *Justice Quarterly* 12(1):113–140.

Morris, Allison, and Loraine Gelsthorpe. 1991. "Feminist Perspectives in Criminology: Transforming and Transgressing." *Women and Criminal Justice* 2:3–26.

National Victim Center. 1992, April 23. *Rape in America: A Report to the Nation.* Arlington, VA.

Orloff, Leslye E., and Nancy Kelly. 1995. "A Look at the Violence against Women Act and Gender-Related Political Asylum." *Violence against Women* 1(4):380–400.

Owen, Barbara. 1998. *In the Mix: Struggle and Survival in a Women's Prison.* State University of New York Press.

Parrot, Andrea. 1986. *Acquaintance Rape and Sexual Assault Prevention Training Manual.* Department of Human Services Studies. Ithica, New York: Cornell University.

Pearson, Jennifer M. 1993. "Centro Feminil: A Women's Prison in Mexico." *Social Justice* 20:85–128.

Pence, Ellen, and Melanie Shepard. 1988. "Integrating Feminist Theory and Practice: The Challenge of the Battered Women's Movement." Pp. 282–298 in *Feminist Perspectives on Wife Abuse,* edited by K. Yllo and M. Bograd. Newbury Park, CA: Sage.

Pendergrass, Virginia E. 1975. "Innovative Programs for Women in Jail and Prison: Trick or Treatment." Pp. 67–76 in *The Female Offender,* edited by A. M. Brodsky. Beverly Hills, CA: Sage.

Pogrebin, Mark R., and Eric D. Poole. 1997. "The Sexualized Work Environment: A Look at Women Jail Officers." *The Prison Journal* 77(1):41–57.

Pollack, Shoshana. 1994. "Opening the Window in a Very Dark Day: A Program Evaluation of the Peer Support Team at the Kingston Prison for Women." *Forum on Corrections Research* 6:7–10.

Proto-Campise, Laura, Joanne Belknap, and John Wooldredge. 1998. "High School Students' Adherence to Rape Myths and the Effectiveness of High School Rape-Awareness Programs." *Violence against Women* 4(3): 308–328.

Rafter, Nicole H. 1985. *Partial Justice: Women in State Prisons, 1800–1935.* Boston: Northeastern University Press.

Rafter, Nicole H., and Elena M. Natalizia. 1981. "Marxist Feminism: Implications for Criminal Justice." *Crime and Delinquency* 27:81–98.

Richie, Beth E. 1996. *Compelled to Crime: The Gender Entrapment of Black Battered Women.* New York: Routledge.

Roche, Susan E., Katy Biron, and Niamh Reilly. 1995. "Sixteen Days of Activism against Gender Violence" *Violence against Women* 1(3):272–282.

Ross, Robert R., and Elizabeth A. Fabiano. 1986. *Female Offenders: Correctional Afterthoughts.* Jefferson, NC: McFarland.

Russell, Diana E. H. 1984. *Sexual Exploitation: Rape, Child Sexual Abuse, and Workplace Harassment.* Beverly Hills, CA: Sage.

Saltzman, Linda E., L. Rachid Salmi, Christine M. Branche, and Julie C. Bolen. 1997. "Public Health Screening for Intimate Violence." *Violence against Women* 3(3):319–331.

Sanday, Peggy R. 1981. "The Socio-Cultural Context of Rape: A Cross-Cultural Study." *Journal of Social Issues* 37:5–27.

Sarri, Rosemary C. 1987. "Unequal Protection under the Law: Women and the Criminal Justice System." Pp. 427–453 in *The Trapped Woman: Catch-22 in Deviance and Control.* Newbury Park, CA: Sage.

Schupak, Terri L. 1986. "Comment: Women and Children First: An Examination of the Unique Needs of Women in Prison." *Golden Gate University Law Review* 16:455–474.

Schur, Edwin M. 1984. *Labeling Women Deviant: Gender, Stigma, and Social Control.* New York: McGraw-Hill.

Schwendinger, Julia R., and Herman Schwendinger. 1983. *Rape and Inequality.* Beverly Hills, CA: Sage.

Sherman, Lawrence W. 1992. *Policing Domestic Violence: Experiments and Dilemma.* New York: Free Press.

Slote, Kim, and Carrie Cuthbert. 1997. "Women's Rights Network (WRN)." *Violence against Women* 3(1):76–80.

Smart, Carol. 1989. *Feminism and the Power of Law.* London: Routledge and Kegan Paul.

Sommerlad, Hilary, and Peter Sanderson. 1998. *Gender, Choice and Commitment: Women Solicitors in England and Wales and the Struggle for Equal Status.* Aldershot, England: Ashgate Publishing Company.

Sommers, Ira and Deborah R. Baskin. 1994. "Factors Related to Female Adolescent Initiation into Violent Street Crime." *Youth & Society* 25(4):468–489.

Spohn, Cassia. 1990. "Decision Making in Sexual Assault Cases: Do Black and Female Judges Make a Difference?" *Women and Criminal Justice* 2: 83–106.

Spohn, Cassia, and Julie Horney. 1991. "The Law's the Law, But Fair Is Fair: Rape Shield Laws and Officials' Assessment of Sexual History Evidence." *Criminology* 29:137–161.

———. 1992. *Rape Law Reform: A Grassroots Revolution and Its Impact.* New York: Plenum Press.

———. 1993. "Rape Law Reform and the Effect of Victim Characteristics on Case Processing." *Journal of Quantitative Criminology* 9:383–409.

Stanko, Elizabeth A. 1989. "Missing the Mark? Policing Battering." Pp. 46–69 in *Women, Policing, and Male Violence: International Perspectives,* edited by J. Hanmer, J. Radford, and E. A. Stanko. London: Routledge and Kegan Paul.

Stanton, Ann M. 1980. *When Mothers Go to Jail.* Lexington, MA: Lexington Books.

Stark, Evan. 1992. "Framing and Reframing Battered Women." Pp. 271–292 in *Domestic Violence: The Changing Criminal Justice Response,* edited by E. S. Buzawa and C. G. Buzawa. Westport, CT: Auburn House.

———. 1993. "Mandatory Arrest of Batterers: A Reply to Its Critics." *American Behavioral Scientist* 36:651–680.

Steffensmeier, Darrell. 1993. "National Trends in Female Arrests, 1960–1990." *Journal of Quantitative Criminology* 9:411–441.

Sudderth, Lori K. 1998. "It'll Come Right Back at Me: The Interactional Context of Discussing Rape with Others." *Violence and Victims* 4(5):572–594.

Sullivan, Mary, and Deborah I. Bybee. 1987. "Female Students and Sexual Harassment: What Factors Predict Reporting Behavior?" *Journal of the National Association for Women Deans, Administrators and Counselors* 50:11–16.

Tierney, Kathleen J. 1982. "The Battered Women Movement and the Creation of the Wife Beating Problem." *Social Problems* 29:207–220.

Tolman, Richard M. 1996. "Expanding Sanctions for Batterers: What Can We Do besides Jailing and Counseling Them?" Pp. 170–185 in *Future Interventions with Battered Women and Their Families,* edited by J. L. Edleson and Z. C. Eisikovits. Thousand Oaks, Sage Publications.

Tutty, Leslie M., Gillian Weaver, and Michael A. Rothery. 1999. "Residents' Views of the Efficacy of Shelter Services for Assaulted Women." *Violence and Victims* 5(8):898–925.

U.S. Census Bureau. 1999. *Statistical Abstract of the U.S. 1998.* Washington, DC: U.S. Government Printing Office.

Ullman, Sarah E., and Raymond A. Knight. 1992. "Fighting Back: Women's Resistance to Rape." *Journal of Interpersonal Violence* 7:31–43.

Van Voorhis, Patricia, Joanne Belknap, Karen Welch, and Amy Stichman. 1993. "Gender Bias in Courts: The Findings and Recommendations of the Task Forces." A paper presented at the 1993 annual meeting of the American Society of Criminology, Phoenix, AZ.

Vinton, Linda. 1998. "A Nationwide Survey of Domestic Violence Shelters' Programming for Older Women." *Violence and Victims* 4(5):559–571.

Von Cleve, Elizabeth, and Joseph G. Weis. 1993. "Sentencing Alternatives for Female Offenders." Pp. 94–100 in *Female Offenders: Meeting Needs of a Neglected Population,* edited by the American Correctional Association, Laurel, MD.

Walker, Lenore E. 1989. *Terrifying Love: Why Battered Women Kill and How*

Society Responds. New York: Harper Perennial.

Weitzman, Lenore J. 1985. *The Divorce Revolution: The Unexpected Social and Economic Consequences for Women and Children in America.* New York: Free Press.

Wertsch, Teresa L. 1998. "Walking the Thin Blue Line: Policewomen and Tokenism Today." *Women and Criminal Justice* 9(3):52–61.

Whitcomb, Debra. 1991. "Improving the Investigation and Prosecution of Child Sexual-Abuse Cases." Pp. 181–190 in *Abused and Battered: Social and Legal Responses to Family Violence,* edited by D. D. Knudsen and J. L. Miller. New York: Aldine de Gruyter.

Widom, Cathy S. 1989a. "The Cycle of Violence." *Science* 244:160–166.

Widom, Cathy S. 1989b. "Child Abuse, Neglect, and Adult Behavior: Research Design and Findings on Criminality, Violence, and Child Abuse." *American Journal of Orthopsychiatry,* 59(3), 355–367.

Wikler, Norma J. 1987. "Educating Judges about Gender Bias in the Courts." Pp. 227–246 in *Women, the Courts, and Equality,* edited by L. L. Crites and W. L. Hepperle. Newbury Park, CA: Sage.

Wishik, Heather R. 1985. "To Question Everything: The Inquiries of Feminist Jurisprudence." *Berkeley Women's Law Journal* 1:64–77.

Wooldredge, John D., and Kimberly Masters. 1993. "Confronting Problems Faced by Pregnant Inmates in State Prisons." *Crime and Delinquency* 39:195–203.

Zabelina, Tatiana. 1995. "Syostri (Sisters): The Moscos Sexual Assault Recovery Center." *Violence against Women* 1(3):266–271.

Name Index

Page numbers in italics refer to the citations at the end of chapters.

Subject Index